C. S.                August 1988.



A painting could not do you justice – unless it could talk. I do not know where I found you, but it was a wonderful discovery.

With Love

J. P. C. N.

National Portrait Gallery

# *Franz Xaver Winterhalter*

## AND THE COURTS OF EUROPE 1830–70

By Richard Ormond and Carol Blackett-Ord

With contributions by
Susan Foister
Philip Mansel
Delia Millar
Oliver Millar
and Aileen Ribeiro

The exhibition and catalogue sponsored by United Technologies Corporation

Published for the exhibition at the National Portrait Gallery, London
30 October 1987–10 January 1988
and at the Petit Palais, Paris
11 February–7 May 1988

Exhibition organizer: Richard Ormond
Exhibition designer: Barry Mazur


Published by the National Portrait Gallery,
St Martin's Place, London WC2H OHE

Catalogue edited by Rosemary Amos and Gillian Forrester
Art Director: Derek Birdsall RDI
Designed by Alan Kitching
Production by Martin Lee/Omnific

ISBN 0 904017 83 4 (paperback)
ISBN 0 904017 84 2 (hardback)

Typeset in Monophoto Van Dijck 203
and printed in England by Balding + Mansell International Limited
on Parilux matt cream

Front cover: *Pauline Sandor, Princess Metternich* (no. 63)

Photographic Acknowledgements

The exhibition organizers would like to thank the following for making photographs available. All other photographs were provided by the owners of the paintings, or the sources given in the catalogue:

By gracious permission of Her Majesty The Queen figs. 24, 25, 26, 27, 31, 44, 59
A.C.L. – Brussels figs. 34, 38, 39, cat. no. 66; Atelier 53, Paris cat. no. 57; Barnes and Webster, London figs. 9, 43, 47, 49; Christie's, Monaco cat. no. 2; Cliché des Musées Nationaux figs. 18, 19, 20, 21, 22, 23, 35, 45, 46, 58, cat. nos. 14, 17, 18, 19, 21, 22, 23, 25, 53, 56, 64, 65; Courtauld Institute of Art, London fig. 33; Davis-Dunlop Inc., Washington D.C. fig. 36; Founders Society, Detroit Institute of Arts fig. 28; Gauls, Koblenz cat. no. 26; Georg Goerlipp fig. 10, cat. no. 54; Hansjörg Henn figs. 11, 13; J. Hyde, Paris cat. nos. 51, 55, 62; Lauros-Giraudon, Paris cat. no. 1; Andreas Mayer fig. 1; Christoph Mayer figs. 2, 3, 5, 40; Dr Hubert Mayer fig. 6; National Galleries of Scotland cat. nos. 34, 45; Photographie Bulloz, Paris cat. no. 59; Photo Studio Berger, Nyon cat. 58; Prudence Cuming Associates Ltd, London cat. no. 61; Sotheby's, London figs. 14, 29; The Trustees of the Victoria and Albert Museum, London fig. 50; Witt Library, London figs. 17, 48, 57.

# Contents

We hope our British friends will be as pleased as we were to find, in this exhibition, that the art of Franz Xaver Winterhalter goes far beyond the more predictable court portraiture of the mid-1800s to include some of the most impressive work of any period.

It is a pleasure to support such a delightful show and such a beautiful catalogue.

Robert F. Daniell
*Chairman and Chief Executive Officer*
*United Technologies Corporation*

United Technologies companies in the U.K. include:
*Pratt & Whitney*
*Carrier*
*Otis*
*Sikorsky*
*UT Automotive*
*Hamilton Standard*

# Foreword

EXCEPTIONALLY GIFTED, properly ambitious, Winterhalter was unusual among the German artists of his age in being frankly *retardataire*. Completing his artistic education at the Munich Academy in the heady days of Ludwig I's vision of a new Athens for the Bavarian capital, he found alien to his spirit both the nationalistic fervour of king and populace and the high seriousness of the monumental fresco cycles then being executed for the Glyptothek and elsewhere by Cornelius and Schnorr von Carolsfeld. In Rome seven years later he gravitated away from the German *avant-garde* towards the French Academy. Finally, in 1834, installed as court painter to the Margrave of Baden in Karlsruhe, a town in which he had worked with great contentment since 1828, he suddenly left an assured existence to settle in Paris. His aim was to triumph at the Salon as an academic painter, and in this he quickly succeeded. But fate intervened. Louis-Philippe required a portraitist to celebrate the new dynasty, and at the time there were no French painters worth considering for the job (Ingres was in Rome). Winterhalter accepted the position, but was soon trapped by his own facility. His sleek, well-tailored portraits, with their aura of confidence, good breeding and glamour perfectly suited the nineteenth-century *beau monde*, whether noble or *nouveau*.

Louis-Philippe introduced him to Queen Victoria, who took him up in place of the hapless Partridge, and who became his greatest single patron, and for the rest of his life Winterhalter was in constant demand all over Europe as a society portraitist. Queen Victoria thought posterity would place him in the same class as Van Dyck.

Curiously, this glittering career, amply documented though it is, has never been the subject of serious study. Nor previously has there been a full-scale exhibition of Winterhalter's work; the last one to be held of any description was over fifty years ago, at Knoedler's in London in 1936. I am deeply grateful to my former colleague, Richard Ormond, now Director of the National Maritime Museum, who is a leading authority on Victorian painting and the author of pioneer studies of Landseer and (with Leonée Ormond) Lord Leighton, for finding the time in an increasingly busy life to select and catalogue this major exhibition, and to incorporate into it many little known pictures and much original archival research. Most of the works have not been seen in public before. I am no less grateful to Sir Oliver Millar, Director of the Royal Collection, for cataloguing the works from the Royal Collection and for including in his entries the rich documentation available in the royal archives; to Lady Millar, for cataloguing the loans from the Royal Library at Windsor; and to Dr Aileen Ribeiro, who has acted as consultant on dress and wrote the essay on fashion. Dr Susan Foister has co-ordinated the whole enterprise, and Mrs Carol Blackett-Ord, the co-author, has helped greatly with the research. Will Allan, representing the sponsors, has brought characteristic enthusiasm to the project. The catalogue has been edited by Miss Rosemary Amos and Miss Gillian Forrester. The arrangements for the loans have been conducted by Miss Jo Rickards.

It is especially appropriate, and a particular pleasure for me, that the exhibition should be shared with the Petit Palais in Paris; appropriate, of course, because Winterhalter lived for thirty-six years in Paris, and because the Petit Palais, built for the 1900 World Exhibition, is the city museum devoted to nineteenth-century painting. This is the first time that the Gallery has shared an exhibition with a French museum, and I am greatly indebted to Mlle Thérèse Burollet, the Conservateur-en-Chef of the Petit Palais, who, since her appointment, has done so much to transform and enliven that institution, and to her colleagues, notably Mlle Roselyne Hurel, for their enthusiasm, ready co-operation and (where needed) diplomacy.

A comprehensive exhibition such as this could not be achieved without the great generosity of the many owners who have very kindly agreed to lend us their treasures, and the Trustees and I wish to express our warmest gratitude to them all. Her Majesty The Queen has graciously lent an unprecedented number of works from the Royal Collection. Her Majesty Queen Elizabeth The Queen Mother and His Majesty The King of the Belgians have also graciously lent important works. Other works have been lent from collections in Austria, France, Germany, Poland, the Soviet Union, Spain and the United States as well as in this country.

The Trustees and I are extremely grateful to United Technologies Corporation for its most generous sponsorship which has made the exhibition possible.

*John Hayes*
*Director, National Portrait Gallery*

## Acknowledgements

The Exhibition has resulted from a research project which goes back five years. During that time we have received assistance, advice and information from a wide range of institutions and individuals. To all of them we owe a great debt, for piece by piece they have enabled us to chart the course of Winterhalter's life and art.

Among those to whom we owe most are Michael Alexander and Donald MacAndrew. The first wrote an important article on the artist, promoted his idea of the exhibition, and shared his enthusiasm with us. The second allowed us access to his own transcript of many of the source materials on which this catalogue is based, from a lifetime of study devoted to the artist. Our debt is scarcely less to the members of the Winterhalter family, who held so many of the vital original documents on the artist, and who co-operated so generously with us, foremost among them Dr Hubert Mayer. The task of deciphering and translating many of the German documents fell to David McLintock, whose timeless persistence is here gratefully acknowledged. Among others who have been of special assistance are the Hon. Michael Tollemache, who made vital contacts for us with owners of Winterhalter's paintings; Mrs Lada Grodzicka, the daughter of Tancred Borenius, organizer of the 1936 exhibition at Knoedler's; Armin Panter, currently engaged in Germany on a doctoral dissertation on Winterhalter at the University of Karlsruhe; Mlle Roselyne Hurel of the Petit Palais, who has been of great assistance in our searches for documents in the French archives and in communicating with owners of paintings in France; Barry Mazur, the designer of the exhibition, who has cheerfully tackled the numerous problems associated with fitting one of the largest exhibitions ever staged by the Gallery into a specially extended but limited space to produce a characteristically distinguished setting for Winterhalter's pictures; Alan Kitching, designer of the elegant catalogue; and Margaret Beck and Penny Dearsley our exemplary typists.

*Richard Ormond*
*Carol Blackett-Ord*

The National Portrait Gallery would also like to thank the following individuals and institutions who contributed in many different ways to the organization of the exhibition and preparation of the catalogue:

Lady Abdy
Sir Valentine Abdy, Bt.
The Duke of Alba
Mme Véronique Alemany
Mrs J. Alexander
Mr Colin Anson
The Comte d'Aspremont Lynden
The Duc d'Audiffret-Pasquier
Mrs Brenda Auslander
Dr Jörn Bahns
Mr Brian Barder
Herr G. Bartoschek
Mrs Bauer-Schichtegeroll
Miss Susan Baxter
Baron Christian de Beaugrenier
Count and Countess A. Benckendorff
Professor Albert Boime
M. Edward Borowski
Dr Helmut Börsch-Supan
The Hon. Christopher Brett
Prince de Chimay
Dr Andrew Ciechanowiecki
Mme Bernadette Cordier
Miss E.H. Cuthbert
Mrs Victoria Dannreuther
Herr Hansjakob Diggelmann
Herr Ernest Ludwig Dihl
Miss Frances Dimond
Dr Franz Dirnberger
Miss R.J. Doubzova
Axel Graf Douglas
The Marchioness of Douro
M. Jacques Duval
Mr Simon Endsor
Mr Oliver Everett
Mr G.I. Fedosov
Mme E.B. Ferry
Mrs Angela Brown Fischer
The Marquis de Forbin
Mr Antony Ford
Fabius Frères Antiquaires
Mr C.J. Gregory
Dr Rudolf Griesser
Mr Antony Griffiths
M. Robert Grossmann
Mrs Grundwald
M. P. Guyot de Villeneuve
Dr William Hauptmann
Dr Hans H. Hofstätter
Fürstin zu Hohenlohe-Langenburg
Mr Michael Holcroft
The Comte d'Humières
Dr Volker Illgen
Mr Edward Jackson
Dr Zdzislaw Jagodzinski
Drs T. Th. Kloek
Dr F. van Kretschmar
Mme Labat
M. Michel Laclotte
Mme C. Lanchy
Mlle A. Lefébure
M. Pierre Lemoine
Dr Christian Lenz
Mr Mark Lewis
Prince Antoine de Ligne
Mr Bruce Livie
Dr E.W. Graf zu Lynar
M. Bernard Marbot
Miss Stephanie Mather
Herr Christoph Mayer
Baroness Mayr-Melnhof
Mr Bruno Meissner
Dr Klaus Merten
Dr Hellmut Merz-Jaesrich
Dr Janina Michalkowa
Herr Hans Jürgen Moesch
Mr C. Monkhouse
M. Guy Monrosty
Mr David Moore-Gwyn
Mr J.A.L. Morgan
The Duc de Mouchy
M. Jean-Marie Moulin
Neumeister Münchener Kunstauktionhaus
Miss Lucy Oakley
Mr Robert Oresko
The Comte d'Ornano
M. Hervé Oursel
Mrs R. Page
The Comte de Paris
Miss Elzbieta Pastecka
Señor Ramón Andrada Pfeiffer
Mr Leslie Phillips
M. B. Piotrovsky
Lord Poltimore
The Comte de Pourtalès
Herr Gerhard Rammel
The Duke and Duchess of Ratibor
Mr John G. Rauch Jnr.
The Comte Stanislas Rey
Dr Gottfried Riemann
Mr Joseph Rishel
The Hon. Mrs Roberts
Prof. Philippe Roberts-Jones
Mlle Marie-Dominique Roche
Miss Monique Rodes
Mr G. Stair Sainty
Dr Marie Salaba
M. Jean-Pierre Samoyault
Dr Erich Schleier
Dr Bertold Schmidt
Frau Christa Schmidt
Dr Schneiders
Mr Alexander Schouvaloff
Dr Karl Schütz
Dr Lorenz Seelig
Dr Meinolf Siemer
Mr Michael Simpson
Mr R. Sneyers
Mr W. Staniszewski
Dr C. Sternberg
Mr Robert G. Stewart
Dr Vitali Suslov
Colonel P. Taton
Dr Rudolf Theilmann
Albert Fürst von Thurn und Taxis
Prince de la Tour d'Auvergne Lauraguais
M. Treister
Ms Ann Tzeutschler Lurie
The Marquise de Vanssay
Mlle Martine Vermeire
M. Dominique Vieville
Herr Horst Vey
Mr Adrian Ward-Jackson
Herr Volker Westphal
Colonel P. Willing
Prof. K.H. Winterhalter
Drs B. Woelderink
Miss Lucy Wood
Mrs Donald Workman
Baronne A. van Ypersele de Strihou
Count Adam Zamoyski
Dr Jürgen Zimmer
Dr Werner Zimmerman

# List of Lenders

Numbers given below refer to catalogue numbers

Her Majesty The Queen 15, 27, 28, 29, 30, 31, 33, 36, 37, 38, 40, 42, 43, 44, 48, 89, 90, 91, 93
Her Majesty Queen Elizabeth, The Queen Mother 24
Musée de Picardie, Amiens 1
The Artemis Group 49
Nationalgalerie der Staatlichen Museen, Berlin DDR 88
Baron de Bussière 62
Cleveland Museum of Art 4
Musée national du château de Compiègne 53, 56, 64
Augustinermuseum, Freiburg-im-Breisgau 6
Joachim Egon Fürst zu Fürstenberg, Donaueschingen 54
The Right Hon. The Earl of Harewood 35
The Earl of Jersey 41
Staatliche Kunsthalle, Karlsruhe 5, 11, 86, 87, 95, 96
Collections royales, Château de Laeken 16, 66
The State Hermitage Museum, Leningrad 73, 74, 75
J. Paul Getty Museum, Malibu 20
Lord Middleton 47
Prince Louis Murat 51
Metropolitan Museum of Art, New York 52
LL AA II Le Prince et La Princesse Napoléon 58
National Trust for Scotland, Brodick Castle 45
Allen Memorial Art Museum, Oberlin 84
Musée Jacquemart-André, Paris 59
Musée d'Orsay, Paris 65
Lady Lever Art Gallery, Port Sunlight Trustees of the National Museums and Galleries on Merseyside 32
Private Collections 3, 7, 8, 9, 10, 12, 13, 25, 39, 46, 47, 50, 55, 61, 63, 69, 76, 80, 82, 83, 85, 92, 94
Le Comte de Pourtalès 57
Savitskoy Gallery, Penza 60
Prince Alexander Sayn-Wittgenstein-Sayn 26
The Sutherland Trust 34
Musée national du château de Versailles 14, 17, 18, 19, 21, 22, 23
Kunsthistorisches Museum, Gemäldegalerie, Vienna 78, 79
National Museum, Warsaw 67, 68, 70, 71, 72, 77, 81

# Notes and Abbreviations

Both exhibition and catalogue are arranged in seven sections under the headings of the courts for which Winterhalter worked, with the exception of the first section, *Early Works*, which includes portraits painted at the Court of Baden, and the final section, *Drawings, Watercolours and Prints*. Within each section the exhibits are arranged in chronological sequence around the dated works. However, since Winterhalter worked for more than one court at the same time, the sequence of sections cannot be strictly chronological, and the apportioning of works to the various courts must necessarily be an artificial one (for instance English sitters have been placed under *The Court of Queen Victoria* even where the portraits were executed abroad). The divisions are therefore intended to serve only as an indication of the main *foci* of Winterhalter's patronage during his career; full details of his movements between the courts of his patrons will be found in the Chronology (pp. 13–16).

Some paintings could be included only in one showing of the exhibition, and this is indicated as follows:
* London only † Paris only

The contributors to the catalogue entries are identified by the following initials:

| | |
|---|---|
| CBO | Carol Blackett-Ord |
| SF | Susan Foister |
| PM | Philip Mansel |
| DM | Delia Millar |
| OM | Oliver Millar |
| RLO | Richard Ormond |

Except where stated, all exhibits are oil on canvas. Sizes are given in centimetres only, height preceding width; not all exhibits have been measured by the compilers.

Catalogue entries for portraits are preceded by biographies of the sitters. Where more than one portrait of the same sitter is included in the exhibition, the biography precedes the entry for the first portrait of the sitter exhibited and cross-references to the further portraits are included. Where there is no biography the number of the entry giving the biography is indicated.

References to the principal engraved versions of Winterhalter's works are included, but the listing of prints is not intended to be exhaustive.

LITERATURE

Any attempt to catalogue Winterhalter's works must take as a starting-point Franz Wild's *Nekrologe und Verzeichnisse der Gemälde von Franz & Hermann Winterhalter*, Zurich 1894. This is referred to in the catalogue as Wild, 1894. A fully annotated version of Wild's catalogue is appended to this catalogue (see pp. 226–39).

References to manuscript sources in the Royal Archives, Windsor Castle, have not been given in full for works in the Royal Collection: full references for these works will be found in Oliver Millar, *Victorian Pictures in the Collection of Her Majesty The Queen* (forthcoming). Please note that in English and foreign references, the place of publication will be included only where this is not the capital city.

The following abbreviated references have been used for published works:

| | |
|---|---|
| Collins-Baker, *Windsor* | C.H. Collins-Baker, *Catalogue of the Principal Pictures in the Royal Collection at Windsor Castle*, 1937. |
| Ormond | Richard Ormond, *Catalogue of Early Victorian Portraits in the National Portrait Gallery*, 2 vols., 1971. |
| Millar, *Victorian Pictures* | Oliver Millar, *Victorian Pictures in the Collection of Her Majesty The Queen* (forthcoming). |
| Wild, 1894 | Franz Wild, *Nekrologe und Verzeichnisse der Gemälde von Franz & Hermann Winterhalter*, Zurich 1894. |

Abbreviations used for manuscripts are as follows:

| | |
|---|---|
| Diary, Hayter | Copy of later transcript of the painter's diary in possession of his descendants. |
| Journal | Queen Victoria's Journal, Royal Archives, Windsor Castle. |
| Winterhalter *Album* | Unpublished annotated album of photographs, chiefly of works by F.X. Winterhalter, compiled in 1891 as an inventory of Hermann Winterhalter's estate and still in the possession of the descendants of F.X. Winterhalter. |
| Winterhalter Family Papers | Uncatalogued MS letters, papers and diaries still in the possession of the descendants of F.X. Winterhalter. |
| WRA | Royal Archives, Windsor Castle. |

EXHIBITIONS

The following abbreviations are used for exhibitions:

| | |
|---|---|
| Baden, 1873 | Kunsthalle, 'Winterhalter', October 1873, catalogue reprinted in Wild, pp. 54–7. |
| Karlsruhe, 1965 | Badischer Kunstverein, 'Romantiker und Realisten', 20 June–15 August 1965. |
| London, 1936 | M. Knoedler & Co. Inc., 'Winterhalter', 3–19 December 1936, catalogue by Tancred Borenius. |
| London, 1956–7 | Royal Academy, 'British Portraits', winter exhibition, 1956–7, catalogue by Ellis Waterhouse and others. |
| London, 1977 | Royal Academy, 'This Brilliant Year: Queen Victoria's Jubilee, 1887', 19 March–10 July 1977, catalogue by Jeremy Maas. |
| Menzenschwand, 1973 | Town Hall, 'Franz Xaver Winterhalter', commemorative exhibition, 8 July 1973. |
| Paris, 1928 | Galeries Jacques Seligmann et Fils, 'Winterhalter (Portraits de Dames du Second Empire)', 25 May–15 June 1928. |
| Philadelphia, 1978–9 | Philadelphia Museum of Art, 'The Second Empire 1852–1870: Art in France under Napoleon III', 1 October–26 November 1978. (The Detroit Institute of Arts, 15 January–18 March 1979; Grand Palais, Paris, 24 April–2 July 1979), catalogue by Kathryn B. Hiesinger, Joseph Rishel and others. |

# Chronology of Winterhalter's life and European events

| | *Winterhalter's life* | *European events* |
|---|---|---|
| 1805 | 20 April: born in Menzenschwand, sixth child of Fidel Winterhalter, a farmer and resin producer, and of Eva Mayer. | 21 October: Battle of Trafalgar.<br>2 December: Battle of Austerlitz.<br>26 December: Baden created a Grand Duchy. |
| 1809 | | 10 July: Nazarene painters in Rome form Brotherhood of St Luke. |
| 1814 | | 11 April: Napoleon I abdicates; Louis XVIII becomes King of France.<br>1 November: Congress of Vienna. |
| 1815 | | 18 June: Battle of Waterloo. |
| 1818 | Apprentice in studio of Karl Ludwig von Schüler, Freiburg-im-Breisgau. | 29 August: Liberal constitution in Baden. |
| 1819 | Under Schüler, makes engravings for the publishing house of Herder. Schüler becomes Director of Institute of Arts established by Herder, and takes apprentices with him. Winterhalter joined by his brother Hermann. | 24 May: Queen Victoria is born. |
| 1820 | | 29 January: George III dies, succeeded by George IV. |
| 1821 | | 5 May: Napoleon dies on St Helena. |
| 1823 | Leaves Herder Institute for Munich. Lodges there with Ludwig Albert von Montmorillon. Contributes lithographs to Piloty and Selb's *Taffel Werk*. | |
| 1824 | Receives a grant to study in Munich; Hermann joins Winterhalter there. | 16 September: Louis XVIII dies, succeeded by Charles X. |
| 1825 | Student at Munich Academy. Joins studio of Josef Stieler. July: receives pension of 200 florins from Grand Duke of Baden for executing a drawing annually. | 1 December: Tsar Nicholas I succeeds Tsar Alexander I of Russia. |
| 1827 | Travels in Germany studying art. | |
| 1828 | Based in Munich; visits Karlsruhe. | |
| 1829 | Drawing Master to Sophie Guillemette, Grand Duchess of Baden. | |
| 1830 | Moves to Karlsruhe; lodges with Dr. J. Albert Wich, no. 8 Innerer Zirkel. | 26 June: George IV dies, succeeded by William IV.<br>27–29 July: Revolution in France; Charles X abdicates.<br>7 August: Louis-Philippe of Orléans elected King of France.<br>18 November: Independence of Belgium declared.<br>Revolutionary risings in Brunswick, Hesse and Saxony.<br>Margrave Leopold of Baden succeeds his brother Ludwig to become Grand Duke of Baden. |
| 1831 | Paintings include Leopold, Grand Duke of Baden (nos. 3, 96) and Sophie Guillemette, Grand Duchess of Baden (nos. 4, 69, 95). | 4 June: Leopold of Saxe-Coburg elected King of Belgium. |
| 1832 | Travels to Italy on a bursary partly funded by Grand Duke Leopold. | |
| 1833 | Studies in Rome. His *poste restante* address: Caffè Greco, via Condotta. Paintings include *Roman Genre Scene* (no. 5) | |

| | *Winterhalter's life* | *European events* |
|---|---|---|
| 1834 | August: returns to Karlsruhe where appointed Court Painter to Grand Duke Leopold. December: leaves for Paris. | 30 June: German Confederation forms committee for political investigations. |
| 1835 | Paris address: 17 rue des Petits Augustins. First exhibit at Salon, *Portrait de Femme*. | Baden joins *Zollverein*. |
| 1836 | Paris address: 15 rue des Petits Augustins. Paintings include *Il Dolce Farniente* (no. 9). Passport: *à la Légation de Bade*, 23 April. | |
| 1837 | Paintings include *The Decameron* (fig. 16). | 20 June: William IV dies, succeeded by Queen Victoria. |
| 1838 | Paris address: 34 rue de Lille. Paintings include Queen Louise-Marie of the Belgians with the Duke of Brabant (Her Majesty The Queen) and Princess Clementine of Orléans (Private Collection). | Louis-Napoleon settles in England. |
| 1839 | Paris studio address: 1 rue de Labruyère. Paintings include King Louis-Philippe (no. 17) and Leopold I, King of the Belgians (Royal Collections, Belgium). Decorations: 5 May, Knight of the Légion d'Honneur; Knight of the Order of King Leopold I. | Invention of photography by Daguerre and Fox Talbot. |
| 1840 | Hermann joins Winterhalter in Paris. Paintings include Leopold I (no. 14) and Self-portrait with Hermann (no. 11). Decorations: Cross of the Commander of the Order of King Leopold. | 10 February: marriage of Queen Victoria to Prince Albert of Saxe-Coburg-Gotha. |
| 1842 | Paintings include Queen Marie-Amélie (no. 19), Queen Victoria (no. 27) and Prince Albert (no. 28).<br>June–September: Buckingham Palace and Windsor Castle. | |
| 1843 | July–September: Buckingham Palace and Windsor Castle. | |
| 1844 | Paris studio address: 29 rue Notre Dame-de-Lorette. Paintings include *The Reception of King Louis-Philippe at Windsor Castle* (fig. 18).<br>November–December: Windsor Castle. | |
| 1846 | Paintings include *The Royal Family* (fig. 26) and Albert Edward, Prince of Wales (no. 31).<br>September–December: Windsor Castle. | |
| 1847 | January: Windsor Castle.<br>May–June: exhibition of Winterhalter's paintings at St James's Palace. | |
| 1848 | At outbreak of Revolution in Paris, goes to Brussels. August: Geneva. | 21–24 February: Revolution in Paris; Louis-Philippe abdicates.<br>10 December: Louis-Napoleon elected President of the Republic.<br>Revolutions in Sicily, Venice, Parma, Milan, Vienna, Berlin; revolts in Prague, Warsaw, Cracow.<br>Pre-Raphaelite Brotherhood formed. |
| 1849 | March: leaves Brussels for England (passport: from Brussels to England via France, 21 March); stays at Buckingham Palace.<br>May: Osborne House; June: Buckingham Palace; October: Windsor Castle.<br>Returns to Paris. | 28 March: Frederick William IV of Prussia elected 'Emperor of the Germans'.<br>11–13 May: Military revolt in Baden. |

| | *Winterhalter's life* | *European events* |
|---|---|---|
| 1850 | 14 February: created member of Akademie Royale des Beaux-Arts, Amsterdam.<br>June–July: Osborne House and Buckingham Palace. Passport: Paris to Baden, 15 July. | |
| 1851 | May–June: Buckingham Palace. Paintings include *The First of May* (Her Majesty The Queen). Berckmüller draws up plans for modernization of Adler Inn, Menzenschwand. | 1 May–15 October: Great Exhibition in London at Crystal Palace in Hyde Park.<br>2 December: Louis-Napoleon's *coup d'état* in Paris. |
| 1852 | April–June: Buckingham Palace and Windsor Castle. Berckmüller negotiates marriage between Winterhalter and Marie Scheffel in Karlsruhe; engagement broken in July. Winterhalter travels to Spain with Eduard Magnus. Paintings include Queen Isabella of Spain (Palacio Réal, Madrid) and *Florinda* (no. 38). | 23 January: Orléans family banished from France.<br>1 December: Napoleon III declared Emperor of France. |
| 1853 | Spring: invited to paint Empress Eugénie, Paris. Paintings include state portraits of Napoleon III and Empress Eugénie (figs. 33 and 34), finished in December. Passport: Baden to Paris, 22 July. | 29–30 January: Napoleon III marries Eugénie de Montijo, Countess of Teba. |
| 1854 | Created *Peintre Attitré de la Cour de Napoleon III*. Paintings include Empress Eugénie (no. 50) and Empress Eugénie à la Marie Antoinette (no. 52). | Crimean War begins. |
| 1855 | June: Buckingham Palace. Paintings include: *Empress Eugénie Surrounded by Her Ladies in Waiting* (no. 53). On the Salon Awards Jury with Ingres and Delacroix. | 2 March: Tsar Nicholas I of Russia succeeded by Tsar Alexander II.<br>April: visit of Emperor and Empress of France to England.<br>May 15: *Exposition Universelle*, Paris.<br>August: visit of Queen Victoria and Prince Albert to Paris. |
| 1856 | April–May: Buckingham Palace.<br>22–29 November: invited to Palace of Fontainebleau. Paintings include Empress Alexandra Feodorovna (The Hermitage, Leningrad). Passports: Paris to Austria, 14 July; Paris to Strasbourg, 15 July. Also visited Baden, Warsaw and Wildbad. | 25 February–30 March: Peace Congress of Paris.<br>16 March: Birth of Prince Imperial. |
| 1857 | Paris address: 2 rue de la Chaussée d'Antin. Studio address: 64 rue de la Rochefoucauld. June: Buckingham Palace. July: exhibition at Baden of Winterhalter's paintings from Grand Duke's collection. August: raised to *Officier de la Légion d'Honneur*. Paintings include Empress Marie Alexandrovna of Russia (no. 73); Empress Eugénie (fig. 36); Empress Eugénie with Prince Imperial (no. 58). Also visited Menzenschwand, Brückinau and Geneva. | 6–10 August: Visit of Emperor and Empress of France to England. |
| 1858 | Decorations: Knight of the Order of St. Anne, third class (Russian Empire). Passports: Switzerland to Germany, 24 April; Germany to Paris, 28 September. Visits Interlaken. | 21 July: Napoleon III and Cavour meet at Plombières to prepare unification of Italy. |
| 1859 | Paintings include Queen Victoria in Coronation robes and Prince Albert (both Her Majesty The Queen). Decorations: Order of the Red Eagle, third class (Prussia). Passports: England to Germany (no date); Paris to Baden, May; London to France, 21 June. Work begins on Villa Trianon, Baden. | 4 June: Battle of Magenta.<br>24 June: Battle of Solférino. |
| 1860 | Passports: Germany to Baden, 31 July; Karlsruhe to France, September; England to France, 9 October; Germany to France, 13 October. | |

| | *Winterhalter's life* | *European events* |
|---|---|---|
| 1861 | Villa Trianon, Friedricksgasse, Baden, completed. | Outbreak of American Civil War. Emancipation of serfs granted in Russia. 18 February: Victor-Emanuel II proclaimed King of Italy. 18 December: Death of Prince Albert. |
| 1862 | Paintings include Empress Eugénie in Mourning (fig. 37) and the Family of the Princess Royal (Her Majesty The Queen). Passport: Germany to Italy, 28 June. Sells Villa Trianon to Auffrm'Ordt family. | London World Exhibition. 23 September: Bismarck appointed Prussian Premier. |
| 1863 | Paintings include Queen Sophia of the Netherlands (Rijksmuseum, Amsterdam) and Duchess of Brabant (fig. 39); Passports: Germany to Paris, 11 May; Germany to Italy, 8 July. Also visits Brussels, Baden and Stuttgart. Fidel Winterhalter dies in May. | 8 February: Prussia allies with Russia to suppress Polis rising. |
| 1864 | Summer: visits England to paint wedding portraits, Prince (Her Majesty The Queen) and Princess of Wales (no. 48). Vienna, Schönbrunn, to paint 2 portraits of Empress Elizabeth (Kunsthistorisches Museum Gemäldegalerie, Vienna and fig. 43). 23 November: awarded Order of Franz Joseph. Passports: Baden to France, 21 June; Baden to Germany, 23 June. | 30 October: Peace of Vienna. |
| 1865 | Paintings include Franz Joseph I, Emperor of Austria and Empress Elizabeth (nos. 78 and 79). Passport: Baden to Paris, 4 July. | October: Bismarck and Napoleon III meet at Biarritz. 9 December: Leopold I of Belgium dies, succeeded by Leopold II. |
| 1866 | | August: Peace treaties between Prussia and Württemberg, Baden, Bavaria and Austria. |
| 1867 | Passport: a permit of 3 June, signed by Empress Eugénie, allowing Winterhalter to travel to 'Germany, Italy, etc.' Visits Menzenschwand. | 1 April: Opening of *Exposition Universelle*, Paris. 19 June: Emperor Maximilian of Mexico shot. |
| 1868 | Lengthy visit to Munich. Paintings include Self-portrait (Uffizi, Florence). | |
| 1870 | January: Nice. September: takes a cure at Kur, Switzerland. | 19 July: France declares war on Prussia. 2 September: Napoleon III capitulates at Sedan. 4 September: Revolution in Paris; Republic proclaimed. 19 September: Siege of Paris begins. |
| 1871 | July: included in Kurliste, Bad Petersthal with Tsar, Tsarina and the Russian contingent. 23 November: moves with Hermann to no. 4 Friedricksplatz, Karlsruhe. | 18 January: William I proclaimed German Emperor at Versailles. March: Napoleon III exiled to England. 10 May: Franco-German peace treaty at Frankfurt. 31 August: Thiers elected French President. |
| 1873 | January–April: Karlsruhe. June–July: a guest of von Metzler family Frankfurt. 8 July, 6 p.m.: dies of typhus at Diakonissen Krakenhaus, Frankfurt. Buried in Frankfurt Cemetery (fig. 52). Exhibition at Kunstverein, Frankfurt, immediately following death. October: retrospective exhibition at Kunsthalle, Baden. Decorations: another Order of Franz Joseph presented posthumously, on 7 October. | 9 January: Napoleon III dies. 15 September: Germans evacuate France. |

Richard Ormond

# *Introduction*

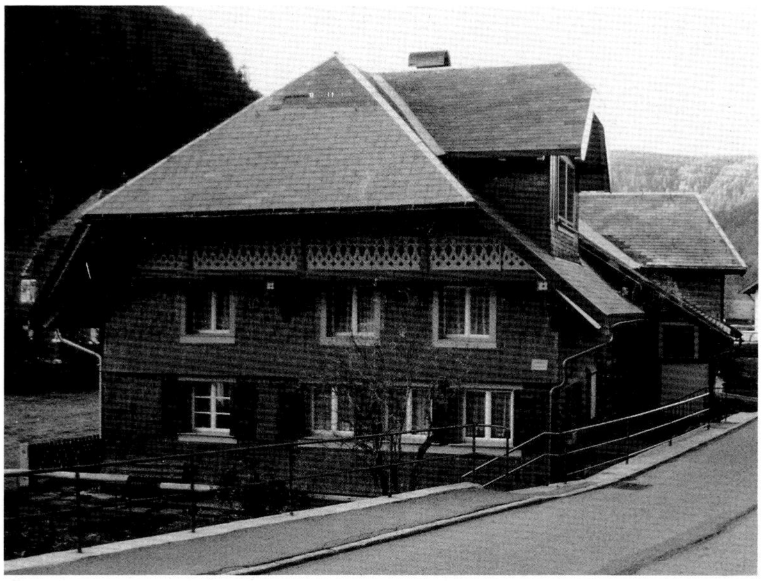

Figure 1
F.X. Winterhalter's birthplace, Menzenschwand in 1987
Photograph by A. Mayer

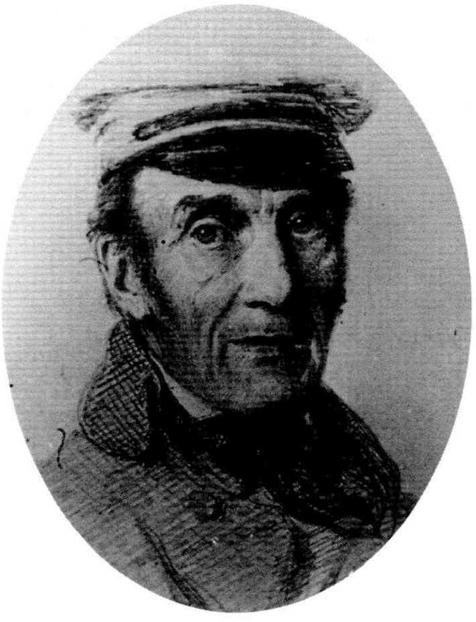

Figure 2
F.X. Winterhalter:
*Fidel Winterhalter*
Pencil drawing
Private Collection

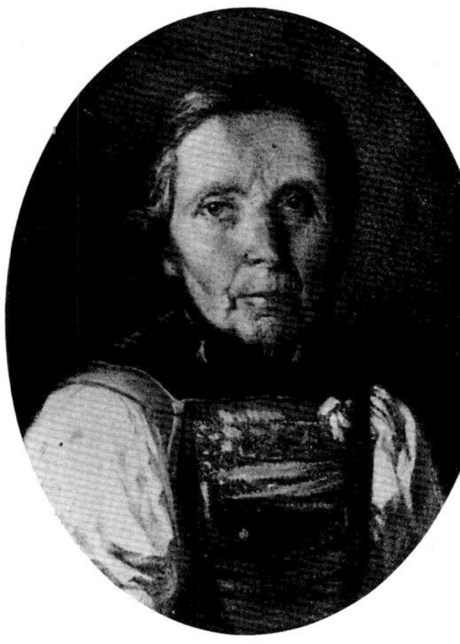

Figure 3
F.X. Winterhalter: *Eva Mayer*
Watercolour, 15.5 × 12.3 cms
Private Collection

FRANZ XAVER WINTERHALTER was born in Menzenschwand, a small village in the upper reaches of the Black Forest, on 20 April 1805.[1] Though considerably altered, the Winterhalter family house still stands to this day in the village (fig. 1), and the painter is commemorated by a public memorial and a room at the local inn named in his honour.

He was the sixth child of Fidel Winterhalter (fig. 2), a farmer and resin producer in the village, and his wife, Eva Mayer. Fidel had been born in 1773, the natural child of a servant girl from Menzenschwand, Anna Schlageter, and took the name of the elderly man to whom she was hastily married off; Matthias Winterhalter. According to family legend, the real father of the boy was one of the monks from the nearby Benedictine monastery of St Blasien which owned much of the land in the district. Some support to this theory is given by the evidence of considerable education in Fidel's letters, and because of the help later extended to his son by the priest of Menzenschwand, Father Joseph Berthold Lieber, a former inmate of the monastery. Fidel's mother returned to Menzenschwand on the death of her elderly husband in 1785, and subsequently married a local gunmaker, Jacob Benedict Laule. In 1790, Fidel himself married Eva Mayer (fig. 3), a member of a long established Menzenschwand family, when she was twenty-five and he was sixteen-and-a-half.

One explanation for Fidel's extremely early marriage was the risk that unmarried men ran of being pressed into military service. In 1791, Fidel secured a permit to sell watches to members of the German community in Bohemia; the Black Forest was famous at the time for watchmaking. A few years later, he was settled as a dairy farmer at Eschberg on land belonging to the monastery. By 1815, the family was back in Menzenschwand at no. 21 Hinterdorf, where Fidel ran a smallholding, and in summer operated as a resin producer in the nearby forests with an assistant, Franz Xaver Wild.

Four sons and four daughters were born to Fidel and his wife between 1791 and 1808, of whom only four survived beyond infancy: Justina (1793–1867); Theresia (1799–

1863); Franz Xaver, known in youth as Xaver (1805–73); and Hermann, or Fidel as he had been christened (1808–93). In 1824, Justina married Hieronymous Mayer, the owner of the Adler Inn at Menzenschwand, who was considerably older than her. He was lazy and unreliable, and by 1830 the Inn was effectively being run by Justina (already the mother of several children), and by her father. The younger sister, Theresia, was more fortunate in her choice of husband: Katejan Wild was the owner of a small trading company, and a modest capitalist.

The Winterhalter family was clearly a united one. The passionate interest shown by Fidel in the careers of his sons, and his anxious solicitude for them long after they had grown up, is evidence of this. So is the reciprocal interest shown by Winterhalter himself in events at home. Year after year he returned to Menzenschwand, followed the fortunes of his sisters and their children, and contributed financial assistance. His character had been formed by the independence, conservative outlook, simple morality and deeply-held Catholic beliefs of the rural community in which he had been raised. These qualities continued to exert a determining influence on him throughout his life.

Franz Xaver and Hermann were both taught in Menzenschwand at the local Pfarr-schule by the priest, Father Lieber. Lieber was interested in the arts, and had acquired his own modest picture collection. He encouraged the two brothers to draw, nurtured their talent and drew their work to the attention of a local grandee, Daniel Seligmann, Baron Eichtal (fig. 4),[2] who ran a textile factory in the former monastery buildings of St Blasien. His father had been a wealthy banker, ennobled for his services to the Bavarian state. The son became one of the leading industrialists in the Grand Duchy of Baden, and a prominent figure at court in Karlsruhe.

The rich and influential Eichtal promoted the young Winterhalter's career as a Royal portraitist, and made the vital early contacts for him. Later gossips, seeking the motive for Eichtal's sponsorship of this young artist, came to the conclusion that it was he who was the natural father.[3]

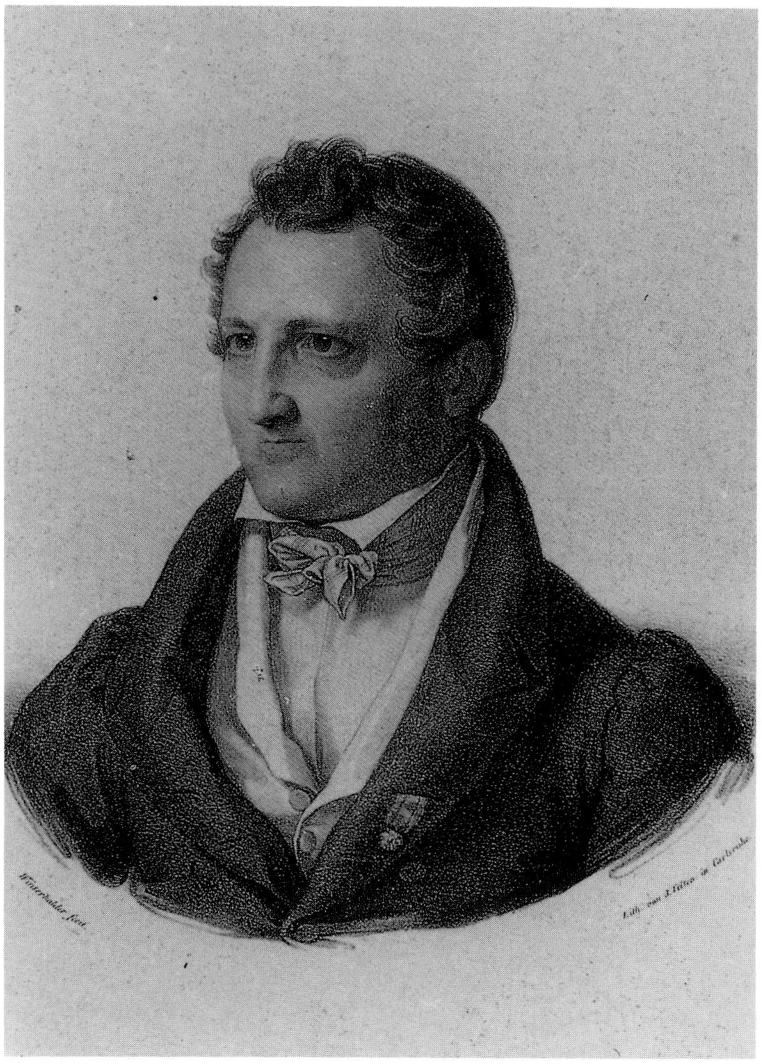

Figure 4
J. Velten after F.X. Winterhalter:
*Daniel Seligmann, 2nd Baron Eichtal*
Lithograph, 47.5 × 34.5 cms
Generallandesarchiv Karlsruhe

Between them, Father Lieber and Eichtal persuaded Fidel Winterhalter to allow his elder son (fig. 5) to train professionally as an artist. They may well have helped to raise the initial premium necessary to apprentice him for four years, and to pay for his board and instruction. He left Menzenschwand in 1818 at the age of thirteen to study drawing and engraving in the studio of an established Freiburg artist, Karl Ludwig Schuler (1785–1852).

Housing the Catholic metropolitan church of the Upper Rhine, the picturesque mediaeval town of Freiburg-im-Breisgau was the nearest centre of any substance to Menzenschwand. Founded in the twelfth century by the Dukes of Zahringen, it then formed part of the Grand Duchy of Baden. Apart from its proximity to the Black Forest, it was an obvious place to send the young Winterhalter, for it had a strong artistic tradition. The town was a well-known publishing centre, and Schüler had made his name as an illustrator and printmaker. Winterhalter, like several other Black Forest art students, was sent to Freiburg to learn a skill and earn a living. He was to be an engraver before he was a painter.

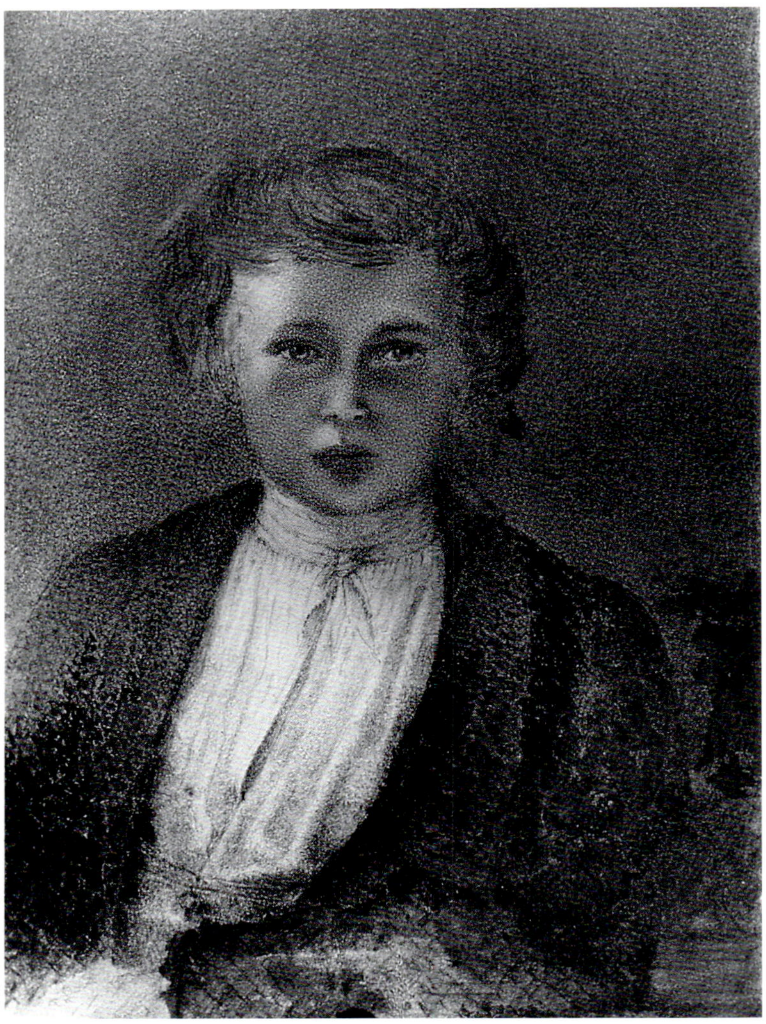

Figure 5
F.X. Winterhalter: *Self-portrait*, c.1817–18
Pencil drawing, 18 × 22 cms
Private Collection

Within a year of the young Winterhalter's arrival, Schüler was appointed as Director of the Institute for the Arts established by the publishing house of Herder. His eight apprentices went with him, and boarded at Herder's, to become part of a team of engravers and lithographers producing the illustrated books for which Herder was famous. The young Winterhalter wrote to his parents of the bullying he suffered from the other apprentices, of the bad language they used, of Bartholomaus Herder's rages at their ingratitude and of his own determination to be a religious painter. He worked on copper-plate engravings of peasant scenes, religious subjects for bible illustrations and on lithographic reproductions of famous works of art. His artistic training was not neglected, and there are several surviving drawings by him from plaster casts of Classical busts – some dated 1818 (fig. 6), as well as animal studies and sporting scenes. In 1819, Winterhalter was joined by his eleven-year-old brother Fidel, or Hermann, as he would become known. Their lives were simple and circumscribed. 'Since we are always busy learning, both on Sundays and weekdays, I had to write you a letter in extreme haste in order to satisfy you', Winterhalter confided to his ever-anxious parents in a letter of 26 March 1820:

> *'I have been to Madame Herder and asked her for money. The reason was this: we send to Strasbourg for all our* crayons et sauce, *Fidel and I, for one fl and eight gr; and we have had our shoes mended. She gave me a thaler. As long ago as carnival we lost our cook and the maid, and so until now we have had to remain without a maid and do all things ourselves eg. fetching water and doing the dishes and everything connected with meals, having to carry it all up three flights from the bottom kitchen. However we shall be without a maid only until Easter, and then we shall get another, which is a great joy to everybody as things are a little squalid in the bottom kitchen.'*[4]

By 1822, the two brothers were living in lodgings in the town and beginning to draw from life. Winterhalter's surviving life studies show a stronger grasp of form, and a surer technique, than his naive and schematized drawings of busts. His closest friend at the time was Heinrich Frank (*fl.* 1820–30) the son of a wine merchant in Freiburg, whose name frequently occurs in the correspondence between Fidel Winterhalter and his sons.

Winterhalter's sense of his own achievement and his self-evident talent, coupled with an ambition to get on, soon made him restive at the Herder Institute. He wanted to pursue his career in less restrictive and provincial surroundings, and he was encouraged in his desire to move by Baron Eichtal. The irascible Herder, however, was not prepared to release his gifted apprentice without a fight. In a letter to Fidel of 7 October 1822, he stood by the terms of the contract, arguing that he had done more for Winterhalter than he deserved: 'For some time now the disgusting ingratitude of my apprentices has made me positively ill, and it gets worse and worse . . . the revolutionary conduct in my Institute I will not tolerate. I would sooner dismiss all my ungrateful and unwilling apprentices at once than allow myself to be played with. The parents are very much to blame.'[5] In the event, a compromise was worked out. Winterhalter would be allowed to leave the following year, while Hermann was tied down by an exacting apprenticeship of eight years.

The decision that Winterhalter should train in Munich had been taken on Eichtal's advice and with his support. Winterhalter finally left the Herder Institute early in 1823. An emotional letter of farewell from a young priest who taught there, Father Josef Haïss, and who had taken a great liking to him, is dated 23 January 1823. Haïss warned him to be sincere, God-fearing and diligent, to avoid the company of inferiors, and not to raise himself in the world by a liaison with a fashionable woman ('you will only come a cropper'), and to steel himself against desire and lust.[6] Winterhalter was said to have carried the letter with him wherever he went, an indication of his simple and pious outlook on life that changed little with age.

By the spring of 1823, Winterhalter was back in Menzenschwand, making portraits of the locals, shooting grouse and snipe and enjoying the pleasures of the countryside. Later in the year, he set out for Munich with his friend, Heinrich Frank. They took lodgings in Munich at a hostel run for young artists by Ludwig Albert von Montmorillon (1794–1854), an engraver and lithographer, whose father had been a French *émigré* at the time of the Revolution. Winterhalter had met him once at Herder's, and he was known to Schüler and Eichtal. Winterhalter's earliest surviving letter from Munich, dated 15 April 1824, reveals his rising expectations. It had been decided that Hermann should join him in Munich, after a second fracas with Herder, and the older brother wrote to advise his father as to what things Hermann should bring with him:

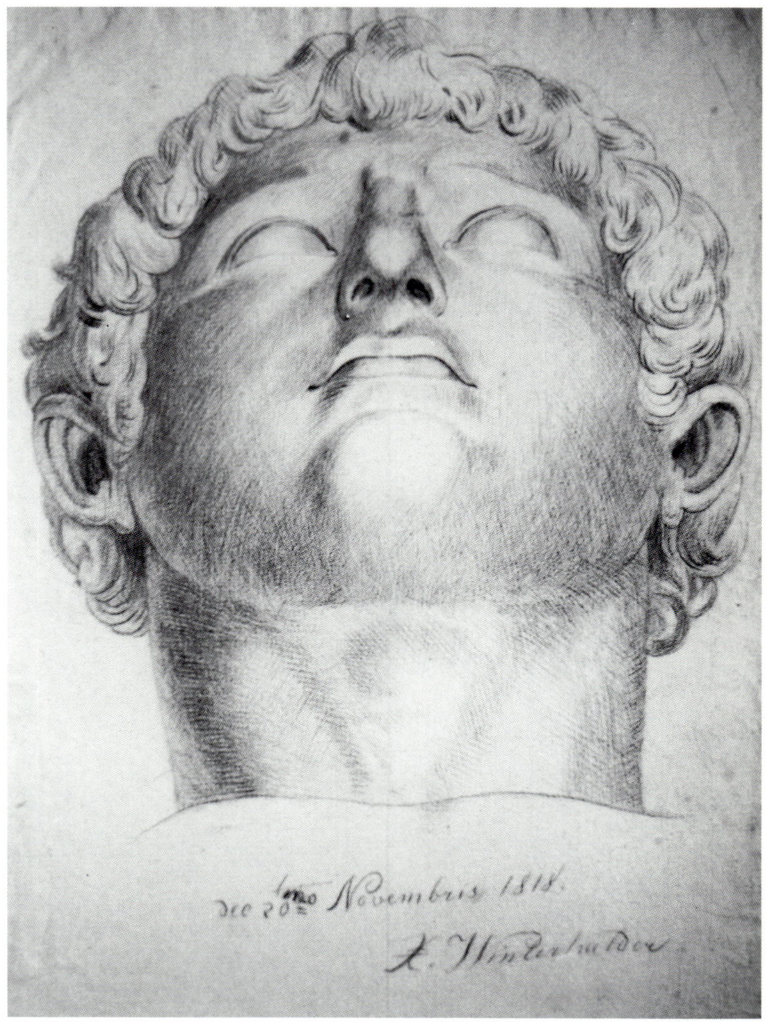

Figure 6
F.X. Winterhalter: *Study of a cast*, 1818
Chalk drawing, 35 × 21 cms
Private Collection

*'His shirts must be of fine linen. The best you can do and must do is to ask Frank's sisters to cut them out and sew one of them as a pattern. They must have many pleats and very fine collars. For you must not imagine that things are the same here as they are at home or in Freiburg: here one has to be very well dressed simply to be ordinary. But my brother, through us, is going to become acquainted with people of such station. It is happening to us more and more every day, and at the same time our business is very good. It is natural: where the common people give a guilder, the important people give a thaler, and they are no better informed. He will see for himself how good things are. If he has got decent waistcoats at home he should bring them and his coat, too. He might also have some boots made in Freiburg, so that they are not Menzenschwand clodhoppers; they must be elegant boots.'*[7]

Through Montmorillon, Winterhalter got work as a lithographer which enabled him to keep himself, as well as earning small sums from portrait commissions. Over twenty lithographs by him from this Munich period are known, mostly after the work of other artists. By 1825, he had joined the Munich Academy where he continued to draw from life. He had also joined the studio of the fashionable portrait painter, Josef Stieler (1781–1858). Stieler is remembered today for the set of court beauties, commissioned by Ludwig I, which still hang at Nymphenburg (fig. 7). His smooth, neo-Classical style, with its pretty effects of lighting and colour, exercised a decisive influence on Winterhalter's art and led him firmly in the direction of portraiture. The introduction to Stieler seems to have come from Eichtal, and it was the latter who urged him to stay in the studio of the older painter when he was contemplating a move to Paris. Winterhalter must have been useful as an assistant, and he is also known to have lithographed several of Stieler's portraits.[8]

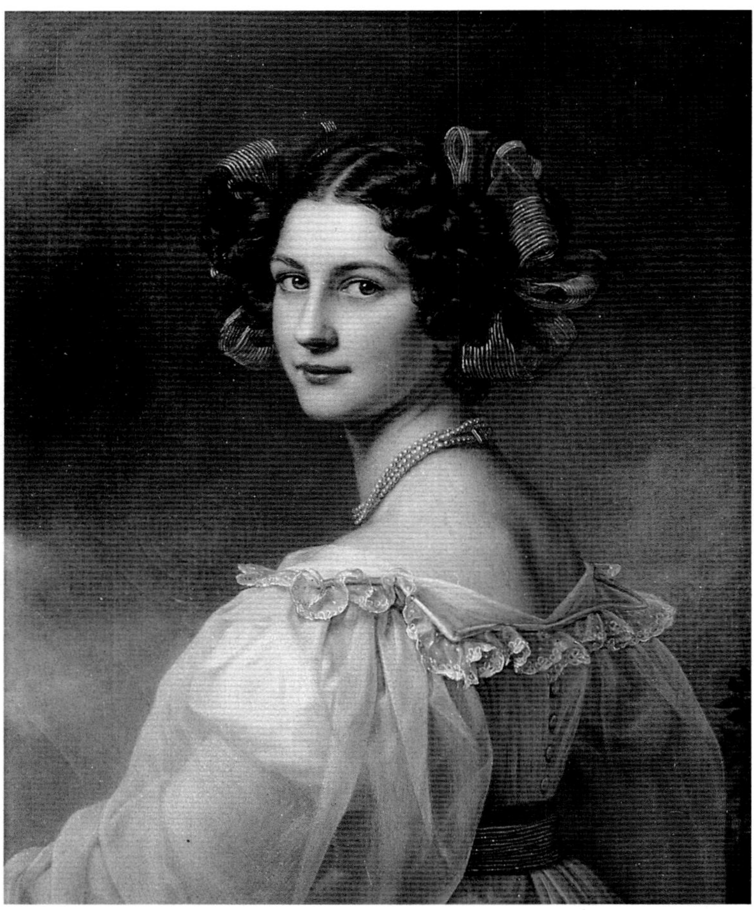

Figure 7
J. Stieler: *Auguste Strobl*, 1827
72.5 × 59.2 cms
Schloss Nymphenburg, Munich

Winterhalter arrived in Munich at a momentous period of its history. The new King, Ludwig I, was a Maecenas of the arts, intent on turning his capital into a new Athens. Architects were commissioned to design prestigious public buildings in the Classical style and artists employed to decorate them. Two of the leading luminaries of German art, the Nazarenes Peter Cornelius (1783–1867) and Julius Schnorr von Carolsfeld (1794–1872), together with Cornelius's protégé, Wilhelm Kaulbach (1805–74), came to Munich in the 1820s to carry out monumental mural schemes (fig. 8), and their achievements raised Munich's prestige to unparalleled heights. Cornelius took up the post of Director of the Munich Academy in 1825, soon after Winterhalter had begun to study drawing and painting there.

It is indicative of his taste that Winterhalter should have found little inspiration in the excessive naturalism and religious intensity of Nazarene painting. He turned away instinctively from the new aesthetic creed and the nationalistic fervour which supported it. Stieler, and Cornelius's predecessor at the Academy, Peter von Langer (1756–1824), had been trained in Paris. Their work continued to enshrine the lessons of French neo-Classical painting which provoked such a strong counter-reaction in German artistic circles in the 1820s. Winterhalter's preference for French art, his rejection of the movement towards the unification of Germany, and his instinctive dislike of radicalism and idealism, cut him off from the enthusiasms of many of his fellow students. He had been trained in the 'bread-and-butter' world of engraving and publishing; he had come up the hard way, and must have looked at current aesthetic theories with a sceptical eye.

Winterhalter's career in Munich is documented in a handful of letters he wrote home, and in a sequence of twenty-seven letters written by his father to him and his brother between 1824–8. Fidel Winterhalter took a possessive interest in the activities of his two sons, whom he likened to Leonardo and Raphael. He bombarded them with advice, made every effort to promote their careers at a distance, discussed their prospects with Lieber, Eichtal, Schüler and other friends, visited them from time to time and kept them in touch with all the happenings at home. Births and marriages are recounted in detail, the problems of the Adler Inn, his own business of resin extraction, land distribution and village life. The impassioned energy which these letters exhibit is touching in someone of such simple origins, and they help to explain the strong bond which continued to draw both brothers back to Menzenschwand.

In July 1825, Winterhalter received a modest and welcome acknowledgement of his progress. He was given a pension of 200 florins by the Grand Duke of Baden in return for executing an annual drawing, 'for which, however, the ambassador thinks I shall be paid. Even if I am not – it is a piece of great good fortune for me all the same. Oh, I am so happy, and so is my brother . . .' (letter to his parents, 20 July 1825).[9] Writing later in the same year (3 December 1825), Winterhalter described the work he was doing:

> *'I have drawn a few other portraits, partly because I have been paid for them, partly because I had to do them out of complaisance and courtesy. But now I am going to work continuously at the portrait for the Grand Duke. By the 8 February he has to have it in the room. When this is finished* I must *attend the Academy and work diligently under the direction of the new director, Cornelius, if I am in time to have good references, and how necessary these are for Karlsruhe! For academic study is what really matters, and if in time I should wish for favour from the court, or an appointment, they would look for an* academic education. *So now we have to sit down and work like schoolboys beside a crowd of others. We now have one hour's lecture on anatomy every afternoon from three o'clock till four. We often have to tear ourselves away violently from our lithography, for although we are earning money, the actual* learning *is not making progress. When my drawing is finished, for the Grand Duke, I will* quite definitely *paint both portraits.'*[10]

Predictably, Fidel Winterhalter took a keen interest in the subject of the stipend. 'There is nothing undignified in asking the receipt of a stipend', he wrote to his son who had expressed doubts; 'firstly was it not agreed from the first that you might expect one and secondly have you not earned it by your hard work?' In December 1825, while on a visit to Karlsruhe in connection with his land, Fidel endeavoured to thank the Grand Duke in person, but the crowd was too large 'for me to broach my business'. In May 1826, he was writing to let his son know he might expect an extension if he was 'tactful', and in the following spring he advised him to go with Eichtal to Karlsruhe to solicit a renewal of the

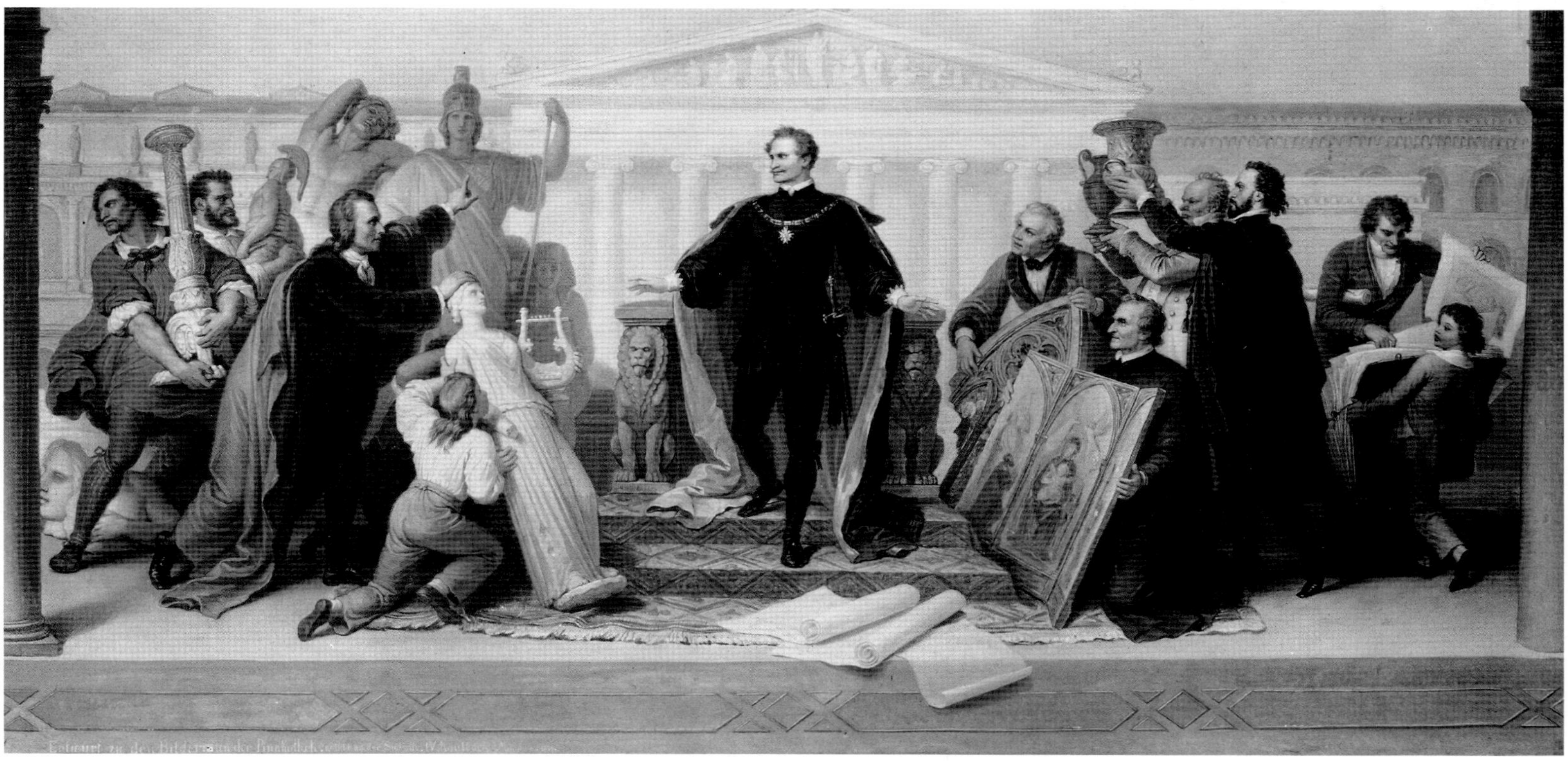

Figure 8
W. von Kaulbach: *Ludwig I*, 1848
78.5 × 163 cms
Neue Pinakothek, Munich

stipend which he would need for the expenses of a journey to Italy. By February 1828, Fidel was still urging him to visit the city in person with his drawings and portraits: 'Herr Lieber says that on St. John's Day [24 June] the *Landtag* [Parliament] will be opened, which will be especially convenient, for in Karlsruhe no more passionate lover of the arts exists than Director Palmenburg, a brother of the Munich ambassador.'[11]

Winterhalter does not appear to have visited Italy at this time, but he did travel in Germany to look at works of art. In a letter to his father in 1827, he describes a two month trip he had taken to Landshut, Nuremburg, Ravensburg, Bamburg and finally to Pommersfelder, the famous Rococo palace of the Prince Bishop. 'By God! An artist needs to see other men's work if he would himself create', he wrote sententiously. In the same letter, he went on to describe his friends and activities in Munich.[12] There was a breach with Heinrich Frank, who had gone off to Leipzig and later to Rome. His place had been taken by Anton Graeffle (1807–89), a Freiburg painter who was to become one of Winterhalter's assistants and a lifelong friend. Other companions of this period included the well-known genre painter Johann Baptist Kirner (1806–66), the sculptor Ludwig von Schwanthaler (1802–48), and Karl Schüler, the son of his old teacher in Freiburg. The common link was invariably Herder, a connection which Winterhalter still found claustrophobic: 'We have here Res, August Treschor, Gerspacher', he wrote in this same letter of 1827, 'and soon doubtless the whole blessed [Herder] crowd will come and this will speed our departure [to Italy] as we don't wish to revive more bitter memories than we can help.'[13]

In the summer of 1828, Winterhalter visited Karlsruhe and began to cement his relations at court. He had already received patronage from the Grand Duke, Ludwig, but it was to the latter's half-brother, Prince Leopold, and his beautiful wife, Sophie, that the artist now owed his advancement.

Karlsruhe was a political and cultural backwater, and the spirited Sophie must have found the presence of a talented young artist a distraction from the stifling provincialism of court life. Early in May 1829, she was writing warmly to him:

> *'I have completed only the drawing which you helped me begin, and I have done a few more sketches from memory. Part of the trouble was that my eyes pained me, which naturally persuaded me to spare them, and then time was often too short, which has prevented me from thanking you earlier in the last few days. However you need not fear that I shall give up drawing, for as soon as I have a free moment, I at once sit down at my drawing table, which is always there ready to receive me. This week I intend to begin copying your beautiful drawing. If, as you write, you can perhaps find a few other things which are not too difficult for my small talent, I should be very pleased if you would be so good as to send me them. Please accept once more my hearty thanks and the assurance of my special esteem.'*[14]

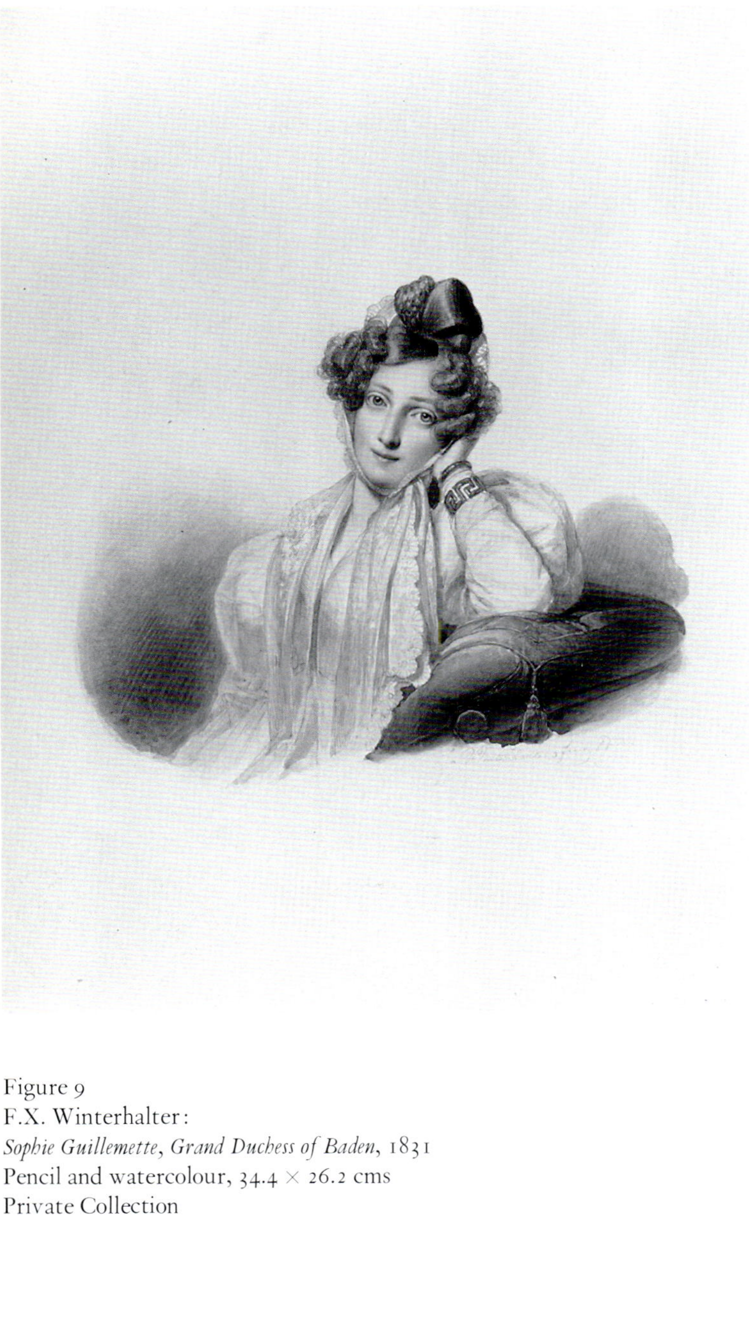

Figure 9
F.X. Winterhalter:
*Sophie Guillemette, Grand Duchess of Baden*, 1831
Pencil and watercolour, 34.4 × 26.2 cms
Private Collection

Leopold succeeded his brother on 30 March 1830. Trained as a soldier, and unexpectedly succeeding as Grand Duke of Baden through a succession of early deaths in the family, Leopold proved a competent ruler during a period of upheaval and change. His wife, Sophie, daughter of Gustav IV of Sweden, was cultivated, intelligent and beautiful and she exercised a benign influence over her husband. It was no doubt at her instigation that Winterhalter was employed on Royal commissions, an early instance of his adroitness in cultivating the feminine interest at court.

Winterhalter's only life-size commission was the 1831 state portrait of Leopold in military uniform (no. 3). A conventional exercise in the style of the French portraitist, Baron Gérard, it reveals the artist's lack of experience on the scale of life. Much more successful were the small cabinet-sized portraits he painted of the Grand Duke and his family.

A companion pair of small threequarter-lengths of Leopold and Sophie date from 1831 (see nos. 95, 96), he in military frock-coat beside a table of documents, she in fur tippet seated by a balustrade before a stormy sky. To the same period belong portraits of Leopold's brother, Prince Wilhelm and his wife, Princess Elizabeth, and a pretty composition of Leopold's three children. There are several drawings and watercolours of Sophie (fig. 9), her children and her brothers-in-law, Wilhelm and Maximillian. Many of these served as the source of prints as Winterhalter capitalized on his skills as a lithographer to earn extra income. Of all his Baden commissions, it is his two Romantic representations of Sophie *à la campagne* (for one, see no. 4) which are beautiful and touching. In these exquisite works he imparted a sense of her beauty, tinged with melancholy, in a style reminiscent of the Austrian Biedermeier painter, Ferdinand Waldmüller (1793–1865).[15]

Winterhalter came to Karlsruhe each year for a specified period (fig. 10), but his base was Munich. 'We are still living at the old jogtrot', he told his parents in a letter of 16 January 1830, 'and perhaps that is best. We both keep painting portraits but otherwise nothing else . . . . I expect I shall be coming to Karlsruhe in three months' time, but I am not yet certain. I still have to write and ask if I may come'.[16] Evidently he did come to Karlsruhe that year, for a portrait of Eichtal's son-in-law, Karl Josef Berckmüller (1800–79), is dated 1830 (no. 1). This Romantic characterization is rooted in the tradition of French portraiture, with its strong modelling, simple lucid shapes and tight surface. To the same year belongs his sensitive study of Luise Fries (Kurpfälzisches Museum, Heidelberg), sister of the landscapist Ernst Fries, painted in Munich. Another portrait in the same vein is that of the writer, Karl Spindler (no. 2). More typical of Winterhalter's commissioned works are the companion half-lengths of Franz von Steiger of Baldenburg and Thal, Royal Bavarian Court of Appeal Councillor in Meiningen, and his wife (Private Collection).

On his visits to Karlsruhe in the 1830s, Winterhalter lodged at the house of the court physician, Dr J. Albert Wich, at no. 8 Innerer Zirkel. Dr Wich and his family were

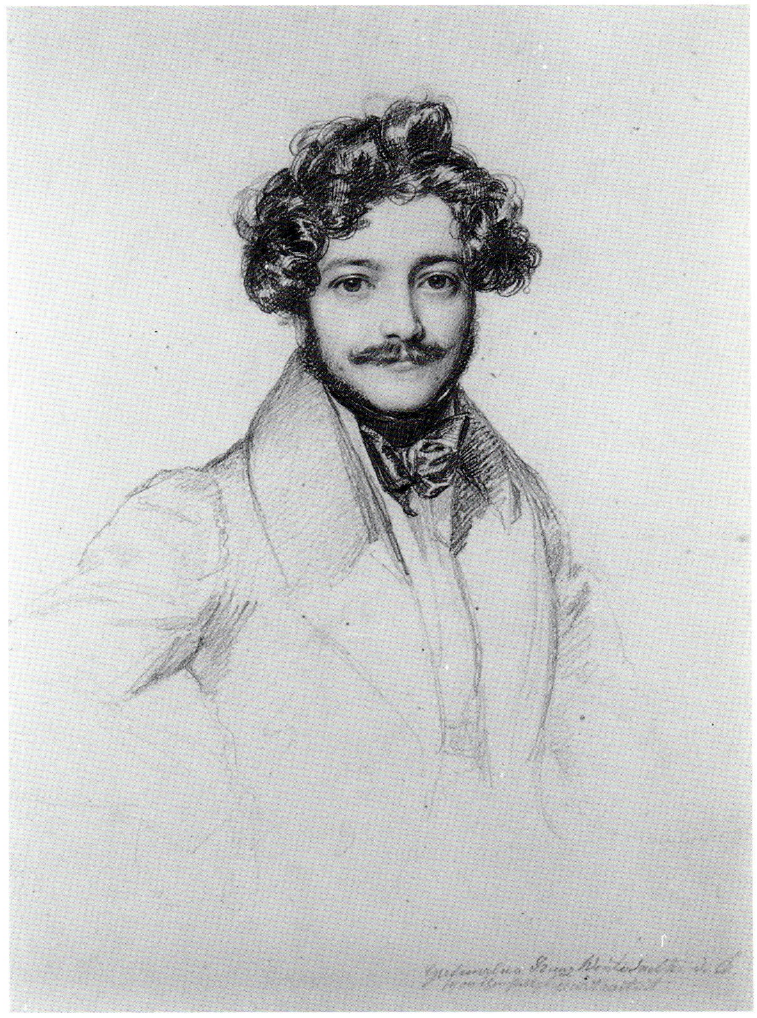

Figure 10
F.X. Winterhalter: *Self-portrait*, *c.*1831
Pencil drawing
Private Collection

the subject of a charming group of watercolours and drawings (nos. 86, 87), which demonstrate the precision and vitality of Winterhalter's draughtsmanship at this period. He had been trained as a graphic artist long before he was a painter, and these delicate studies have a fluency and directness often lacking in the early oils. If the finished watercolours are sometimes overworked, the pencil studies have a springiness of outline combined with fine cross-hatching that anticipates a freer style of painting. In 1832, Winterhalter painted the Grand Duke's mistress, Katharina Werner, recently married to the Count of Langenstein. Two years later, he visited the romantic Schloss Langenstein, which he recorded in a dashing watercolour (no. 85), and where he painted the Countess's young son (no. 8).

Late in 1832, Winterhalter set out on his long postponed visit to Italy, in part funded by Grand Duke Leopold, arriving in Rome early in 1833. No serious German artist could consider his education complete without a visit to Rome, the centre of a large, polyglot community of artists. Winterhalter had a number of friends in Rome, including the portrait painter Eduard Magnus (1799–1872), and the genre painters, August Heinrich Riedel (1799–1883) and Johann Baptist Kirner. A drawing by the architect, H.W. Schülz, dated 4 March 1833 (fig. 11), includes the painter among a group of convivial drinking companions. Winterhalter did not, however, share the fervent idealism or nationalism common to so many German artists in Rome. In matters of taste he leaned, by instinct, towards Horace Vernet (1789–1863) and the French Academy, rather than to Johann Friedrich Overbeck (1789–1869) and the Nazarene sphere, earning the nickname of 'der Französische' among his contemporaries. His introduction to Vernet came from Count Jenison (fig. 12), the Bavarian ambassador in Paris, whose portrait he painted in 1837 (Neue Pinakothek, Munich). Vernet kept open house at the Villa Medici, and the young German assiduously cultivated his friendship.

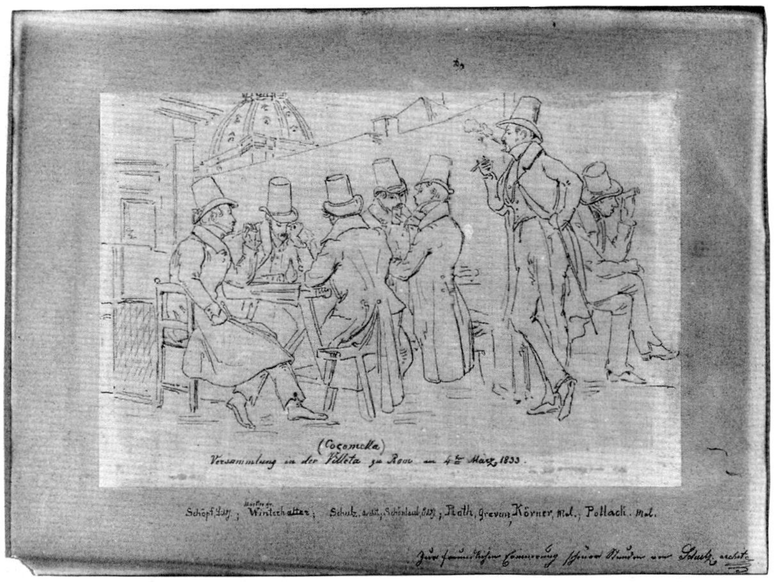

Figure 11
H.W. Schülz: *Artists at the Valetta, Rome*, 1833
(Winterhalter is second from left)
Drawing, 15.5 × 10.5 cms
Private Collection

There is no doubt of the liberating effect which Italy had on Winterhalter's imagination. In his only surviving letter from Rome, written from the Caffè Greco, on 12 March 1833, he wrote of his delight in the country: 'I will be glad all my life that I came here.'[17] His pencil was never still; a surviving sketch-book (Winterhalter Family Collection) includes copies from the Old Masters, figure studies, landscapes (fig. 13), and ideas for compositions. Six of his drawings after Michelangelo's figures of prophets and sybils in the Sistine Chapel were later lithographed by Josef Anton Selb and published in a portfolio by Anton Werder in Munich. Freed for the first time from the pressures of lithographic work and portrait commissions, he raised his sights to academic composition and embraced new subject matter.

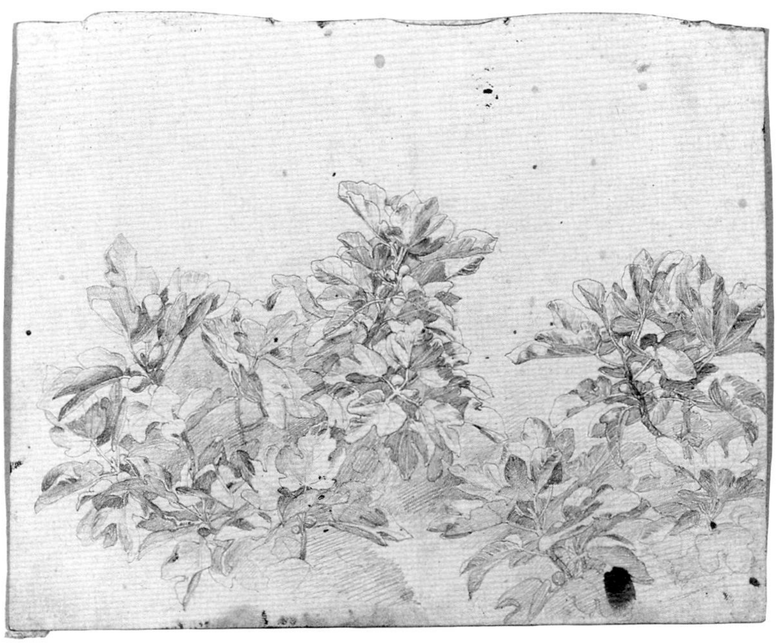

Figure 13
F.X. Winterhalter: *Study of fig branches*, *c.*1833
Drawing, 24 × 19 cms, Private Collection

The apparently simple, sensual, uncomplicated lives of the Italian peasants of the south, resplendent in native costume, provided excellent copy for Romantic, Northern painters in love with the Mediterranean. It was easy to overlook the poverty they endured, and the eccentric,

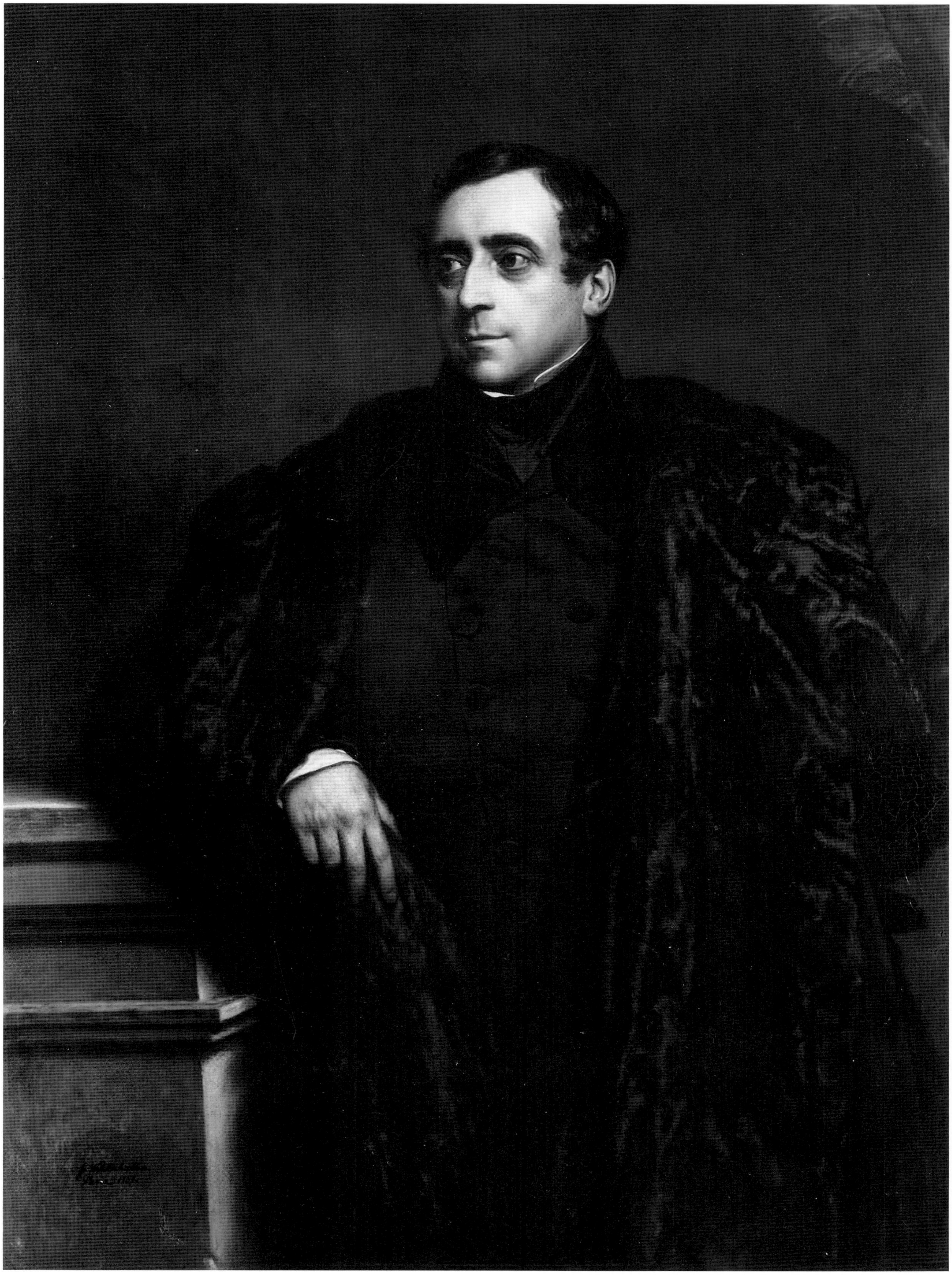

Figure 12
F.X. Winterhalter: *Franz Oliver, Graf von Jenison-Walworth*, 1837,
131 × 98 cms, Neue Pinakothek, Munich

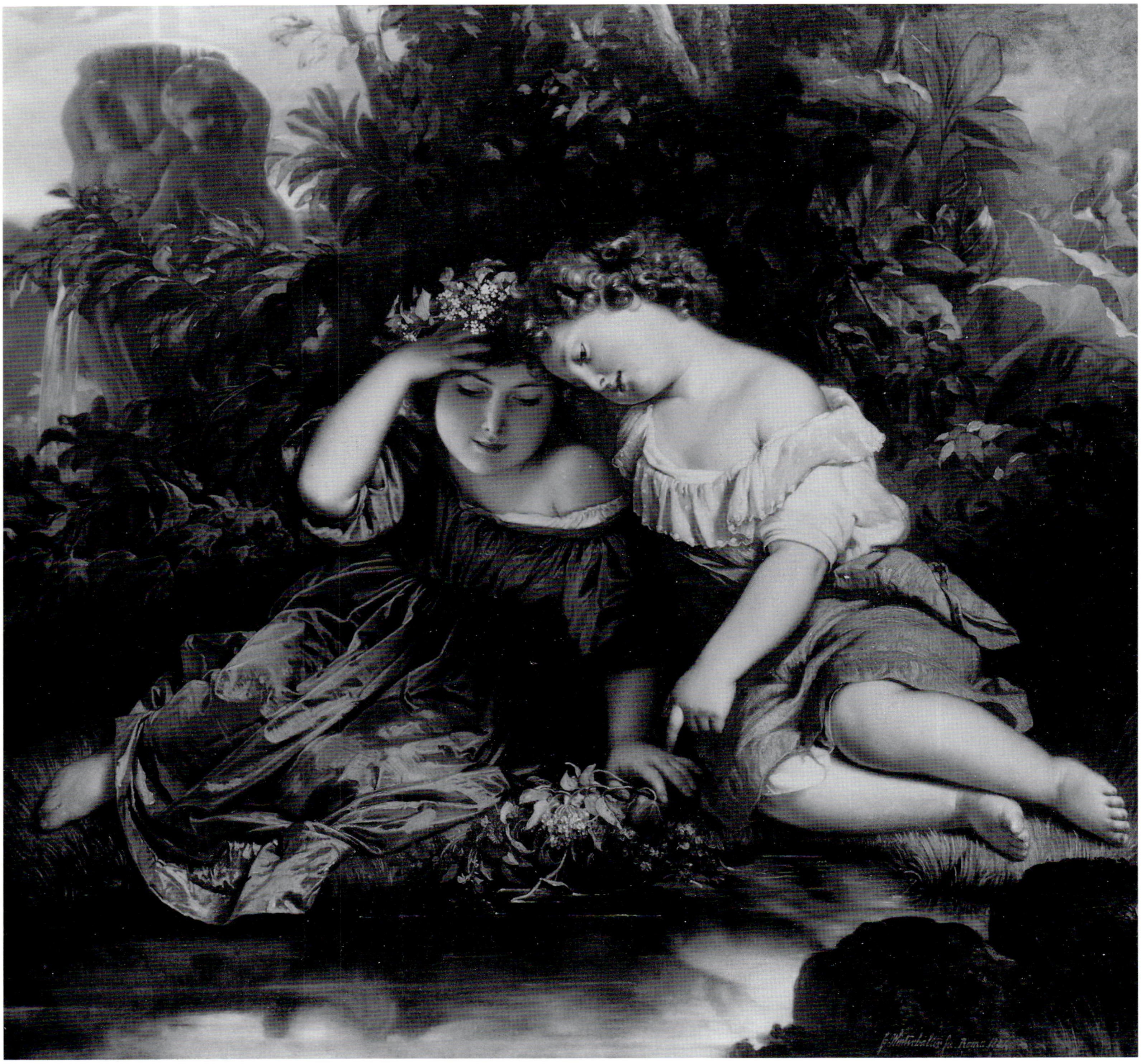

Figure 14
F.X. Winterhalter: called *Princess Colonna seen by a Garden Pool*, 1834, 99 × 108.5 cms approx., location unknown

oppressive rule of the Neapolitan Court, in the search for the picturesque. Numbers of German painters, and those of other nationalities, devoted themselves to this popular and profitable genre, among them Winterhalter's friends, Riedel and Kirner. Winterhalter threw himself into this enchanted world with enthusiasm, developing a new richness of palette, a new fluency of technique and subtle effects of lighting. The *Roman Genre Scene* (no. 5) is inscribed 'Rome 1833', but the distant view of the sea is surely the Bay of Naples. The theme of the picture is Spring, youth, music and beauty.

The pose of the young girl by the well, in another picture of this date (no. 6) is consciously statuesque, though the effect is softened by the underlighting on the face, and the beautifully rendered textures of the costume. The view beyond is again the Bay of Naples. Classical illusion is played up more obviously in the picture of two children watching their reflections in the pool by which they sit (fig. 14). A Classical vase in the background, with sculpted *putti*, suggests an antique analogy to the children in the foreground, themselves arranged like a frieze. The picture is dated 'Rome 1834', and one of the children is said to be the future Princess Colonna.[18]

Winterhalter left Rome early in 1834, returning to Karlsruhe not only with saleable pictures but with plans for several large-scale pictures in his mind. Events in his life moved rapidly. In August 1834, he was appointed court painter to the Grand Duke, no doubt as a result of his Italian trip. Portraits of Ludwig, Count of Langenstein (no. 8), of his old patron, Baron Eichtal, and others dating from 1834, suggest that he was fully employed at court.

Then suddenly, in December, Winterhalter packed his bags and departed for Paris, settling at no. 17 rue des Petits Augustins, an area in which he would reside for the next thirty-six years. He had made his decisive move, not within Germany, but to the capital of a foreign country. We can only guess at the reasons for this dramatic transformation. Even with the support of patrons, the chances of success for a foreign painter, in a city not short of native talent, were decidedly risky. Instinct must have told Winterhalter that his sympathies lay overwhelmingly with French painting, and that the prospects of patronage for a court painter were much greater in this cosmopolitan centre than in any of the German capitals. Paris would be his testing-ground.

Within months of arrival, Winterhalter had sent his first contribution to the Salon, a portrait of an unidentified woman. During 1835, he was devoting his energies to a more substantial contribution. *Il Dolce Farniente* (no. 9), a dreamy siesta scene set in Naples and staffed by an unusually large cast of handsome girls and beautiful young men, was a full-scale academic composition, dressed up as a genre scene. The source of the picture is not to be found in the peasant scenes of Riedel and Kirner, but in Raphael and his nineteenth-century interpreters (fig. 15). The harmonious disposition of the figures on two levels, the studied poses, and the mood of dreamy reverie, were inspired by Raphael's

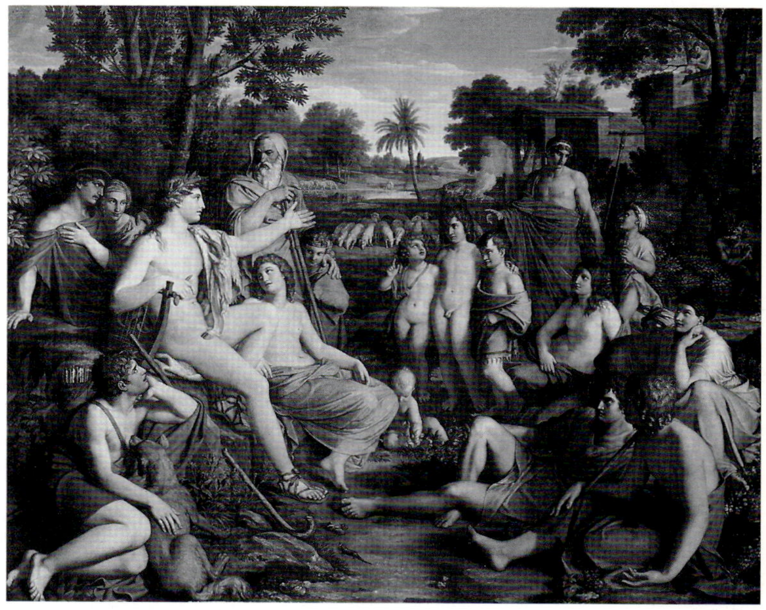

Figure 15
G.C. Schick: *Apollo and the Shepherds*, 1806–8
178.5 × 232 cms
Staatsgalerie, Stuttgart

*Parnassus*. Winterhalter was creating a Golden Age in modern dress, with exotic Italian props, and here lay the secret of its success. When the Salon of 1836 opened, *Il Dolce Farniente* scored an immediate success; it was widely noticed in the press and it established its author as an up-and-coming man.

Winterhalter painted a number of other Italian genre scenes at this period, later issued as a series of successful lithographs by F. Girard, which helped to introduce his work to a wider audience. At the 1837 Salon, he followed up his earlier success with *The Decameron*, a picture of Boccaccio's circle of storytellers (fig. 16). The recipe was the same as before, a tightly controlled academic composition in the style of Raphael, this time in a picturesque historical setting. Once again he scored a success. Some critics complained of his facile approach to history, his fashion-

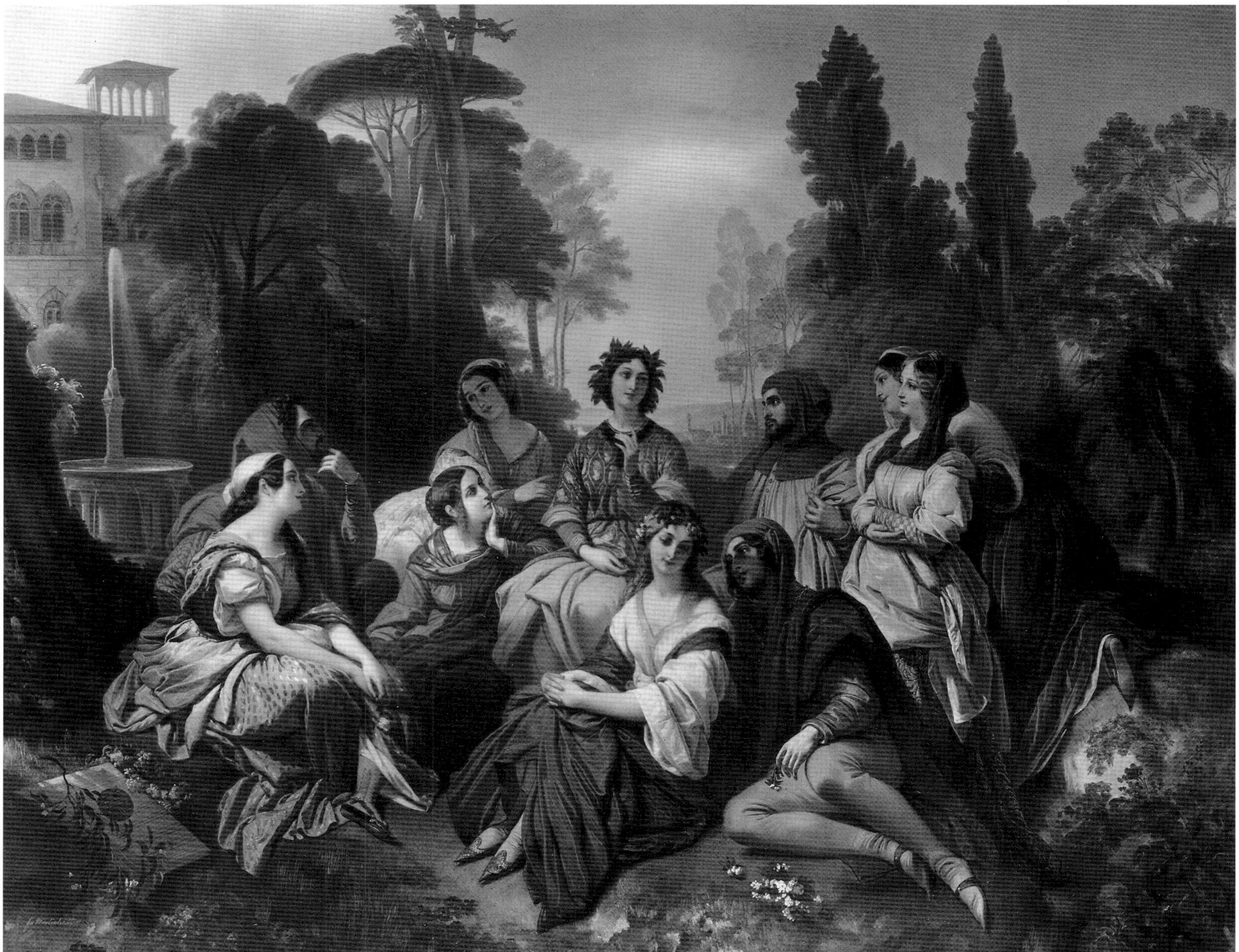

Figure 16
F.X. Winterhalter: *The Decameron*, reduced version, *c*.1837, 81.5 × 116 cms, Staatliche Kunsthalle Karlsruhe

plate models and the pasteboard setting, but the picture went down well with the public. It was decorative and colourful and, as Théophile Gautier perceptively noted some years later, it formed a welcome contrast to the violent productions of the Romantic School.[19] The picture was sold for 10,000 francs to a wealthy wool merchant and philanthropist, the Deputé Paturle, a fact sufficiently well publicized to reach the ears of Baron Eichtal, who relayed it at once to Menzenschwand.

Winterhalter showed a second Italian genre scene at the Salon of 1837, as well as two portraits. One of these, a woman in white, is certainly the portrait called *Madame Delong* and dated 1837, which appeared on the art market in 1972 (fig. 17). The style is altogether weightier than Winterhalter's earlier German portraits. The heavily-draped figure, leaning her head on her hand in a pose of melancholy, fills the picture space with her smooth and sonorous forms. The head-on-hand recurs in the portrait of Princess Leonilla Sayn-Wittgenstein-Sayn (no. 26), another self-conscious essay in Classical design. A comparable male portrait of this period is that of Count Jenison (see fig. 12, p. 26).

Winterhalter owed his reputation as the 'darling' of the Salon to his subject pictures. The time now came to show the other side of his talent. His major contribution to the Salon of 1838 was a portrait of the Prince de Wagram with his young daughter (no. 10), one of a pair of whole-lengths of the Prince and his wife. In the same year, he painted Louise-Marie, Queen of the Belgians, and her son; portraits of her husband, King Leopold I, followed later, with a state portrait in 1840 (no. 14). Louise-Marie was the daughter of the French King Louis-Philippe, and it was probably through this connection that Winterhalter came to the notice of the French Court.

Winterhalter had arrived on the Paris scene at a fortunate moment. Following the Revolution of 1830, Louis-Philippe revealed a reverence for the past achievements of his country which he hoped to emulate. At Versailles, he had established a national pantheon, transforming part of the palace into a museum, and filling it with pictures of personalities and events famous in French history. It was within this framework of historiography that he decided to commission a series of full-length portraits of himself and his family. He was an unusually proud father, and his sons were encouraged to play a prominent part in public and military affairs. The idea of a set of portraits, a dynastic portrait gallery which would satisfy the demands of official imagery, naturally appealed to the King.

It is difficult to know the reasons which lay behind the choice of Winterhalter. According to one legend, it was the Queen who decided to give the young artist a chance and commissioned a portrait of herself, the success of which made his reputation. The portrait of the Queen, however, was painted three years after that of the King, and there is no evidence to show that she had any interest in the artist. It was the King himself, with his strong dynastic sense, who

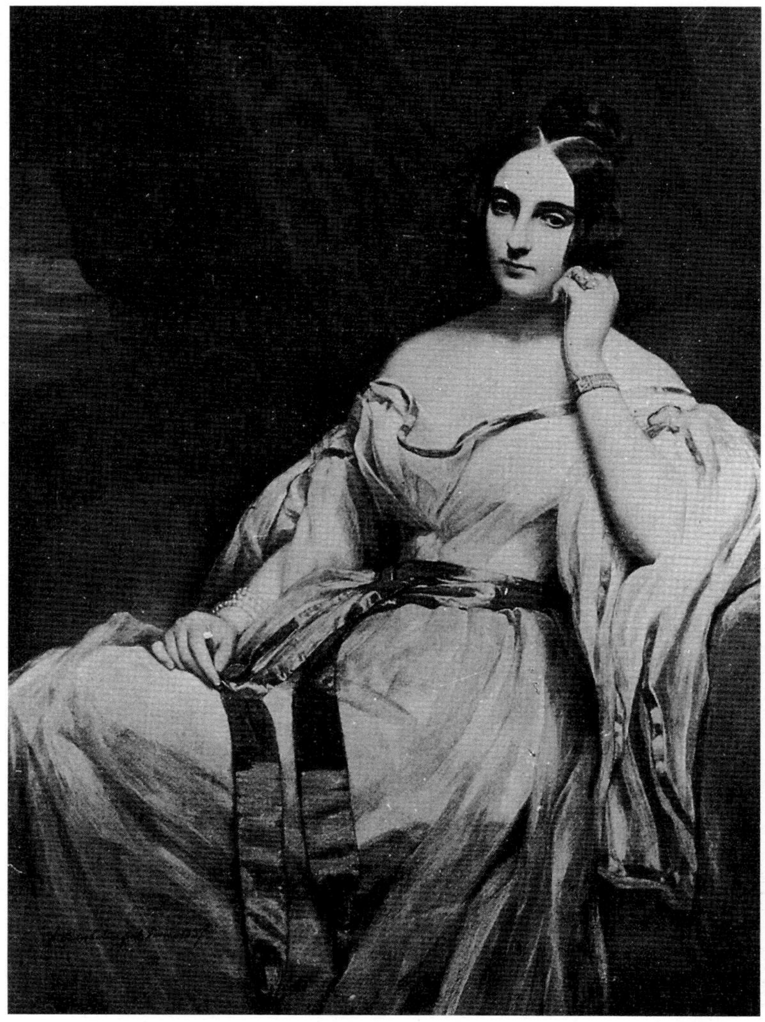

Figure 17
F.X. Winterhalter: *Madame Delong*, 1837
130 × 97.5 cms
Private Collection

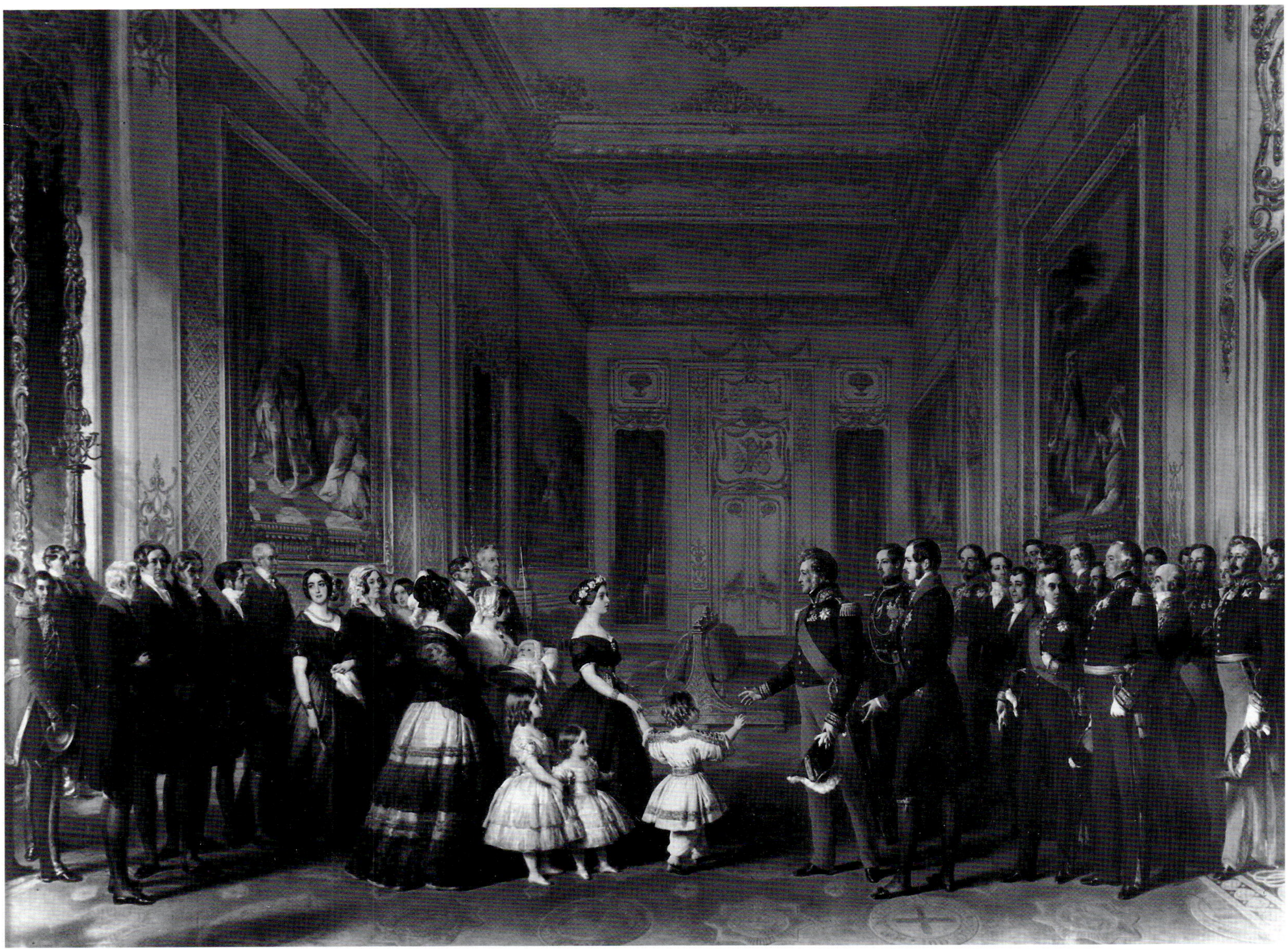

Figure 18
F.X. Winterhalter: *The Reception of King Louis-Philippe at Windsor Castle*, 1844
345 × 480 cms
Musée national du château de Versailles

must have taken the lead in selecting his court portraitist. The field was not a wide one. The older generation of portraitists was dead; J. L. David in 1825; Baron Gros in 1835; François Gérard in 1837. Of the big names in French art at the time, few were interested in undertaking official portrait commissions. Winterhalter's chief rivals were men of second rank, Amaury-Duval (1808–85), Louis Boulanger (1806–67), Auguste Charpentier (1813–80) and Claude-Marie Dubufe (1790–1864). For a foreigner to take the prize after only four years in Paris is a tribute to the court's nose for talent, and evidence of the influence which the artist could call on to support his case.

Winterhalter executed more than thirty commissions for Louis-Philippe. The state portraits of the King and Queen (nos. 17, 19, 1839 and 1842 respectively) were copied many times for préfectures, mairies and embassies, reproduced on Sèvres porcelain and popularized as prints. They became the accepted images of the Royal couple, and Winterhalter the established painter at court.

A set of whole-lengths of the King's sons and daughters, as well as their spouses and children, was painted over the course of the next six years, and this was supplemented by portraits of other Royal personages, among them the King's sister, Madame Adélaïde, and the Duchess of Kent. Apart from a few items in Château d'Eu, the country residence of the King in Normandy, Winterhalter's portraits were hung in the Royal apartments at Versailles. There is almost no trace, in Winterhalter's work for the French Court, of the informal canvases of family life, and his swift *ad vivum* sketches – so popular with Queen Victoria and Prince Albert. His employment was restricted to formal portraiture.

Winterhalter's largest commission came in 1844, when he was asked to record the King's reception at Windsor Castle on the occasion of his state visit to England (fig. 18). A smaller group portrait of the two Royal families in the small cabinet-room at Château d'Eu, the Salle Victoria (no. 24), followed in 1845. The King was painted again in 1845 at the request of Queen Victoria for a portrait in court dress (fig. 19). The artist's one Royal commission for a picture other than a portrait, was an historical representation of a scene of French history, Eléanore de Guyenne taking the vow. This work was never finished (if it was ever begun), and the sum of 2,400 francs allocated for it was withdrawn. For the thirty pictures or so listed as painted for the King in his accounts (which are by no means comprehensive), Winterhalter received over 70,000 francs (approximately £3,500). When the sum raised through the mass-production of copies is taken into account (800 francs apiece), as well as the copyright in prints, it is clear that Winterhalter was not only successful but also rich. The award of the Légion d'Honneur in 1839 put the stamp of Royal approval on his achievement.

The first three Royal commissions, those of the King (no. 17), his daughter-in-law, the Duchesse d'Orléans with the infant Comte de Paris (no. 18), and his daughter, Princesse Clémentine, set the tone for those to follow. The King, in the

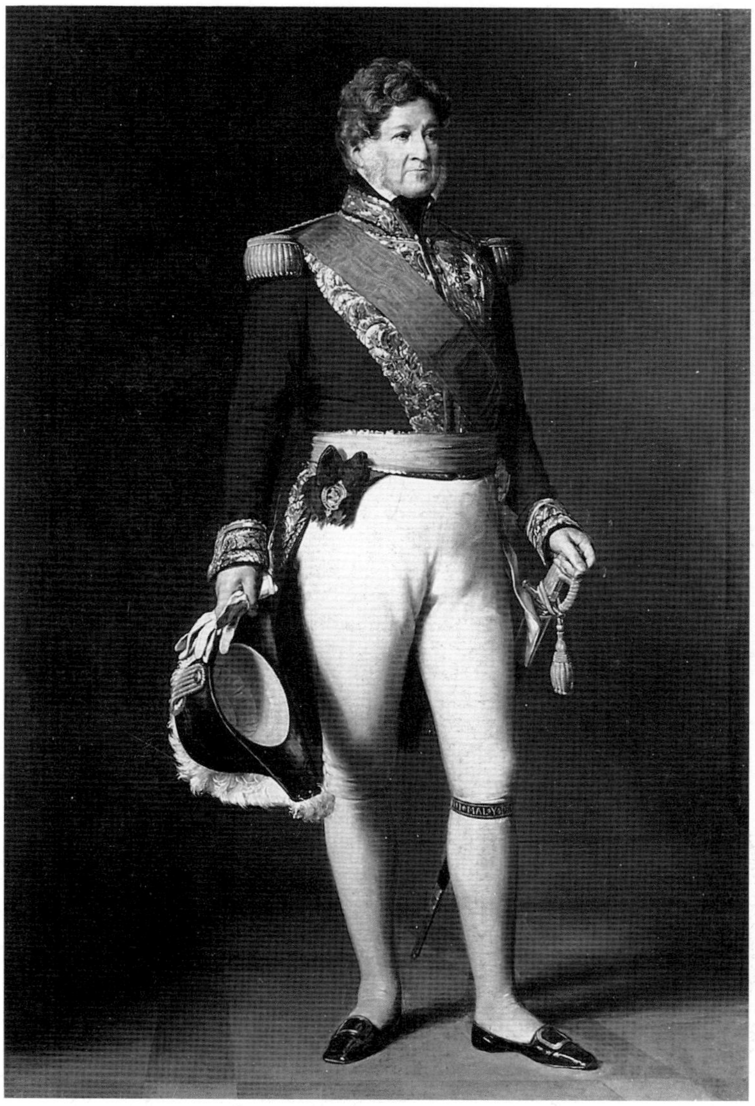

Figure 19
F.X. Winterhalter: *King Louis-Philippe*, 1845
218 × 150 cms
Musée national du château de Versailles

uniform of Lieutenant-General of the Kingdom, rests his hand on the charter of 1830. A lush floral carpet and heavy damask curtains complete the furnishings of a room whose back wall is a view of the terrace at St Cloud, seen grandly from on high. No effort is made to harmonize the Palace interior and the idealized landscape. One is abruptly set against the other. What holds the two together is the solidly four-square representation of the King himself. Winterhalter's contribution to the Renaissance-inspired language of Royal portraiture was to apply the gloss of realism.

For the King, he chose a sober uniform of blue and grey; for the Duchesse d'Orléans, a froth of creamy satin, muslin and lace. Feminine allure in the Duchesse's picture is contrasted with the masculine power of command in that of the King. The portrait of Princesse Clémentine shows the sitter in white, posed this time entirely out of doors beside a terrace and urn of flowers. Once established, the formula was easily repeated. One after another, the great ladies of the court posed for Winterhalter in bell-shaped dresses silhouetted against a landscape of park and sky (fig. 20). Flesh is enamelled, costumes are smooth and unyielding, accessories bear an assertive gleam. It is brilliant, efficient painting, but without much charm. The old fare better; the Queen posed indoors with quiet dignity (no. 19), and the King's sister, Madame Adélaïde, a characterful old soul, in bonnet and shawl (Versailles).

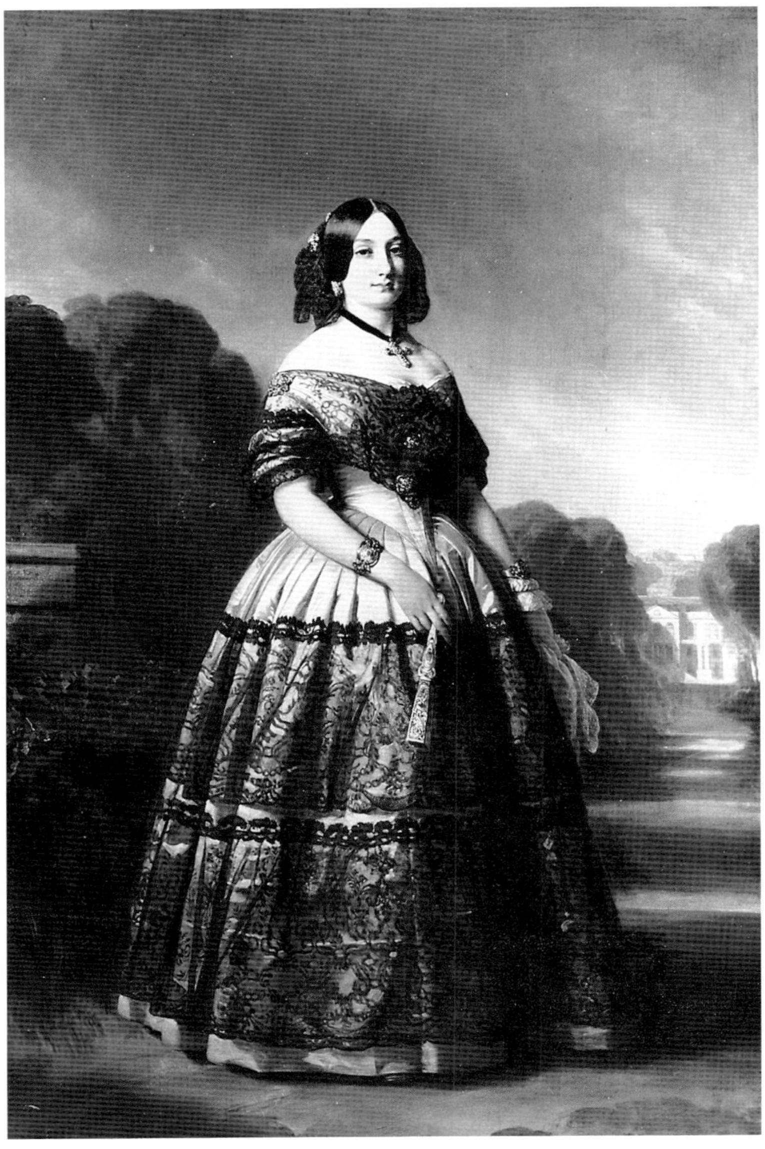

Figure 20
F.X. Winterhalter:
*Dona Marie-Louise-Ferdinande de Bourbon, Duchesse de Montpensier*, c.1847
215 × 136 cms
Musée national du château de Versailles

A rare glimpse of the artist at work is provided by Jules Janin in an account published in 1844. Winterhalter and the medallist, Jean Auguste Barré (1811–96) were invited to Neuilly to portray the beautiful young Duchesse de Nemours. While the medallist slowly traced her profile in wax, the painter 'throws upon the canvas the charming head; he proceeds like a man who improvises with wonderful readiness . . . "Madam" said he "Your Royal Highness is released from me; I have finished". "But it is impossible" cried Barré. "Look then" replied Winterhalter. And in fact there was the faithful likeness of the Duchesse de Nemours . . . "That I may not trouble Your Royal Highness", said Winterhalter, "I will take away the portrait, I will paint the dress at home"'.[20]

For the King's sons, Winterhalter chose the theme of military prowess, leaning heavily on the repertoire of images invented by Sir Thomas Lawrence for his set of Allied Commanders in the Waterloo Chamber at Windsor Castle. The Duc de Nemours (no. 21) commands the field in a stormy landscape, four-fifths sky. Winterhalter's powers of characterization, never very considerable, were incapable of transforming his well-groomed sitters into heroes. The most sympathetic of the Dukes is unquestionably Orléans, seen before a panorama of Paris (fig. 21). He is sensitive and self-questioning, by contrast with the facile elegance of his brothers. Winterhalter's portrait is close in mood to Ingres' memorable characterization of the Duc (fig. 22), and both were painted in the year of his death, 1842. Winterhalter's most convincing military portrait of this period was *Maréchal*

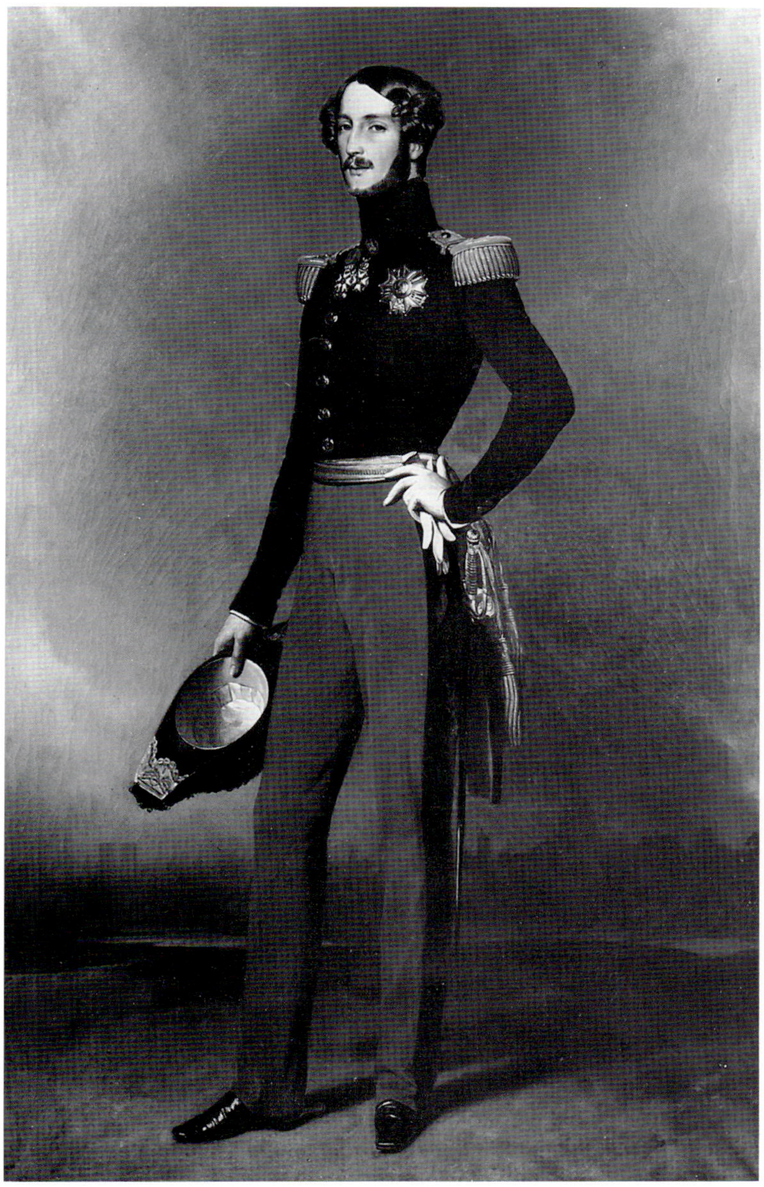

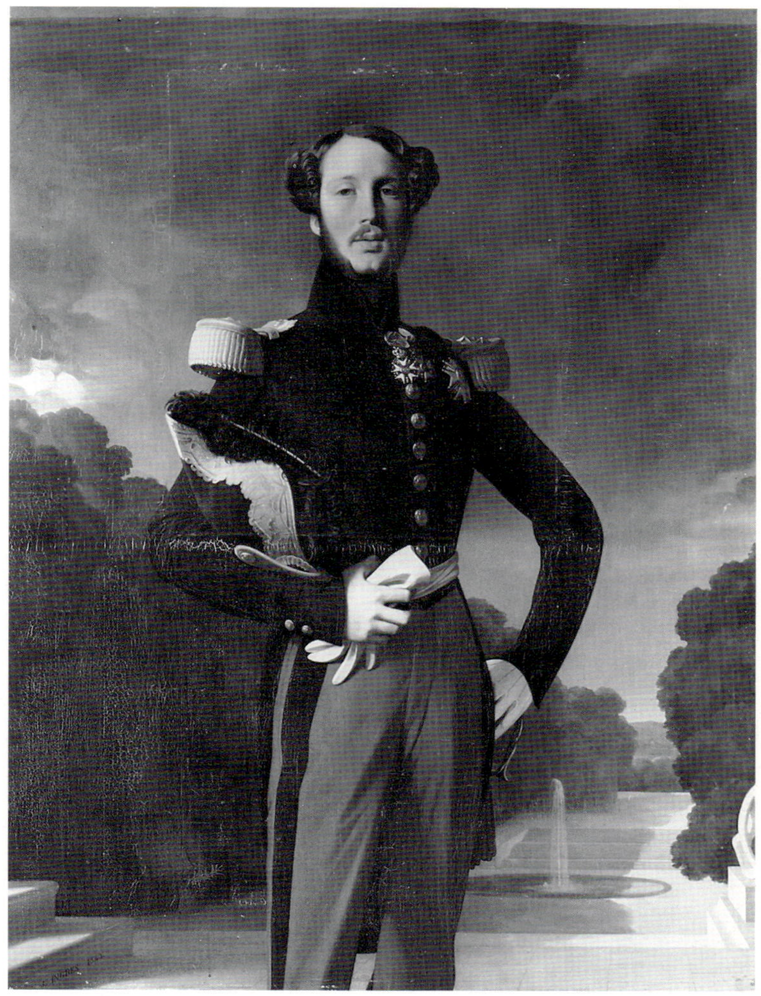

Figure 22
J.A.D. Ingres:
*Ferdinand-Philippe-Henri, Duc d'Orléans*, 1842
156 × 120 cms
Musée national du château de Versailles

Figure 21
F.X. Winterhalter:
*Ferdinand-Philippe-Henri, Duc d'Orléans*, 1842
218 × 140 cms
Musée national du château de Versailles

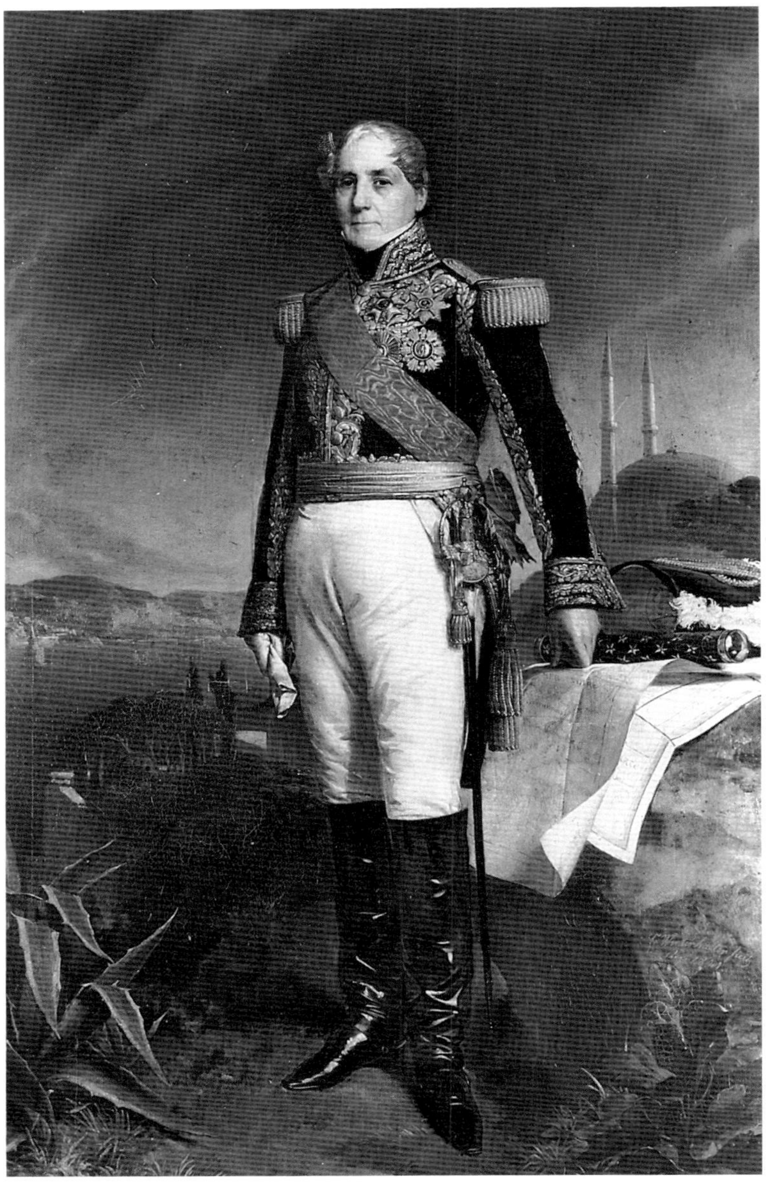

Figure 23
F.X. Winterhalter:
*François-Horace, Comte Sébastiani, Maréchal de France*, 1841
215 × 139 cms
Musée national du château de Versailles

*Sébastiani* (fig. 23), commissioned for the Salle des Maréchaux at the Tuileries. There is a quiet authority to this Napoleonic veteran, an outstanding administrator and Minister for Foreign Affairs, standing before a view of Constantinople, where he served as ambassador.

Royal patronage established Winterhalter's reputation, but cut him off from his artistic roots. The critics, who had loudly hailed the appearance of *Il Dolce Farniente* and *The Decameron*, condemned the artist two years later as a Royal 'toady'. He had abandoned his passport as a painter and could no longer be taken seriously. The attitude was to persist throughout the artist's career, condemning his work to a category of its own in the hierarchy of painting. Arthur Stevens reviewed Winterhalter at the Salon of 1863: 'Everything has been said about this artist's talent. His colleagues lost interest in him long ago. For them, he no longer exists but he has retained his noble clientele. He specialises in painting the queens and princesses of the whole world; every august head appears to require consecration by Winterhalter's brush.'[21]

Winterhalter himself regarded the first of his Royal commissions as a temporary intermission before he returned to the proper business of subject painting and the fold of academic respectability. He failed to reckon the price of success. Once started, nothing would stem the demand; it spread out from Paris to embrace the rest of Europe. The move from Germany to France had been one kind of exile, the treadmill of court portraiture was a longer and more profound exile.

From 1839 onwards, Winterhalter painted an average of three to four formal portraits each year for Louis-Philippe. They included not only the King's children, but his grandchildren as well; the Comte d'Eu, son of the Duc de Nemours (no. 23); Princess Charlotte, Leopold's daughter (no. 15); and the infant Prince of Württemburg (Versailles). They were among the first in a long line of Royal children to be portrayed with a sympathy and charm not seen since Van Dyck. The sequence of Royal commissions culminated with his huge picture celebrating the King's reception at Windsor Castle during the state visit of 1844 (see fig. 18, p. 32). In essence a processional picture, it is static and strangely airless. The setting is the Grand Reception Room at Windsor, a chamber designed by Sir Jeffrey Wyatville for George IV, and decorated with six Gobelins tapestries representing the story of Jason and the Golden Fleece. Queen Victoria thought the group 'successful in parts'. She commissioned a copy of the whole on a reduced scale, as well as a separate picture of herself and her children from it, and another of Sir Robert Peel standing beside the Duke of Wellington (no. 30) whose likenesses she considered 'so good'.[22] (All Royal Collection.) A second group of the two Royal families squeezed into the Galerie Victoria at the Château d'Eu on the return state visit of 1845 was a sequel to the first, but painted on a more intimate scale (no. 24).

Louise-Marie, Queen of the Belgians, had first introduced Winterhalter to her father, Louis-Philippe. She was also responsible for arranging his first visit to the English Court, describing him to Queen Victoria in a letter of 16 May 1842 as 'an excellent man full of zeal for his art, of goodwill, obligingness and real modesty' (WRA Y/977/78). Between 1842 and 1871, Winterhalter painted more than a hundred works in oil for Queen Victoria and Prince Albert, including four pairs of state portraits, the great family piece, sequences of their children at various ages and in various guises, infants, highlanders, and débutantes, portraits of the ever-growing army of relatives that meant so much to the Queen, and quantities of delightful, informal sketches.

He came to England every summer or autumn for a stay of six to seven weeks, sometimes longer, in the early years when commissions were plentiful, and painted at Buckingham Palace and Windsor Castle, but rarely elsewhere in England. He made few contacts socially or professionally outside the Royal circle, and exhibited only a token number of pictures at the Royal Academy. He understood English but spoke it brokenly, joining a small and select group of German retainers at court.

The nature of Winterhalter's appeal to the British Royal family is not difficult to explain. His portraits were elegant, refined, lifelike and pleasingly idealized. He invested the traditional imagery of monarchy with romance and a fresh brand of naturalism. He captured the spirit of kindness and idealism which inspired the Royal couple as parents and rulers. The Queen, whose chief concern was that portraits should be like, was easily satisfied. The more knowledgeable Prince Albert, however, responded to the academic and technical virtuosity of his compatriot.

Local talent was unable to compete with the suave, cosmopolitan style of the newcomer. Queen Victoria had little time for the older generation of painters favoured by her uncle, William IV. She considered the portraits of herself by Sir David Wilkie (1785–1841) and Sir Martin Archer Shee (1769–1850) to be singularly unlike and turgidly old-fashioned.[23] Of the younger generation, Sir George Hayter (1792–1871) was her favourite. He first painted the Queen in 1833, long before her accession, and his coronation portrait of her was widely applauded. His star began to wane as his ambitious later ceremonial groups failed to find purchasers. From being early in 1838 'out and out the best portrait painter in any opinion',[24] he rapidly slumped in her estimation. Hayter was not a member of the Royal Academy, nor, interestingly enough, was another of the Queen's protégés, John Partridge (1790–1872). In choosing her own portraitists, it seems that she deliberately turned her back on the established Academy painters. Her eventual choice of a foreigner confirms her preference for outsiders. Partridge painted a dashing picture of Prince Albert in Hussar uniform, but the companion work of the Queen in evening dress, found less favour. Partridge, like Hayter, was out. The way was clear for Winterhalter.

With his first pair of threequarter-length portraits of Queen Victoria and Prince Albert (nos. 27, 28), Winterhalter struck exactly the right note. The Queen is dressed in a white ball-gown cut low at the shoulders, and she holds a spray of roses. The background of threatening sky, novel in its effect, underscores the tender mood of the picture. What pleased the Queen most was its likeness to herself, the beauty of its accessories and its fluent technique. The portraits by Hayter and Partridge looked stylized in comparison. Prince Albert's portrait was blander, an essay in military rhetoric like those of Louis-Philippe's sons, but it had the merit of making him look dashing and attractive.

Of Winterhalter's first experience at the English Court, there are two records. The first occurs in a letter from the artist to his parents, written on his return to Paris in November 1842:

> *'I returned from London last month, had a most satisfactory stay, enjoyed myself enormously. I painted the portraits of the Queen of England and her husband, the Prince Albert of Saxe-Coburg. And afterwards a picture of the little Princess, and that of Albert's sister-in-law, wife of the Heir Apparent of Saxe-Coburg, and daughter of our Grand Duke of Baden. Later again the Duke of Beaufort, which I will finish in Paris. I have promised to return to London next April to paint more portraits. Life in London is expensive, but I am better paid there than in Paris, so on the whole it is preferable. . . . My brother returned from Normandy a few weeks ago, he had a commission to paint a portrait there. . . . When you next see M. von Eichtal give him many greetings from both of us, and tell him that although we seldom write to him, we hope we will always be good friends, and will never forget him.'*[25]

The second is a contemporary account of the artist painting the Princess Royal in 1842:

> *'In a corner of the throne room whose windows, with one exception have been darkened, the arrangements for painting a picture "by command" are faithfully displayed. A portrait of the Princess Royal is in the act of being taken, and* Winterhalter *is the fortunate artist chosen for the occasion. In a chair, placed on a table, the mother's "first born" is seated: near her stands the Dowager Lady Lyttleton whose duty it is . . . to endeavour by appropriate conversation, to keep her attention from flagging. A rose gathered by Her Majesty is presented to the little Princess. . . . Meantime H.M. and the Prince seat themselves at a convenient distance . . . and, as the work proceeds they politely cheer the painter, and assure him of their confidence by many generous compliments. . . . On these happy occasions no state etiquette is observed.'*[26]

Winterhalter earned 300 guineas for his 1842 portraits of Queen Victoria and Prince Albert, and they were the beginning of a large and lucrative practice. He came back to London in the summer of 1843 to tackle a pair of whole-lengths, showing his Royal patrons in garter robes. In contrast to the tone of *majesté bourgeoise* which characterized his French Royal portraits, Winterhalter now invoked the full panoply of Royal tradition. The pose of Prince Albert (fig. 24) bears some similarity to Van Dyck's Charles I in coronation robes (fig. 25), though in reverse. The portrait of Queen Victoria, posed full-face in billowing robes against a corner of Buckingham Palace, is grandiose in conception. She confided to her *Journal*: 'the originals are beautiful, so well painted and his backgrounds are so cleverly managed.'[27]

Other portraits from this summer foray (July to September) include a whole-length portrait of the Duchess of Kent commissioned to hang at Versailles, a portrait of the infant Prince of Wales with plumed hat and ball (Royal Collection) and the 'surprise' oval head of the Queen with unbraided hair painted for Albert's birthday (no. 29), and destined for his dressing-room. In 1844, King Louis-Philippe was formally received (see fig. 18, p. 32). In 1845, there was a commission for a new pair of whole-lengths of the Royal

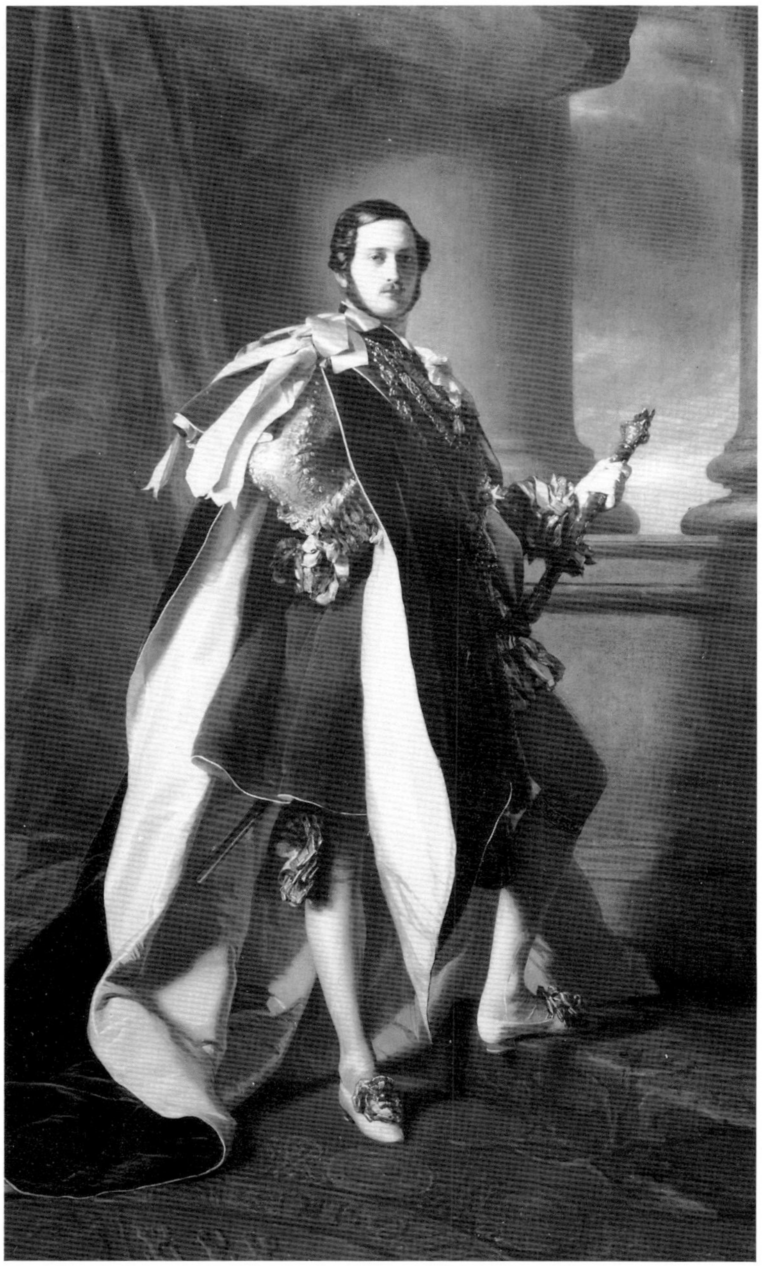

Figure 24
F.X. Winterhalter: *Prince Albert*, 1843
274.3 × 162.6 cms
By gracious permission of Her Majesty The Queen

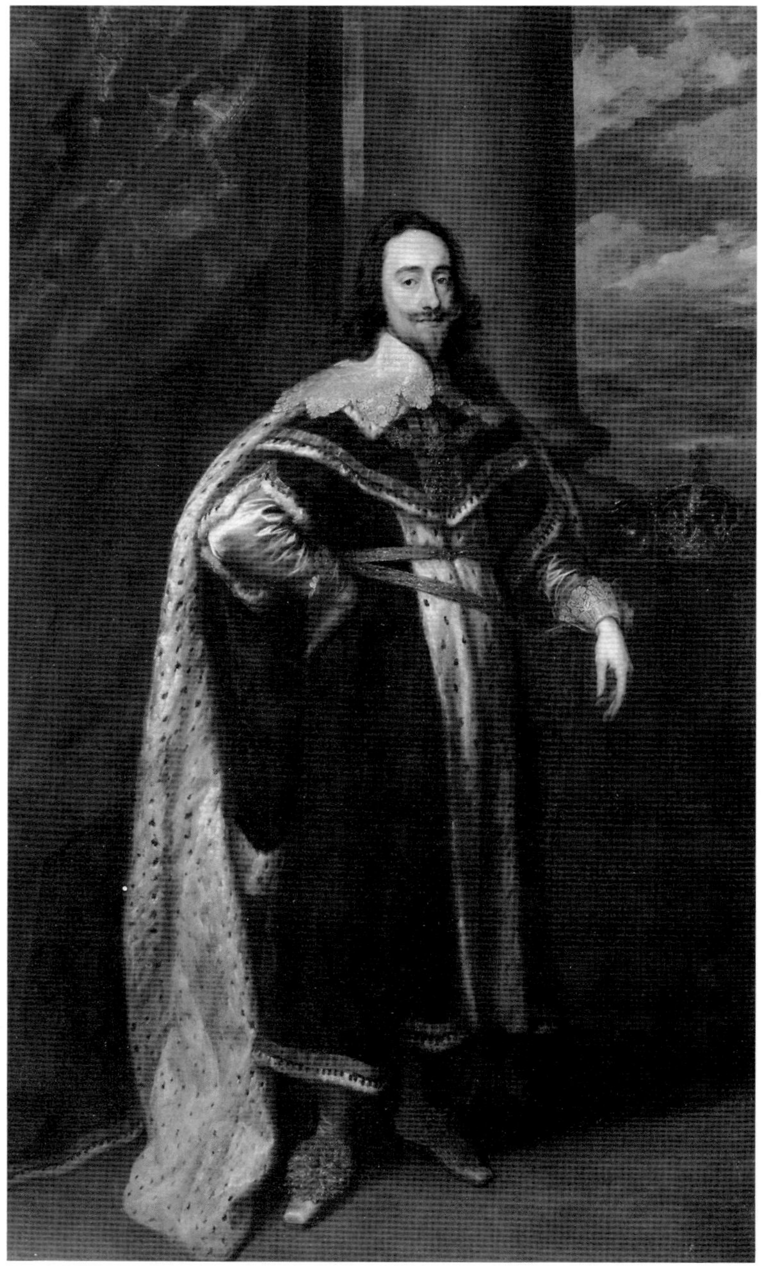

Figure 25
Van Dyck: *Charles I*, 1636
248.3 × 153.6 cms
By gracious permission of Her Majesty The Queen

couple, he in uniform, she in a ball-gown. The year 1846 was Winterhalter's *annus mirabilis*: a new set of whole-lengths ordered by Sir Robert Peel (no. 32); the stunning picture of the Prince of Wales in a sailor suit (no. 31); and the family group (fig. 26). In no other work did Winterhalter so eloquently pay tribute to the charisma and idealism of his Royal patrons. No other work of the period displays his gift for design and his painterly fluency. Set obliquely to the picture plane and dominating the space, the Royal parents sit on a magnificently carved gilt sofa. The Queen, looking out at us, has her arm round the shoulders of her eldest son, while Albert, turned sharply in profile, protectively watches the tottering steps of his second son, Prince Alfred. On the right, the infant Princess Helena looks up at us with beguiling charm, supervised by her two older sisters, Victoria, the Princess Royal, and Princess Alice. All is peace,

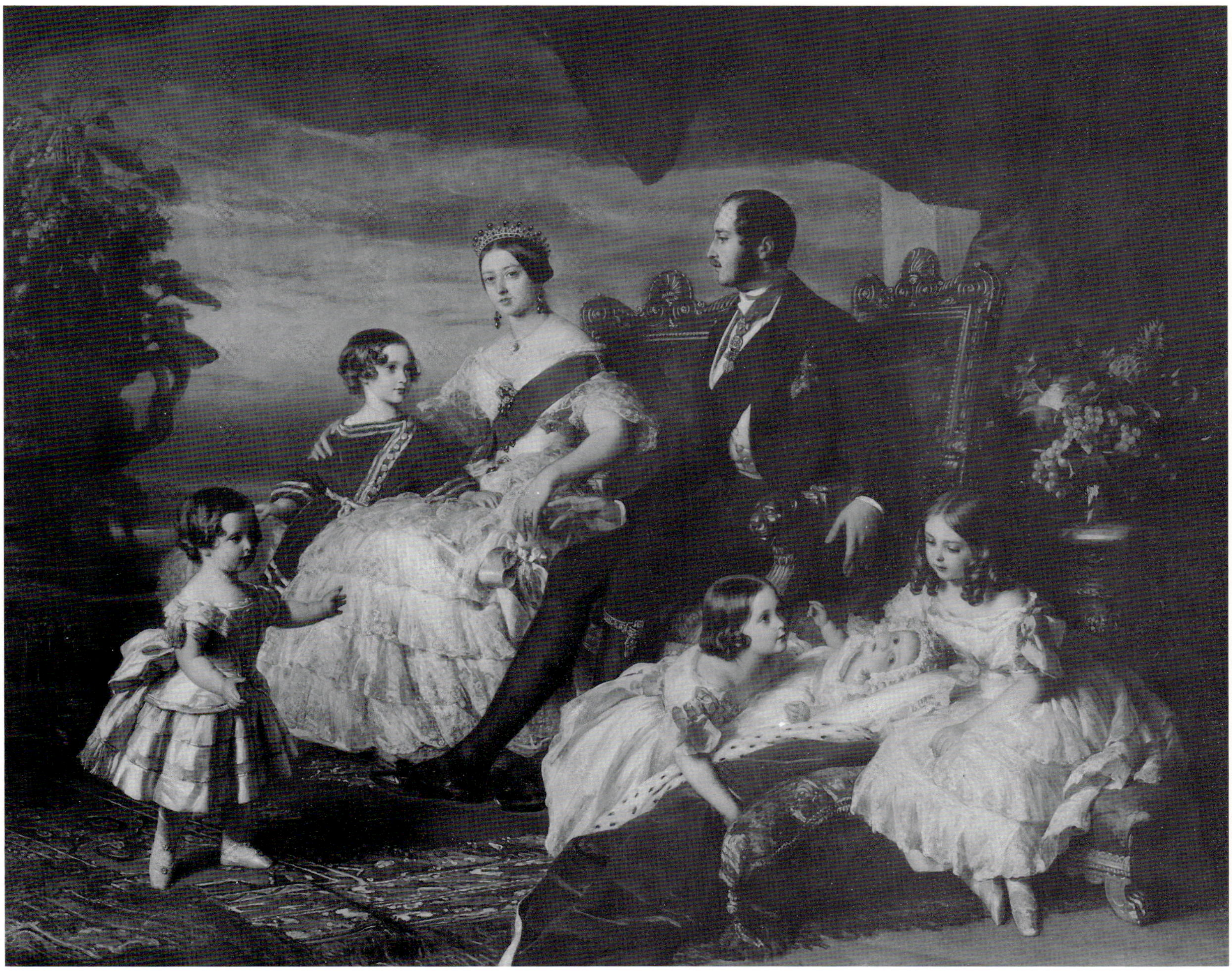

Figure 26
F.X. Winterhalter: *The Royal Family*, 1846, 249.5 × 316 cms
By gracious permission of Her Majesty The Queen

harmony, concord, wealth, fecundity, obedience, happiness. The Palace interior gives way to a view of sky and sea – we are at Osborne House (where the picture was to hang) rather than Buckingham Palace – and this vista adds a note of freedom and expansiveness to the scene.

The picture's antecedents again lie with Van Dyck, with his family picture of Charles and Henrietta Maria, and the group of their five children (fig. 27), from which the motif of the two girls and the baby is borrowed, together with the vase and the still life of fruit. There are some excellent passages in Winterhalter's picture; the children especially seem to breathe and live. They are tenderly observed and delicately painted. What is lacking is rhythm and energy in the composition as a whole. The figures of Queen Victoria and Prince Albert are almost cut-outs, unrelated to the space as a whole, or to the vividly realized children in front. Winterhalter's limitations are only too apparent, but he was the only painter in England who could have begun to orchestrate a composition of this complexity on the scale of life.

As far as the Queen was concerned, this was Winterhalter's masterpiece. No other picture by him gave her such pleasure, and she alluded to it on several occasions.

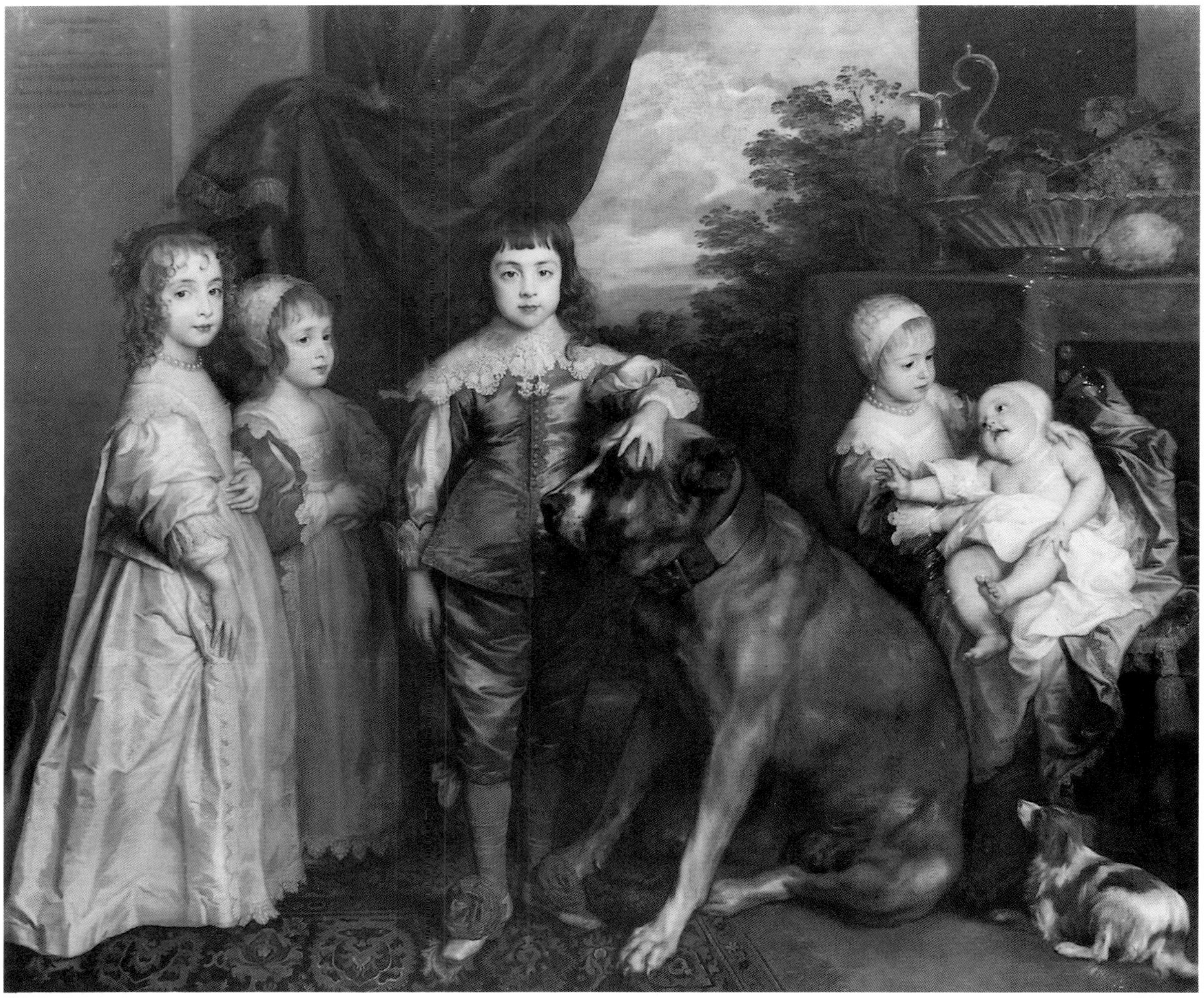

Figure 27
Van Dyck: *The Five Eldest Children of Charles I*, 1637
163.2 × 198.8 cms
By gracious permission of Her Majesty The Queen

Here is her description at the time of its completion: 'we went over to see Winterhalter's picture which is a "chef d'oeuvre" – like a Paul Veronese: such beautiful, brilliant, fresh colouring, and we were enchanted with it.'[28] A later comment is similarly enthusiastic: 'it is so like and so powerfully painted, so beautiful in colouring and design.'

The family picture and other Royal commissions, including the Prince of Wales in sailor suit, were put on exhibition at St James's Palace in the spring of 1847. This was Winterhalter's first and last one-man-show in England. During the two months it was shown, between May and June, over one hundred thousand people visited the exhibition, evidence of Winterhalter's popularity with the public. In London, however, as in Paris, the art critics were generally silent. No reviews appeared in the *Art Journal*, *The Times* or other prominent papers. The notice in *The Athenaeum* voiced the anti-German sentiment which Winterhalter's work invariably provoked in the English press: 'The Queen and Prince, though likenesses, are yet sensual and fleshy visions of those distinguished persons . . . The work is diffuse and unemphatic; while there is a coarseness in the details – such an odour, we may say, of paint, and such a want of taste – as make us frankly rejoice that it is not from the hand of an Englishman.'[29]

The Royal couple recognized what they owed to an artist who could translate their vision of family life into reality so faithfully and so well. His painting aside, he fitted easily into court life, made his contribution to social occasions, provided the Queen with her first lessons in oil painting, advised the Prince on the arts, helped to secure pictures for him and became, in short, a friend. His simplicity of manner and absence of affectation appealed to the Queen, who liked plain speaking and directness in those around her. She calls him such an 'interesting man', 'so good natured and straightforward'.[30] His visits to Windsor Castle and Buckingham Palace were eagerly awaited. The Queen never ceased to be fascinated by watching him paint, his skill in catching likeness, his wizardry with the brush. She was used to the vagaries of the artistic temperament, and expected painters to be unreliable. The methodical Winterhalter, turning portraits out like clockwork, was a paragon.

Royal portraits dominated Winterhalter's work during the 1840s, but not exclusively so. In spite of the pressures exerted on him by the demands of the French and English Courts, he found time to continue his normal practice as a portrait painter in Paris. His sitters were drawn almost exclusively from the highest aristocratic circles in Europe, who found his style irresistible. To a long list of French grandees, were added famous titles from Germany, Belgium, Russia and Poland: Count Mensdorff, the Duchesse d'Audiffret Pasquier, the Princesse de Chimay, Princesse Michel Galitzine and Count Bobrinsky, to take a few names at random. A popular format for these portraits was the oval threequarter-length. With women, the formal effect of the bell-shaped crinoline was off-set by floral accessories and Romantic skyscapes. His male sitters, invariably dressed for the outside world, were characterized with greater severity. Winterhalter's natural affinity with the young found renewed expression in his portraits of children, which have a natural ease and charm (nos. 70, 71, 72).

There are few similarities between Winterhalter's dashing pictorial style and the prevailing character of French portraiture during the 1840s. There, an austere neo-Classical orthodoxy prevailed. The portraits by Ingres and his School have a static, timeless quality, a severity and simplicity of form, and a lack of adornment, alien to the Romantic spirit of the German painter. Leading neo-Classicists, like Ary Scheffer (1795–1858), Hippolyte Flandrin (1809–64) and Henri Lehmann (1814–82) painted portraits intermittently, their sitters generally drawn from a narrow range of patrons; they never aspired to fashionable success in this branch of art. Flandrin's *Comtesse de Cambourg* (fig. 28) is an essay in formal design, showing marbled flesh against black costume, almost bare of jewellery or accessories. Such a style did not command universal approval, nor did it travel easily abroad. French artists painting in a more Romantic style tended to be followers rather than rivals of Winterhalter. The portrait of Princesse Pauline de

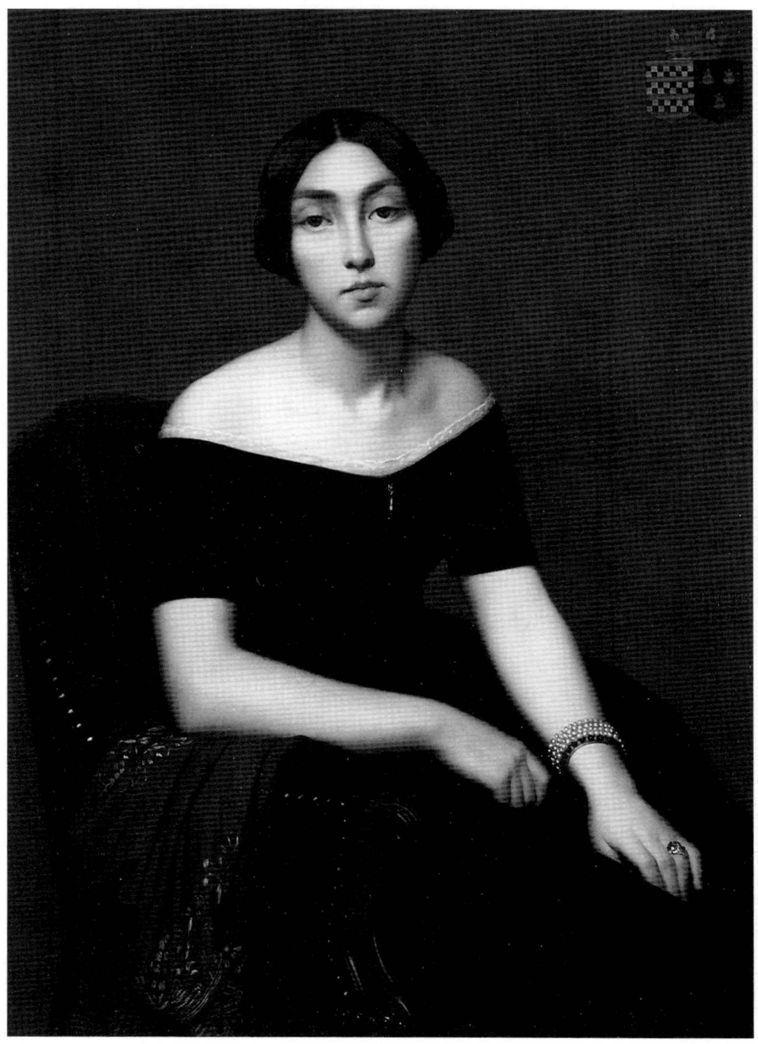

Figure 28
H. Flandrin: *Madame Louis Antoine de Cambourg*, 1846
100.3 × 76.2 cms
The Detroit Institute of Arts

Talleyrand-Périgord (fig. 29) by Claude-Marie Dubufe (1794–1864) is a weak imitation of Winterhalter's court ladies, and for his male portraits Dubufe adopted a format developed by Winterhalter for the Royal princes.

To maintain a prolific portrait practice requires a highly-organized studio. Of the practical details of Winterhalter's working life, however, we know hardly anything. The Salon catalogue gives no more than a bare list of addresses: no. 17 rue des Petits Augustins in Montparnasse in 1835, no. 15 in 1836, no. 34 rue de Lille round the corner in 1838, no. 1 rue de Labruyère, north of the Opera House in 1839, no. 29 rue Notre Dame-de-Lorette in the same district in 1844. No. 15 rue des Petits Augustins appears to have been his residence, the two addresses north of the river simply working studios. No. 15 was also the home of his brother, Hermann.

It is extraordinarily difficult to disentangle the lives and personalities of the two brothers, so closely were they intermeshed. From childhood, the younger had reflected a mirror image of the elder. Studying together, living together, practising together, they had become inseparable. When Franz moved to Munich, Hermann followed; there was the same double move to Karlsruhe, and later still to Paris. For himself, Hermann had little ambition; he knew his limitations as a painter, and his lack of confidence in the world of high society. His sacrifice, if sacrifice it can be called, was offered in the interests of a common Winterhalter cause, and it was made easier by the admiration he felt for his elder brother. Franz was the leader, Hermann the follower, but it should not be assumed from this that Hermann was a weak and colourless character. There is ample evidence, especially after Franz's death, to show that he was an independent and sturdy individual with his own pronounced views on life. If he remained a background figure so far as the world of fashion was concerned, at home the two men were on terms of robust equality. It could not have been otherwise to survive a lifetime with so little apparent friction.

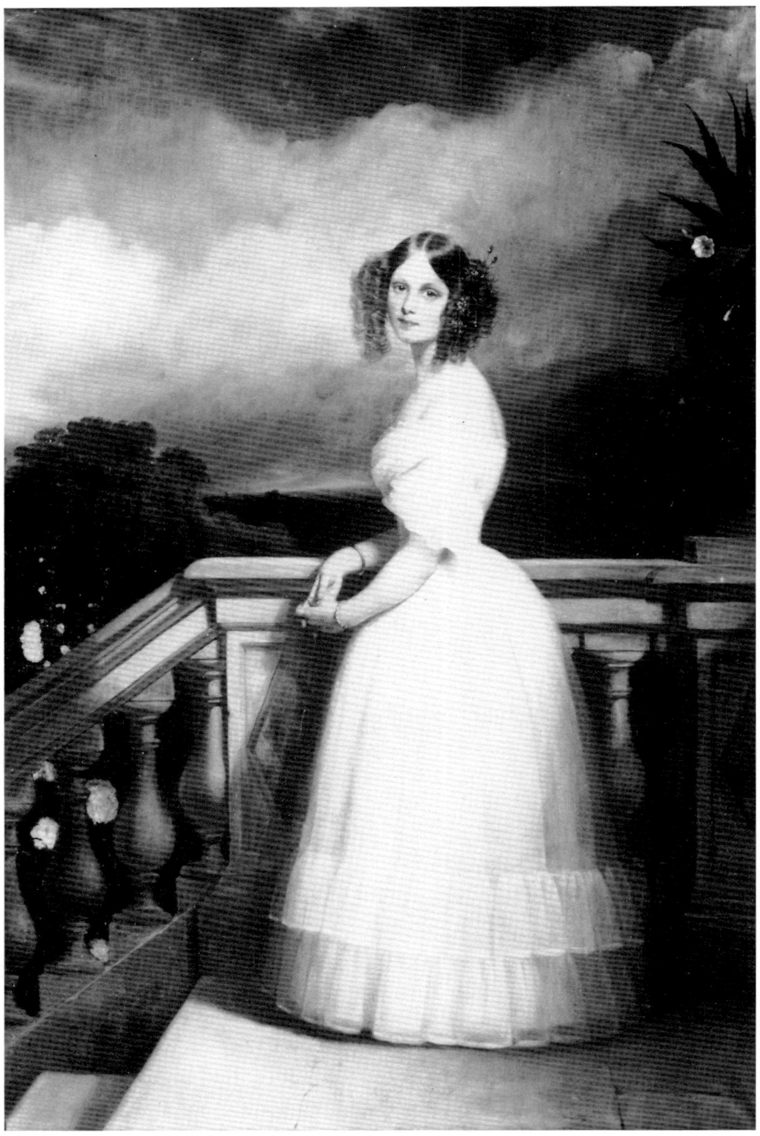

Figure 29
C.-M. Dubufe: *Pauline, Princesse de Talleyrand-Périgord*, c.1840
212 × 145 cms
Location unknown

Nothing illustrates the character of the relationship between the brothers so tellingly as the double portrait at Karlsruhe (no. 11). Winterhalter, in student cap and shirt sleeves, looks up from his sketch-book to confront us with a charming smile. Hermann leans affectionately on his brother's shoulder and looks down, too, with a smile, as if enjoying the same pleasantry. The mood of the portrait is one of easy familiarity and relaxed good humour. Only two or three years separate the oil from the double self-portrait drawing of 1841 (fig. 30). The latter is formal and conventional by comparison. Franz with his arm over a chairback looks confidently out at the world, while behind him, Hermann gazes into space with an abstracted air. Both are fashionably dressed, in well-cut morning coats, high stocks and gloves.

Without Hermann's support, Winterhalter's task would have been immeasurably more difficult. The business side of the practice, the organization of the studio, the vast production line of replicas, the publication of prints, the manufacture of frames, and the delivery of pictures, fell on

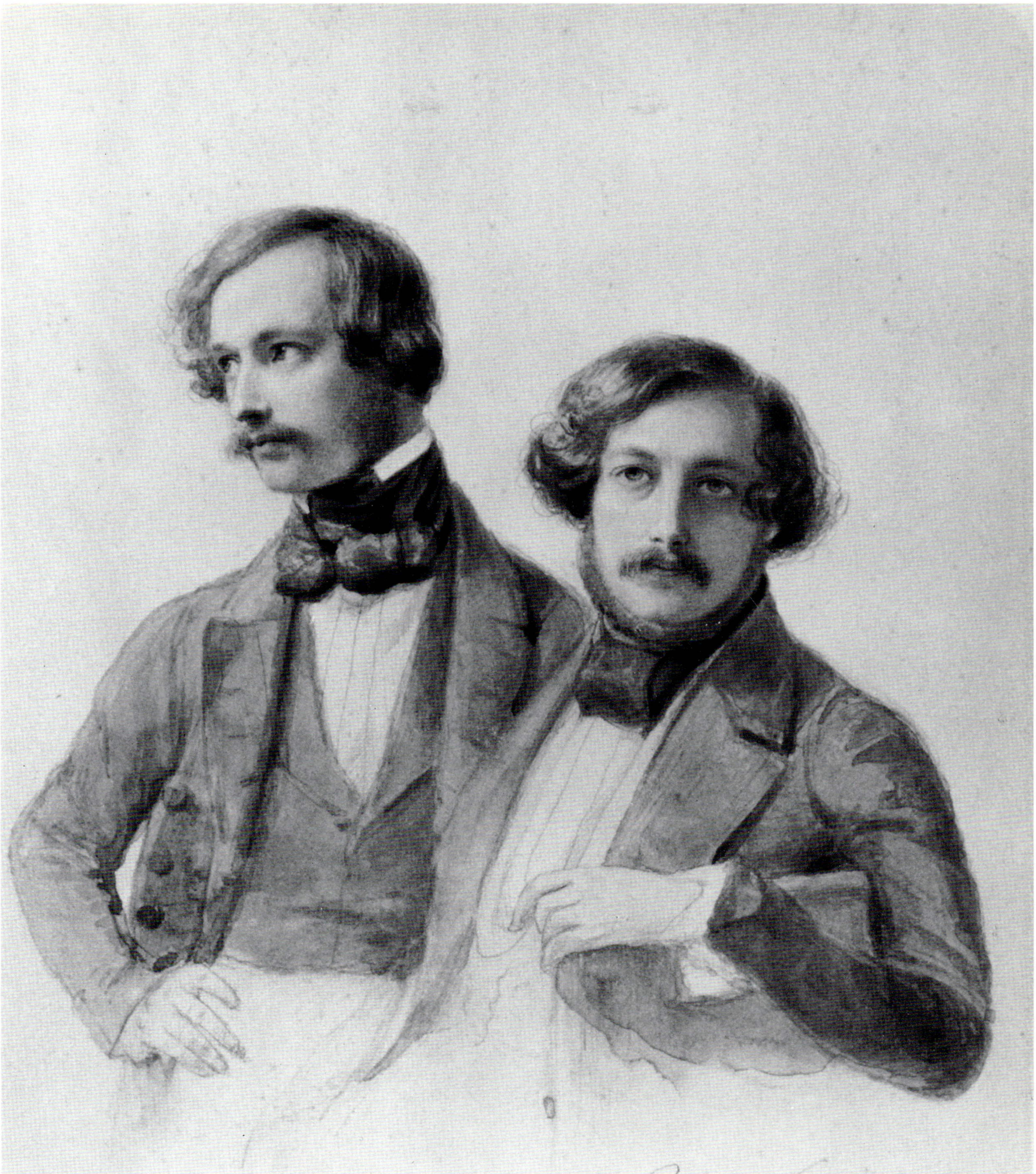

Figure 30
F.X. Winterhalter: *Hermann and Franz Winterhalter*, 1841
Pencil and watercolour, 29 × 23 cms, private collection

the shoulders of the younger man. He was reliable and loyal. Less important portrait commissions were pushed his way; he painted and exhibited charming studies of models, his most individual form of expression; but his chief energies went to aid the development of his brother's career. When Winterhalter went off on his travels to European capitals, he would leave Paris with complete assurance that all was well at home.

Hermann was supported in the studio by assistants, who helped in the task of copying and who probably contributed to the painting of dresses and accessories. Prominent among these assistants were two German artists, both of whom were to have independent careers. Albert Graeffle (1807–89) was a native of Freiburg who had trained with the Winterhalters in Munich. He followed them to Paris, and kept himself going with studio work. In 1846, he won success at the Salon with a theatrical composition, *The Battle of Armenius* (Karlsruhe, Kunsthalle), and in 1859 he moved back to Munich. In the early 1860s, he was employed at the English Court, painting Queen Victoria and the Crown Prince and Princess of Prussia, no doubt on Winterhalter's recommendation. The second assistant, Louis Coblitz (1814–63) was younger and, like Graeffle, a product of the Munich Academy. He worked and exhibited in Paris from 1842–6, before returning to his native Mannheim. Those artists, described later on as working in Winterhalter's studio, like the genre and sporting artist, Charles Boutibonne (1816–97), and the portraitist, Richard Lauchert (1823–69), seem to have been pupils rather than copyists. In 1853, the Grand Duchess Sophie wrote a warm letter of recommendation for Josephine Ludwig asking the artist to look after her until 'she has to some extent found her legs in Paris'.[31] Two years later Prince Wilhelm of Baden wrote asking Winterhalter to sponsor another woman artist, Emma Gaggiotti Richards (1825–1912).[32]

Socially, as well as professionally, the two brothers were remarkably self-sufficient and self-contained (figs. 31, 32). Success and wealth did not alter their modest and contented life-style. Social climbing was alien to their upbringing; they had no desire to cut a dash in the fashionable world of Paris; they remained loyal to old friends in Germany and to a limited circle of acquaintances in Paris. A letter of 12 July 1841 from Winterhalter to an architect friend in Munich is full of news of mutual friends, including the diplomat Count Jenison, the painter, J.B. Kirner, and Baron Eichtal's son, Charles.[33] Among Winterhalter's French friends was the flamboyant marine artist, Théodore Gudin (1808–80), and the genre painter and orientalist, Alexandre Decamps (1803–60). He had first become friends with the wealthy and well-connected Gudin at the French Academy in Rome, and they continued to meet regularly in Paris and London. When, in 1844, Gudin married the daughter of Lord James Hay, aide-de-camp to the Duke of Wellington at Waterloo, Winterhalter painted a fan for him as a wedding present.

For all his success and popularity, Winterhalter continued to live simply and abstemiously. He had become an

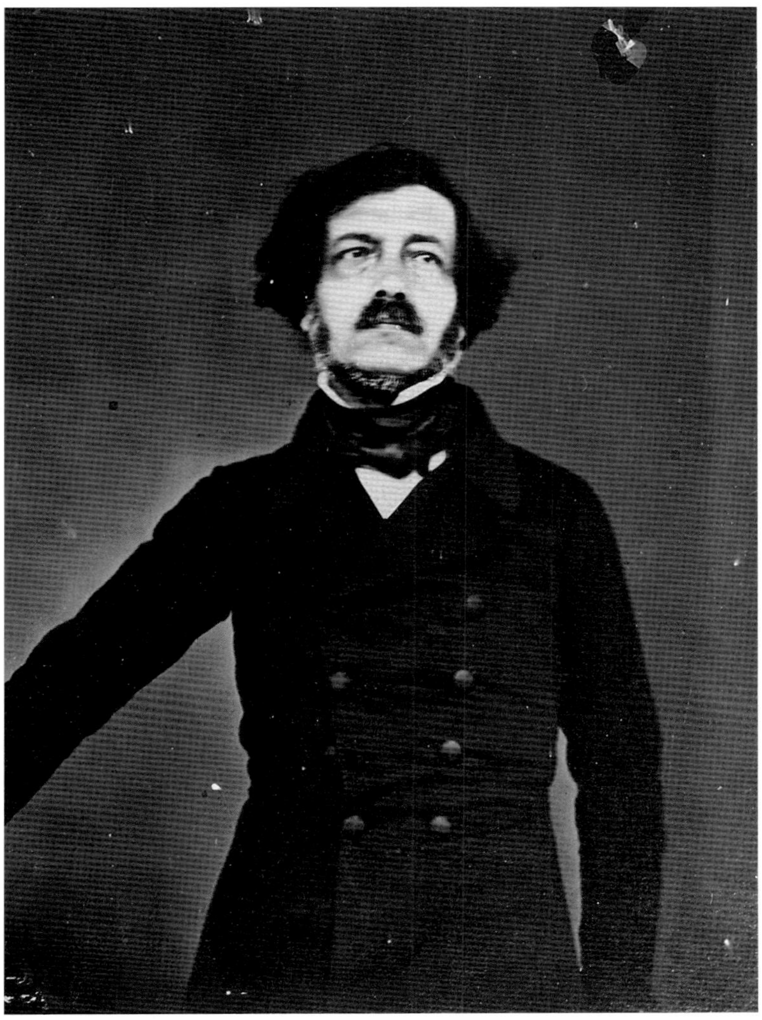

Figure 31
Dr. E. Becker: *F.X. Winterhalter*, 1854
Photograph
By gracious permission of Her Majesty The Queen

international celebrity through his portraits of Royalty, but he continued to believe that this was only a temporary phenomenon. To a friend in Holland he confided in a letter of 8 August 1846: 'Soon I will have done with the entire royal family, [of France] and then should end the period of portrait painting for me, and I shall be able to resume my way in the arts which derive their inspiration from the imagination, a pleasure which one cannot enjoy as a portrait painter.'[34]

Two years later Winterhalter's wish was almost granted, but not in a way he could have foreseen. The Revolution of 1848 swept away the Orléanist monarchy, whose patronage had established him, and with it the world he knew and admired. The Revolution realized all the worst fears of this deeply conservative man, with his reverence for order and authority. The events which he was forced to witness in Paris, as the mob took control of the city, overturned the army and forced the abdication of the King, appalled him. He withdrew to Switzerland, probably staying with relatives or friends in the German-speaking cantons, where Black Forest entrepreneurs were well-established. In August he went to Geneva, and later that same year to Brussels, where he was occupied with commissions. The following March Winterhalter crossed to England, which seemed like a welcoming haven after the storms ravaging Europe. He confided his experiences to Queen Victoria: 'We talked of France and Germany and the horrors of the past year; and he said that what he saw at Paris had made a terrible impression upon him, and that he had been unfortunate enough to come in for a revolution in almost every place! The fate of the French Royal Family and the behaviour of Germany is what distresses him most.'[35]

Professional pride prevented him from giving up or giving way to despair. He had commitments to fulfill, portraits to paint. He was still in demand. Persistence saw him through from the fall of one dynasty to the rise of another. Paris remained his home, but in the wake of the Revolution he was much abroad. His trip to England in 1849 was unusually prolonged, five months in the spring and summer, a further month in the autumn.

He returned again in 1850 and 1851, painting some of his most inventive and original portrait groups during this tense and unsettled time. There are no precedents for the groups of Queen Victoria's children in Highland dress (no. 33), which show the artist in high Romantic vein, nor for the vivacious double portrait of the Queen with her cousin, Princess Victoire (no. 37), nor for the tender cabinet-picture of her seated on the terrace at Osborne House with Prince Arthur (no. 36). The baptism of this favourite son was the occasion for another experimental group, *The First of May* (Royal Collection), which shows the Royal couple in the guise of a Holy Family, with the aged Duke of Wellington as an adoring magus. The appearance of the Crystal Palace in the background serves to unite religion and modern technology in an uneasy allegory suggested to the artist by Prince Albert.

In France, a temporary lull in portrait commissions gave

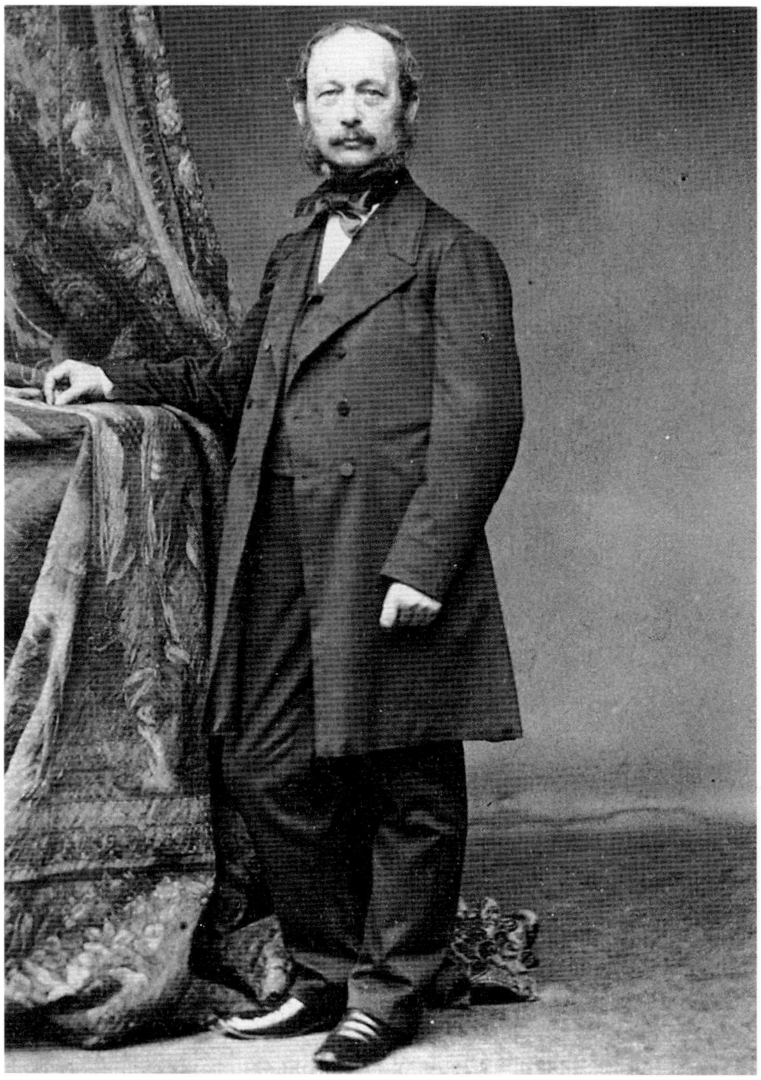

Figure 32
R.J. Bingham: *Hermann Winterhalter*, c.1868–70
Photograph
Private Collection

Winterhalter the chance to assert his creative independence. He embarked once more on a major subject painting. *Florinda* (no. 38) is not a fateful picture, but a joyous and sensual celebration of female beauty. It was inspired by an ancient Spanish ballad entitled 'La Cava'. King Rodrigo came across the beautiful Florinda while she was bathing with her companions, fell in love with her, and seduced her. To avenge this affront, her father brought a Moorish army to Spain. Rodrigo was killed in battle, and Spain came under the rule of the Moors.

According to more modern legend, *Florinda* represents the leading courtesans of the Second Empire in thinly veiled disguise. Winterhalter is said to have planned both this picture and the later group, *The Empress Eugénie Surrounded by her Ladies-in-Waiting* (no. 53) in deliberate contrast; erotic demi-monde on the one hand, chaste court beauties on the other. The legend, alas, is false. The Second Empire had not begun when Winterhalter painted his picture, and its protagonists are certainly professional models rather than ladies of the town. Nevertheless, the picture can be seen as the herald of Winterhalter's return to the Paris scene, and it marks the beginning of a new and triumphant phase of his career. He sent the picture in the first instance to the Royal Academy, his one major contribution to that august institution in the year of the Great Exhibition. Admired for the beauty of its form and its sonorous colour, it was bought by an enthusiastic Queen Victoria as a present for Prince Albert. A year later a version of it went to the Salon, Winterhalter's first showing there for more than six years.

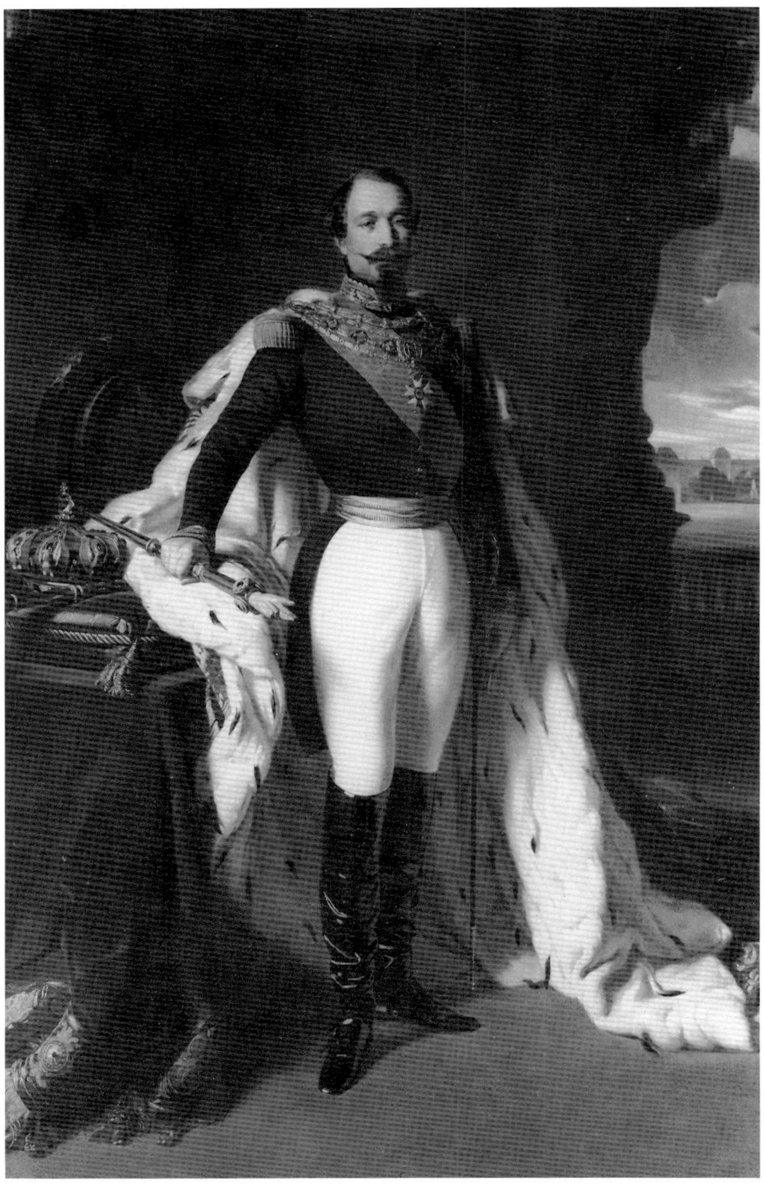

Figure 33
Studio of F.X. Winterhalter: *Emperor Napoleon III*, 1853
254 × 152 cms approx.
By courtesy of the Crown Estate Commissioners

At the moment when *Florinda* made its début in Paris, Winterhalter fell in love, in Karlsruhe. Of earlier romances, the record is almost silent, but it would be surprising if there had been none. His latest conquest was Marie von Scheffel (1829–57), an intense young woman half his age (twenty-three to his forty-seven). Her father was an established architect in Karlsruhe, her mother a playwright and literary hostess, her brother Victor a prominent novelist. She herself wrote and painted. It was Winterhalter's old friend, the architect Karl Josef Berckmüller, who acted as marriage broker. In his view, Winterhalter needed the comfort of a wife and family, while the flighty Marie would enjoy wealth and stability through marriage to a celebrity. It seemed an ideal arrangement. Spurred on by Berckmüller, Winterhalter proposed to Marie in the spring of 1852 on one of his fleeting visits to Karlsruhe

Marie's parents were less than enthusiastic about a suitor living in Paris, who travelled to European courts where their daughter would not be received. Marie had her own reservations in the form of a second lover, Major Frederick Keller, a forthright but penurious soldier of forty who had seen active service during the revolutions of 1848–9, and had served as aide-de-camp to Grand Duke Leopold. For weeks she havered between the two men. Passion decided the issue in Keller's favour. Her brother, who thought Keller too ordinary and prosaic for her, wrote disconsolately: 'If Keller loves you, and is truly noble, he will not demand your hand at the price of your soul.' He could not understand why she had broken with Winterhalter, whom he had never met, and attributed her rejection to his age. Winterhalter's letter to Marie of 15 July 1852, anticipating defeat, reveals a disappointing absence of ardour:

> *'I was so happy last night, and now today am overcome by the profoundest melancholy – a melancholy I can ill support . . . impossible for me to await, as he [Berckmüller] bids me do, your final decision in Baden while I am in this mood. On the other hand, I am now so near to you, that were we to meet, I have not the strength to accept from you words of a final parting, I cannot expel you from my heart. But however you decide I will always remain* your *loving friend – Winterhalter.'*[36]

After rejecting Winterhalter, Marie took some time before she accepted Keller's proposal; in the end she broke with him as well. Her brother wrote perceptively in March 1853, 'Deep in my heart I wonder if you have been over hasty, motivated *par dépit*, caused by some disappointment you had with the other man'. Unable to find the peace and happiness she craved, Marie began to show symptoms of the mental imbalance to which her family was prone (her brother Karl was shut up with a keeper, one of her uncles was in an asylum). She died from typhus on 10 February 1857, at the age of twenty-seven.

Winterhalter's heart remained in his work. On 4 May 1853, the *Badische Landszeitung* announced that he had been invited to Paris, 'in his official capacity' to paint the Empress Eugénie's portrait. Winterhalter had performed this service for the Orléans family when the Tuileries was their home. Other times, other faces! It may seem strange that the court painter of an overturned dynasty should be employed by the dynasty succeeding it, but the connection between art and politics is rarely straight-forward. Napoleon III set out to mobilize the best artistic talents of the time in the service of the state irrespective of past loyalties.

Artists were regularly invited to the famous series of week-long parties given four or five times a year at Compiègne, when the Emperor and Empress entertained a gathering of distinguished guests from all walks of life. Winterhalter was invited to Compiègne in 1853, before the *séries élégantes* had begun, the first artist to be so honoured. The invitation was no doubt a result of the commission he had received to paint the state portraits of the Imperial couple. These were finished in December 1853 at a cost of 24,000 francs. The originals are missing, and the mechanical forms and surfaces of the copies serve only to blunt the eye (figs. 33, 34). So huge was the reproduction business that special request forms were printed to cope with the demand from préfectures, consulates and embassies. The portraits were engraved, transferred to Sèvres porcelain, woven into tapestry, made into miniatures, interpreted in sculpture, to become universal talismans of the Second Empire. The formula of robes and regalia, pillars, drapes and palace parks, was so familiar to Winterhalter that one senses how

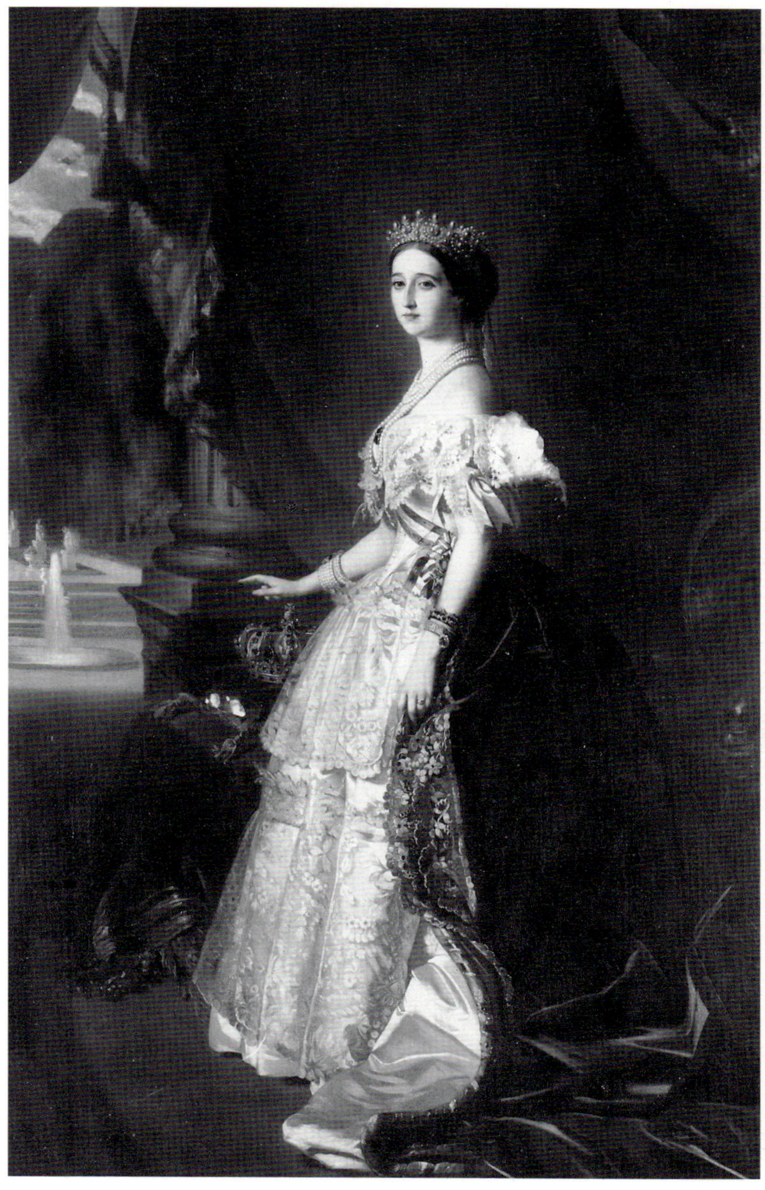

Figure 34
After F.X. Winterhalter: *The Empress Eugénie*, 1853
236 × 152 cms
Château de Belœil

little involved he was with either sitter. Where Hippolyte Flandrin reveals such penetrating insight into the complex personality of the Emperor in his 1861 portrait (fig. 35), Winterhalter is content with the superficial trappings of power. The man himself is blandly impersonal. Significantly Winterhalter painted only one other portrait of Napoleon (no. 56), and commissions for official ceremonial groups went to other painters: the Prince Imperial's baptism to Thomas Couture (Compiègne); the reception of the Siamese ambassadors to J.L. Gérôme (Versailles).

It was as painter extraordinary to the Empress that Winterhalter left his mark on the Second Empire. With unerring judgement she had selected him as the artist best able to do justice to herself and the ladies of the court, and she treated him generously. According to an anonymous contemporary source, she gave orders for a studio to be constructed in the attics of the Tuileries: 'she decorated this with rich stuffs and objects of art. Here artists showed her their works and here Royalty sat for them. Winterhalter created his portrait of the Prince Imperial in this room, and Flandrin his of the Emperor.'[37] While at work on his official state portrait of the Empress, Winterhalter was painting a second, far more intimate picture of her seated (no. 50), and a third in fancy-dress costume (no. 52). In 1855, Winterhalter painted his masterpiece, *The Empress Eugénie Surrounded by her Ladies-in-Waiting* (no. 53). They sit in a pastoral setting of woodland and park, gathering flowers: roses and camellias, clematis and most of all, lilac, the Empress's favourite flower and emblem, of which she wears sprays in her hair. Pausing from their work, the nine women form themselves into a harmonious circle. Their spreading dresses, subtly contrasting in shade, form rivers of satin, lace and gauze which suggest all the beauty of the female form. The scene is radiant and refulgent, a beguiling vision of the world of fashion transferred into a *fête champêtre*, a *tableau vivant* of Diana and her acolytes, Titania and her fairies, an allegory of the Muses, a celebration of Spring and fertility (the Empress was already pregnant). Winterhalter had painted large-scale groups before, but never with such ease and refinement, such glowing colour and exuberant panache.

When the picture was finished, it was unveiled before the Emperor and Empress at the Tuileries. Reporting the occasion to Winterhalter, Princess Metternich assured him that it had 'enchanted *both* their Majesties. The likeness and then the admirable conception were appreciated by all'.[38] The picture was subsequently exhibited at the 'Exposition Universelle' in 1855 to a mixed critical reception. Théophile Gautier singled it out as Winterhalter's most important work, sensing the influence of English painting in the artist's flirtatious and brilliant style; preoccupied by elegance, the artist had failed to make use of the rich colouristic possibilities of the subject.[39] Gustave Planche called it an inferior *Decameron*, 'quite simply the parody of a Watteau', and 'a bizarre composition' that defied all the laws of painting.[40] Such strictures had little effect on the immense popular success of the group, which remains Winterhalter's single

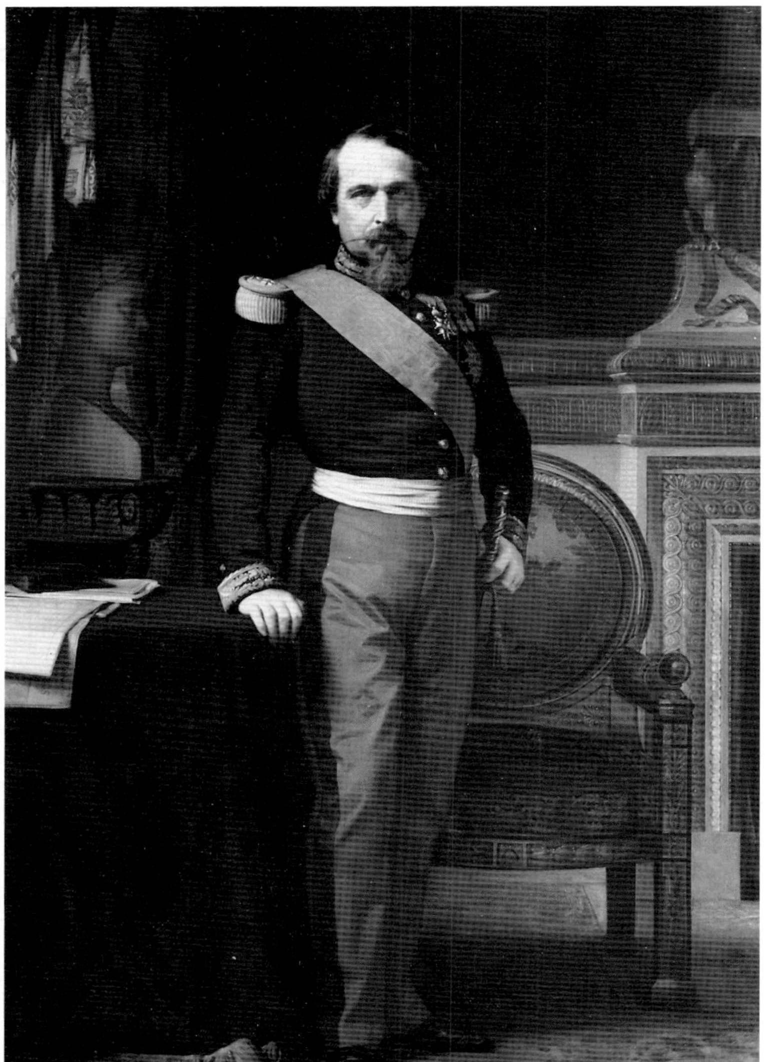

Figure 35
H. Flandrin: *Emperor Napoleon III*, 1861
212 × 147 cms
Musée national du château de Versailles

most famous work. In Vienna, the room at the Kunstverein where the picture was shown during the spring of 1856 became so crowded that tickets had to be issued. Both the Emperor Franz Joseph and the Empress Elizabeth paid a long visit to the exhibition and, according to one journalist, 'the charming female figures from Winterhalter's brush are the main topic at all the tea parties and salons'.[41]

Winterhalter was awarded a first-class medal at the 'Exposition Universelle' of 1855. He had been a member of the jury that selected paintings for the famous exhibition, together with many of the great names in French painting; Ingres, Delacroix, Henri Lehmann and Horace Vernet. Delacroix's only recorded reference to Winterhalter is scarcely complimentary, but it shows that they were on terms of familiarity. They met in Baden-Baden in September 1855: 'As I was on my way back I met Winterhalter; he is not a bad fellow, but a terrible bore. He insisted on our having a glass of beer together and I went along with him.'[42]

Winterhalter's reign at the French Court lasted for ten years. The 1855 group was followed in 1857 by informal threequarter-length oval portraits of Napoleon III and Eugénie that appear to be companion works. The portrait of the Emperor (no. 56) has only recently been reattributed, and it offers a pleasant informal view of him altogether more sympathetic than the bombastic state portrait of 1854. The portrait of the Empress (fig. 36) seated out of doors in a straw hat, is a bravura performance. Confident in the power of her charm, she dazzles the onlooker. The portrait was commissioned by the Empress herself, and was given by her to Count Bacchiochi.

The portrait of the Empress holding the Prince Imperial (no. 58), painted the following year, was an official

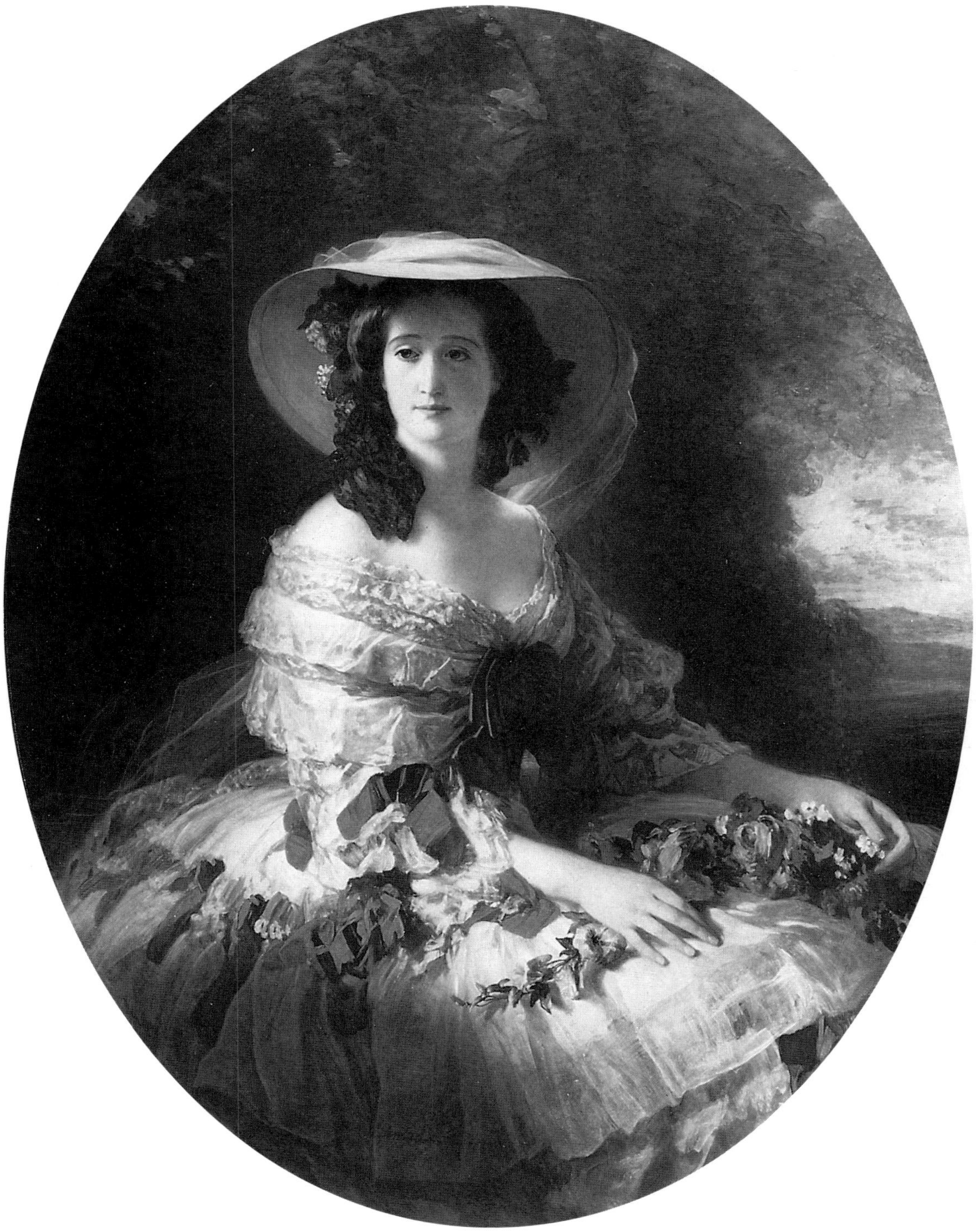

Figure 36
F.X. Winterhalter: *The Empress Eugénie*, 1857, 138 × 109 cms approx.
By courtesy of the Hillwood Museum, Washington D.C.

commission from the Surintendant des Beaux-Arts. Flamboyant beauty is replaced here by maternal solicitude. The simple and noble lines of the composition, emphasized by the plain velvet dress, focus attention on the tender relationship between mother and child. This is one of Winterhalter's most touching portraits of the Empress.

It is divided from the last of his whole-lengths of her by an interval of four years. During that time, the Empress had endured much personal suffering and sorrow, and Winterhalter makes no attempt to disguise the marks of it. The appealing beauty of the young mother gives way to the mature and decided features of a middle-aged woman in the late seated portrait of 1862 (fig. 37). Status and rank are underscored by regal dress, Baroque throne and heraldic arms. What raises the portrait to a higher imaginative plane is the change in the personality of the Empress herself.

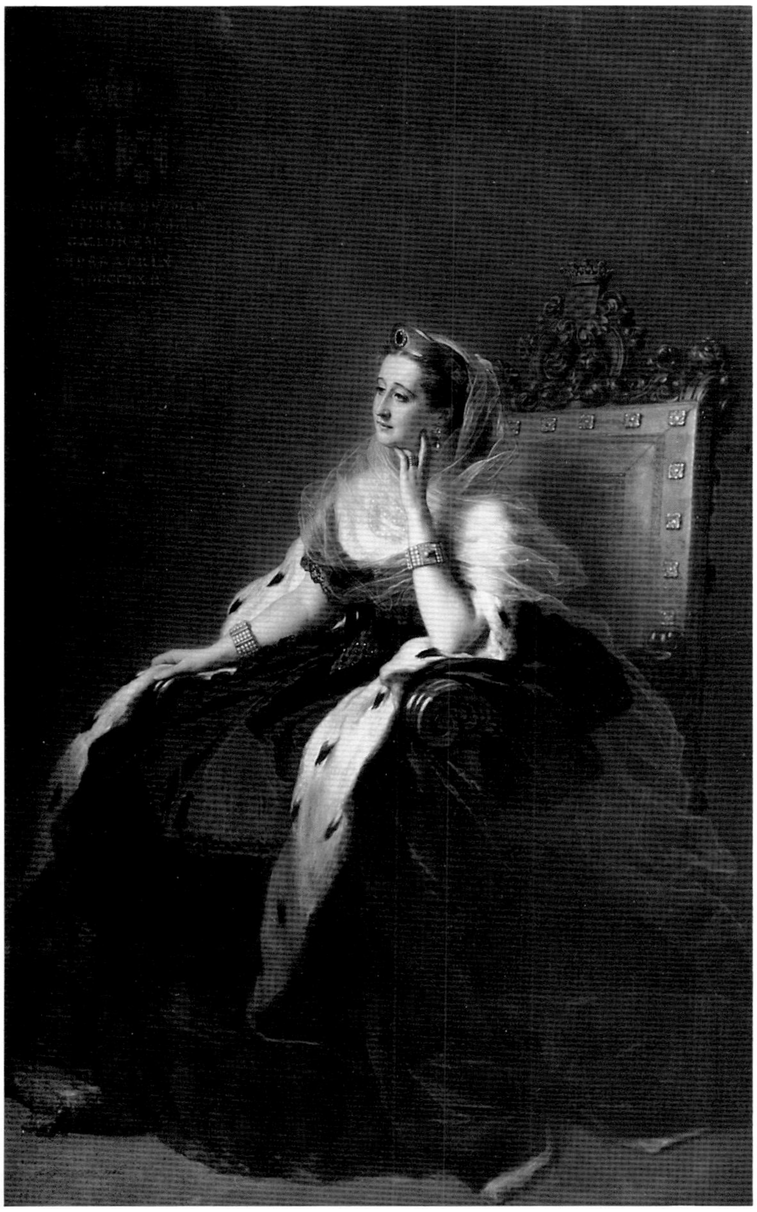

Figure 37
F.X. Winterhalter: *The Empress Eugénie*, 1862
229 × 146 cms
Collection of the Dukes of Alba, Palacio de Liria, Madrid

Winterhalter rarely allowed himself such penetrating characterization, but his long association with the Empress had intensified his feelings of admiration and sympathy for her. She had been and would remain the most exceptional of his sitters, and he put all the resources of his art into this last tribute to her.

Winterhalter's two letters to an unidentified member of the Empress's suite about this portrait, and the profile sketch of 1861, deserve to be quoted in full, for the light they throw on the relationship between artist and sitter:[43]

> *'My dear friend, I should like to ask H. M. the Empress the favour of giving me one more sitting to complete the picture. The background too is not yet quite finished. Should she approve the arms and the inscription which I should like to incorporate in the background, I would request her to describe them to me precisely. I have incorporated them thus.*

*[SKETCH]*

*I should have to have the arms and their colours, then it would soon be finished. As for the price of the portraits, I should request most humbly that Her Majesty would decide it herself, since they are fantasy pictures, indeed the profile is only a variation on the popular theme. Perhaps the Empress wishes to see my picture first, but if she is prepared to grant me a sitting at once, I request a dress which is made in such a way that I can see her arms.*
*And now, dearest friend, I beg you to lay my deepest reverence at Her Majesty's feet, and please accept the assurance of my old friendship and devotion, with which I remain*
*Yours sincerely,*
*F Winterhalter*
*19 Feb 62*
*Please let me know in good time when the Empress is coming, so that everything is in order.'*

*'My dear friend, Since I am being asked by all and sundry whether the portrait of the Empress which I have now completed is going to the exhibition in London, I feel I must ask you to speak to Her Majesty about this; perhaps she would find it not displeasing herself. At all events she ought now to order a frame as soon as possible, with a crown on it I think. Would you be so kind as to speak to Her Majesty about this and let me know her commands.*
*Excuse me for giving you this trouble.*
*I am afraid of being immodest if I repair so often to the Tuileries to ask for an audience.*
*In old friendship and with great respect,*
*Yours sincerely,*
*F Winterhalter'*

The Empress's recorded comments on Winterhalter's work are merely conventional expressions of praise. The only tangible expressions of her regard are a gold watch and an ormolu clock given by her to the artist which are still in the possession of the Winterhalter family. It is clear, however, that the Empress valued his creative talent as highly as Queen Victoria, if not more so.

The artist recorded her beauty and grandeur in an unforgettable sequence of images from his early state portrait of 1854, to the last head-and-shoulders at Compiègne painted exactly ten years later. When Eugénie went into exile in England it was with Winterhalter's portraits that she chose to surround herself – a recollection of her past glories. In the division of property that followed the Emperor's abdication, the French state eventually agreed to release to her the famous group of herself and the ladies of her court, and it hung resplendently in the Empress's home at Farnborough Hill in Surrey until her death. For reasons perhaps of convenience, the frame of the picture remained in France, and it was not until the purchase of the painting at the sale of the Empress's pictures in 1927 by the authorities at Malmaison, that frame and picture were reunited.

Outside the Imperial Court, Winterhalter continued to fulfil a wide range of international obligations. In 1852, he travelled to Spain with his friend Eduard Magnus to paint a flamboyant state portrait of Queen Isabella (Royal Palace, Madrid). In 1854 followed portraits of King Pedro of Portugal and his brother, the Duke of Oporto, the Belgian Prince de Chimay, Princesse Murat, Queen Victoria's Indian protégé the Maharajah Duleep Singh (no. 40), and her son, Prince Leopold, William I of Prussia, and the artist's old patron, the widowed Sophie of Baden (no. 69), elegant and beautiful to the end. In 1856, he briefly visited England, executing a set of watercolours of the Queen and her family.

The most extensive journey of 1856, however, was much further afield, to Warsaw. His patrons in Paris had included many of the great Polish families, the Potockis, Krasinskis and Branickis, who were closely linked by ties of marriage and friendship. These Francophile families were well-established in Parisian society, and noted for their beauty, wealth and taste. Winterhalter found them congenial spirits. In 1853, he painted the charming Van Dyckian group of Countess Elizabeth Krasinska (*née* Branicka), the beautiful and intelligent wife of the poet, Sigismund Krasinski, and her three children (no. 67). In the following year he painted two portraits of Katarzyna Potocka (*née* Branicka), one of them in oriental dress (no. 68). Three delightful studies of Potocki children followed in 1856 (nos. 70, 71, 72), together with a sequence of oval heads, of Anna and Maria Branicka, Jadwiga Branicka (*née* Potocka) (no. 77), Zofia Odescalchi (*née* Branicka), and Countess Krasinska. This last sitter was the subject of a separate threequarter-length in 1857. (Most of the portraits listed here belong to the National Museum, Warsaw.) Polish patronage was still going strong a decade later when Winterhalter painted Countess Branicka (*née* Marie Sapicka) (Philadelphia Museum of Art), Roza Potocka (National Museum, Warsaw) and Zofia Zamoyska (*née* Potocka) (no. 81).

The year of the Poles was 1856, 1857 the year of the Russians. In the summer of that year, Winterhalter went to Bad Brückinau, a spa town in Upper Bavaria, to paint the Tsar and Tsarina (no. 73). Writing from Jugenheim in Germany, on 26 July 1857, the Tsarina's lady-in-waiting, Countess Tolstoi, acknowledged the arrival of these two works:

> *'I displayed them skilfully and in a good light, and only then did their Majesties enter. I wanted to see the first impression in order to report it to you, my dear Monsieur Winterhalter. Well, you must be satisfied, for both the Emperor and the Empress were delighted and did not know which of the two portraits to prefer, each being thrilled. But there was a still bigger exhibition and among the numerous guests was the King of Prussia, who greatly admired your work and told us that you painted him in two sittings. Opinions on the likeness of the two portraits were divided, as is usual, but the enthusiasm for the beauty of the painting was universal and unanimous. As I looked at the beautiful pictures I myself thought I was once again in the beautiful Peterstal, where we have spent so many lovely days. I only wish that you will not forget them and that the memory of them may one day bring you to St Petersburg, where you will find the same friends again.'*[44]

The Tsarina set a trend among the ladies of her court. Everyone wanted to be painted, and over the course of the following three years, Winterhalter received sittings from a succession of Russians; Princess Youssoupova, Grand Duchess Marie Nicolaievna and Countess Bobrinskaia in 1857, Countess Chouvalova, Madame Naryschkina (no. 75) (all five in The Hermitage, Leningrad), and Princess Bariatinsky in 1858, from Princess Troubetskoï (no. 61), and Countess Lamsdorff (Metropolitan Museum, New York) in 1859. There were later Russian commissions throughout the 1860s.

No portrait painter has ever enjoyed such extensive Royal patronage as Winterhalter. One has to go back to the age of Rubens and Van Dyck to find court painters operating in a similar international network of contacts. In both periods, recognized masters could transcend the normal barriers of country and culture with a style that was recognized universally. The links through marriage and friendship between the Royal houses of Europe were very close in the nineteenth century; Queen Victoria's epithet as the grandmother of Europe was almost literally true. A painter who established himself successfully in one court had the possibility of recommendations to other courts at the highest and most personal level.

The secret of Winterhalter's success was not simply one of good connections. His portraits gained currency because they flattered the self-esteem and pretensions of his patrons. He breathed life into the tired and debased conventions of Royal imagery. His monarchs and consorts were staged in settings of princely magnificence, but they remained refined and elegant figures of their own time. Winterhalter's style was suave, cosmopolitan and above all plausible. There were persistent innuendos about the need to employ a foreign artist at court, especially in England, but, in reality, Winterhalter had little opposition to overcome. The realistic trends of much Victorian portraiture were singularly ill-suited to the conventions of Royal iconography. Most portraitists felt ill at ease with the idiom and practised it rarely. Like a court jeweller, Winterhalter supplied rarefied artefacts to a specialized market which he knew intimately. He was an expert operating in a world of amateurs.

One other important factor underlying the widespread recognition of Winterhalter's work was the fact that it originated in Paris. Though he remained incorrigibly German in his habits and temperament, his painting represented that quality of high style and elegance, peculiarly French, to which other countries had always aspired. French taste continued to be a touchstone of excellence, as it had been throughout the eighteenth century and the Empire. In architecture, painting and the decorative arts, people took their cue from developments in Paris. Among the highest classes in Germany, Poland and Russia, the passion for things French exercised a pervasive influence. With the prestige of French art behind him, Winterhalter came armed with impeccable credentials.

The courts of Europe rewarded the artist for his services with appropriate marks of respect. He did not aspire to emulate the worldly achievements of Rubens and Van Dyck. He was first and foremost a professional painter, not a courtier. The honours he received were correspondingly modest: the Order of St Anne, third class, from the Russian Court; the Royal Order of the Red Eagle, third class, from the Prussians; the Imperial Franz Josef Order from the Austrians; the Comenthur Cross from the Württembergs. The rank accorded to him was similar to that of a minor court official. Only in France was he given higher recognition, becoming a chevalier of the Légion d'Honneur in 1857.

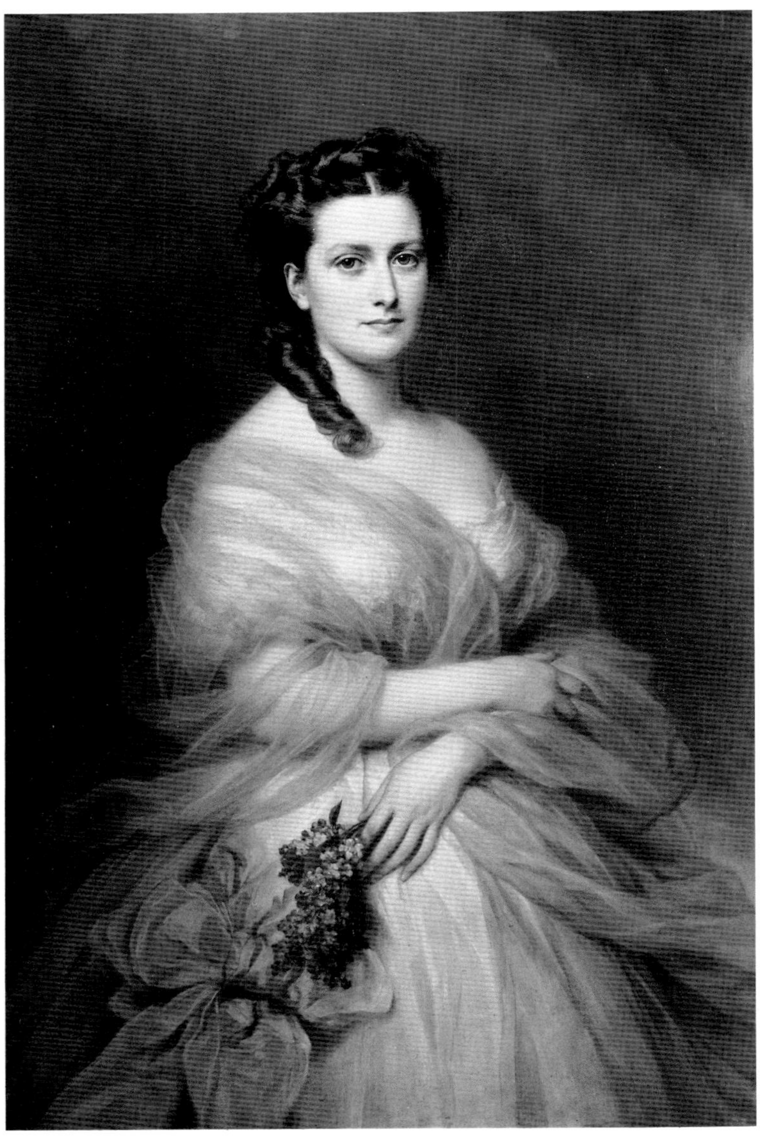

Figure 38
F.X. Winterhalter: *Princess Anna Murat, Duchesse de Mouchy*, 1862
114 × 80 cms
Château de Belœil

Winterhalter came into his own as a portrait painter during the Second Empire and there is no doubt that he painted his best work during the last two decades of his life. He matched this style to the luxury and relaxed moral atmosphere of the age, its hedonism and high living, its elegant fashions and sophisticated taste, its energy and gaiety. His female sitters of the 50s and 60s inhabit a different psychological climate from their predecessors of the 40s. They are not reticent and reserved, but knowing, alluring and eager for life.

Winterhalter's style was in tune with Second Empire taste. Like much of the architecture and applied art of the time, his painting was superficially neo-Rococo. His frothy and elegant creatures could invite comparison with the work of Watteau, Fragonard and Greuze. He was helped by the revival of eighteenth-century fashions and hairstyles, and by the use of filmy materials like lace and tulle in contemporary dress-making. His portraits transmitted qualities of lightness, movement and elegance associated with eighteenth-century painting, without becoming remotely imitative. Rococo was less a style to follow than a series of chic references to play up contemporary fashions.

In 1853, Théophile Gautier wrote of Winterhalter's official portraits: 'he made many such paintings in the corner of which sparkles with glittering facets a handsome rococo console, sculptured and gilded, with a pillar draped in a red velvet curtain in the background. Monbro would have found nothing at fault in the console, nor Délille in the materials; the figures of cream cheese and beaten pink charmed the models. Everyone was satisfied.'[45] Ten years later, Arthur Stevens voiced the same charge of superficiality: 'Winterhalter, we must concede, does show some taste in the portraits, a fashionable arrangement, if I may say so. How much affectation, how many tantalising coquetries have been displayed in the cause of popularity! All the magnificence of fashion plates has been achieved but there is no unity, no simplicity. Whoever contemplates the portraits admires the model's attire but does not seek out the head first, in other words the intelligent part. Bearing and gesture reveal nothing restful – where is grandeur, life, truth?'[46]

Winterhalter's later female portraits can be broadly distinguished by type and pattern. The choice of a particular format was determined partly by the function of the portrait, partly by the age and status of the sitter, and partly by the artist's sense of what would suit best. The question of size was secondary since that was determined by price. Certain favourite poses recur in whole-length and in threequarter-length form, though similarity is often disguised by the use of different backgrounds and accessories. *Lady Middleton* (no. 47) is a classic example of the full-face standing figure. In Winterhalter's portraits of the 1840s, the rigid effect of the crinoline is emphasized by the smooth unbroken fall of the material. Here the effect is relieved by the textural contrast between the delicate flounces and gatherings of the muslin ball-gown and the rich heavy folds of the velvet train, divided symmetrically down the middle. The same contrast of light dress and dark train can be seen in the earlier portrait of the Empress Eugénie (see fig. 34, p. 47), but the impact there is weakened by the less frontal pose of the sitter and the weakly gesturing hand. Lady Middleton's crossed hands, contained within the outline of the figure, convey the impression of interior calm and self-command. The sitter scarcely needs the supporting column and drapes to assert her claims to nobility.

The pose of Lady Middleton is repeated verbatim in contemporary whole-lengths of Queen Olga of Württemberg (Stuttgart) and of an unidentified woman, known only through a contemporary photographic reproduction by R.J. Bingham. Crossed hands are common to all three portraits, and may be said to denote the type.

At first glance the Duchesse de Mouchy (fig. 38), dressed simply in white, appears to belong to a different world from the remote grandeur of Lady Middleton. Her crossed hands are, however, the clue to what is, in essence, the same pose, though the pyramid shape of the whole-length figure has now become an hourglass. Other threequarter-length examples of the crossed-hands type include the Countess Bobrinskaia (The Hermitage, Leningrad), and the unidentified lady in black with fur cape known from a Bingham photograph. It can be identified on a still smaller scale in the half-length of the Duchesse de Morny (no. 64).

An alternative format favoured by Winterhalter for standing figures was the profile view, contrasting the ballooning line of the bustle, with the slender lines of shoulder, neck and head. The genesis of the type can be traced back to the fancy-dress picture of the Empress Eugénie dressed as Marie-Antoinette (no. 52), where the figure resembles the shape of a bell with curved handle. The same effect of domed dress and elegant carriage is conveyed by the famous portrait of the Princess Troubetskoï (no. 61), though with one significant difference. She turns to face the spectator with a very direct look, as if to dispel any suggestion that she belongs to the world of Arcadian make-believe. The landscape is pastiche Fragonard, as the dress is pastiche *Louis Seize*, but the Princess herself is vividly real and modern.

Later examples of the profile view include the threequarter-length portraits of the Duchess of Brabant (fig. 39) and of Princess Alexandra (no. 48), and the whole-lengths of the Empress Elizabeth (no. 79) and Lady Mary

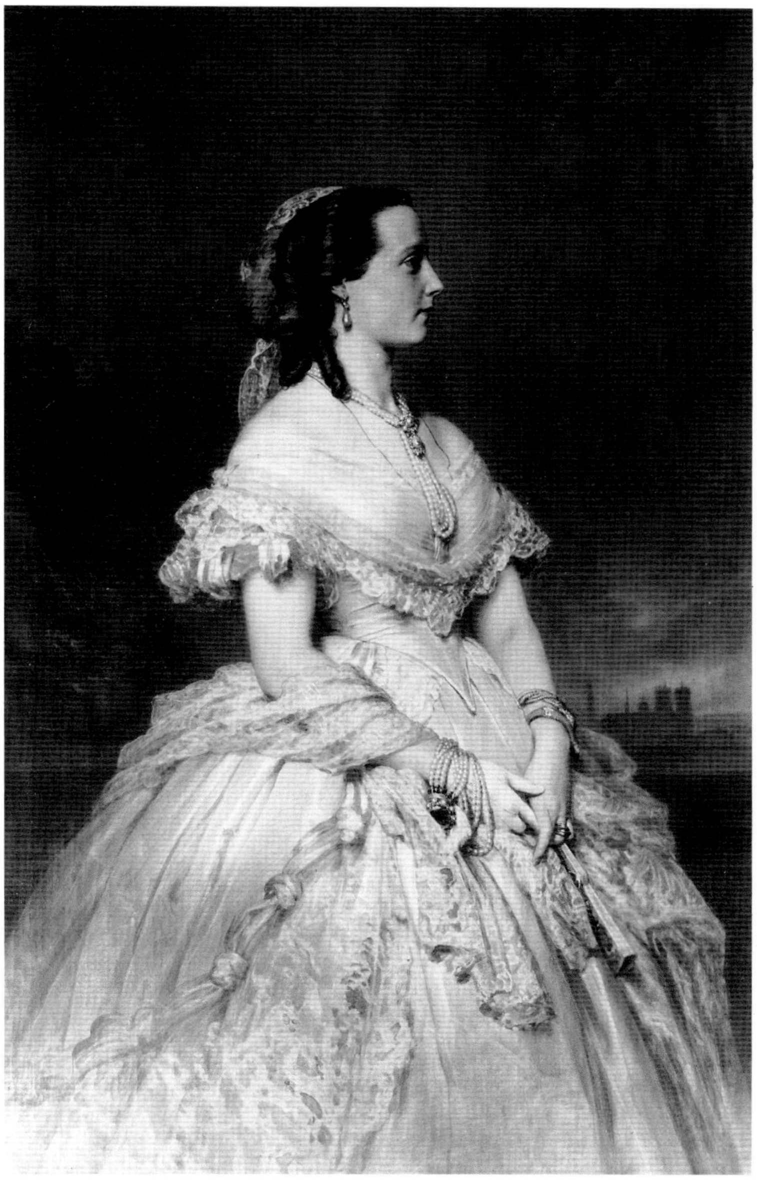

Figure 39
F.X. Winterhalter:
*Archduchess Marie of Austria, Duchess of Brabant*, 1863
157 × 106 cms
Collections Royales, Belgium

Douglas-Hamilton (fig. 40). The pose of Princess Alexandra is slightly more threequarter view than that of Princess Troubetsköi. She turns her head less sharply and there is no park scene behind her, but the shape of the dress and the treatment of the upper figure follow the same pattern. The Empress Elizabeth looks out over her shoulder, as if momentarily pausing in her walk, the soft gauze of her over-dress still moving in the breeze. The pose emphasizes the beauty of her head, and shoulders, and the swaying, sinuous grace of her figure. Lady Mary makes no such appeal to the spectator. Shielding her eyes with her fan she gazes seawards over hill and loch with the fearless look of a commander.

Winterhalter's repertoire of poses includes seated as well as standing figures. The late portraits of Queen Victoria (1859, Buckingham Palace) and the Empress Eugénie (see fig. 37, p. 50), are as potent and impressive as anything he had painted. Queen Victoria rests her hands on the arms of her chair in a gesture of Royal authority. She is raised on a dais, her crown outlined against a distant view of Westminster Abbey and the Houses of Parliament. Billowing dresses are a feature of all Winterhalter's seated portraits. The 1854 seated portrait of the Empress Eugénie (no. 50) is the prototype for a group showing the sitter threequarter view, often looking inwards: examples are the Countess Chouvalova (The Hermitage, Leningrad) and the Duchess of Alba (Duke of Alba). Princess Youssoupova (fig. 41), and the Countess Lamsdorf (Metropolitan Museum, New York) represent the conventional full-face pose, bust and head rising vertically from the perfect semicircle of the dress. Madame de Jurjewicz (no. 62) and Princess Obolensky (Private Collection) are more expansive in composition and more sensual in mood. Both ladies lean back, filling the space top as well as bottom, with one arm crooked to fondle a lock of hair.

Though Winterhalter was always constrained by the conventions of formal portraiture, his art became more daring and inventive as the Second Empire proceeded. His amazing portrait of Princess Anna of Hesse (fig. 42) represents the ultimate expression of his virtuosity. It is difficult to believe that tulle can assume such convoluted forms, or that it could be painted with such gossamer-like delicacy, appearing to weave about the sitter with a life of its

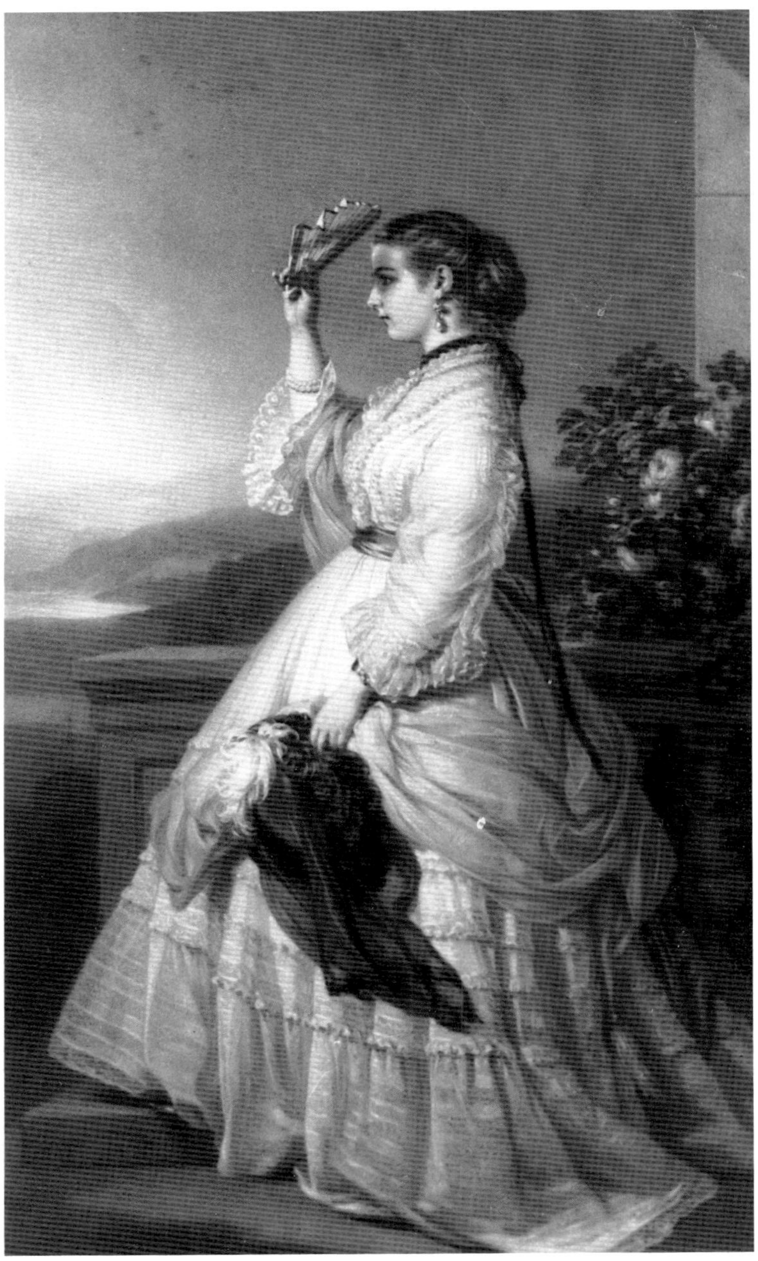

Figure 40
After F.X. Winterhalter:
*Lady Mary Douglas-Hamilton*
Engraving: location unknown

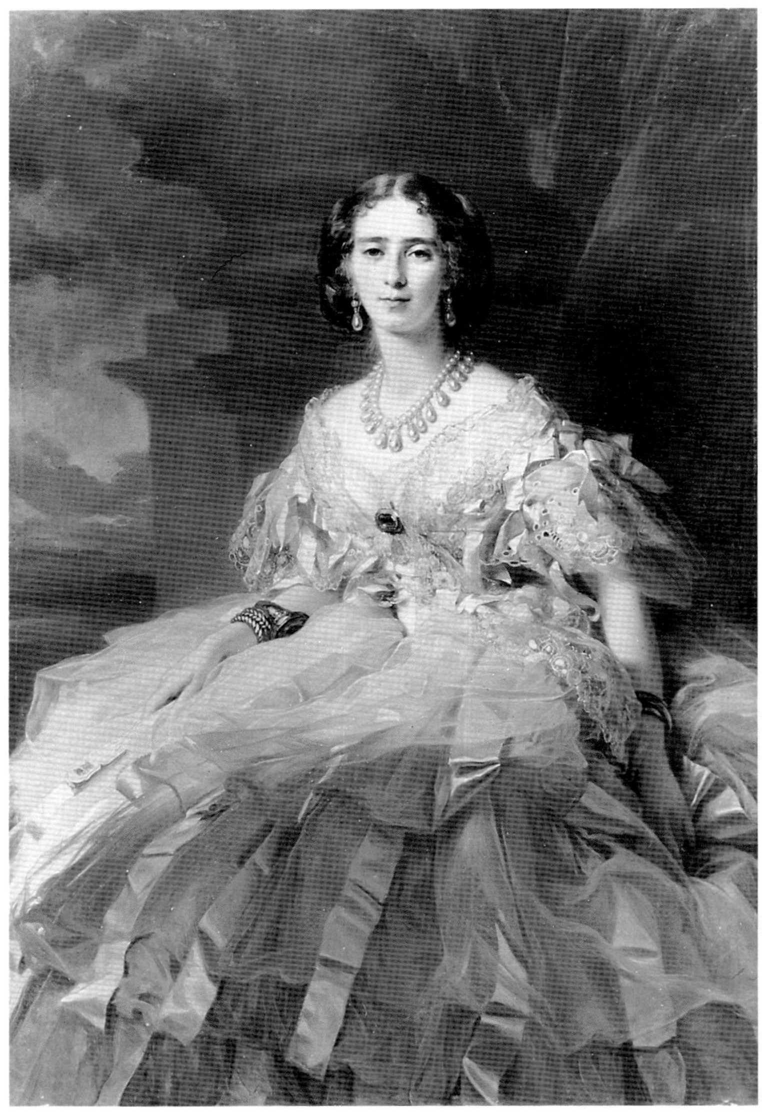

Figure 41
F.X. Winterhalter:
*Princess Tatiana Alexandrovna Youssoupova*, 1858
147 × 104 cms
The Hermitage, Leningrad

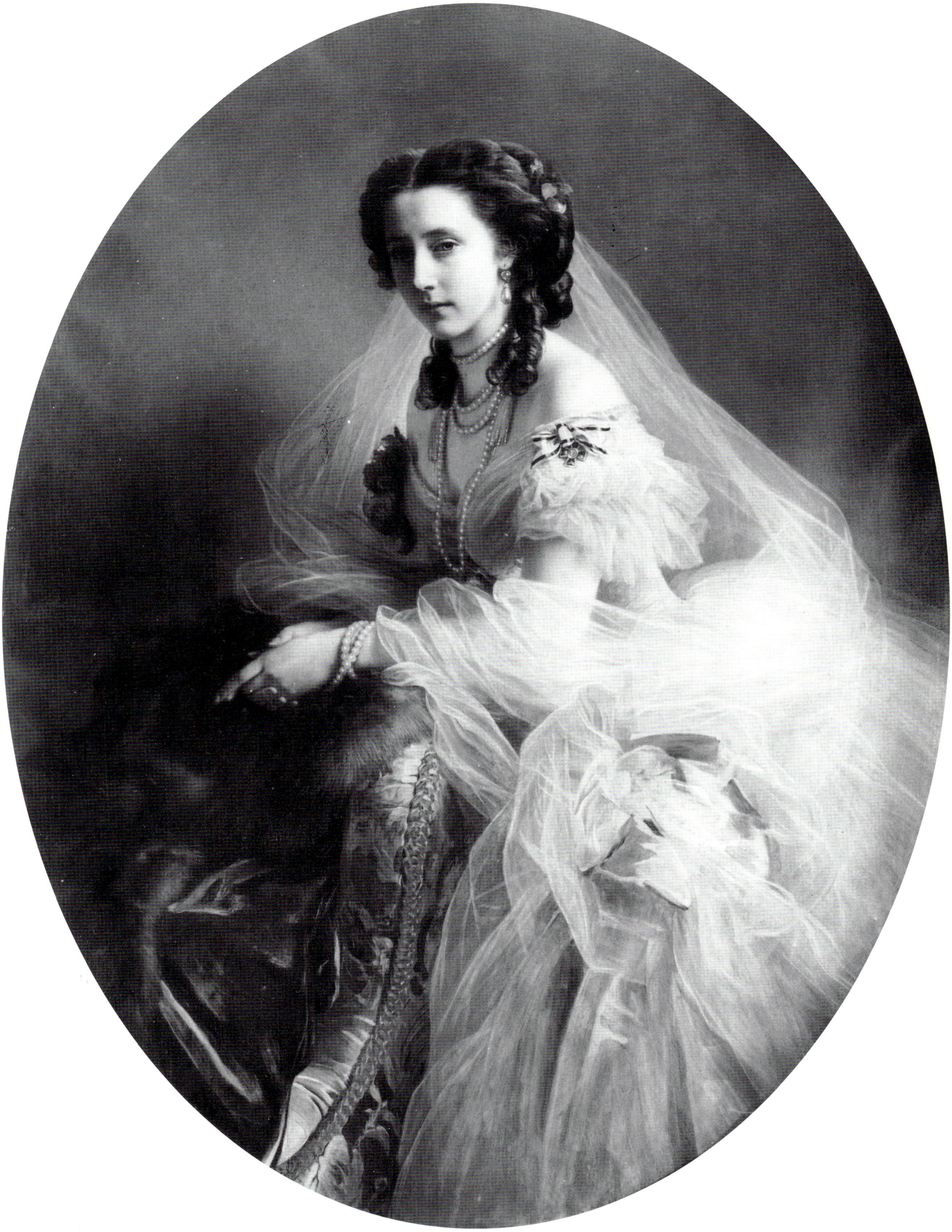

Figure 42
F.X. Winterhalter: *Princess Anna von Preussen, Landgräfin von Hesse*, 1858
147 × 115.5 cms, Schloss Fasanerie Museum, Fulda

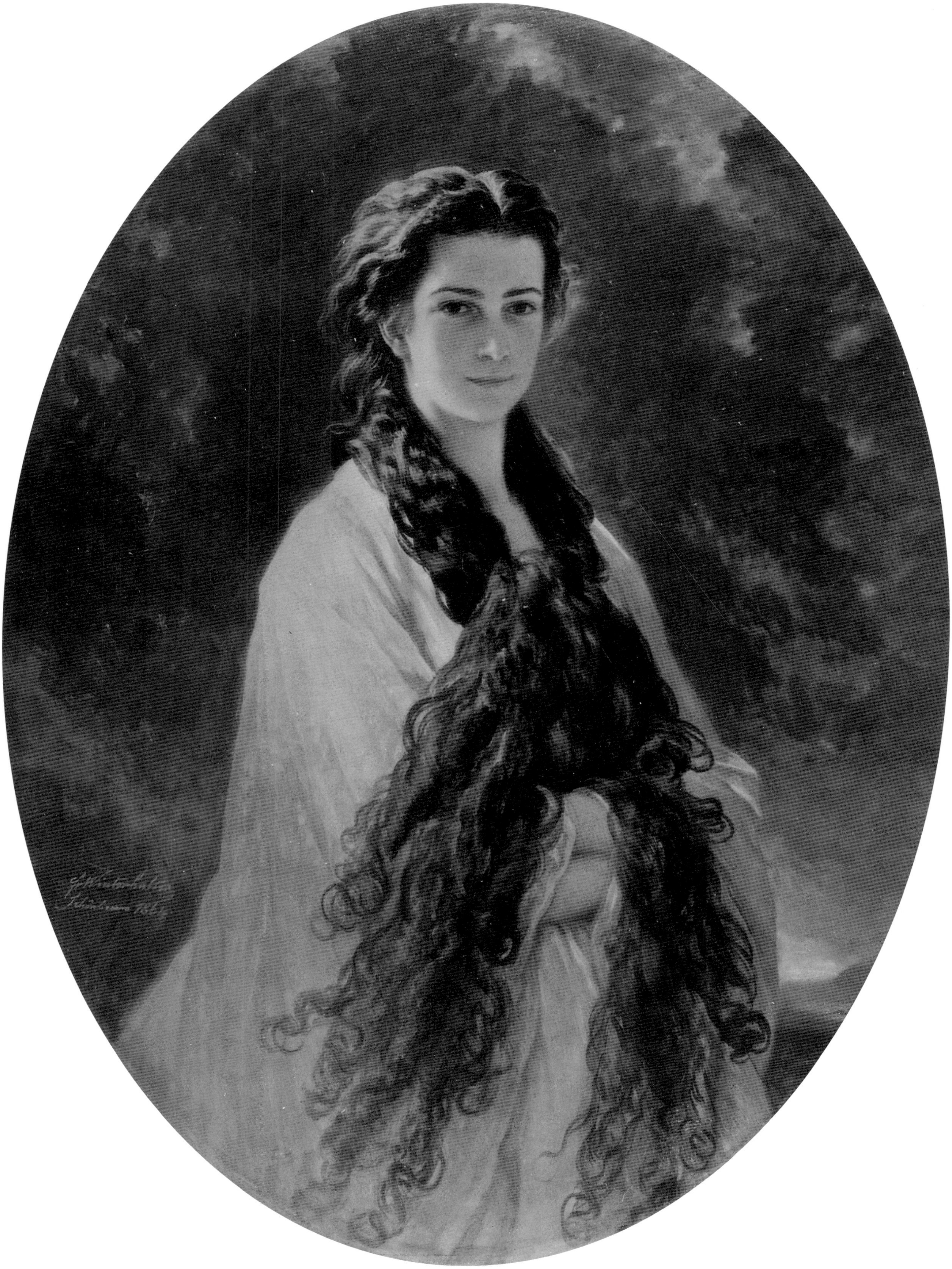

Figure 43
F.X. Winterhalter: *Elizabeth, Empress of Austria*, 1864, location unknown

own. The Princess leans her arms on the back of a chair in an attitude of studied informality, the extended index fingers of her clasped hands, like the intelligent and quizzical expression of her features, perhaps posing a question.

The chair-back motif is repeated in a portrait of Madame Rimsky-Korsakov (Penza, USSR) (no. 60), and in a portrait of Countess Branicka (Philadelphia Museum of Art). A second portrait of Madame Rimsky-Korsakov (no. 65) is one of Winterhalter's boldest and most sensual depictions of female beauty, comparable to the female studies by the realist master, Gustave Courbet (1819–77). Suddenly interrupted in the act of undressing, she clasps a long tress of hair to her bosom in a gesture of modesty. The sense of arrested movement, the unguarded look of the sitter, and the provocative details of her *déshabillé*, impart an extraordinary vitality to the image. The only pictures to compare with it are those of the Empress Elizabeth, painted in the same year. In the portrait in Vienna (no. 79), she is posed in profile in a loose wrap, her hair, famous for its length, reaching below her hips. In the second portrait (fig. 43), she stands full-face with folded arms, her hair knotted loosely at the neck falling in great strands.

Winterhalter continued to paint groups and he remained popular as a painter of children. His set of heads of Queen Victoria's children are freshly observed and wonderfully vivid (fig. 44); they well stand comparison with Gainsborough's earlier sequence of George III's sons and daughters. Among the artist's Russian and Polish commissions are several of children which deserve wider recognition for their very direct and natural qualities (nos. 70, 71, 72). Winterhalter clearly liked young children and responded to their personalities with instinctive sympathy.

As a chronicler of men, Winterhalter occupies a lower level of achievement. His male sitters inspired few original or memorable compositions. He could do the formal parade portrait competently enough, but rarely with much enthusiasm. The 1859 portrait of the Prince Consort (Royal Collection, Buckingham Palace), companion to the seated Queen Victoria, shows the sitter wearing the uniform of the Rifle Brigade, one foot placed before the other, his left hand resting on his sword hilt. The whole-lengths of King Karl of Württemberg (Staatsgalerie, Stuttgart) and the Emperor Franz Joseph (no. 78) are similar in idea and design. Heroics in the manner of Sir Thomas Lawrence's (1769–1830) portraits have given way to prosaic court formality. Only in the portrait of Duleep Singh (no. 40), which is a variant on the same theme, does Winterhalter strike sparks. Here the curved scimitar is used for dramatic effect, to play up the exotic appearance of this Sikh prince in full regalia. The painting, with its scintillating effects of light and colour, matches the romantic glamour of its subject. Duleep Singh is something of an exception. The majority of Winterhalter's male portraits are modest and unpretentious threequarter-lengths and half-lengths.

As a portraitist, it is relatively easy to relate Winterhalter to the society of his time. As an artist, he remains

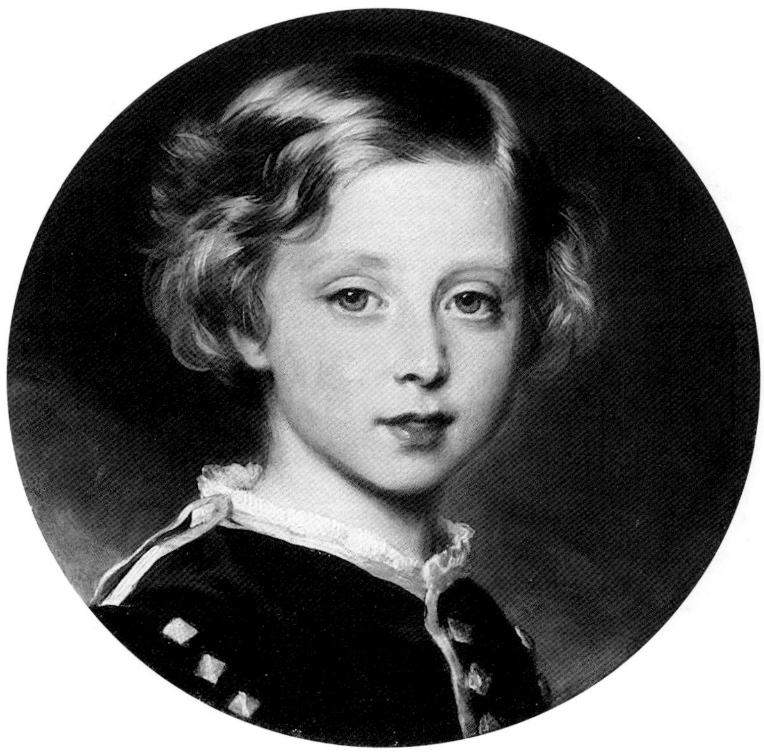

Figure 44
F.X. Winterhalter: *Prince Leopold*, 1859
Roundel, 34.3 cms
By gracious permission of Her Majesty The Queen

a difficult figure to place. There are few painters with whom to compare him, and he does not fit into any of the current schools or orthodoxies. His early affinities were neo-Classical, but experience had long since turned him away from the idealized art of Ingres and his followers. As they exercised such a pervasive influence over French portraiture during the middle decades of the century, it is worth exploring the comparison. The famous portrait of Madame Moitessier by Ingres (see *Fashion in the Work of Winterhalter*, fig. 54, p. 67) is marked by formality of design, smooth rendering of surface, even light, hallucinatory colour and an atmosphere of extreme stillness. Winterhalter's Princess Youssoupova (see fig. 41, p. 54), by contrast, is all movement, chiaroscuro, suggestion and sensibility. Ironically it is the Classicizing Ingres, rather than the fashionable Winterhalter, who provides the better record of contemporary dress.

It is a truism to say that the portraits by Winterhalter's French contemporaries tend to be more rooted in the experience of real life than his aspired to be. The portrait of Madeleine Rohan by Paul Baudry (fig. 45) reflects the realist tendencies emerging in the work of the younger generation. It is, however, far closer in spirit to Ingres than to Winterhalter, in its studied analysis of form and design, its restrained treatment and truth to appearance. French portraiture was moving into a sombre, sub-fusc phase, dominated by tonal values. Léon Bonnat (1833–1922), Carolus-Duran (1837–1917) and Fantin-Latour (1836–1904) may be taken as representatives of the new trend. Winterhalter was not immune to these developments. His portraits of the later 1860s are often surprisingly direct (no. 80).

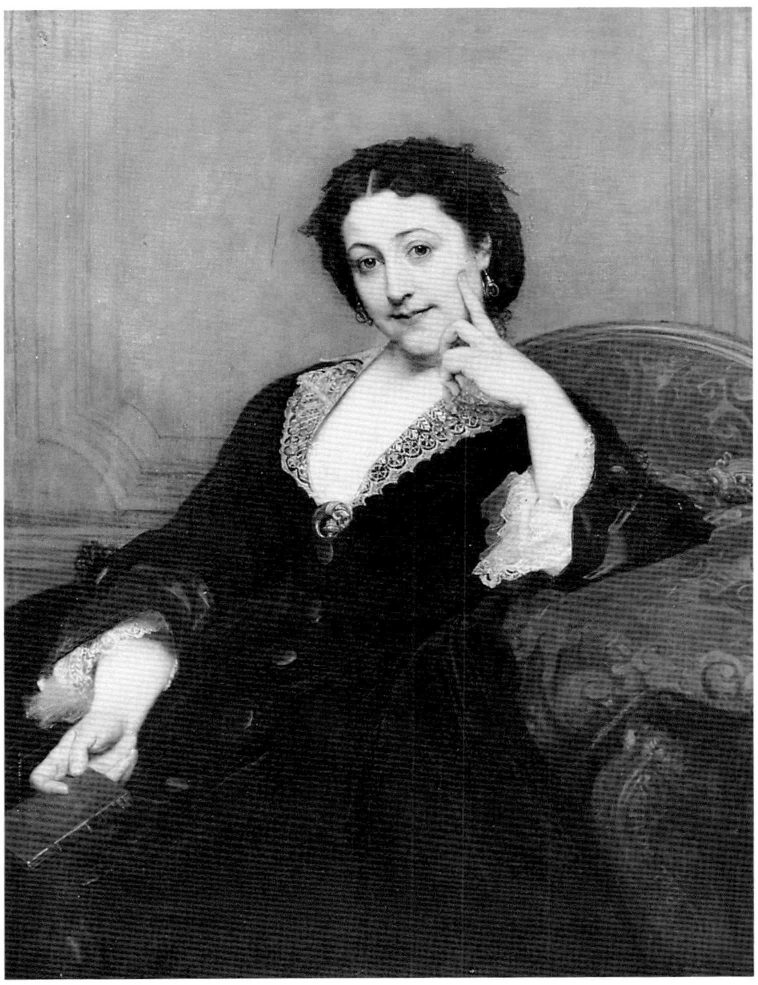

Figure 45
P. Baudry: *Madeleine Rohan*, 1860
106 × 84 cms
Musée d'Orsay, Paris

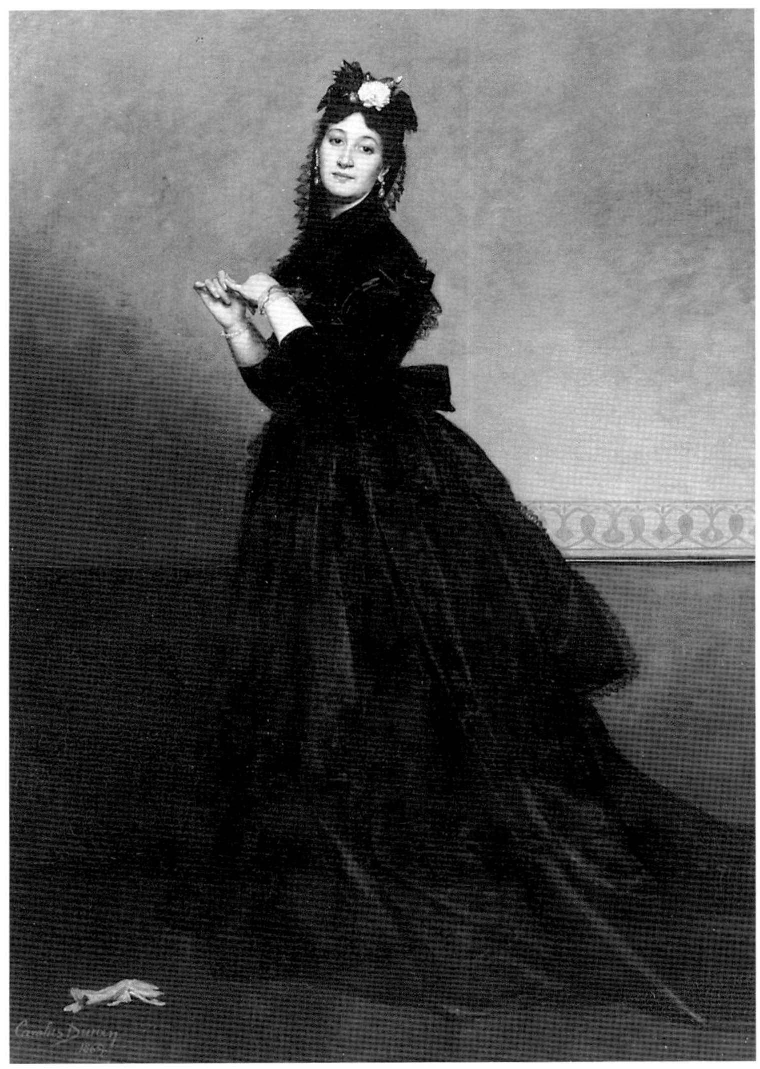

Figure 46
E.A. Carolus-Duran: *La Dame au Gant: Madame Carolus-Duran*, 1869
228 × 164 cms
Musée d'Orsay, Paris

Carolus-Duran's *Femme au Gant* (fig. 46) is placed before a modern setting of dado and wall; Winterhalter's *Princess Woronzova* (fig. 47) inhabits an elegant Van Dyckian landscape. The first was hailed as a masterpiece of modern art when it appeared at the Salon of 1869. The second would have been regarded as Romantically old-fashioned by the same public. Yet the similarity between the two figures, both dressed in dark outdoor costume, is very marked, not only in terms of pose and type, but more subtly in terms of psychology. Carolus-Duran became the embodiment of fashionable portraiture in the 1870s and '80s. Through him the elegant and cosmopolitan spirit of Winterhalter's art would be transmitted to the next generation of international portraitists, John Singer Sargent (1856–1925) Giovanni Boldini (1845–1931), J. Sorolla (1863–1923) and Philip de Laszlo (1869–1937). The line between the fashionable styles of the Empire and the Belle Epoque is tenuous, but without Winterhalter it would be scarcely traceable at all.

Of Winterhalter's more immediate influence there is less to be said. In France, his closest imitator was Edouard Dubufe (1820–83) whose father, Claude-Marie, had copied his style in the 1840s. The younger Dubufe enjoyed wide patronage in Paris and London, and closely modelled his work on that of the older artist (fig. 48). In Germany, Richard Lauchert (1823–69) and Heinrich von Angeli (1840–1925) followed the lead of their compatriot and pursued international careers. The real successor to Winterhalter in Germany, however, and an artist of considerable ability, was Franz von Lenbach (1836–1904). In England, there are traces of Winterhalter's influence in the early portraits by Frederick Leighton (1830–96), but in general his style had little impact.

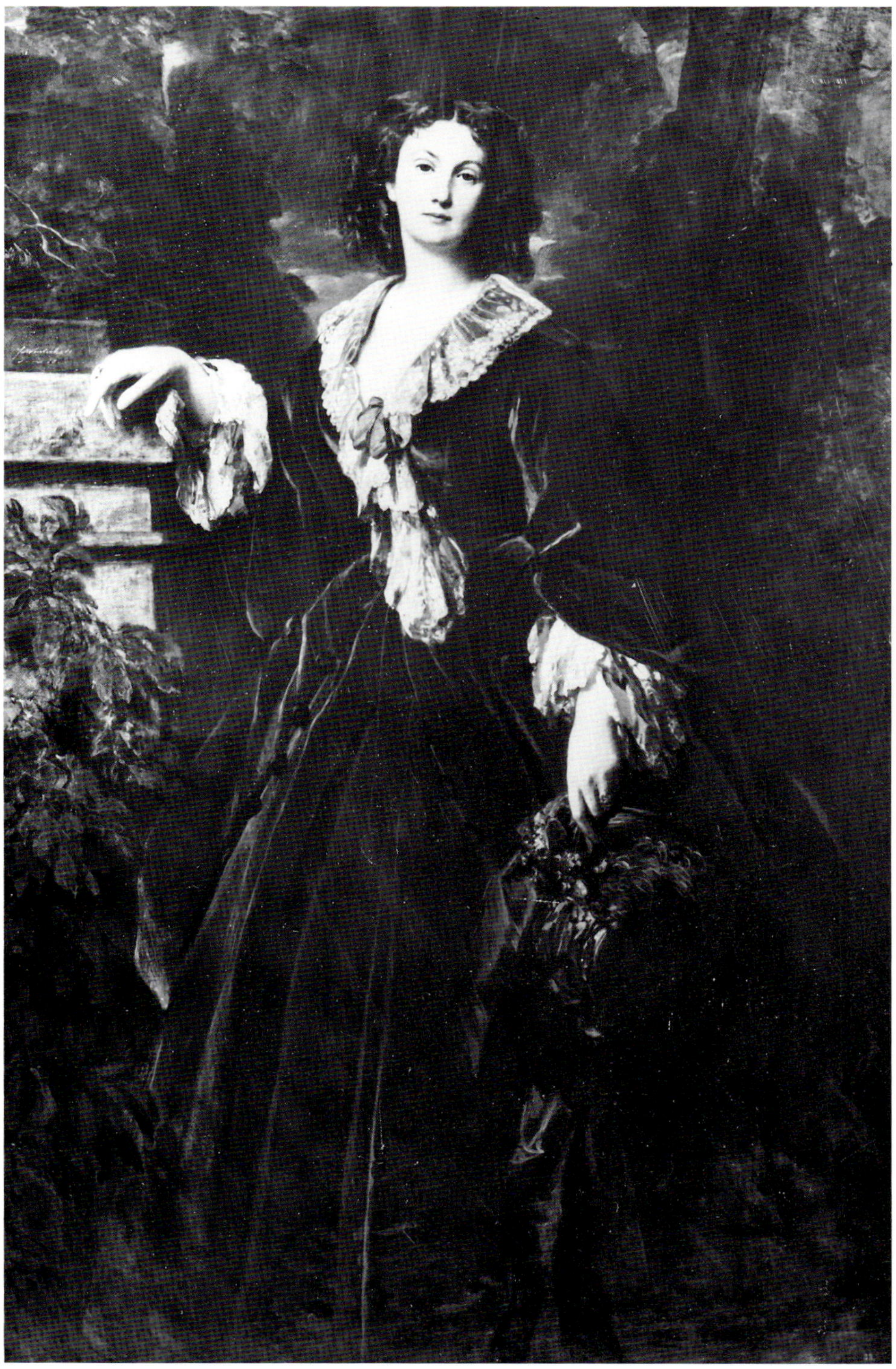

Figure 47
F.X. Winterhalter: *Princess Maria Woronzova*, c.1859
Destroyed

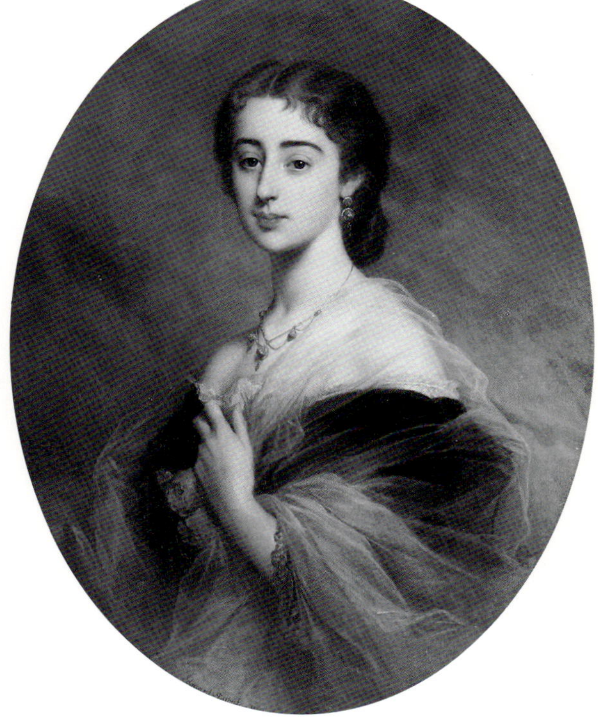

Figure 48
E. Dubufe: *Bene Garofalo, Mrs Clare Ford*, 1860
86.3 × 67.3 cms approx.
Collection Sir Brinsley Ford, CBE, FSA

In view of his long and productive career, surprisingly few details survive to document Winterhalter's studio practice and working methods. It is known that he painted very rapidly and very fluently. The absence of preliminary studies or drawings suggests that he designed most of his compositions straight on the canvas. One exception is *The Empress Eugénie Surrounded by her Ladies-in-Waiting* (no. 53), for which a number of sketches survive (no. 54). Once a design was established, it seems probable that the head was finished first, and the costume and background added afterwards. Studio assistance may have been used for these subsidiary parts, but there are few signs of empty or repetitive passages. His portraits have a unity of effect which would make such collaboration difficult. Few descriptions survive to reveal how he posed his sitters, or the way in which he painted them. While he was capable of painting a head in a single sitting, five or six seems to have been the norm. The choice of costume must invariably have been his, since his conception of a portrait depended so heavily on it. In a letter referring to a sitting, perhaps for the portrait of 1860 exhibited here (no. 63), Princess Metternich wrote to him: 'I am at your disposition from Thursday onwards. I shall then appear with the desired coiffure and several small items, and also flowers; I will leave my head to your care, and I for my part will pose as well as I possibly can, otherwise I shall wish for nothing else.'[47]

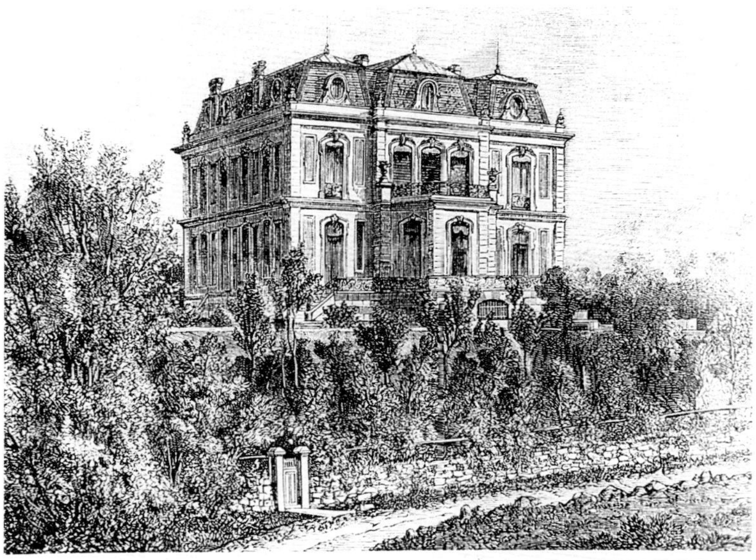

Figure 49
The Villa Trianon, Baden
Engraving

Winterhalter might have been expected to capitalize on his reputation by making his sitters pay heavily for the privilege. In fact, his prices remained remarkably stable, and they are consistent with those charged by other leading portraitists of the time. The market was firmly established, and it was not worthwhile for an artist, however famous, to risk pricing himself out of it. In 1842, the threequarter-length portraits of Queen Victoria and Prince Albert (nos. 27, 28) had cost 150 guineas each. A decade later they would have cost 200 guineas, with corresponding prices for a half-length and whole-length of 100 and 300 guineas respectively. These sums are identical to prices charged by Sir Francis Grant, the leading English portraitist of this time. Winterhalter's income from portraiture, including copyright fees, is likely to have been a little less than £5,000 per annum. This was a substantial income by any standards, but it did not match the vast sums earned by successful subject painters from the late 1850s onwards.

Winterhalter sought respite from the pressures of a busy portrait practice in holidays abroad, in Italy, Switzerland and above all, in Germany. He remained firmly attached to his native country by past ties and deep family affections. He and Hermann travelled regularly to Karlsruhe, Baden-Baden and the Black Forest. They remained in constant touch with their father, and they continued to support him and their sisters on a generous scale. In the autumn of 1851, for example, Winterhalter sent a remittance of 3,000 francs to his father (5,000 the year before), and 6,000 francs to each sister; to Theresia for the education of her sons; to Justina for a new kitchen at the Adler Inn. During the ensuing decade, Winterhalter supervised the rebuilding of the entire Inn, to the plans of Berckmüller. 'It simply can't remain as it is now, the light ought to come from the roof to the stairs', he wrote to his father on 23 October 1859, 'Herr Berckmüller has shown me how this could be arranged, & how the doors to the big guest-room should be large. . . . You must do all that Herr Berckmüller says. His plans are practicable, and cannot be improved upon'.[48]

A desire to put down roots himself led Winterhalter to build his own villa in 1859 at Baden-Baden, which had remained his favourite summer resort. In October the magazine *L'Artiste* announced that the villa would be very pretty and very 'sérieuse', and that it would cost at least 100,000 francs, 'just about the price of five of his paintings'. His architect, Monsieur Olive, was French, his agent, Herr L. Lang, a local man. Letters from both followed Winterhalter about Europe, requesting advice on this or that detail of building, discussing plans for the garden, urgently demanding money. The house (fig. 49), built between 1859 and 1861, was a dignified two-storey building, of symmetrical design, faced with stucco. Inside, it was well-appointed with parquet floors, marble fireplace and mirrors. 'It is necessary for me to know whether you want the rooms executed in the style of the exterior,' wrote Lang in 1860, 'which means the ceiling and the walls rendered with stucco and painted or gilded: or whether you want the walls papered'.[49] Situated in the Friedricksgasse (now Winterhalterstrasse), Winterhalter's Villa Trianon was one of several new houses springing up in this fashionable spa town. It was sufficiently imposing to be singled out for special mention in contemporary guide-books. Then having expended so much time and effort on the enterprise, Winterhalter quite suddenly sold the house at the end of 1862, to the Auffm-Ordt family, before it was completely finished. Hermann told his father that it had proved over-large and expensive to run, and that the stream of visitors had proved burdensome. In truth, the itinerant Winterhalter was too incurably restless to settle anywhere for long.

By the 1860s, Winterhalter's career had reached a high plateau. There were no peaks to be climbed. With few startling developments or changes in style, he continued to pursue his career as a portraitist. His last subject picture, a study of Susannah and the Elders (fig. 50) was executed in 1860. Inspired by Titian and Rubens, it produces much the same erotic frisson as the nude models in *Florinda*. Winterhalter had never entirely abandoned subject painting. His picture of *Spring* (*Der Frühling*) (no. 39) is a reminder of his imaginative powers, and the Winterhalter *Album* contains several studies of idealized models.

As Winterhalter's work for the French Court came to an end, new sitters appeared on the scene. In 1861, he painted the King and Queen of Prussia, and the following year, in Berlin, a large group of Crown Prince Frederick of Prussia with his wife Victoria, the Princess Royal, and their children. In the summer of 1864, he undertook wedding portraits of the Prince and Princess of Wales (no. 48) on his

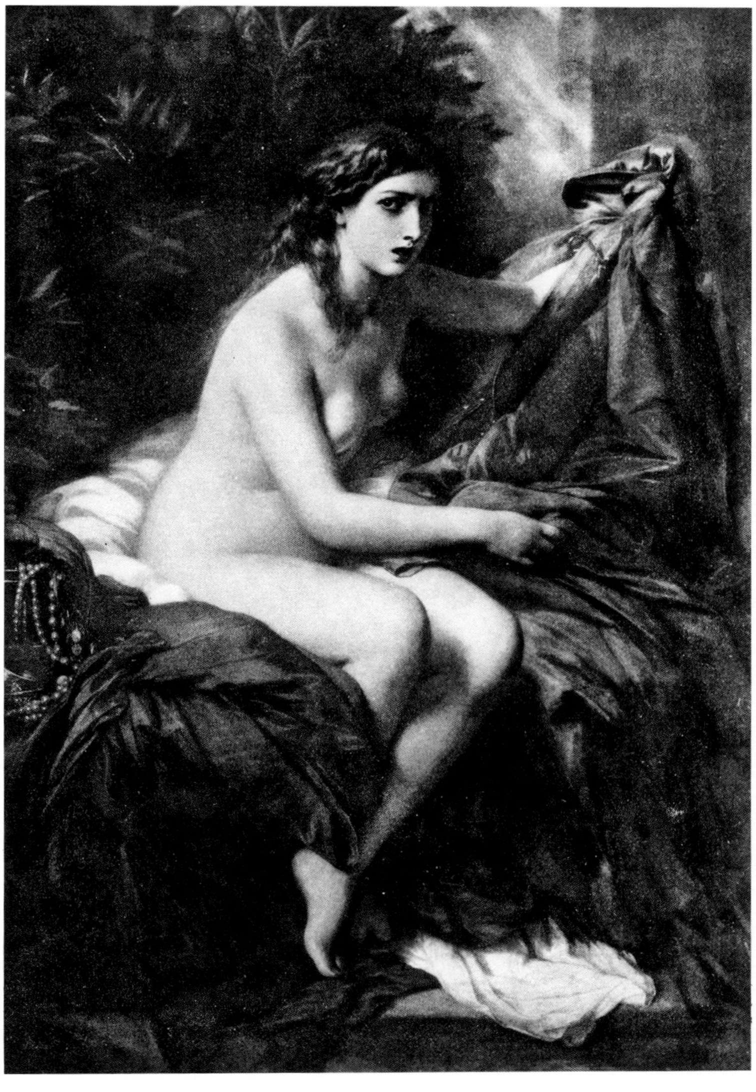

Figure 50
F.X. Winterhalter: *Susannah and the Elders*
Location unknown

last visit to England, and in the autumn of that year he travelled to Vienna to execute the state portraits of the Emperor Franz Josef I and the Empress Elizabeth (nos. 78, 79). He was given an apartment at Schönbrunn, together with a studio, where he carried out private portrait commissions. In 1865, he went to Rosenau in Coburg at the request of Queen Victoria to paint Prince Alfred and his two sisters, Princess Louise and Princess Helena (all Royal Collection).

As the Second Empire approached its zenith, Winterhalter's world contracted. The reminiscences of the art critic, Friedrich Pecht, provide an invaluable insight into his life at this time:

> *'Formerly he had had a small pale head with black hair its chief attraction, now the locks were silver-grey. He had withdrawn from French society and associated almost exclusively with Germans. They formed a small circle round him, which met at his table for the excellent cooking of Mère Morel, to whom he introduced me. I later spent most of my evenings there. Winterhalter was always high spirited, and when we left the restaurant we went to the Grand Café to enjoy our demi-tasse, after which we would stroll along the boulevards till late at night. He would tell comic stories about his own youth, and his time in Italy, the very last thing he would do would be to boast about his high acquaintances and sitters, as so many others did. His criticisms of works of art were individual, never depreciative. . . . Though depreciatively nicknamed "the Frenchman" he remained always a German, for all his love of French manners and Paris. Yes, it was touching to see how he could not suppress his German nature.'*[50]

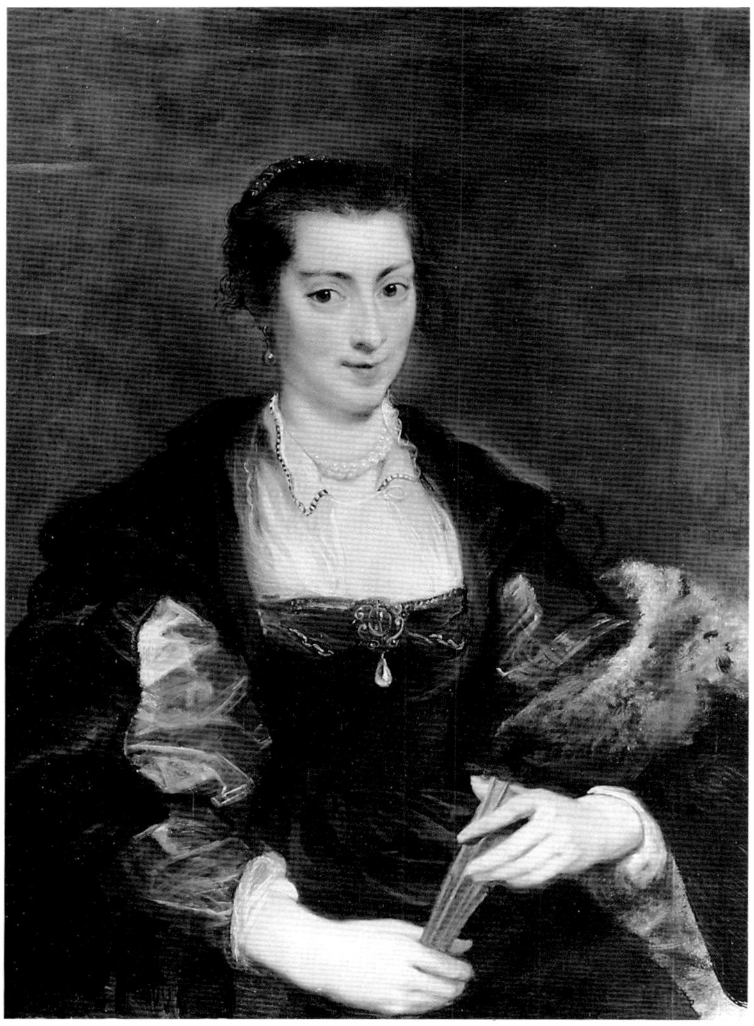

Figure 51
P.P. Rubens: *Isabella Brandt*, 1620
97.3 × 71.5 cms
Staatliche Museen Preussischer Kulturbesitz, Gemäldegalerie, Berlin, Dahlem

Pecht's impression is confirmed by another contemporary, W. Landgraf:

> *'I made Winterhalter's personal acquaintance in Paris in 1863. Never did a royal portrait painter correspond less to the conception one has of such a favourite of rulers. He had remained completely simple, natural and without mannerisms, and even retained something of the southern German rural population about him. His lifestyle, his needs were extremely modest. His correspondingly simple studio contained only one ornament, but naturally the most exquisite and costly: a wonderful large portrait of a woman (lifesize half-portrait) by P. P. Rubens that probably represents his first wife with a fur wrapper over her shoulders.'*[51]

Winterhalter's studio was at no. 64 rue de la Rochefoucauld. Apart from the Rubens portrait (fig. 51), a number of other works of art hung there, including the portrait of a woman attributed to Van Dyck, a portrait of himself by Eduard Magnus, another of August Riedel by L. Pollak, a view of Rome by Pinelli, and gardens of the Château d'Eu by Simon Fort, a Capri house by C. Carelli, and a storm at sea by Andreas Achenbach. Among paintings by himself were studies of models, his picture of Spring (no. 39), and copies after Titian and Guido Reni. There is no contemporary view of the studio, but it was photographed during his occupancy of one of his successors, the English landscapist, William Horton, around 1906.

Winterhalter's residence was at no. 2 rue de la Chaussée d' Antin on the right bank. He moved there from the nearby rue Basse-du-Rempart in 1858 when his apartment building was demolished. Among his neighbours was a collector of musical instruments and the composer, Rossini, whose music the artist deeply admired. The faithful Hermann now lived on his own at no. 68 rue de l'Arcade. He had begun to strike out more independently, developing a modest portrait practice of his own during the 1850s. A diary of sitters for the period 1852–5 reveals details of his rate of work. Between December 1852 and June 1853, he was at work on thirteen female portraits. Of his chief sitters for this period, Madame Manuel, Madame Say and Madame Heine, none sat less than twenty times, and he never received more than one sitter a day.[52]

As he grew older, Winterhalter's links with France weakened, while the siren call of his native Germany grew stronger. Paris had been the centre of his professional life, the source of the art and culture he most admired, but it had never claimed him spiritually. His affections remained centred around his family. When his younger sister, Theresia Wild, died early in 1863, he wrote to his father that the news 'has stricken us sorely. We didn't even know she was sick . . . God give her peace. Even though we must all follow her soon, it is difficult to accustom oneself to the temporary loss of one of the family. We hope to come to you soon, but we are still bound by many orders'. His elder sister, Justina Mayer, suffered a series of strokes, and was semi-paralysed. 'Oh that Justina were well again', Winterhalter wrote feelingly to her son-in-law, Baptist Schlageter; but she never recovered, dying in 1867. Fidel himself was failing. 'Nothing could have given us a better send-off for the New Year than a letter in your hand', wrote Hermann to his father in January 1863: 'It is a sure sign that you are well, thanks be to God. . . . The red wine that my brother sent you is said to bring health – It is an excellent brand known as Bordeaux – which is pronounced Bordo – but it does not stand keeping in the cold.'[53] By May, Fidel was dead, at the age of eighty-nine, a proud and devoted father to the end.

As the older generation died out, Winterhalter continued to take a keen interest in the activities of his nephews and nieces. Justina's elder daughter, Wilhelmina, was running the Adler Inn, now a prosperous concern and popular with tourists, with her husband, Heinrich Mayer. Her younger daughter, Frederika, was married to an entrepreneur, Johann Baptist Schlageter. He was responsible for building an inn at Hohenschwand on the Feldberg in the Black Forest, later run by Theresia's eldest daughter, Justina. Winterhalter stayed there in September 1866, but was unable to attend Justina's marriage to Augustin Mayer in November, though he sent his best wishes. Of Theresia's six remaining children, Hermann was an artist, Oskar a doctor, Karl a farmer, Balbina the wife of her cousin Peter Mayer, Franz Xaver and Pankranz watchmakers in Switzerland.

When Justina's husband, Augustin, requested a loan of 20,000 florins in 1870, to help buy an inn at Säckingen, Winterhalter replied to Baptist from Nice:

> *'I doubt if Augustin is capable of such an enterprise. But if I give him the 20,000 florins the others will have the right to demand as much too, so that to be fair I should have to part with 100,000 florins. And then who knows what kind of a muddle you might get into should things go wrong? I could only do it that way if I have your consent that I give 20,000 florins to you all as a gift, and under the condition that you loan it to Justina and she pay you the interest. But please understand that I really cannot give all my nephews and nieces 20,000 florins. It would be safer if I were to invest the money and give you the interest.'*[54]

The purchase of the inn went ahead, and Winterhalter followed the plans of the rebuilding with close attention. He was also involved with another of Baptist's enterprises, a new paper and cellulose factory at Neustadt, Schwarzwald, spending increasingly large sums of money for both projects right up to the time of his death.

A glimpse of Winterhalter in the late 1860s is provided by three letters he wrote to Friedrich Pecht in 1867.[55] The latter had written a critique of painting at the French 'International Exhibition' which Winterhalter was anxious to read: 'You were going to send it to me care of a beautiful Munich lady', he wrote from Bad Ems in June 1867, 'but since the beautiful ladies who take walks here are not labelled like wine bottles I have not yet been able to identify her'. In a later letter of 2 October 1867, written from Paris, he wrote to congratulate Pecht on 'the courage and bravery with which you fight for the dignity of art and seek to put everything in its proper place and explain to people why. And I believe they will not contradict you – they would almost be ashamed to! For you speak after all only for the honour of art, and this art criticism of yours is the most respectable I have yet heard. And then the thing is quite amusing and the "videndo dicere verum" comes across very well in it. Yesterday I was at the exhibition again and came across your book twice in the possession of bankers' families'. In the same letter, Winterhalter spoke of his unsettled life, and the peregrinations which had prevented him from visiting Pecht in the Bavarian Tyrol, 'as we first had to go home to the Black Forest. We got as far as Rheinegg, but then had to turn back and go in search of two pictures'.

Winterhalter was in Switzerland taking a cure, when news came of the outbreak of war between France and Prussia, the early disastrous battles, and finally of Napoleon's capitulation at Sedan (2 September 1870). The Second Empire was swept away. Instead of returning to Paris, at the end of the holiday, he and Hermann headed for Karlsruhe instead. The transition was smooth and without trauma, a natural culmination of Winterhalter's growing preference for Germany over France, an enforced early retirement. He was still officially credited to the Baden Court; all the orders and honours he had received had always been formally approved at Karlsruhe before acceptance. He and Hermann fitted back into provincial court life, taking an apartment at no. 4 Friedrichsplatz, the elegant and spacious circle designed by Berckmüller. 'We are quite happy here', Winterhalter told Baptist in November 1871, 'though naturally we miss many things. It is very uncomfortable for one thing. Perhaps we should put more furniture into this apartment. Anyway we mean to stop here. But if it is a question of work we must go to some other town. Here we get no orders and see no prospects of any coming'.[56]

Occasional interruptions to their quiet regime served to remind them of the world of high fashion they had left behind. In 1871, they were guests of the Tsar and Tsarina at Bad Petersthal, a popular spa, with a glittering company of European Royals. Winterhalter's later letters, however, reveal little sign of nostalgia or regret for the past. Workhorse though he was, he seems content to have hung up his brushes and mahl-stick, and to have accepted retirement naturally. His friend, Stallmeister Meyer, Master of the Stables to Queen Victoria, found this transition more painful. Writing to Winterhalter in January 1872, he poured out his heart:

*'The Queen looked after us like a loving mother. Altogether, Winterchen, the way in which everything was arranged, the consideration in all respects, the marks of friendship shown by all the other gentlemen at the Court, made leaving England very hard for me, and it is hard for me to accustom myself to living here [Hanover], for I have become alienated from Germany, an alienation to which the narrowness and small-mindedness of the people contributes a good deal. Oh Winterchen, those were really happy days when you used to say; "Meyer, Meyer you must play 'God Safe the Queen' once more or else we shall not get home and Coblitz will eat up all the cheese." I am often assailed by a melancholy which I cannot describe in words. All your beautiful pictures of the Royal Family I have hung just as they were in London.'*[57]

During his last two years of life, Winterhalter found a limited circle of patrons in the banking community of Frankfurt. Among his sitters of this time were Olga von Grunelius and Emma von Passavant. During a visit to the city in the summer of 1873, he contracted typhus, as a result of an epidemic that eventually claimed sixty lives. The speed with which he succumbed to the disease suggests that years of travel and concentrated work had taken their toll of his health. He was rushed from the house of his banking friends, the von Metzlers, to the Diakonissen Krankenhaus, a hospital run by Protestant nuns, but all efforts to save him were in vain. He died on 8 July 1873. His disconsolate brother, Hermann, sent brief details to Baptist Schlageter in a letter of 18 July: 'He had not been feeling well for some time but he didn't go to bed till Friday when he had a burning fever, which brought his life to an end. It is a comfort for me to know that he was unconscious and I think without pain. I ask you to tell all our relatives of this so irreplaceable loss in my name, as I am at present quite unable to do it. I have to stay here to attend the funeral.'[58]

Winterhalter lies buried in the cemetery in Frankfurt under an imposing tomb topped by an angel designed by O. Sommer (fig. 52). Funds for the maintenance of the tomb have long since evaporated and the tomb is now maintained by the city authorities. By the terms of Winterhalter's will, his fortune of 4 million francs was divided equally between his brother and the children of his two sisters. One notable benefaction of 50,000 francs established a foundation for the support of youth of Menzenschwand and two neighbouring villages 'who wish to learn useful trades, arts and sciences'.

In European capitals the news of his death was greeted with official expressions of regret, as of the passing of a court dignitary rather than a great artist. Obituaries were brief and few. Winterhalter belonged to an age that was rapidly fading from people's memories. The figures of the Second Empire whom he had chronicled had died or disappeared from public gaze. Few of those who had made him famous were there to remember, or to mourn him. The widowed Queen Victoria was one, the exiled Empress Eugénie perhaps another. To the first, he was the artist of those happy early years with Prince Albert. In letters to her daughter, the Crown Princess Frederick, Queen Victoria poured out her feelings. His death was 'terrible . . . quite irreparable. . . . His works will in time rank with Vandyck. He painted you all from your birth. There was not another portrait painter like him in the world, – it seems like a bit of former days, *Gone*! . . . With all his peculiarities I liked him so much'.[59]

In Karlsruhe, obsequies were elaborate and heart-felt. It was from this city that he had set out as an unknown young painter forty years before, and to which he had returned as a European celebrity. His beloved Baden honoured him with an exhibition in October 1873. Exhibits from local collections, those of the Grand Duke of Baden, the Prince of Fürstenberg, the King of Württemberg and various private individuals, were complemented by loans from further afield. Queen Victoria lent four pictures, the early portraits of 1842 of herself and Prince Albert, Duleep Singh and *The First of May*. No biographer came forward to chronicle the dead man's achievement. In 1894, Winterhalter's nephew Franz Wild published a brief memoir, with an invaluable check-list of portraits (see Appendix), but the artist had to wait a further forty years before a reawakening of interest in the Second Empire brought his work once more to prominence with exhibitions in London and Paris in 1936. His name had become associated with fashionable court portraiture. Little was known about him personally, and his art was not taken seriously. It is only after a further lapse of time that his style can be set in context, his career documented, and the full range of his achievement fairly judged.

1. I am indebted to Dr Mayer, a descendant of Winterhalter's sister, Theresia, and to Donald MacAndrew, for information on the Winterhalter genealogy, and for details of the artist's early life.
2. For Baron Eichtal, see *Neue Deutsche Biographie*, 4, 1959, p. 386.
3. See the letter from Victor Scheffel to his sister, Marie, of 18 September 1852. 'I learned from Lotsch that W. is the son of the late Herr von Eichtal.' (*Scheffel in Italien*, ed. Dr W. Zentner, Karlsruhe, 1929.)
4. Winterhalter Family Papers.
5. Winterhalter Family Papers.
6. Winterhalter Family Papers.
7. Winterhalter Family Papers.
8. A review in the *Kunstblatt* for 10 April 1826 complimented Winterhalter for his plates of the Royal family and the Duchess of Leuchtenburg, as well as those after Paris Bordone and Van Dyck.
9. Winterhalter Family Papers.
10. Winterhalter Family Papers.
11. Winterhalter Family Papers.
12. Winterhalter Family Papers.
13. Winterhalter Family Papers.
14. Winterhalter Family Papers.
15. For a listing of Winterhalter's portraits belonging to the Grand Duke of Baden, see G.F. Kircher, *Zähringer Bildnissammlung im Neuen Schloss zu Baden-Baden*, Karlsruhe 1958, pp. 104 (no. 508), 107 (nos. 529–30), 109 (no. 543), 110 (no. 548), 114 (nos. 570, 572), 115 (no. 575), 116 (no. 580), 121 (no. 613), 141 (no. 714). Watercolours of Leopold's brothers, Wilhelm and Maximillian (1829) are at Schloss Langenburg and Karlsruhe. Prints after these, and other untraced portraits, will be found at the Generallandesarchiv Karlsruhe.
16. Winterhalter Family Papers.
17. Winterhalter Family Papers.
18. Donna Maria, daughter of the Marchese di Villafranca and future Princess Colonna, was born in 1823.
19. 'Salon de 1853', *Feuilleton de la Presse*, 6 July 1853.
20. *Heath's Picturesque Annual for 1844*, London.
21. A. Stevens, *Le Salon de 1863*, Paris, 1866, p. 142.
22. Queen Victoria's Journal, WRA, QVJ, 8 November 1844.
23. Wilkie's portrait of Queen Victoria, 1840, is in the Lady Lever Art Gallery, Port Sunlight; that of her by Shee, 1842, belongs to the Royal Academy, London.
24. Queen Victoria's Journal, WRA, QVJ, 8 May 1837.
25. Winterhalter Family Papers.
26. B. Adams, 'London Interiors 1841–44', *London Illustrated*, 1983.
27. Queen Victoria's Journal, WRA, QVJ, 13 February 1843.
28. Queen Victoria's Journal, WRA, QVJ, 18 December 1846.
29. *The Athenaeum*, 8 May 1847, p. 496.
30. Queen Victoria's Journal, WRA, QVJ, 24 June 1851.
31. Winterhalter Family Papers.
32. Winterhalter Family Papers.
33. Letter to Franz Jakob Kreuter, Winterhalter Family Papers.
34. Letter to M. Mazel, coll. Bibliothek der Eidgenössischen Technischen Hochschule, No. HS234, Zürich.
35. Queen Victoria's Journal, WRA, QVJ, 23 March 1849.
36. Winterhalter Family Papers. Text contributed by D. MacAndrew
37. Text contributed by D. MacAndrew.
38. Winterhalter Family Papers.
39. *Les Beaux-Arts en Europe*, 1855, pp. 145–6.
40. *La Revue des Deux Mondes*, 25, 1855, pp. 403–4.
41. *Kunstblatt*, Karlsruhe, 21 March 1856, communicated by D. MacAndrew.
42. E. Delacroix, *Journal*, 27 September 1855 ed. J.L. Vaudoyer and A. Joubin, 1960.
43. Bayerische Staatsbibliothek, Munich, texts communicated by Armin Panter.
44. Quoted in *Die Pyramide*, 4, 1935.
45. 'Salon de 1853', *Feuilleton de la Presse*, 6 July 1853.
46. A. Stevens, *Salon de 1863*, p. 144.
47. Winterhalter Family Papers.
48. Winterhalter Family Papers.
49. Winterhalter Family Papers.
50. F. Pecht, *German Artists of the 19th Century*, Nördingen 1885.
51. *Daheim*, no. 38, 1908, p. 12.
52. Winterhalter Family Papers.
53. Winterhalter Family Papers.
54. Winterhalter Family Papers.
55. Stadtische Bibliothek, Landeshauptstadt, Munich.
56. Winterhalter Family Papers.
57. Winterhalter Family Papers.
58. Winterhalter Family Papers.
59. WRA, Add. U32 and Z/27.70.

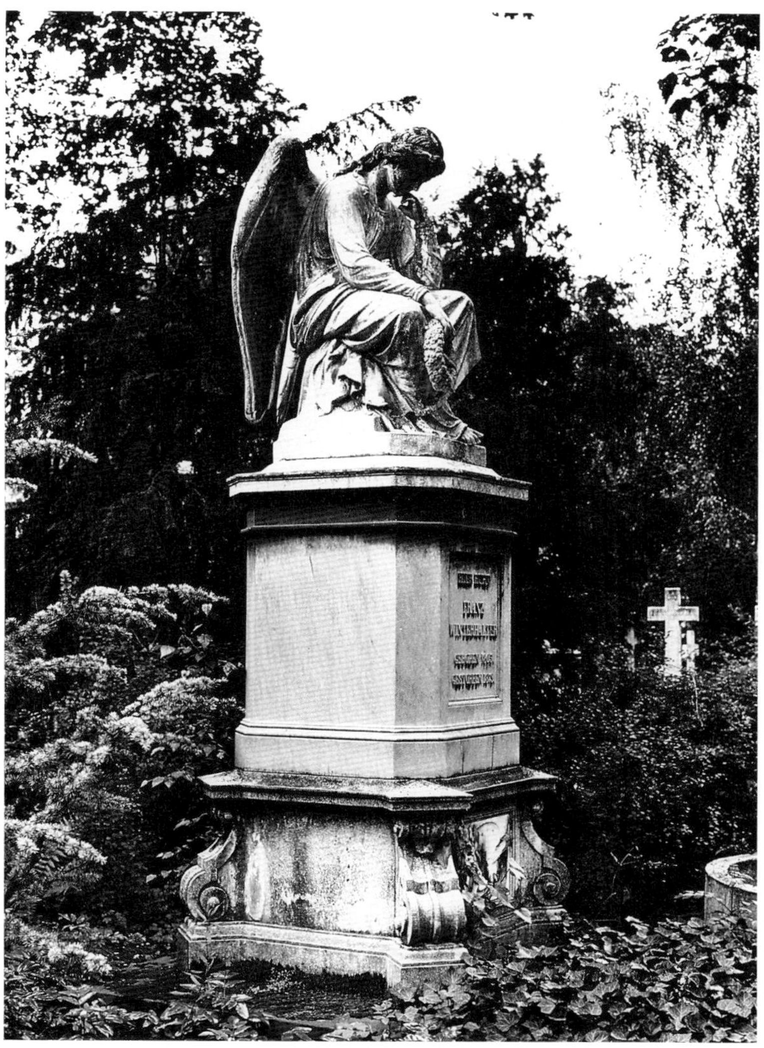

Photograph by K. Meier-Ude

Figure 52
O. Sommer: F.X. Winterhalter's grave, Frankfurt Cemetery

# Fashion in the Work of Winterhalter

*Aileen Ribeiro*

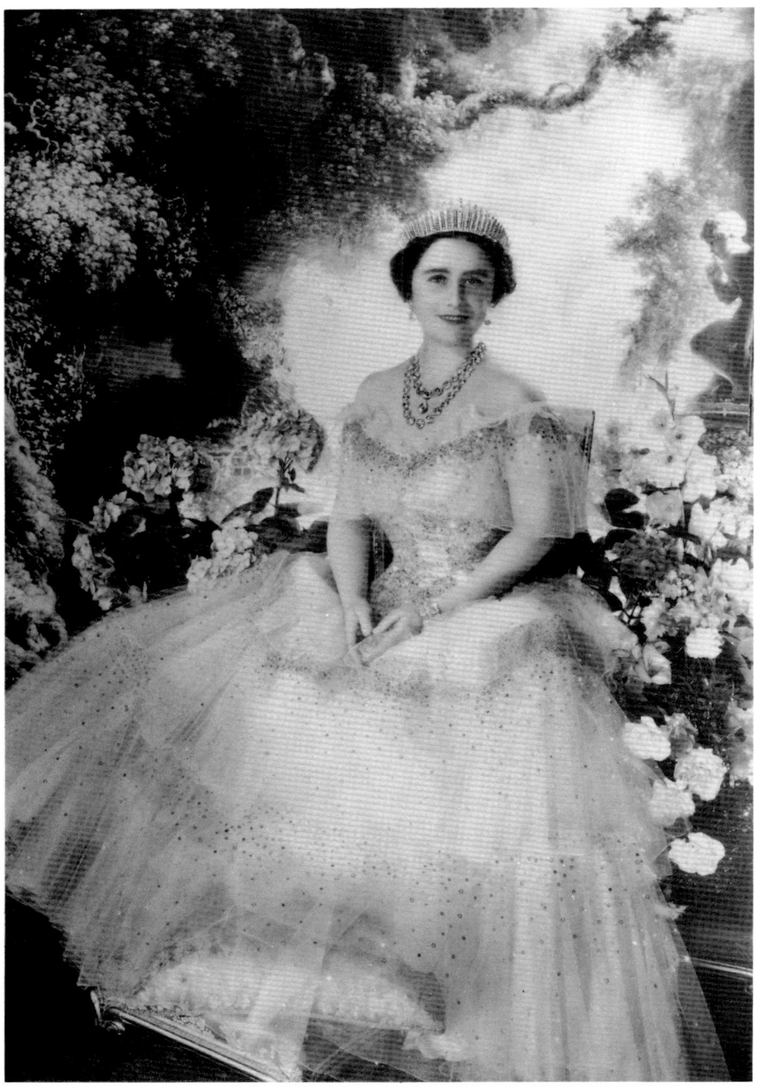

Figure 53
Cecil Beaton: Her Majesty Queen Elizabeth, The Queen Mother, 1939
Photograph
National Portrait Gallery, London

According to the couturier, Norman Hartnell, it was King George VI who drew his attention to the sumptuous Royal Winterhalters as a source of inspiration for the formal costumes he was to design for Queen Elizabeth for the state visit to Paris in the summer of 1938. Using shades of white as a guide (this was a traditional mourning colour for Royal ladies, and the Queen's mother had just died), Hartnell chose satin, lace, tulle and flowers in homage to Winterhalter, and with the same Romantic, fairy-tale effect. Winterhalter inspired a style of dress – a floating, glittering crinoline – which came to be associated with the Queen, and which was recorded by Cecil Beaton (fig. 53), far more skilful a 'society' artist than any contemporary painter in his ability both to capture a likeness and to promote a Romantic image – a tradition going back to the Royal portraits of Van Dyck.

Winterhalter, too, was able during his highly successful career, to paint an accurate likeness while subtly enhancing the features of his sitters, and to record in what resembles photographic detail, every item of costume and uniform. Although we tend to be dazzled by his skill in the meticulous depiction of female plumage, it is worth noting how well he copes with masculine dress. Men had the opportunity of being painted in military uniform, and while this could sometimes look slightly absurd, it could also be rather dashing, as with Edouard André's Hussar-inspired scarlet, green and gold of the Guides de la Garde Impériale (no. 59). Court uniform was regarded as somewhat Ruritanian, and is rarely depicted in portraiture, but formal evening dress, while restrained in colour, showed off the figure to perfection. Although many artists and writers claimed that men were in a kind of perpetual mourning in their dark clothes – 'si triste, si éteint, si monotone' in the words of Théophile Gautier (*De la Mode*, 1858) – they could, with the help of a good English tailor, look as elegant as any cavalier painted by Van Dyck. Prince Albert, depicted by Winterhalter in 1846 in his evening dress (no. 32) with his black coat, white waistcoat, tight black pantaloons and flowing black cloak, is a good example.

As we know comparatively little about Winterhalter's studio organization, it is difficult to say how far he dictated the choice of costume worn by his sitters or, indeed, how much of the dress was actually painted by himself or his assistants. He may have suggested which Worth dress his fashionable ladies should wear, or how they might drape a court train, or what head-dress would suit them best. Unlike Van Dyck, we get no sense of personal preference, artistic dictatorship or invented costume. Winterhalter paints what is before his eyes – real costume; even the vaguely oriental *déshabillé* seen in *Florinda* (no. 38) is based on actual fabrics and garments such as white linen shifts and Indian silks, and the somewhat sentimentalized Italian peasant girls are dressed in their Sunday best. Winterhalter depicts textiles with a virtuoso skill, whether it is the pleats and open-work on the shift seen in the *Young Italian Girl by the Well* (no. 6), or the rich Brussels lace and embroidered net which dominate the costume worn by Queen Marie-Amélie (no. 19). He dwells with pleasure on the tactile surfaces of velvet, fur, lace, foaming tulle, and on glossy wings of hair, decorated with flowers. Jane Austen often observes in her novels that white is a colour which suits every woman, and it is used with flattering effect over and over again in Winterhalter's portraits of fashionable ladies of all ages. Black, too, set off a fine complexion, and the artist paints the sloping, gleaming bottle-neck shoulders of the Duchesse de Vallombrosa rising from her black silk dress trimmed with Chantilly lace.

Winterhalter faithfully records, through his stylish female portraits, the changing fashions of forty years; no artist, other than J.-A.-D. Ingres, covered so long a period with equal devotion to the religion of high fashion. His career starts with the exuberant, rather doll-like fashions of the 1830s with their tight-waisted dresses with puffed sleeves and the curious curled and segmented hairstyle seen, for example, in the portrait of Sophie, Grand Duchess of Baden (no. 4). The Biedermeier prettiness of the 1830s gives way to the demure style of the 1840s, when women in their pointed bodices and dome-shaped skirts seem to be almost muffled up in face-framing bonnets and capacious shawls. There is a kind of bourgeois sobriety in dress of this decade, best typified by the court of Louis-Philippe; the meeting of the French Royal family with Queen Victoria and Prince Albert at the Château d'Eu in 1845 (no. 24) is also an encounter of two courts in sartorial harmony, a rich yet comfortable dowdiness.

It is in the 1850s that Winterhalter really comes into his own as a fashion artist, with the arrival of an Imperial Court in France, and the re-emergence of a sense of style and splendour. Although the Empress Eugénie, in her private life, preferred fairly simple clothes – Winterhalter paints her in 1857 holding the baby Prince Imperial and dressed in a red jacket and skirt (no. 58) – in her public life, she had to be seen to outshine any other Royal lady, and to lead a court which recalled the glitter and grandeur of that of the first Napoleon. With her long neck, perfect bust and shoulders, she looked her best in low-necked evening gowns and was painted by Winterhalter in 1854 in frothy lace and tulle, in one of her trousseau ball-dresses by Palmyre, with camellias in her hair and bosom (no. 50). It was Winterhalter who, as official artist to the court, captures the hot-house luxury and the sheer opulence of the lavish *toilettes* obligatory at the Tuileries, and at the *séries élégantes*, the fashionable house-parties held at the Château de Compiègne, where different outfits were needed for the morning, the afternoon, for dinners, receptions, and balls – each costume with its complementary accessories, fans, gloves and jewellery.

Throughout the 1840s and into the 1850s, the skirts of fashionable women had been getting larger, often distended with *jupons de crinoline* (horse-hair petticoats) or with whalebone hoops. The increased skirt area demanded large patterned printed silks, to be seen, for example, in Ingres' portrait of Madame Moitessier of 1856 (fig. 54), or light

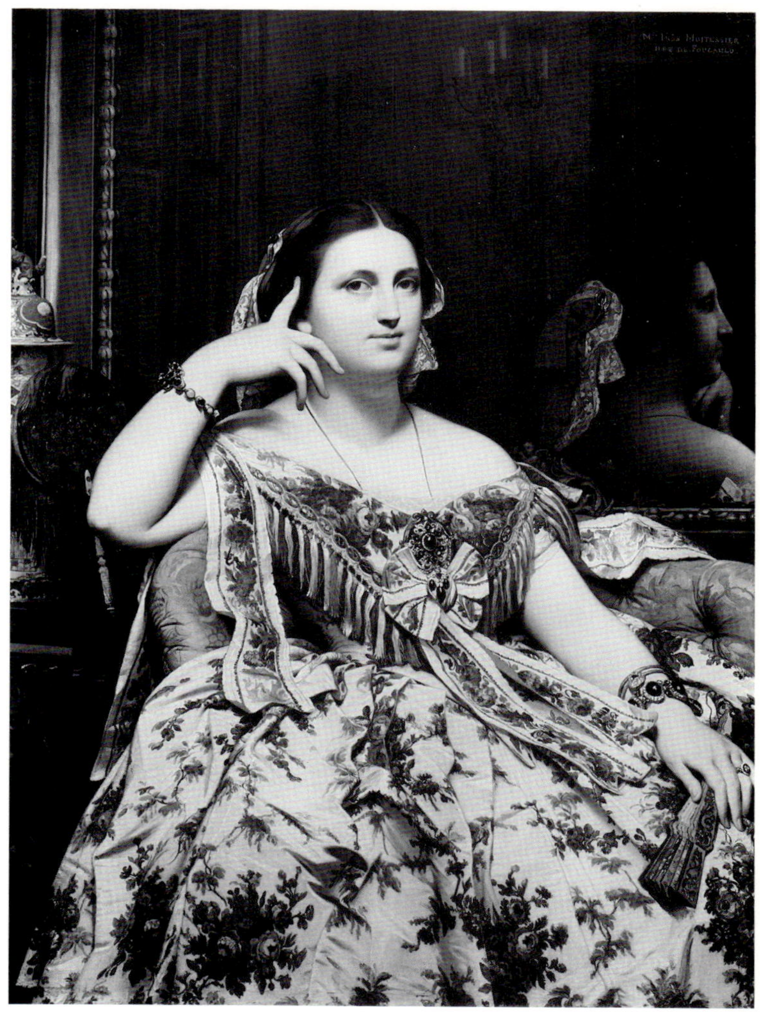

Figure 54
J.-A.-D. Ingres: *Madame Moitessier*, 1856
120 × 92.1 cms
National Gallery, London

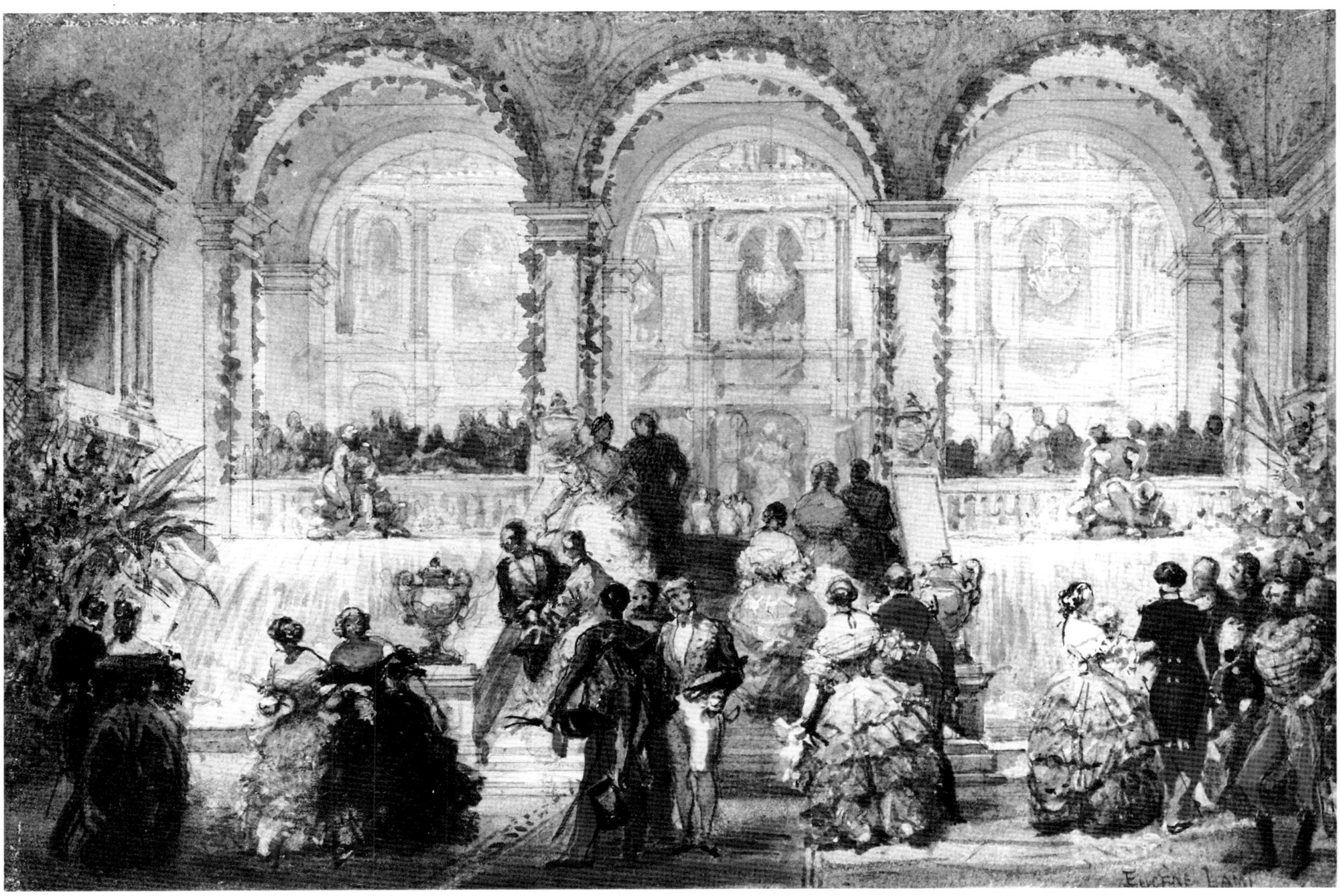

Figure 55
E. L. Lami: *Bal à l'Hôtel de Ville*, *1855*
Watercolour, 12.5 × 19.5 cms
Collection Musée des Arts Décoratifs, Paris

floating material like printed muslin arranged in flounces, one example being Winterhalter's portrait of Queen Victoria, seated on the terrace at Osborne House with the baby Prince Arthur (no. 36). During the 1850s, light gauzy fabrics like tulle (a machine-made silk net) and tarlatan (a transparent muslin, usually stiffened) rivalled lightweight silks like taffeta in popularity. Ball-gowns, like those depicted in Eugène Louis Lami's *Bal à l'Hôtel de Ville, 1855* (fig. 55), could take hundreds of yards of fabric for their trimmings alone – the ruches, ribbons, drapes, ruffles and flounces which could so easily make an over-enthusiastic lady look like an over-decorated tea-cosy. Such fabrics have to be used with restraint, as can be seen in the elegant but not over-elaborate prettiness of Winterhalter's group, *The Empress Eugénie Surrounded by her Ladies-in-Waiting* of 1855 (no. 53); the Empress, wearing a dress of white tulle over white silk, trimmed with lilac ribbons which echo the lilac in her hair, sits with her ladies who almost float around her in layers of silk, tulle and lace, like a Worth-designed *fête champêtre*.

In 1855, however, Charles Frederick Worth did not have Royal patronage, and could not have made the dresses in this picture, although it is possible that the fabrics came from Maison Gagelin, the most famous silk merchant in Paris, for whom Worth worked, and who had supplied the trousseau for the Empress. It was not until 1858 that Worth, with the help of a Swedish partner, was able to set up on his own, and it was not until 1860 that he obtained the custom of the chic Princess Pauline Metternich who was adventurous enough to defy convention by patronizing that unheard-of innovation, a 'man-milliner'. Worth made her an evening dress of white tulle woven with silver, and trimmed with daisies with pink hearts placed in bunches of grass and veiled with tulle. As the Princess records in her memoirs, the Empress was captivated, and the next day Worth was summoned to an audience in the Tuileries. He supplied the Empress with court dress, evening dress and fancy-dress, and became the virtual dictator in matters of high fashion, not just in France, but elsewhere in a world rapidly opening up through improved communication and travel.

At times, it seems almost as if Worth and Winterhalter were working as a team, with the same ideas of the beautiful and the sublime; this is not surprising when we realize that many of Worth's clients were painted by Winterhalter and they wished to be depicted in their very expensive finery, usually evening dress, which was Worth's forte. The focal point of Worth's designs, as can be seen in his sketch-books from the 1860s and early 1870s, now in the Victoria and Albert Museum (fig. 56), was a vast skirt held out over the cage crinoline of metal which had been invented in 1856, and which was, with its swaying side-to-side motion, one of the most seductive of all feminine modes until its disappearance in 1868. Like many artists, Worth disliked the often violently bright aniline dyes coming into fashion in the late 1850s, preferring white dresses with small touches of colour; garlands, spots, and stripes on white were as popular for

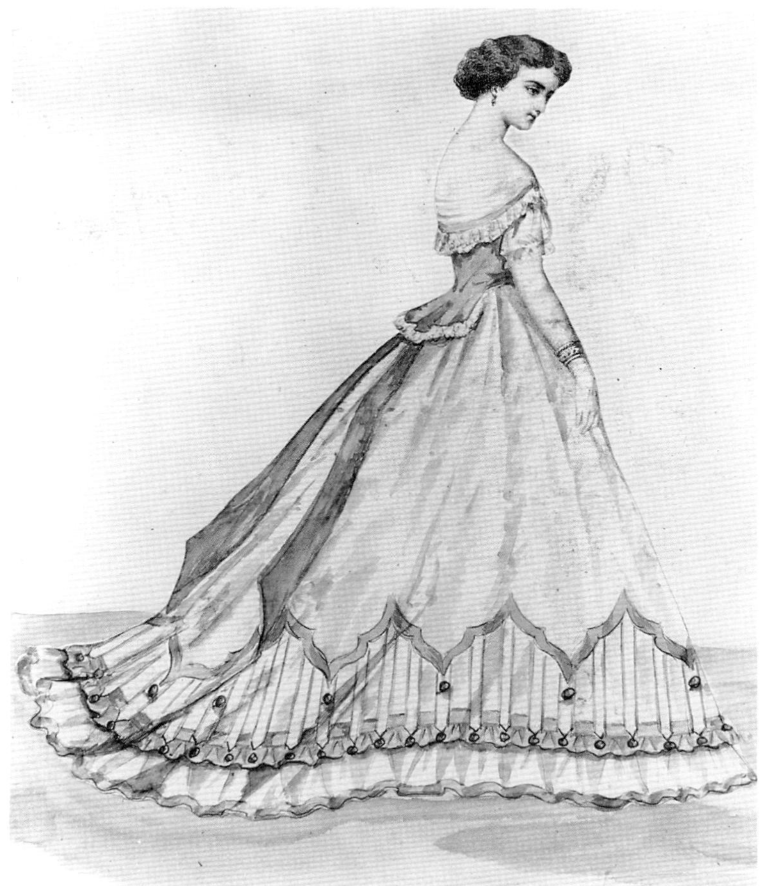

Figure 56
C.F. Worth: Costume design
Watercolour and lithograph, 24.2 × 20.5 cms
The Trustees of the Victoria and Albert Museum

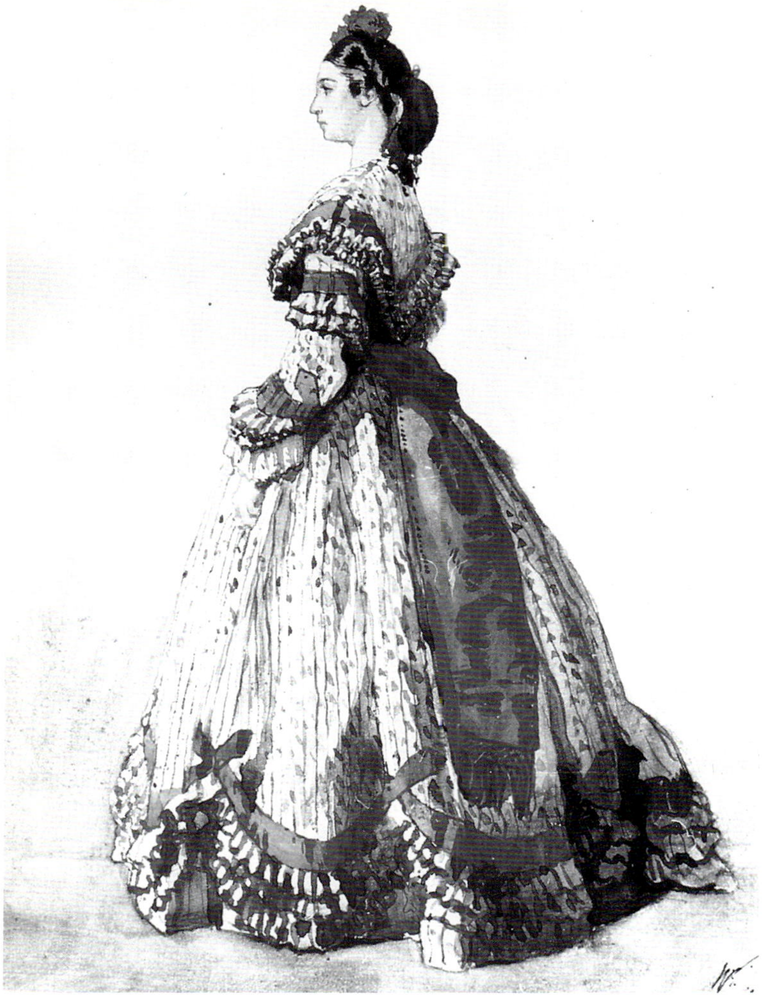

Figure 57
F.X. Winterhalter: *A Lady-in-Waiting to the Empress Eugénie*
Watercolour, 28 × 21.5 cms
Private Collection. The dress is by Worth

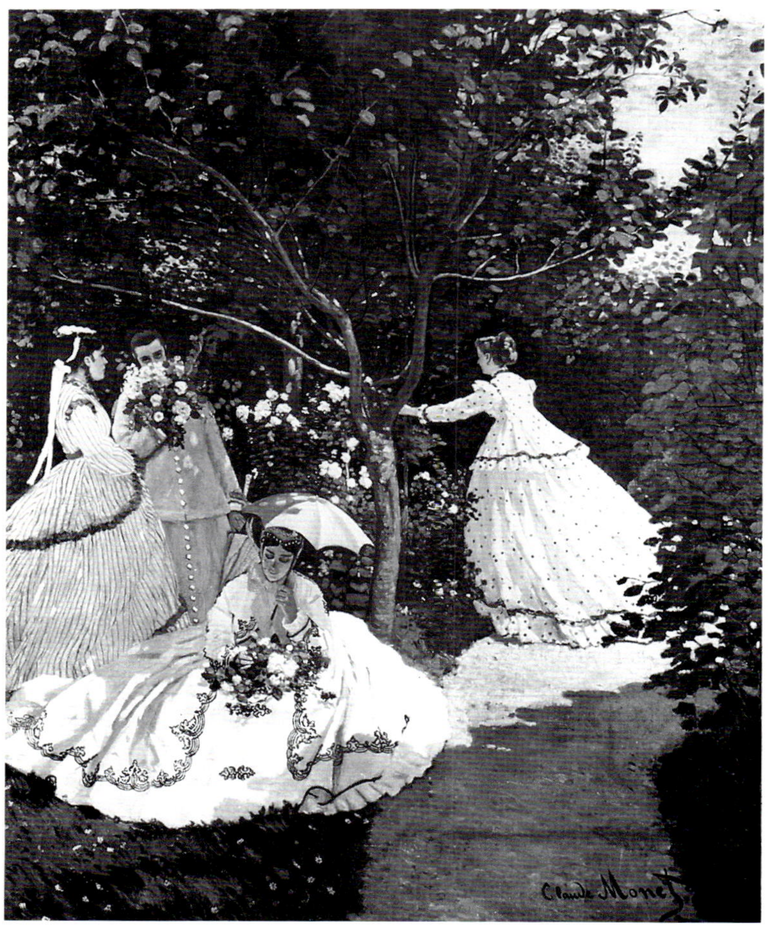

Figure 58
C. Monet: *Femmes au Jardin*, 1867
255 × 205 cms
Musée d'Orsay, Paris

Worth and Winterhalter (fig. 57) as they were for Claude Monet (fig. 58).

White was also *de rigueur* for court, and Worth had to think up endless variations of style and fabric; satin, brocade, velvet and lace were all popular (the sewing machine, well-established in the dress-making business in the 1860s, made it possible to produce large numbers of elaborately trimmed gowns in record time), but the most popular fabric of all was tulle. No matter that the floating cobweb material crumpled badly and was immensely fragile, it made women look like ethereal visions, especially when painted by Winterhalter. Tulle could be elegantly simple, veiling and flattering the sitter as it does with Pauline Sandor, Princess Metternich (no. 63) and the Duchesse de Morny (no. 64), or contorted into an over-elaborate style as seen in the candy-floss puffs of the Countess Musina-Pushkina's dress (no. 74). In the 1860s, Worth popularized spangled tulle, the most stunning example being the costume worn by Elizabeth, Empress of Austria in her portrait by Winterhalter (no. 79); acknowledged by the Empress Eugénie as 'the loveliest crowned head in Europe', the glitter on Elizabeth's dress is echoed by the brilliant diamond stars in her long hair.

Court dress was another *tour de force* for Worth; it consisted of a lavishly trimmed evening gown, and a long train which had been established as part of court dress in France in 1854 – at the court of Louis-Philippe, ladies just wore *très-grande toilette*. Worth also provided court dress for other countries (some of the most luxurious for the Russian Court), and he may have designed the imposing costume worn by Lady Middleton (no. 47), painted by Winterhalter in Paris in 1863. It is a triumph of character for the sitter not to be overwhelmed by the vast, crinolined dress of white satin swagged with tulle, and the purple train edged with Honiton lace. Winterhalter also painted the Empress Eugénie in court dress, the skirt of her gown decorated with great flounces of Brussels lace; the white dress with a coloured train (worn on state occasions), was inspired by court costume under the first Napoleon.

This was undoubtedly a political decision, to link the court of Napoleon III with that of his admired predecessor, but there was also a trend towards reviving the dress of the past. Worth, who had the English taste for historical fancy-dress, designed many of the outfits for the *bals costumés* held during the winter months in the Tuileries Palace, and for the Watteau-inspired *fêtes champêtres* organized by Princess Metternich at St Cloud. At the French Court, it was the eighteenth century which was fashionable; the brothers Goncourt helped to make the period in vogue, and the Empress had her apartments in the Tuileries decorated in Rococo style. The influence of the Rococo, with its self-conscious charm and frivolity, can be seen in Winterhalter's portrait of Eugénie in eighteenth-century dress of yellow taffeta trimmed with black bows, blue ribbon, pearls, fringes and tassels, her powdered hair trimmed with flowers, ribbons and a feather aigrette (no. 52). Ironically identifying with Marie-Antoinette, the Empress wore at a ball in the Tuileries in 1866, a costume copied from a portrait by Vigée-Lebrun of the French Queen in crimson velvet furred with sable, with high-piled hair and a feathered toque.

In a more domestic vein, Queen Victoria's Court also enjoyed a love of dressing up. In 1851, the Queen held a 'Restoration Ball' when everyone had to dress up in costume of the time of Charles II. With more concern for splendour than for accuracy, Prince Albert wore a coat of brocaded orange satin, the sleeves turned up with red velvet embroidered in gold and silver, breeches of crimson velvet with pink satin bows and gold lace, and lavender stockings. Victoria's dress (now in the Museum of London) was a grey watered silk trimmed with gold and silver lace, with an underskirt of cloth of gold trimmed with embroidery and silver fringe. Both Queen and Consort are portrayed in this finery by Winterhalter (fig. 59). Their troupe of children ensured the success of *tableaux vivants* and fancy-dress parties, and Winterhalter's delightful watercolour of the Princess Royal and Princess Alice (no. 91) depicts the two girls in their eighteenth-century-style *bal poudré* costumes, like a miniature Octavian and Sophie from 'Der Rosenkavalier'.

Mannered poses and elegant costumes are the hall-mark of portraits by Winterhalter. His is not the world of informality, of the simple looped-up walking costumes popularized by the Empress Eugénie as she promenades along the beach, with her ladies, in the canvases of Eugène Boudin (fig. 60). Winterhalter is not concerned with the way costume moves, but with the details of the dress itself, with women on show in the glory of their splendid *toilettes*. He is an artist forever identified with the fairy-tale life for the lucky few at court, and in high society, during the Second Empire. An English newspaper correspondent in 1867, describing the Empress Eugénie at a ball, sitting in a bower surrounded by her ladies, summed up the effect made on him by saying 'there was the prettiest picture, – a Winterhalter it should have been'. This was the world that ended really for him with the surrender of Napoleon III to the Prussians at Sedan in September 1870.

In what might be regarded as a commentary on so many Winterhalter portraits, are the following words by Hippolyte Taine from *Notes on Paris* (1867); ostensibly attacking the all-consuming female interest in fashion but, I suspect, really captivated in spite of himself, he says:

> *'A perfect toilette is equal to a poem. There is a taste, a choice in the placing and the shade of each satin ribbon, in the pink silks, in the soft silvered satin, in the pale mauve . . . beneath their coverings of guipure, their puffings of tulle, and the ruches which rustle with every motion. Shoulders and cheeks wear a charming tint in this luxurious nest of blonde and lace. This is the only poetry left to us . . . what art, what appeal to the eye in these white waists which fit the figure so closely, in the chaste freshness of these glistening silks.'*

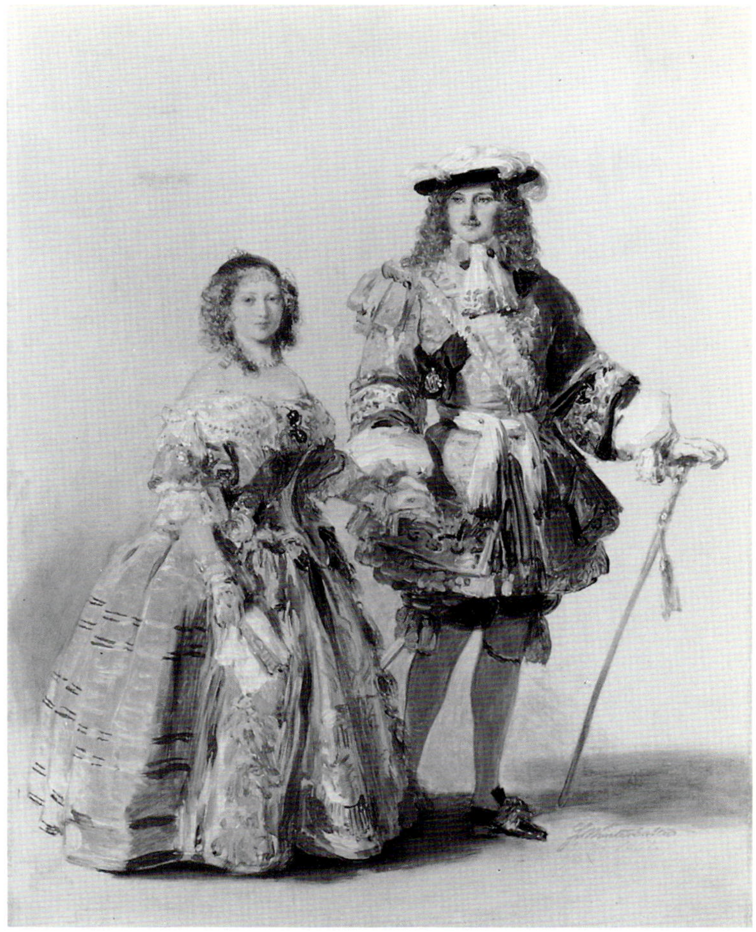

Figure 59
F.X. Winterhalter: *Queen Victoria and the Prince Consort*, 1851
57.5 × 45.7 cms
Reproduced by gracious permission of Her Majesty The Queen

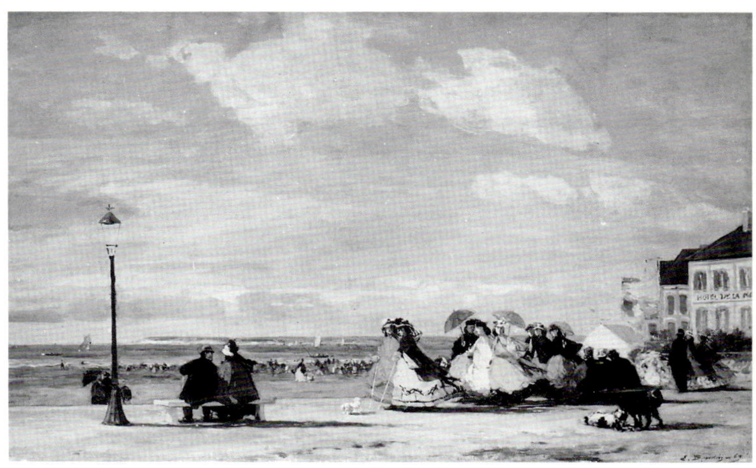

Figure 60
E. Boudin: *The Empress Eugénie on the Beach at Trouville*, 1863
Oil on panel, 34.2 × 57.8 cms
The Burrell Collection, Glasgow Museums and Art Galleries

# Early Works

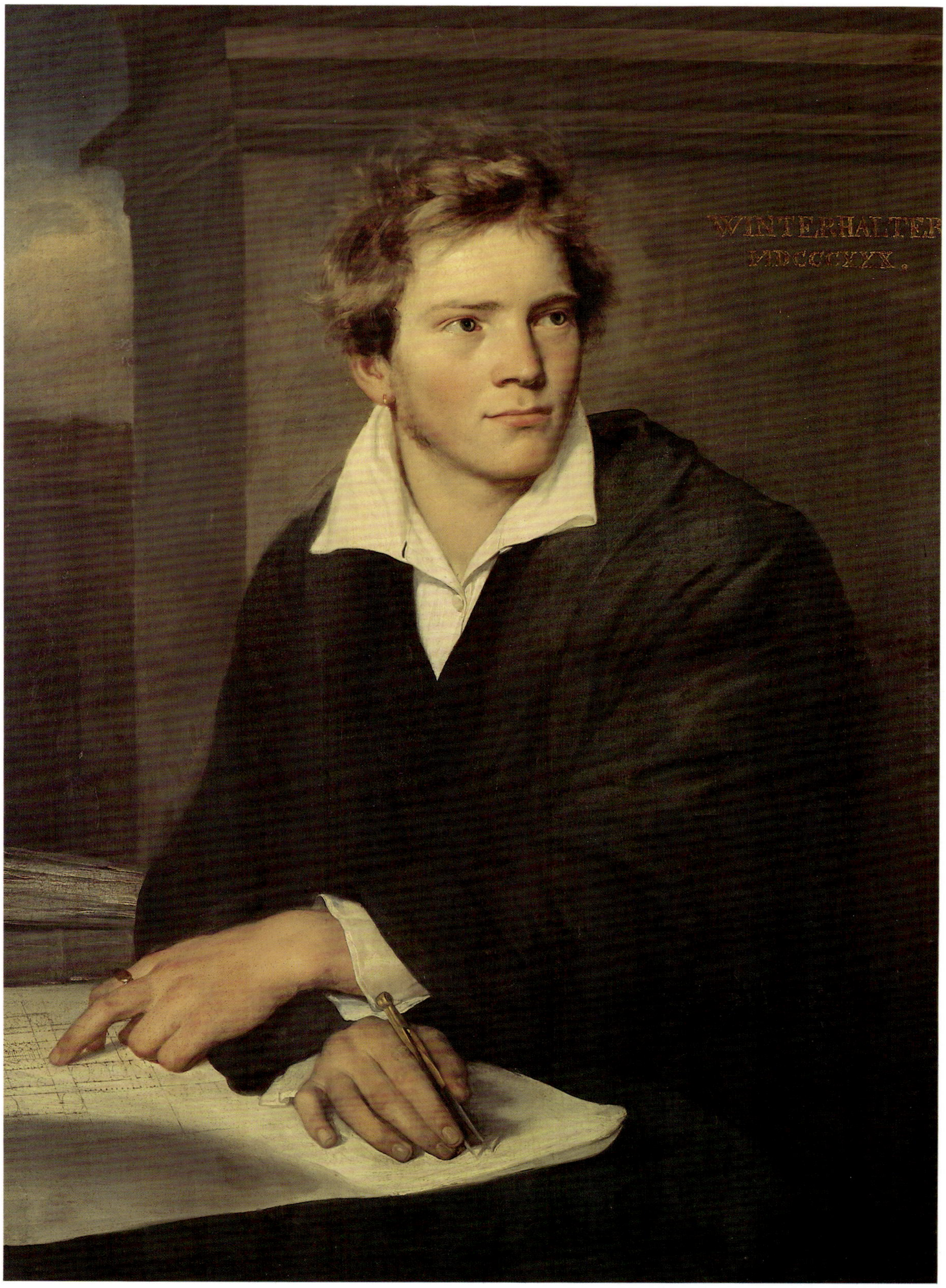


PORTRAIT OF A YOUNG ARCHITECT, PROBABLY KARL JOSEF BERCKMÜLLER 1830 (no. 1)

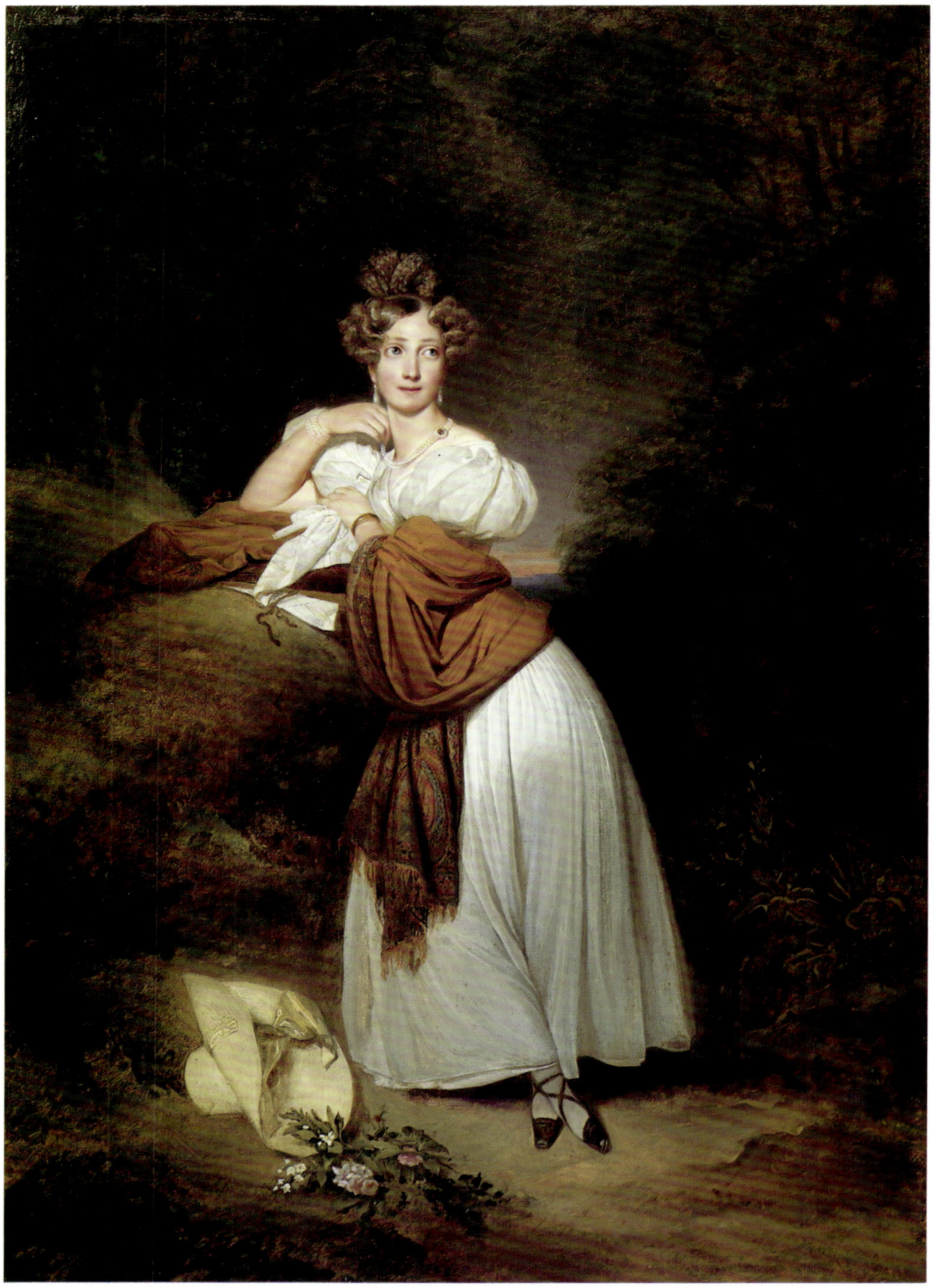

SOPHIE GUILLEMETTE, GRAND DUCHESS OF BADEN (no. 4)

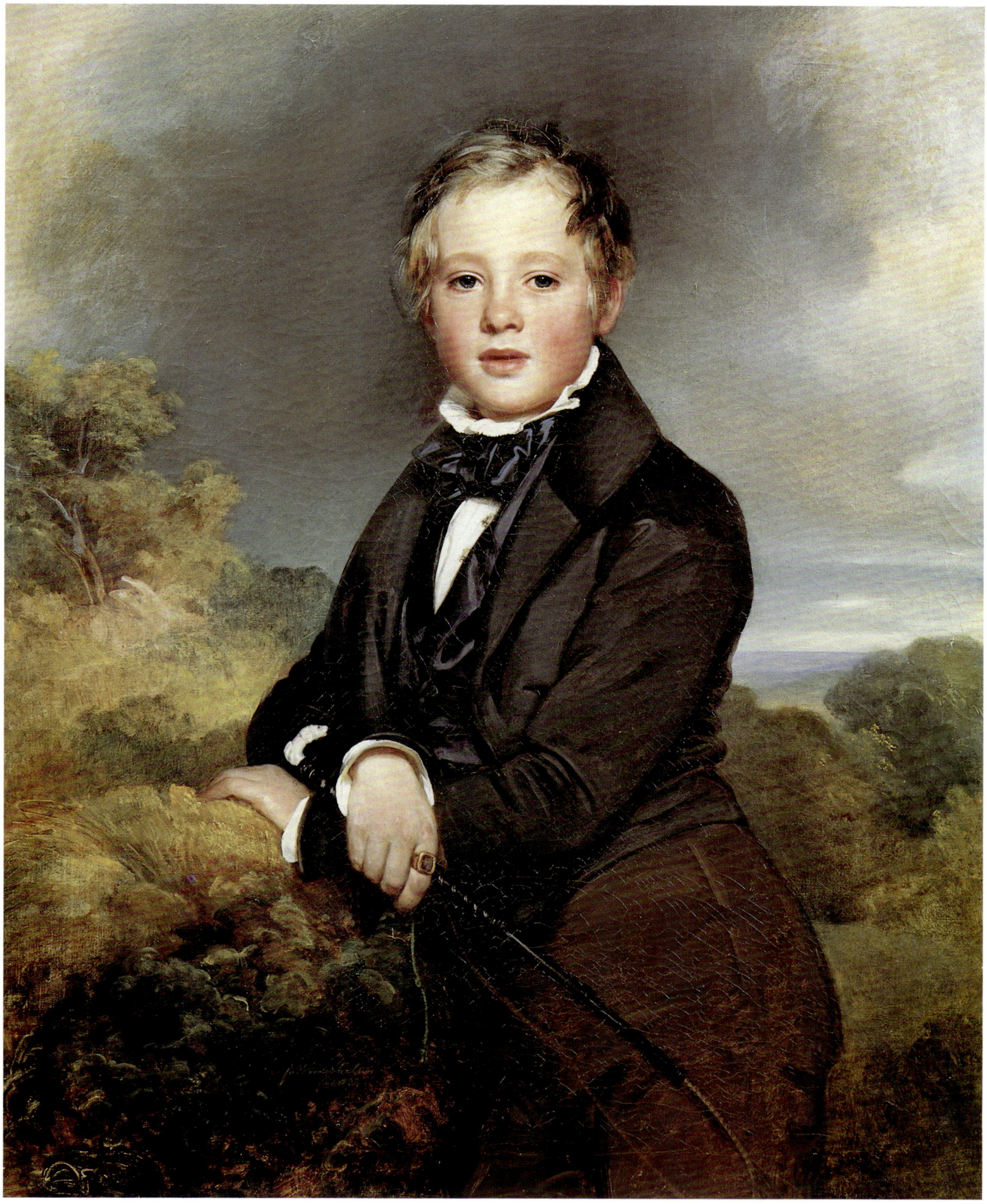

LUDWIG, GRAF VON LANGENSTEIN 1834 (no. 8)

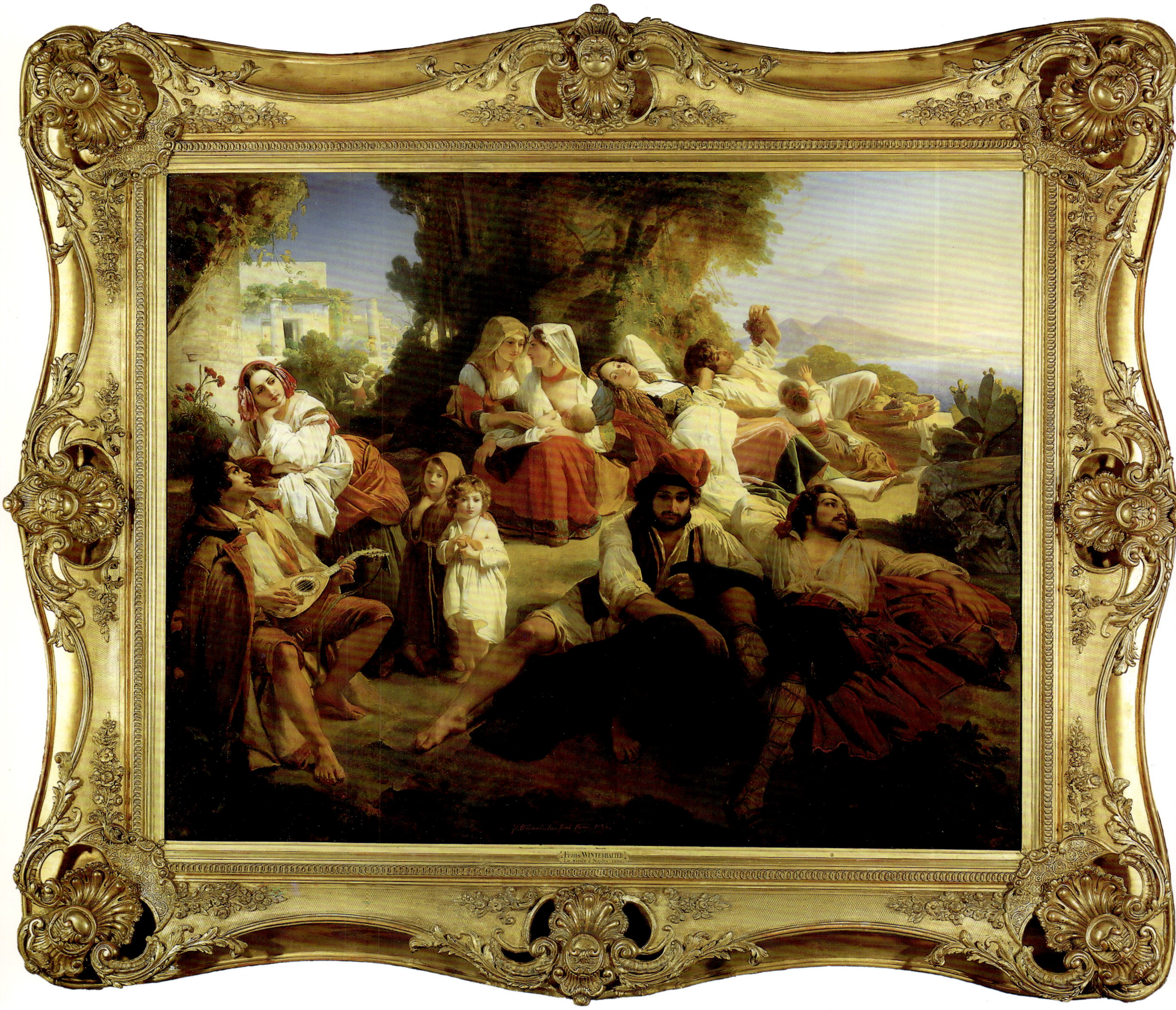

*Il Dolce Farniente* 1836 (no. 9)

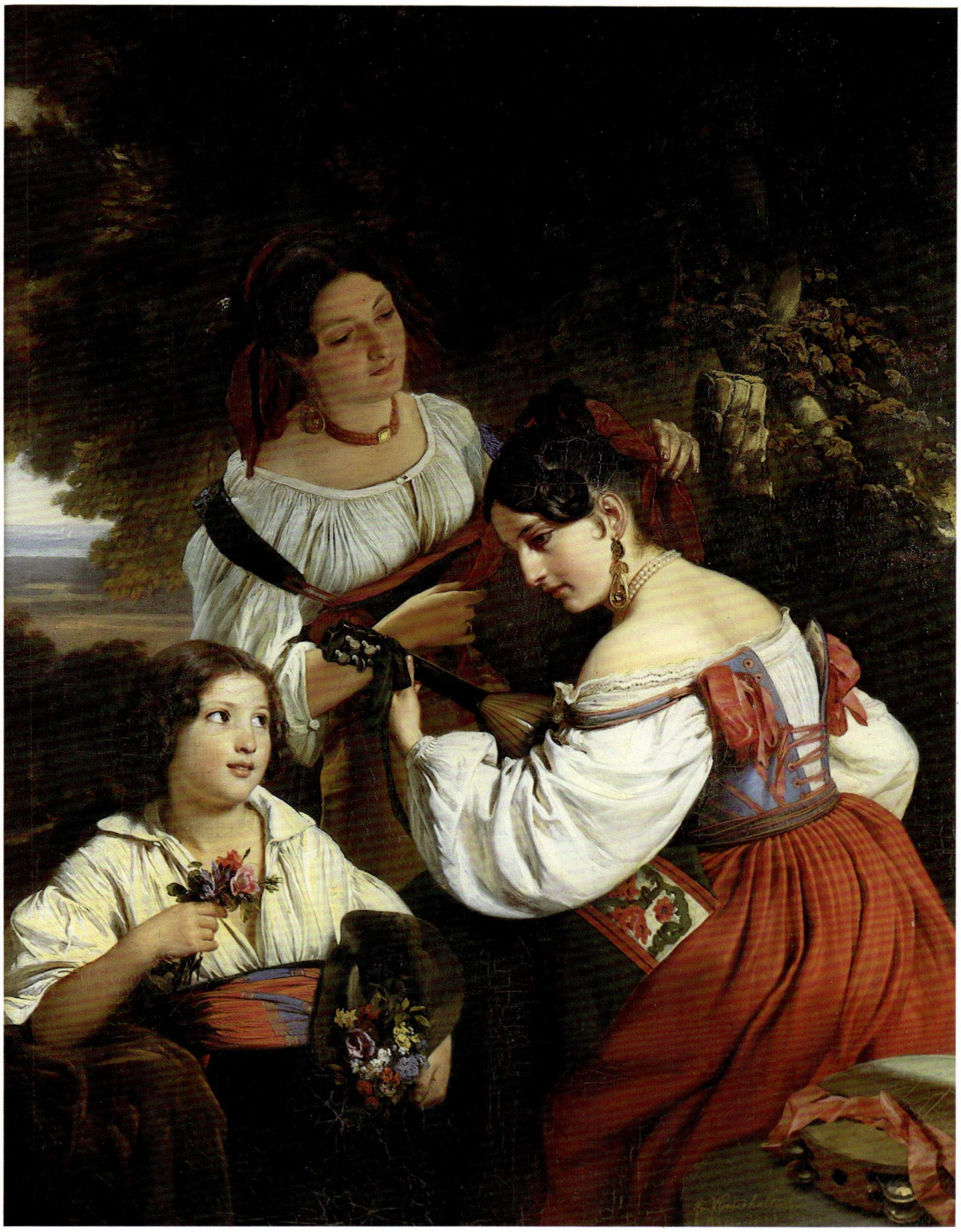

ROMAN GENRE SCENE 1833 (no. 5)

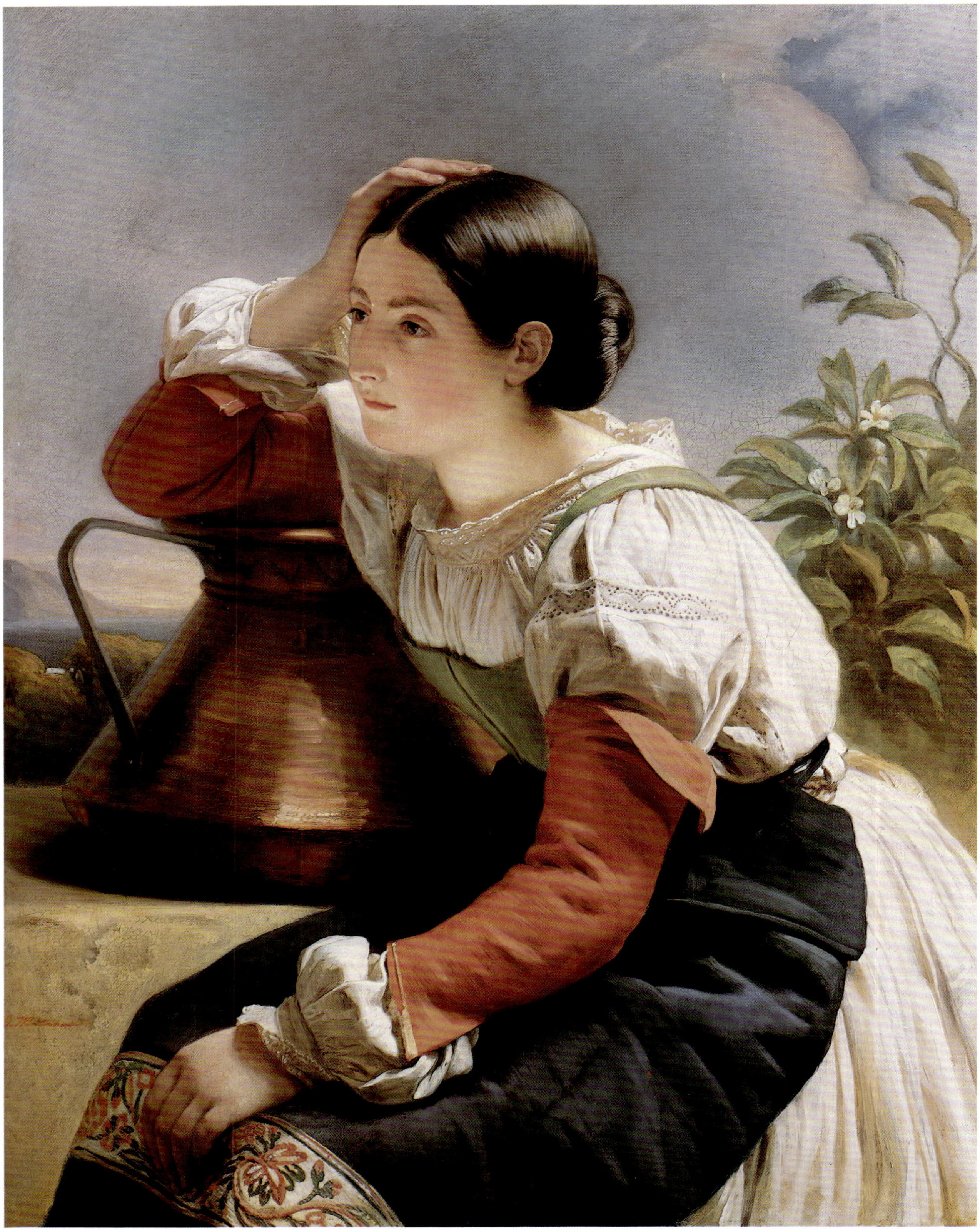

YOUNG ITALIAN GIRL BY THE WELL (no. 6)

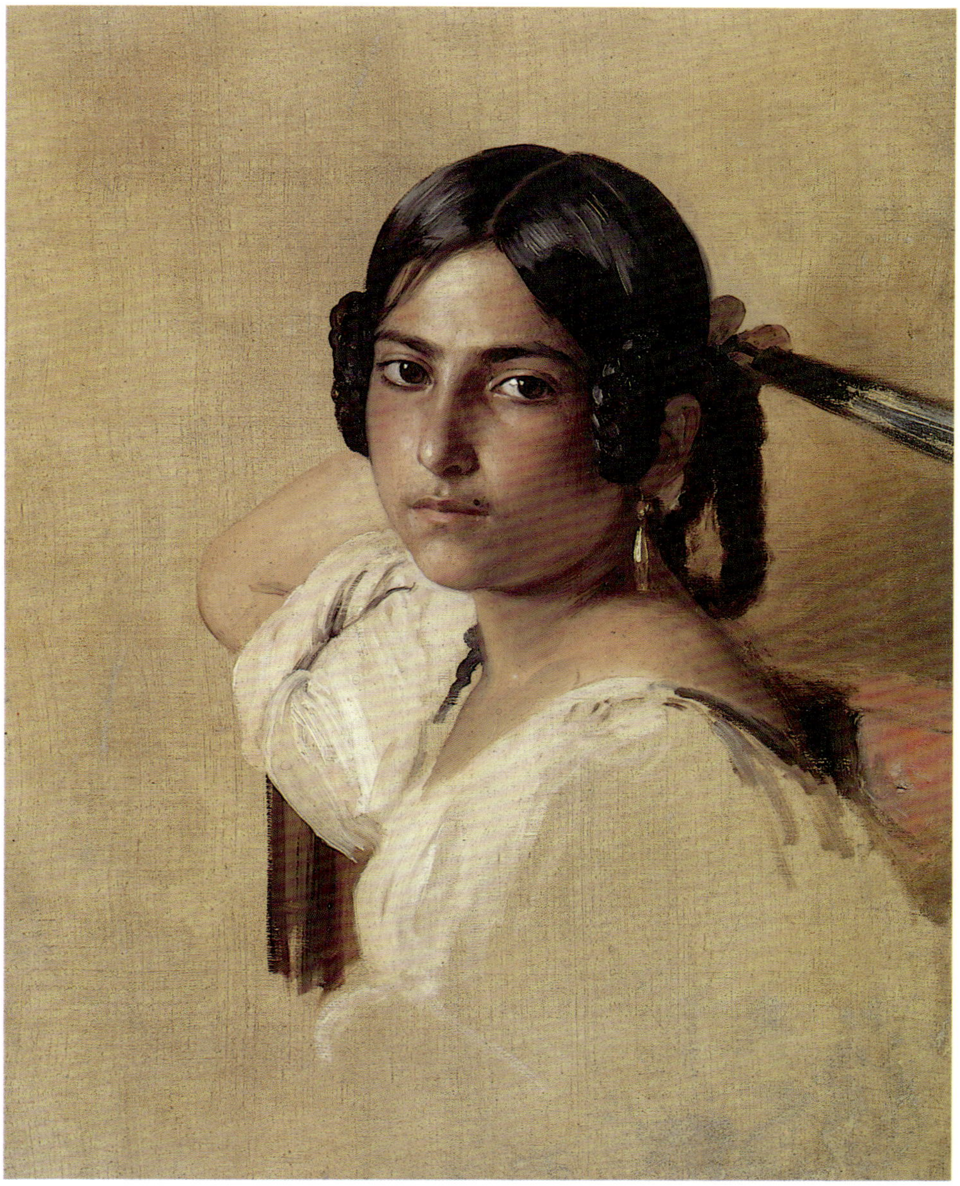

STUDY OF AN ITALIAN GIRL (no. 7)

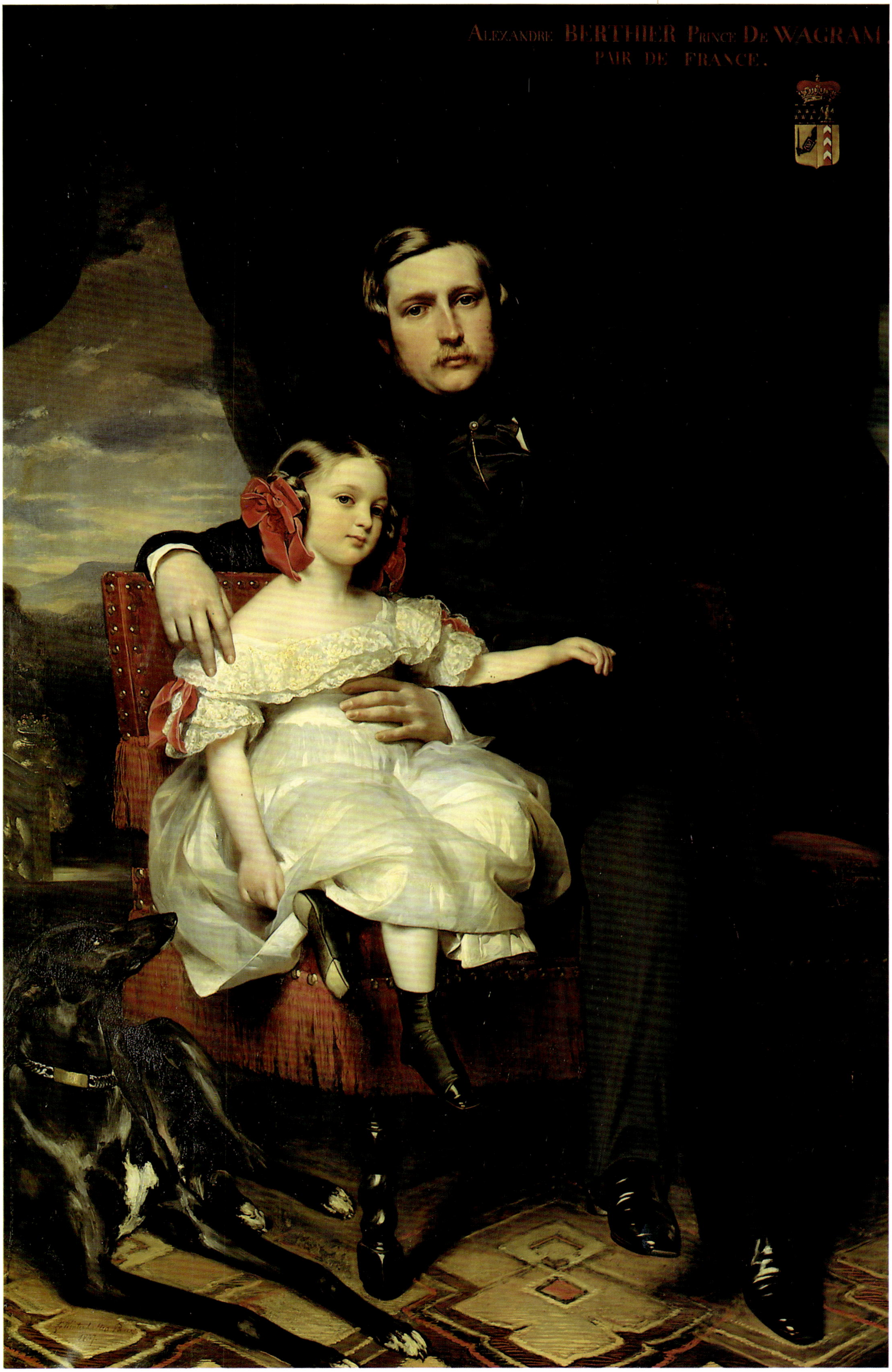


NAPOLEON-ALEXANDRE-LOUIS-JOSEPH BERTHIER,
PRINCE DE WAGRAM AND HIS DAUGHTER MALCY-LOUISE-CAROLINE-FRÉDÉRIQUE 1837 (no. 10)

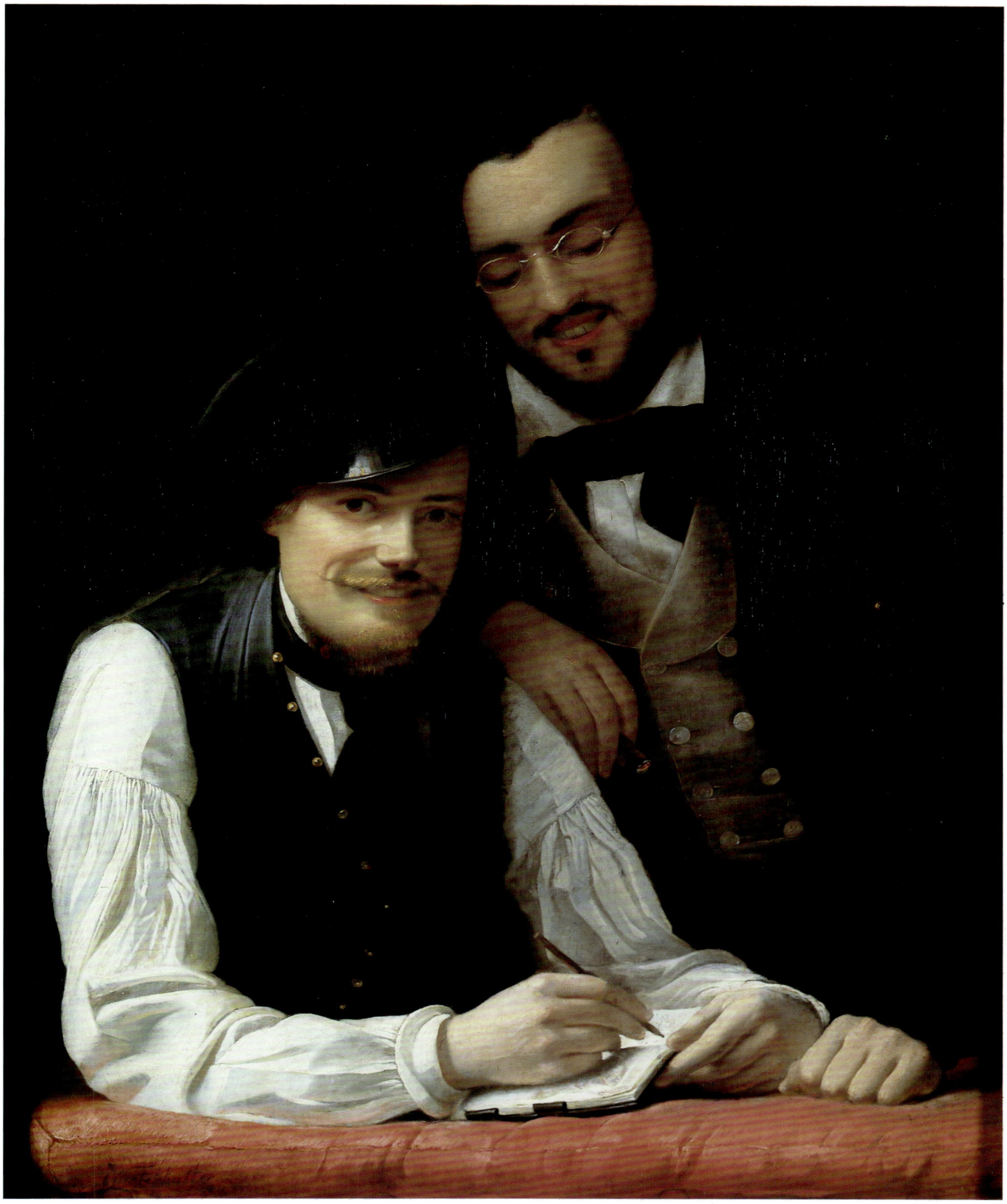

SELF-PORTRAIT OF THE ARTIST WITH HIS BROTHER HERMANN 1840 (no. 11)

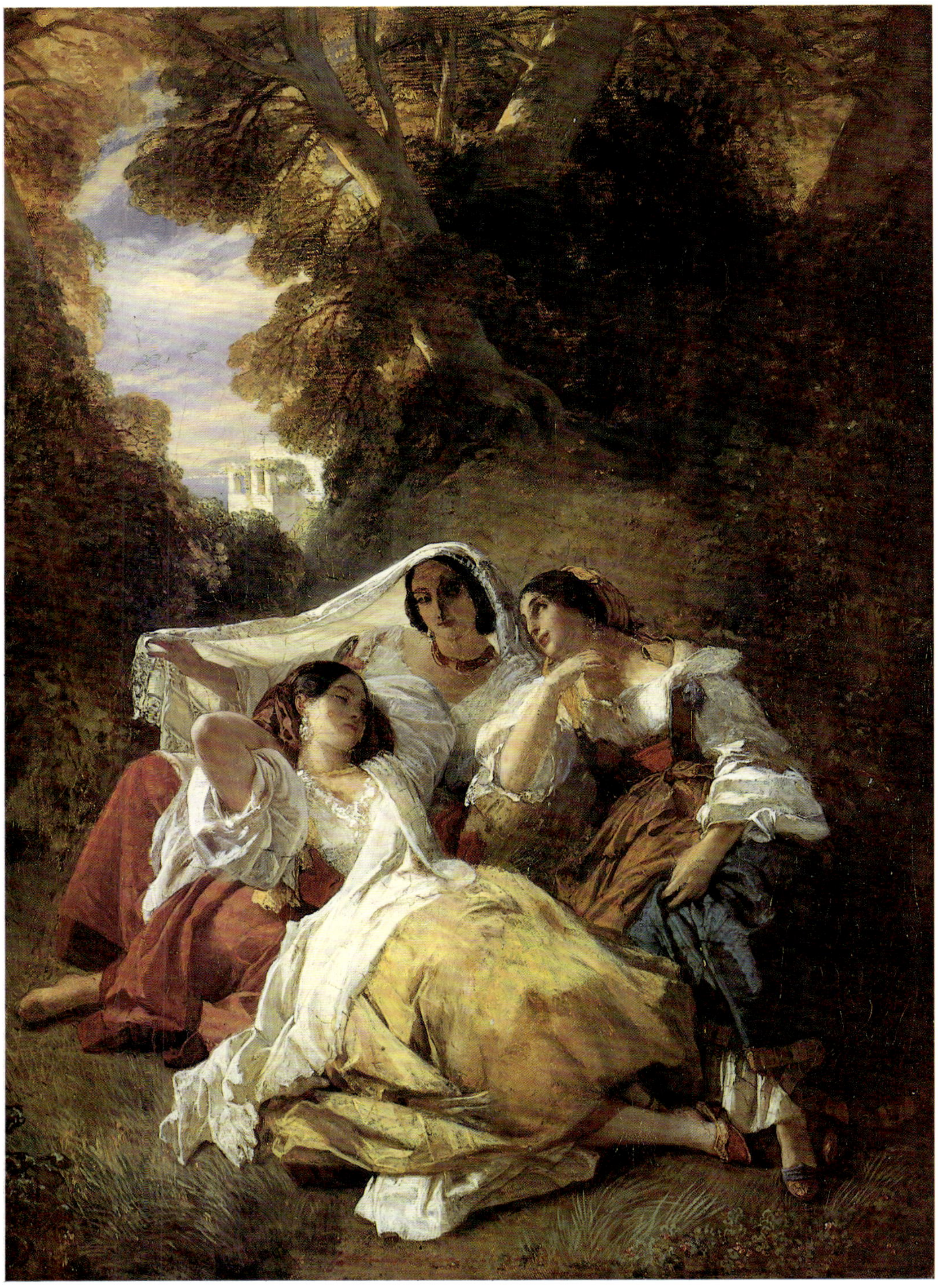

*La Siesta* 1841 (no. 12)

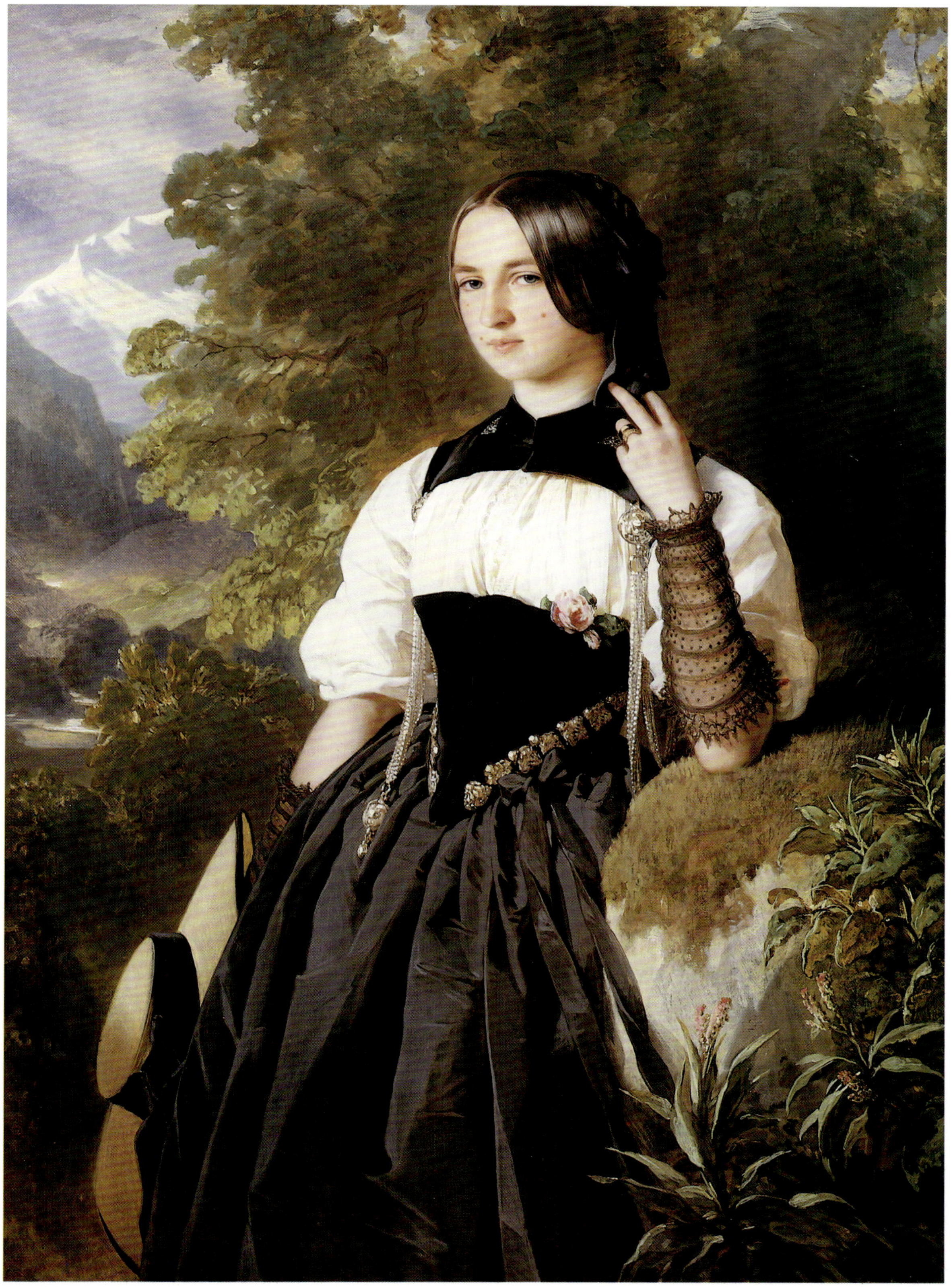

A SWISS GIRL FROM INTERLAKEN (*La Bernoise*) (no. 13)

# The Court of Leopold I

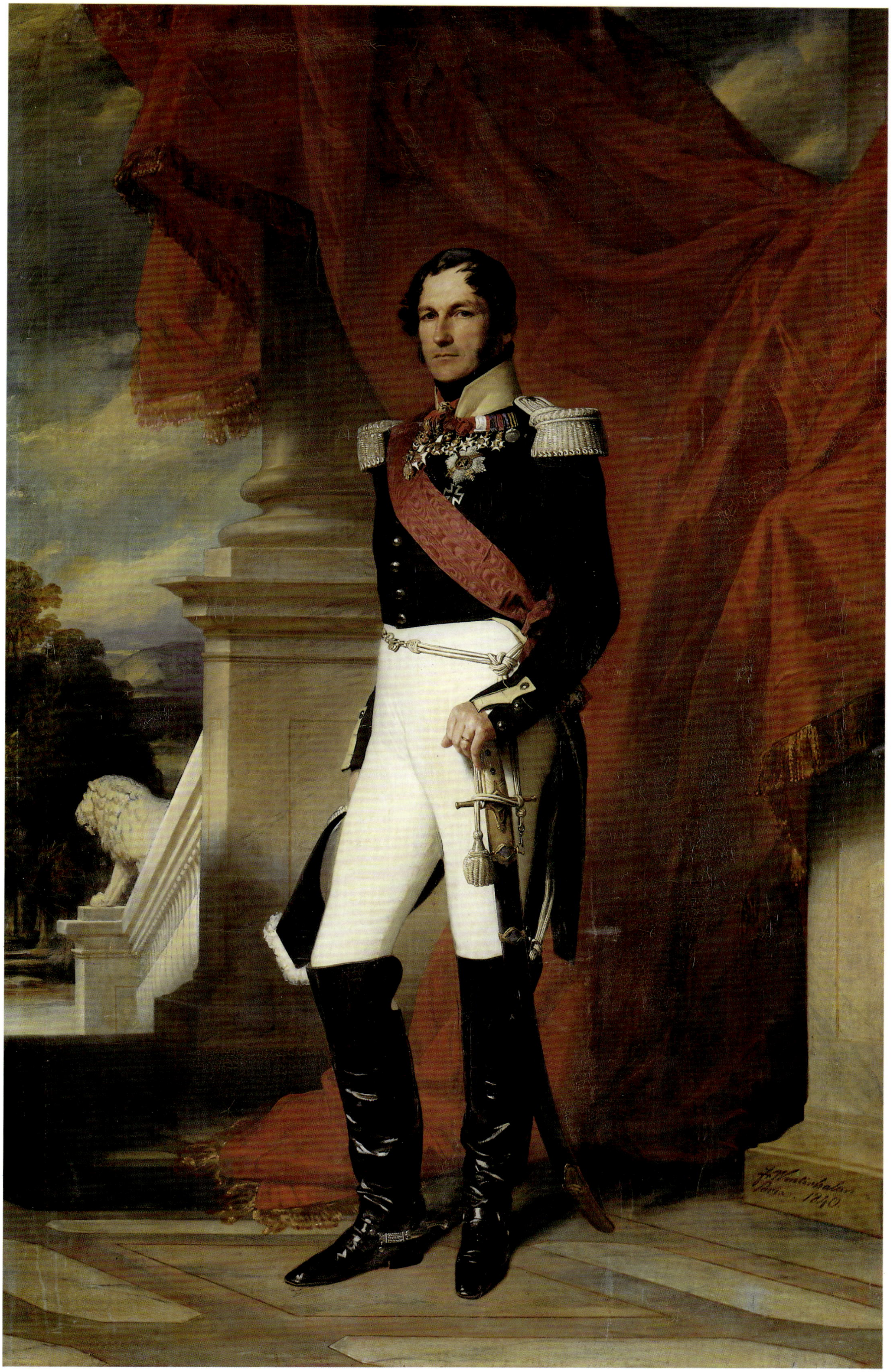

LEOPOLD I, KING OF THE BELGIANS 1840 (no. 14)

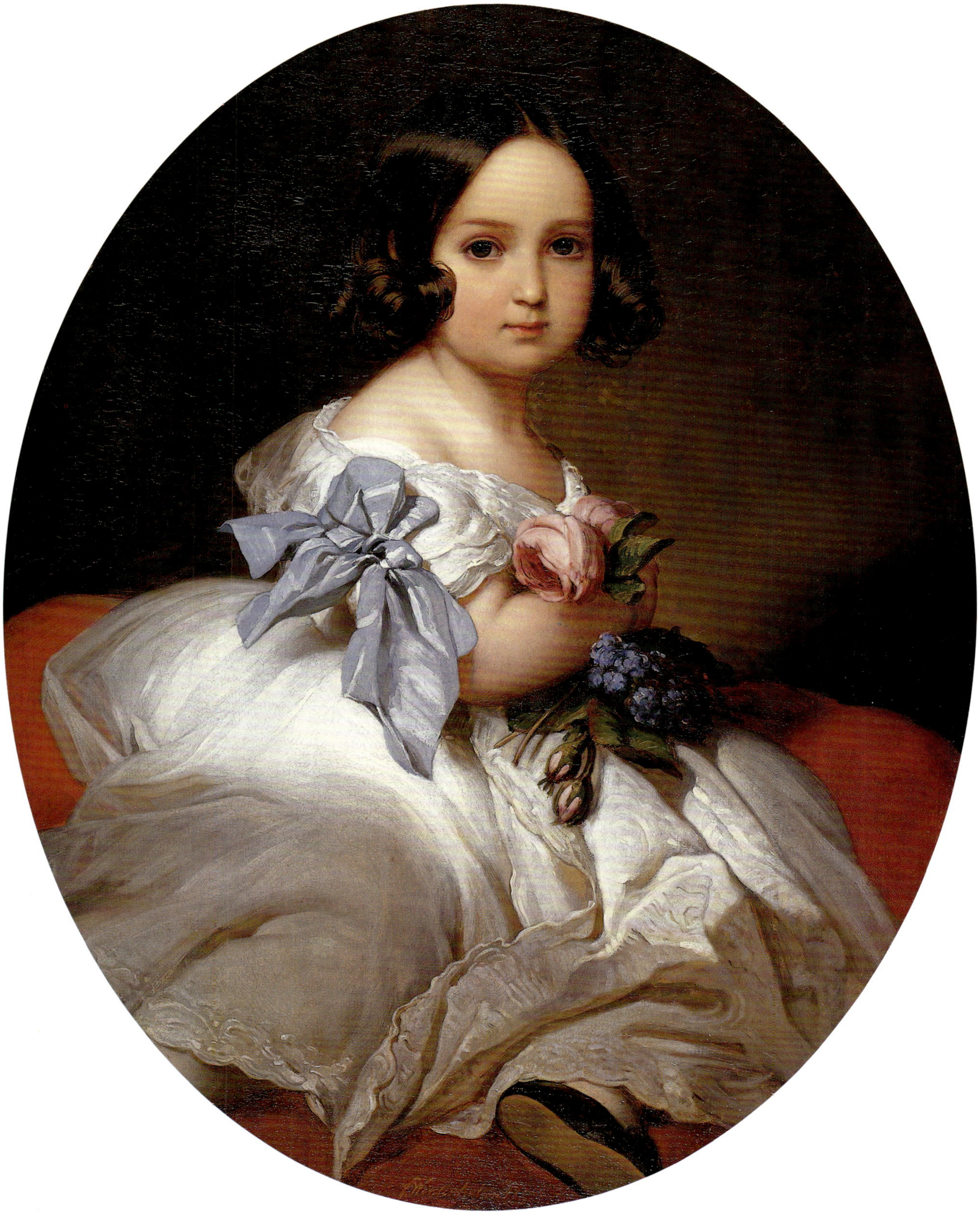

PRINCESS CHARLOTTE OF BELGIUM 1842 (no. 15)

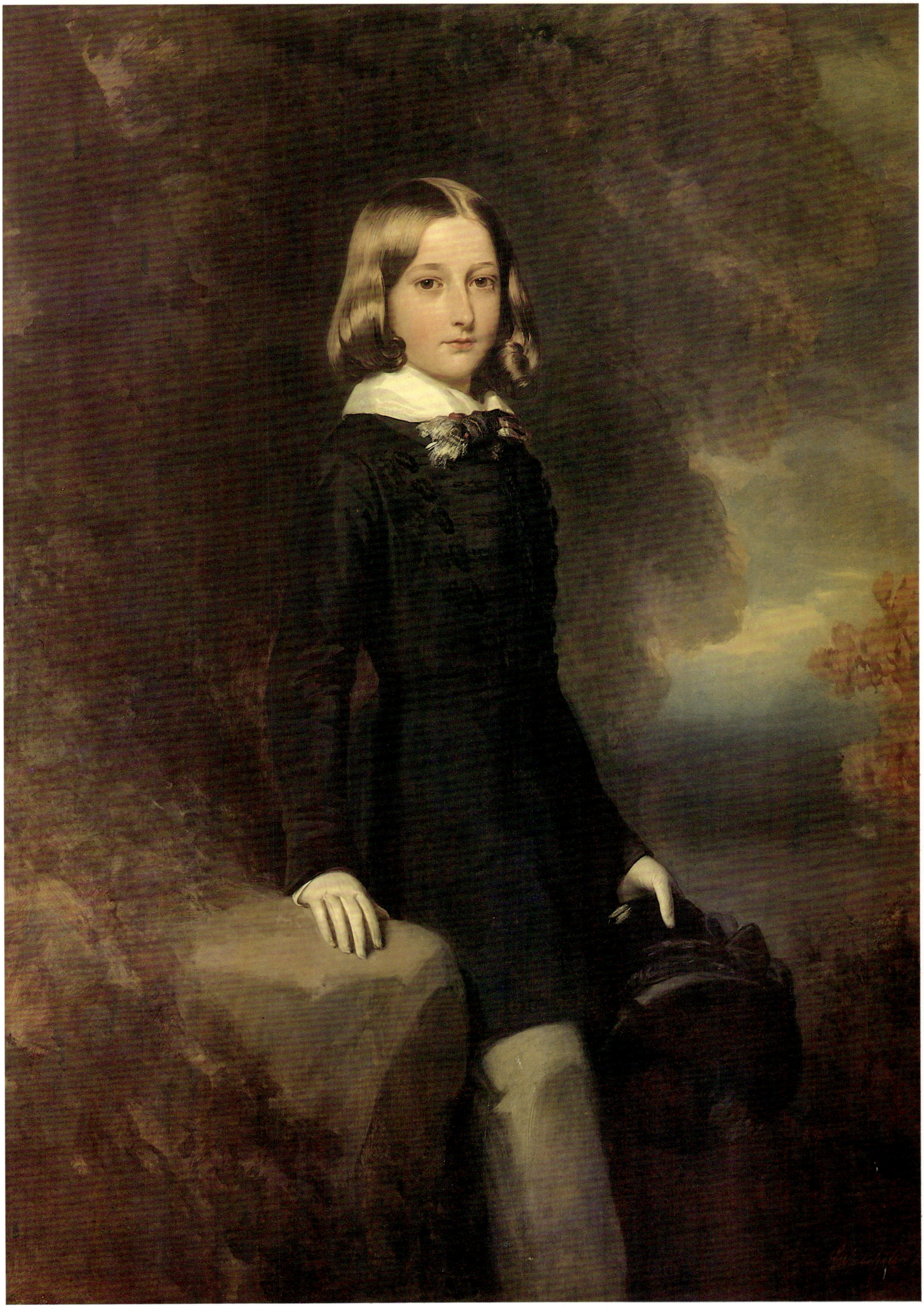

LEOPOLD, DUKE OF BRABANT (no. 16)

# The Court of Louis-Philippe

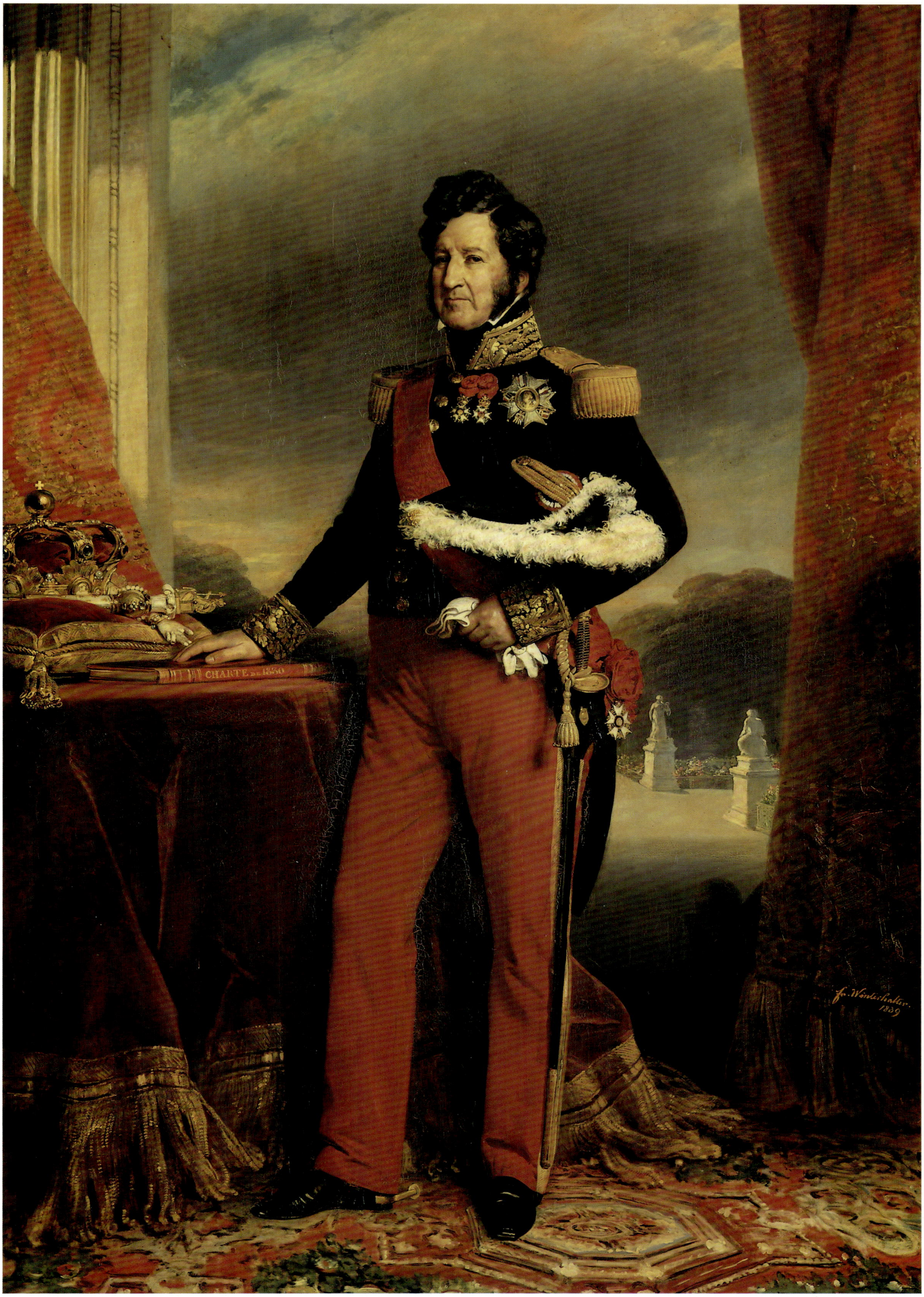

KING LOUIS-PHILIPPE 1839 (no. 17)

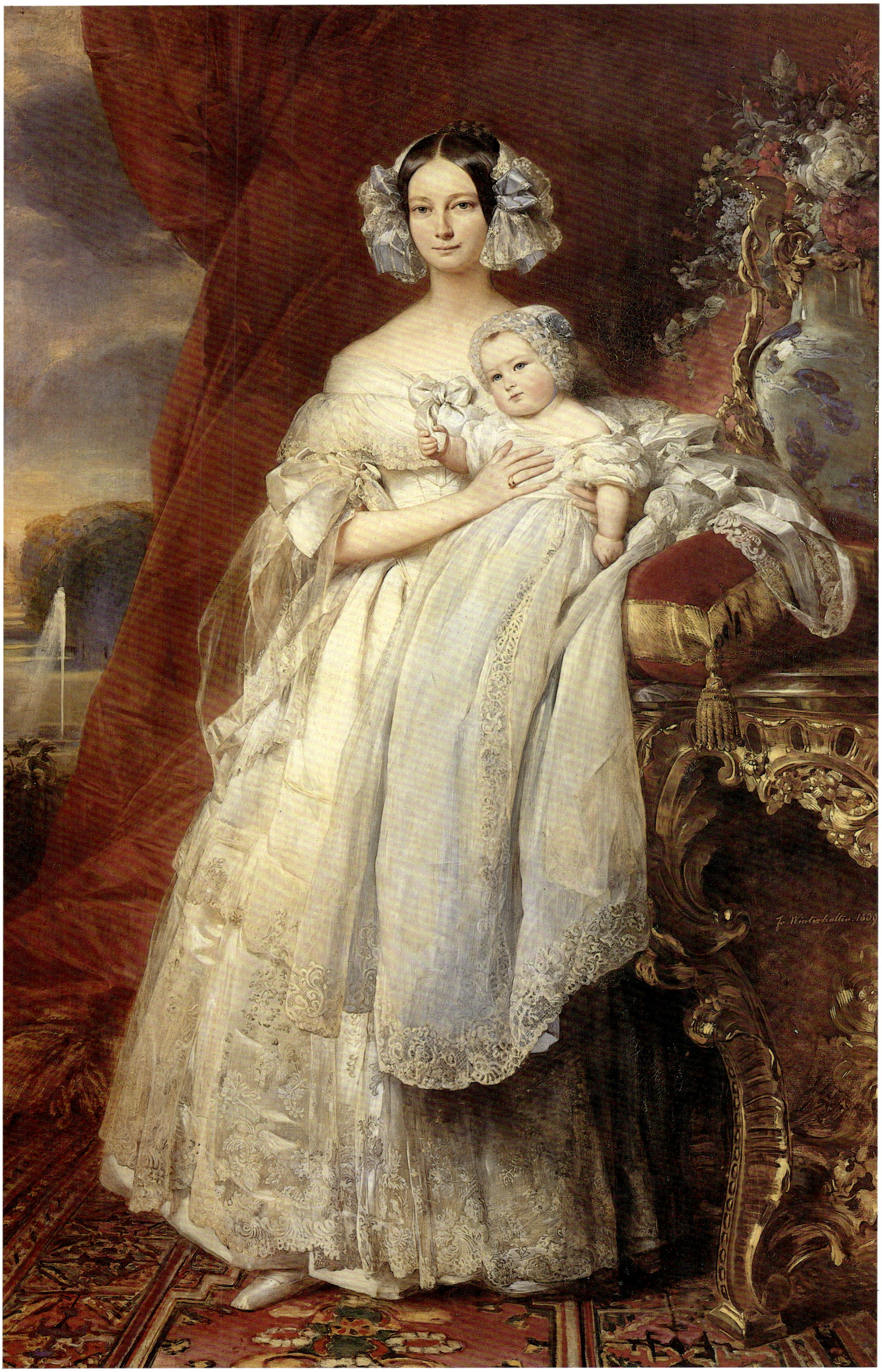

HÉLÈNE-LOUISE-ELIZABETH DE MECKLEMBOURG-SCHWERIN,
DUCHESSE D'ORLÉANS WITH PRINCE LOUIS-PHILIPPE-ALBERT D'ORLÉANS, COMTE DE PARIS 1839 (no. 18)

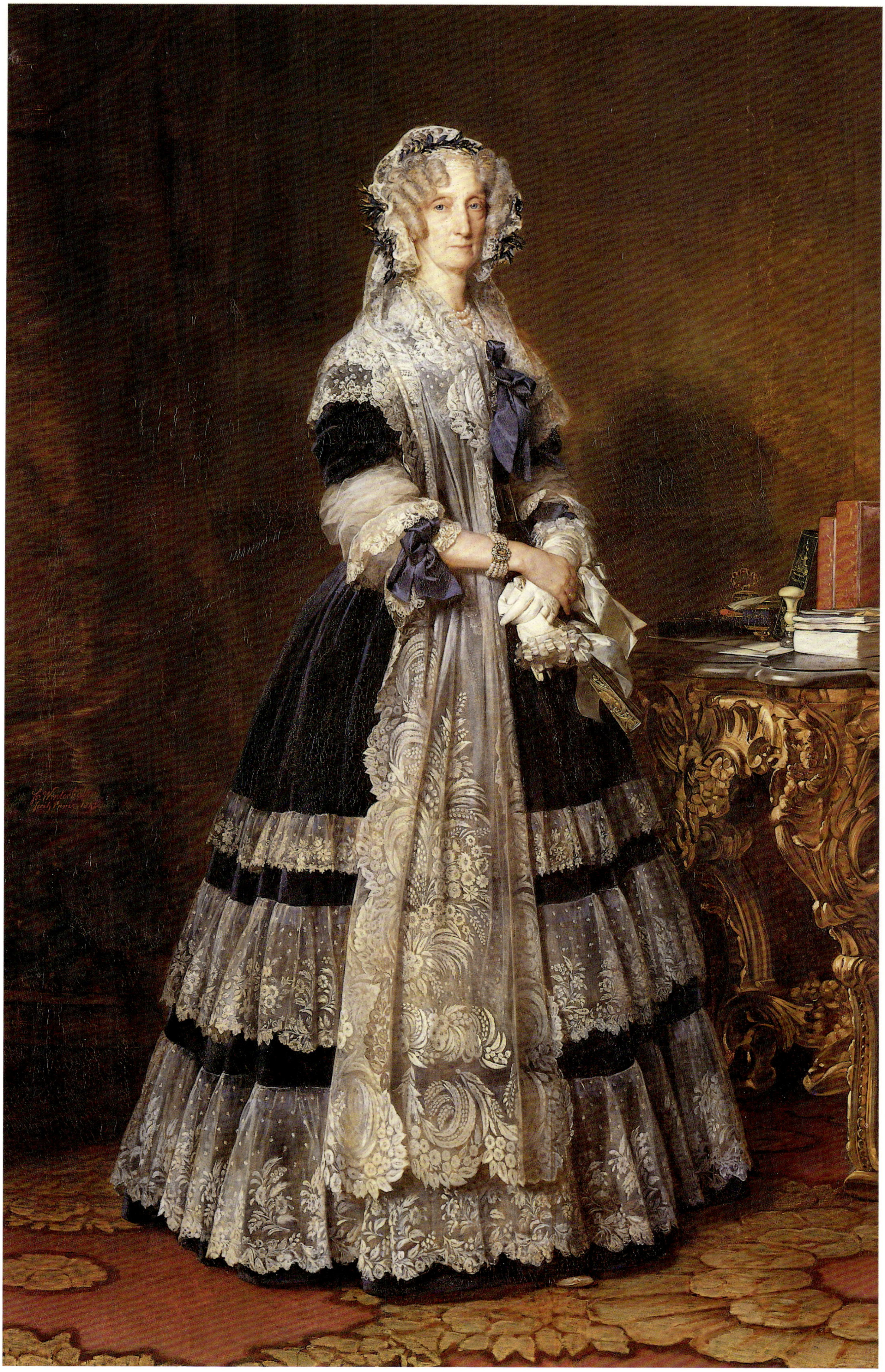

QUEEN MARIE-AMÉLIE 1842 (no. 19)

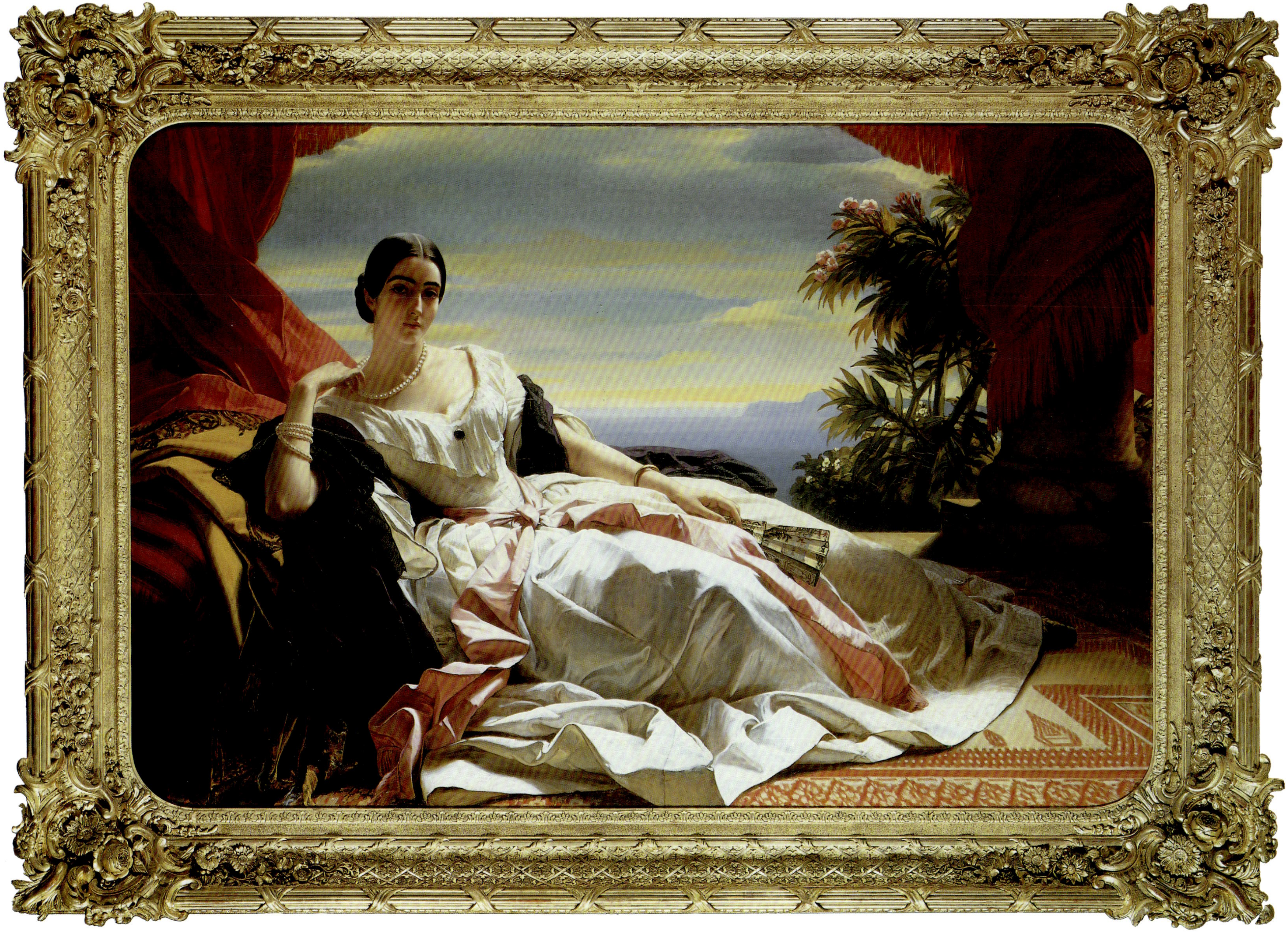

PRINCESS LEONILLA OF SAYN-WITTGENSTEIN-SAYN 1843 (no. 20)

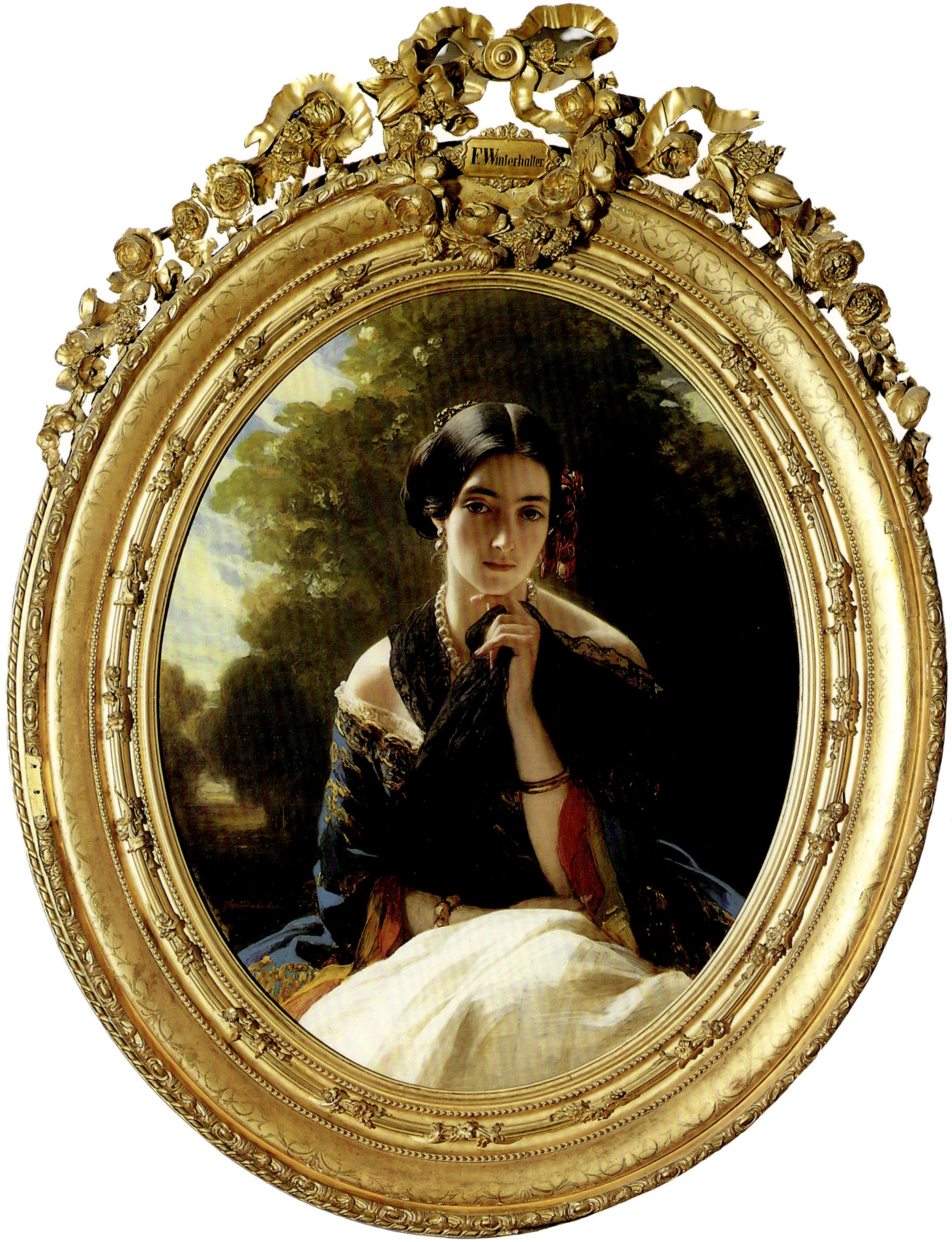


PRINCESS LEONILLA OF SAYN-WITTGENSTEIN-SAYN (no. 26)

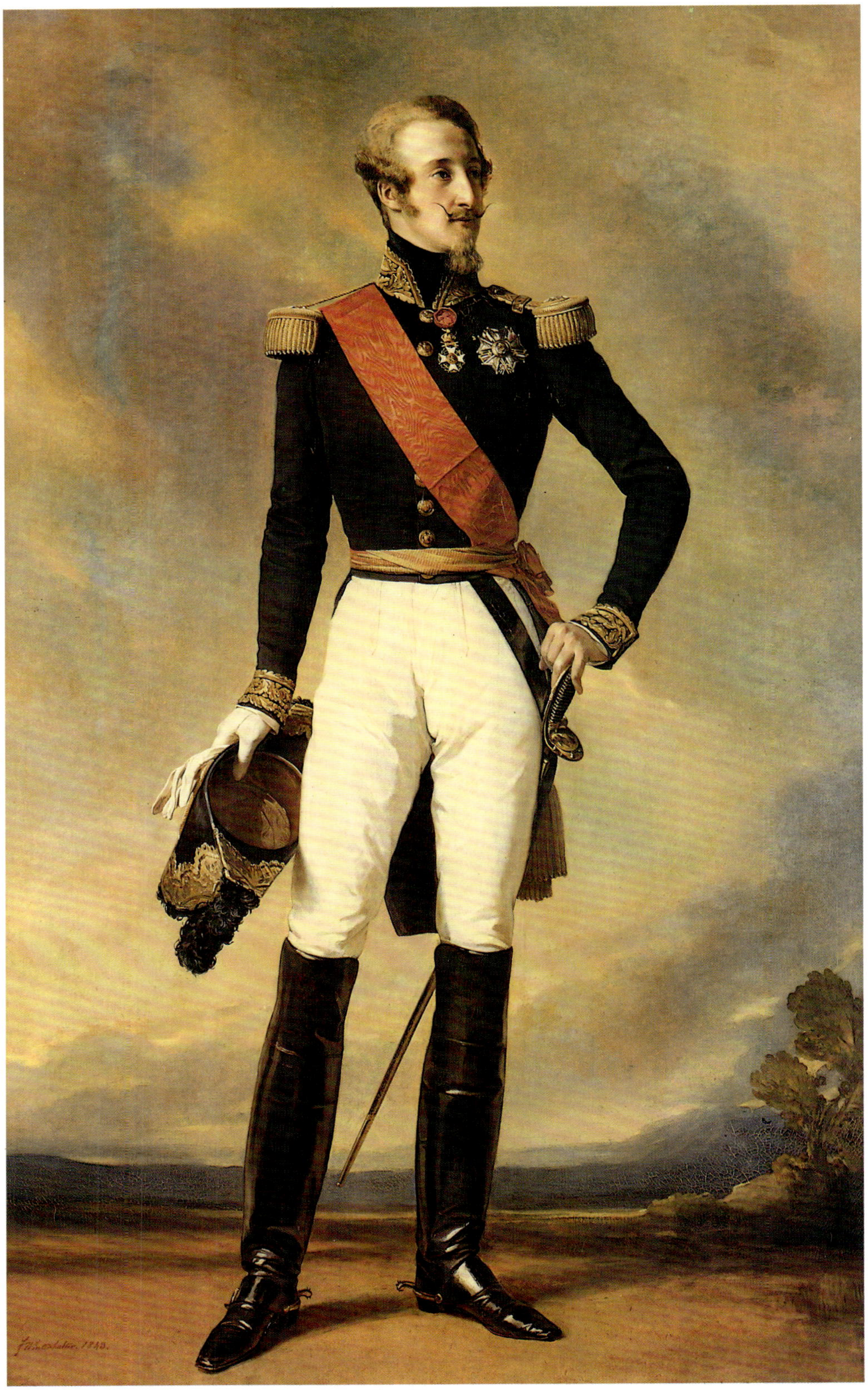

LOUIS-CHARLES-PHILIPPE-RAPHAEL D'ORLÉANS, DUC DE NEMOURS 1843 (no. 21)

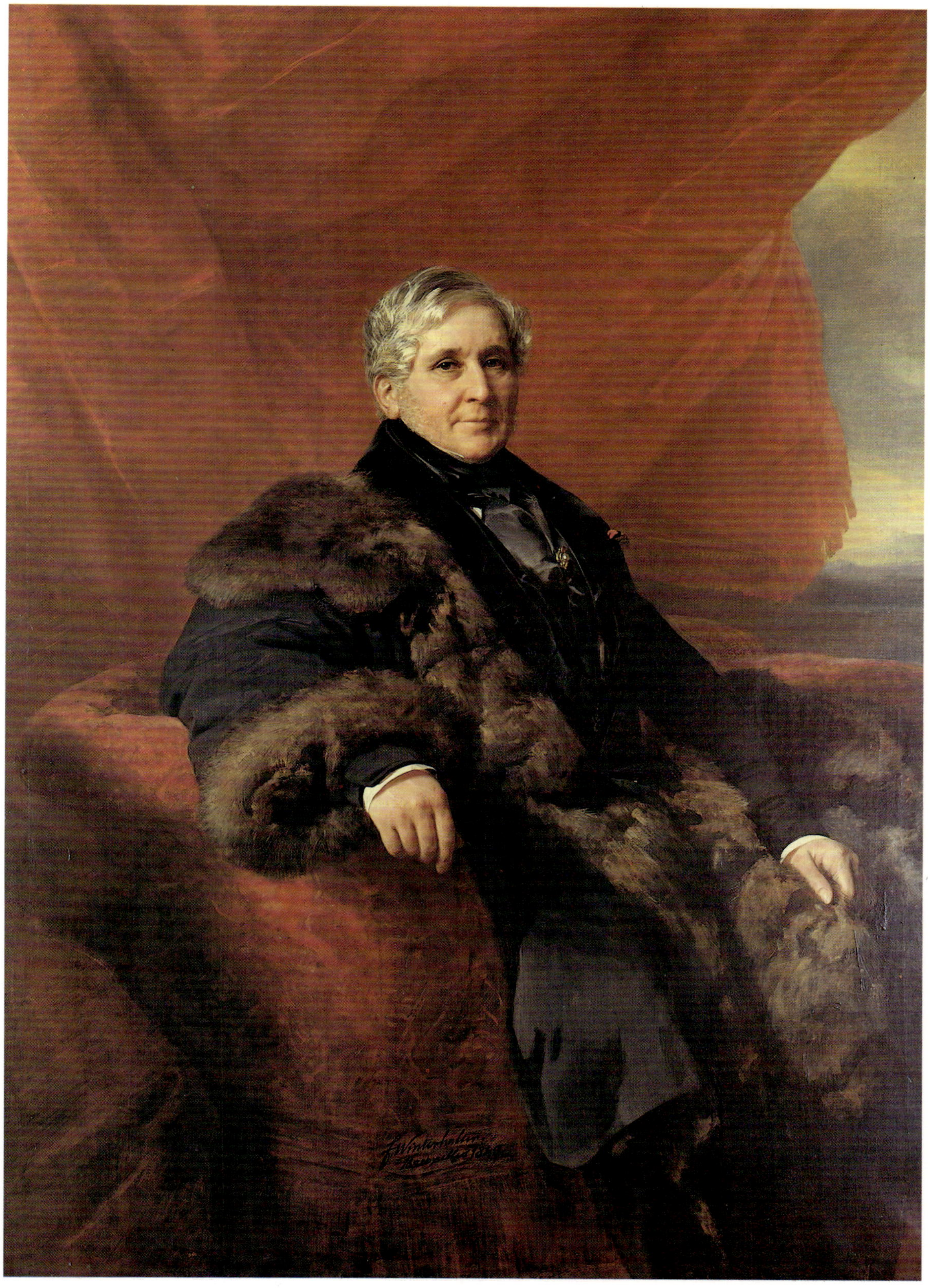

CHARLES-JÉRÔME, COMTE POZZO DI BORGO 1849 (no. 25)

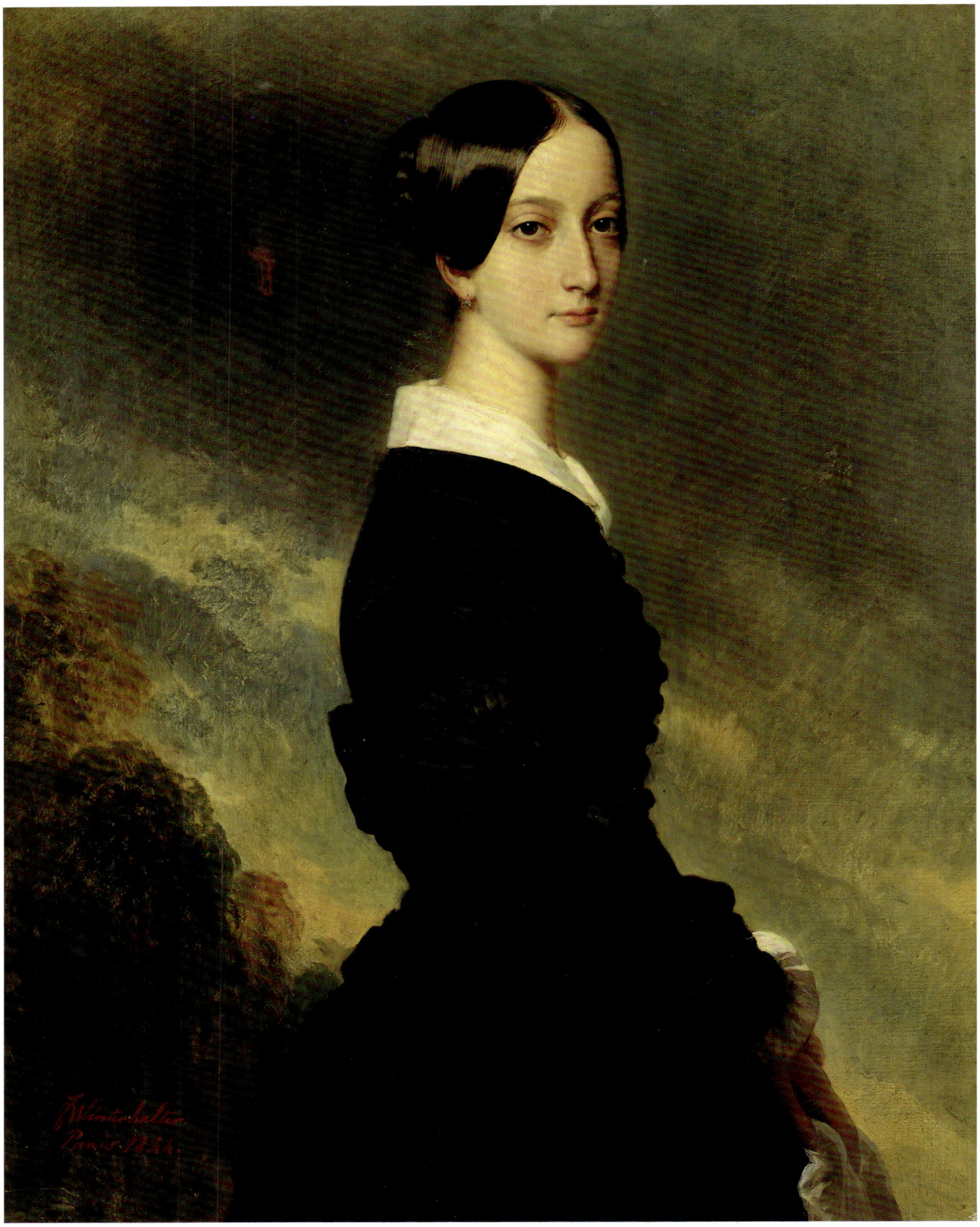

FRANÇOISE-CAROLINE-GONZAGUE, PRINCESSE DE JOINVILLE 1844 (no. 22)

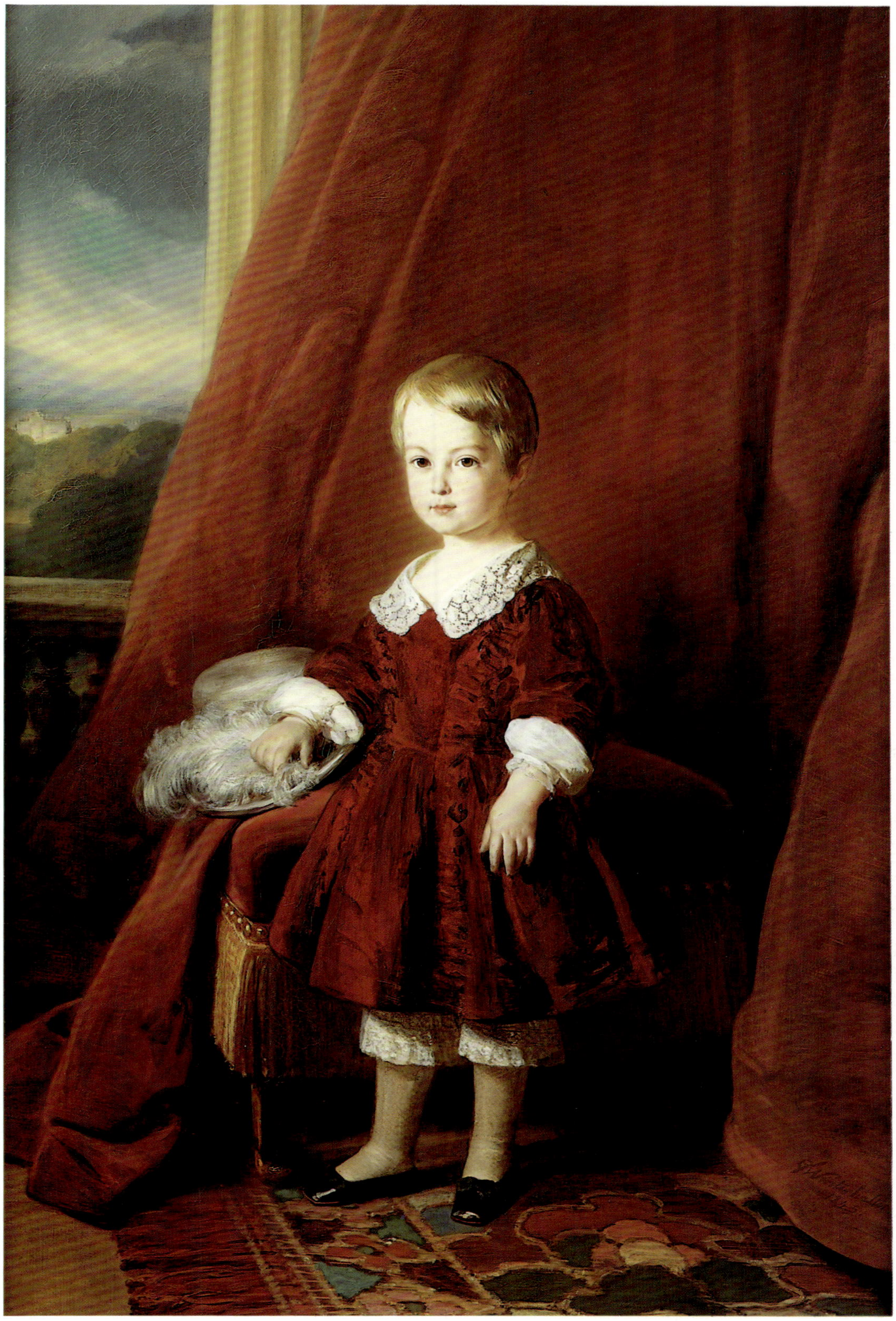

LOUIS-PHILIPPE-MARIE-FERDINAND-GASTON D'ORLÉANS, COMTE D'EU 1845 (no. 23)

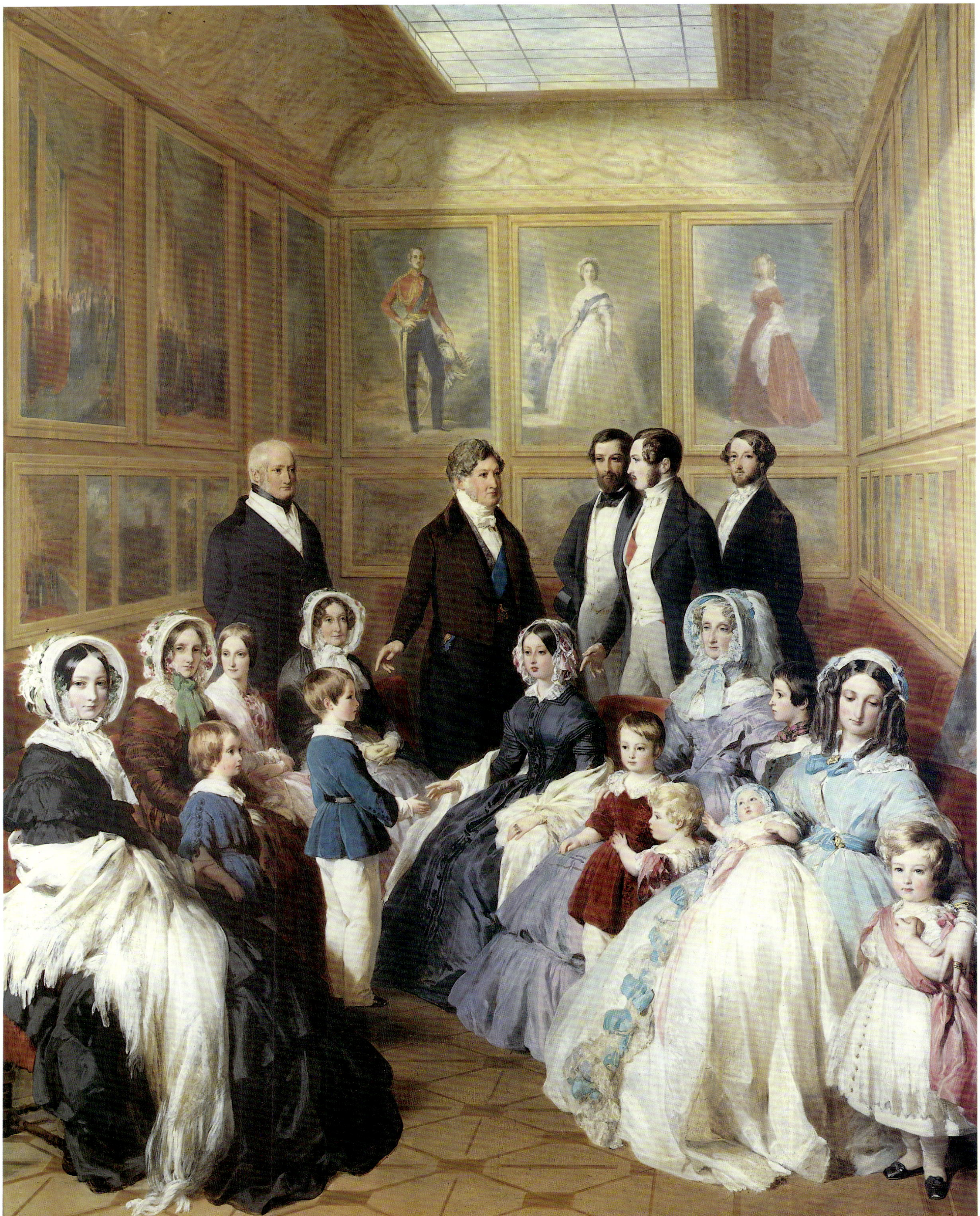

QUEEN VICTORIA AND PRINCE ALBERT
WITH THE FAMILY OF KING LOUIS-PHILIPPE AT THE CHÂTEAU D'EU 1845 (no. 24)

# The Court of Queen Victoria

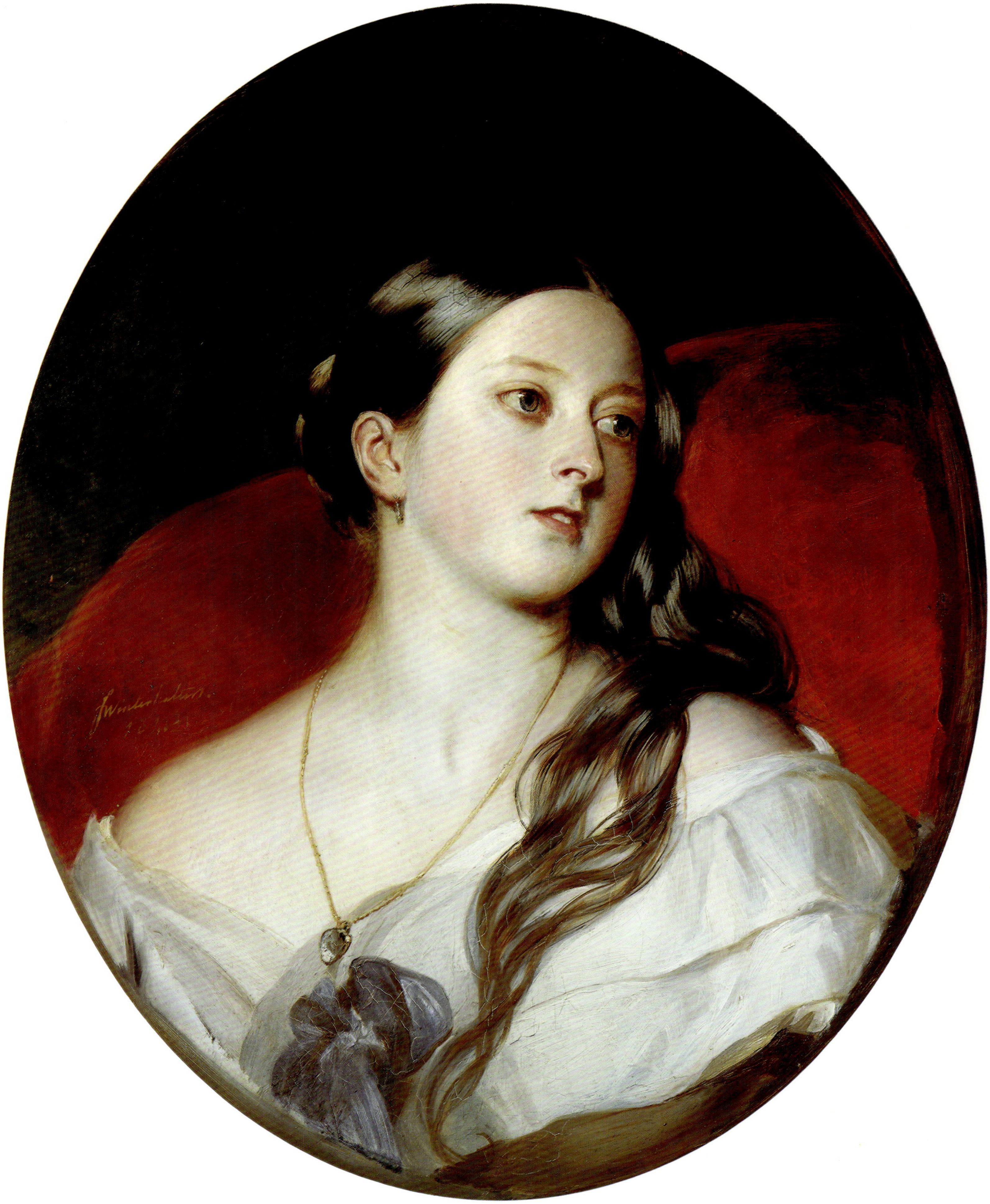

QUEEN VICTORIA 1843 (no. 29)

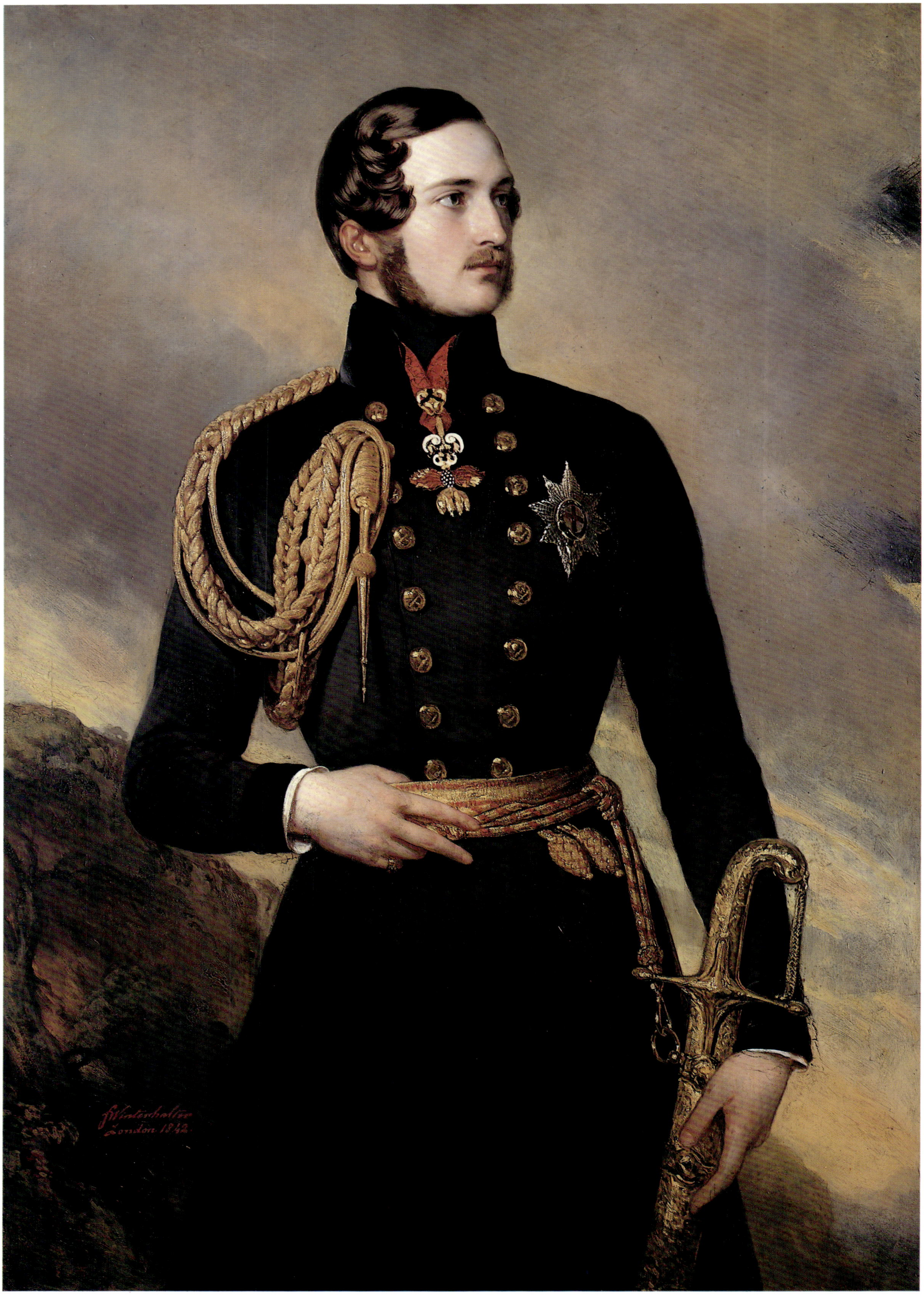


PRINCE ALBERT 1842 (no. 28)

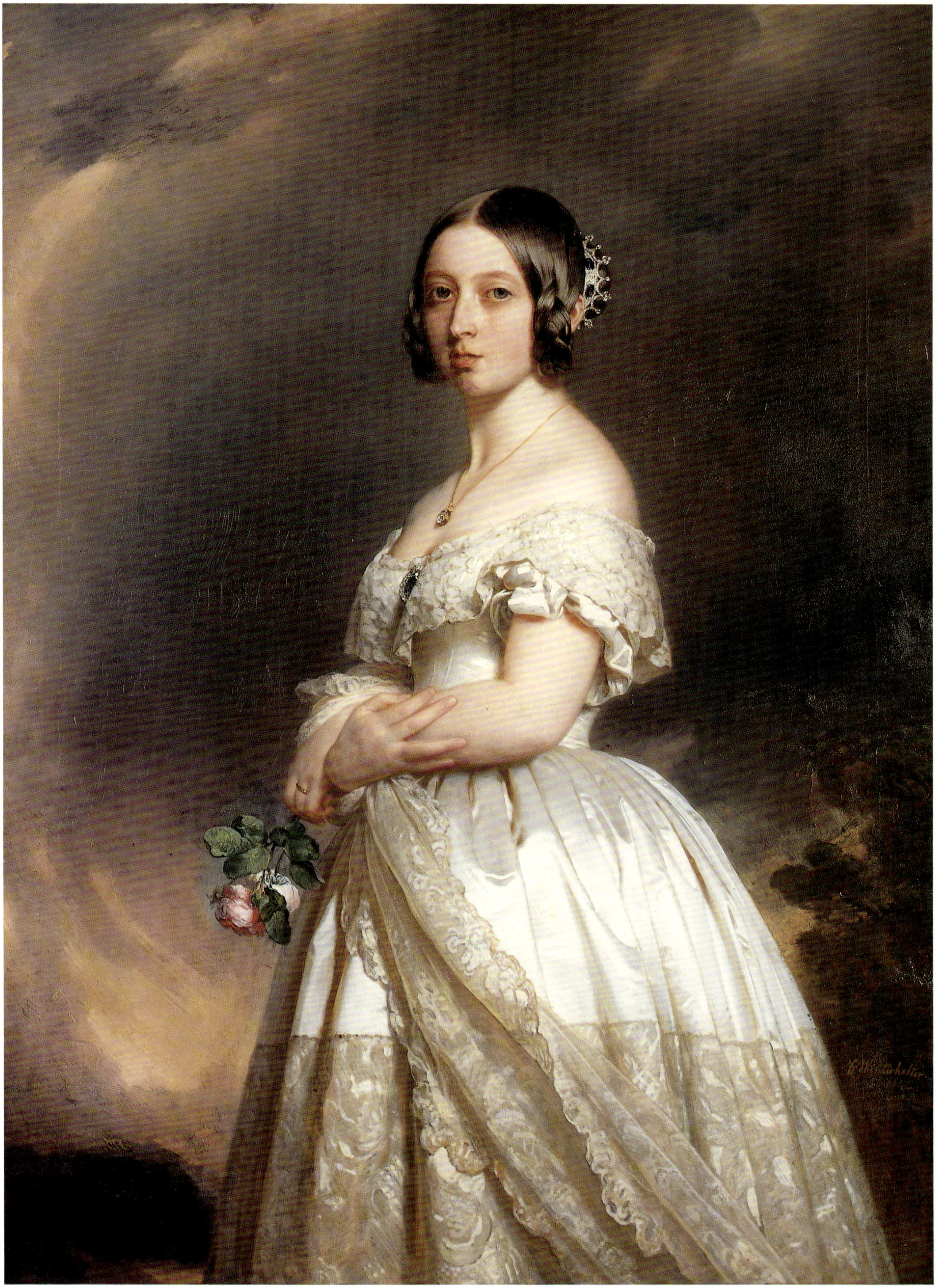

QUEEN VICTORIA 1842 (no. 27)

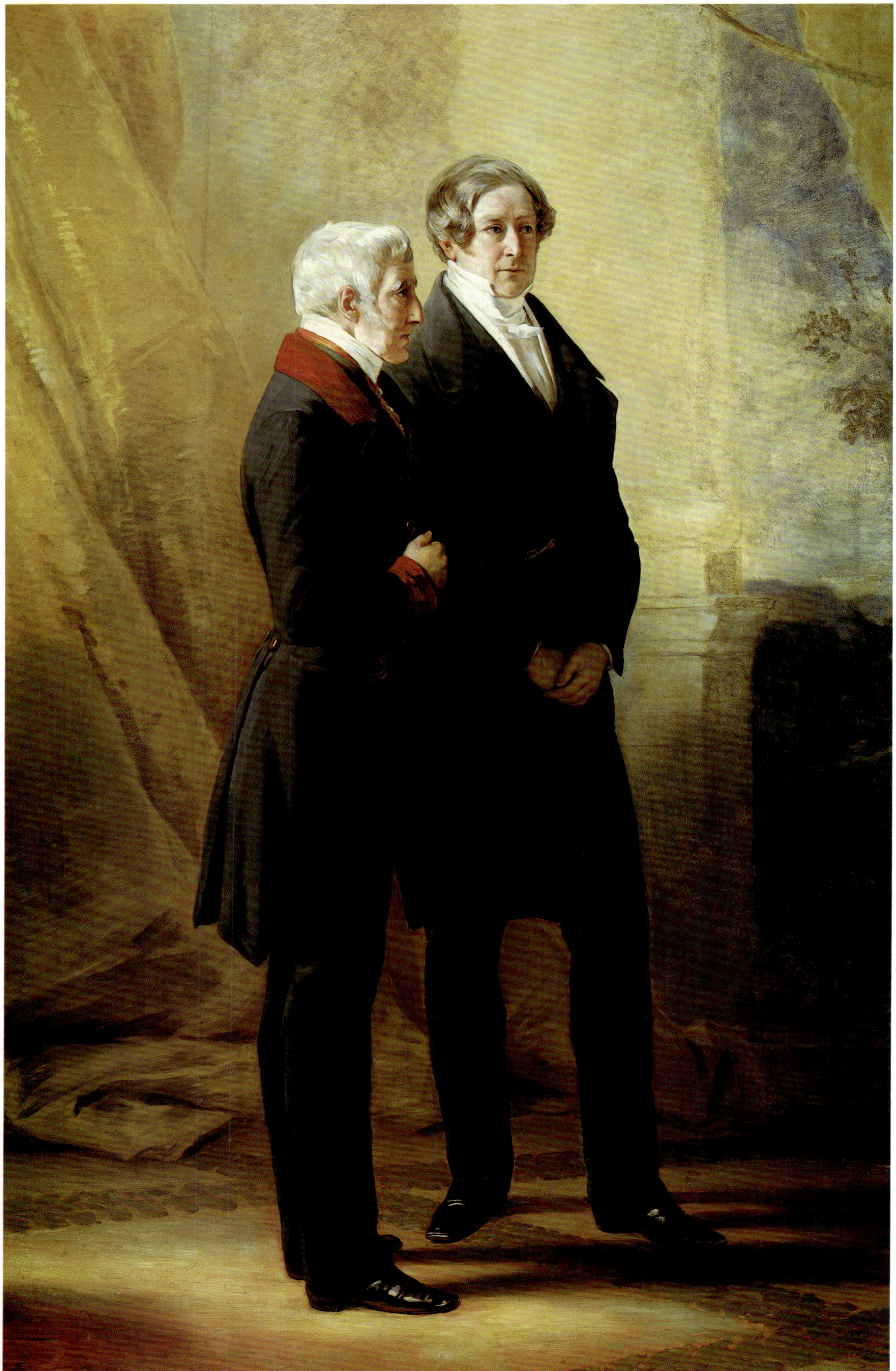

ARTHUR WELLESLEY, 1ST DUKE OF WELLINGTON, WITH SIR ROBERT PEEL 1844 (no. 30)

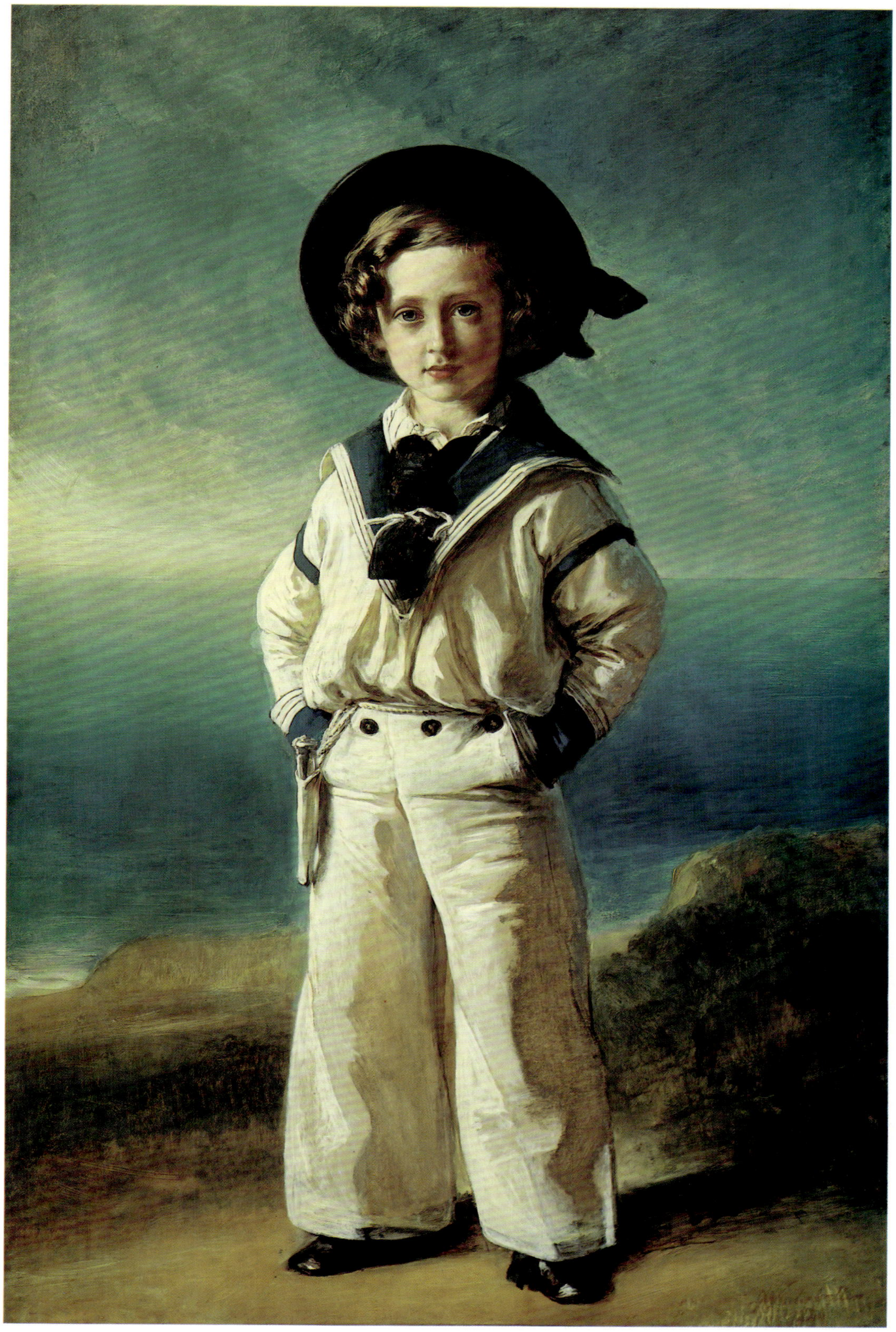

ALBERT EDWARD, PRINCE OF WALES 1846 (no. 31)

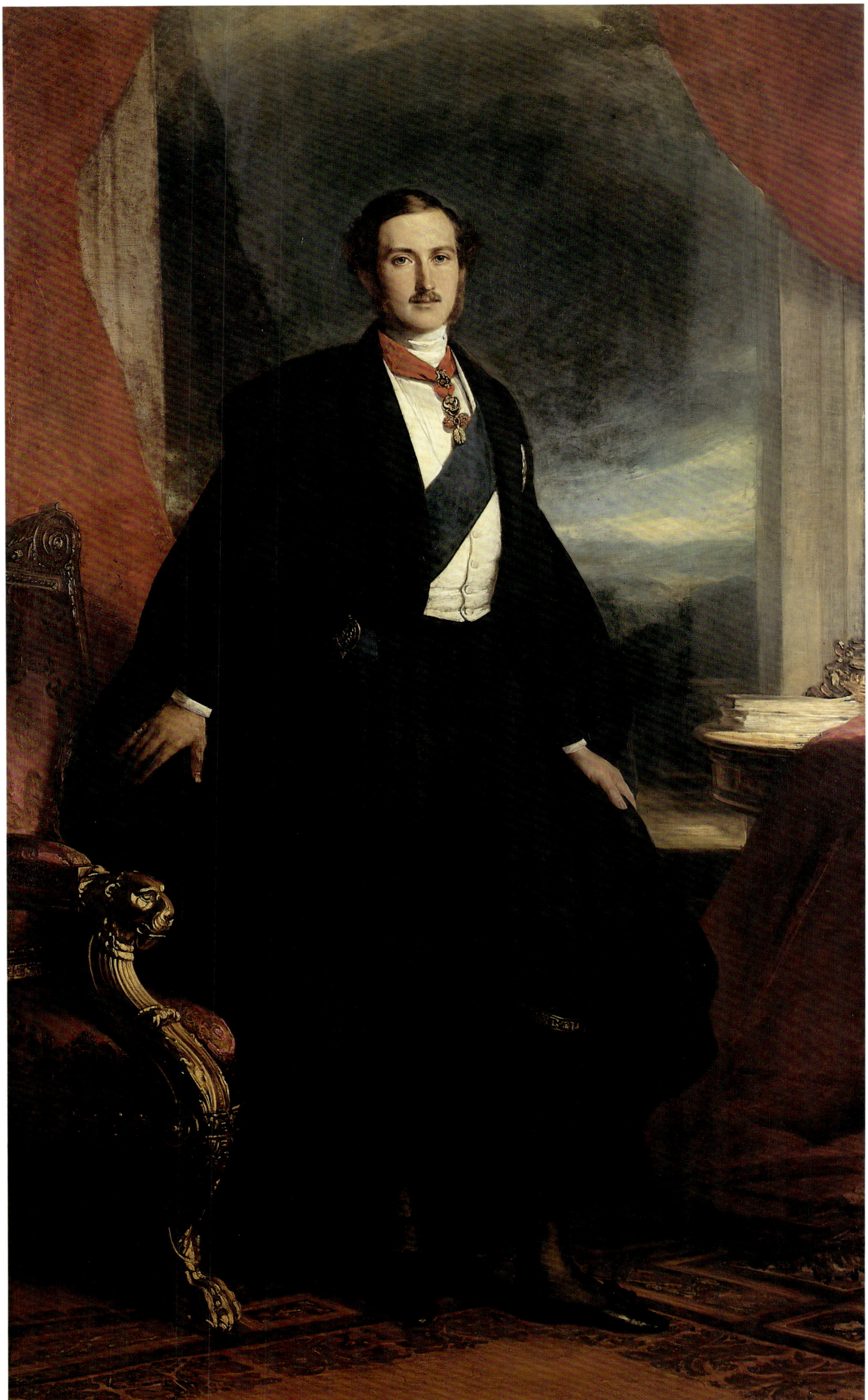

PRINCE ALBERT 1846 (no. 32)

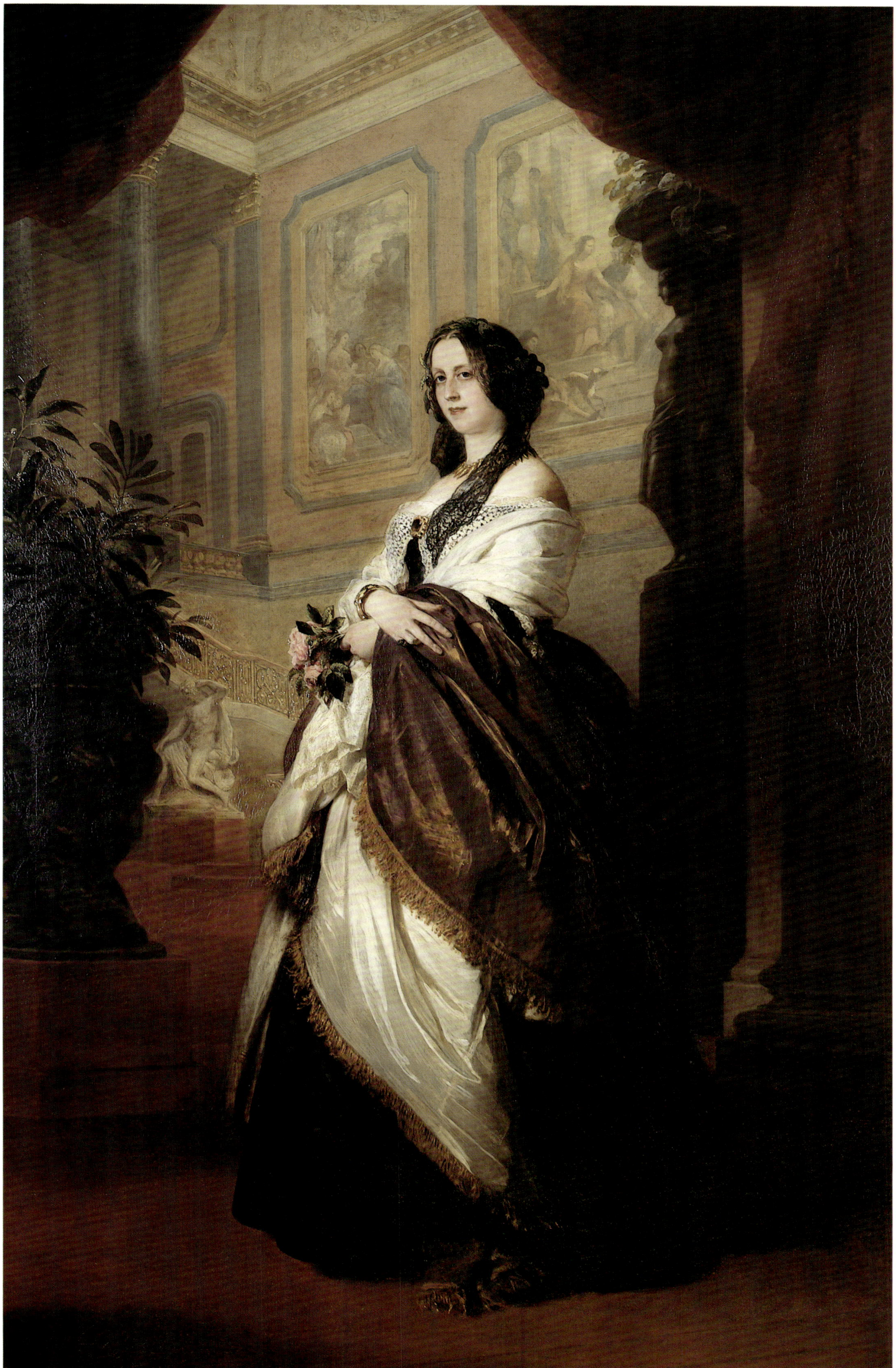

HARRIET HOWARD, DUCHESS OF SUTHERLAND 1849 (no. 34)

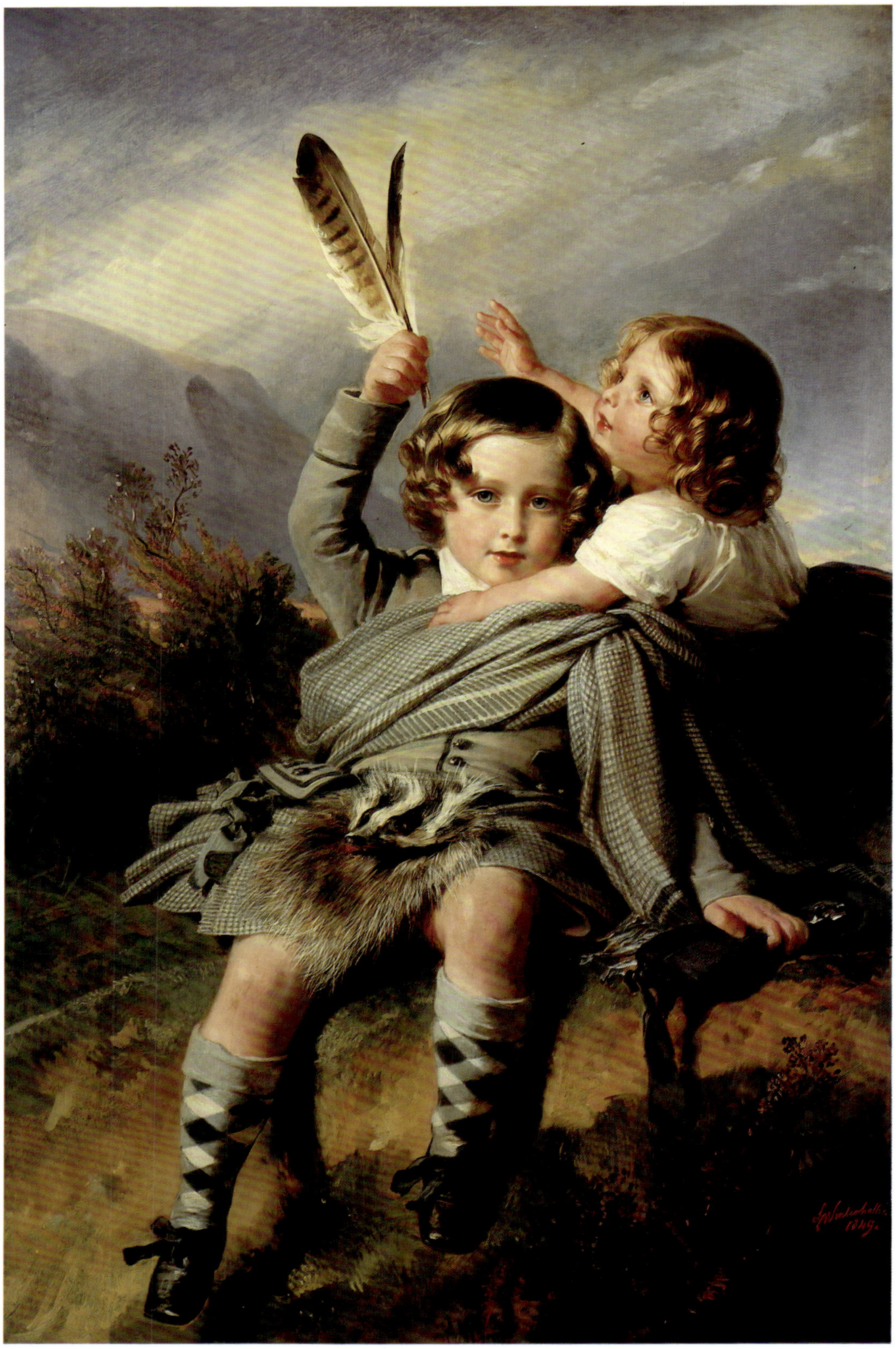

PRINCE ALFRED AND PRINCESS HELENA 1849 (no. 33)

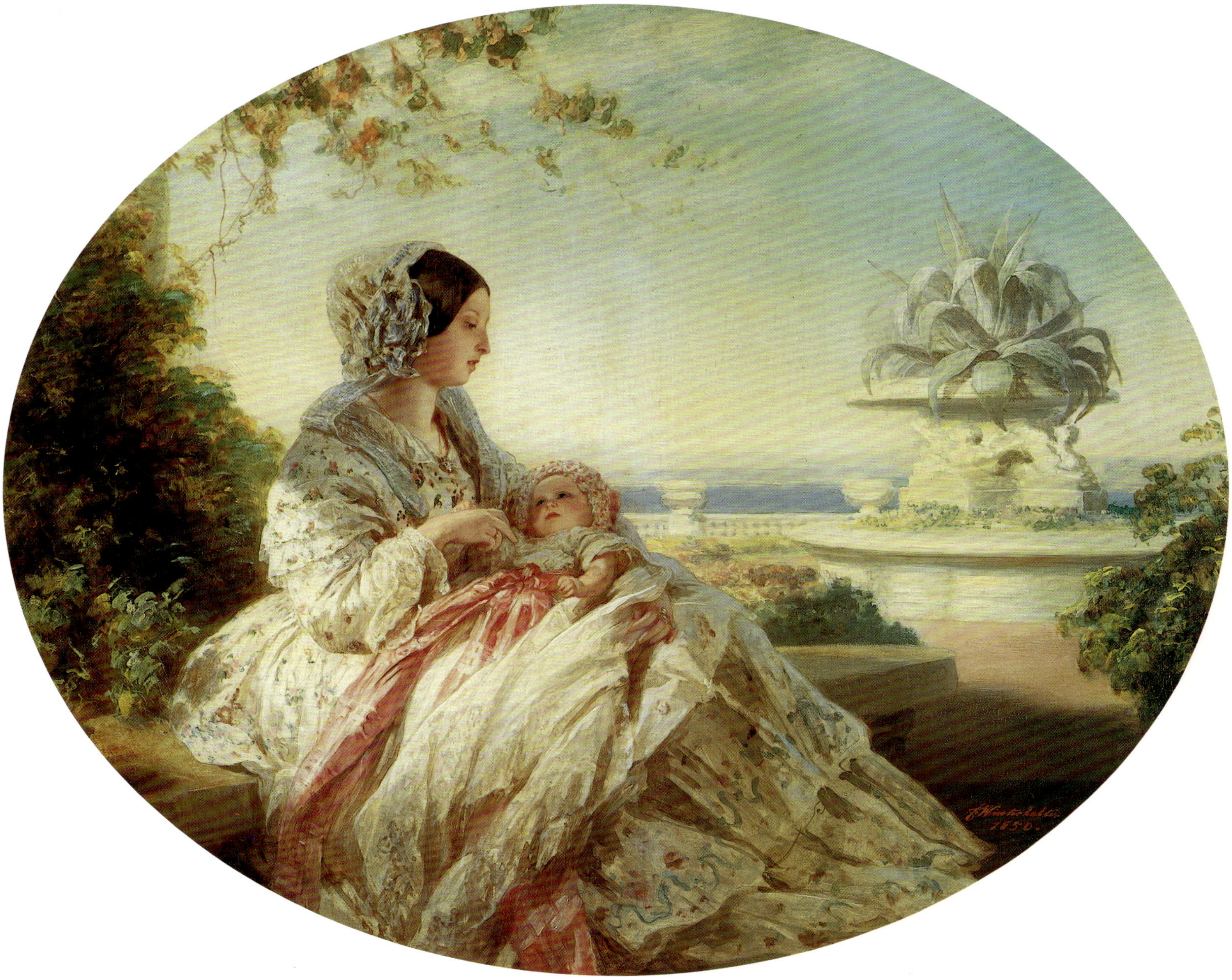

QUEEN VICTORIA WITH PRINCE ARTHUR 1850 (no. 36)

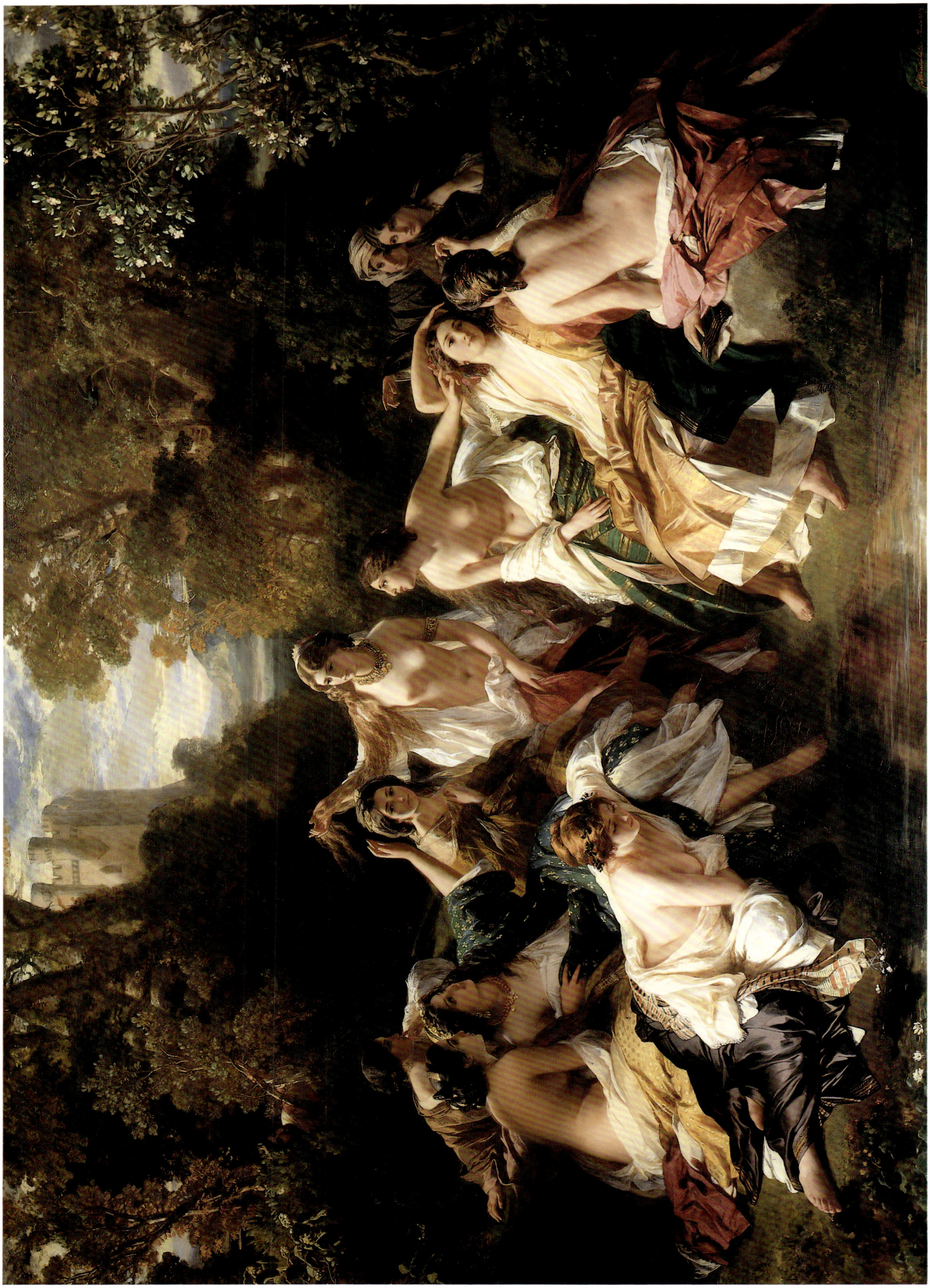

*Florinda* 1852 (no. 38)

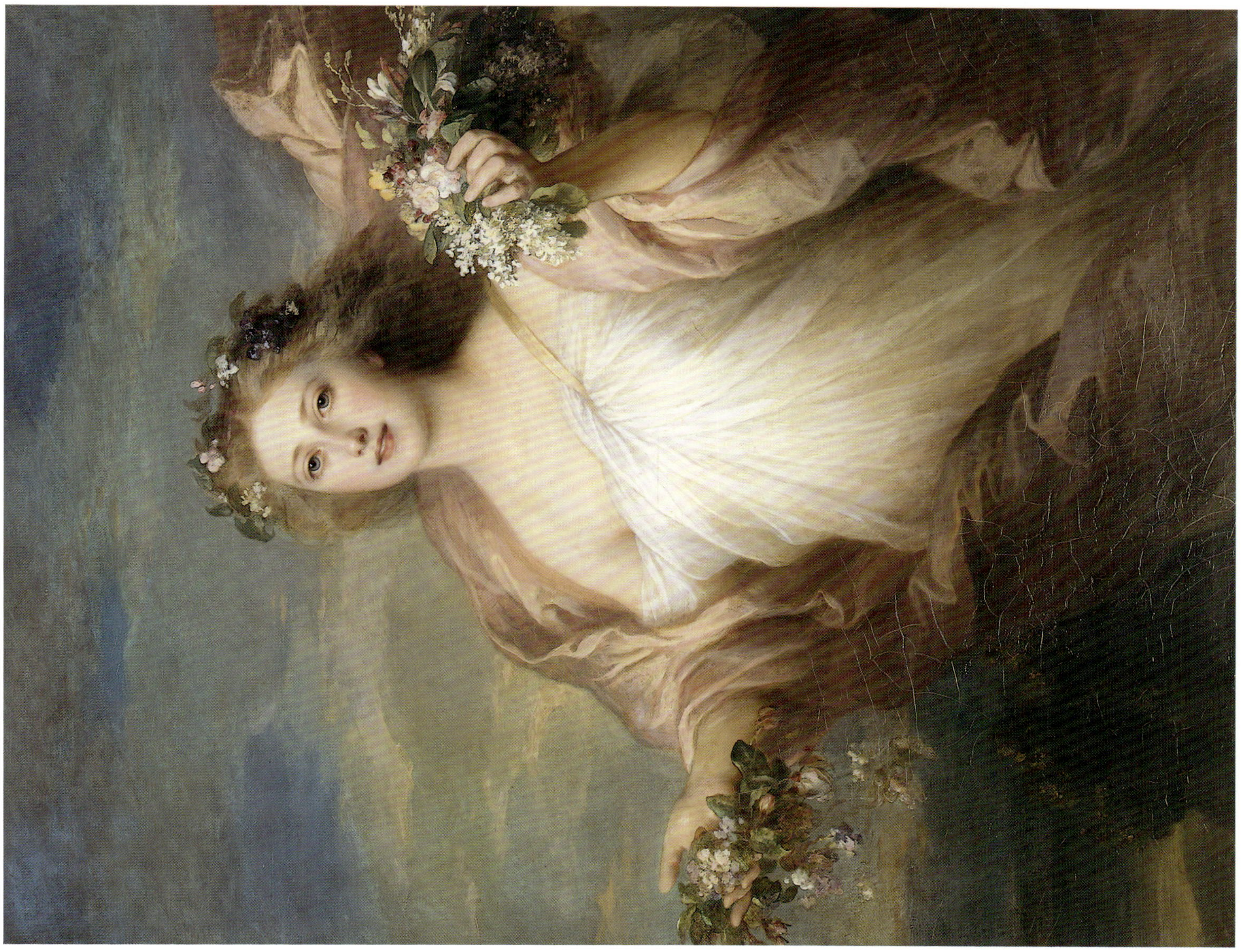

SPRING (*Der Frühling*) (no. 39)

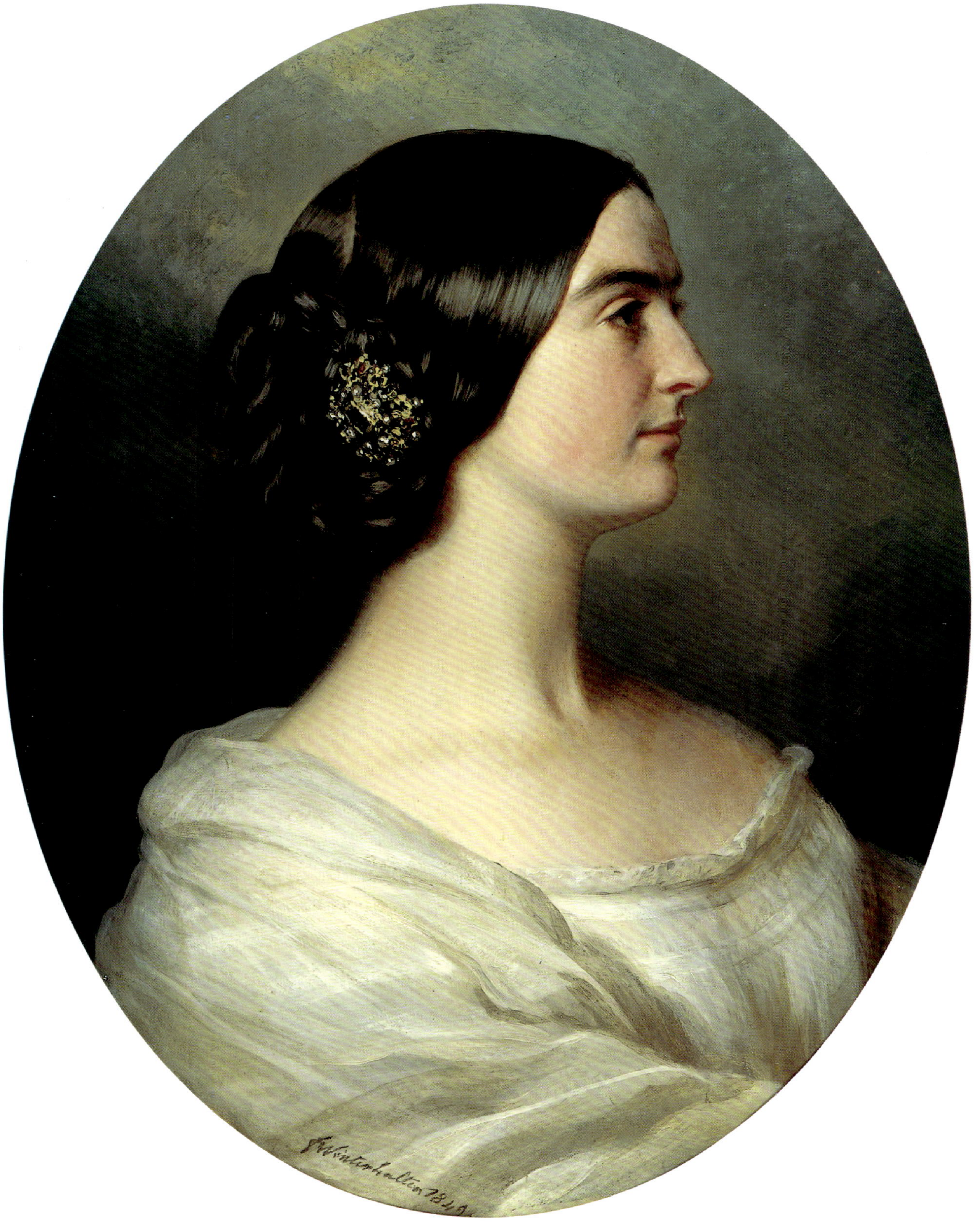

CHARLOTTE STUART, VISCOUNTESS CANNING 1849 (no. 35)

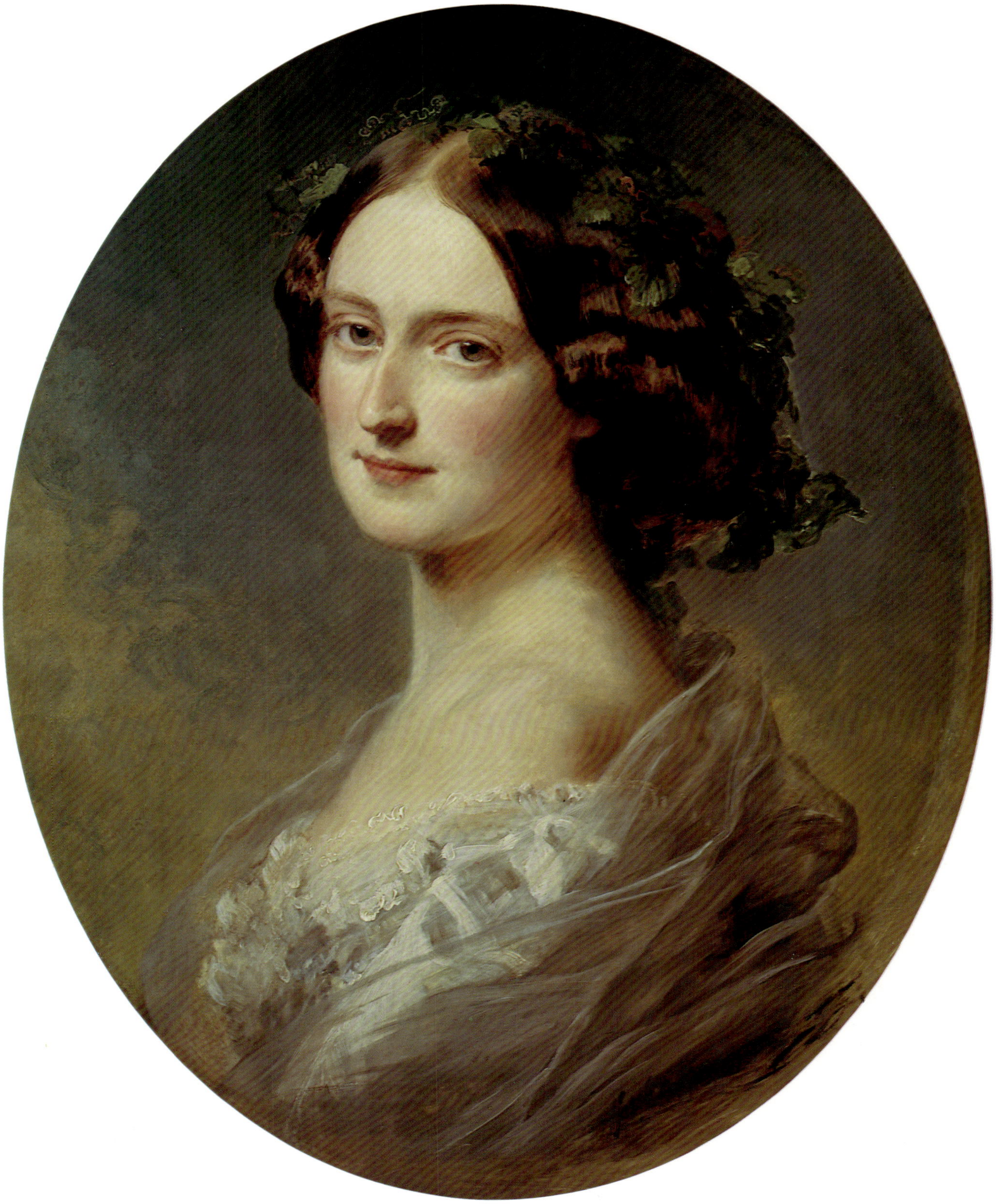

LADY CLEMENTINA AUGUSTA WELLINGTON CHILD-VILLIERS (no. 41)

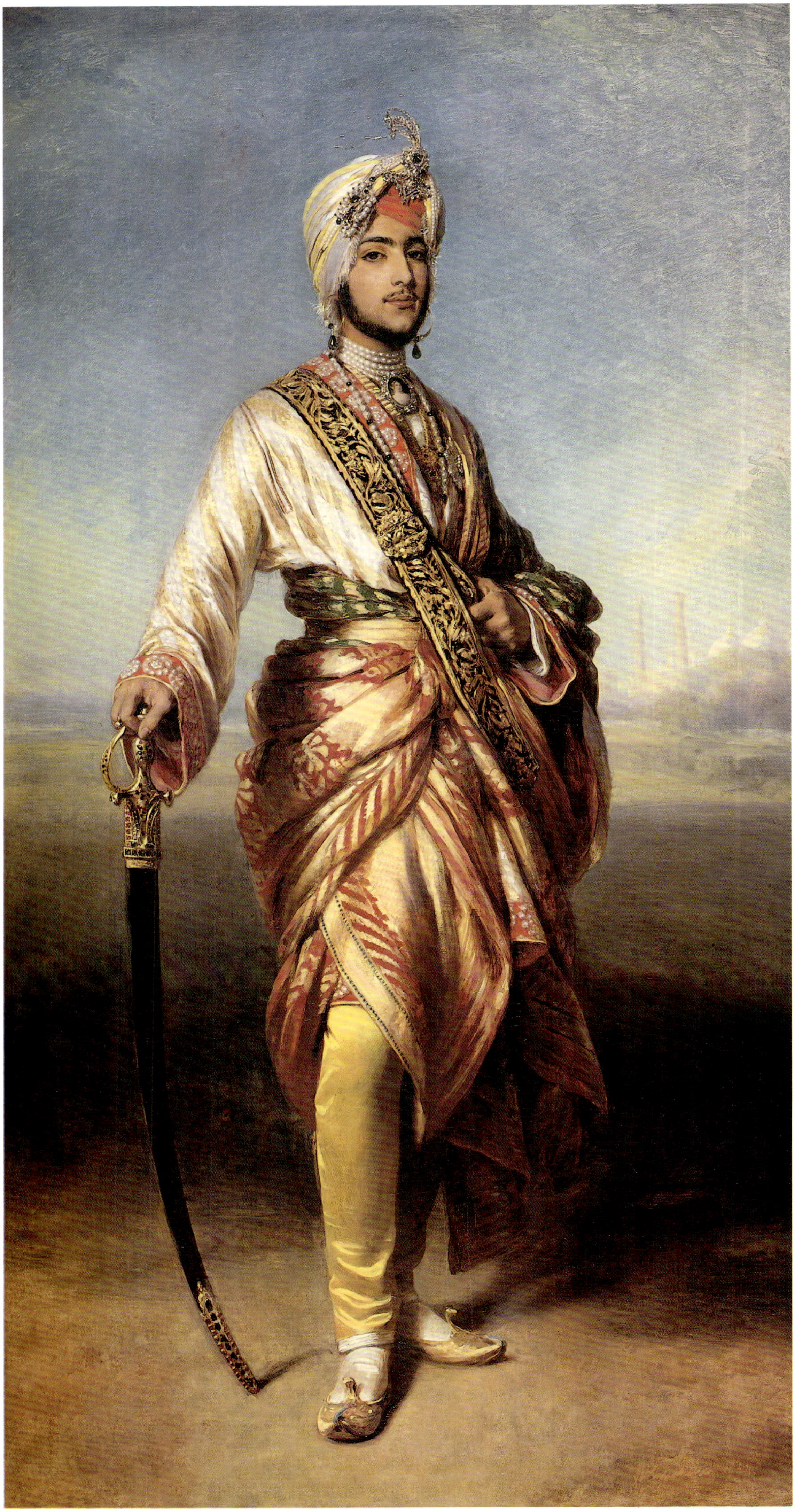

THE MAHARAJAH DULEEP SINGH 1854 (no. 40)

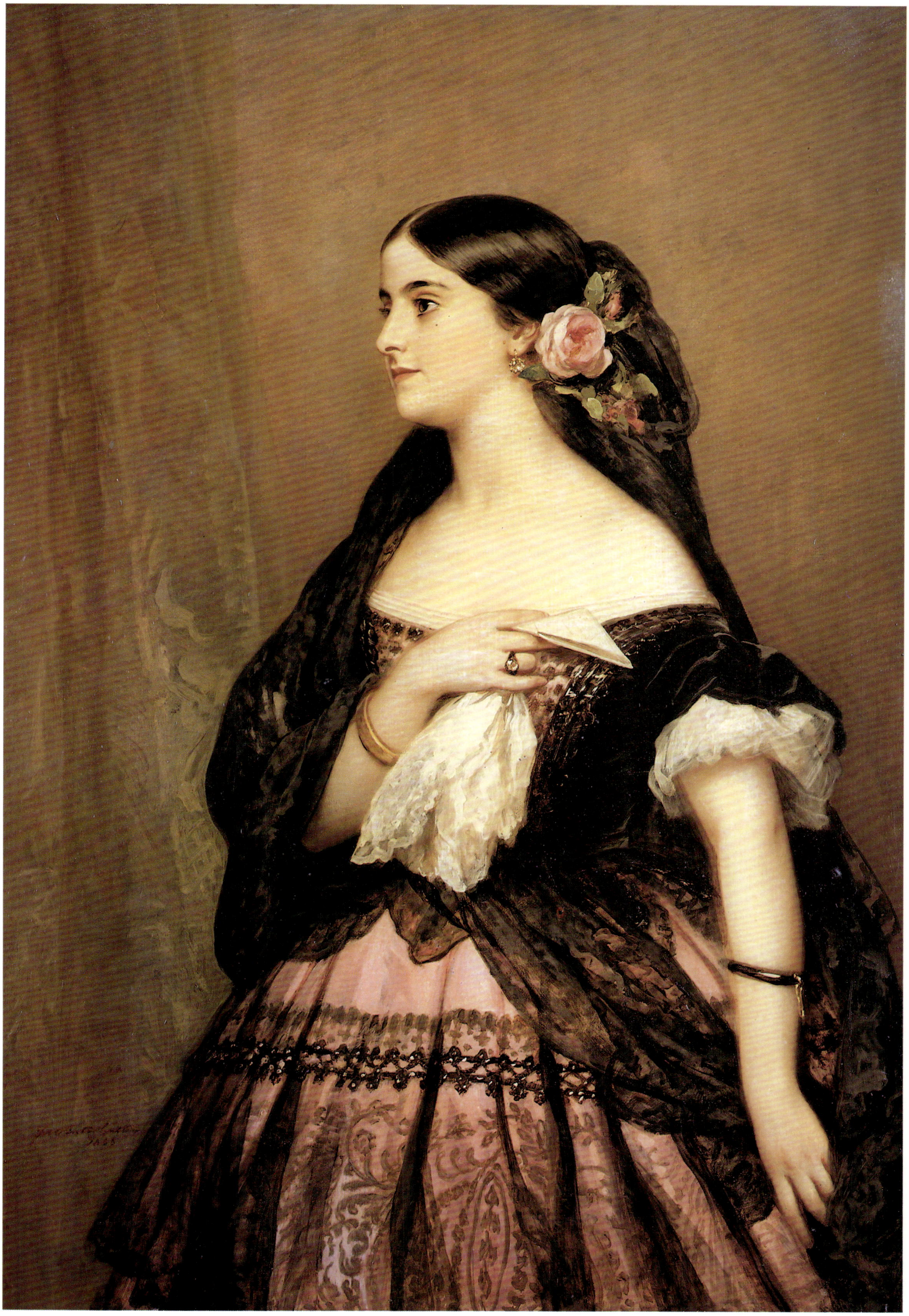

ADELINA PATTI 1863 (no. 46)

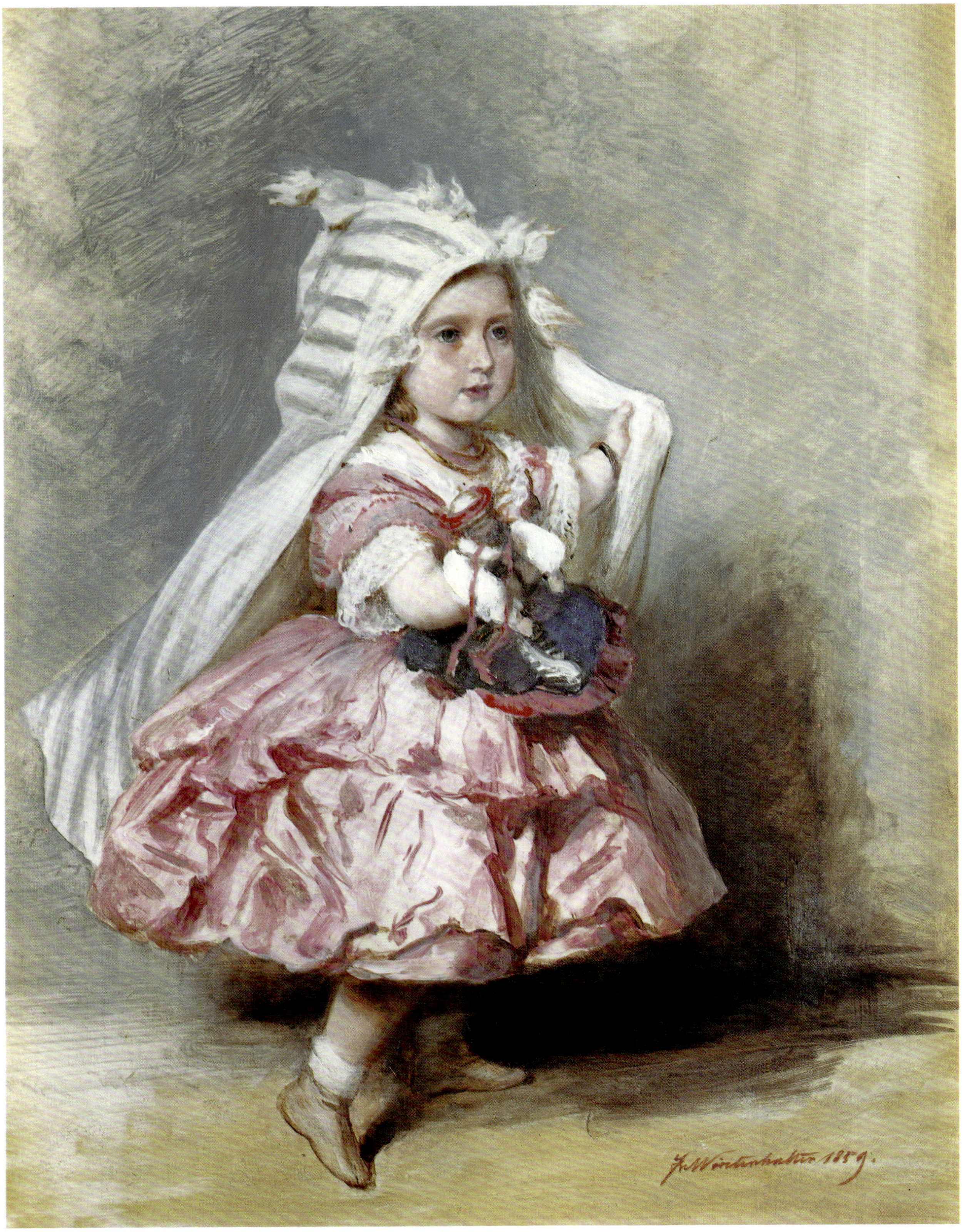

PRINCESS BEATRICE 1859 (no. 42)

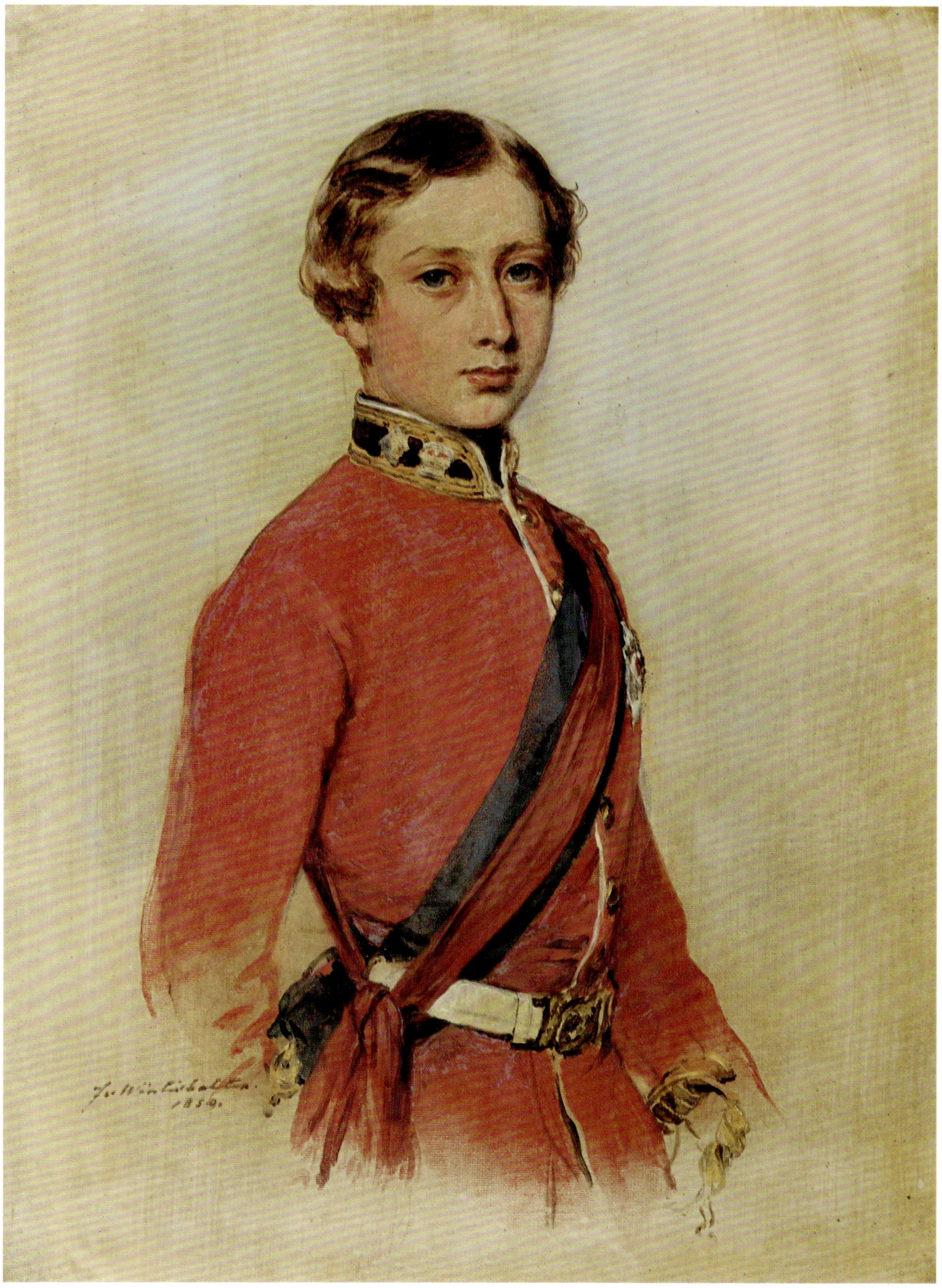

ALBERT EDWARD, PRINCE OF WALES 1859 (no. 43)

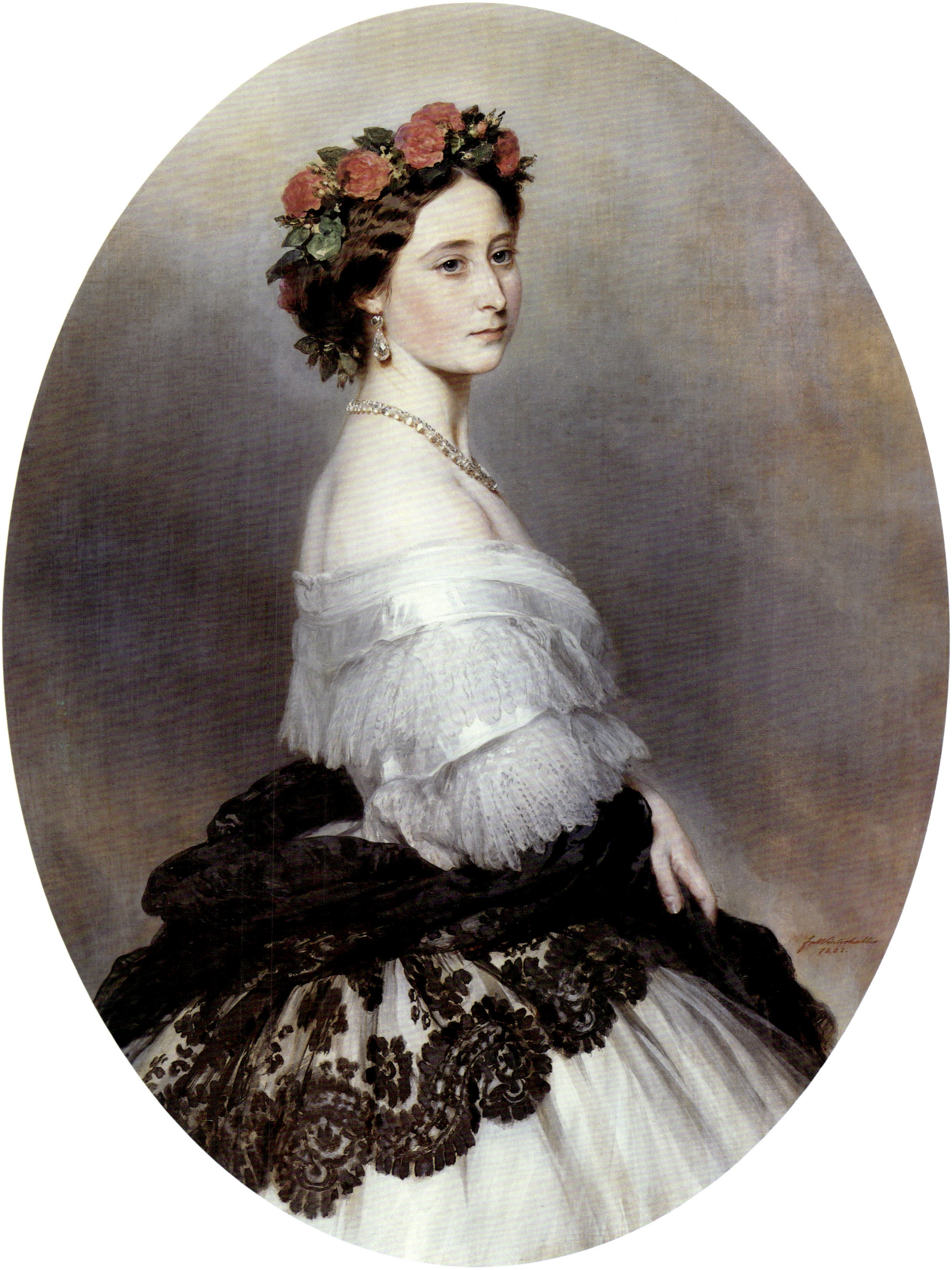

PRINCESS ALICE 1861 (no. 44)

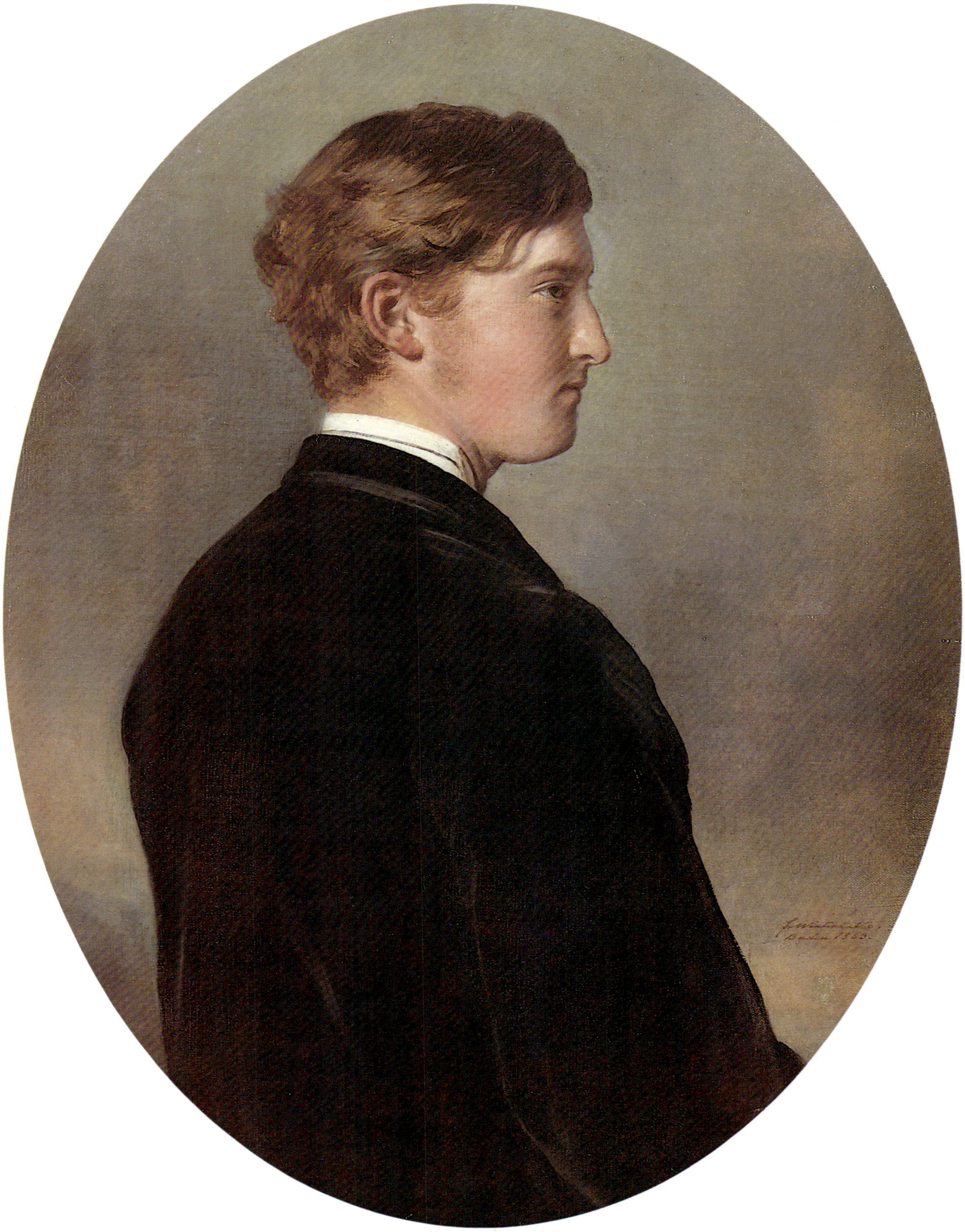

WILLIAM DOUGLAS-HAMILTON, 12TH DUKE OF HAMILTON 1863 (no. 45)

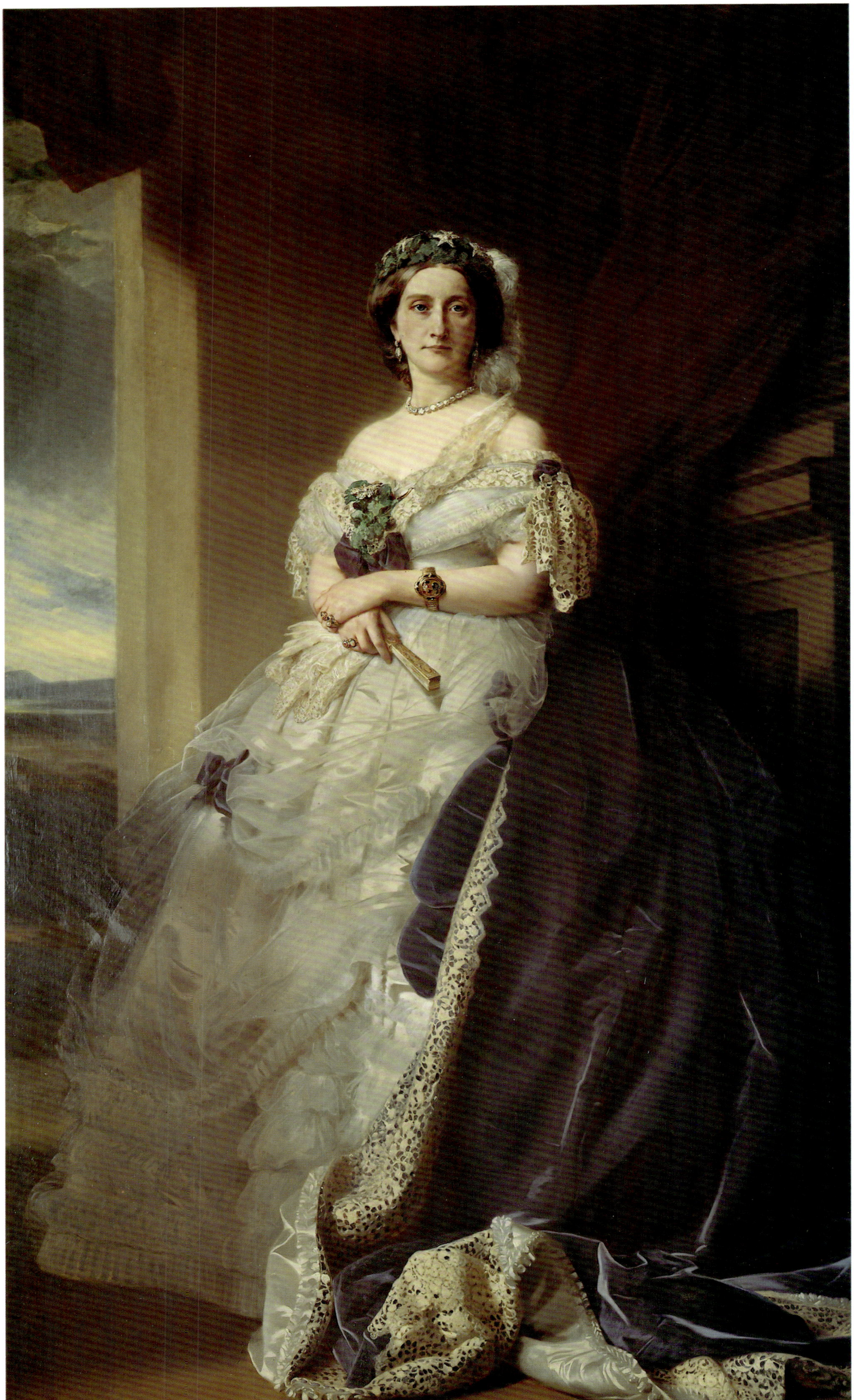

JULIA LOUISA BOSVILLE, LADY MIDDLETON 1863 (no. 47)

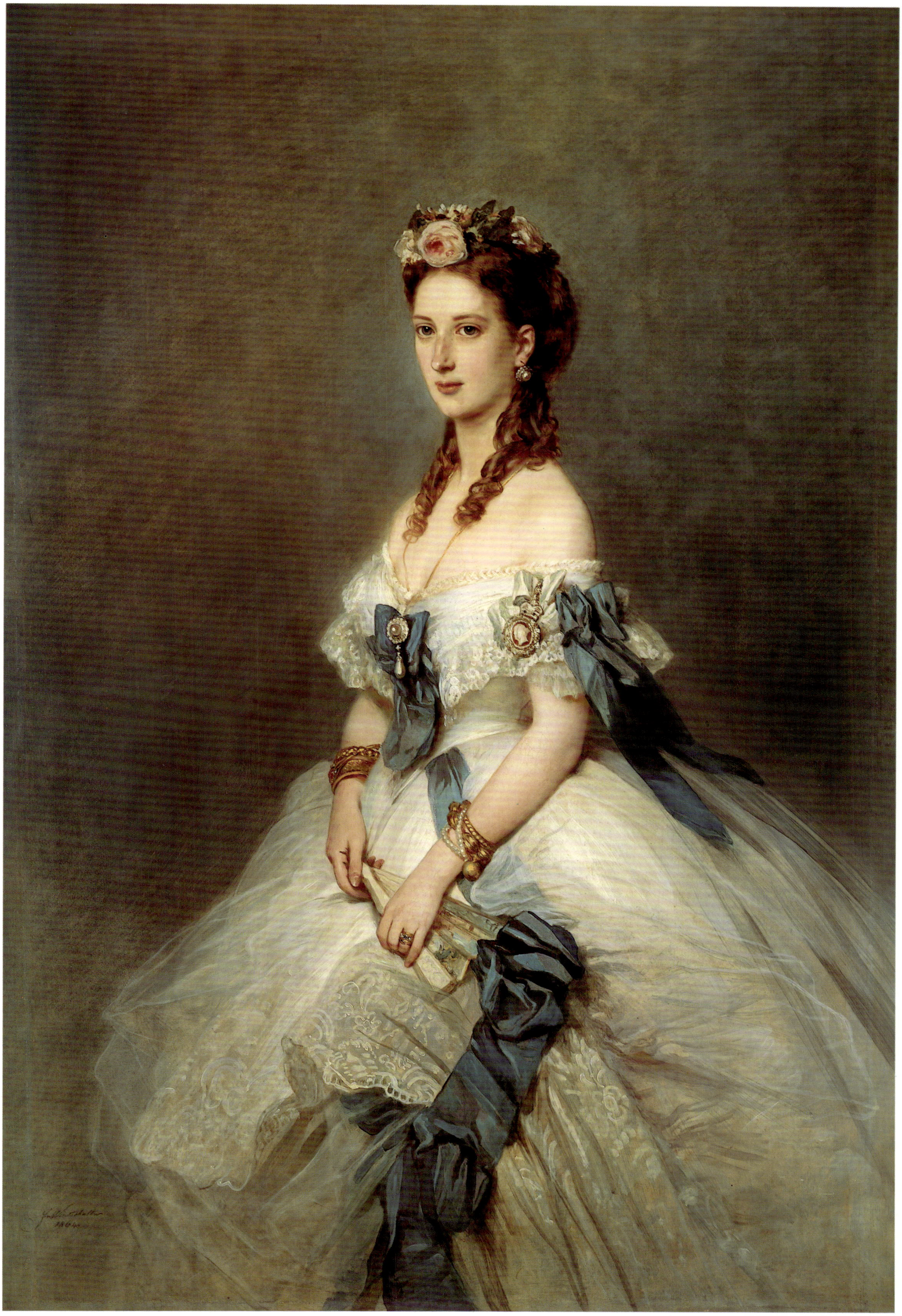

ALEXANDRA, PRINCESS OF WALES 1864 (no. 48)

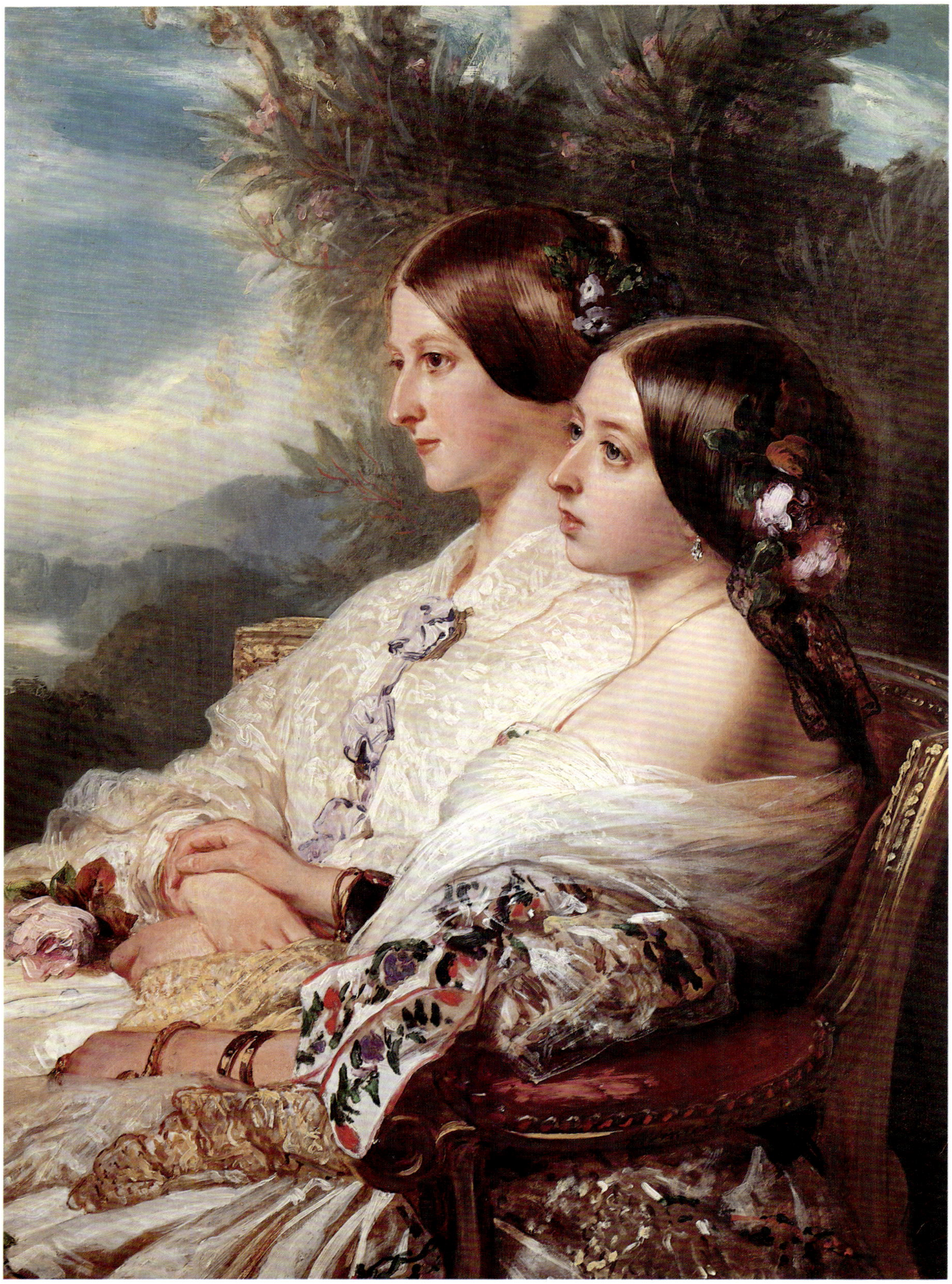

THE COUSINS: QUEEN VICTORIA AND VICTOIRE, DUCHESSE DE NEMOURS 1852 (no. 37)

# The Court of Napoleon III

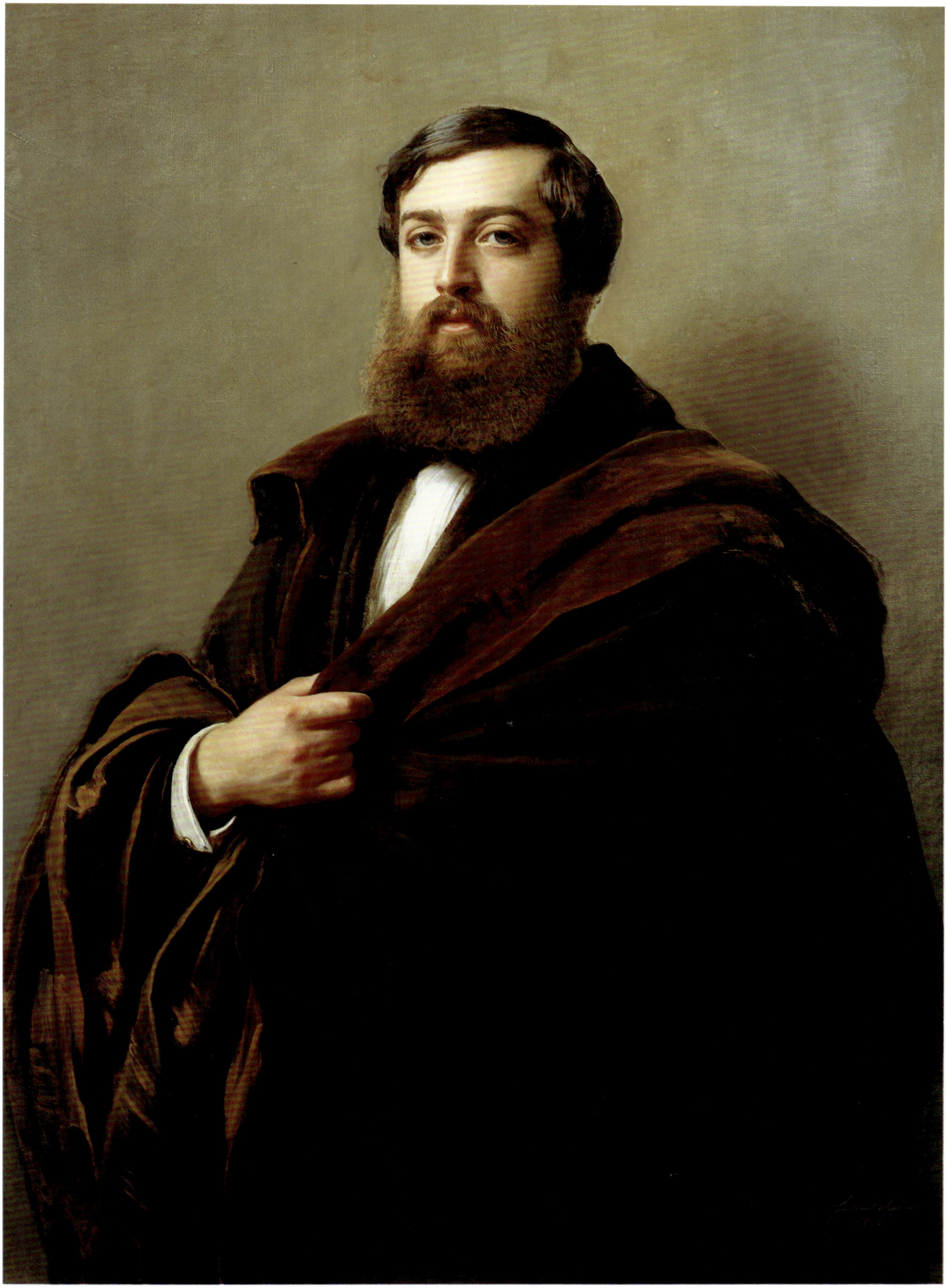

ALFRED-ÉMILIEN, COMTE DE NIEUWERKERKE 1852 (no. 49)

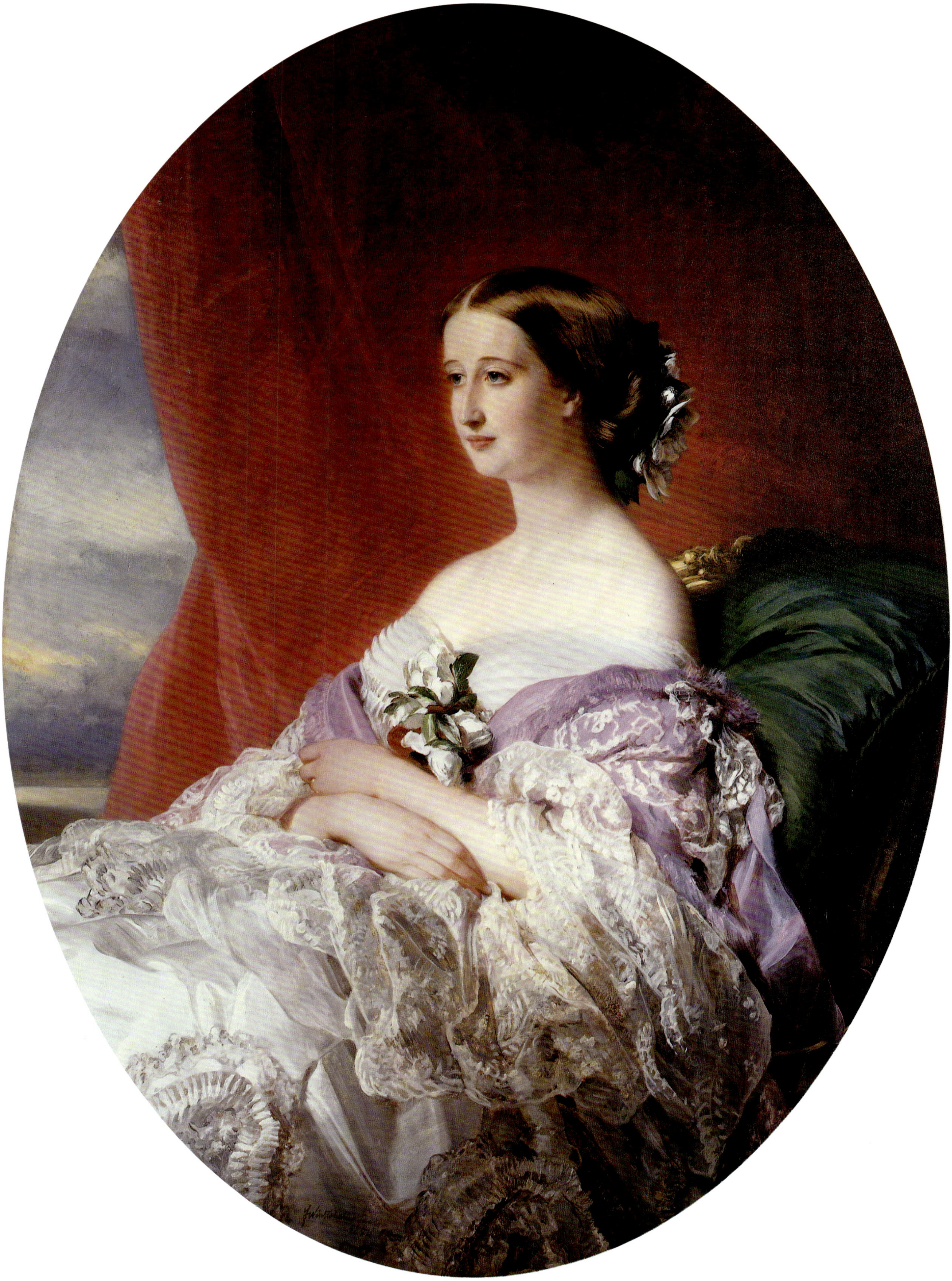

THE EMPRESS EUGÉNIE 1854 (no. 50)

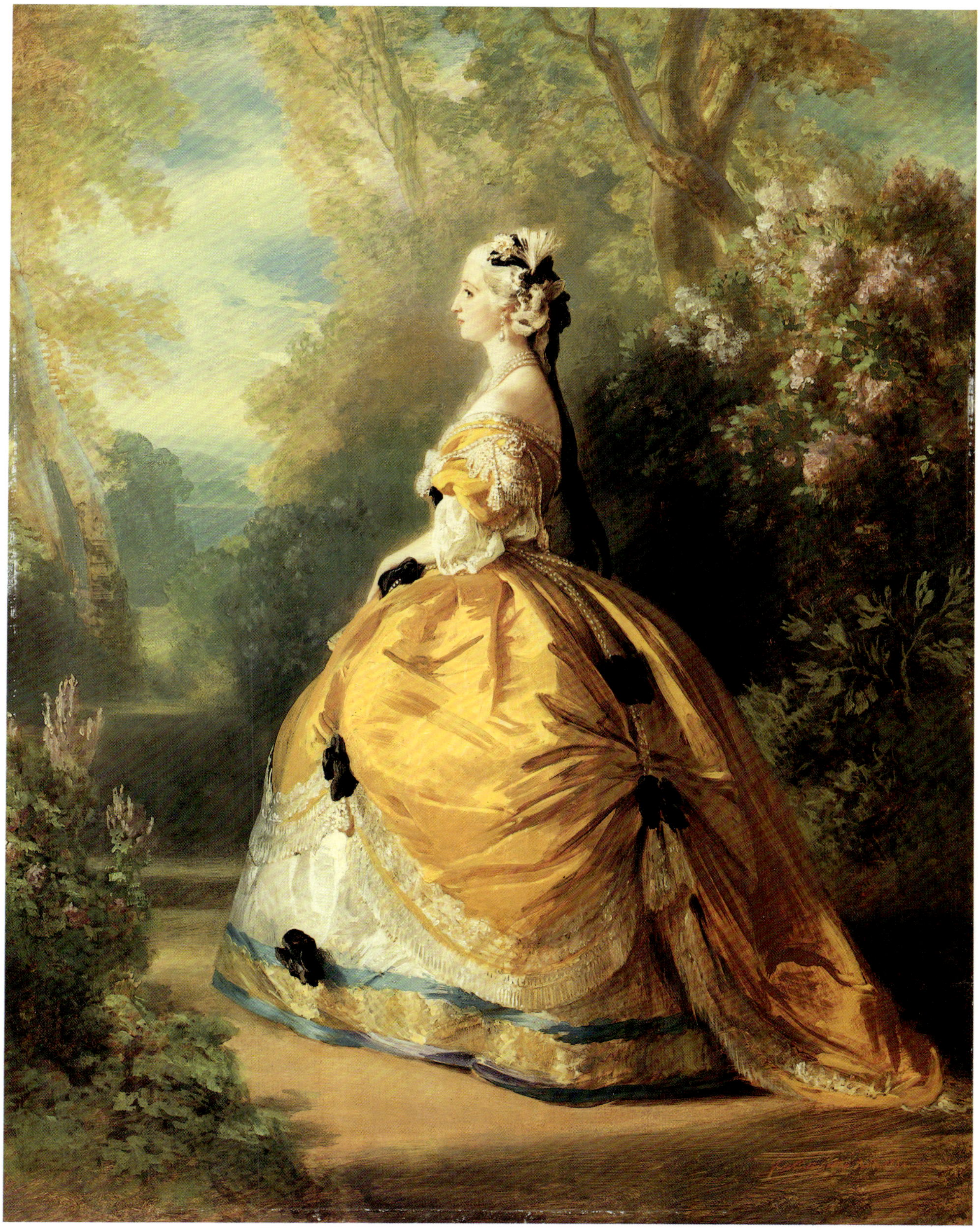

THE EMPRESS EUGÉNIE À LA MARIE-ANTOINETTE 1854 (no. 52)

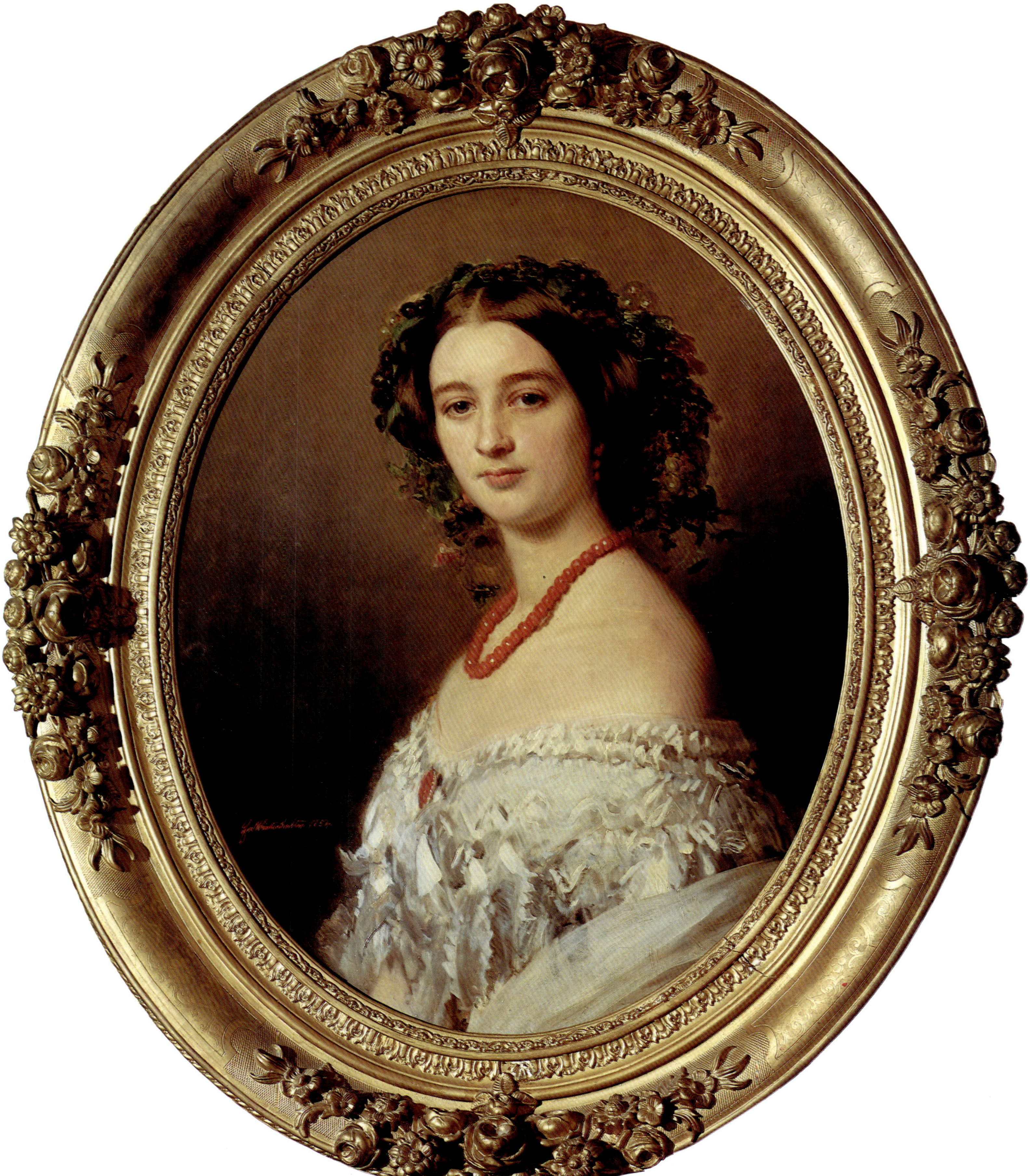

MALCY-LOUISE-CAROLINE-FRÉDÉRIQUE BERTHIER DE WAGRAM, PRINCESSE MURAT 1854 (no. 51)

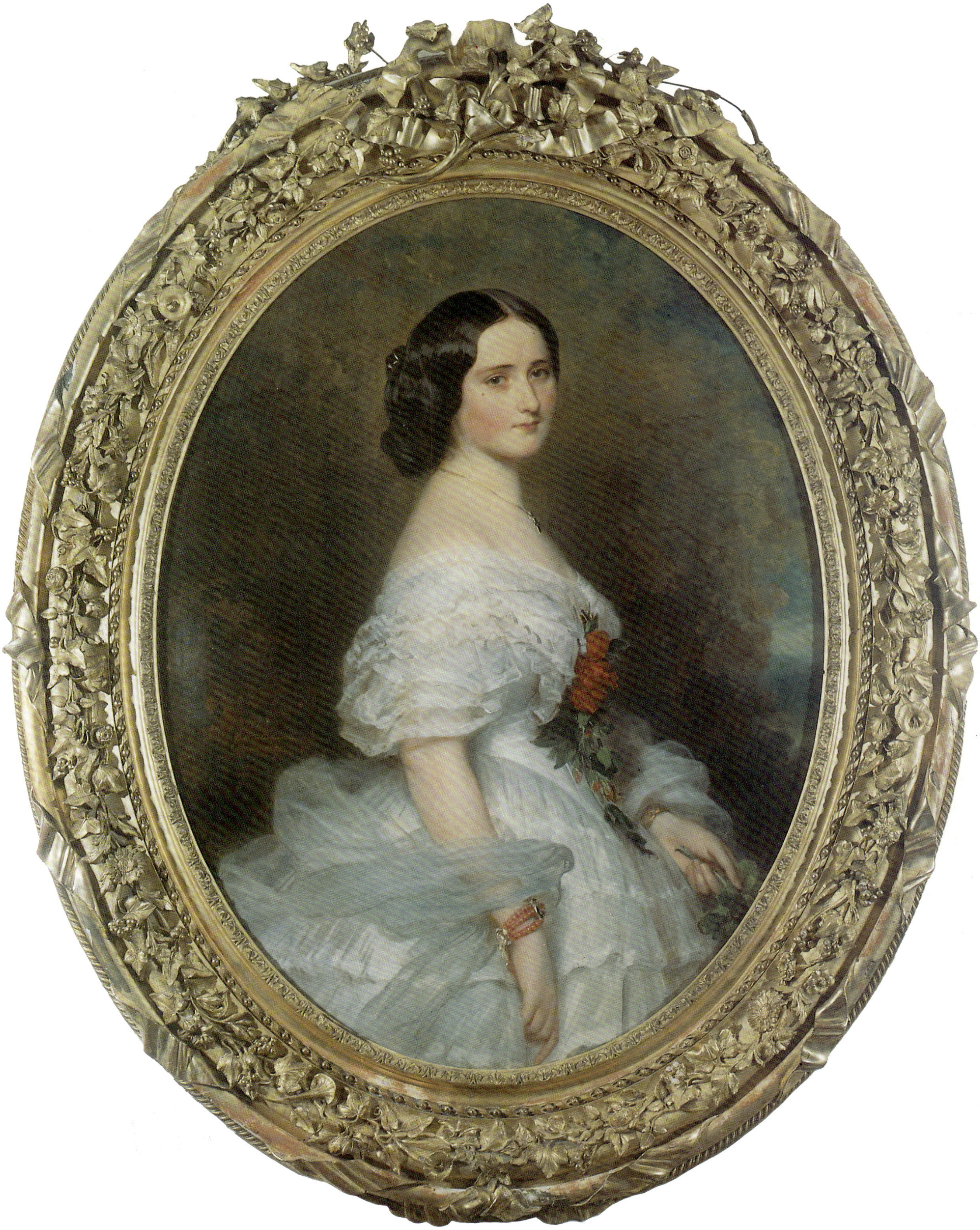

ANNA DOLLFUS, BARONNE DE BOURGOING 1855 (no. 55)

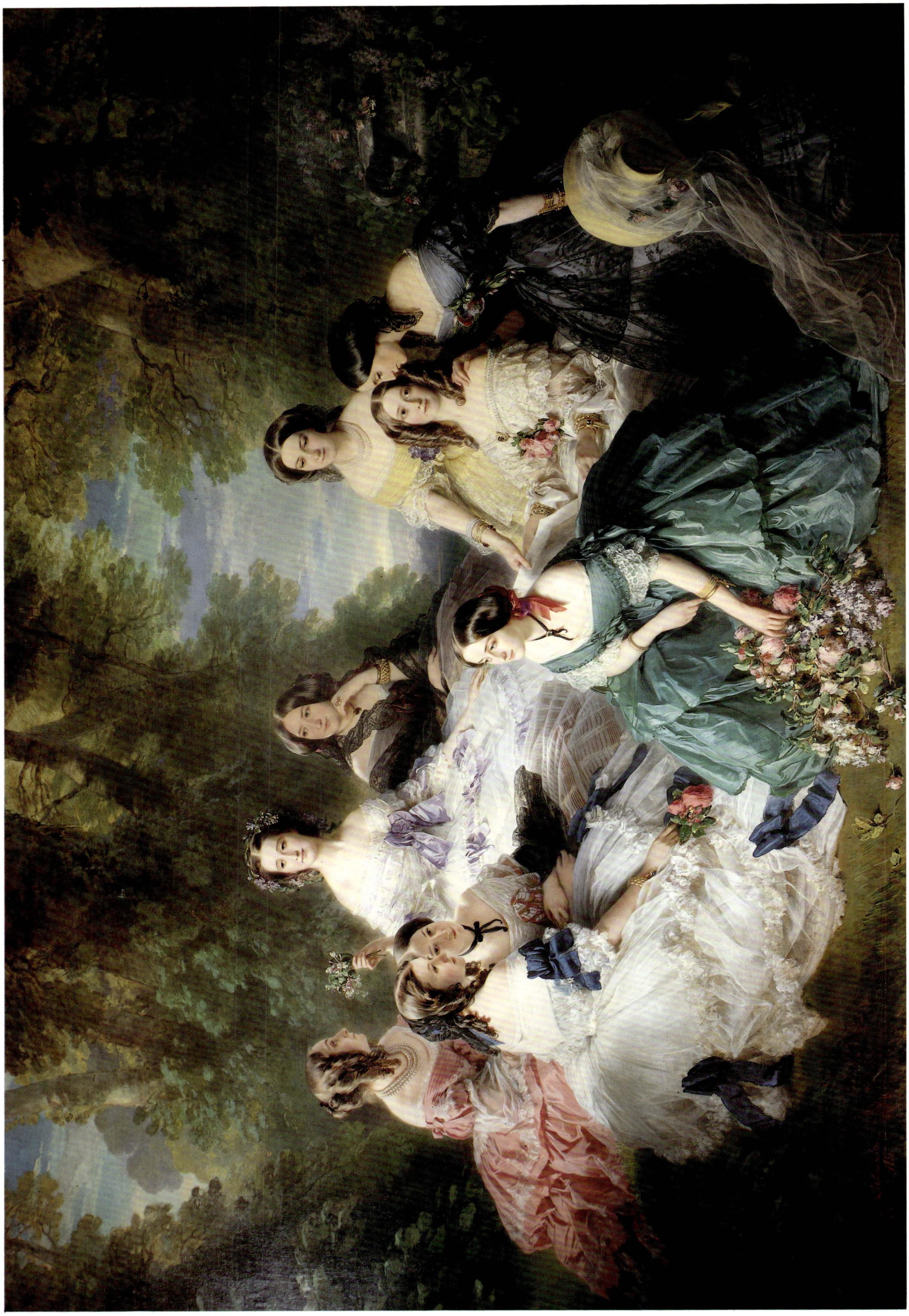

THE EMPRESS EUGÉNIE SURROUNDED BY HER LADIES-IN-WAITING 1855 (no. 53)

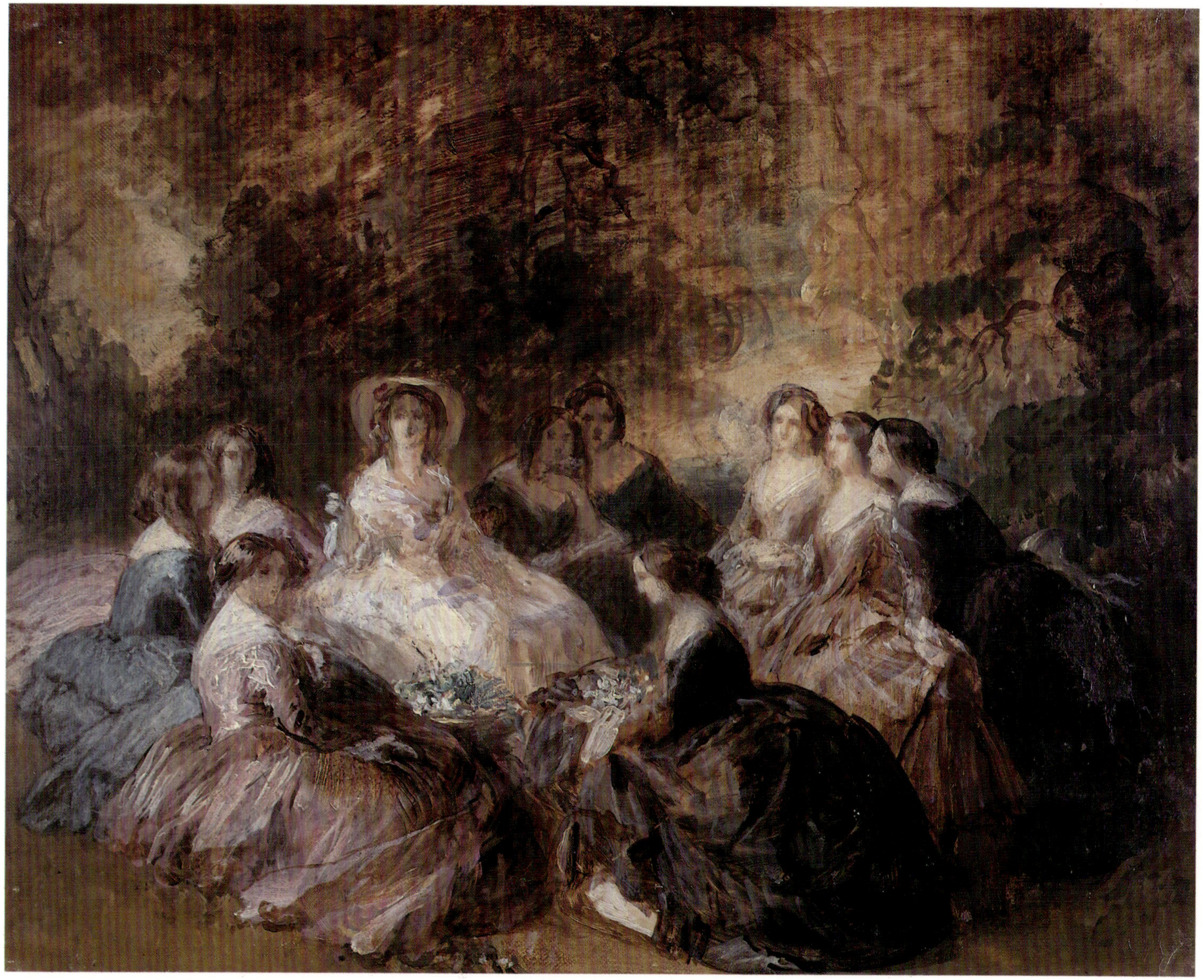

THE EMPRESS EUGÉNIE SURROUNDED BY HER LADIES-IN-WAITING 1855 (no. 54)

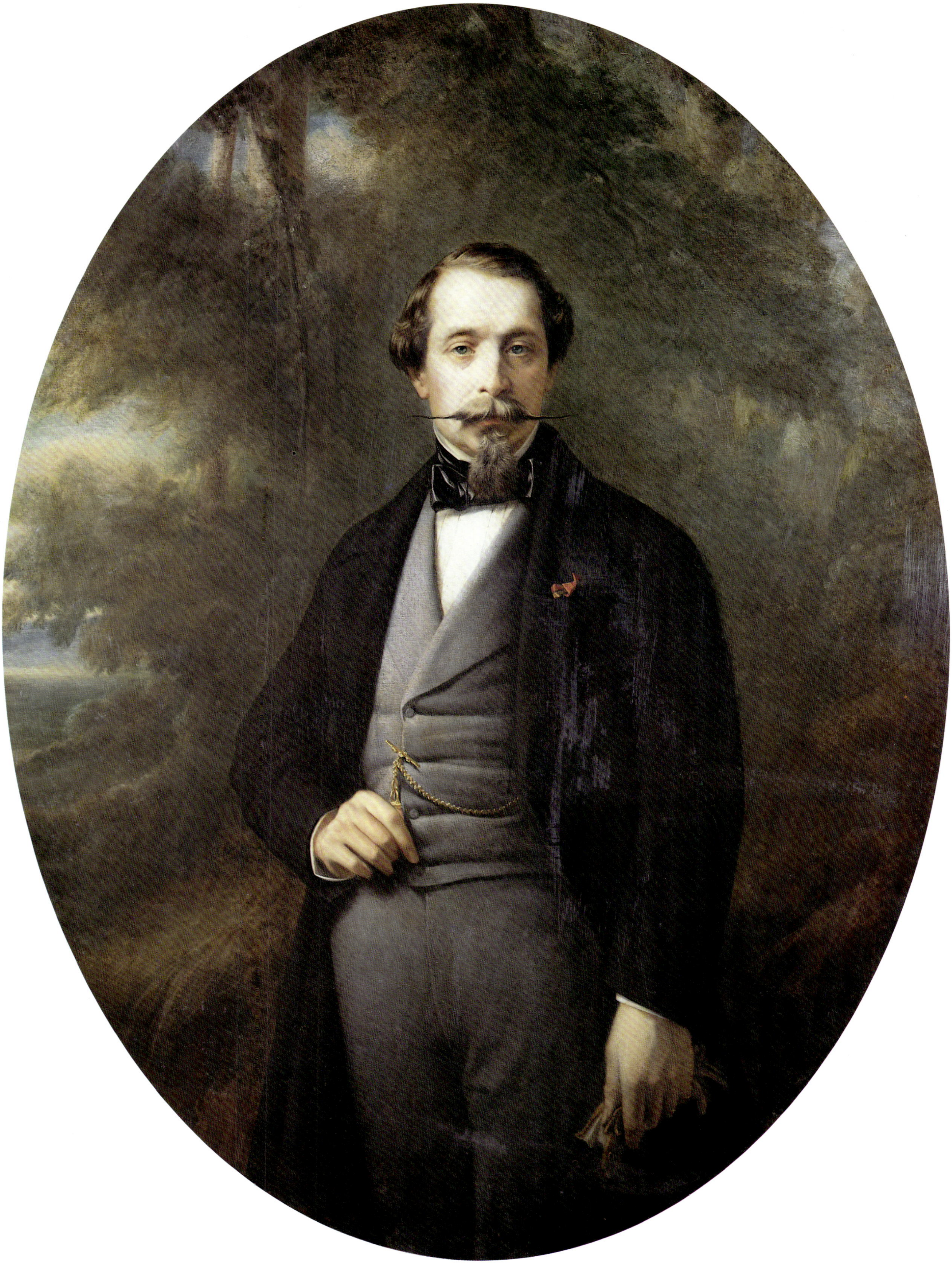

EMPEROR NAPOLEON III (no. 56)

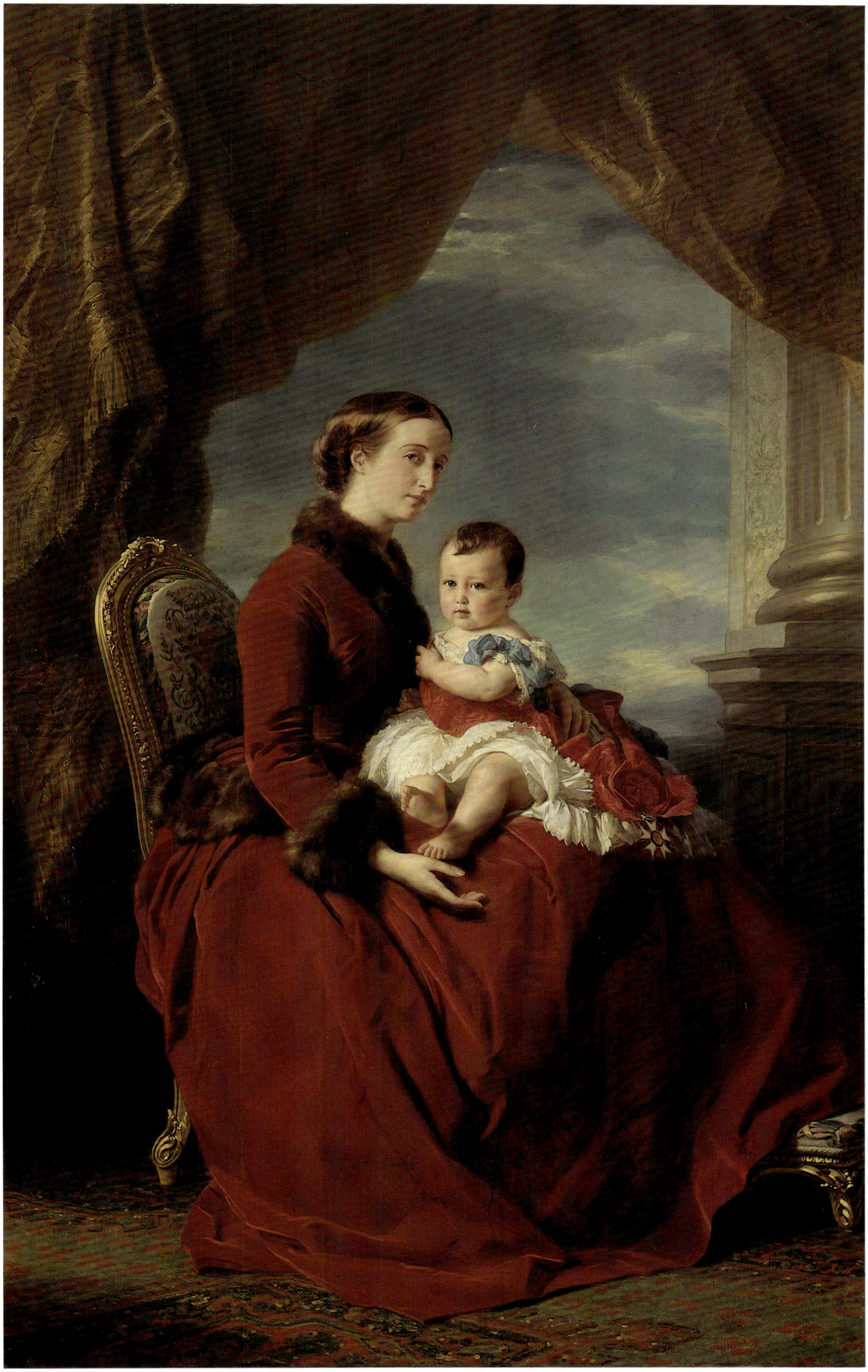

THE EMPRESS EUGÉNIE HOLDING LOUIS NAPOLEON, THE PRINCE IMPERIAL ON HER KNEES 1857 (no. 58)

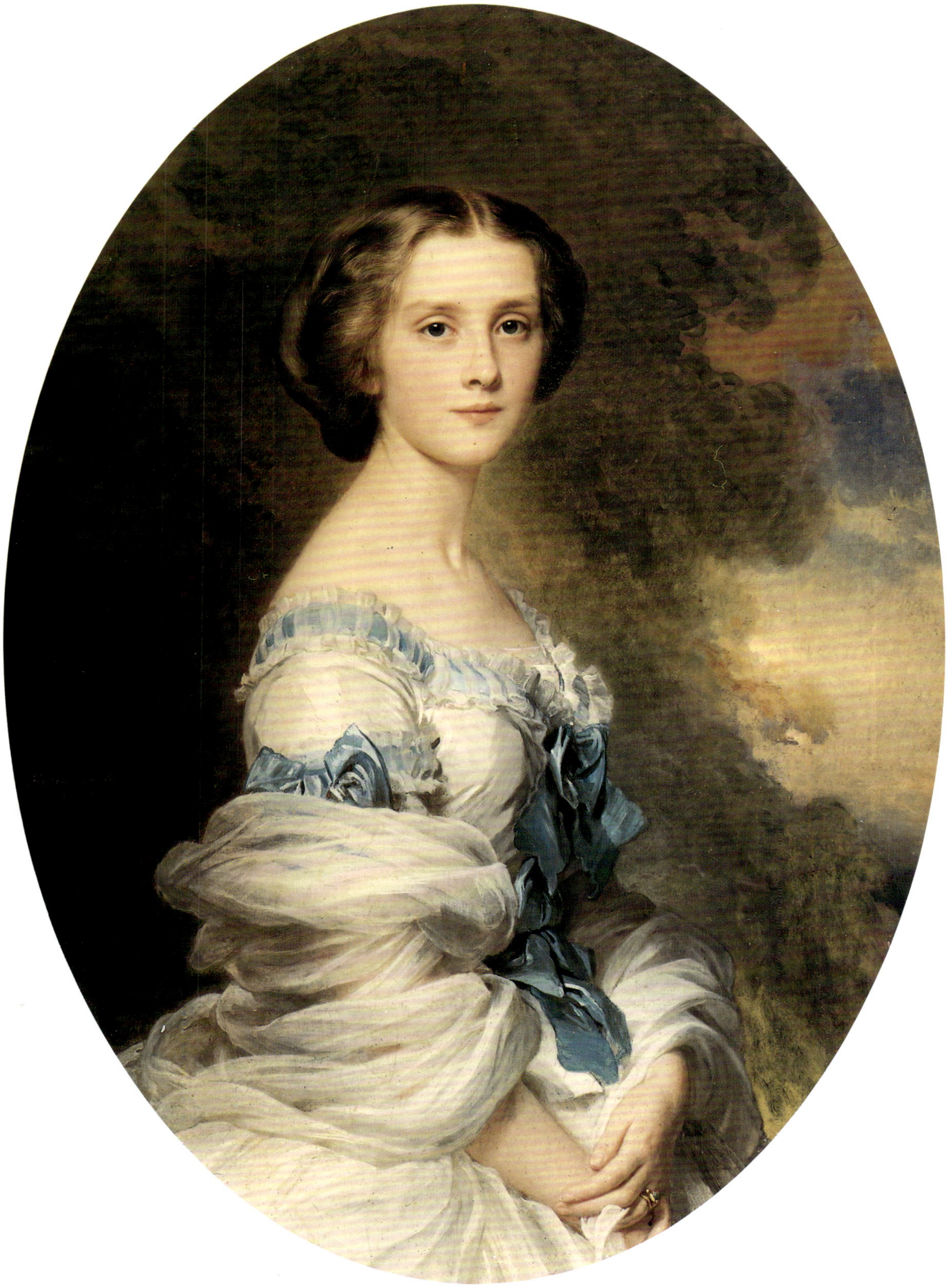

MÉLANIE DE BUSSIÈRE, COMTESSE EDMOND DE POURTALÈS 1857 (no. 57)

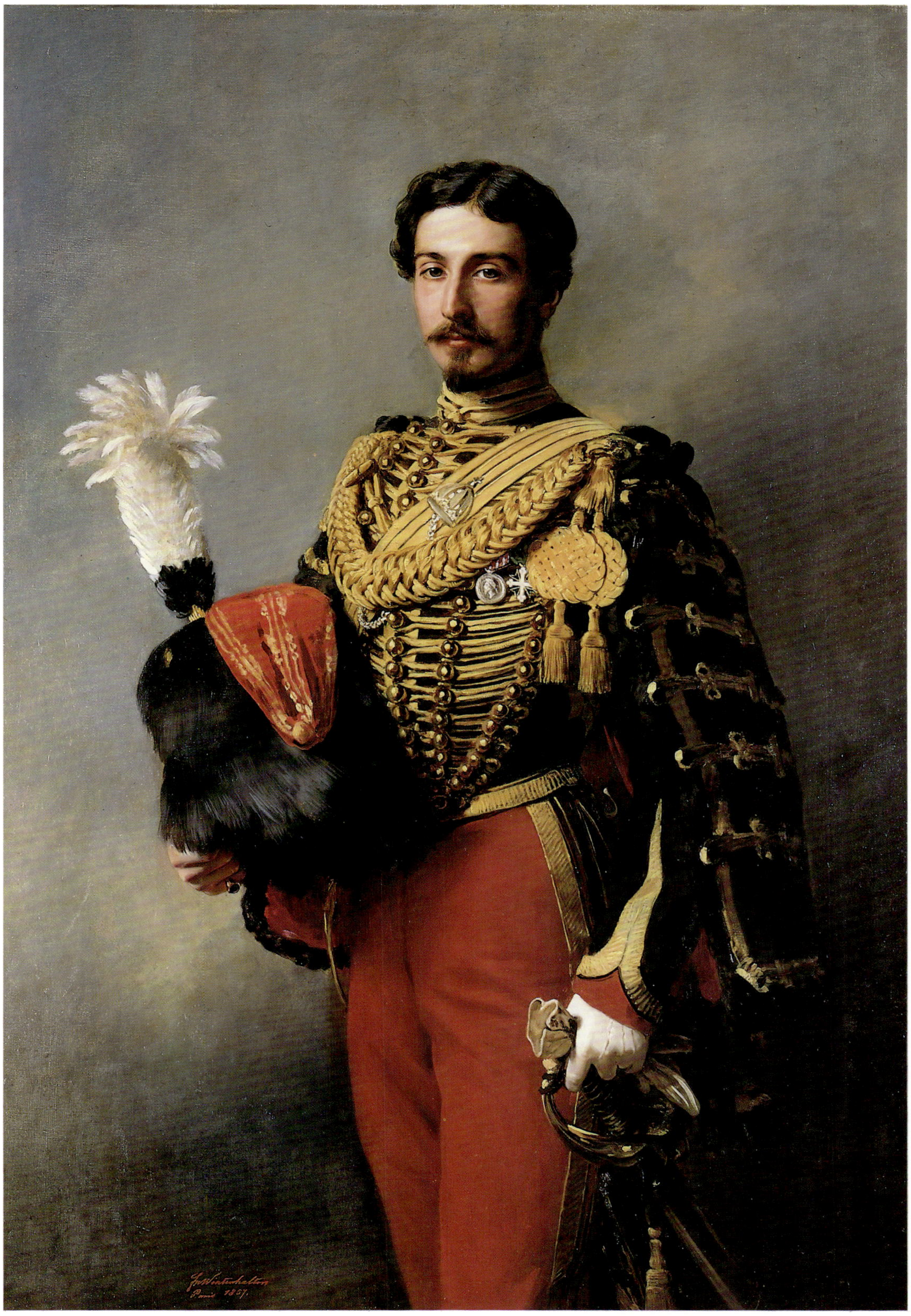

EDOUARD ANDRÉ 1857 (no. 59)

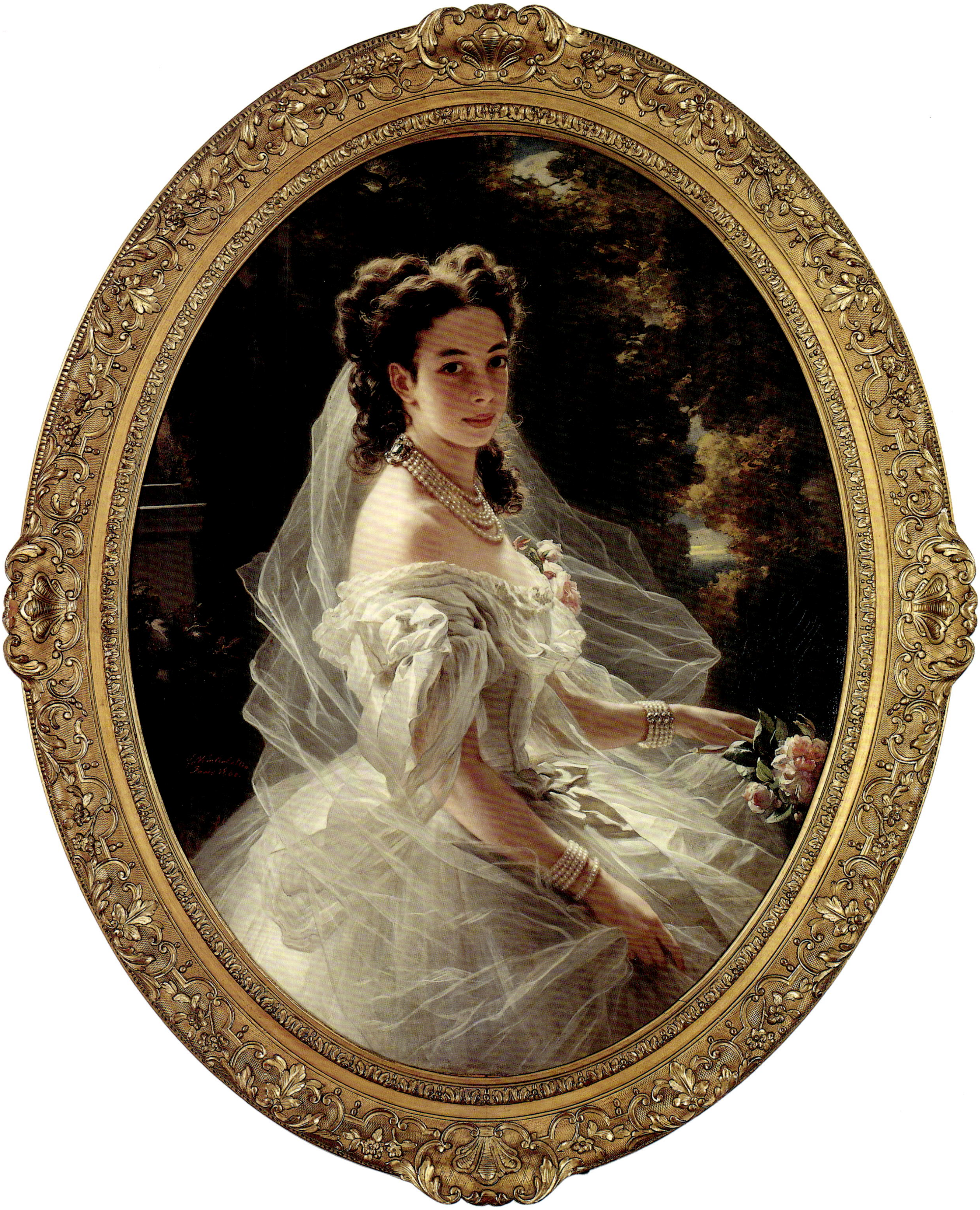

PAULINE SANDOR, PRINCESS METTERNICH 1860 (no. 63)

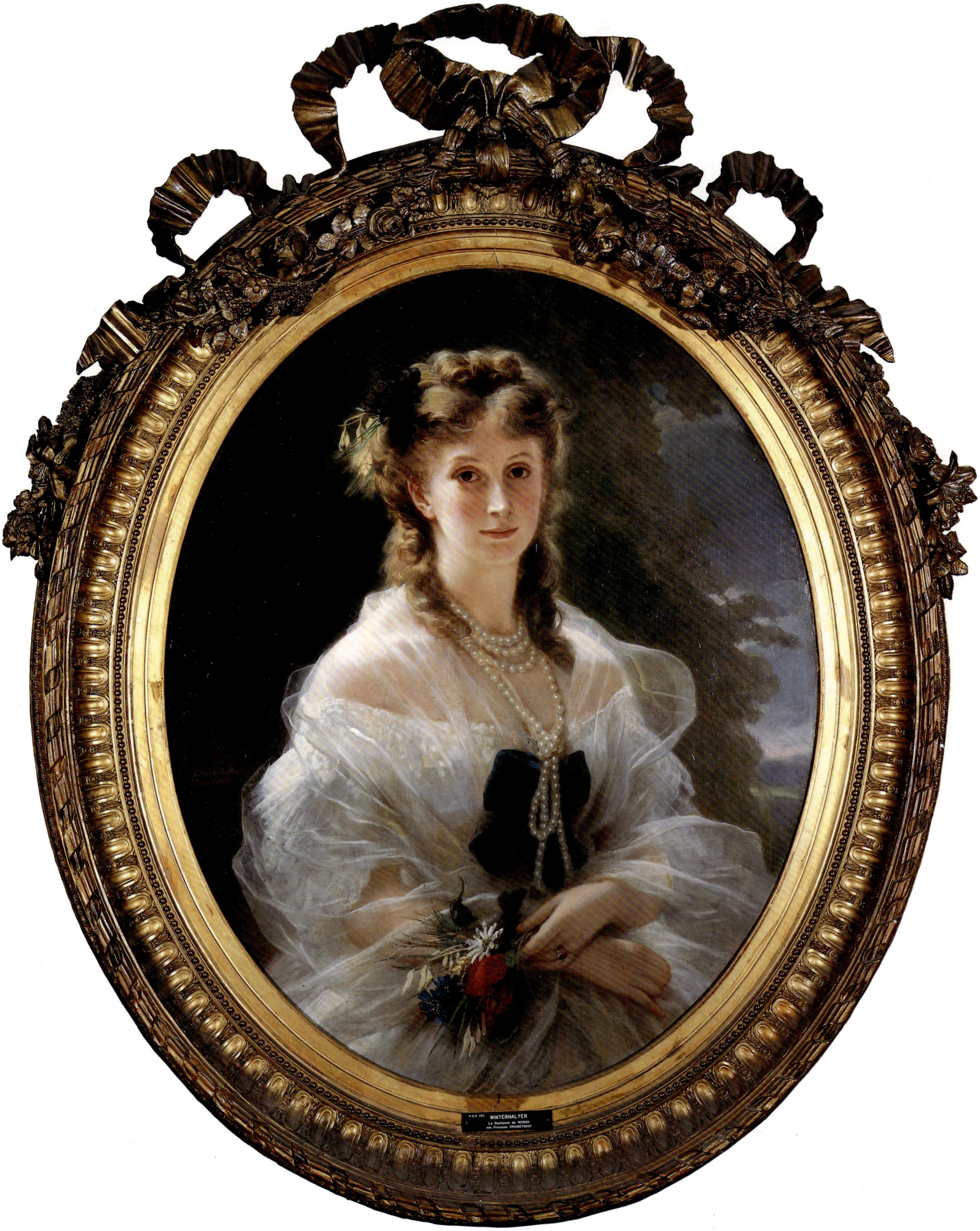


PRINCESS SOPHIE TROUBETSKOÏ, DUCHESSE DE MORNY 1863 (no. 64)

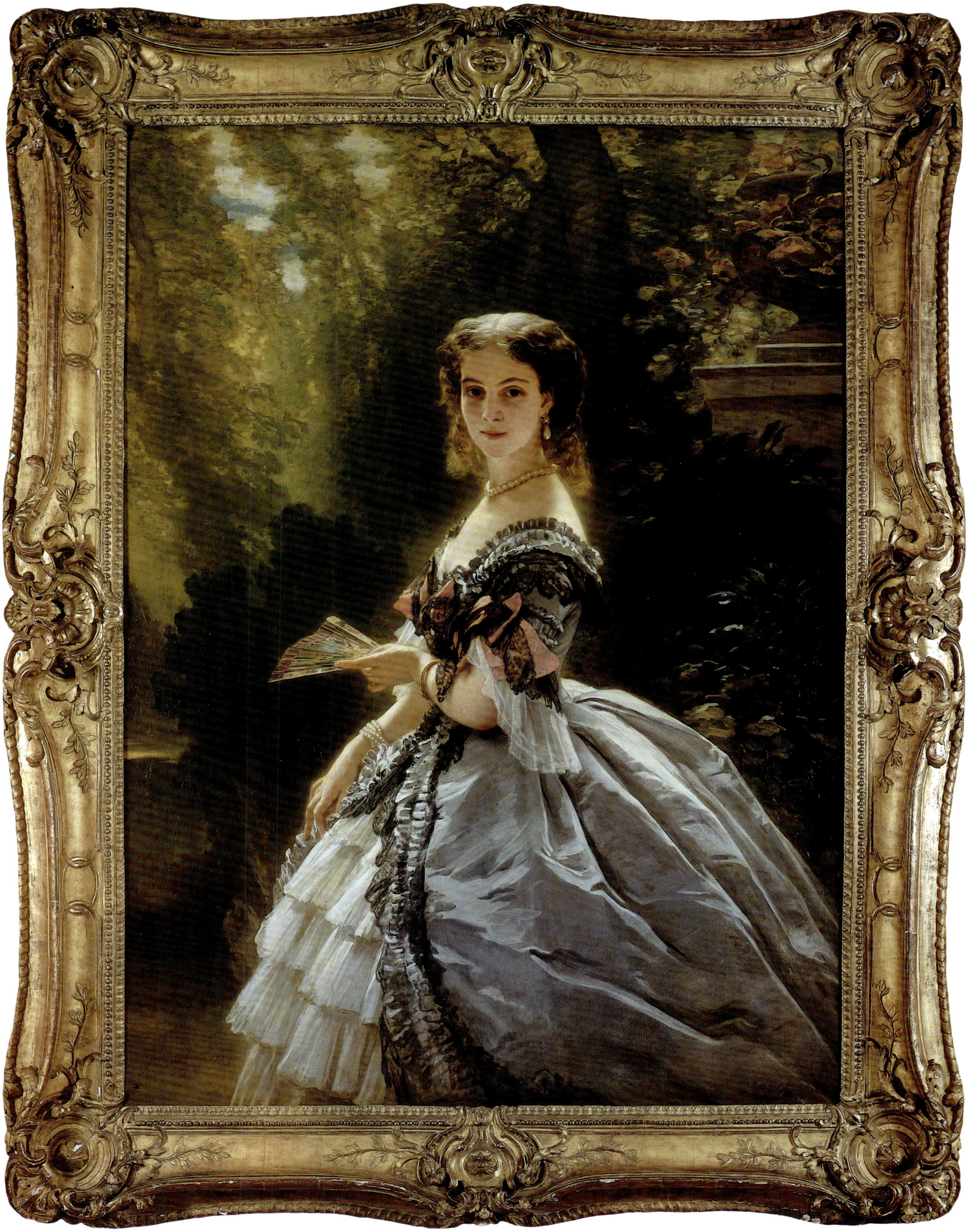

PRINCESS ELIZABETH ESPEROVNA BELOSSELSKY-BELOSENKY, PRINCESS TROUBETSKOÏ 1859 (no. 61)

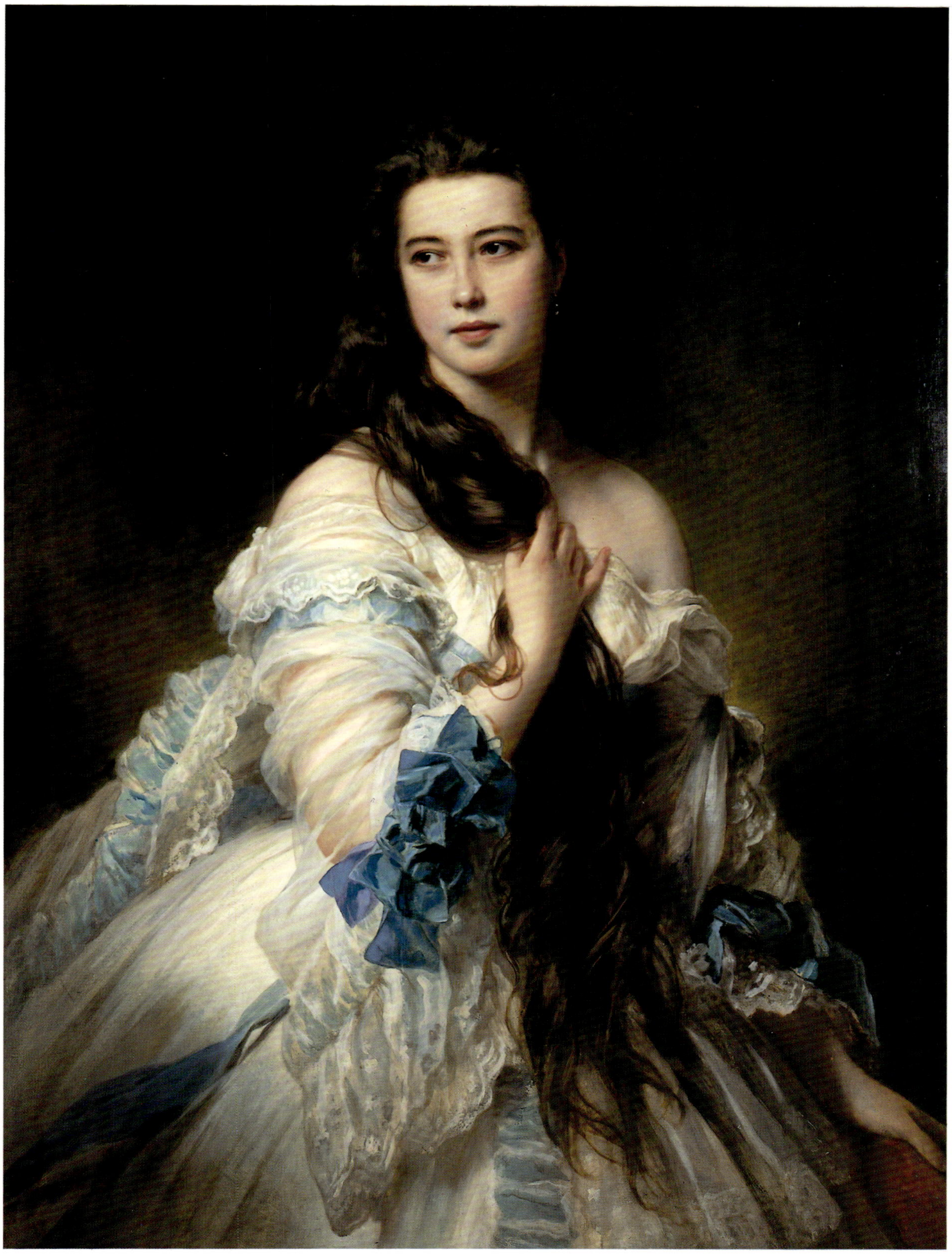

BARBE DMITRIEVNA MERGASSOV, MADAME RIMSKY-KORSAKOV 1864 (no. 65)

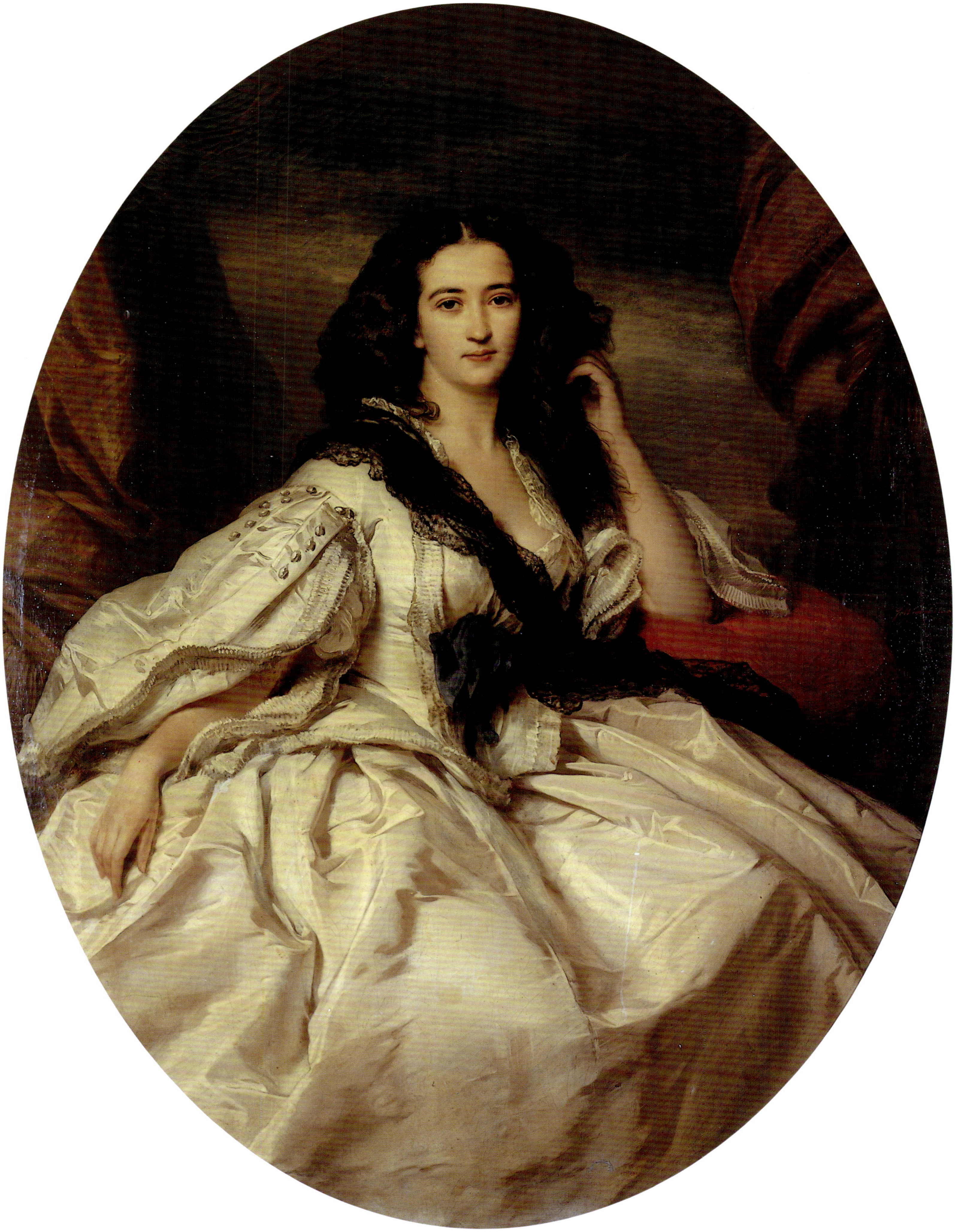

WIEŃCZYSLAWA BARCZEWSKA, MADAME DE JURJEWICZ 1860 (no. 62)

# Other Courts

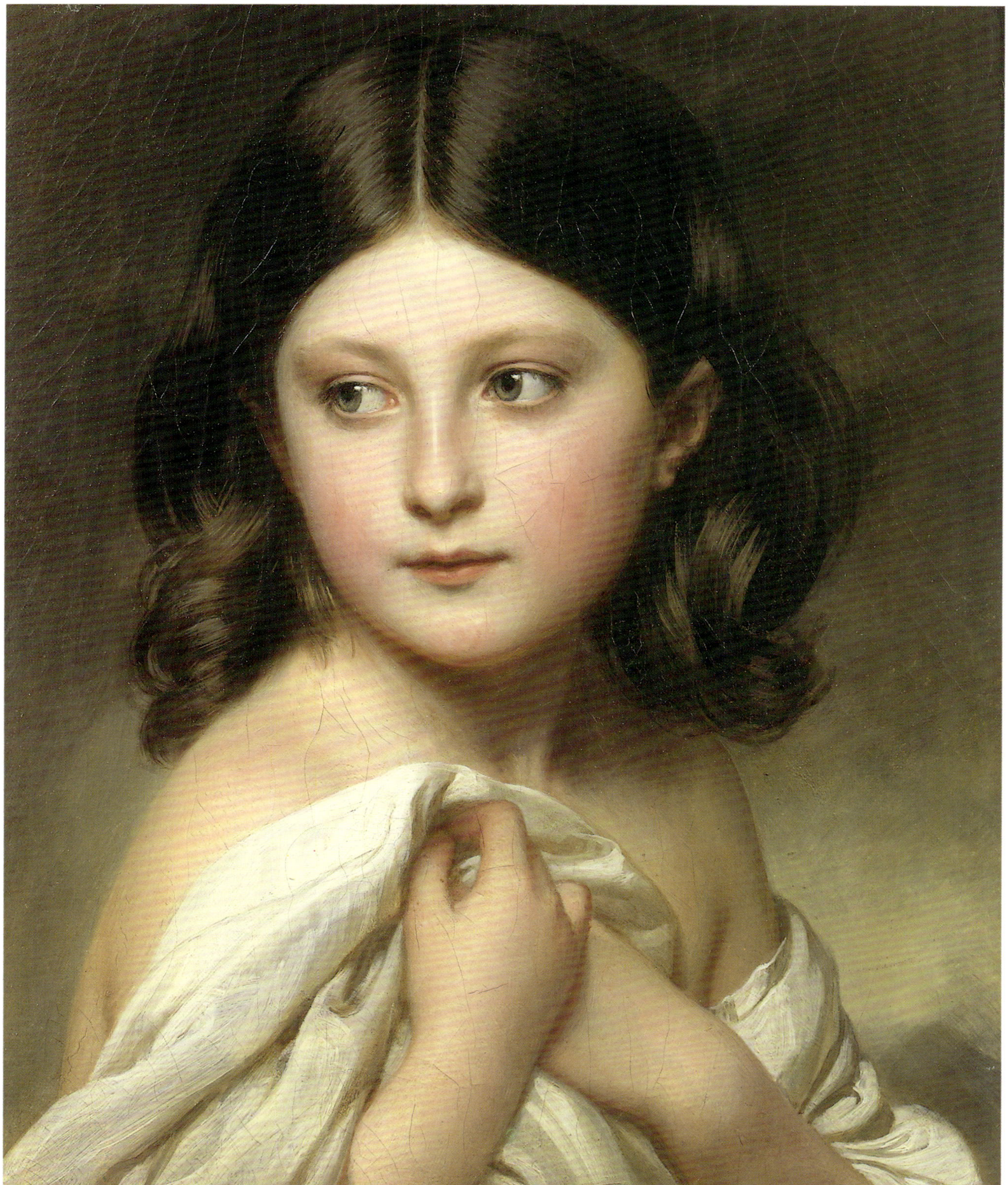

A YOUNG GIRL CALLED PRINCESS CHARLOTTE (no. 66)

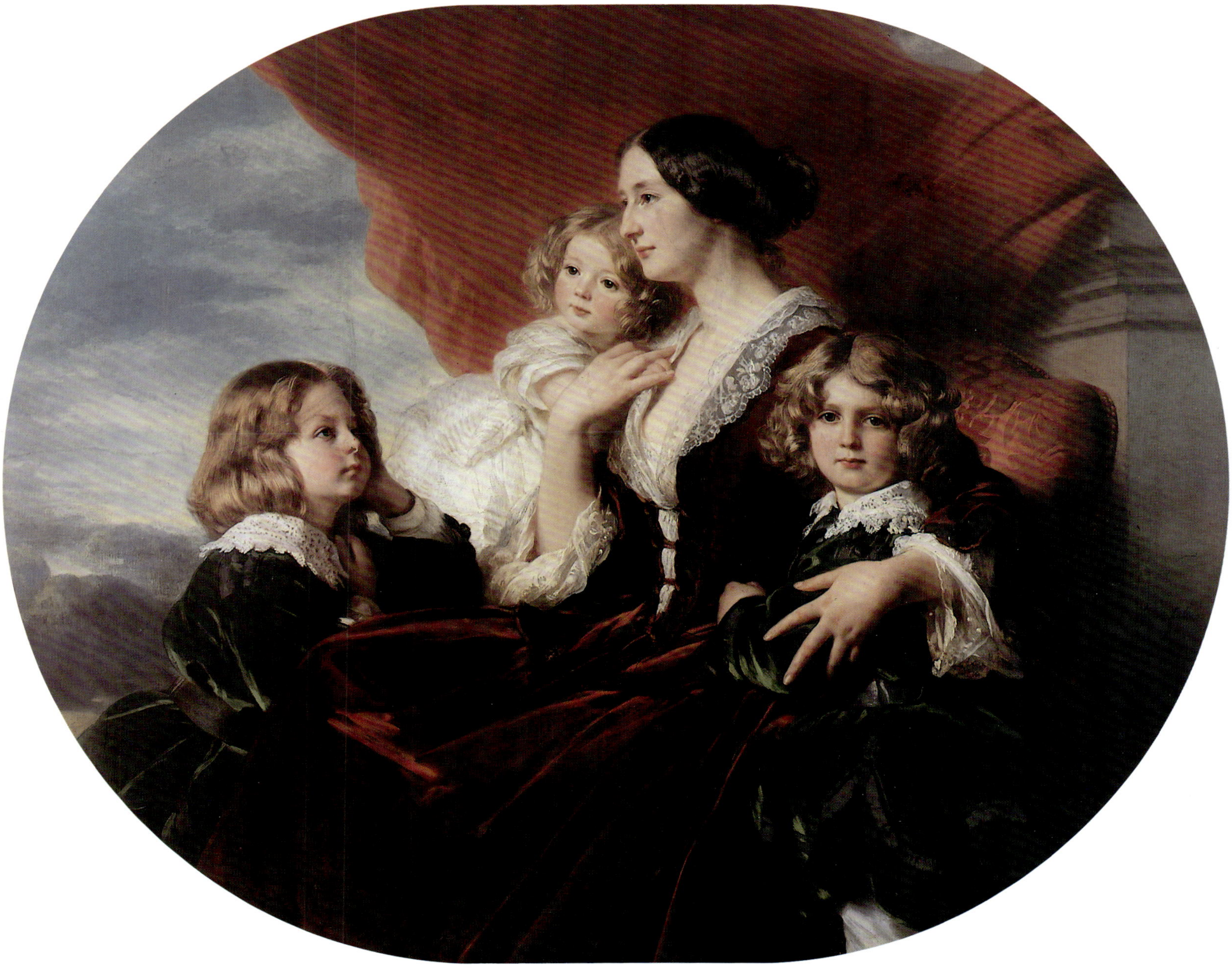

ELZBIETA BRANICKA, COUNTESS KRASINSKA AND HER CHILDREN 1853 (no. 67)

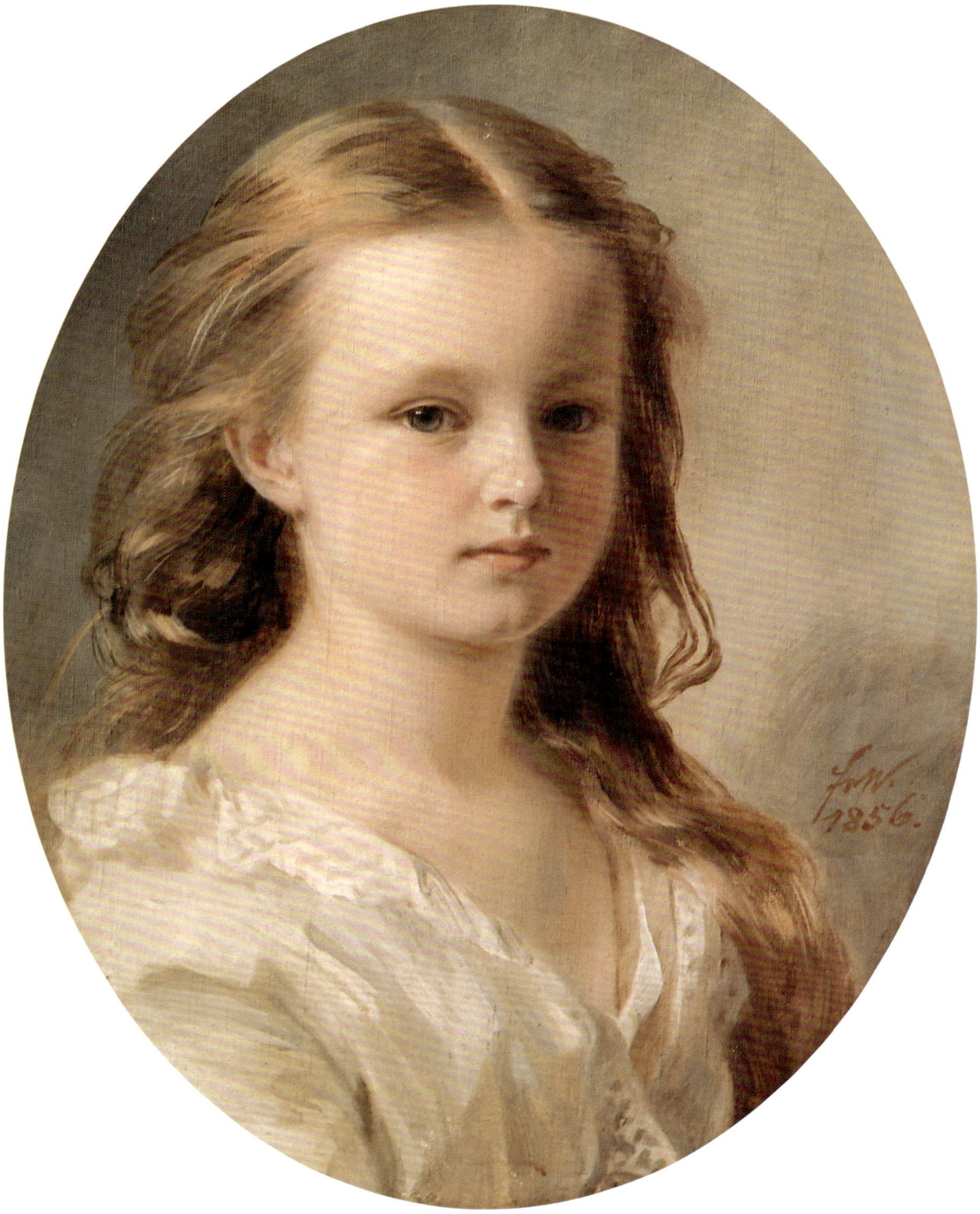


ROZA POTOCKA 1856 (no. 70)

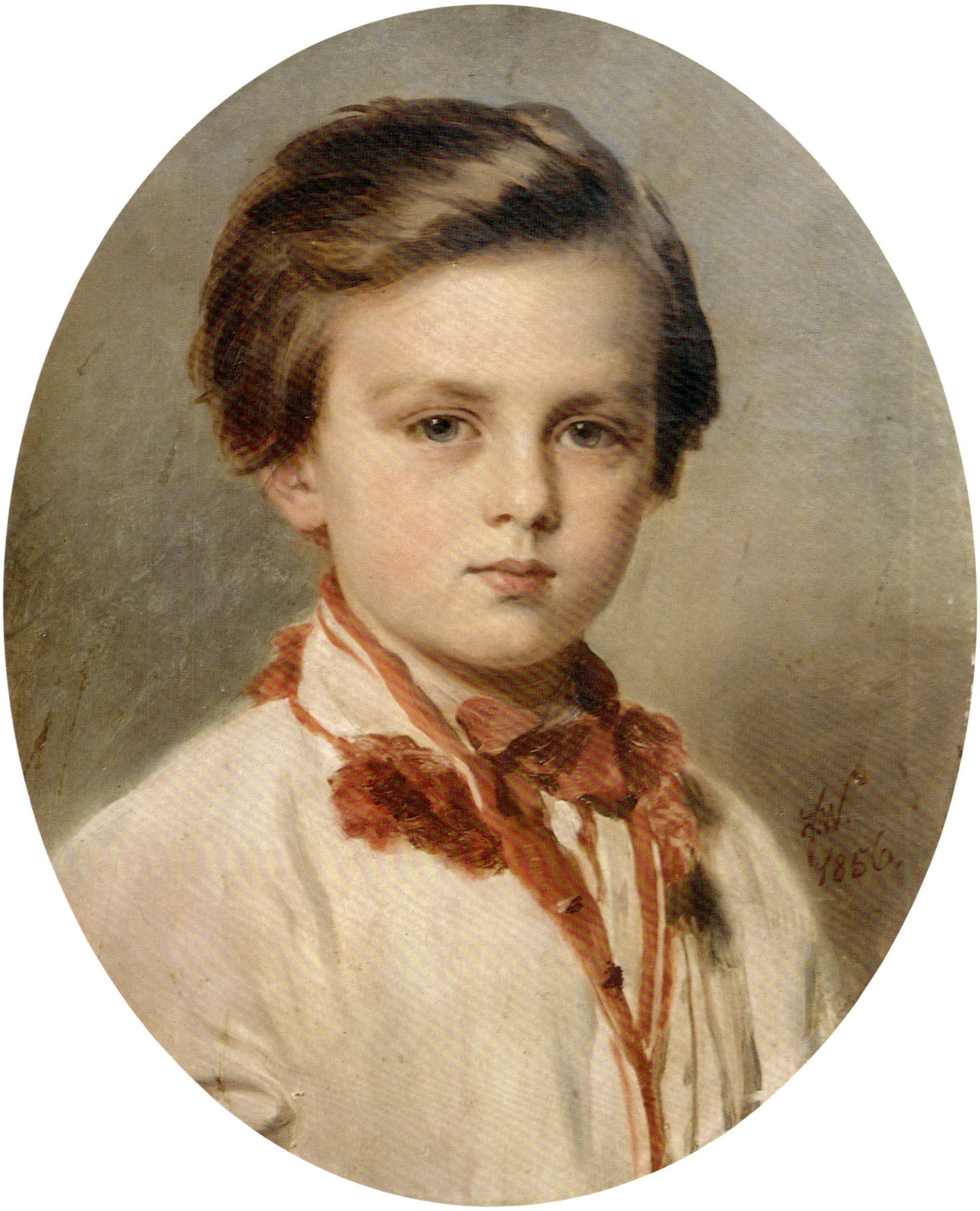

ARTUR POTOCKI 1856 (no. 72)

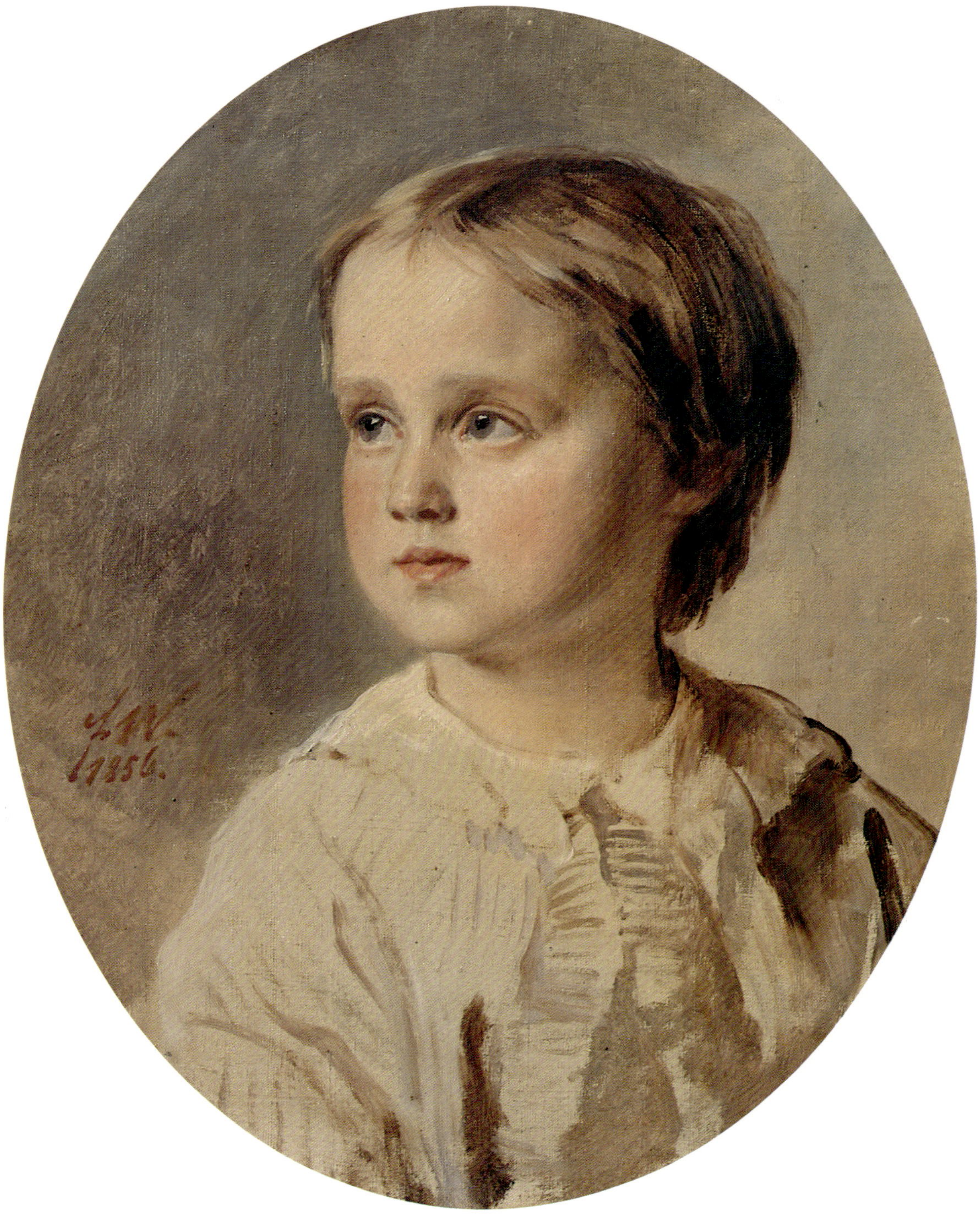

ZOFIA POTOCKA 1856 (no. 71)

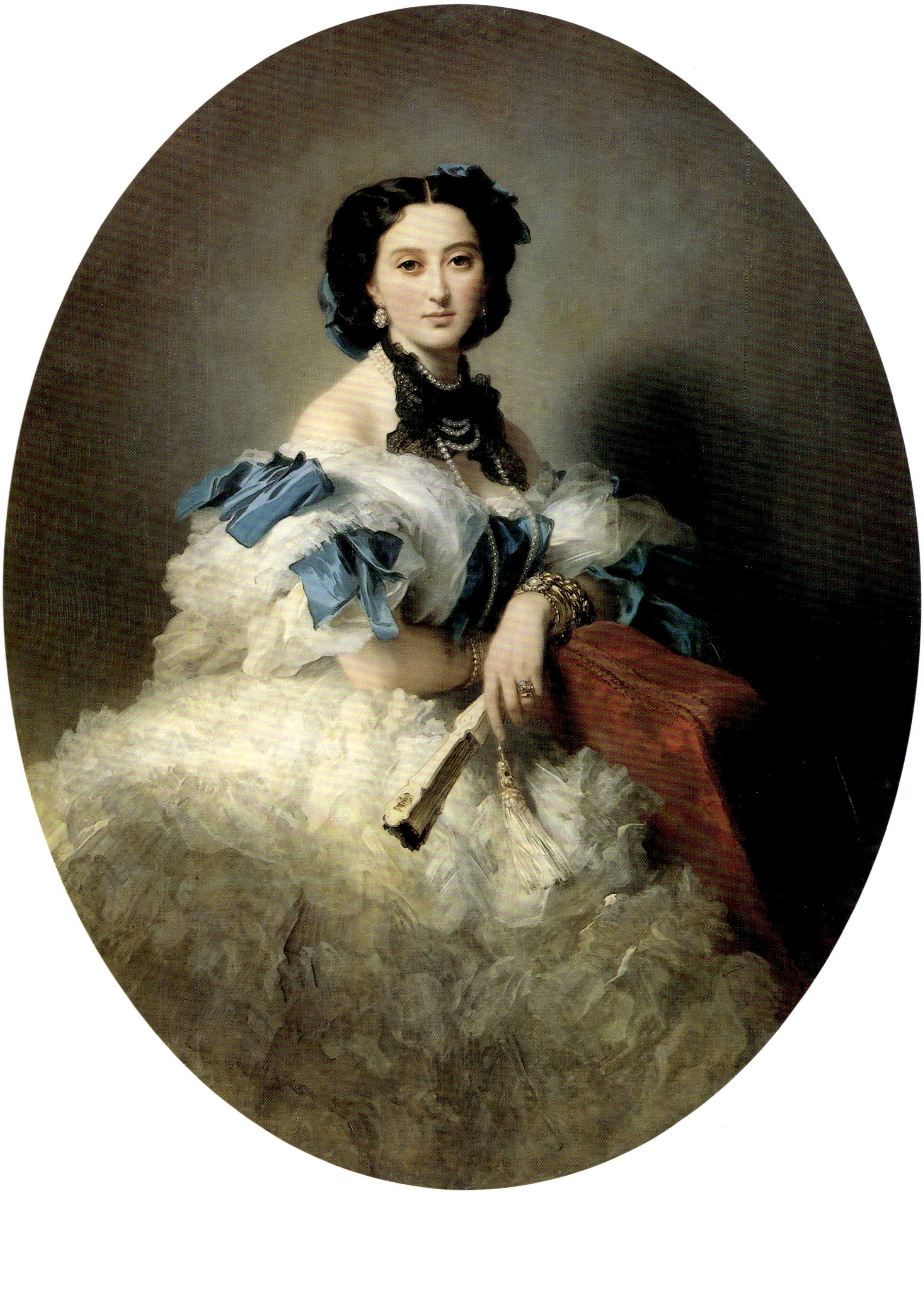

COUNTESS VARVARA ALEKSEYEVNA MUSINA-PUSHKINA (no. 74)

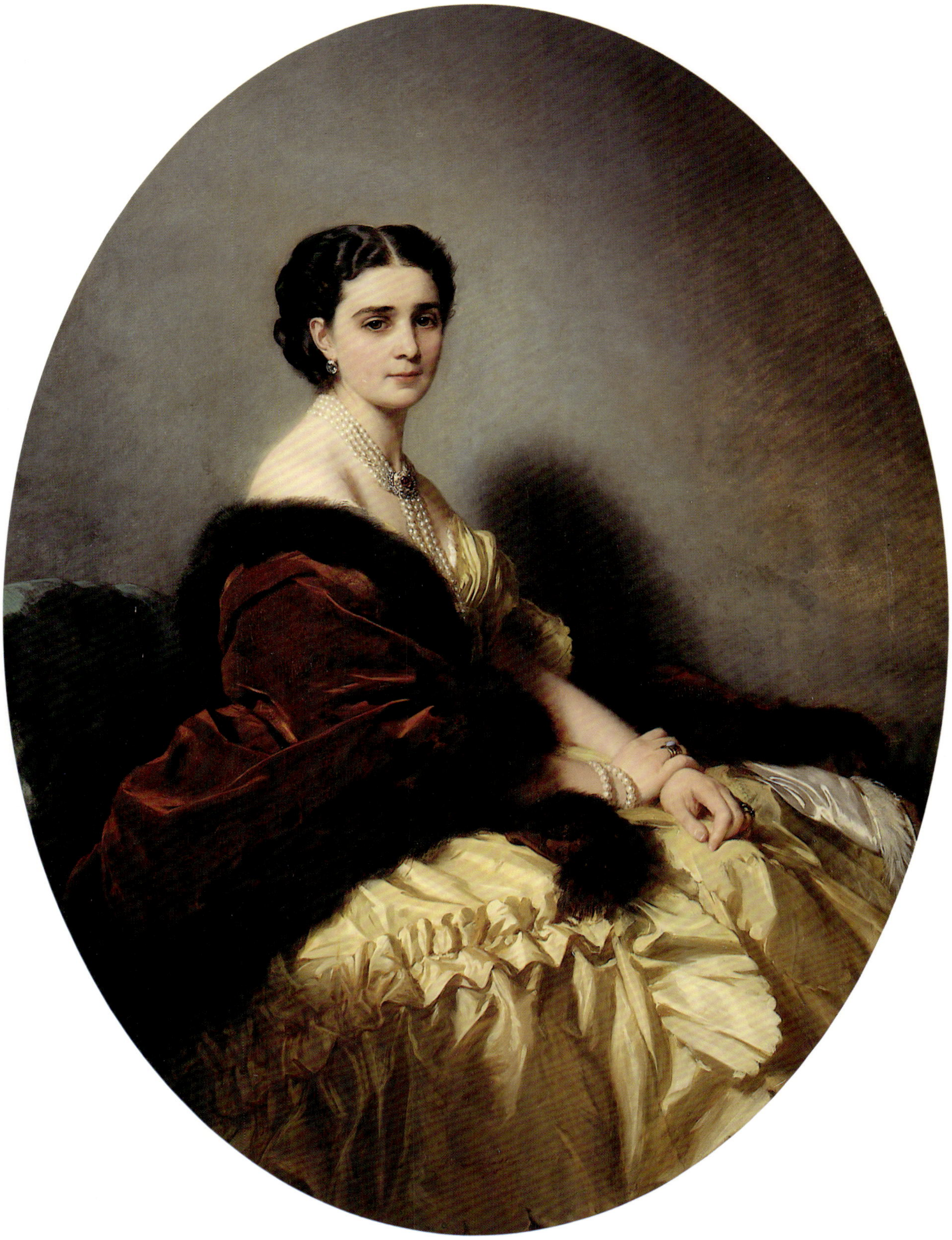

MADAME SOFYA PETROVNA NARYSCHKINA 1858 (no. 75)

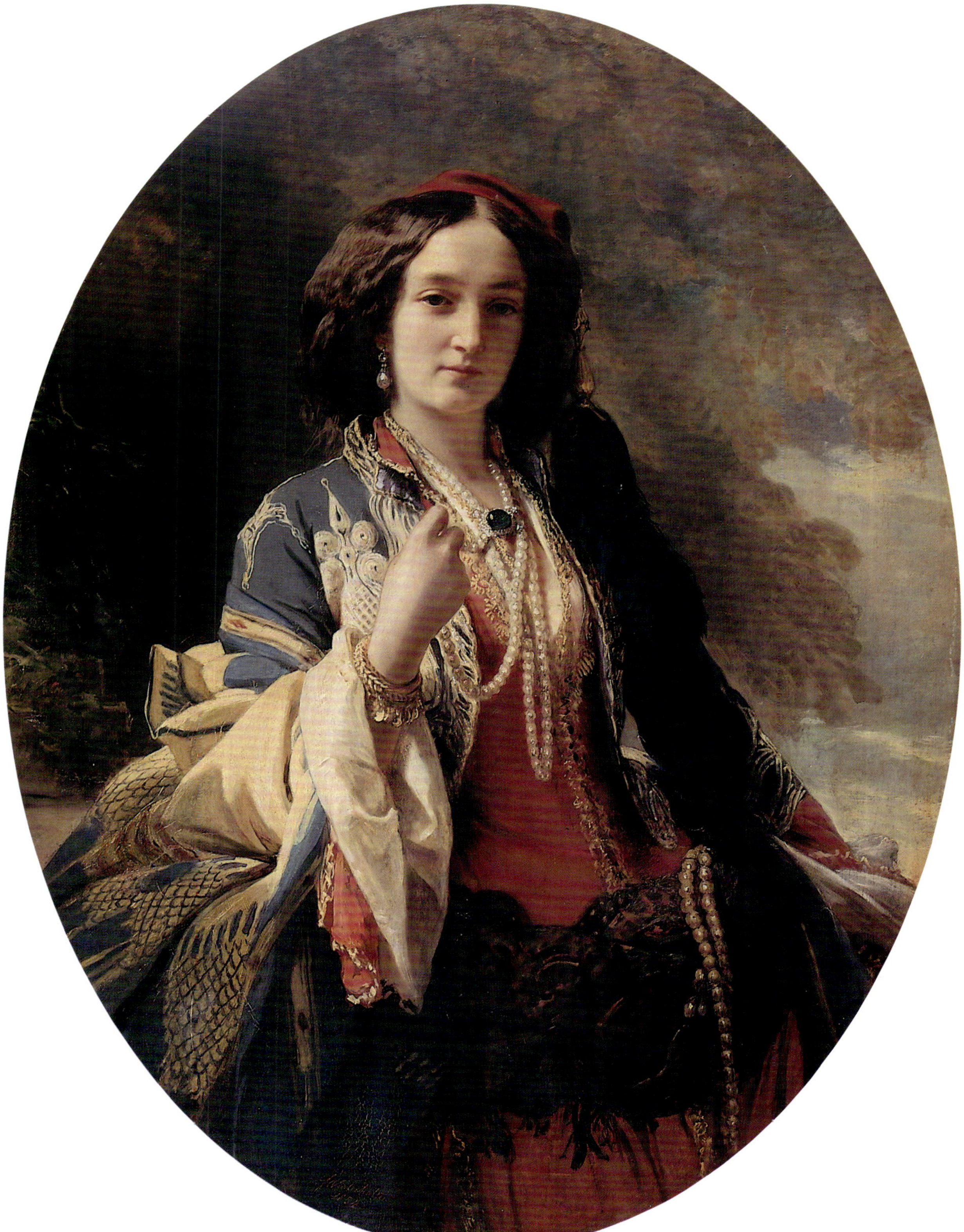

KATARZYNA BRANICKA, COUNTESS POTOCKA 1854 (no. 68)

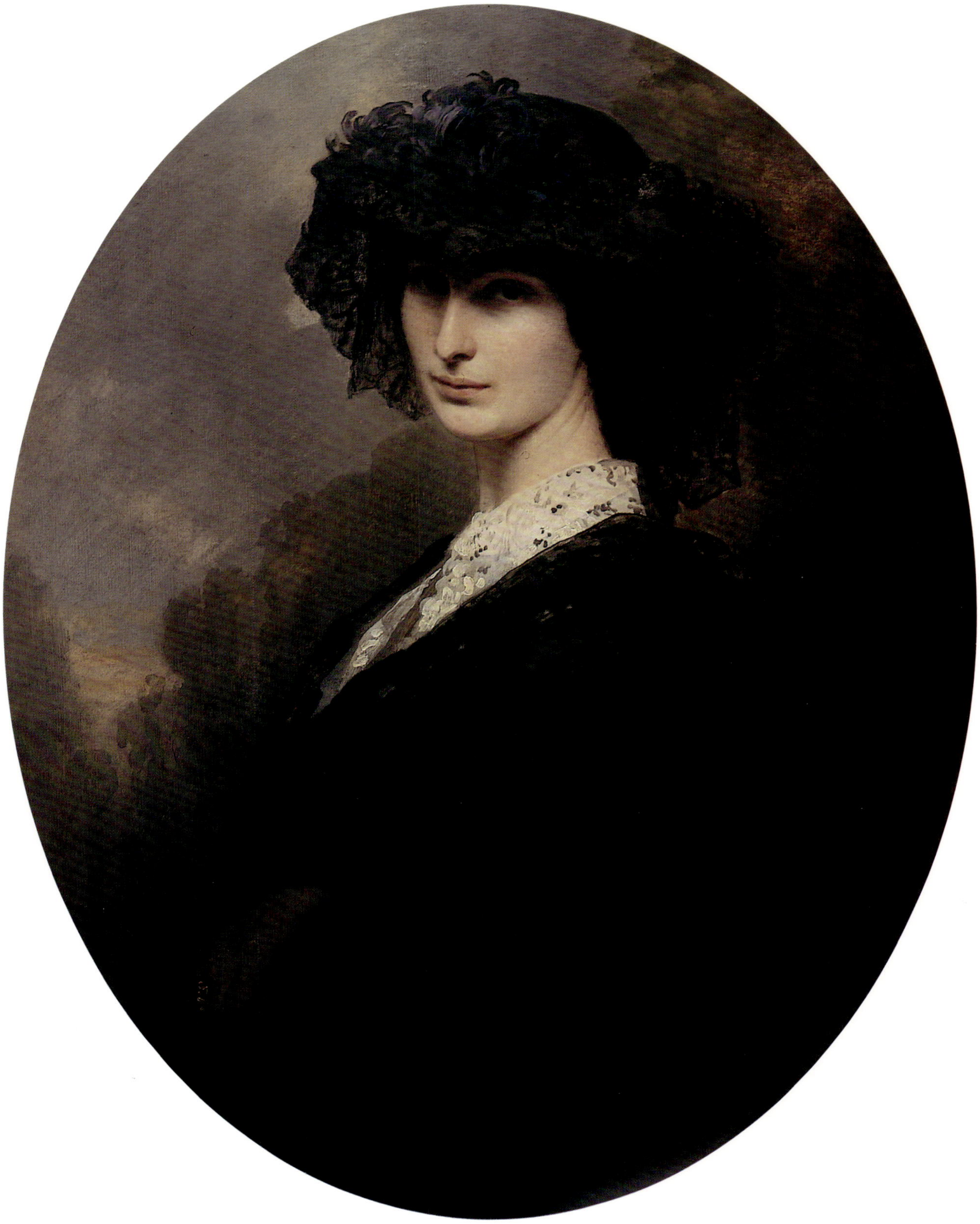

JADWIGA POTOCKA, COUNTESS BRANICKA (no. 77)

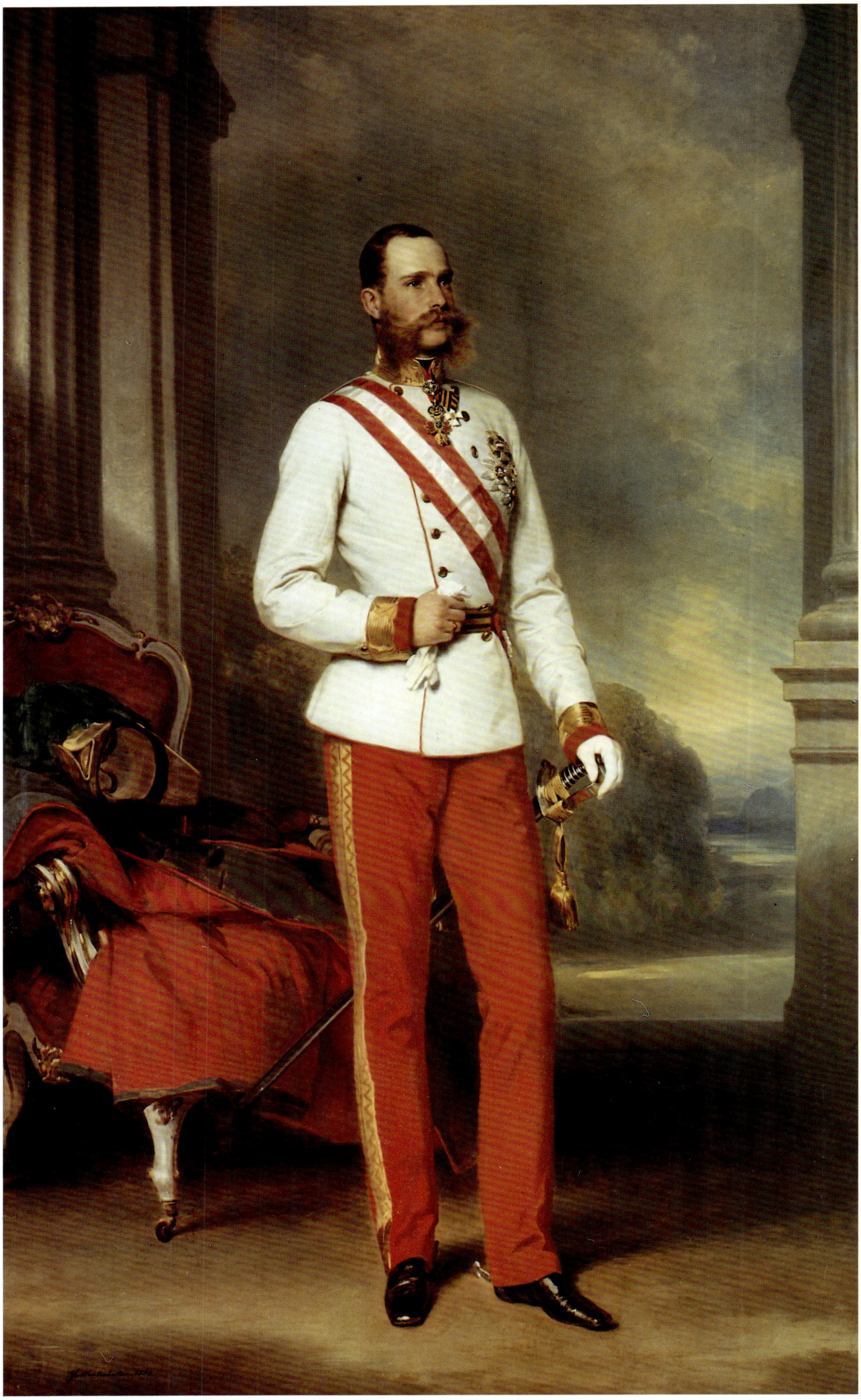

FRANZ JOSEPH I, EMPEROR OF AUSTRIA 1865 (no. 78)

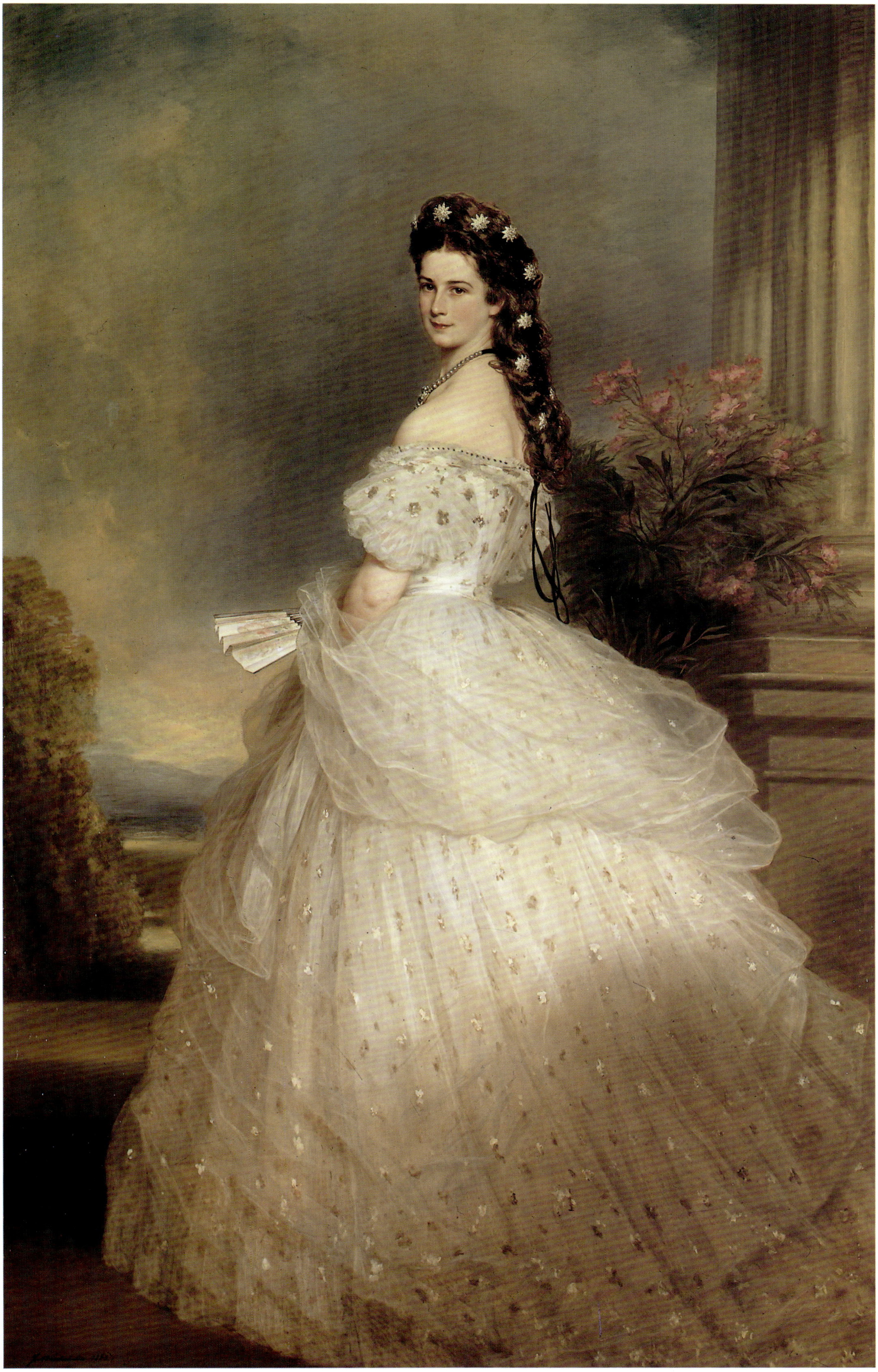

ELIZABETH, EMPRESS OF AUSTRIA 1865 (no. 79)

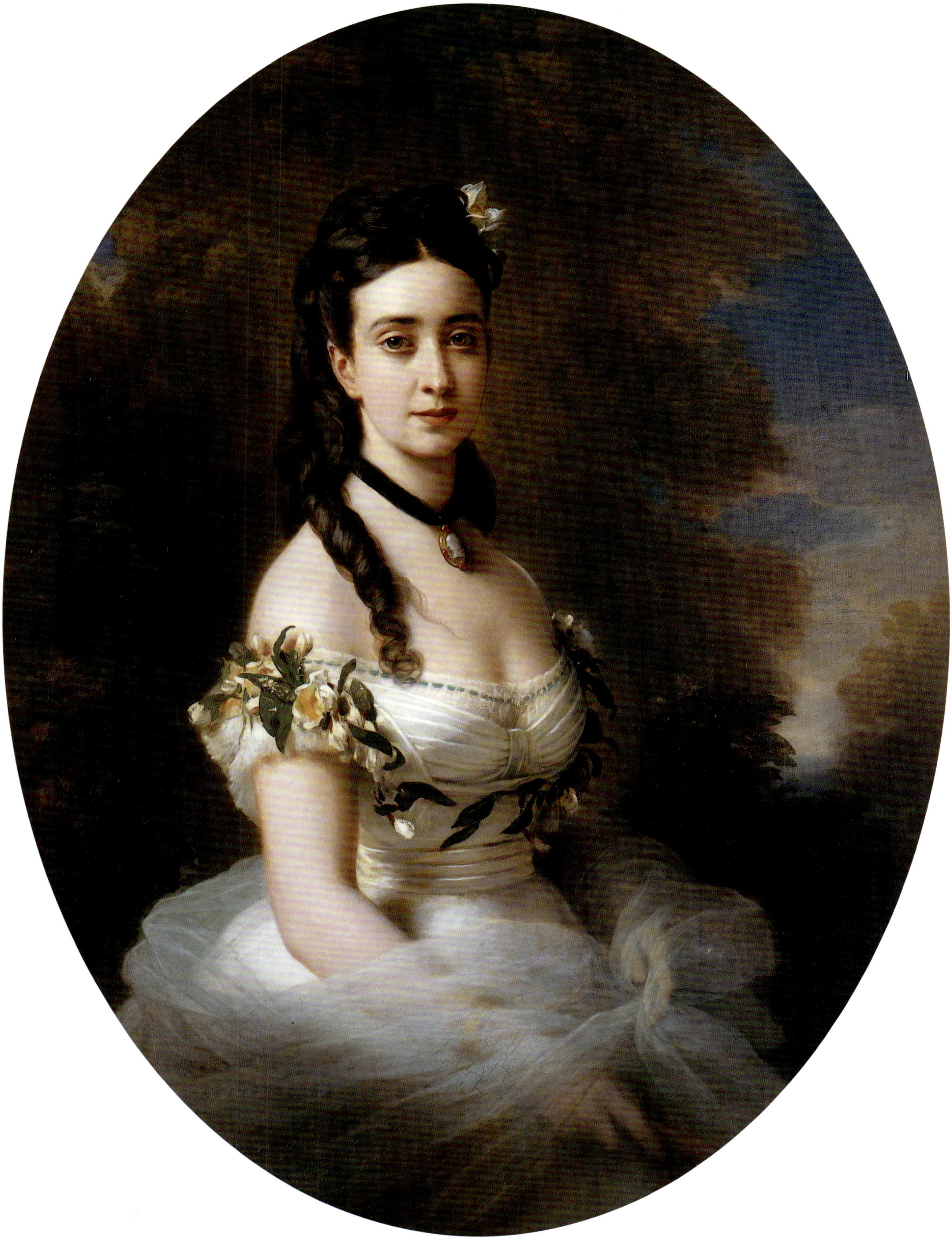

AN AMERICAN LADY (*Die Amerikanerin*) (no. 80)

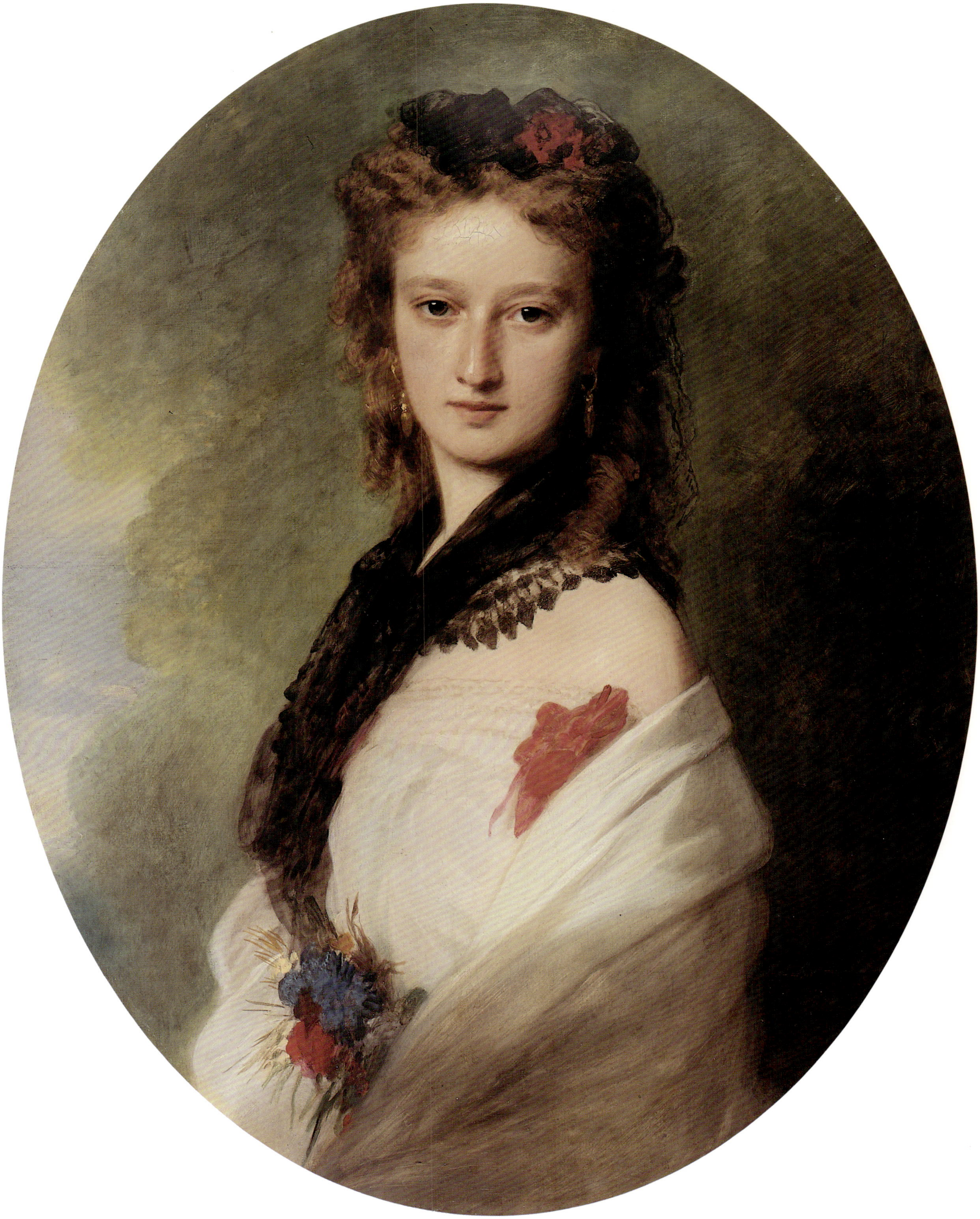

ZOFIA POTOCKA, COUNTESS ZAMOYSKA 1870 (no. 81)

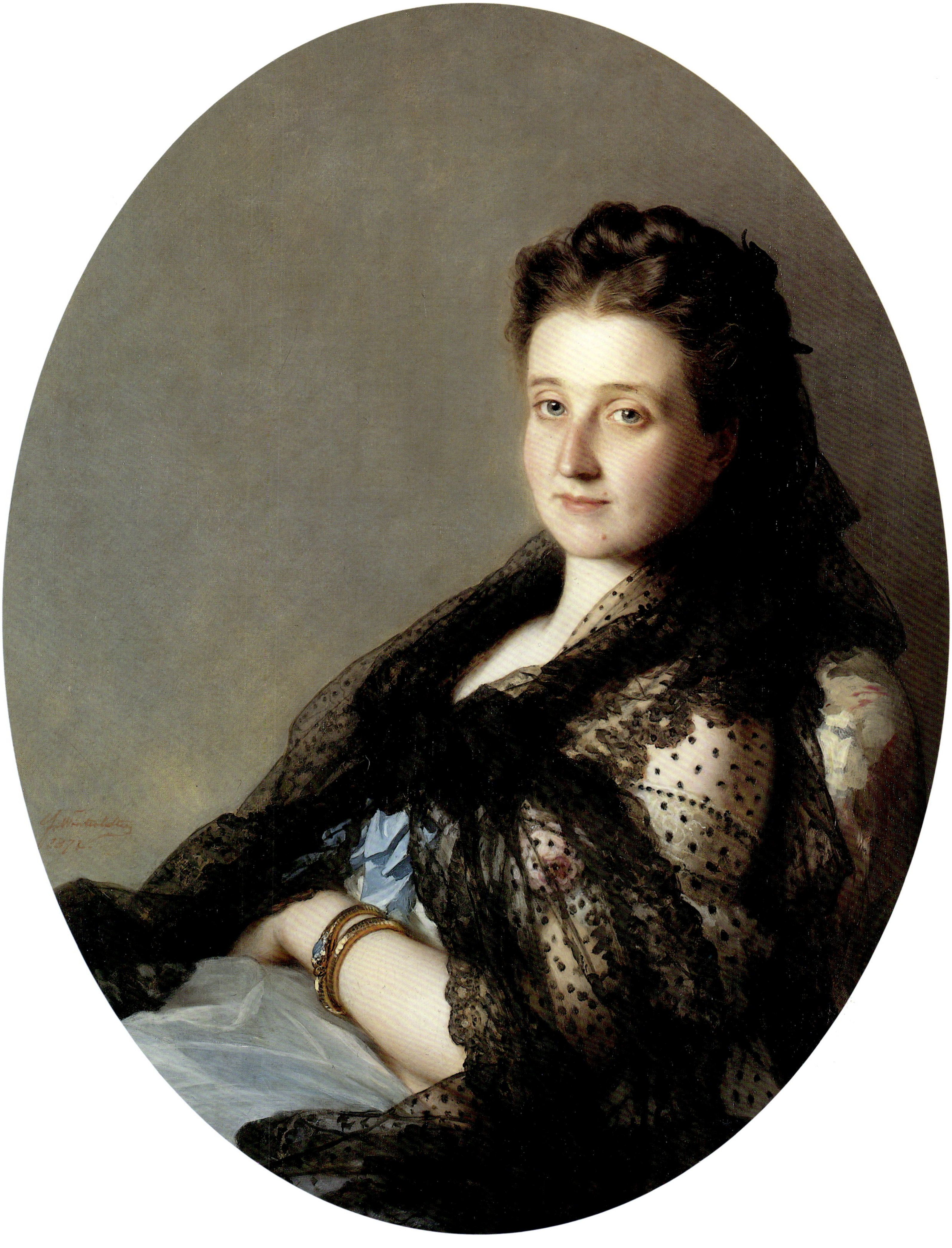

UNIDENTIFIED LADY 1872 (no. 82)

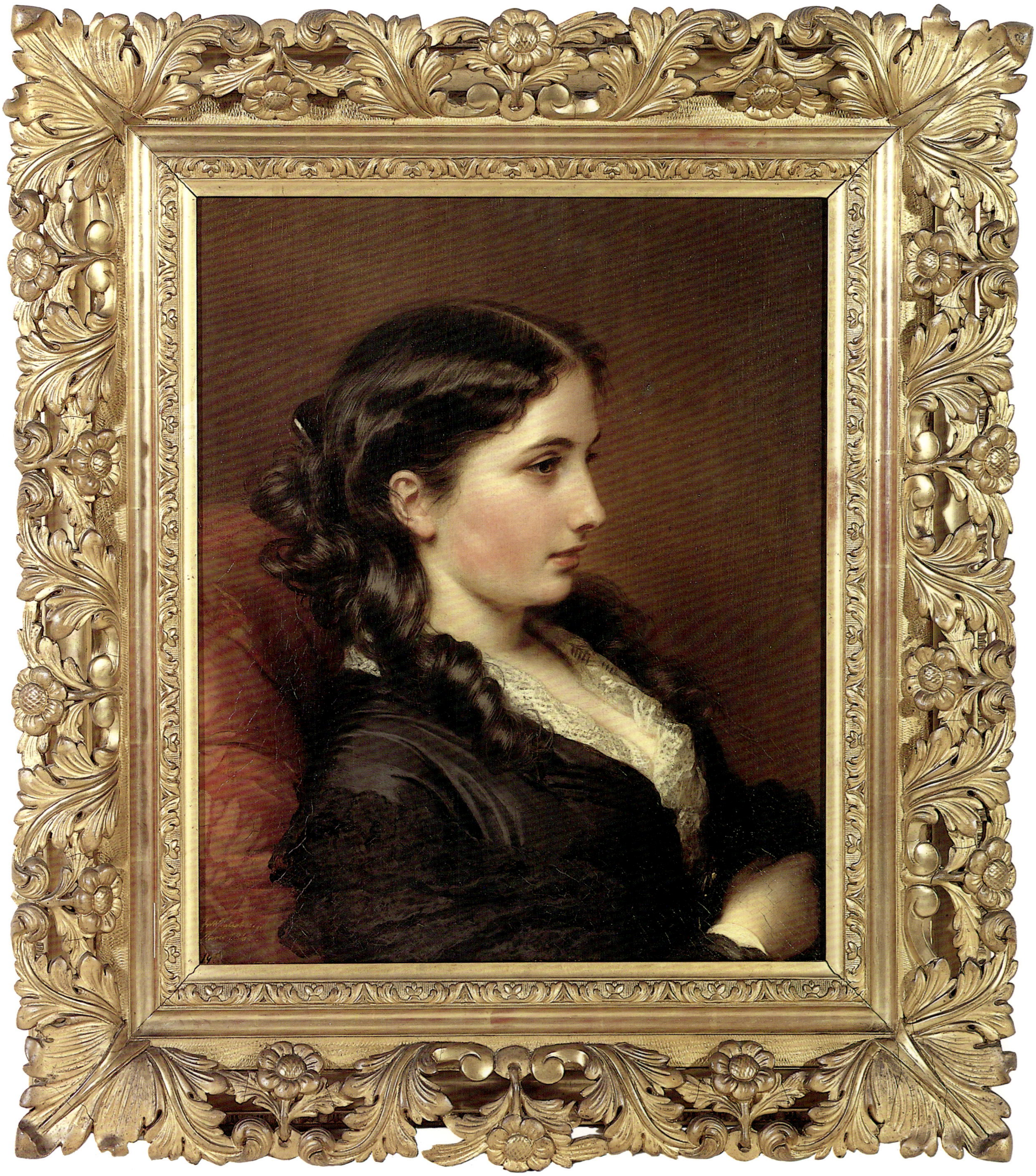

STUDY OF A GIRL IN PROFILE 1862 (no. 76)

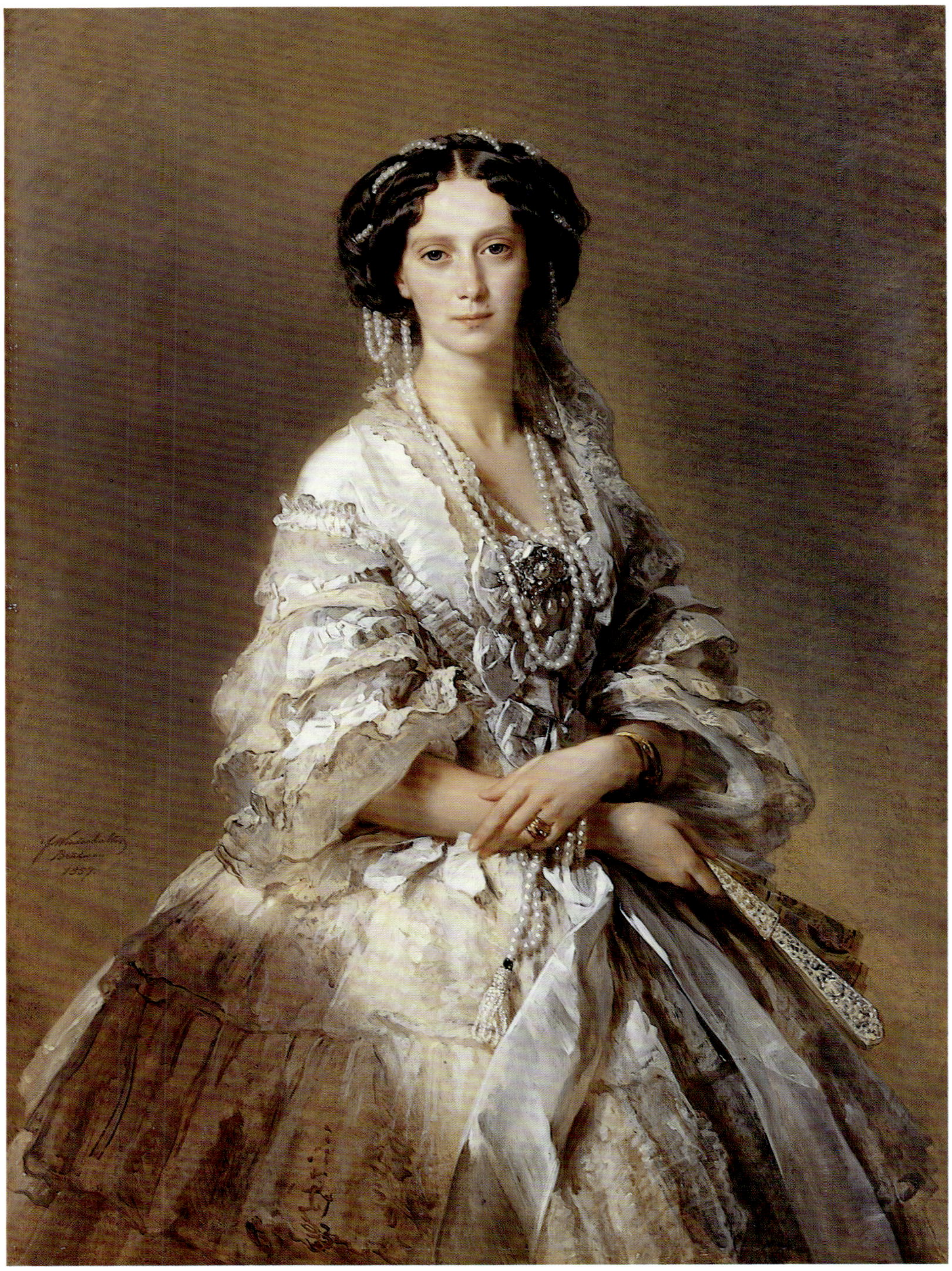

THE EMPRESS MARIA ALEXANDROVNA OF RUSSIA 1857 (no. 73)

# Drawings, Watercolours and Prints

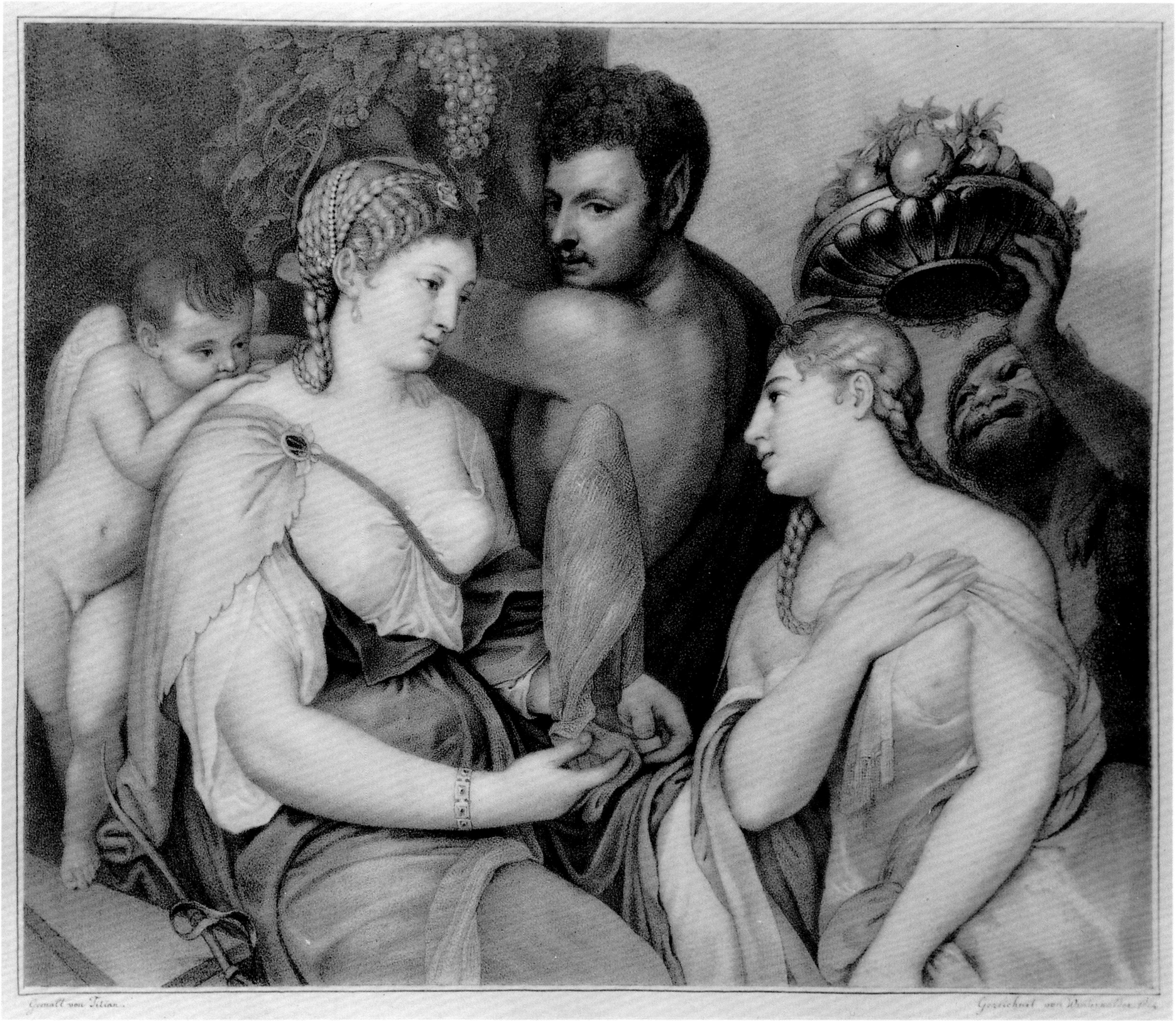


MYTHOLOGY AFTER TITIAN 1824 (no. 83)

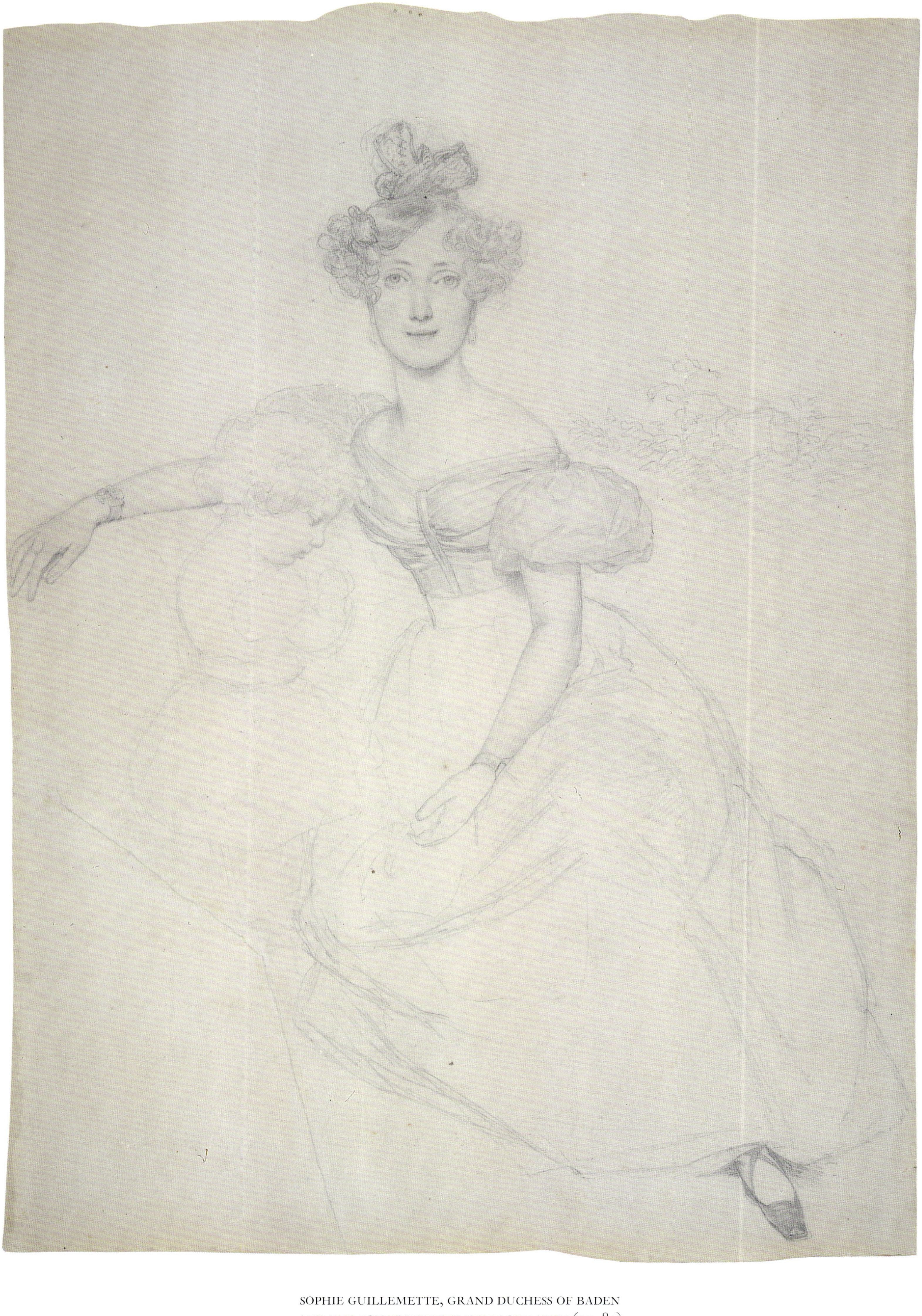

SOPHIE GUILLEMETTE, GRAND DUCHESS OF BADEN
AND HER SON PRINCE WILHELM OF BADEN (no. 84)

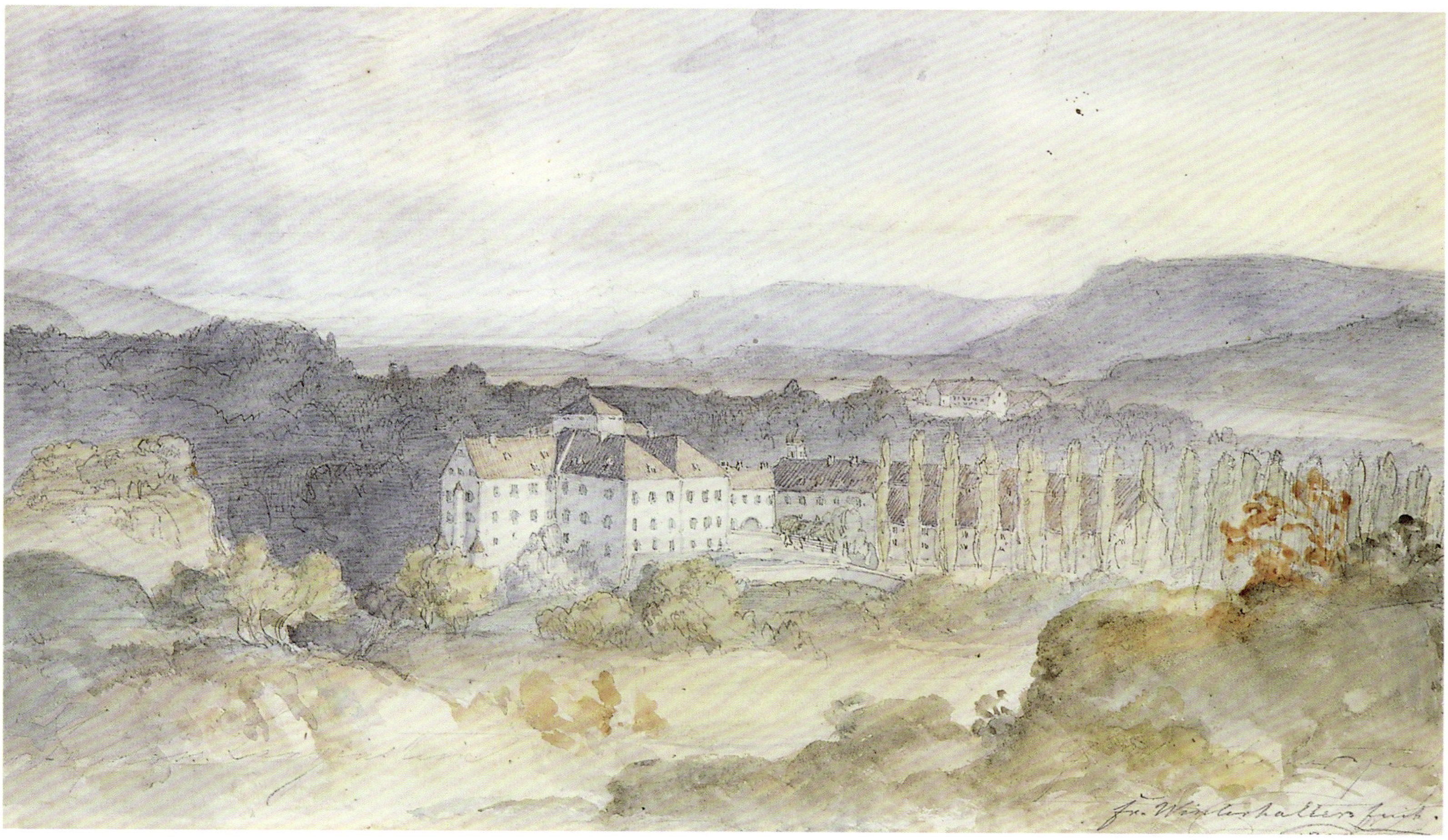


SCHLOSS LANGENSTEIN (no. 85)

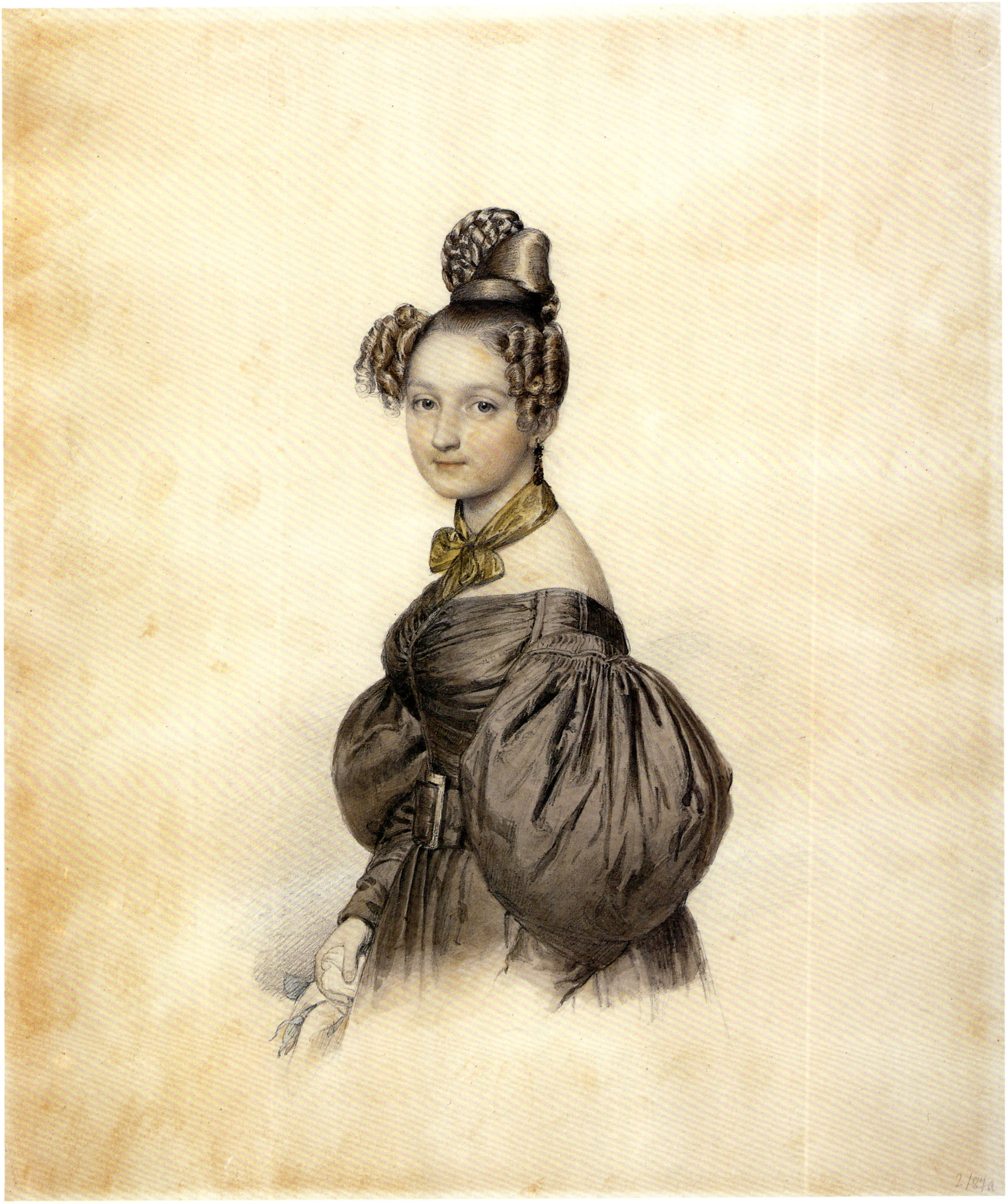


PAULINE WICH, BARONESS SEUTTER VON LÖFZEN 1833 (no. 87)

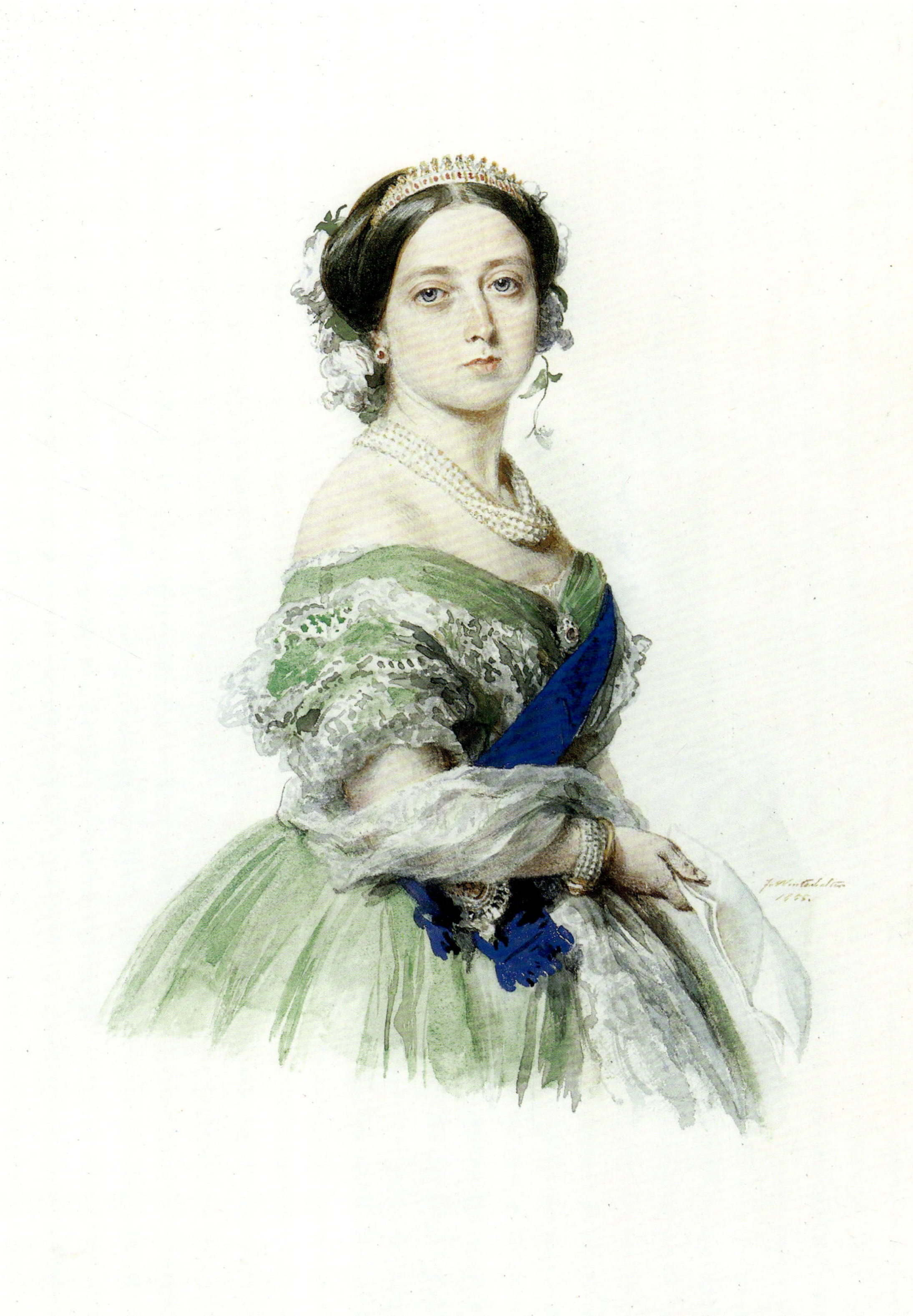

QUEEN VICTORIA 1855 (no. 93)

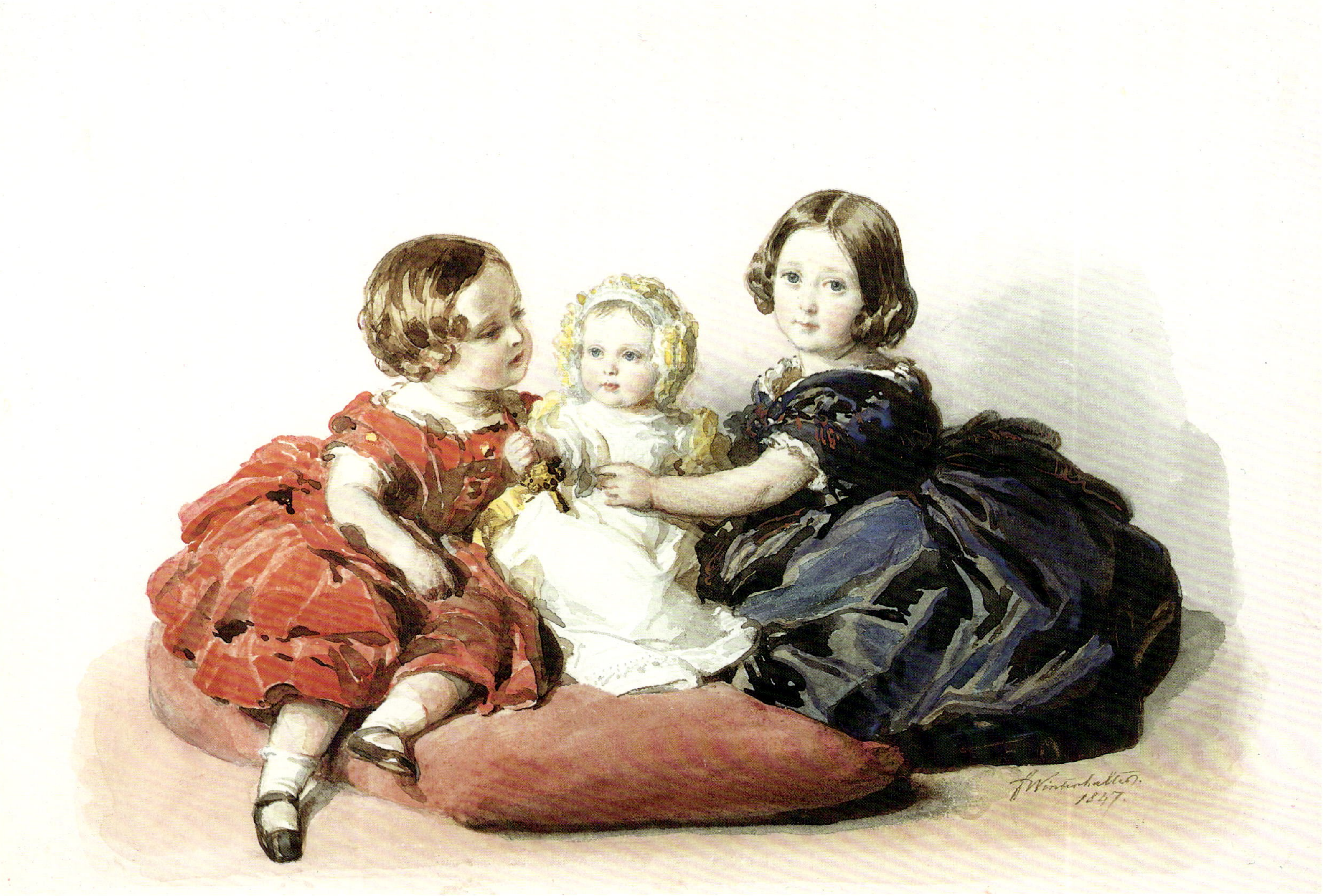

PRINCESS ALICE, PRINCE ALFRED AND PRINCESS HELENA 1847 (no. 89)

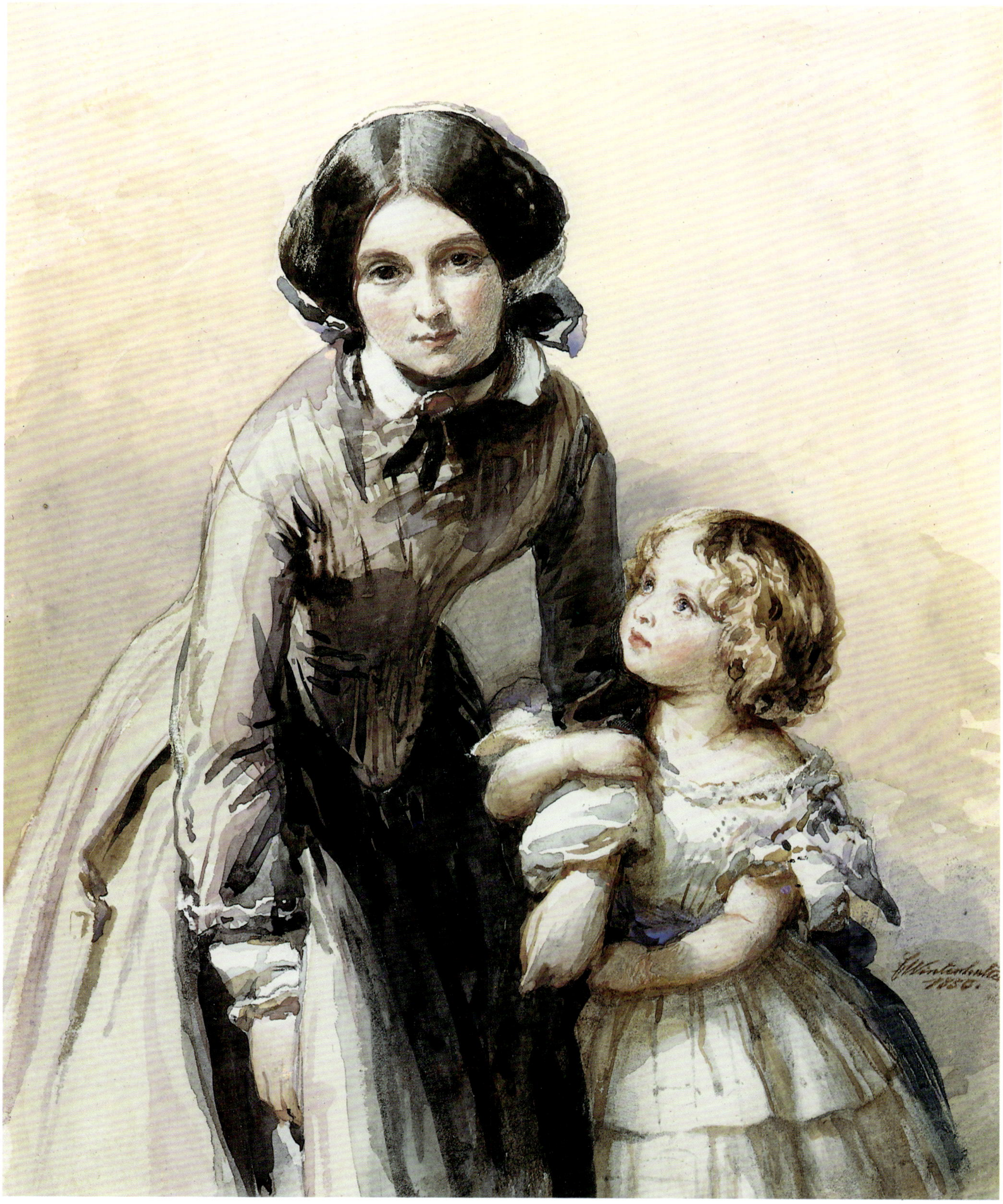

PRINCESS LOUISE WITH HER NURSEMAID ELIZA COLLINS 1850 (no. 90)

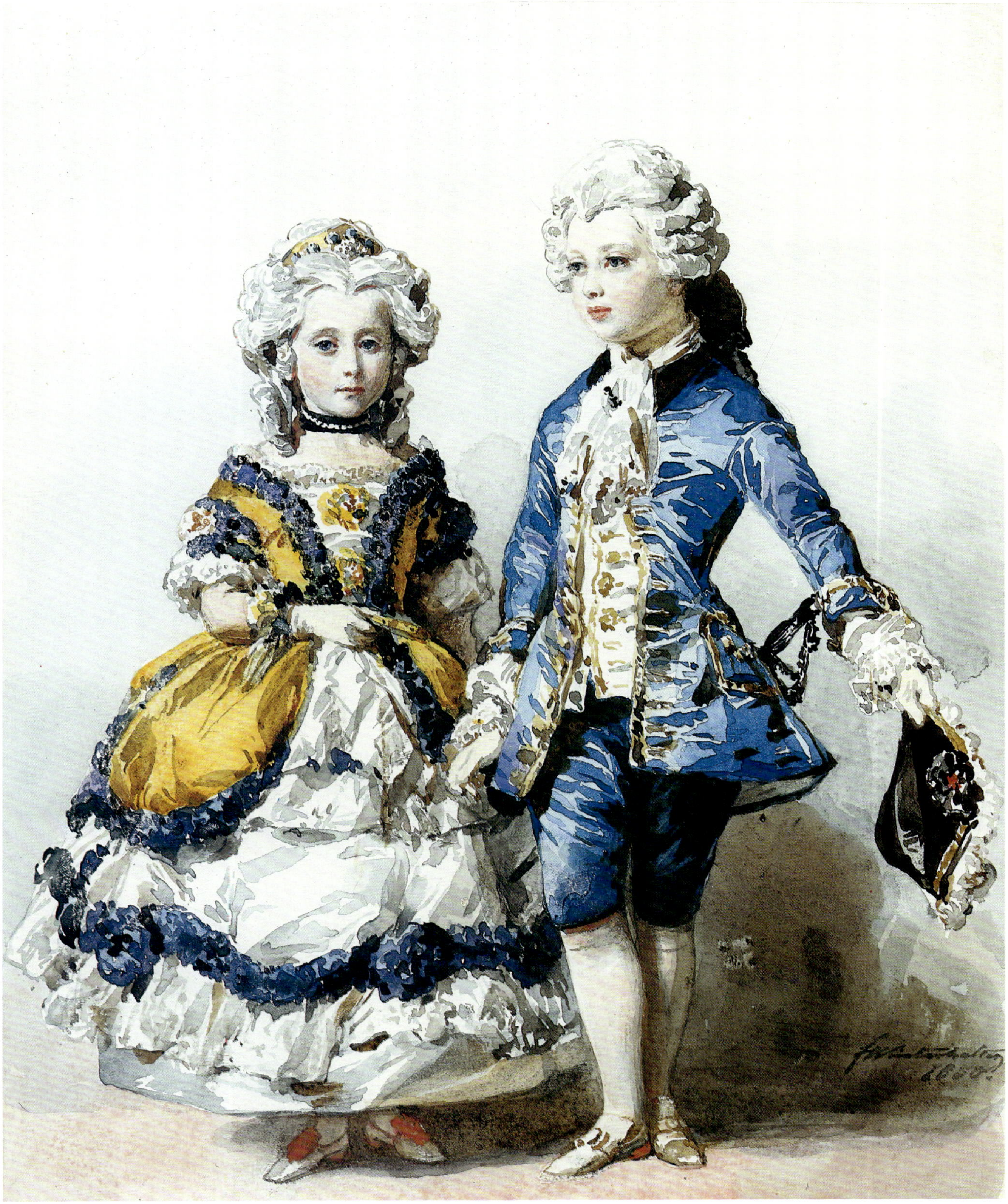

VICTORIA, PRINCESS ROYAL AND PRINCESS ALICE
IN EIGHTEENTH-CENTURY COSTUME 1850 (no. 91)

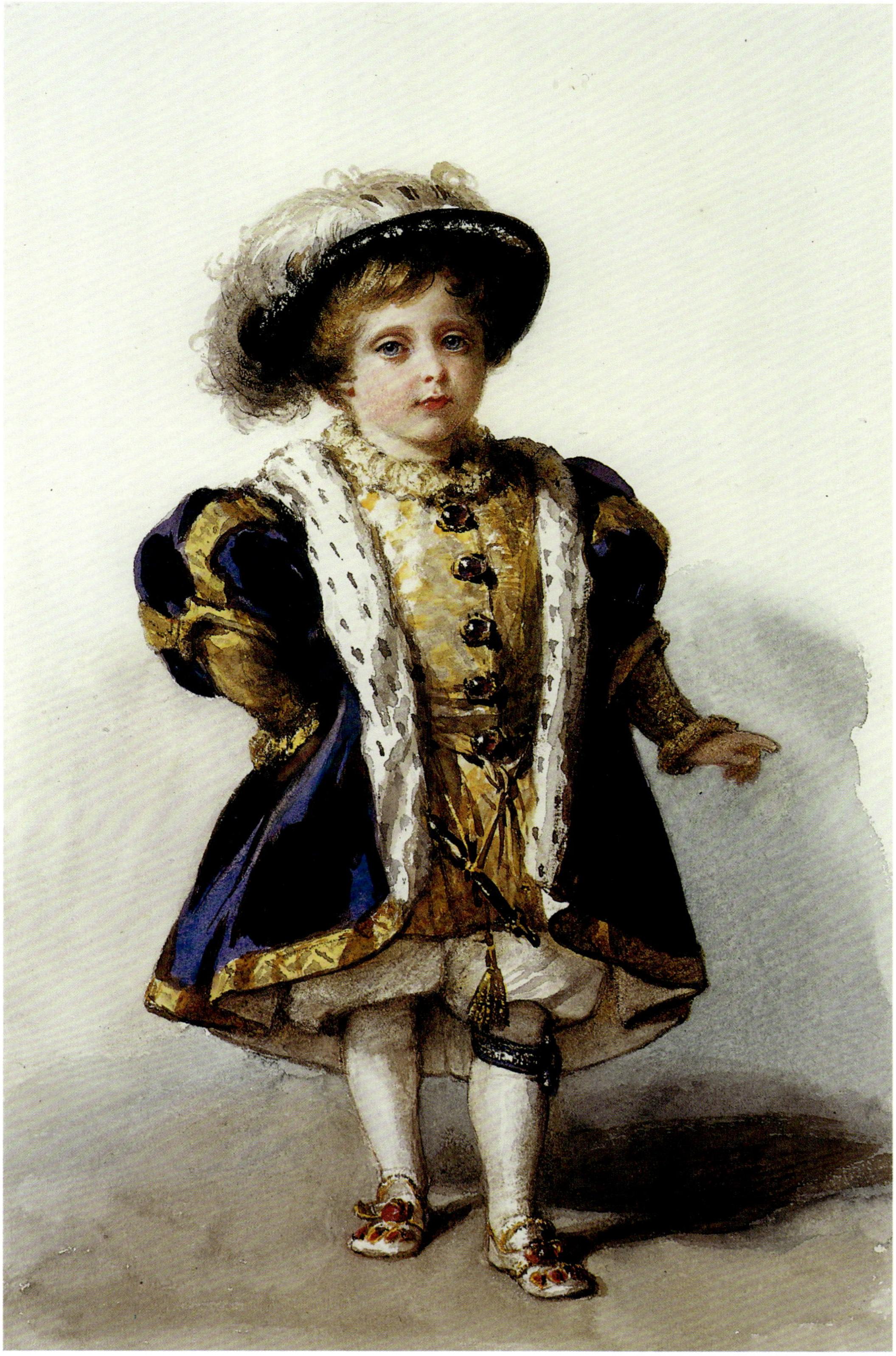

PRINCE ARTHUR DRESSED AS HENRY VIII (no. 92)

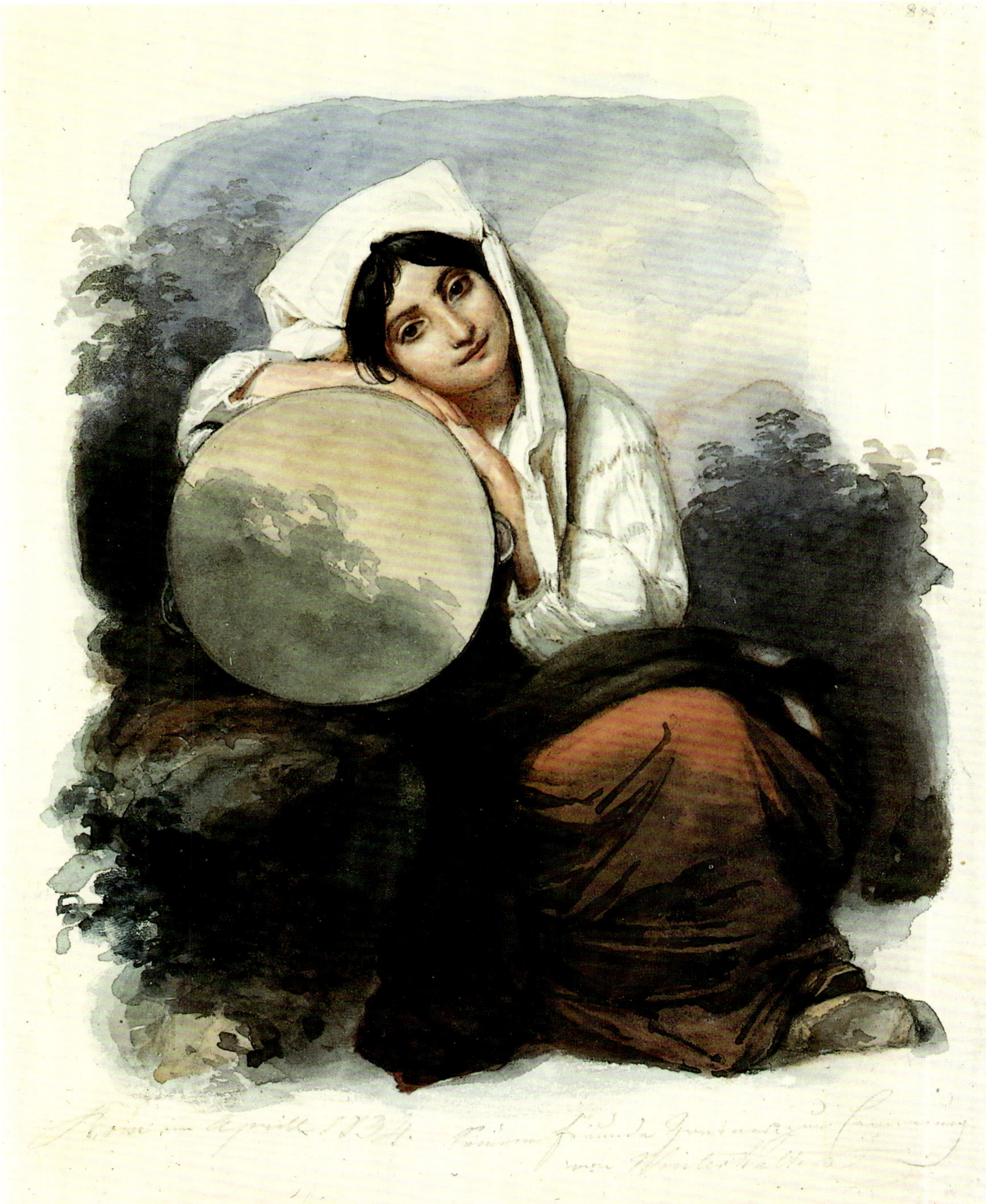

ITALIAN GIRL RESTING WITH A TAMBOURINE 1834 (no. 88)

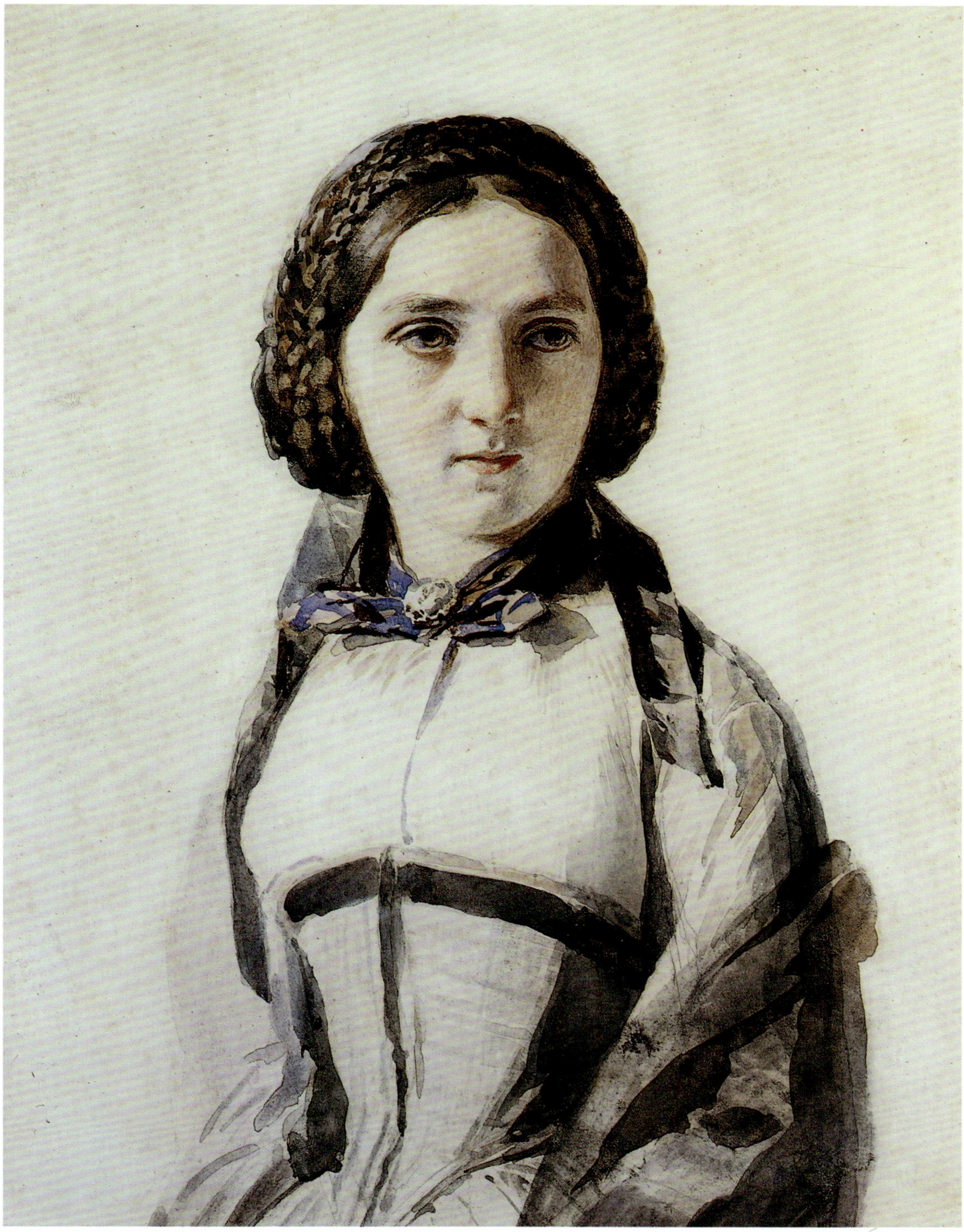

THE DAUGHTER OF MR AEBI (no. 94)

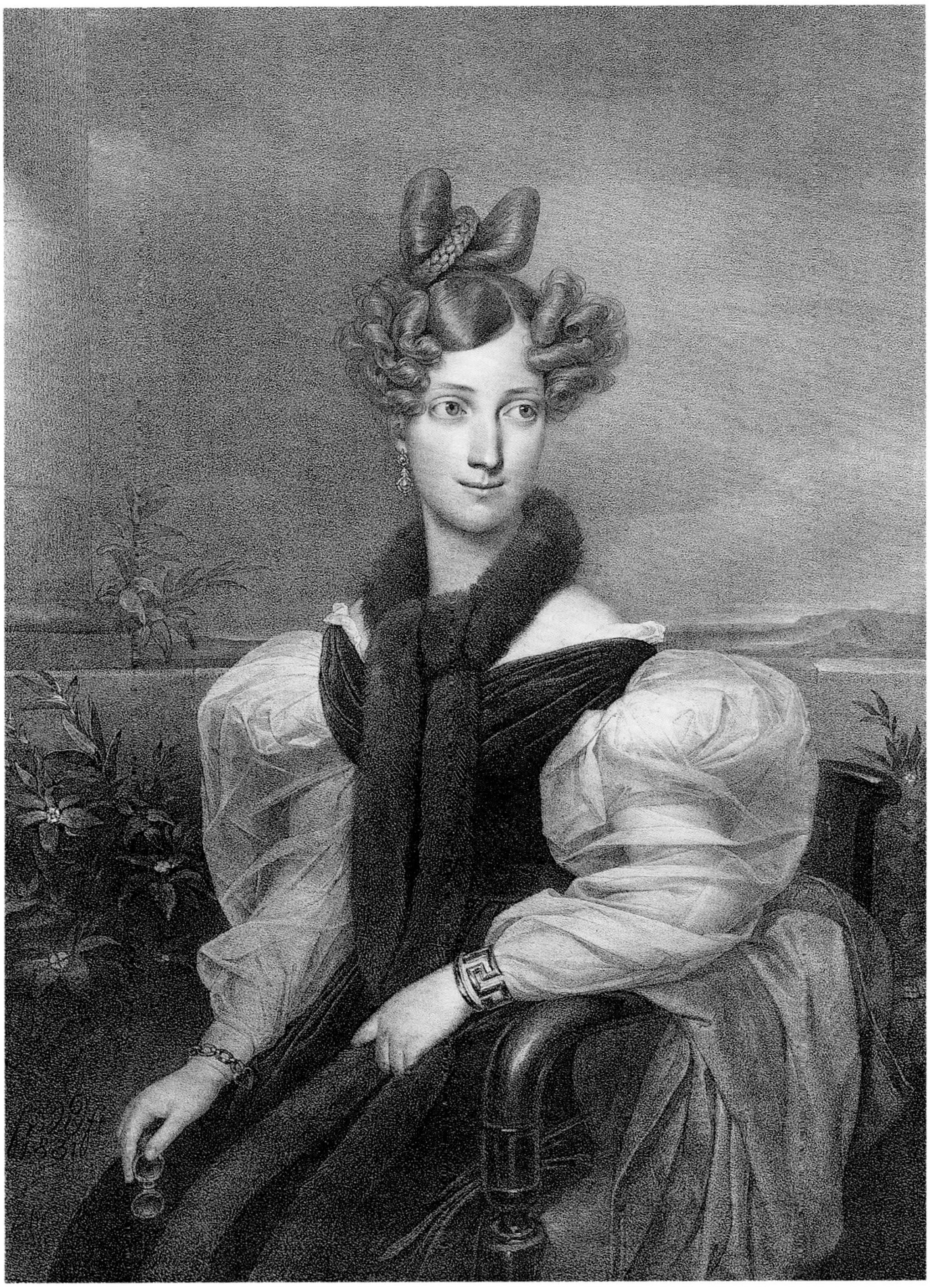

SOPHIE GUILLEMETTE, GRAND DUCHESS OF BADEN (no. 95)

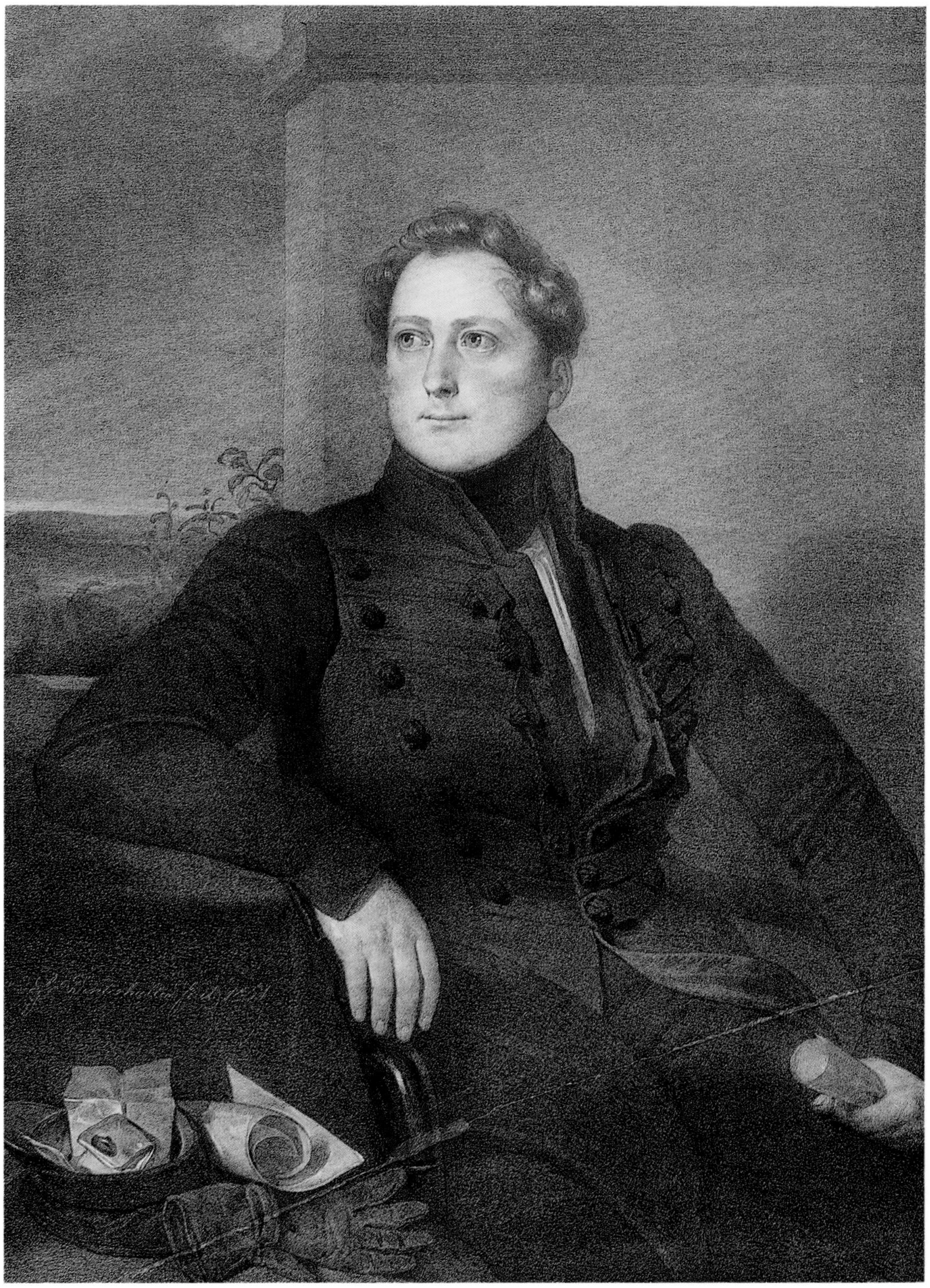

LEOPOLD, GRAND DUKE OF BADEN (no. 96)

# *Catalogue*

I

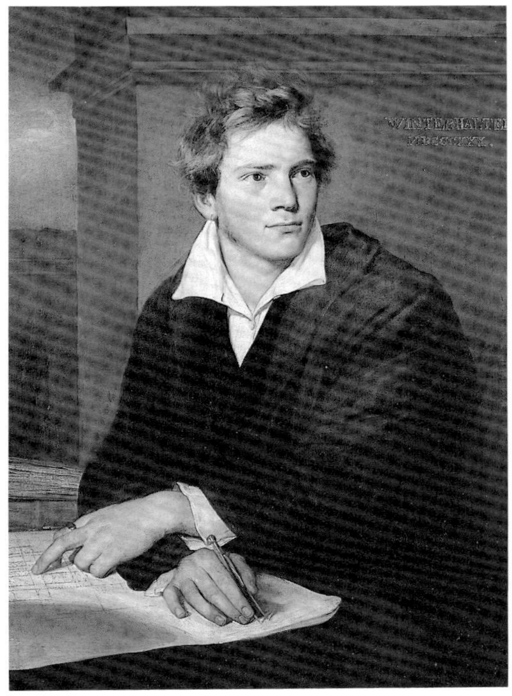

PORTRAIT OF A YOUNG ARCHITECT, PROBABLY KARL JOSEF BERCKMÜLLER (1830)

*Karl Josef Berckmüller (1800–79) was the son of a prominent builder of Karlsruhe, the capital of the Grand Duchy of Baden. He was, himself, to become a government architect. One of his most important works was the building to house the Grand Ducal Collections on the Friedrichsplatz in Karlsruhe.*
PM

96 × 72.3 cms
Signed and dated, upper right:
WINTERHALTER/MDCCXXX
*Musée de Picardie, Amiens*

*Provenance*: Gift of Maréchal Leclerc de Hautecloque, 1945, inv. no. 3276.
*Exhibitions*: Possibly Karlsruhe, Kunstausstellung, 1832, no. 82; Karlsruhe, 1965, no. 57.
*Reviews*: 'Oeffentliche Kunstausstellung in Karlsruhe im Mai 1832', *Kunstblatt*, no. 82, 11 October 1832, p. 325.
*Bibliography*: Introduction, p. 25.
See colour plate p. 73.

The architect is poised, as if explaining a point on the plan before him, with his head turned to the right. The attributes of his profession, a ground plan and a set of calipers, are in front of him, but attention is focused upon a fine study of hands. The diagonals of the crossed hands are echoed in the sitter's splayed open collar. An atypical form of signature, with Roman letters and numerals, appears as though carved into the architectural background.

There are good grounds for identifying the sitter in the portrait as Winterhalter's close friend, Karl Josef Berckmüller. He had qualified as an architect the previous year, and had further established himself by marrying the daughter of Baron Eichtal, Winterhalter's great benefactor. The picture appears to be the *Portrait of a Man*, shown at the Public Art Exhibition at Karlsruhe in May 1832 (no. 82). It received qualified praise in *Kunstblatt*, 11 October 1832:

> '*Mannliches Porträt, von Winterhalter. Der Künstler hat hier die entschiedenen Züge eines männlich schönen Angesichtes mit großer Kühnheit und Sicherheit, gleichsam* alla prima *wiedergegeben. Die Aehnlichkeit ist so sprechend, daß man das Original selbst zu sehen glaubt. Man muß bei diesem Porträte, wie bei allen des Herrn Winterhalter, seinem großen Talente für die Bildnißmalerei Gerechtigkeit widerfahren lassen; aber ungerügt können wir es nicht lassen, daß diese flüchtige Malerei des gerühmten schönen Talentes unwürdig ist.*'[1]

Differing circumstances were to bring Winterhalter and Berckmüller together again over the years. Apart from serving as a go-between during the romantic attachment of Winterhalter for Marie Scheffel, Berckmüller was also the exacting Head Planning Officer to whom all plans for Winterhalter's new villa at Baden had to be submitted (see Introduction, p. 61). In 1873, Berckmüller lent two oil paintings to the Winterhalter exhibition at Karlsruhe; a portrait of Baron von Eichtal (no. 39), and a genre painting (no. 40).
CBO

1. 'The artist has reproduced here, as it were *alla prima*, the firm features of a handsome male face with great boldness and assurance. The likeness is so vivid that one believes one is seeing the original. With this portrait, as with all Mr Winterhalter's portraits, one must acknowledge his great talent for portraiture; but we cannot fail to comment adversely on the fact that this hasty manner of painting is unworthy of the great talent we have praised . . . .'

## 2

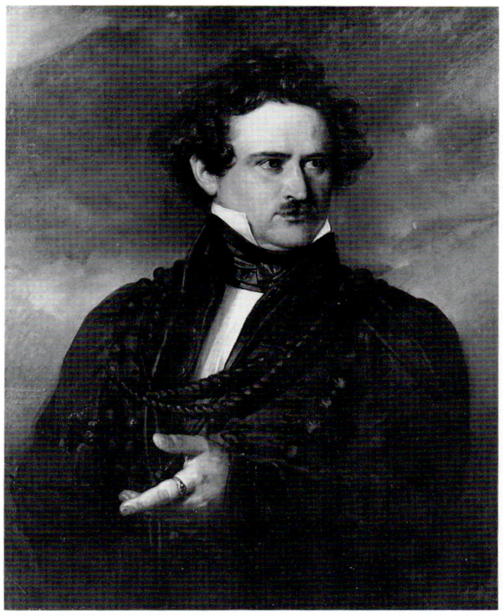

KARL SPINDLER (1830)
(Not exhibited)

*After several years in pursuit of a career on the stage, Karl Spindler (1796–1855) turned his attention to literature. He wrote 101 historical novels and was known as 'the German Walter Scott'. Between 1827 and 1832, he was resident in Munich where he knew Winterhalter. In 1832, he moved to Baden-Baden, and died in 1855.*
PM

70 × 58 cms
Signed and dated, lower left: *FX Winterhalter Munchen 1830*
*Private Collection*

*Provenance*: In the collection of Herr Rissler, Baden 1873; sold Christie's, Monaco, 15 June 1986, lot 110.
*Exhibitions*: Baden, 1873, no. 36.
*Bibliography*: 'Kritik über die Winterhalter-Ausstellung', Wild, 1894 (reprinted from *Karlsruher Zeitung*, 7 October 1873); Introduction, p. 25.
Not reproduced in colour.

Spindler is shown at half-length against a blue sky interspersed with light clouds, his head turned to the right, his left hand gesturing in the opposite direction; he wears a black Hussar's uniform.

This strikingly vigorous portrait of the writer, Karl Spindler, must have been painted when Spindler was resident in Munich between 1827 and 1832, at the same time that Winterhalter had made his base there. The Hussar's uniform which Spindler wears reinforces his self-consciously artistic pose, giving the sitter a more Romantic air which is perhaps borne out by the carefully tousled hair. The sense of movement implicit in the half-length pose with its jutting hand, in which the sitter is silhouetted against the sky, was not to be repeated in Winterhalter's considerably more formal male portraits executed during his long career. The portrait of Spindler seems to indicate that Winterhalter's male portraiture could have taken an entirely different direction. When the painting was exhibited in Baden in 1873, the critic of the *Karlsruher Zeitung* wrote that: 'Ein Bild aus der frühesten Zeit, das Porträt des Novellisten Spindler, lässt schon vollständig den grossen Meister erkennen.'[1]
SF

1. 'One painting from his earliest days, the portrait of the novelist Spindler, already carries the marks of a great Master.'

## 3

LEOPOLD, GRAND DUKE OF BADEN (1831)*

*The Margraves of Baden had ruled parts of south-west Germany since the early Middle Ages. The end of the Holy Roman Empire and an alliance with Napoleon enabled them to quadruple their territory and, in 1806, assume the title of Grand Duke. Leopold (1790–1852), who succeeded in 1830, was a son of his father's second morganatic marriage. His right to the throne had only been recognized in 1819.*

*Like most of his family, he was liberal, and governed according to the constitution which had been granted in 1818. Nevertheless, a violent revolution broke out in 1849 and had to be suppressed by the Prussian army.*
(See no. 96)
PM

232 × 150 cms
Signed and dated, lower right: *Fr. Winterhalter fec. 1831*
*Private Collection*

*Provenance*: Originally executed for the Karlsruhe Museum Society; on deposit prior to 1914 with Karlsruhe Gallery (cat. no. 522); in 1930, returned to Margraves of Baden; by descent to the present owner.
*Exhibitions*: Possibly Baden, Salon of the Konversation Haus, 'Karlsruhe Zeitung', 22 July 1857; Baden, 1873, no. 1.
*Bibliography*: Wild, 1894; G.F. Kircher, *Zähringer Bildsammlung im Neuen Schloss zu Baden Baden*, Karlsruhe 1958, p. 104; Introduction, p. 25.
*Prints after*: Lithograph by S. Meier, printed by J. Velten and Lemercier, Paris; slight variant of present picture; undated.
Not reproduced.

Leopold, Grand Duke of Baden, is portrayed at full-length against a landscape background. He wears a dark blue coat with silver epaulettes, white knee breeches and black boots, with the yellow sash of the Order of the House of Baden over his shoulder, and on his left breast the cross of the Order of the Zahring Lion, the star of the Order of the House of Baden and the star of the Karl Friedrich Order of Merit. In his left hand, he carries a plumed hat.

One of at least two portraits of Leopold known to have been painted by Winterhalter, this is the more formal and less successful representation. In a second, smaller portrait of the same year (present whereabouts unknown, but recorded in a lithograph, no. 96), Leopold is shown seated. Here he stands somewhat stiffly, a slight disproportion between the elongated legs and arms and short square torso and head detracting from the intended grandeur of the placing of the upper part of the body against the sky. The similarity between the head here, and that of no. 96, suggests that a single sitting served both compositions. This portrait may have had a pendant of the Grand Duchess Sophie, recorded only in the 1873 exhibition at Baden. The lithograph by S. Meier shows a slightly altered hairstyle and coat.
SF

4

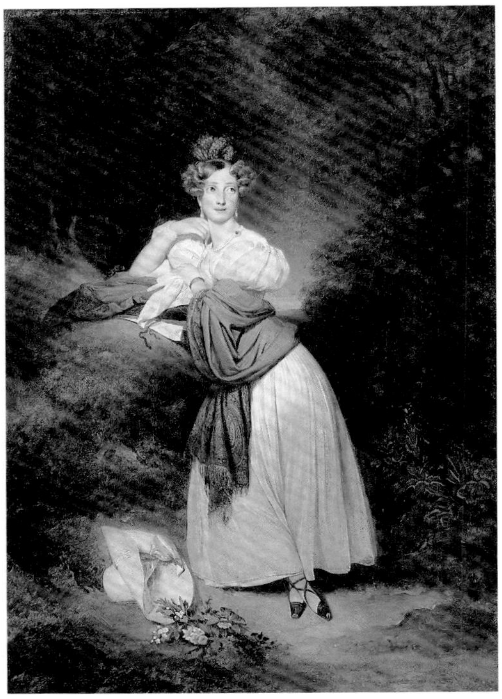

SOPHIE GUILLEMETTE, GRAND DUCHESS OF BADEN*

*Grand Duchess Sophie (1801–65) was a daughter of King Gustavus IV Adolphus of Sweden, whose catastrophic foreign and domestic policies had led to his deposition and exile in 1810. Her mother was a princess of Baden, where she was brought up. Her husband, the Grand Duke Leopold, was also her great-uncle. She was amorous, ambitious and less liberal than her husband.*
(See nos. 69, 84, 95)
PM

39.5 × 29 cms
Illegible signature and date, lower left: *183(?)*
*The Cleveland Museum of Art, The Thomas L. Fawick Memorial Collection*

*Provenance*: Christie's, London, 24 November 1978, lot 74; Hazlitt, Gooden & Fox Ltd, from whence acquired for the Thomas L. Fawick Memorial Collection (Cleveland Museum of Art), 1979, inv. no. 79.43.
*Exhibitions*: Cleveland Museum of Art, 'The Year in Review for 1979', 1980, no. 40.
*Reviews*: *The Bulletin of the Cleveland Museum of Art*, 67, 1980, no. 3, p. 59.
*Bibliography*: Introduction, p. 25.
See colour plate p. 74.

In this small whole-length portrait, Grand Duchess Sophie of Baden stands in a white dress in a landscape. She is in the fashionable attire of the early 1830s, with broad puffed sleeves, ankle-length skirt and laced pumps. A brown paisley shawl accentuates her hourglass silhouette, while her hairstyle culminates in an elaborate plaited 'Apollo' knot. She leans against a mossy boulder on which a portfolio of drawings has been laid, and flowers spill out of an upturned bonnet at her feet. Formally, the portrait encapsulates the perfect polish of Biedermeier taste, and yet the scene is also deeply Romantic: the beauty of the young woman is rendered poignant and vulnerable against the threatening dark of the forest.

As well as court painter at Karlsruhe, Winterhalter was the Grand Duchess's drawing-master. A warm friendship appears to have developed between the two, judging by Sophie's letters to Winterhalter (see nos. 69 and 84). The sitter's features, dress and hairstyle are very similar to those in the double portrait with Prince William of 1832 (Private Collection), which suggests a date of around 1832 for this painting.

A portrait of Grand Duchess Sophie was auctioned in 1917 by Rudolf Bangel in Frankfurt am Main (30–31 January 1917, no. 278, illustrated plate II).
CBO

5

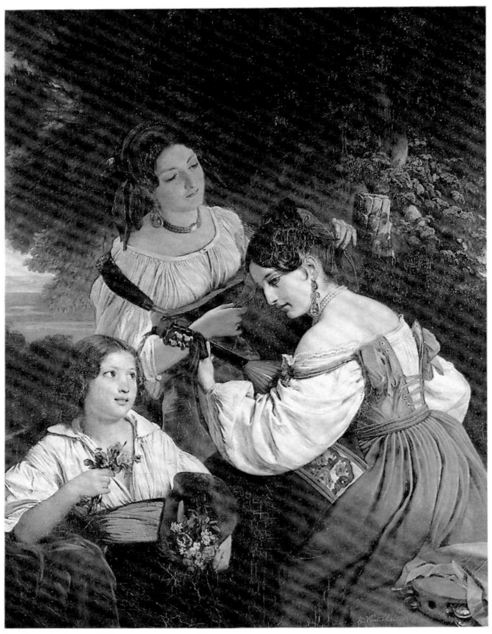

ROMAN GENRE SCENE (1833)*

60.5 × 50.5 cms
Signed, dated and inscribed, lower right:
*Fr. Winterhalter fec./Roma 1833*
*Staatliche Kunsthalle Karlsruhe*

*Provenance*: Transferred with the Private Collection of Grand Duke Leopold of Baden, 1853, inv. no. 523.
*Exhibitions*: Karlsruhe, Badischer Kunstverein, 1835, no. 523; Baden, 1873, no. 7; Menzenschwand, 1973, no. 3.
*Reviews*: 'Oeffentliche Kunstausstellung in Karlsruhe 1835', *Kunstblatt*, no. 60, 28 July 1835, p. 249.
*Bibliography*: Wild, 1894, no. 7; F. von Boetticher, *Malerwerke des 19 Jahrhunderts*, 2, Leipzig 1901, no. 25, p. 1027; J.A. Beringer, *Badische Malerei im neunzehnten Jahrhundert*, Karlsruhe 1922, p. 20; A. von Schneider, *Badische Malerei des 19. Jahrhunderts*, 1935, p. 59, pl. 32a; E.C. Conte Corti, 'Winterhalter, Ein deutsch-französischer Maler', *Velhagen und Klasings Monatshefte*, 53/2, 1938–9, col. pl. p. 130; A. von Schneider, *Thieme-Becker*, 36, 1947, p. 87; *Deutsche Meister 1800–1850 aus der Staatlichen Kunsthalle Karlsruhe*, Karlsruhe 1964, no. 43; A. von Schneider, *Badische Malerei des 19. Jahrhunderts*, 2nd edn. 1968, p. 83, pl. 81; C. Sternberg, *Geschichte des Karlsruher Kunstvereins*, Karlsruhe 1977, p. 56; Introduction, p. 29.
*Prints after*: Lithograph by Léon Noël, 1836.
See colour plate p. 77.

The mandoline player is the centre of attention. On the left a young boy offers her a posy from flowers held in a hat, while a second woman arranges the player's head-dress. White peasant blouses accentuate the triangular composition which is interwoven with a secondary, circular rhythm of hands. The child's alert expression off-sets the pensiveness of the women; a tambourine has been laid aside in favour of the softer notes of the mandoline, while dark foliage closes the background leaving a glimpse of sea to the left. A broken capital adds a note of Romantic decay. Altogether, a sleepy, sensual atmosphere hangs over the scene.

There are many virtuoso details such as the way in which the player's shoulders emerge from her blouse, the painting of her bejewelled ear, her half-unlaced bodice and the subdued lighting of the second woman's face, but the overall execution remains piecemeal and experimental. In particular, the angle of the player's arm in relation to the neck of the mandoline is uncertain, as is the woman's right arm in relation to her body.

Winterhalter arrived in Rome early in 1833 from Karlsruhe; Grand Duke Leopold partly sponsored the trip and no. 5 was to be part of his picture collection. Some of Winterhalter's pencil sketches of Italian peasants survive (Stadtische Museum, Freiburg-im-Breisgau, nos. G 37/4a–m), though none relate directly to no. 5. The *Roman Genre Scene* belongs to the body of works that Winterhalter painted in the mid and late 1830s, which includes no. 6, *Young Italian Girl by the Well*, no. 9, *Il Dolce Farniente*, 1836, no. 7, *Study of an Italian Girl* and no. 88, *Italian Girl Resting with a Tambourine*, 1834.

The painting was exhibited at the Karlsruhe Art Exhibition of 1835, and was well-reviewed in *Kunstblatt*. The critic offered his interpretation of the scene, and continued:

> *'Der lyrische Moment ist so geschlossen. Ein schöneres Kleeblatt gibt es nicht leicht. Der Kopf des älteren Frauenzimmers ist im Helldunkel gehalten. Kein Meister neuerer Zeiten dürfte Winterhalter in der Wahrheit und Klarheit des Helldunkels übertreffen. Dieser Kopf hier ist in dieser Hinsicht und vielleicht auch was den Ausdruck betrifft, so wohlgelungen, daß sich die Blicke des Beschauers kaum wieder davon wegwenden können.'*[1]

In 1832, the Karlsruhe Kunstverein began to distribute a work of art annually amongst its members. Winterhalter's *Roman Genre Scene* was the choice for 1836. The artist, who was in Paris by then, recommended the lithographer Léon Noël with outstanding results: it was said that no finer reproduction was ever sent out by the Kunstverein.
CBO

1. 'The lyrical moment is so self-contained. One will not easily find a more beautiful clover leaf. The head of the older woman is done in chiaroscuro. Probably no modern master surpasses Winterhalter in the truth and clarity of his chiaroscuro. This head here is in this respect – and perhaps also in respect of expression – so successfully executed that the viewer can hardly turn his gaze away from it.'

6

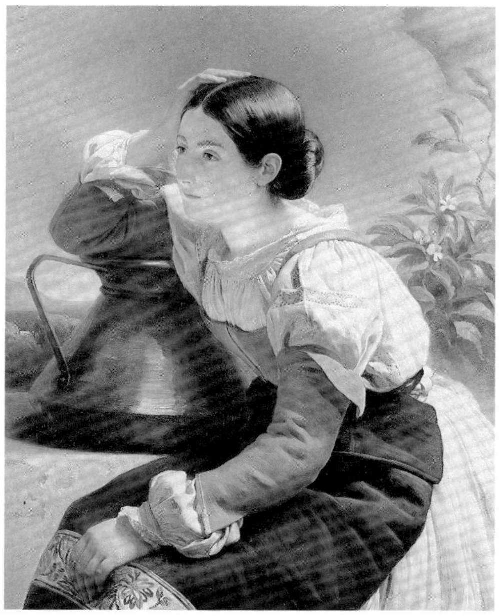

YOUNG ITALIAN GIRL BY THE WELL

92 × 74 cms
Signed, to left: *F.X. Winterhalter*
*Augustinermuseum Freiburg-im-Breisgau*

*Provenance*: Olga Nikolajewna, later Queen of Württemburg; Duchess Vera of Württemburg; Galerie Bruno Meissner, Zürich; acquired by the Museum, 1976, inv. no. M 76/7.
*Bibliography*: B.N. (probably Benedict Nicolson), 'Swiss Antique Fair', *The Burlington Magazine*, 118, 1976, pp. 180–1; P. Thornton, *Authentic Decor*, 1984, p. 291, repr.; Introduction, p. 29.
See colour plate p. 78.

The traditional identification of the model as Vittoria Caldoni, the daughter of a winegrower from Albano, is almost certainly incorrect. Vittoria was discovered in 1820, and she became the rage in Rome, sitting to most of the leading artists of the time. A portrait of her aged sixteen by Friedrich Overbeck of 1821 is in the Neue Pinakothek in Munich. By the time that Winterhalter might have painted her, she would have been in her late twenties.

The model in the picture appears much younger. She rests her right arm on a copper pitcher placed on a stone ledge, and day-dreams with her head framed by her arm against a blue sky. There are branches of orange blossom to the right, and a coastal view in the distance. Sunlight plays along her back, illuminating her face with a reflected glow. The pleats and open-work of the full white dress are carefully picked out. Coral red sleeves are pulled over the arms, the green bodice is separate from the padded blue apron; the three colours of the costume reappear on a strip of embroidery on the apron. The broad masses of colour and the bold 'S'-shaped design are counterbalanced by a number of exquisite changes in texture: it is one of Winterhalter's most accomplished genre paintings.

The work is not dated, but belongs stylistically to the group of peasant scenes which Winterhalter painted in Italy *c.*1833–4. By the mid-1850s, the painting was hanging in the closet of the Villa Berg, near Stuttgart, the Italianate country residence built for Crown Prince Karl of Württemburg and his wife, Olga. For a view of the closet showing the position of the picture, see the watercolour by A. Kappis, collection Graphische Sammlung Staatsgalerie, Stuttgart (repr. P. Thornton, *Authentic Decor*, 1984).

RLO
CBO

7

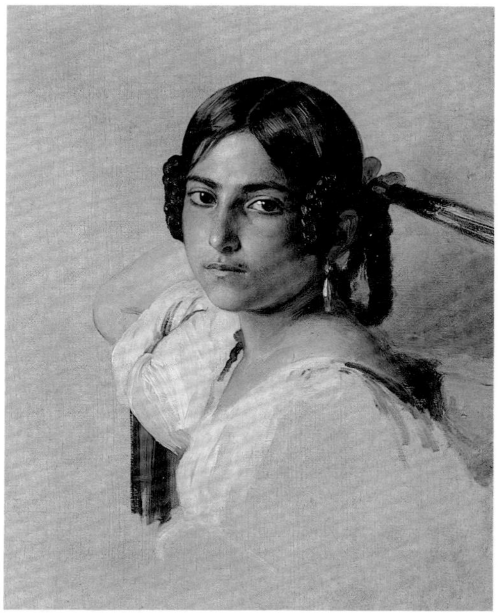

STUDY OF AN ITALIAN GIRL

57 × 46 cms
*Private Collection*

*Provenance*: The artist; his brother, Hermann; thence by family descent.
*Bibliography*: O.E. Sutter, 'Franz Xaver Winterhalter', *Daheim*, no. 25, 1936, p. 370, repr.
See colour plate p. 79.

This fresh and charming study of a model holding a fan behind her head belongs to the period of the artist's Italian genre scenes, *c.*1833–4 though it does not appear to relate to them directly. It is reproduced in the Winterhalter *Album*, the 1891 inventory of Hermann Winterhalter's estate (Winterhalter Family Papers), no. 17. Three or four similar studies are shown in the *Album*, one at least from the same model.

RLO

8

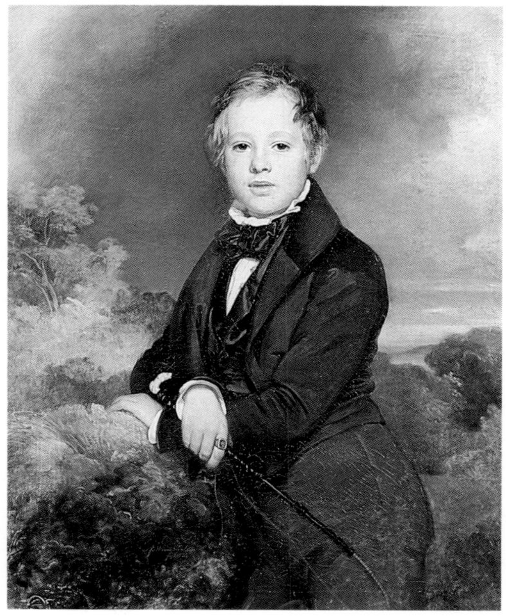

LUDWIG, GRAF VON LANGENSTEIN (1834)

*The Grand Duke Ludwig of Baden (1763–1830) was extremely fond of his mistress, the actress Katharina Werner. He gave her Schloss Langenstein near Baden-Baden, besides several other properties, contracted a morganatic marriage with her, and made her Countess of Langenstein. Their son, Ludwig, Count of Langenstein (1820–70), travelled extensively, never married and is buried in Langenstein.*

PM

96.3 × 79.5 cms
Signed and dated, bottom left: *fr. Winterhalter/ fecit 1834*
*Private Collection*

*Provenance*: By descent in the family.
*Bibliography*: Introduction, pp. 26, 29.
See colour plate p. 75.

The boy leans cross-legged against a rock and turns a full gaze upon the spectator. He wears a black satin waistcoat under a short, waisted black jacket with a high shawl collar, dark brown trousers and carries a riding crop in his right hand. The landscape is sketched in autumnal colours against a sky of massing grey clouds. Winterhalter has captured the youthful vitality of his subject with great aplomb. The boy's tousled hair, ruddy cheeks and parted lips combine to create an image of exceptional freshness and charm.

In 1832, Winterhalter painted the Count's mother, Katharina, Countess of Langenstein, as a buxom young woman in a white dress with puffed sleeves (Private Collection). It was not until his return from Italy, early in 1834, that Winterhalter painted her son, Count Ludwig. In an undated letter from Winterhalter to the Countess of Langenstein, the artist apologises for not having finished the portrait of her son (the letter was lost after the Second World War). A smaller half-length portrait of Katharina's daughter, Countess Louise, also dating from 1834, is in the same Collection.

CBO

9

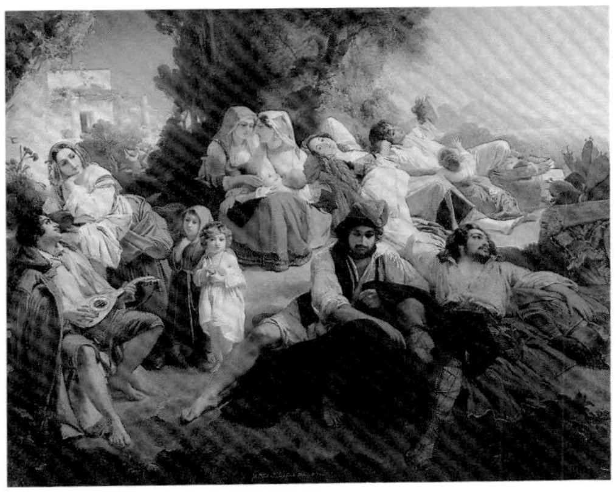

*IL DOLCE FARNIENTE* (1836)

160 × 200 cms
Signed, dated and inscribed, bottom centre:
*Fr. Winterhalter fecit Paris 1836*
*Private Collection*

*Provenance*: M. Asse by 1843; acquired in Paris by a Brussels collector, during the period 1864–74; by descent in the family; Artemis Group, London 1984.
*Exhibitions*: Paris, Salon, 1836, no. 1851.
*Reviews*: Roger de Beauvoir, 'Salon de 1836', *Revue de Paris*, 2$^{e}$ série 28, 1836, pp. 249–50; Alfred de Musset, 'Salon de 1836', in *Mélanges* from *Oeuvres Complètes*, p. 868; Victor de Nouvion, 'Salon de 1836', *La France Littéraire*, 1836, p. 310; 'Der Pariser Salon 1836', *Kunstblatt*, no. 49, 1836, pp. 206–7.
*Bibliography*: Wild, 1894, no. 496; H. Holland, *Allgemeine Deutsche Biographie*, 43, 1897, pp. 497–9; F. von Boetticher, *Malerwerke des 19 Jahrhunderts*, 2, Leipzig 1901, no. 5, p. 1026; A. Bürgin, 'Badische Bildnisse, Europas Hofmaler: F.X. Winterhalter', *Neustädte Zeitung*, no. 243, 21 October 1933; E.C. Conte Corti, 'Winterhalter, Ein deutsch-französischer Maler', *Velhagen und Klasings Monatshefte*, 53/2, 1938–9, pp. 129–140; Artemis Group Annual Report, 1984–5, p. 24, repr.; Introduction, pp. 29, 30, 36.
*Prints after*: Engravings by F. Girard, pub. Goupil and Vibert, 1843, and by Abel Lurat, pub. Goupil, 1863.
See colour plate p. 76.

This is the largest and most ambitious of the Neapolitan genre scenes inspired by Winterhalter's visit to Italy from 1833–4. Ostensibly a scene of the siesta hour during the grape-picking season, it is, in reality, a peasant version of the *fête champêtre*, in which the figures abandon themselves to the pleasures of the senses. The figures, in clumps of twos and threes, are grouped into a loose triangle, the rich tones of the men in the foreground leading back to the pale-complexioned women in the middle-ground, while the buildings and Vesuvius in the background shimmer still more whitely.

All the figures share a grave idealized beauty, whilst retaining an immediate human appeal: the children are lovable, the women attractive and sensual, the men refined and good-looking. A soulful young man on the left croons to the girl leaning thoughtfully beside the well; her beauty was particularly noted by many critics. The children link this pair to that of the mother feeding her baby, watched by a friend in the centre of the design. An odalisque with loosened hair, in the pose of a Niobe, reclines with her head propped on her hands, a pose echoed in that of the young man to her right playing with a child. The composition ends rather abruptly with the two men in the foreground, one gazing out intensely, the other gazing skywards. The relation between these two figures and those further back is an uneasy one. A great tree in the centre divides the view of a white terraced house, and hillside on the left, from the sweep of the Bay of Naples on the right. The dramatic use of light and brilliant colour intensifies the startling impact which the painting makes when first seen.

The picture must have been painted from a series of careful studies and with the aid of professional models. It is, in essence, an academic arrangement of individual studio poses. No precise drawings for it are known, but studies of comparable Neapolitan figures occur in sketches and sketch-books (see no. 7).

Engravings after two related pictures by Winterhalter show similar subjects. In one, dated 1838 (engraved by F. Girard, pub. Jeannin, Paris), nine figures are variously occupied in gathering grapes, conversing and dancing. In the other, dated 1836 (engraved by F. Girard, pub. Rittner & Goupil, Paris; exhibited 1837 Salon), a group of four women at a well listen to a young man singing. In all these pictures, labour is associated with music and pleasure, workers in harmony with their surroundings and occupations. The atmosphere is dreamy, sensuous and indolent.

*Il Dolce Farniente* was Winterhalter's first significant contribution to the Salon following his move to Paris, and the advent of this young German painter was greeted with enthusiasm. There was nothing original about Winterhalter's choice of a genre scene set against the Bay of Naples. What appealed to the French public was the use of the Classical formula, laced with northern introspection, and the brilliant virtuosity with which he carried it off. Winterhalter deliberately distanced himself from his German contemporaries in Italy too, and his work is more sheerly decorative by comparison. The reporter from *Kunstblatt*, sent to cover the 1836 Salon, noted approvingly: 'Eine sehr günstige Aufnahme fanden zwei Bilder unsers Landmanns Winterhalder';[1] he objected to 'ein zugelblicher Farbenton',[2] but praised 'einer reinen Zeichnung, einer zarten Behandlung und eines gefälligen, graziösen Ausdrucks.'[3] But a note of moralizing creeps into the German review: 'Da ist Italien . . . kurz mit dem ganzen Zubehör einer leiblichen und geistigen Kraft, welche das Farniente lähmt und erschlafft, wenn nicht Religion und Liebe sie aus dem gewöhnlichen Fahrgleise des Lebens herausreissen.'[4]

Several French critics, including Victor de Nouvion, likened the artist to the nineteenth-century French landscapist and genre painter, Léopold Robert: '. . . le faire et les types de Léopold Robert, avec plus d'abandon et de naturel.'[5] The poet and critic, Alfred de Musset, gave a rapturous description of the painting; 'Le *Far-Niente*, de M. Winterhalter, me plaît tellement, que je n'ose dire jusqu'à quel point.'[6] Another reviewer, Roger de Beauvoir, dwelt on the contrast between timeless southern indolence and modern haste; here, Winterhalter has evoked a Golden Age, and the painting is 'un véritable poème.'[7] In general, the reviews are interspersed with snatches of Italian folksongs, and critical standards are literary rather than properly aesthetic.

A second version of the picture, 130 × 163 cms, dated 1837, is in The Hermitage, Leningrad. It is probably identical with the *Festive Gathering of the Grape at Naples*, recorded in the dining-room of the Empress Alexandra Feodorovna at Novotsarskoeseloe Palace, 1856.

A watercolour copy, measuring 30.4 × 60.9 cms, by Hermann Winterhalter, is in a Private Collection.

RLO
CBO

1. 'Two pictures by our compatriot Winterhalder [*sic*] were very well received.'
2. '. . . rather too yellowish colouring.'
3. '. . . fine qualities of clean drawing, sensitive treatment and a pleasing and graceful expressiveness.'
4. 'Here is Italy . . . with all the appurtenances, in short, of a physical and spiritual strength, which becomes languid and paralysed by *farniente* unless it is torn out of the even tenor of day-to-day life by religion and love.'
5. '. . . the style and the characters of Léopold Robert, but with added freedom and simplicity.'
6. 'I hardly dare say how greatly I like M. Winterhalter's *Far-Niente*.'
7. '. . . a veritable poem.'

## 10

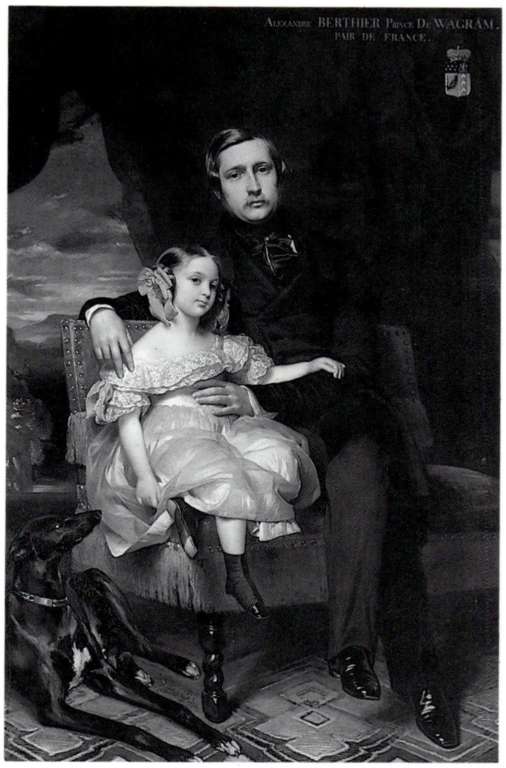

NAPOLEON-ALEXANDRE-LOUIS-JOSEPH BERTHIER, PRINCE DE WAGRAM AND HIS DAUGHTER MALCY-LOUISE-CAROLINE-FRÉDÉRIQUE (1837)

*The Prince de Wagram (1810–87) was the son of Napoleon's indispensable Chief of Staff, Marshal Berthier, created Prince de Wagram in recognition of his contribution to the Emperor's victory over Austria at Wagram in 1809. The second Prince devoted himself to his magnificent estate at Grosbois, south-east of Paris, and to hunting and racing: he was not an active Bonapartist. His daughter (1832–84) married a first cousin of Napoleon III, Prince Joachim-Napoleon Murat, in 1854, two years after the proclamation of the Second Empire.*
PM

186 × 138 cms
Signed, dated and inscribed, bottom left:
*fr. Winterhalter*
*Paris/1837*
*Private Collection*

*Provenance*: Prince de Wagram; Prince de La Tour d'Auvergne Lauraguais.
*Exhibitions*: Paris, Salon, 1838, no. 1798.
*Reviews*: F. Mercey, 'Salon de 1838', *La Revue des Deux Mondes*, 1838, p. 393; G. Planche, 'Salon de 1838', *Etudes Sur l'Ecole Française*, 1831–52, pp. 123–4; V. Schoelcher, 'Salon de 1838', *La Phalange*, 1838, p. 140; T. Thoré, 'Salon de 1838', *Revue de Paris*, 1838, p. 271.
*Bibliography*: Wild, 1894, no. 17; H. Holland, *Allgemeine Deutsche Biographie*, 43, 1897, pp. 497–9; Introduction, p. 31.
See colour plate p. 80.

The Prince de Wagram is seated with his daughter, Malcy-Louise-Caroline-Frédérique (see no. 51) on a Louis XIII–style double seat. He wears a black double-breasted frock coat and black trousers with an instep strap under his shoe. His black silk cravat is held with a pearl pin. The girl wears a white silk and muslin frock, the bodice trimmed with lace, with crimson velvet bows at the sleeves and in her hair. With one leg tucked under her, she lays a trusting hand on her father's sleeve. A greyhound looks up from the left, a symbol of fidelity and an allusion to family devotion.

The painting marked a turning point in Winterhalter's career in France. Hitherto, he had been celebrated for his genre work. At the 1838 Salon, Winterhalter showed three paintings, two of which were portraits: one of an anonymous lady (*Mme D. d'A*, probably Dubois d'Angers), the other of the Prince de Wagram. Henceforth, Winterhalter's professional competence as a portrait painter was recognized. He could treat a life-size subject, and handle realism or affecting charm with equal success. The King took note, and at the Salon the following year Winterhalter showed four Orléans portraits, all 'commandes ordonées par le Roi', which included one of Louis-Philippe himself (no. 17).

At the 1837 Salon the reviews were, on the whole, favourable. T. Thoré may have been mildly sarcastic: 'Jusqu'ici personne n'avait accomodé un drap si luisant et des souliers si bien vernis. Il était réservé à M. Winterhalter, avec son portrait du Prince de Wagram, de vaincre M. Dubufe.'[1] (*Revue de Paris*.) G. Planche criticized certain parts, but ended in qualified approval:

> *'Le portrait de M. le prince de Wagram ne manque pas de réalité. La tête de l'enfant placé sur le genou [sic] du prince se recommande par sa fraîcheur; mais le buste de la figure principale est plein de roideur, et donne à la toilette entière un caractère d'immobilité. Cependant cet ouvrage mérite de grands éloges, et si M. Winterhalter exécute seulement une douzaine de portraits tels que celui du prince de Wagram, il ne peut manquer d'acquérir bientôt les qualités destinées à compléter son talent.'[2]*

V. Schoelcher, on the other hand, dwelt on the picture at length and was broadly enthusiastic:

> *'Le portrait de M. de Wagram avec sa fille par M. Winterhalter, est bien entendu; c'est un tableau, et non pas seulement une ressemblance. Les accessoires se justifient avec la position des personnages; l'harmonie du sujet et des détails, trop souvent négligés dans les portraits modernes . . . sans doute la peinture est trop brillantée, trop privée de repos; elle manque de corps, et a un peu l'aspect d'un métal verni; mais elle est colorée, elle a de l'élégance, de la distinction, et, sous le rapport du dessin, on ne trouve guère à reprendre que la jambe de l'enfant, qui est trop forte.'[3]*

In 1838, Winterhalter painted a pendant to the portrait of the Prince (Private Collection, France). Format and furnishings are similar, and the composition, showing the Princesse de Wagram with her son, somewhat symmetrical with no. 10.
CBO

1 'Until now, nobody had rendered such shining cloth and such highly polished shoes. It was left to M. Winterhalter, with his portrait of the Prince de Wagram, to outshine M. Dubufe.'
2. 'The portrait of the Prince de Wagram does not lack realism. The child's head, laid on the Prince's knee, is particularly appealing in its freshness, but the main figure's chest is very stiff, and lends an element of immobility to the attire as a whole. The work does, however, merit great praise, and if M. Winterhalter produces a mere dozen portraits such as that of the Prince of Wagram, he cannot help but soon acquire the qualities needed to perfect his talent.'
3. 'The portrait of M. de Wagram with his daughter, by M. Winterhalter, is well-executed; it is a painting, not just a likeness. The details are justified by the positioning of the figures: harmony of subject with detail, a matter all too often neglected in modern portraits. . . . Certainly the painting is too glossy, too tiring to the eye, it lacks depth, and slightly gives the impression of a varnished metal; but it is colourful, it has elegance, and distinction, and, as far as the drawing is concerned, the only thing that could be at all criticized is the child's leg, which is too large.'

## 11

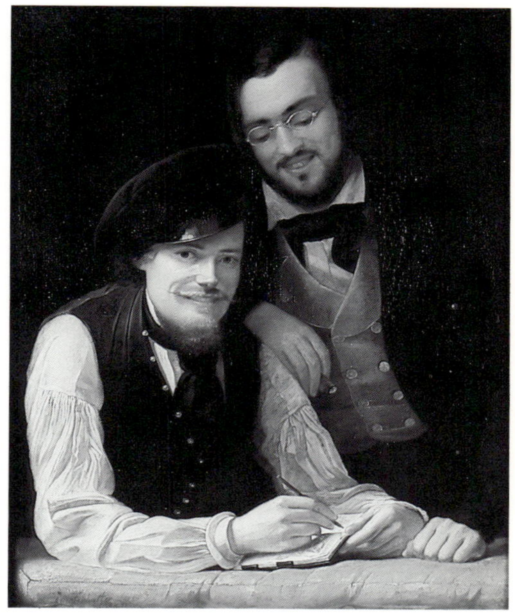

SELF-PORTRAIT OF THE ARTIST WITH HIS BROTHER HERMANN (1840)*

84.5 × 71.5 cms
Signed, dated and inscribed, bottom left:
*F. Winterhalter./Paris 1840*
*Staatliche Kunsthalle Karlsruhe*

*Provenance*: On German art market, *c.*1927; collection Henri de Marguerie-Bourdariat, 1928; acquired by Staatliche Kunsthalle Karlsruhe, 1960, inv. no. 2461.
*Exhibitions*: Paris, 1928, no. 23; Karlsruhe, 1965, no. 61; Menzenschwand, 1973, no. 1.
*Reviews*: Armand Dayot, *L'Art et les Artistes*, no. 87, May 1928, p. 263, repr.
*Bibliography*: E. Waldmann, *Die Kunst des Realismus und des Impressionismus im 19. Jahrhundert*, Propyläen-Kunstgeschichte, 15, 1927, p. 75, p. 229, repr.; F. Neugass, *Oberrheinische Kunst*, 3, 1928, p. 179; E.C. Conti Corte, 'Winterhalter, Ein deutsch-französischer Maler', *Velhagen und Klasings Monatshefte* 53/2, 1938–9, p. 138, repr.; L. Bruhns, *Deutsche Künstler in Selbstdarstellungen*, (*Blaue Bücher*), Königstein, Leipzig 1943, p. 83, repr.; A. von Schneider, *Thieme-Becker*, 36, 1947, p. 88; E. Baader, *Badischer Heimat*, 3, 1960, p. 371, repr.; *Deutsche Meister 1800–1850 aus der Staatlichen Kunsthalle Karlsruhe*, Karlsruhe 1964, no. 44, repr.; J. Lauts, *Jahrbuch I*, 1964, p. 23, note 22; C. Helmholt, *Frankfurter Allgemeine Zeitung*, 7 July 1973, p. 31, repr.; Introduction, p. 42.
See colour plate p. 81.

Winterhalter is seated with his sketch-book, smiling directly at the spectator. His younger brother Hermann, also a painter, leans easily against him, smiling. The artist wears a blue peaked student cap, dark blue waistcoat and a white shirt with pleated sleeves set in low to the arm. Light falls sharply from the left illuminating the sensitive study of the brothers' hands, which rest on a strawberry-coloured cushion. Hermann stands in the shadow cast by his brother, and his grey double-breasted waistcoat and dark frock coat merge into the background. The cigar in his right hand does not dispel the scholarly, introspective impression conveyed by his spectacles and downcast eyes. The portrait plays with the possibility that the artist may not be sketching his own reflection, but taking the viewer's. The composition is admirably compact, and the figures interlock like jigsaw pieces.

Winterhalter sent for his brother to join him in Paris in 1840, and this double portrait is probably a private exercise to mark their reunion. Franz must have been confident of enough work for two, and needed Hermann's help with commissions for the Musée du Roi. Hermann Winterhalter was a talented genre painter, portrait painter and Salon exhibitor in his own right. He collaborated closely with his brother, executing details of costume and props, and helping with the production of copies.

There are self-portrait drawings of Winterhalter aged about twelve or thirteen (Private Collection), and as a dapper young man about court in Karlsruhe, *c.*1831 (see Introduction, fig. 10). The work which most closely resembles the painting as a composition is a double self-portrait drawing of self-conscious urbanity, *c.*1841 (see Introduction, fig. 30). An early self-portrait in oils belonging to the family descendants was destroyed by fire; a later self-portrait of *c.*1868 was commissioned for the famous series of artist's self-portraits in the Uffizi Gallery, Florence; copies of this are in the Kunsthalle Karlsruhe, two Private Collections, and elsewhere. The fresh candour of the 1840 double portrait sets it outside the mainstream of Winterhalter's production; it also gives us a glimpse, on canvas, of the professional and emotional bond between the brothers.

There are portraits of Winterhalter by Count d'Orsay (drawing, 1843 or 1845, Private Collection) and Prince Albert (Her Majesty The Queen, Osborne), as well as photographs by Dr Becker, 1854 (Royal Photographic Collection, Royal Library, Windsor Castle, see Introduction, fig. 31), L. Caldesi (carte de visite, National Portrait Gallery), and Jabez Hughes (Royal Photographic Collection, Royal Library, Windsor Castle).

CBO

## 12

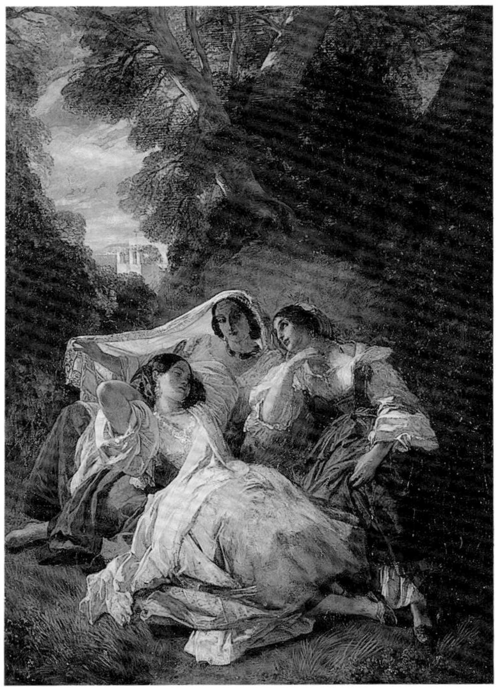

*LA SIESTA* (1841)

55.9 × 43.2 cms
Signed, dated and inscribed, bottom centre:
*fr. Winterhalter Paris 1841*
*Private Collection*

*Provenance*: Queen Victoria; Duke of Connaught, after 1876; Lady (Victoria) Patricia Ramsay.
*Exhibitions*: London, 1977, no. 5.
*Bibliography*: A. I. Durrant, *Catalogue of the Paintings, Sculpture and other Works of Art at Osborne, 1876*, n.d., no. 188, p. 12.
*Prints after*: Engravings by H. Cousins, pub. E. Gambart, 1848; H. Louis, pub. Goupil and Vibert; H. Jazet, pub. Goupil, 1860.
See colour plate p. 82.

In this fancy picture, three young women (referred to as 'trois femmes napolitaines' in the 1876 *Catalogue*) are resting in the shade from the brilliant Mediterranean sun. At the centre, one of them holds out her veil as an awning over the second one, asleep against her, with her head nestled in her arms; the girl on the right leans over to complete the triangular composition. Forked tree-trunks provide a corresponding triangle overhead, while on the left we are given a glimpse of the sea and a sunlit pergola – the stock-in-trade of Winterhalter's earlier Italian genre pieces.

Winterhalter's last important Italian genre scene was *The Decameron*, painted *c.*1837 (see Introduction, fig. 16); after that he appears to have been too busy with Royal portrait commissions to do much else. The intervening seven years in Paris made a considerable impression on his style. The paint work is much looser, the figures less sculptural and the scale quite intimate, when compared to his Italian scenes of the 1830s. The principal new influence is likely to have been Delacroix, who was exhibiting Orientalist scenes at the time, however different in intention.

Queen Victoria bought the picture from Winterhalter for £200 in 1841 and had it hung in her dressing-room at Osborne, where it remained until at least 1876, before being given to Arthur, Duke of Connaught, possibly as a wedding present in 1879. The wooden cross-bar of no. 12 is stamped: *Osborne Inventory 1873 no. 188/VR/Queen's personal property.* On 22 December 1841, she wrote in her Journal: 'To-day I got from Paris a beautiful picture by Winterhalter which I had ordered. It is quite small, representing a "Siesta", three lovely Italian girls, with one of them asleep.' This is the earliest reference in the Journal to the acquisition of a Winterhalter by the Queen; it is also an instance of the Queen's predilection for this type of fancy picture, which was to be more amply satisfied by the acquisition of *Florinda* (no. 38), eleven years later.

CBO

## 13

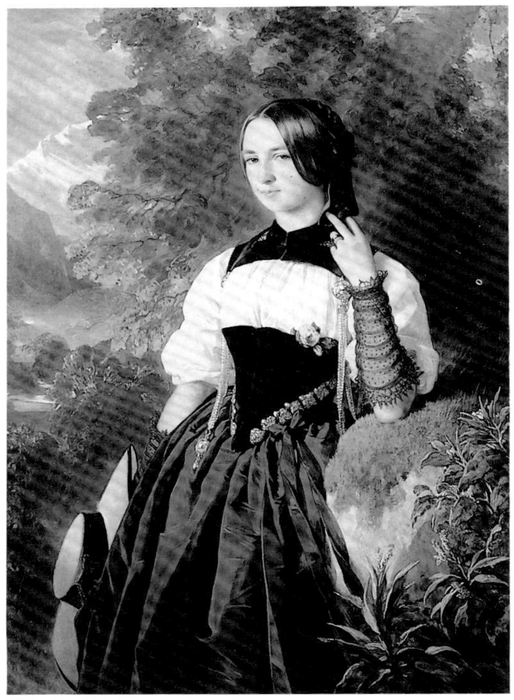

A SWISS GIRL FROM INTERLAKEN (*LA BERNOISE*)

126 × 93 cms
*Private Collection*

*Provenance*: The artist; his brother, Hermann; thence by family descent.
*Bibliography*: Wild, 1894, p. 53.
See colour plate p. 83.

The Swiss girl is wearing the traditional regional costume of the Canton of Berne: a black velvet over-bodice held together with jewelled straps, and with a decorated, pointed waist, worn over a white chemise, a dark silk skirt with ribbons at the waist and black net mittens. She stands beside a bank, holding a straw hat in one hand and raising one hand to her head. Behind her rises a snow-covered ridge of the high Alps. Dating from the 1840s, the picture continues the theme of Winterhalter's Italian genre scenes, though the model here is an incarnation of the spirit of the mountains, rather than of the soft and luxurious south. The identity of this beautiful model is not known, but family tradition links her with the daughter of a banker in Berne, to whom the artist is said to have been engaged. The portrait is reproduced in the Winterhalter *Album*, 1891, no. 51 (see no. 7).

RLO

14

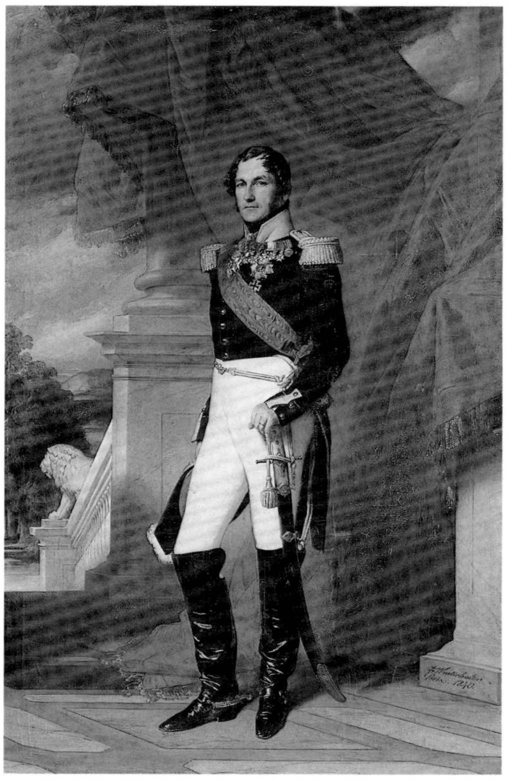

LEOPOLD I, KING OF THE BELGIANS (1840)†

*Leopold I (1790–1865), the younger son of the Duke of Saxe-Gotha and uncle of Queen Victoria, had a spectacular career, helped by his excellent judgement and startling good looks: Napoleon remembered him as 'the handsomest young man I saw in the Tuileries'. He married the Prince Regent's daughter, Princess Charlotte, heir to the throne of the United Kingdom, in 1816. After a few months of happiness, she died in childbirth. To the annoyance of his father-in-law, who called him 'le Marquis peu à peu', Leopold continued to live in England. Having refused the throne of Greece, he consented to become King of the Belgians after their revolt against the Netherlands in 1830. Despite innumerable obstacles, including the hostility of much of the aristocracy, he founded a monarchy which remained stable even during the year of revolutions in 1848. He gave advice to Queen Victoria and refuge to Prince Metternich. By his second wife, Louise, the eldest daughter of King Louis-Philippe, he was father of Leopold II (no. 16) and the Empress Charlotte of Mexico (no. 15).*

PM

27 × 181 cms
Signed, dated and inscribed, lower right:
*fr Winterhalter/Paris. 1840*
*Musée national du château de Versailles*

*Provenance*: Commissioned by Louis-Philippe for the Musée du Roi; inv. MV 6510.
*Bibliography*: Wild, 1894, p. 37, no. 60; Introduction, p. 31.
*Prints after*: Engraved by Léon Noël, 1844, and G. Levy.
See colour plate p. 85.

King Leopold is depicted whole-length, looking to the left, wearing the full dress uniform of a Belgian general in mounted order. The decorations on his dark blue coat include the Grand Cross of the Order of Leopold I with the crimson sash, the insignia of the Légion d'Honneur and the Iron Cross of Prussia. The King's left hand rests on the hilt of a heavy cavalry sabre, carried by a gold and red Morocco sword-belt with a double sling. He stands on a terrace against a swagged red curtain, the impression of grandeur accentuated by the steep perspective of the balustrade and the column behind.

Winterhalter first painted King Leopold in Paris in 1839, a half-length, *en habit bourgeois* (Wild, no. 36) (Belgian Royal Collections, Argenteuil). Earlier, in 1838, he had painted the Queen of the Belgians (who was also Louis-Philippe's daughter) and her son (Her Majesty The Queen). It was presumably Queen Louise-Marie's recommendation, together with Winterhalter's Salon success, which prompted Louis-Philippe to use Winterhalter for the portraits for the Musée du Roi. In any event, no. 14 was commissioned by Louis-Philippe a year after his own state portrait in 1839 (no. 17). A sketch for the composition survives which the finished portrait closely follows (oil on panel, 39.5 × 33.5 cms, Private Collection, Belgium). As well as the 1839 and 1840 portraits of King Leopold, Winterhalter painted an important whole-length of the King wearing the Order of the Garter in 1846 (Her Majesty The Queen; various versions and copies in Belgium).

Versions of the 1840 portrait *en cuirassier* are at the Château de Beloeil, Belgium, signed and dated 1843, and the Hôtel de Ville, Brussels. There are two copies after the Winterhalter at the Palais de Bruxelles, one by J. Geirnaert. A threequarter-length version of no. 14 (signed and dated 1841, and inscribed *Paris*) belongs to Her Majesty The Queen; another shortened version is at Schloss Ehrenburg, Coburg.

Winterhalter included a reference to the portrait of King Leopold in his list of Orléans commissions: 'Portrait en pied du Roi des Belges pour Versailles – 1500 fr.' (Winterhalter Family Papers.) In 1840, in recognition of his merit, the artist was awarded the Cross of the Commander of the Order of King Leopold.

CBO

# 15

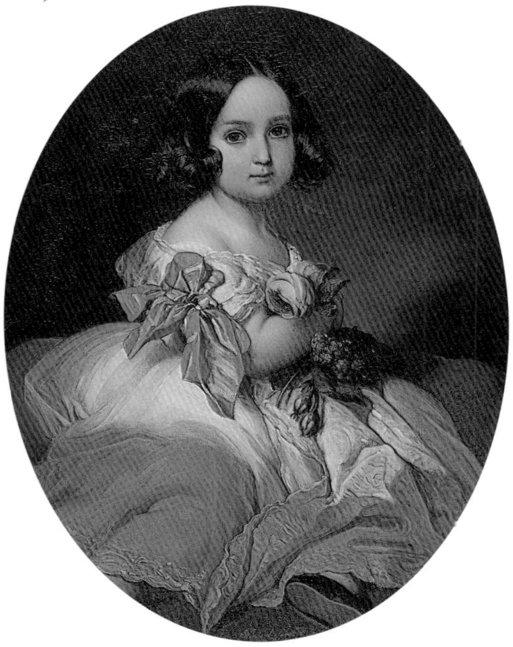

PRINCESS CHARLOTTE OF BELGIUM (1842)

*Called* la beauté de la famille *by her father Leopold I, who adored her, Princess Charlotte (1840–1927) married the Archduke Maximilian of Austria, younger brother of Franz Joseph, in 1857. Clever, energetic and proud, she did her best to help her husband when he was Viceroy of Lombardy-Venetia, 1857–9, and Emperor of Mexico, 1864–67. As his position in Mexico grew weaker, she returned to Europe to persuade France and Austria to send help, but her failure drove her insane. She spent her last years in the Château de Bouchout in Belgium, where she died in 1927, sixty years after her husband was shot in Mexico.*
PM

72 × 58.4 cms, oval
Signed and dated, bottom centre: *F Winterhalter 1842.* On the back of the original canvas was an inscription giving the names of artist and sitter and the date, 1842.
*Her Majesty The Queen*

*Provenance*: Given to Queen Victoria by the Queen of the Belgians at Christmas, 1842; placed in the Queen's Sitting-Room at Buckingham Palace.
*Bibliography*: Wild, 1894, no. 72; Introduction, p. 36; Millar, *Victorian Pictures*.
See colour plate p. 86.

Princess Charlotte is depicted full-length, seated on a red cushion in a white frock with pale blue ribbons, holding hyacinths and roses in her arms.

On 22 December 1842, the Queen of the Belgians wrote to Queen Victoria:

> 'Your great kindness *for us and Charlotte and your amiable wish so often expressed to have her picture by Winterhalter lithographed led me to believe, the picture itself might be agreable to you. Your Uncle is not quite satisfied with it, but I must confess, I think the head* very like *and quite in the character of the Child. The Drawing of the figure is not good, but unfortunately Drawing is not the strong part of Winterhalter.*' (WRA)

On 13 March 1843, Queen Victoria wrote to the Queen of the French that she was charmed with the portrait of Princess Charlotte that '*ma bonne Louise*' had sent to her (ibid.).

A version is at Versailles (MV 5104), and another, signed and dated 1842, in the Belgian Royal Collections (at Argenteuil).
OM

# 16

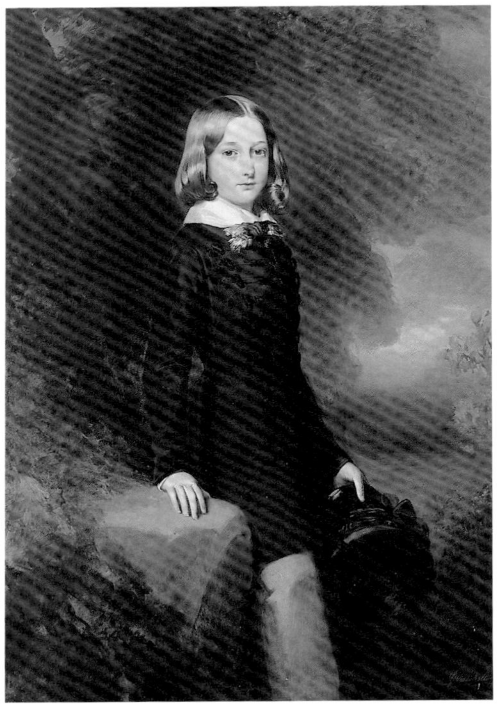

LEOPOLD, DUKE OF BRABANT

*Leopold I of the Belgians wrote to Queen Victoria, 28 December 1838, of his son and heir at the age of three: 'he is very original and very sly. I often call him the little tyrant because nobody knows so well how to* faire aller le monde'. (The Letters of Queen Victoria, *eds. A.C. Benson and Viscount Esher, 3 vols., 1908, vol. 1, p. 140.) Leopold (1835–1909) became King of the Belgians in 1865 and Sovereign of the Congo in 1885.*
PM

142 × 101 cms
Signed, lower right: *F Winterhalter*
*Collections royales, Château de Laeken, Belgium.*

*Provenance*: King Leopold I, listed in inventories of 1864 and 1869; King Leopold II, listed in 1898 inventory; sold France 1908; 1950 restored to Prince Baudouin by Mrs Laurent Meeus, according to whom it had previously been in the collection of Baroness Vaughan.
*Bibliography*: Wild, 1894, no. 101 (date given as 1843).
See colour plate p. 87.

The Duke is shown against a landscape background, his right hand resting on a rock. His black coat, and the tasselled black cap he holds, give him a fashionably military air, and around his open white collar he wears a loosely knotted tartan cravat.

The Duke of Brabant had already been painted by Winterhalter with his mother, Queen Louise-Marie, in 1838 (Her Majesty The Queen). This portrait was painted as a pendant to two other portraits of the Belgian Royal children, Philippe, Count of Flanders and Princess Charlotte, commissioned from Winterhalter by King Leopold I, which were to be begun on 15 July 1844 (WRA). All three portraits have similar dimensions and have evidently always been hung together. A copy made for Leopold II is at Château d'Argenteuil; head and shoulders replicas of the portraits of both the Duke and his brother were sent to Queen Victoria and are dated 1844 on the reverse (Her Majesty The Queen).
SF

17

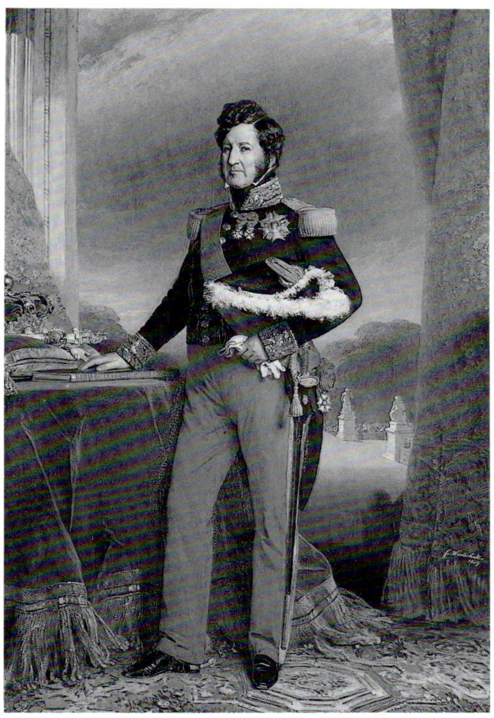

KING LOUIS-PHILIPPE (1839)

*Louis-Philippe (1773–1850) was one of the most intelligent monarchs of his day. He had experience of poverty and exile as well as power and palaces. After he ascended the throne in 1830 at the age of fifty-seven, he lived so simply that he was known as* 'le roi citoyen'. *Throughout his reign, he exercised immense influence over the choice of ministers and the conduct of policy. His peaceful foreign policy and cooperation with the conservative powers of Europe were reasons for his loss of popularity.*
(See no. 24)
PM

260 × 190 cms
Signed and dated, lower right (on curtain):
*fr Winterhalter./1839*
*Musée national du château de Versailles*

*Provenance*: Commissioned by Louis-Philippe for the Maison du Roi, 1839; State Collection, Versailles, inv. no. MV 5219.
*Exhibitions*: Paris, Salon, 1839, no. 2126; Paris, Archives Nationales, 'Louis-Philippe, l'homme et le roi', 1974, no. 321.
*Reviews*: A. Decamps, 'Beaux-Arts. Salon de 1839', *Le National*, 13 May 1839; A. Barbier, *Salon de 1839*, 1839, pp. 125–6; J.A. Dréolle, *Journal de l'Institut Historique*, 1839, pp. 151–2; Laurent-Jan, *Salon de 1839*, 1839, p. 19; Prosper Mérimée, *La Revue des Deux Mondes*, 1839, pp. 224–5; E. Souvestre, *Revue de Paris*, 1839, p. 47.
*Bibliography*: Wild, 1894, no. 46; H. Holland, *Allgemeine Deutsche Biographie*, 43, 1897, pp. 497–9; A. Dayot, 'A propos de Winterhalter', *L'Art et les Artistes*, no. 87, May 1928, p. 256; Introduction, p. 33.
*Prints after*: Engraving by A. Bridoux; lithograph by Léon Noël, 1845.
See colour plate p. 89.

The King is shown in the uniform of a lieutenant-general: a black coatee, decorated on the collar and cuffs with a double row of gold oak-leaf lace and heavy bullion epaulettes bearing three silver stars on a crescent; deep scarlet pantaloons with double gold lace stripe; black boots with gilt brass box spurs; short sword (*épée*) with gold hilt, tassel and scabbard ornaments; white and gold sash round the waist; scarlet sash of the Légion d'Honneur over right shoulder; black felt cocked hat with tricolour cockade, gold loops and ostrich feathers; white gloves. The orders are the insignia of the Légion d'Honneur and the Order of Leopold I of Belgium. Louis-Philippe's right hand rests on the *Charte de 1830*, the constitutional compact between King and people underlying the settlement of 1830. Displayed beyond, on a tasselled cushion, are the crown, sceptre and hand of Justice.

The figure of the King is framed by a richly draped table, a strongly patterned carpet and a heavy curtain with floral motifs on the right. These luxurious interior accessories are thrown into relief by the outdoor vista which dramatically opens up behind. The upper part of the King's figure is silhouetted against the sky, as if to emphasize the high and lonely sphere he occupies. Below, bathed in warm sunshine, is a view of the park at St Cloud, with flower-beds, trees and two life-size statues.

Two earlier whole-length portraits of Louis-Philippe at Versailles, by Horace Vernet, 1832 (MV 5222), and Baron Gérard, 1834 (MV 5210), also show him with the *Charte*. Bombastic and flamboyant, they belong to a tradition of Royal iconography already passing out of fashion. Winterhalter's solidly composed and level-headed portrayal struck a new and convincing note. The King's pear-shaped head and lined features were all too familiar to the French public, through the medium of caricature. Winterhalter invests the figure of the King with dignified self-importance, while at the same time providing an index to his perplexed, wary and watchful personality.

The King himself was clearly delighted. The portrait became the basis for numerous copies by other artists which were widely distributed. Documents relating to these commissions can be found in the Archives du Louvre. Winterhalter's fee for the commission, 'Portrait en pied du Roi pour Versailles – 12,000 frs' is recorded in two manuscript lists of French Royal portraits (Winterhalter Family Papers). In 1842, the King presented Queen Victoria with a miniature after the 1839 state portrait by François Meuret (Royal Library, Windsor Castle). Other versions of the Meuret miniature are in the Wallace Collection, London (M 280), and Sotheby's, 9 June 1986, lot 87.

In 1841, Winterhalter painted a second portrait of Louis-Philippe, using the same face pattern, but showing him differently dressed, standing before a view of the Galerie des Batailles at Versailles (Musée du Louvre, inv. no. RF 1975.26). This formerly belonged to the Czartoryski family. In 1845, Louis-Philippe sat again, in Garter Costume, for a whole-length portrait commissioned by Queen Victoria (Her Majesty The Queen). A second version of this new type is at Versailles (MV 5211).

The 1839 portrait was one of four portraits of the Orléans family exhibited at the 1839 Salon. Opinion among the critics was divided. One camp remained ardent admirers of Winterhalter's virtuosity, while the other could not forgive him for abandoning genre painting. A. Decamps declared in *Le National*: 'Jamais la figure du modèle [Louis-Philippe] n'avait été peinte avec tant de caractère et de vérité . . . c'est véritablement un portrait historique.'[1] For A. Barbier, an establishment man: 'Il y a du sens et du bon goût, par le temps qui court, à presenter la royauté sous cet aspect si noble et si simple . . . .'[2] (*Salon de 1839*.) Whereas J.A. Dréolle, writing in *Journal de l'Institut Historique*, dismissed the four portraits altogether: 'M. Winterhalter n'a fait que des portraits cette année. Oh! pourquoi n'a-t-il pas continué à nous bercer dans ses délicieuses villes italiennes?'[3] And E. Souvestre, in *Revue de Paris*, warns: 'M. Winterhalter est précisément sur le bord de ce précipice doré au fond duquel M. Dubuffe a dressé son chevalet. Qu'il y prenne garde.'[4]
RLO

1. 'Never before had the model's face been depicted with such character and accuracy; . . . it is indeed a historic portrait.'
2. 'It is sensible and in good taste, nowadays, to portray Royalty in this noble and yet unpretentious light.'
3. 'M. Winterhalter has done nothing but portraits this year. Oh! why has he not continued to pamper us with his exquisite Italian towns?'
4. 'M. Winterhalter is right on the edge of that golden abyss at the bottom of which M. Dubuffe has set up his easel. May he beware.'

18

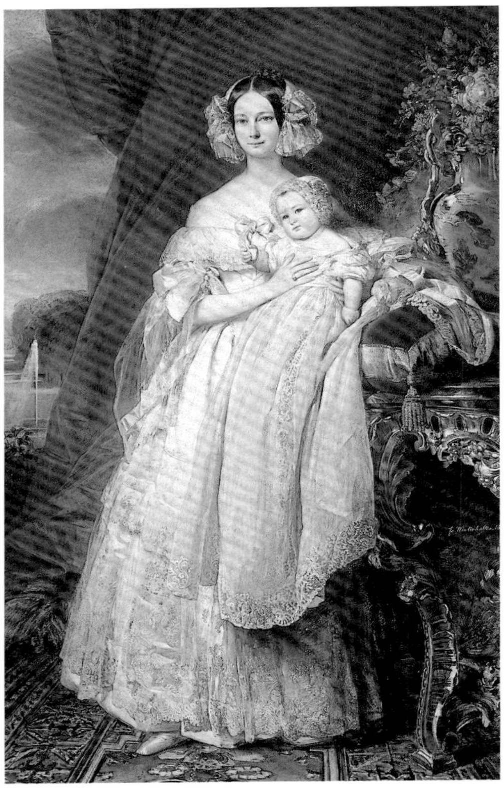

HÉLÈNE-LOUISE-ELIZABETH DE MECKLEMBOURG-SCHWERIN, DUCHESSE D'ORLÉANS WITH PRINCE LOUIS-PHILIPPE-ALBERT D'ORLÉANS, COMTE DE PARIS (1839)

*Intelligent and Protestant, Princesse Hélène of Mecklembourg-Schwerin (1814–58) married the Duc d'Orléans, eldest son of King Louis-Philippe, in 1837. This picture commemorates the birth, a year later, of their son, who was given the title of Comte de Paris (1838–94). After her husband's death, the Duchesse d'Orléans upheld his liberal principles within the family circle. On 24 February 1848, with extraordinary courage, she took the Comte de Paris and her second son, the Duc de Chartres, to assert her son's right to the throne in the Chamber of Deputies. She was forced to leave by an armed crowd yelling 'Deposition!' Thereafter she lived in Germany, with occasional visits to the rest of the family in England, until her death in 1858.*
(See no. 24)
PM

215 × 140 cms
Signed and dated, to right: *fr. Winterhalter. 1839.*
*Musée national du château de Versailles*

*Provenance*: Commissioned by Louis-Philippe for the Maison du Roi, 1839; State Collection, Versailles, inv. no. MV 5201.
*Exhibitions*: Paris, Salon, 1839, no. 2127; Paris, Maison Victor Hugo, 'Maturité de V. Hugo', 1953; Chicago, Toledo, Los Angeles, San Francisco, 'Treasures of Versailles', 1962, no. 102; Paris, Archives Nationales, 'Louis-Philippe. l'homme et le roi', 1974, no. 444 (repr. p. 107).
*Reviews*: A. Decamps, 'Beaux-Arts. Salon de 1839', *Le National*, 13 May 1839; A. Barbier, *Salon de 1839*, 1839, pp. 125–7; J.A. Dréolle, *Journal de l'Institut Historique*, 1839, pp. 151–2; Laurent-Jan, *Salon de 1839*, 1839, p. 19; Prosper Mérimée, *La Revue des Deux Mondes*, 1839, p. 225; E. Souvestre, *Revue de Paris*, 1839, p. 47; Charles Blanc, *Revue du Progrès*, 1839, p. 477.
*Bibliography*: Wild, 1894, no. 31; C. de Ris, *Catalogue de Versailles*, 1881, no. 4995; *Connoisseur*, 31, 1911, p. 137, repr.; *Souvenirs de la Princesse de Ligne*, 1923; Introduction, p. 33.
See colour plate p. 90.

This is the first in the series of whole-length portraits of his daughters-in-law ordered by the King. The slight figure and doll-like features of the young Duchesse are set off by a dazzling cream satin gown trimmed with Brussels lace, which is a triumph of subtle textural effects. Her smooth hair, drawn into a coil at the back, is framed by a matching head-dress of lace with blue ribbons. The young Comte de Paris, in white christening robes and a cap, is propped on a red and gold tasselled cushion.

The Duchesse gently holds him while he plays with a bow in her corsage. Dynastic considerations determined the display of the heir, and the Duchesse exhibits little of the maternal feeling so strongly expressed in the later portrait of the Empress Eugénie holding the Prince Imperial (see no. 58). The bell-shaped figures of mother and son are contrasted with sumptuous accessories: an ornate gilt console table of Rococo design; a ceramic vase with ormulu mounts of similar period, with a bouquet of flowers spilling out of it; a rich patterned carpet and a heavy damask curtain swagged back to reveal a distant view of the park of St Cloud, punctuated by a single jet of water from a fountain. The composition, and the type of accessories used, have their source in eighteenth-century Royal portraiture; the portrait of Marie Leczinska, Louis XV's Queen by Carle van Loo (Musée du Louvre, Paris) offers a typical example. What Winterhalter contributes to this tradition is naturalism conveyed through the sensual treatment of materials, and the subtle evocation of atmosphere. However grand his female models may be, Winterhalter always manages to endow them with Romantic tenderness and fragrance.

The Duchesse d'Orléans appears almost overawed by the opulence of the surroundings which enclose her. She was a retiring personality, 'pas jolie mais très agréable' ('not pretty but very pleasant'), in the words of the Princesse de Ligne: 'Belle tournure, mais Allemande' ('a fine figure, but German') (*Souvenirs*).

Two manuscript lists of French Royal portraits painted by Winterhalter (Winterhalter Family Papers) record a 'portrait en buste' of the Duchesse and her son (3000 frs), a separate portrait of the Duchesse 'en buste' (1200 frs), and a copy of the whole-length (3000 frs), but not the original. A copy of the double portrait belongs to the Fondation St Louis at Amboise, and another is at Fontainebleau (MV 5224). In 1842, Winterhalter painted a portrait of the Comte de Paris with a view of Notre Dame behind (Private Collection). The portrait of the Duchesse and her son was one of four Royal commissions exhibited at the Salon of 1839. Reviewers were not, in general, impressed by the brilliant display of effects: 'Il a déployé un tel luxe d'étoffes et de mobilier que la figure est ce qu'on voit le moins.'[1] (*Revue du Progrès*.) A. Decamps, more provocative in *Le National*, judges the portrait not bad, though at first glance it looks like a midwife's shop-sign ('une enseigne de sage femme'). However there remained a few critics who shared the views of the female section of the public. A. Barbier, for example, in his *Salon de 1839* writes: 'C'est dans toutes ses parties une admirable peinture, et qui jouit auprès des dames d'une faveur toute particulière, à cause d'un certain point d'Angleterre qui les éblouit et les enchante.'[2]
RLO

1. 'He put forth such a wealth of materials and furniture as to make the face the thing one saw least of all.'
2. 'It is in every way an admirable painting, and one which has become a special favorite with the ladies, owing to a certain type of Brussels lace which dazzles and enchants them.'

19

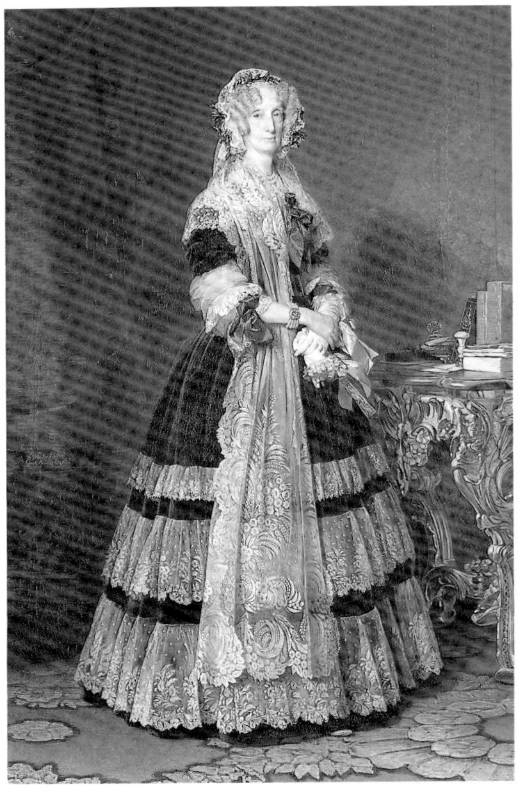

QUEEN MARIE-AMÉLIE (1842)

*The daughter of Ferdinand IV, King of Naples, Marie-Amélie (1782–1866) married the future King Louis-Philippe in Palermo in 1809, when they were both exiles during the Napoleonic Wars. Conservative, religious and a devoted wife, mother and grandmother, Queen Marie-Amélie did not enjoy being Queen of a revolutionary monarchy after 1830. Nevertheless, she was a strong character and supportive of her husband. She marked passages for him to read in the newspapers, prepared documents for him to sign, and advised resistance during the Revolution of 1848. She died in exile in England.*
(See no. 24)
PM

215 × 140 cms
Signed, dated and inscribed, to left:
*fr. Winterhalter/fecit, Paris 1842*
*Musée national du château de Versailles*

*Provenance*: Commissioned by Louis-Philippe for the Maison du Roi, 1841; State Collection, Versailles, inv. no. MV 5111.
*Exhibitions*: Paris, Salon, 1842, no. 1876; Paris, 1928, no. 2; Chicago, Toledo, Los Angeles, San Francisco, 'Treasures of Versailles', 1962, no. 100.
*Reviews*: Théophile Thoré, under pseudonym George Dupré, in 'Salon de 1842', *Revue du Progrès*, p. 225; Auguste Dupouy, *Le Monde Illustré*, 2 June 1928, p. 355; Armand Dayot, *L'Art et les Artistes*, no. 87, May 1928, p. 254.
*Bibliography*: Wild, 1894, no. 68; E.C. Conte Corti, 'Winterhalter, Ein deutsch-französischer Maler', *Velhagen und Klasings Monatshefte*, 53/2, 1938–9, p. 132; J. Richardson, *History Today*, 23 May 1973, p. 331; Introduction, pp. 33, 34.
*Prints after*: Engravings by Sandoz and by H. Grevedon, pub. Lemercier.
See colour plate p. 91.

This is one of the most dignified of Winterhalter's early Royal portraits, and sympathetic characterizations of the elderly French Queen. She stands very firm and straight, the conical outline of her dress strongly emphasized against a neutral background, her crossed hands suggesting quiet resignation. The skirt of her grey velvet dress is trimmed with flounces of white Brussels lace, beautifully rendered, and her fichu and veil, held in place by a crown of artificial flowers, are of the same material. The stole is embroidered net of very high quality. She wears a pearl bracelet bearing a head of the King, probably one of the many painted by F. Meuret after the 1839 state portrait (no. 17). She carries a glove and a fan in her left hand; her right is empty. The gilt console table is similar in design to that of the Duchesse d'Orléans with her son (no. 18). Books, writing materials and a seal are visible on top. The carpet has a broad floral pattern.

Unlike the portrait of the King, that of the Queen includes no outward symbols of Royalty, and it is altogether simpler in idea. It was painted as a pendant to the whole-length portrait of the King's influential sister, Madame Adélaïde (Versailles, MV 5101), another image of dignified age. Both works were commissioned in 1841 and finished early in 1842, appearing at the Salon in that year. Critical response, as usual, was mixed. The irreverent and caustic Thoré did not mince matters: '. . . entrons dans le Salon des figures de cire: Voici le portrait de la reine, par M. Winterhalter. La tête est si petite, que la femme paraît avoir six pieds de haut. En effet, la tête est un détail de mince importance dans un portrait! M. Winterhalter est trop occupé des atours et des accessoires pour songer à la personne dont on l'a chargé de peindre la ressemblance.'[1] (*Revue du Progrès.*)

According to the two manuscript lists of French Royal portraits which he painted (Winterhalter Family Papers), the artist received 1500 frs for this portrait, and a similar sum for a copy, possibly the picture now at Fontainebleau. Another copy is in the Palacio Réal, Madrid. A replica of no. 19 was sold at the Hôtel Drouot 10–11 March 1971, lot 22. Other portraits of the Queen by Winterhalter are a pencil drawing, half-length, seated to the right, 20 × 13.5 cms, once the property of M. Delpechin, secretary to Louis-Philippe (sold Hôtel Drouot, 9–10 February 1938, lot 66), and a watercolour 30 × 19 cms (sold Hôtel Drouot, 8–10 May 1911, lot 394). A watercolour of Marie-Amélie with two of her grandsons is recorded (Private Collection), and she also appears among the group of English and French Royal families at Château d'Eu (no. 24). A terracotta statuette of the Queen by J.J. Pradier (collection A. Roth, London) appears to derive from the 1842 portrait.

A miniature after no. 19 by F. Meuret was given to Queen Victoria, who recorded the gift in her *Journal*, 13 January 1844: 'I have written a letter of thanks to the dear excellent Queen of the French for 2 very kind ones I received from her, together with a most lovely miniature of herself by Meuret after Winterhalter. It is full-length, beautifully painted, and excessively like. It is a pendant to the one the King sent me of himself in '42.'

RLO

1. 'We turn now to the waxworks room. Here, the portrait of the Queen, by M. Winterhalter. The head is so small as to make the woman seem six foot tall. Indeed, the head is a matter of minor importance in a portrait! M. Winterhalter is far too busy with the finery and the details to consider the person whose likeness he has been commissioned to paint.'

## 20

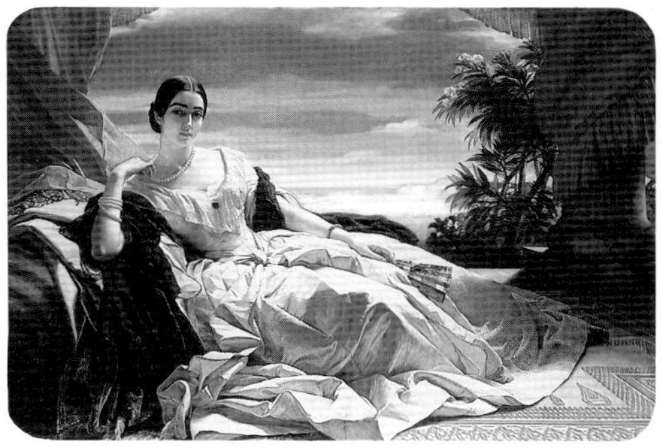

PRINCESS LEONILLA OF SAYN-WITTGENSTEIN-SAYN (1843)

*Leonilla Bariatinsky (1816–1918), a member of one of the most influential families of the Russian nobility, married one of the Tsar's aides-de-camp, Ludwig, Prince of Sayn-Wittgenstein-Sayn, in 1834. Her beauty caused a sensation at court, but her husband fell from favour, perhaps because of his liberal treatment of his serfs. They retired to Germany where her husband became a member of the Prussian Upper House and built a neo-Gothic castle on the family estates on the Rhine. He died in 1866.*

*The Princess, who had converted to Catholicism, preferred Rome and Paris, where she witnessed the pillage of the Tuileries in 1848. She held a monarchist and Catholic Salon, and died at the age of one-hundred-and-two at her villa of 'Monabri' on Lake Geneva.*
(See no. 26)
PM

142 × 212 cms
Signed, dated and inscribed (on base of pillar to right): *fr Winterhalter/Paris 1843*
*The J. Paul Getty Museum*

*Provenance*: By family descent; on loan to Neue Pinakothek, Munich, 1980–5; subsequently purchased by Artemis Group; purchased by the Museum, 1986, inv. no. 86. PA.534.
*Bibliography*: Wild, 1894, nos. 79, 80; A. von Schneider, *Die Pyramide*, 4, 1935; Catalogue of Neue Pinakothek, Munich 1981, p. 369; Artemis Annual Report, 1985–6, p. 26, repr.; Franz Prinz zu Sayn-Wittgenstein-Sayn, *Die Wittgenstein, Geschichten aus einer alten Familie*, Munich 1979, p. 162, repr.; Alexander Fürst zu Sayn-Wittgenstein-Sayn, *Sayn-Ort und Fürstenhaus*, Bendorf-Sayn 1979, p. 145, repr.
See colour plate p. 92.

The Princess is shown in an exotic setting, possibly painted *en souvenir* of the Wittgenstein Palace in the Crimea. Dressed in a luxuriant gown of ivory silk moiré, with a deep purple mantle and a pink sash, she holds a fan in one hand, and fingers a necklace of large pearls with the other; a matching rope is wound round her wrist. Propped up against a striped silk bolster, she reclines in eastern fashion on a white oriental rug with patterned border. The background opens up into a distant view of sea and islands, observed from the high vantage point of the terrace. Similar dramatic juxtapositions of figure and landscape, inside and outdoors, occur in Winterhalter's contemporary series of portraits of the French Court. The view is framed by a fringed red curtain, which is wound round a marble pillar on the right-hand side, suggesting the tent or awning of a seraglio. Potted oleanders add a decorative touch to the design.

The Princess was a celebrated beauty and personality, and Winterhalter exploited the occasion to create a work that transcends the normal conventions of portraiture. The picture is quite unique in his oeuvre, both in conception and format. All the resources of his art were employed to create an icon of beauty, an imaginative work of art which would endow the sitter with the timeless values of David's *Madame Récamier* of 1800 (The Louvre, Paris) or Ingres' *Grande Odalisque* of 1819 (The Louvre, Paris). The figure represents a recasting in portrait form of motifs explored earlier in the Italian fancy pictures like *Il Dolce Farniente* (see no. 9), and it shares the same dreamy and exotic mood. The oval of the face, repeated in the sleek line of the hair and the arched eyebrows, is drawn with cool precision. The indolent gesture of the hand fondling the pearls, with the beautifully observed details of wrist and elbow, reinforces the sensuality of the model's shadowed eyes and the 'come hither' tilt of her head. No less sensual is the contrast of the smooth alabaster flesh tones with the rich materials of silk and velvet. From the twisted curtain at the far top corner, the composition spreads out and down in a diagonal ripple of agitated drapery patterns. A strong light source from the right throws the folds of the dress into deep, almost sculptural, relief. The folds have a life and character of their own, like the angular Gothic drapery of a fifteenth-century Flemish madonna.

The rendering of texture and material is a virtuoso performance, a throw-back to the intensive naturalism of Winterhalter's German and Italian period. Amid the riot of stuffs, the Princess remains the still centre around which the composition revolves, her flawless head and sleek locks, softly backlit, outlined against an expansive vista of sky.

It is not certain exactly when Winterhalter met the Wittgensteins. The misdating of the smaller portrait (no. 26) to 1833, has led to suggestions that they first met in Rome. The introduction may have come through Horace Vernet, whose magnificent equestrian portrait of the Princess out hawking still belongs to the family. A letter from the Princess's mother, Princess Bariatinsky, may possibly refer to the big picture:

> *'St. Petersburg, 7./19. Januar Lieber Herr Winterhalter! Ich habe lange gebraucht, mein Versprechen zu erfüllen, und doch geschah es nicht aus Undankbarkeit. Mein Mann, der in Russland mit Ihrer Majestät, der Kaiserin, mehr als einen Monat nach meiner Ankunft eingetroffen ist, war ganz entzückt von dem reizenden Portrait unserer Tochter. Alle, die es sehen, finden es bezaubernd und bewundern es. Ich habe es stets vor Augen und schulde Ihnen herzlichen Dank für den schönen Anblick, den es mir gewährt. Das Modell trägt mir auf, sie Ihrer Erinnerung zu empfehlen. Sie selbst behält eine sehr angenehme Erinnerung von den Sitzungen in der Rue de la Rochefoucauld. Nehmen Sie, bitte, lieber Herr Winterhalter, meine besten Grüsse entgegen . . .'*[1]

According to Wild, Winterhalter painted two whole-length portraits of the Princess in 1843. A copy of the present picture is in a Private Collection.

RLO

1. 'St Petersburg, 7./19. January / Dear Mr Winterhalter, It has taken me a long time to keep my promise, yet the reason was not ingratitude. My husband, who arrived in Russia with Her Majesty the Empress more than a month before my arrival, was quite delighted with the charming portrait of his daughter. All who have seen it think it enchanting and admire it. I have it constantly before my eyes

and owe you hearty thanks for the beautiful sight it affords me. The model requests me to commend her to your remembrance. She herself retains very pleasant memories of the sittings in the Rue de la Rochefoucauld. Please accept, dear Mr. Winterhalter, my best regards. E. Bariatinsky.'

(*Cf.* A. von Schneider, 1935, and Franz Prinz zu Sayn-Wittgenstein-Sayn, p. 162, and Alexander Fürst zu Sayn-Wittgenstein-Sayn, p. 145)

## 21

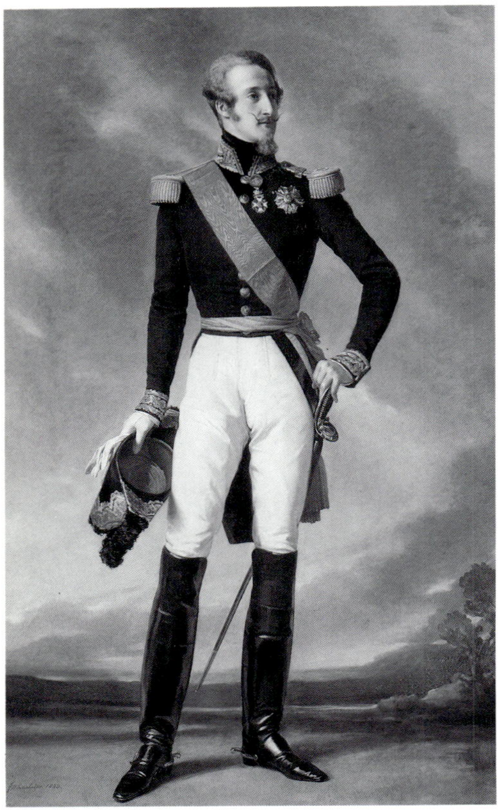

LOUIS-CHARLES-PHILIPPE-RAPHAEL D'ORLÉANS, DUC DE NEMOURS (1843)

*The second son of King Louis-Philippe, the Duc de Nemours (1814–96) was less glamorous and more conservative than the Duc d'Orléans. In the words of Madame de Boigne, a celebrated Orléanist hostess: 'His handsome face and his cold appearance gave him a reputation for haughtiness. He was not even popular with the army.'* (Recollections of a Great Lady, *1912, p. 234.*)

*His unpopularity may have contributed to the rejection of the dynasty when he escorted the Duchesse d'Orléans and the Comte de Paris to the Chamber of Deputies on 24 February 1848. A devoted son to his mother, Queen Marie-Amélie, in exile, he returned to France after the fall of the Second Empire and died at Versailles in 1896.*
PM

215 × 140 cms
Signed and dated, bottom left: *fr Winterhalter. 1843*
*Musée national du château de Versailles*

*Provenance*: Commissioned by Louis-Philippe for the Maison du Roi, 1843; State Collection, Versailles, inv. no. MV 5114.
*Exhibitions*: Paris, Salon, 1844, no. 1797.
*Reviews*: Louis Peisse, 'Salon de 1844', *La Revue des Deux Mondes*, 1844, p. 364; Saint-Martin, 'Salon de 1844', *La Revue Indépendante*, 1844, p. 431; Théophile Thoré, *Le Salon de 1844*, 1844, p. 74.
*Bibliography*: Wild, 1894, no. 84; Introduction, p. 34.
*Prints after*: Lithograph by Léon Noël; engraving by Pannier.
See colour plate p. 94.

The Duke is shown in general's uniform similar to that of his father (no. 17), except that he is in mounted order with white leather pantaloons and black jacked boots with gilt brass spurs. He wears the sash and star of the Grand Cross of the Légion d'Honneur and the Commander's Cross of the Order of Leopold I of Belgium. His hat has black ostrich feathers, instead of white, worn only by commanders-in-chief or corps commanders. His stance, legs parted, one hand crooked on his sword hilt, the other clasping hat and glove, suggests heroic fortitude. The diagonals of sash, jutting arm and sword introduce an element of elegant contraposto to the pose. The heroic mood of the picture is strengthened by the dramatic lighting, playing on the planes of forehead and cheek, and throwing the far side of his face into shadow. The low horizon line, bleak and empty landscape, and lowering expanse of sky, emphasize the solitary magnificence of the commander, awaiting destiny on the field of battle. The King and his sons all chose to be depicted as soldiers in order to enhance their role as protectors of the realm. There is no doubt that they enjoyed soldiering and took their duties seriously. Winterhalter's series of King's sons are similar in mood and format, and trace their inspiration to Sir Thomas Lawrence's famous set of portraits of allied leaders commissioned by George IV for the Waterloo Chamber at Windsor Castle.

Winterhalter's style is smoother and more polished than that of Lawrence; his subjects less energetic and more self-doubting.

In 1839, Winterhalter painted a threequarter-length portrait of the Duke, now lost; this may be the original for a younger portrait of Nemours, now at Compiègne (inv. LP 6237. inv. 383684, after Winterhalter). In 1840, he also painted a whole-length of the Duchesse de Nemours (Versailles, MV 5116). Copies of the 1843 portrait of the Duke are at Schloss Ehrenburg, Coburg, the Palais de Bruxelles and the Musée de L'Armée, Paris (half-length). A studio of Winterhalter portrait of the Duke was sold at the Hôtel Drouot 10–11 March 1971, lot 23.

The 1843 portrait appeared at the Salon the following year, where it was noted by Saint-Martin in *La Revue Indépendante*: 'M. Winterhalter . . . le peintre chéri, exclusivement protégé de la cour, nous a donné un *Duc de Nemours* frais, rose, coquettement impertinent comme un mousquetaire du temps de la régence. C'est un gentil badigeonnage sans solidité, un style équivoque, bien bon pour l'aristocratie bourgeoise de l'époque.'[1] Louis Peisse (*La Revue des Deux Mondes*) called it a skilful effort, if somewhat insipid for a military portrait. Théophile Thoré noted, in *Le Salon de 1844*, that the pose is derived from Ingres' portrait of the Duc d'Orléans, criticized the lack of proportion and concluded: 'Ce n'est pas la botte bien vernie, mais la tête bien intelligente qui fait l'homme.'[2]
RLO

1. 'M. Winterhalter . . . the darling among artists, coveted by the court, has given us a fresh, rosy *Duc de Nemours*, with all the coquettish impertinence of a regency musketeer. It is a pleasant, insubstantial daub, lacking consistency, equivocating in style, perfectly suited to the bourgeois aristocracy of the period.'
2. 'It is not the highly-polished boot but the highly-intelligent look that makes the man.'

## 22

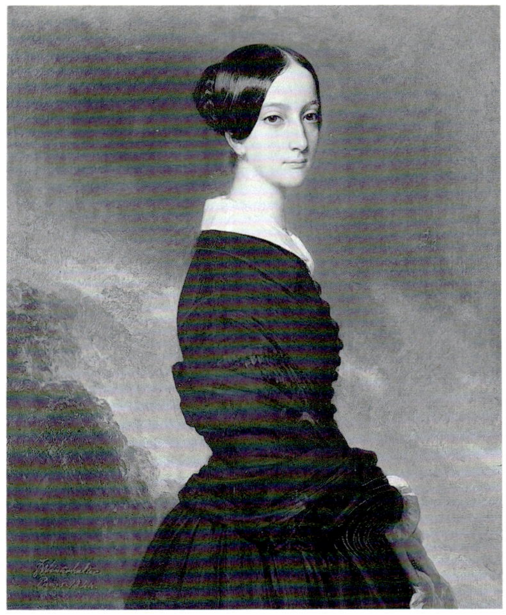

FRANÇOISE-CAROLINE-GONZAGUE, PRINCESSE DE JOINVILLE (1844)†

*The Prince de Joinville, a son of Louis-Philippe, met Françoise (1824–98), a daughter of the Emperor Pedro I of Brazil, while commanding a French ship on a cruise in the South Atlantic. He brought her back as his bride to France in 1843. She was graceful and natural and found it hard to accustom herself to the tedium of the Orléans family circle. Lady Canning wrote in 1843, after an evening at the Château d'Eu: 'she gets dreadfully bored and now and then jumps up as if unable to stand it'. However, she adored her handsome but unfaithful husband. According to Madame de Boigne, a friend of Queen Marie-Amélie, 'her love for her husband was always the mainspring of her life'. They had no children.*
PM

92 × 74 cms
Signed, dated and inscribed, lower left: *f Winterhalter/Paris 1844*
*Musée national du château de Versailles*

*Provenance*: Commissioned by Louis-Philippe for the Maison du Roi in 1844; inv. MV 5117.
*Exhibitions*: Paris, 1928, no. 4; Neuilly, 'Neuilly et le Brésil', 1968, no. 12.
*Bibliography*: Clément de Ris, *Catalogue de Versailles*, 1881, no. 5106, p. 784; E. Bellier, *Dictionnaire Général des Artistes de l'Ecole Française*, vol. 2, 1885, p. 724; Bénézit, vol. 10, 1976, p. 762.
*Prints after*: Engraved by Grevedon, 1847.
See colour plate p. 96.

Princesse de Joinville appears threequarter-length, standing to the right, with hands clasped and turned to the spectator. She wears a modest black silk day dress and shawl. The sloping shoulders, low-set sleeves, pointed waist and dome-shaped skirt are all typical of the 1840s. So, too, is the hairstyle, which is parted centrally and looped smoothly over the ears into a plaited knot at the back. The dark figure is profiled with Ingres-like purity of line on a landscape. Judging from a contemporary description (July 1843), Winterhalter had captured the Brazilian Princesse exactly: 'La Princesse de Joinville, gazelle éffarouchée, taille ravissante, des yeux de velours; sans être régulièrement jolie, elle etait remplie d'attraits.'[1]

Chronologically, no. 22 falls between the two whole-lengths that Winterhalter painted of the Prince and Princesse for the Château d'Eu. In 1843,

Louis-Philippe commissioned the portrait of the Prince de Joinville, a brooding figure in admiral's uniform (Versailles, MV 5105), one of the set of his sons destined for the Versailles Museum (see also *Duc de Nemours*, no. 21). The pendant to this whole-length was painted three years later and shows the Princesse in a pink-and-black lace dress, graceful yet formal, standing in a park (Versailles, MV 5106); it was much copied (Versailles; Fondation St Louis, Amboise). The earlier portrait is a relatively intimate characterization of a member of the Orléans family.

In one of his lists of commissions for the French Royal Family, Winterhalter notes a 'Portrait en buste de la Psse. de Joinville – 1200. fr', and on the other one, 'Copie en buste de la p^sse.^ de Joinville – 1,200 fr' (both Winterhalter Family Papers). No. 22 is not listed by Wild.
CBO

1. 'The Princesse de Joinville, a shy gazelle, with a ravishing figure and velvet eyes; although not a regular beauty, she was nevertheless full of attractive features.' (*Souvenirs de la Princesse de Ligne*, 1923, p. 76.)

## 23

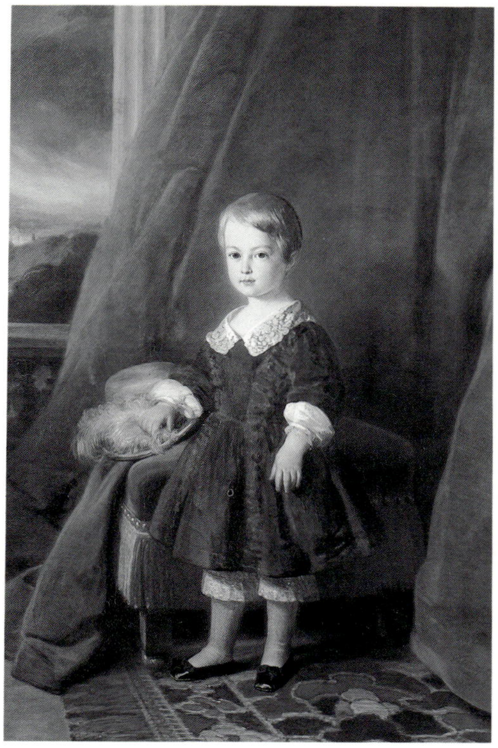

LOUIS-PHILIPPE-MARIE-FERDINAND-GASTON D'ORLÉANS, COMTE D'EU (1845)

*The Comte d'Eu (1842–1922), the eldest son of the Duc de Nemours, was the favourite grandson of Queen Marie-Amélie, who helped to bring him up after his mother's death. He married Isabella, daughter and heiress of the Emperor Pedro II of Brazil, in 1864. His personal unpopularity contributed to the fall of the Brazilian monarchy in 1889. He died in France in 1922.*
(See no. 24)
PM

147 × 100 cms
Signed and dated, lower right:
*fr Winterhalter/1845*
*Musée national du château de Versailles*

*Provenance*: Commissioned by Louis-Philippe for the Maison du Roi in 1845; State Collection, Versailles, inv. no. MV 5118.
*Exhibitions*: National Portrait Gallery, Smithsonian Institution, Washington, D.C., 'Masterpieces from Versailles', 1983, no. 40 (repr.); Tokyo, Kyoto, 'Exposition d'art français au Japon', July 1954–April 1955; Neuilly, 'Neuilly et le Brésil', 1968, no. 18; Florence, Palazzo Pitti, 'Capolavori da Versailles', 1985, no. 47 (repr.).
*Bibliography*: Introduction, p. 36.
See colour plate p. 97.

Louis-Philippe's three-year-old grandson stands by a *tabouret*, his arm resting on a large plumed hat. The child wears a dark tunic dress with a Honiton lace collar and lace-trimmed white pantaloons, and patent leather pumps. A red curtain is drawn aside to reveal a pillar, balustrade and (possibly) a view of the Château d'Eu to the left. A boldly patterned carpet adds colour to the foreground.

Winterhalter has used the same formula for Louis-Philippe's grandson, as he did in his 1843 portrait of the Prince of Wales (Her Majesty The Queen); an infant by a stool, a feathered hat and a heavy background curtain. However, the mannered whimsicality of the earlier English work has been banished, and Winterhalter succeeds in conferring upon his sitter, in this case, a quaint but undeniable air of dignity.

Both child portraits appear to have been inspired by Velasquez's moving depictions of infant princes and infantas, in stiff court dress, standing by tasselled cushions against a curtain background. Prince Balthasar Carlos (Wallace Collection, London) and Prince Felipe Próspero (Kunsthistorisches Museum, Vienna) both offer good analogies.

Winterhalter appears to have done no other portraits of the Comte d'Eu. This portrait is adapted, with slight variations, for inclusion in the group at Château d'Eu (no. 24), also painted in 1845.
CBO

24

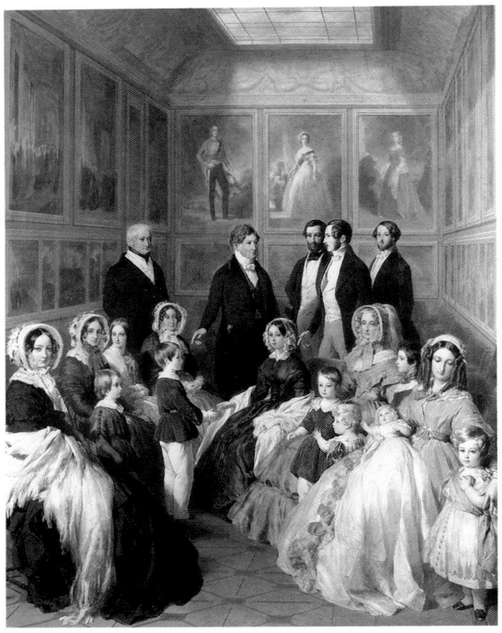

QUEEN VICTORIA AND PRINCE ALBERT WITH THE FAMILY OF KING LOUIS-PHILIPPE AT THE CHÂTEAU D'EU (1845)

220.7 × 177.8 cms
Signed and dated, lower right: *F Winterhalter. 1845*
*Her Majesty Queen Elizabeth, The Queen Mother*

*Provenance*: Painted for the King of the French; subsequently in the possession successively of the Duc de Nemours at Bushy Park and of the Duc d'Alençon at Belmont, Wimbledon; stated to have passed into the possession of Alençon's grand-daughter who was married to the Marquis de Chaponay-Morance; later in the collection of Mrs Derek Fitzgerald and sold by her at Sotheby's, 9 July 1947, lot 140; bought by Agnew's for Her Majesty Queen Elizabeth, The Queen Mother.
*Exhibitions*: Paris, Salon, 1846; London, 1936, no. 20.
*Bibliography*: Introduction, pp. 33, 36; Millar, *Victorian Pictures*.
See colour plate p. 98.

The setting is the Galerie Victoria in the Château d'Eu, which the Queen described during her visit (Journal, 8 September 1845): 'A pretty room, full of pictures representing our last visit here, & also the King's visit to Windsor.' One of the large pictures on the left wall is almost certainly Winterhalter's picture of the reception of Louis-Philippe at Windsor (see Introduction, fig. 18); the small picture nearest to the spectator on the same wall probably represents the King entering St George's Hall with Queen Victoria for the State Banquet held during the King's visit to Windsor. The three full-lengths hanging on the end wall are versions of Winterhalter's portraits of the Queen and Prince Albert and the Queen of the Belgians.

In the Galerie Victoria, the King of the French is presenting his grandsons to Queen Victoria. The King wears the ribbon of the Garter; the Queen is seated in the centre of the composition. Behind the King, on the left, stands the Prince of Salerno; in front of the King stands François, Prince de Joinville, Prince Albert and Augustus, Prince of Saxe-Coburg-Gotha. In the left foreground sits the widowed Hélène, Duchesse d'Orléans; in front of her stand her two sons, Robert, Duc de Chartres, and his elder brother, Louis, Comte de Paris, who extends his hand to Queen Victoria. On the left of the Duchesse are seated the Princess of Salerno, the Duchesse d'Aumale and Madame Adélaïde. On Queen Victoria's left is seated the Queen of the French. In front of her stands Gaston, Comte d'Eu; the smaller child beside him is his brother, Ferdinand, Duc d'Alençon. The boy in profile to the left, by the shoulder of the Queen of the French, is Philip, Prince of Württemberg. In the foreground on the right sits Princesse Clémentine, wife of Augustus, Prince of Saxe-Coburg-Gotha, with her two sons, Philip and (in her arms) Augustus.

The painting was made for the King of the French. The Queen of the Belgians wrote to Queen Victoria on 30 September 1845: 'I don't know if you know that Winterhalter is painting a picture *de la presentation* of my Father's grandsons to you. They say it is delightful.' (WRA.) On 19 October, she wrote again. She did not believe the picture had been begun, but she had been told that the 'various Sketches' were delightful (ibid.).

Drawings at Windsor, attributed to Guglielmo Faija, record the portraits in no. 24 of the King of the French (R.L. 133327) and Princesse Clémentine and her sons (R.L. 13329). A watercolour of the Galerie by François Joseph Nolau, very similar to the view in no. 24, is in the Louvre (inv. 31480).
OM

25

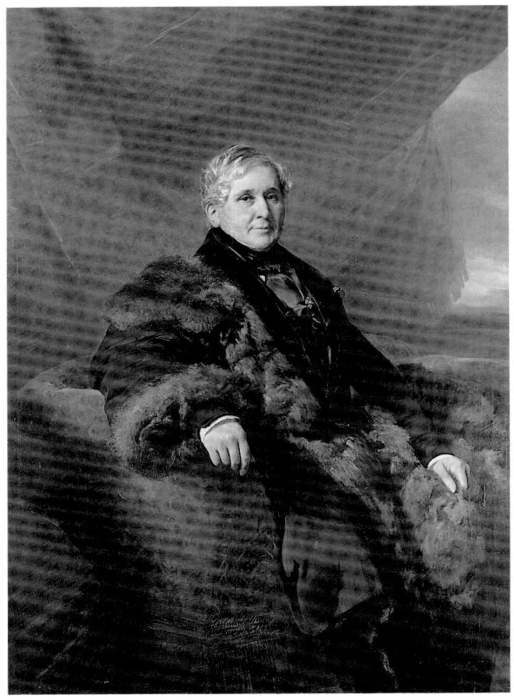

CHARLES-JÉRÔME, COMTE POZZO DI BORGO (1849)

*Comte Pozzo di Borgo (1791–1879) was cousin and heir of the Russian ambassador to Paris from 1814 to 1834, a Corsican noble and personal enemy of Napoléon, also called Pozzo di Borgo. He served in the French army in the 1820s but, like many officers, resigned in 1830 rather than take the oath to King Louis-Philippe. He married a member of the Legitimist aristocracy, Mademoiselle de Crillon, and continued his family's hostility to the Bonapartes. He was made a Duke by the King of the Two Sicilies in 1852.*
PM

158 × 116 cms
Signed, dated and inscribed, bottom centre: *f. Winterhalter./Bruxelles 1849*
*Private Collection*

*Provenance*: By descent to the present owner.
*Bibliography*: Wild, 1894, no. 146.
*Prints after*: Lithograph by Léon Noël, 1852, printed by Lemercier.
See colour plate p. 95.

The Comte is dressed in a black formal suit, with a black silk cravat held in place by a pearl pin, and wearing a fur-lined travelling coat. In his button hole is the knotted ribbon of the Légion d'Honneur. He is seated in a red upholstered armchair against a background of red drapes.

In deference, perhaps, to his model's Italian nationality, Winterhalter appears to have used Titian's portrait of Pope Paul III, 1545–6 (Kunsthistorisches Museum, Vienna and The Hermitage, Leningrad) as the starting-point for the pose in this portrait. The impression, largely owing to the great bulk of the costume (see also the Comte de Nieuwerkerke, 1852, no. 49), is one of majestic authority. Apart from the head, the outstanding feature is Winterhalter's rendering of the lustrous sable. Fur is used to striking effect in Winterhalter's portrait of Count Jenison in 1837 (see Introduction, fig. 12), and in the half-length portrait of the chemist *Frédéric Kuhlmann* of 1869 (Musée des Beaux-Arts de Lille). Titian may have been one influence (*cf. Pietro Aretino*, 1548, Frick Collection, New York) and Rubens another (see Introduction, fig. 51). In any case, throughout his career Winterhalter often chose to use fur for sumptuous decorative effects in his male portraits.

According to Wild, Winterhalter painted the Count and Countess on a second occasion, *c.*1860 (no. 428, location unknown). A whole-length portrait of Louise Victurnienne Valentine de Crillon, the Comtesse Pozzo di Borgo, painted in Paris in 1849 and pendant to no. 25, is still in the same collection. A half-length oval portrait of the Comtesse by Winterhalter was lithographed.

CBO

## 26

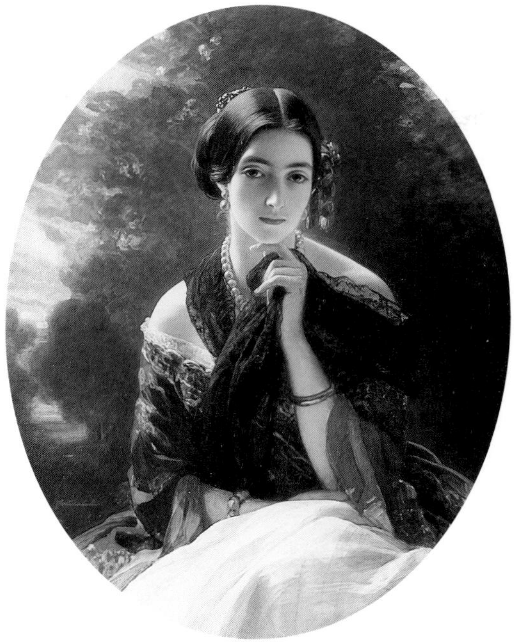

PRINCESS LEONILLA OF SAYN-WITTGENSTEIN-SAYN
(For biography, see no. 20)

97 × 79 cms, oval
Signed, lower left: *F.X.Winterhalter*
*Prince Alexander Sayn-Wittgenstein-Sayn*

*Provenance*: By descent to present family.
*Bibliography*: Wild, 1894, p. 39; Franz Prinz zu Sayn-Wittgenstein-Sayn, *Die Wittgenstein, Geschichten aus einer alten Familie*, Munich 1979, p. 162, repr.; Alexander Fürst zu Sayn-Wittgenstein-Sayn, *Sayn-Ort und Fürstenhaus*, Bendorf-Sayn 1979, p. 145, repr.; Introduction, p. 31.
*Prints after*: Engraving by Léon Noël, 1850.
See colour plate p. 93.

This second portrait of the Princess Leonilla (see no. 20) is more intimate and direct in characterization. The sitter is shown in a loose bodice, blue lined with scarlet, over a white skirt, with a black lace scarf draped around her shoulders. She wears a necklace of large pearls, and pearl earrings and bracelet. She is seated, with one hand in her lap, the index finger of the other propping up her chin in a quizzical, confiding gesture. As in the earlier portrait, light plays across the face, accenting the nose, chin and cheekbone, while leaving the eyes as deep pools in shadow. There is an intensity to the expression, a dimension of feeling and experience absent from the polished odalisque of the 1843 portrait. The background of foliage, with a vista of trees to the left, is treated more loosely and emotively. The Princess remains a woman of exceptional beauty, but she is no longer inaccessible and enigmatic. The force of her attraction is more immediate.

This portrait may be the one listed by Wild under 1849, together with a portrait of her husband. The latter is presumably the portrait of the Prince, dated 1850, in the same Collection. The suggestion that the portrait of the Princess was executed in 1833 is clearly erroneous, but equally 1849 may be on the late side. A study of the head for the portrait is reproduced in the Winterhalter *Album*, no. 16.

RLO

27

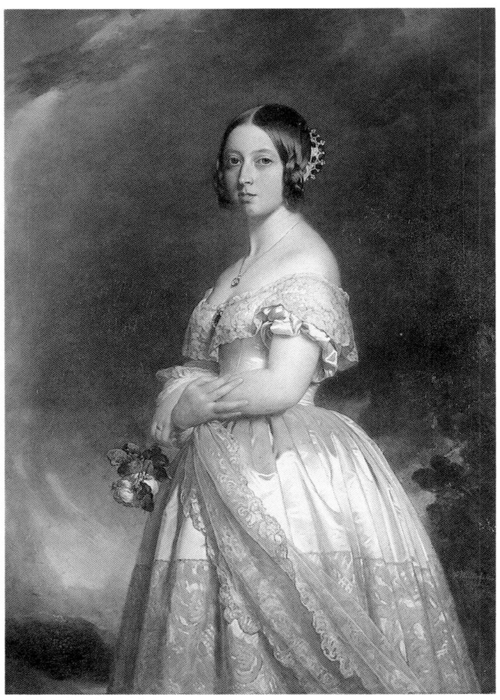

QUEEN VICTORIA (1842)

*Queen Victoria (1819–1901) was one of the most remarkable personalities of her age. She was direct, confident and on occasion, 'hasty and passionate'. She became Queen in 1837 and married her cousin, Prince Albert of Saxe-Coburg-Gotha in 1840; she bore him nine children, and was distraught at his premature death in 1861. She was keenly interested in politics, especially foreign affairs, and held strong views which were not always in sympathy with those of the Prime Minister of the day. She reigned longer than any other British sovereign, and celebrated her Diamond Jubilee in 1897.* (See nos. 24, 29, 36, 93)
PM

133.4 × 97.8 cms
Signed and dated, lower right:
*Fr Winterhalter./1842*
*Her Majesty The Queen*

*Provenance*: Painted for Queen Victoria
*Exhibitions*: London, South Kensington,'Third and Concluding Exhibition of National Portraits', 1868, no. 384; London, 1977, no. 7.
*Bibliography*: Lady Bloomfield, *Reminiscences of Court and Diplomatic Life*, vol. 1, 1883, p. 68; Wild, 1894, no. 73; Collins-Baker, *Windsor*, p. 314; Goodison, *Catalogue of Cambridge Portraits*, vol. 1, 1955, p. 74; Ormond; Introduction, pp. 37, 60, 64; Millar, *Victorian Pictures*.
*Prints after*: Lithograph by F.C. Lewis; prints by F. Forster, 1846, pub. 28 October 1846 and 1 May 1847.
See colour plate p. 103.

Queen Victoria is seen threequarter-length, standing to the left against a landscape background in a white dress, her arms folded, a small bunch of roses in her left hand. In her chignon she wears a little jewelled diadem.

The painting is a pendant to no. 28. It was painted for the Queen who recorded in her Journal sittings on 8, 10, 11, 14, 17 and 25 June 1842. The last she describes as: 'My last sitting. The likeness is perfect and the picture very fine; only my gown and the background have still to be finished.' She sat again on 21 July.

On 31 August, Winterhalter was paid £577.10*s* 'for Portraits & Copies' and on 29 September, £210 for two copies, presumably one of each of the pair (WRA). The payment for the originals is recorded (ibid.) as £157.10*s* for each portrait.

By 4 December, the two portraits had been let into the walls of the White Drawing-Room at Windsor, 'and look so well there' (Journal).

Lady Bloomfield wrote on 24 August 1843, after seeing the pair of 1843, which she thought promised to be good likenesses: 'I find I do not like his former picture of the Queen as much as I did, for it is very cold and leaden in colour; but it is certainly very like, and I think Winterhalter catches the expression of the Queen's mouth better than anybody. It is peculiar, and very difficult to render without being a caricature.' (*Reminiscences of Court and Diplomatic Life*.) Sir George Hayter, who had seen the new portraits as early as 21 June 1842 (Diary), thought the Queen's expression disagreeable and the handling heavy, but described it as exceedingly like. When he saw a pair of replicas on 3 January 1843, he was again impressed by the likeness to the Queen; but the portrait of the Prince he thought a failure as to pose and likeness.

Replicas were commissioned without delay. In 1842, Winterhalter was paid, at £105 each, for copies of the Queen for Baroness Lehzen and Count Mensdorff-Pouilly and for copies of each portrait for the King of the French (WRA). On 30 September, the Queen had sat to Winterhalter again: 'For the last touches to the copies, which are exceedingly good and which I am going to give dear Lehzen.' A pair of copies, signed and dated London 1842, and presumably those given to the King of the French, is at Versailles (MV 4675, 4676). In her Journal, 24 February 1843, the Queen wrote that the King was very pleased with the portraits, which were among those sent over for Versailles; they were priced at £105 each; the Queen and Prince had each paid for their own portrait; and the artist's name is recorded as if he, and not a copyist, had been responsible for them. The Queen of the Belgians described these copies as beautiful and perhaps better than the originals (WRA).

A good pair of replicas, signed and dated 1842, is still in the Fürstenbau in Veste Coburg. In 1843, Melville was paid £30 for a copy of Winterhalter's portrait of the Queen as a Christmas present for the Duchess of Kent (WRA). See no. 28 for a copy of the pendant painted for the Duchess.

Copies of no. 27 are recorded in the collection of the Earl of Hardwicke; in the Examination School, University of Cambridge, by R. Rowe (*Catalogue of Cambridge Portraits*); at Burghley; and in the National Gallery of Art, Washington; in Government House, Sydney; and (formerly) in the German Royal Collection. A copy was sold at Christie's, 20 February 1953, lot 83, another, with a copy of the pendant, 10 July 1953, lot 161, and another at Sotheby's, 8 June 1987 (354). In the copies, the Queen wears the insignia of the Garter and this variant on the original also appears in the engravings by F.C. Lewis and the prints by F. Forster.

The pair of copies sent to the King of the French was the source of the copies on porcelain, made at Sèvres and signed and dated by Adèle de Ducluzeau, 1846 (The Queen), and Antoine Béranger, 1846 (The Prince). They were given to the Queen by the King of the French in the summer of 1846 (WRA) and were set into the walls of the Council Room at Osborne where they remain.

In 1842, copies in enamel were already being made for the Queen for insertion into bracelets to be given to friends (WRA).
OM

28

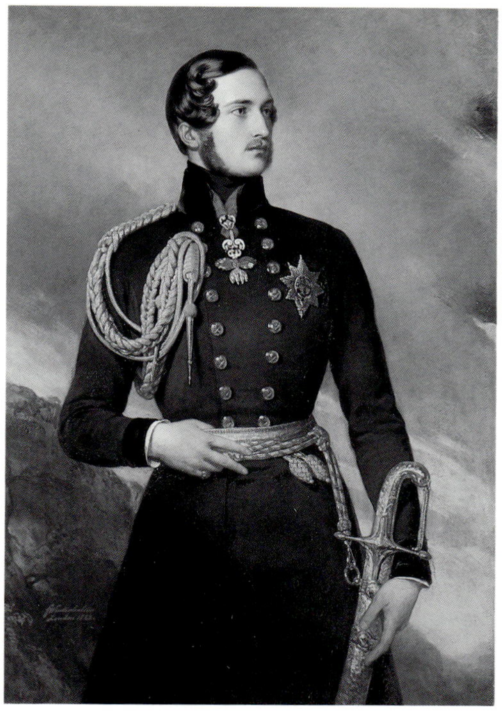

PRINCE ALBERT (1842)

*Prince Albert (1819–61) was the younger son of the Duke of Saxe-Coburg-Gotha, which was a principality in the heart of Germany with a remarkable tradition of artistic patronage. He married Queen Victoria in 1840, and soon established himself as the confidant and adviser not only to Victoria, but to many English politicians. The court became more formal and respectable under his influence, and the Queen less politically partisan. Prince Albert also played a significant role in the arts, as head of the Royal Commission on rebuilding the Houses of Parliament in 1841, and as the instigator of the Great Exhibition of 1851. His death from typhoid in 1861 was a blow from which the Queen never recovered.*
(See nos. 24, 32)
PM

132.7 × 97.2 cms
Signed and dated, lower left: *F Winterhalter/London 1842*
*Her Majesty The Queen*

*Provenance*: Painted for Queen Victoria.
*Exhibitions*: London, 1977, no. 6.
*Bibliography*: Wild, 1894, no. 74; Collins-Baker, *Windsor*, p. 314; Introduction, pp. 37, 60, 64; Millar, *Victorian Pictures*.
*Prints after*: Engraving by A. Lewis pub. 1848; lithograph of the head by F.C. Lewis pub. 1851.
See colour plate p. 102.

Prince Albert appears threequarter-length, standing against a landscape background, wearing a field-marshal's undress uniform with the star of the Garter and the badge of the Golden Fleece, and holding his sword in his left hand. The late Nicolas Dawnay pointed out that 'the scimitar and the dressing gown cord suspension' are not the usual and suggested they might be a Saxe-Coburg-Gotha touch. He also pointed out that in 1843, epaulettes and scales were abolished for field marshals and replaced by the aiguillette on the right shoulder, as it is seen in no. 28; the idea may have come from the Prince Consort.

The painting was done for Queen Victoria as a pair to no. 27. In her Journal, she records sittings for it on 8, 26 and 27 July 1842 and on the last date she described it as '*such* a beautiful picture'. For payments and for the production of replicas and copies of the pair, see no. 27. The Prince paid Melville £30 for a copy for Duke Ferdinand of Saxe-Coburg-Gotha in 1843 and the same sum for a copy for Lord Melbourne. He also paid Melville £30 for a copy of the Duchess of Kent; for the copy of the pendant, see no. 27. A copy was sold at Christie's, 20 December 1962, lot 181.

In 1873, the Queen told Theodore Martin that no. 28 was one of the three portraits of the Prince which she really liked (WRA).
OM

29

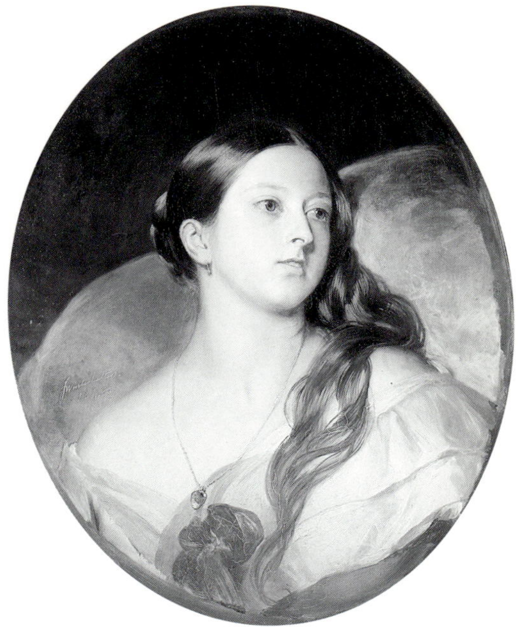

QUEEN VICTORIA (1843)
(For biography, see no. 27)

65.4 × 53.3 cms, oval
Signed and dated, to the left: *F Winterhalter. /1843*. Inscribed on the back with the names of artist and sitter and the date, 1843.
*Her Majesty The Queen*

*Provenance*: Painted for Queen Victoria as a present to Prince Albert; placed in the Prince's Writing-Room at Windsor.
*Exhibitions*: London, 1977, no. 10.
*Bibliography*: Wild, 1894, no. 88; R. Ormond, *The Face of Monarchy*, 1977, p. 196; Introduction, p. 38; Millar, *Victorian Pictures*.
*Prints after*: Engraved by F. Holl.
See colour plate p. 101.

Queen Victoria, head-and-shoulders view, her head turned to the right and resting against a red cushion, a long tress of hair hanging across her naked shoulder.

The portrait was commissioned by Queen Victoria as a present to Prince Albert on his birthday, 26 August 1843. Winterhalter had arrived in London early in July and on 8 July the Queen sat to him 'for a portrait that is to be a surprise for Albert' (Journal). Further sittings are recorded on 10, 13 and 14 July for 'the *secret* picture, which to my joy is succeeding very well'. the Prince was delighted with the picture: 'the surprise was so great, and he thought it so like, and so beautifully painted. I felt so proud and happy to have found something that gave him so much pleasure.' As late as 2 January 1873, she described the portrait as 'my darling Albert's favourite picture' (Journal). She paid Winterhalter £105 for the portrait in 1843 (WRA).
OM

30

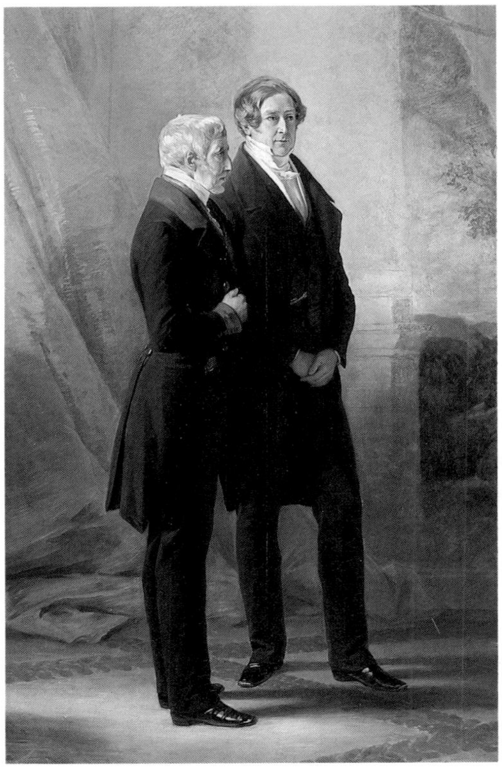

ARTHUR WELLESLEY, 1ST DUKE OF WELLINGTON, WITH SIR ROBERT PEEL (1844)

*After his glorious military career, culminating in the triumph of Waterloo in 1815, Wellington (1769–1852) became a leading Tory statesman, and twice Prime Minister, 1828–30 and 1834. Queen Victoria, as a Whig, at first referred to him as 'this wicked old foolish Duke'; as she mellowed, however, he became 'the best friend we have', and a frequent guest at court. Her feelings for Sir Robert Peel (1788–1850) underwent a similar evolution. She refused him as Prime Minister in 1839 during the Bedchamber Crisis, but came to revere him after he took office in 1841. Peel remained Prime Minister until 1846, when his bill for the repeal of the Corn Laws was passed. He was Prince Albert's favourite politician.*
PM

149.5 × 97.8 cms
Signed, lower right: *F Winterhalter*. Inscribed on the back as copied by Winterhalter from his picture of the reception of King Louis-Philippe; there are markings along the top edge of the canvas which probably indicate a scale.
*Her Majesty The Queen*

*Provenance*: Stated to have been painted for Queen Victoria and to have been purchased by the Lord Chamberlain, 30 June 1851.
*Exhibitions*: London, Royal Academy, 'The King's Pictures', 1946–7, no. 68.
*Bibliography*: Introduction, p. 36; Millar, *Victorian Pictures*.
*Prints after*: Engraving by J. Faed, pub. 31 March 1844.
See colour plate p. 104.

The two men are depicted full-length, the Duke wearing Windsor uniform, standing side by side.

The figures are shown in the same poses and in the same relationship to each other as in the painting of the reception of King Louis-Philippe at Windsor (see Introduction, fig. 18); but they are shown wearing trousers instead of knee-breeches. The details in the background are more defined in the engraving by J. Faed of 1844; on the plate, it is stated that the present picture was painted in 1844.

In 1851 also, Queen Victoria paid Albert Graefle £50 for a copy of Winterhalter's picture of Peel and Wellington (WRA). In the same year, W. Corden painted for the Queen a half-length portrait of Peel, after Winterhalter, as a present to Lady Peel.
OM

31

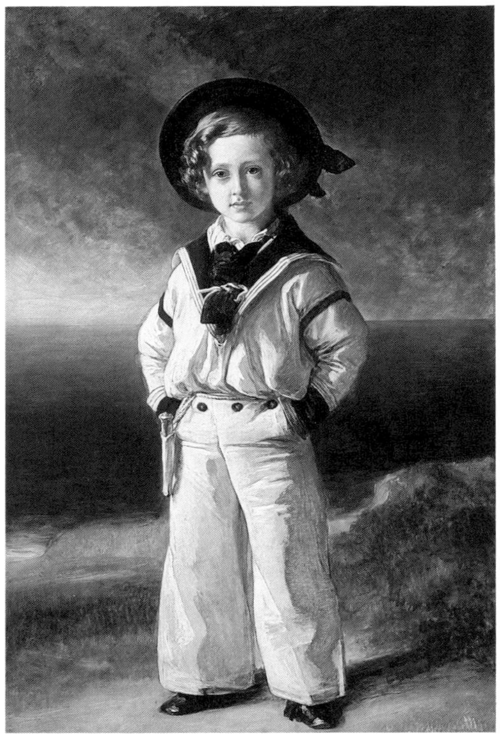

ALBERT EDWARD, PRINCE OF WALES (1846)

*The Prince of Wales (1841–1910), known to his family as Bertie, was neither as clever nor as industrious as his parents. The Queen dismissed him as 'so idle and weak' and later believed that worry over his character had hastened Prince Albert's death. Her dislike of her eldest son became, in Lord Clarendon's words, 'a positive monomania'. The Prince of Wales was obliged to exercise his charm and knowledge of the world in social, rather than public life, until his mother's death in 1901, when he acceded to the throne as Edward VII.*
(See no. 43)
PM

127.3 × 88.3 cms
Signed and dated, bottom right: *F Winterhalter/1846*. Inscribed on the back as painted in December 1846.
*Her Majesty The Queen*

*Provenance*: Painted for Queen Victoria and placed, presumably after the exhibition at St James's Palace, with Winterhalter's portrait of Queen Victoria, Prince Albert and their family of 1846, in the Drawing-Room at Osborne.
*Exhibitions*: London, Royal Academy, 'Kings and Queens', 1953, no. 277; London, 1977, no. 138.
*Bibliography*: Wild, 1894, no. 125; London, 1977, no. 138 (for sailor suit); Introduction, pp. 39, 41; Millar, *Victorian Pictures*.
*Prints after*: Engraving by S. Cousins, pub. Moon on 15 February 1848.
See colour plate p. 105.

Albert Edward is shown at full-length, standing on a grassy path above the sea, his hands in the pockets of his new sailor suit.

The sailor's dress had been made for the Prince of Wales by the ship's tailor who made the dresses for the ratings in the Royal Yacht. He appeared in it on 2 September 1846, during a cruise off the Channel Islands (it is now in the National Maritime Museum). The Prince sat to Winterhalter on 6 October 1846 (but this may have been for the full-length portrait for Sir Robert Peel: see no. 32); another sitting seems to have taken place on 23 December (Journal). Prince Albert's presents to Queen Victoria at Christmas included: 'that lovely full-length picture of Bertie in his sailor's dress, by Winterhalter. It is such a perfect likeness and such a perfect composition.'(ibid.) Sir Robert Peel, shown the portrait on 5 January 1847, described it as 'the prettiest picture he had ever seen'; Lord Liverpool, on 3 February, was no less delighted with it. Winterhalter received £100 for the picture (WRA).

A copy by W. Corden, for which the Queen paid £15, was given to the King of Prussia, the sitter's godfather, in 1847 (WRA); it is now in the collection of the Earl of Southesk. A copy by Koberwein was formerly at Marlborough House. It was still at Marlborough House in 1925, and subsequently passed to Princess Victoire. A copy of the head, in a Private Collection, is stated to have been given by the Queen to Lieutenant Vansittart who was then serving in the Royal Yacht. The engraving by S. Cousins was apparently based on a copy finished under Winterhalter's supervision (WRA). A bronze, apparently based on the figure of the little Prince, was on the art market in 1987.
OM

32

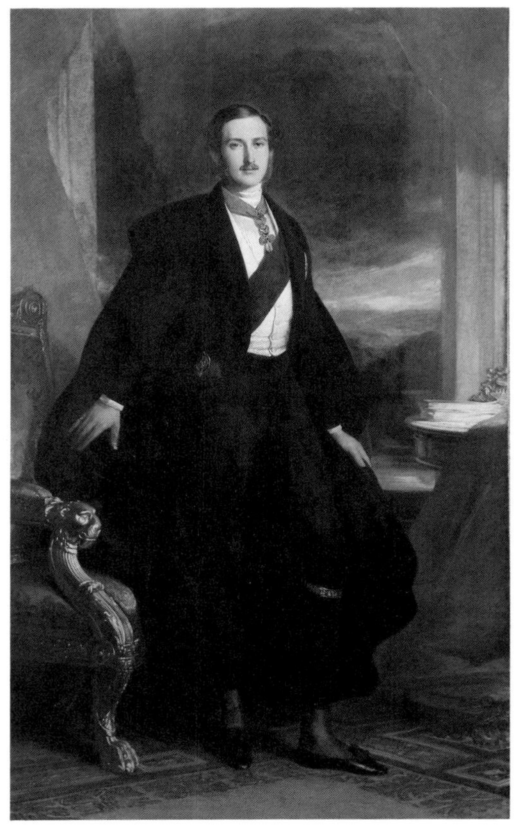

PRINCE ALBERT (1846)
For biography, see no. 28

237.5 × 147.5 cms
Signed and dated, middle right: *Winterhalter/1846*
*Trustees of the National Museums and Galleries on Merseyside, Lady Lever Art Gallery, Port Sunlight*

*Provenance*: Sir Robert Peel; Peel Heirlooms sale, Robinson, Fisher and Harding, 29–30 November 1917, lot 57, where acquired for Sir William Hesketh Lever, later Lord Leverhulme; LL 3525.
*Bibliography*: Wild, 1894, no. 123 (date given as 1843); Merseyside County Council, *Catalogue of Foreign Paintings . . . Lady Lever Art Gallery Port Sunlight*, 1983, pp. 24–5 Introduction, p. 39, Millar, *Victorian Pictures*.
See colour plate p. 106.

Prince Albert is depicted in a tail coat, white waistcoat, black tight-fitting pantaloons, silk stockings, pumps and cloak; he wears the badge of the Order of the Golden Fleece at his neck, the Garter around his leg, and the lesser badge of the Order of the Garter at his hip. He stands in a carpeted interior, between a gilt armchair and two tables, the background of which opens out from the framing columns and drapery to show a distant landscape.

This portrait commission, the last portrait of Prince Albert that Winterhalter was to paint for over a decade, arose through a request from Sir Robert Peel after he had resigned as Prime Minister; in a letter to Queen Victoria of 2 July 1846, he wrote: 'One favour he has to ask of your Majesty. He knows your Majesty will recollect your gracious promise to give to him the portraits of your Majesty and the Prince. He hopes they will be in that simple attire in which, when he has had the frequent happiness of being admitted to your private society, he has seen your Majesty and the Prince.' (*Sir Robert Peel from his Private Papers*, C.S. Parker ed., 1899, vol. 3, pp. 452ff.) Peel requested, in addition, that the portrait of Queen Victoria should include the Prince of Wales.

The Queen consented in her reply of 3 July 1846, and on 30 September she discussed with Winterhalter and Peel 'the pictures we are going to have painted of us for him' (WRA, qv for all subsequent references here). She records sittings which she and Prince Albert gave on 2, 3 and 5 October (although at this period, Winterhalter was also working on his great family group, and some recorded sittings may also be related to this). On 15 October 1846, the Queen saw Winterhalter putting in the background to 'Albert's picture, which is quite Winterhalter's *chef d'oeuvre*, and is the best likeness ever done of my beloved one'. On 5 January 1847, in the room at Buckingham Palace where Winterhalter was painting, the Queen showed Sir Robert and Lady Peel the two portraits, which were framed, but not quite finished; Peel called them 'admirable, beautiful portraits'. The reference in the catalogue of the sale of the Peel Collection to the portraits being presented to Peel on the Queen's visit to Drayton in 1846 is therefore erroneous.

Prince Albert paid Winterhalter £315 for his portrait, while the Queen paid £420 for hers (Her Majesty The Queen). Each paid £210 for a copy of their portrait to be presented to Prince Albert's brother, the Duke of Saxe-Coburg-Gotha; these copies are still in the Ehrenburg at Coburg.

Queen Victoria's delighted reaction to the portraits may be contrasted with the comments of the reviewer in *The Athenaeum* of 8 May 1849, who remarked on what he saw to be a coarseness in Winterhalter's large family group: 'It is as deficient in refinement as two whole-lengths by the same artist; which we saw at Sir Robert Peel's a fortnight ago.'
SF

## 33

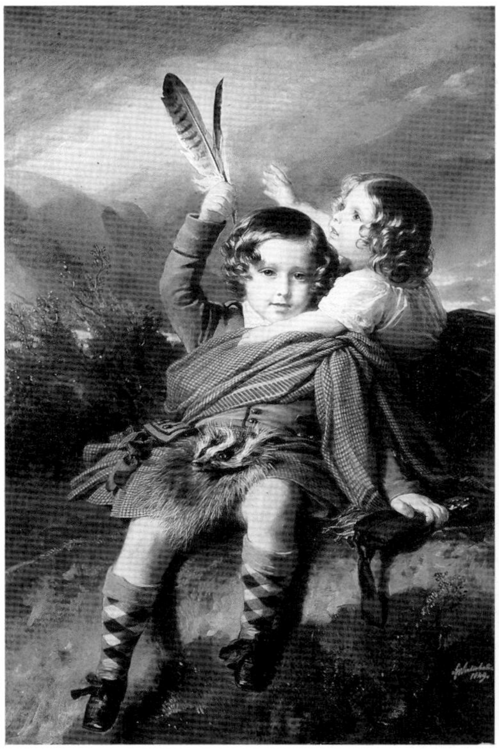

PRINCE ALFRED AND PRINCESS HELENA (1849)

*Prince Alfred (1844–1900), the second son of Queen Victoria, was created Duke of Edinburgh in 1866. He was an active naval officer, and Commander-in-Chief in the Mediterranean, 1886–9. In 1893, he succeeded his uncle, the elder brother of the Prince Consort, as Duke of Saxe-Coburg-Gotha.*

*Princess Helena (1846–1923), the Queen's third daughter, married Prince Christian of Schleswig-Holstein and founded the Princess Christian Nursing Home at Windsor.*
(See no. 89)
PM

127.6 × 87.6 cms
Signed and dated, lower right: *F Winterhalter./ 1849*. Inscribed on the back with the names of artists, sitters and the date, 1849.
*Her Majesty The Queen*

*Provenance*: Given to Queen Victoria by Prince Albert, 24 May 1849; placed in the Queen's Drawing-Room at Osborne.
*Bibliography*: Wild, 1894, no. 151; Introduction, p. 45; Millar, *Victorian Pictures*.
*Prints after*: Engraving by H. T. Ryall, pub. F. G. Moon, 1 November 1850.
See colour plate 108.

Seated together on a bank in the Highlands, the Prince wears Highland dress (his kilt and plaid of a plain grey check), and holds the two feathers from his Glengarry bonnet out of reach of his sister.

The painting was given to Queen Victoria by Prince Albert on her birthday, 24 May 1849: 'A beautiful picture of Affie & Lenchen by Winterhalter, wonderfully like and a charming picture in itself, so prettily grouped.' (Journal; WRA.) Winterhalter was paid £200 for the picture on 10 August 1849. When he saw the picture at Osborne on 29 May 1849, he wished to alter the sky. A small version at Windsor is apparently the *modello* for the composition.

A copy by W. Corden of the head of Prince Alfred was given by Queen Victoria as a birthday present to the Duchess of Kent in 1849; after the Duchess's death, it was given by the Queen, in remembrance of her mother, to Baron Stockmar. It is still in the possession of his descendants near Coburg (WRA).
OM

## 34

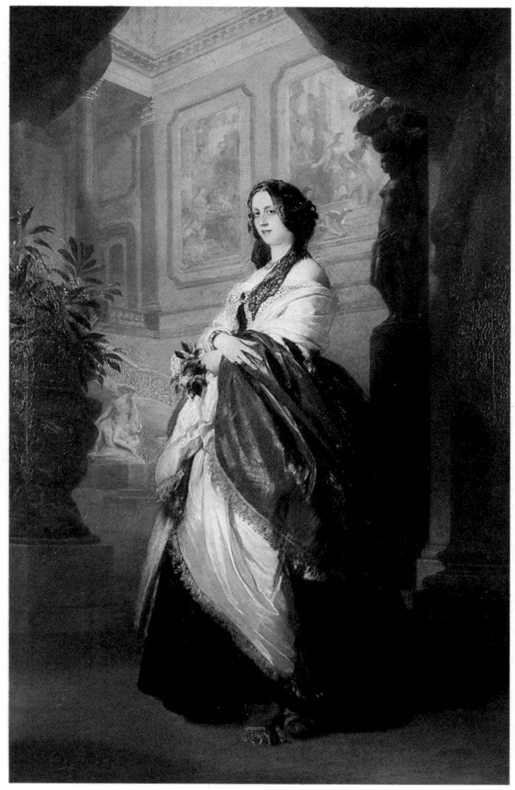

HARRIET HOWARD, DUCHESS OF SUTHERLAND (1849)

*Harriet (1806–68), elder daughter of the Earl of Carlisle, married the Duke of Sutherland in 1823. Her beauty, wealth and splendid receptions in Stafford House provoked her aunt, Lady Granville, to refer to Harriet in a letter dated 23 July 1837 as 'that other queen Harriet the First'. (Harriet, Countess Granville,* Letters, *2 vols., 1894, vol. 2, p. 236.) She was a Whig Mistress of the Robes to Queen Victoria in 1837–41, 1846–52, 1853–8 and 1859–61. The Queen liked the Duchess, although she disapproved of the Duchess's admiration for Gladstone and Garibaldi. The Duchess treated the Queen with such deference that 'the air with which at the Queen's balls she presents her fan and bouquet to her royal mistress' made the wife of the American minister feel thoroughly Republican.*
PM

243.8 × 142.2 cms
*The Sutherland Trust*

*Provenance*: Always in the collections of the Dukes of Sutherland.
*Exhibitions*: Washington, National Gallery of Art, 'Treasure Houses of Britain', 1985, no. 545, pp. 611–2 (repr.).
*Bibliography*: Wild, 1894, no. 159.
See colour plate p. 107.

The Duchess is depicted in rather plain court dress, the effect of casualness reinforced by the way the fringed train is looped up over the arm. She wears black lace lappets in her hair, one of which falls over the Honiton lace collar on her bodice. She stands in the magnificent Staircase Hall at Stafford House,

London, now Lancaster House, decorated by Sir Charles Barry with copies of paintings after Veronese.

The Duke and Duchess of Sutherland evidently developed a taste for Winterhalter's work at a relatively early date. In 1844, they already had at Stafford House a version of Winterhalter's *Decameron* of 1837 (see Introduction, fig. 16) – probably the reduced version now at Staatlich Kunsthalle Karlsruhe. It may have been this picture about which the Duchess wrote to Winterhalter from the Hotel Maurice in an undated letter (Winterhalter Family Papers):

> *'Je ne pense qu'au tableau que j'ai vu l'autre jour et que j'espère bientôt visiter encore une fois. Me trouverez vous bien indiscrète de vous demander vos intentions. Pensez vous le garder auprès de vous – ou a t'il quelque distinction royale? Une idée me revients toujours combien j'aimerai à l'acheter moi même. Si c'est encore possible avec mes économies que je veux faire depuis que je l'ai vu – et puis je voudrais le donner a mon Mari.'*[1]

In a letter dated Windsor, 1 January 1845 (Private Collection, France) to M. Planat in Paris, Winterhalter notes: 'Plusieurs Dames (des très belles) se sont presentées pour portraits entre autres la Duchesse de Sutherland mais – refusées! Ce sera pour la prochaine fois!'[2] The Duchess had evidently to wait until 1849, the date of the present portrait, which Queen Victoria saw being painted at Stafford House on 13 June 1849 (WRA). Although the picture was, according to the Queen, far advanced in the execution of the figure of the Duchess in court dress, at that stage it still lacked its background.

A threequarter-length copy was with Spink 1927, and Newmans, Paris 1936; a head-and-shoulders version was painted by W. Corden for Queen Victoria's birthday on 24 May 1851, while another version with an altered background was painted for Lady Elizabeth Leveson-Gower, wife of the 8th Duke of Argyll and daughter of the sitter (now at Inverary Castle).

SF

1. 'I cannot take my mind off the painting which I saw the other day and which I hope to see again soon. Would it be indiscreet to ask what you intend to do with it. Do you wish to retain it, or is there Royal designation upon it? I am pursued by the idea that I should dearly like to purchase it myself. Is this still possible – I have been economizing ever since I saw it, and I should like to give it to my Husband.'
2. 'Several ladies (and some very beautiful ones) presented themselves for their portraits, amongst them the Duchess of Sutherland, but – all turned away! It will have to be for another time!'

## 35

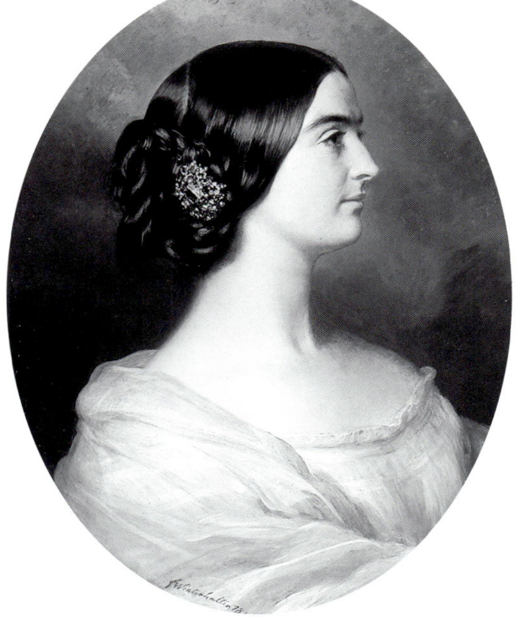

CHARLOTTE STUART, VISCOUNTESS CANNING (1849)

*A daughter of Sir Charles Stuart, formerly British ambassador to France, Charlotte Stuart (1817–61) married the future Earl Canning in 1835. Intelligent, artistic and cosmopolitan, she was a Lady of the Bedchamber of Queen Victoria from 1842 to 1855, when she left for India, where her husband had been appointed Governor-General. Lady Canning admired the Queen and corresponded with her throughout the Indian Mutiny. She died of a fever while travelling with her husband in the Himalayas. Prince Albert missed her because, in his words, 'she was such a distinguished person'.*

PM

61.3 × 48.9 cms, oval
Signed and dated, bottom centre:
*f Winterhalter 1849*
*The Right Hon. The Earl of Harewood*

*Provenance*: Queen Victoria; given to 6th Earl of Harewood by King George V.
*Bibliography*: Wild, 1894, no. 160; T. Borenius, *Catalogue of Pictures & Drawings at Harewood House*, Oxford University Press 1936, p. 56; R. Buckle, *Guide to Harewood House*, 1975, p. 29, repr; C. Allen, *A Glimpse of the Burning Plain*, 1986, repr. frontispiece.
See colour plate p. 112.

Lady Canning is seen wearing a white bodice in this head-and-shoulders view, with her profile to the right of the painting.

It was Queen Victoria who commissioned Winterhalter to paint Charlotte Canning, a Lady of the Bedchamber of whom she was especially fond. On 31 July 1849, she wrote from Osborne House: 'Winterhalter has sent the 2 heads he has painted for me, of Lady Canning & Fanny Jocelyn, which are extremely like. We . . . had a visit from good Winterhalter himself, whom we took to the dining-room to see how his pictures looked hung up, and he was much pleased.' (Journal.)

Comparison with a contemporary daguerreotype by Beard shows the portrait to have been a close likeness. Winterhalter uses a thin line of red, then black paint to accentuate Charlotte Canning's firm features against the sea-blue sky. The focus of attention is the superb Renaissance-style brooch nestling in a coil of glossy black hair. Her neck and shoulders are painted more weakly, however, while the anatomy under the muslin bodice is frankly unresolved. There is a visible *pentimento* at the nape of the neck where Winterhalter has altered the length of the chignon.

CBO

## 36

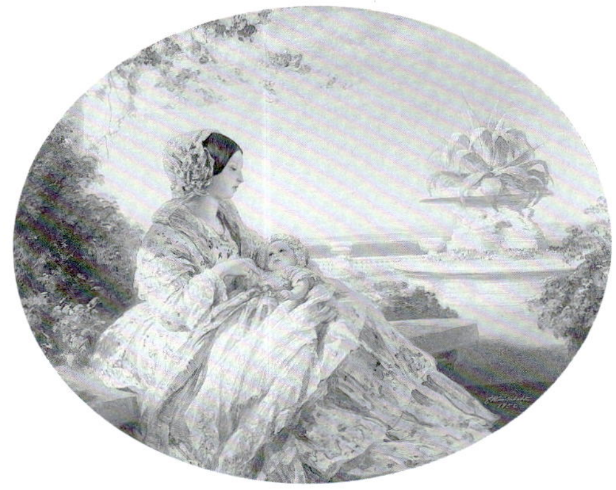

QUEEN VICTORIA WITH PRINCE ARTHUR (1850)

*The Queen described Prince Arthur (1850–1942), who was created Duke of Connaught in 1874, as 'dearer than any of the others put together'. He was intelligent, popular and the most active British Royal soldier of his day. He served in Ireland, Egypt, and the Mediterranean and was Governor-General of Canada from 1911 to 1916. Sir Garnet Wolseley called him 'a first rate Brigadier-General'.*
(See no. 92)

PM

59.7 × 75.2 cms, oval
Signed and dated, lower right: *F Winterhalter/ 1850*. Inscribed on the back with the names of artist and sitters and the date 1850.
*Her Majesty The Queen*

*Provenance*: Painted for Queen Victoria, 1850; placed in the Queen's Sitting-Room at Osborne.
*Bibliography*: Introduction, p. 45; Millar, *Victorian Pictures*.
*Prints after*: Engraving by G. Zobel, pub. 13 January 1852.
See colour plate p. 109.

The Queen is seated on a stone seat on the terrace at Osborne with Prince Arthur in her arms; at some distance is a massive bowl normally filled with flowers but, for artistic reasons, filled by Winterhalter with the broad-leaved plant that in fact grew nearby. In the distance is the sea.

The painting was made for Queen Victoria. She referred to it as 'the lovely little oval picture of Arthur in long clothes lying on my lap, I seated on the terrace here – perhaps one of Winterhalter's most charming pictures', and it was to be one of her presents to Prince Albert on his birthday, 26 August 1850 (Journal). She paid Winterhalter £100 for it in 1850 (WRA).

A copy by Frederick Richard Say is at Osborne (Her Majesty The Queen).

OM

## 37

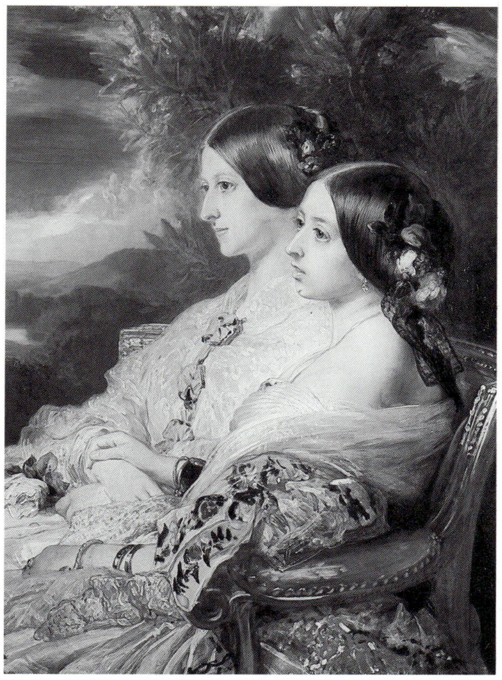

THE COUSINS: QUEEN VICTORIA AND VICTOIRE, DUCHESSE DE NEMOURS (1852)

*The Queen and the Duchesse (1822–57), a Coburg, who had married the second son of Louis-Philippe, were first cousins. The Queen and Prince Albert frequently saw the Duchesse de Nemours after the Revolution of 1848 had forced her to flee to England. They grew to love her 'as a sister'. (Virginia Surtees,* Charlotte Canning, *1975). The Queen wrote after her death: 'She was so dear, so good – one of those pure, virtuous, unobtrusive characters who make a home.'* (ibid.) *Others disagreed. Lady Canning found that 'She is very pretty and nice to look at, but, besides having a tiresome voice, she has nothing to say'* (ibid.).
PM

66.5 × 50.5 cms
Signed and dated: *F Winterhalter 1852*
*Her Majesty The Queen*

*Provenance*: Painted for Queen Victoria; placed in the Queen's Bedroom at Osborne.
*Exhibitions*: National Museum of Western Art, Tokyo, 'English Portraits', 1975, no. 49.
*Bibliography*: Wild, 1894, no. 216; Introduction, p. 45; Millar, *Victorian Pictures*.
See colour plate p. 122.

Seated side by side at half-length on a settee, the Queen's right hand rests on that of her cousin. The Queen wears roses in her hair and a dress of white tulle embroidered with gold and colours, trimmed on the sleeve with ribbons of embroidered cream silk, and a lace shawl. The Duchesse wears a loose, lace mantle fastened down the front with lilac ribbons, the lilac colour echoing that of the flowers in her hair. In the background is a landscape with hills and a broad river.

The portrait was painted for Queen Victoria as a present to Prince Albert. The cousins sat together to Winterhalter on 15 May 1852 (Journal). The Duchesse sat again on 29 June 'for the secret', which was given to the Prince on his birthday, 26 August. In July, Winterhalter was paid £100 for the picture (WRA). There are indications of an alteration to the line of the Queen's brow.

In December 1857, W. Corden was paid £31.10s for two copies (in oil) of the picture. In 1858, he was paid 15 guineas for another copy (WRA).
OM

## 38

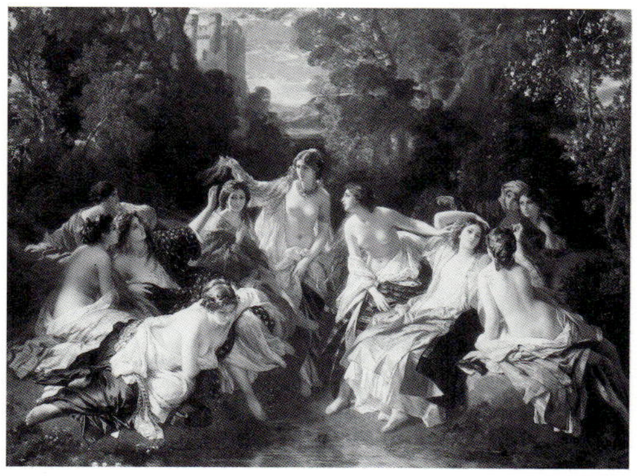

*FLORINDA* (1852)

179.1 × 244.5 cms
Signed, dated and inscribed, lower right:
*Fr Winterhalter. Paris. 1852*
*Her Majesty The Queen*

*Provenance*: Given by Queen Victoria to Prince Albert, 26 August 1852.
*Exhibitions*: London, Royal Academy, 1852, no. 285.
*Reviews*: For no. 38:
'Fine Arts: Royal Academy', *The Athenaeum*, no. 1281, 15 May 1852, p. 551.
For Metropolitan Museum of Art, New York version (Paris, Salon, 1853, no. 1198):
M. Horsin Déon, *Rapport sur le Salon de 1853*, 1853, p. 16; Théophile Gautier, 'Salon de 1853', *Feuilleton de la Presse*, 6 July 1853; L. Boyeldieu-D'Auvigny, *Guide aux Menus Plaisirs – Salon de 1853*, probably 1853, p. 42; Felix Tournachon (Nadar), *Nadar Jury au Salon de 1853, Album Comique*; H. Delaborde, 'Le Salon de 1853' in *Mélanges sur L'Art Contemporain*, 1866, pp. 91ff; Etienne-Jean Delécluze, 'Exposition de 1853', *Feuilleton du Journal des Débats*, 25 June 1853.
*Bibliography*: Wild, 1894, no. 494; W. Landgraf, *Daheim*, no. 38, 1908, p. 12; M. Alexander, *The Sunday Times Magazine*, 18 November 1973, p. 54, repr.; Introduction, pp. 46, 61; Millar, *Victorian Pictures*.
*Prints after*: Engravings by Hermann Eichens, 1857, pub. Goupil and Co., and Lemoine, 1859.
See colour plate p. 110.

The legend of King Rodrigo, last King of the Spanish Visigoths, and La Cava (Florinda) occurs in ballads first published in Spain at the end of the sixteenth century. Interest in the ballad revived during the nineteenth century; in 1814, Robert Southey published his poem 'Roderick, Last of the Goths', while in France the poet Emile Deschamps wrote his 'Romances sur Rodrigue, dernier roi des Goths, imitées de l'espagnol'. The immediate inspiration for the painting of *Florinda*, however, is likely to have been Thalberg's opera 'Florinda', which opened in London in 1851, during one of Winterhalter's summer visits to England.

The incident depicted shows Florinda and her maidens seeking refuge from the heat in the palace garden and removing their clothes to bathe. King Rodrigo, spying through parted branches on the left, falls in love with Florinda, the dark-haired figure to left of centre, still to disrobe. Shimmering silks, Moorish jewellery and a feudal castle set the scene for the Spanish Romance, but it remains a theatrical scene far removed from the original source. Winterhalter's own account of the story is given in a letter to the art critic Friedrich Pecht in 1869:

> *'Mein lieber Herr Pecht!*
> *Sie werden dieser Tage einen Abdruck meiner Florinde erhalten, wie ich Ihnen versprochen habe. Ich will Ihnen hier eine Erklärung des Bildes geben, welches vielleicht nöthig ist.*
> *Rodrigues der lezte der Gothenkönige uberrascht Florinde Tochter des Grafen Julien, als sie ihre Reitze mit jenen ihrer Gespielinnen vergleicht wird von heftiger Liebe zu ihr entbrannt, und verführt sie. Graf Julien, ihr Vater, um sich zu rächen, holt die Mauren aus Afrika herüber, eine 7 tägige Schlacht erfolgt in welcher Rodrigues umkomt und Spanien komt unter die Herrschaft der Mauren, welche 200 Jahre dauert. Die ganze Geschichte ist in einer altspanischen Romanze sehr schön erzählt, welche "La Cava" betitelt ist.'*[1]
> (coll. Stadtbibliothek, Munich)

As with *The Decameron* of 1837 (see Introduction, fig. 16), Winterhalter took a fashionable literary theme and turned it into a fancy picture. *Florinda* was something of a curiosity, however, for it was some twenty years since Winterhalter last painted such a large-scale genre work. There ran a popular rumour at the time that the Empress Eugénie and her ladies-in-waiting had been 'models' for the picture. Eugénie, however, was not married until 29 January 1853, and Winterhalter was far too respectful in character ever to have conceived such an idea. Nevertheless, there is a connection between *Florinda* and the Empress, since *Florinda*'s composition and wooded setting distinctly foreshadow those in *The Empress Eugénie Surrounded by her Ladies-in-Waiting* (no. 53), painted three years later.

On 3 April 1852, Queen Victoria wrote in her Journal from Buckingham Palace: 'On returning from our walk we saw a most beautiful picture by Winterhalter, his [Winterhalter's] favourite work, which I have purchased for Albert's birthday, but which can be no secret as it has to go to the Exhibition [Royal Academy]. It is a most lovely picture containing a group of beautiful women, ½ life-size.' The Queen paid Winterhalter £1000 for the picture in two instalments of £500, paid in 1852 and 1853 (WRA). *Florinda* was given to Prince Albert on 26 August 1852. Placed initially in the Queen's Sitting Room at Osborne House, the picture was later removed to Buckingham Palace.

*Florinda* also made an impression at the Royal Academy. *The Athenaeum* wrote on 15 May 1852:

> *'Of the foreign contributors, Mr. Winterhalter is decidedly entitled to the prize for his* Florinde *(285). . . . It is difficult to avoid overstepping the modesty of nature where so much female beauty of form and nudity are dealt with. Here, however, the Miltonic purity of the artist's mind has elevated the exponent. It is a picture of very great merit; the models are elegant and drawn with learned and decided outline, – the forms are fascinating without being improperly suggestive, the faces are charming, with much beauty of feature, and somewhat sister-like in family likeness. The colouring is gay – every possible tint is enlisted in the rich draperies. A warm light plays about everywhere; and the flesh glows, – although wanting in the nature of Etty and of our English painters, and rather such as French artists admire and aim at.'*

The *Florinde* exhibited at the 1853 Salon was probably the signed version (now Metropolitan Museum of Art, New York). *The Athenaeum* regretted Winterhalter's French types of beauty; conversely, Théophile Gautier in the *Feuilleton de la Presse*, 6 July 1853, deplored the choice of English types:

> *'Le modèle unique semble avoir été une de ces figures de cire moulées sur la Vénus de Canova . . .; c'est l'idéal de la femme tel que peuvent le concevoir Westall, Stephanoff, Carbould et autres illustrateurs des livres d'étrennes de Londres.'*[2]

Gautier also felt that Winterhalter had not exploited the sensual possibilities of the Spanish Romance, and concluded:

> *'Nous ne le tourmenterons donc pas là dessus, et nous accepterons son tableau comme un agréable mélange de chairs soyeuses et d'étoffes lustrées, où l'art sérieux n'a rien à voir,*

*qu'il serait ridicule d'anathémiser formellement. A quoi sert de prendre des carreaux pour foudroyer des papillons? Une épingle suffit.'*[3]

As well as the version at New York (signed, undated, 178.4 × 245.7 cms), a preparatory sketch for *Florinda* is known (oil on canvas, 32.4 × 49 cms, recorded in a Private Collection in 1949); a watercolour of the composition, without the castle or the figure of Roderick, but bearing the monogram F.W., was sold at the Hauswell & Nolte sale, Hamburg, 5 June 1979, no. 230. Related versions by other artists include a copy in oils of *Florinda* by Belli, paid for in 1861, but no longer in the Royal Collection. A signed black chalk drawing (60 × 80 cms), possibly an engraver's drawing, is in a Private Collection.
CBO

1. 'My dear Herr Pecht,
You will shortly be receiving a print of my Florinde, as I promised you. Here I should like to give you an explanation of the picture, which may be necessary.
Rodrigues, the last of the Gothic Kings, surprises Florinde, daughter of Count Julien, as she compares her charms with those of her companions [and] is inflamed by ardent love for her and seduces her. Count Julien, her father, to avenge himself, brings the Moors across from Africa, a seven-day battle ensues in which Rodrigues perishes and Spain comes under the rule of the Moors, which lasts for 200 years. The whole story is told very beautifully in an old Spanish ballad which is entitled "La Cava".'
2. 'The sole model seems to have been one of those wax figures moulded after Canova's Venus . . .; it is the sort of female archetype that appeals to Westall, Stephanoff, Carbould and other illustrators of London's gaudy gift catalogues.'
3. 'We shall not, therefore, slight him on that account, and we shall accept his painting as a blend of silky complexions and shimmering cloths, which has nothing to do with high art, and which it would be absurd to condemn formally. Why use stones to demolish butterflies? A pin will suffice.'

## 39

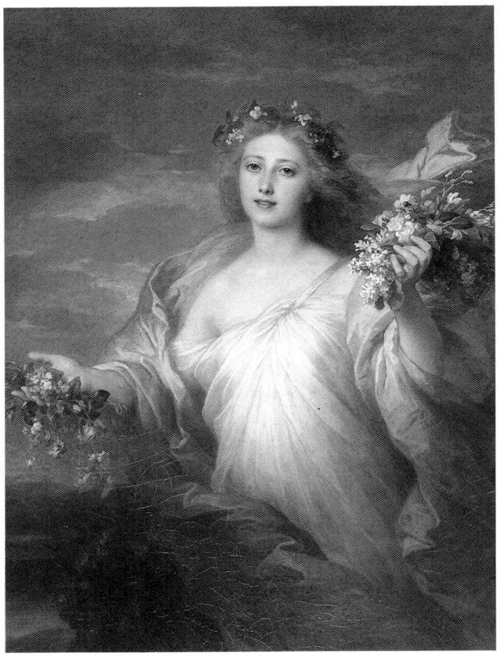

SPRING *(DER FRÜHLING)*

116.5 × 89.5 cms
*Private Collection*

*Provenance*: The artist; his brother, Hermann; thence by family descent.
*Bibliography*: Wild, 1894, no. 492; Introduction, pp. 61, 63.
See colour plate p. 111.

The theme of the young girl with flowers as an emblem of Spring is a recurring one in Western art. The representation of Flora, goddess of flowers, in Classical art, inspired many nineteenth-century sculptors and painters. The pose of Winterhalter's model can be compared to that of the statue of the *Farnese Flora* in Naples who similarly holds a bouquet of flowers in her left hand. Botticelli's *Primavera* was little admired at the time, but representations of Flora and Spring are common in Renaissance and Baroque painting.

The model in Winterhalter's picture holds flowers, including roses and lilac, in her left hand, and wears a wreath of apple blossom in her hair. Romantic skies and floral accessories are familiar components of Winterhalter's portraits, but the model of Spring appears less a creature of flesh and blood than an ethereal being borne on the wind, flowing forward with her offering of flowers and her pink wrap billowing behind. The regular oval features, heavy-lidded eyes and mane of luxuriant hair conform to Winterhalter's conventional ideal of beauty, but are transfigured here by the mysterious, trance-like expression. Lips parted, arms open but tantalizingly out of reach, Spring enshrines the effervescence and transience of beauty.

The picture is one of Winterhalter's rare late subject works, evidently painted for his own pleasure as it does not appear to have been exhibited. It is difficult to date with any precision, but belongs to the period of *Florinda*. It is reproduced in the Winterhalter *Album*, the 1891 inventory of Hermann Winterhalter's estate (Winterhalter Family Papers), no. 4.
RLO

## 40

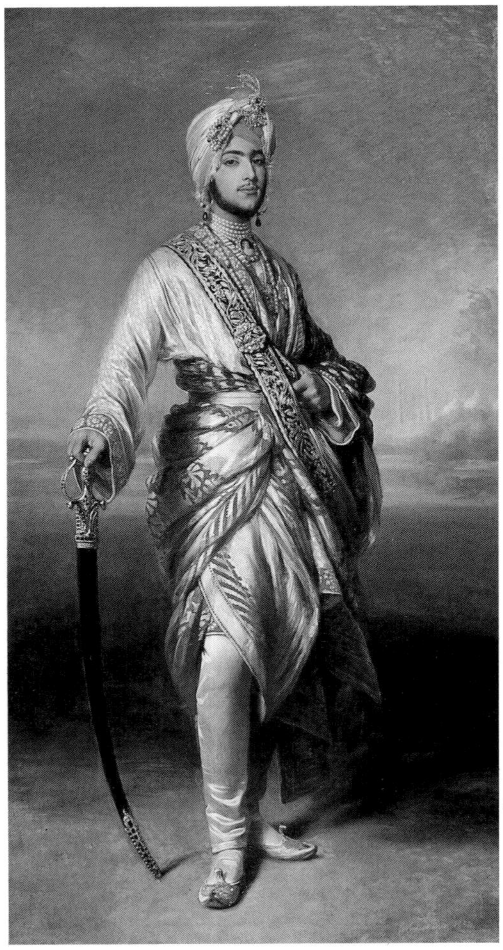

THE MAHARAJAH DULEEP SINGH (1854)

*The Maharajah Duleep Singh (1838–93) was the youngest of the acknowledged sons (although widely believed to be illegitimate) of Ranjit Singh, Maharajah of Lahore, whom he succeeded in 1843. When, in 1849, the British annexed the Punjab, he was forced to resign his sovereignty; at the same period he surrendered 'the gem he called the Koh-i-noor' (the diamond presented to Queen Victoria by the East India Company in 1851 and subsequently set in a tiara for the Queen). He was taken in 1850 to Futteghur, where he became a Christian, and, in 1854, to England, where he was introduced to Queen Victoria. She admired his looks and his manners (she made a number of drawings of him), was touched by his history and remained a sympathetic friend even when, many years after, a combination of financial hardship and a burning sense of injustice induced in the Maharajah a state of schizophrenia, indistinguishable from insanity.*
*He renounced Christianity, became violently anti-British, conceived plans for leading the Sikhs of the Punjab in a revolt against British rule in India and offered his services to the Russians. In 1891, after he had suffered a stroke and begged to be reconciled with the Queen, she met him at Nice: 'I am so glad that we met again & I cld. say I forgave him.'*

203.8 × 109.5 cms
Signed and dated, bottom right: *F Winterhalter 1854*. On the back of the original canvas was an inscription giving the names of artist and sitter and the date, July 1854.
*Her Majesty The Queen*

*Provenance*: Painted for Queen Victoria; placed in the Princesses' Corridor at Buckingham Palace, but transferred to Osborne in 1912.
*Bibliography*: Rev. E. Farrer, *Portraits in Suffolk Houses (West)*, 1908, p. 390; E. Dalhousie Login, *Court Life & Camp Life (1820–1904)*, 1904,

pp. 122–3; M. Alexander and S. Anand, *Queen Victoria's Maharajah*, 1980, pp. 44–9; Introduction, pp. 51, 57, 64; Millar, *Victorian Pictures*.
See colour plate p. 114.

The Maharajah Duleep Singh appears full-length, standing in a landscape in Indian dress, resting his right hand on his sword. He wears a number of the jewels which he had retained at the time when his lands were annexed by the British, including, in his turban, his diamond aigrette and star. (For the miniature of the Queen, see below.)

No. 40 was painted for Queen Victoria. In her Journal for 10 July 1854, at Buckingham Palace, she noted: 'Went to see Winterhalter painting, where we found the Maharajah in his full dress . . . Winterhalter was in ecstasies at the beauty and nobility of bearing of the young Maharajah. He was very amiable and patient, standing so still and giving a sitting of upwards of 2 hours. Winterhalter has got the whole figure beautifully, and the likeness is so good.' On the following day, she was again 'present for a while at the Maharajah's sitting, which went very well. He was again in full dress. The portrait of me, set in diamonds, which he generally wears, was the gift of Lord Auckland to his father, as well as the ring with my miniature which he had on today'. She saw the picture again on 12 July; saw a sitting on the following day; and on 17 July, saw the last sitting the Maharajah was giving: 'the beautiful picture is not entirely finished as regards the dress.' During one of the sittings, the Maharajah was shown the Koh-i-Noor. On 18 July, the Queen wrote to the King of the Belgians that Winterhalter had just painted 'a beautiful picture' of the Maharajah ('not quite 16, short, but *singularly* handsome, gentle, amiable & pleasing') 'in his very peculiar dress' (WRA). According to Lady Login, in this portrait, Winterhalter gave his youthful sitter the height he assumed he would attain in manhood; the Maharajah never, in fact, grew any taller (*Court Life & Camp Life 1820–1904*). Winterhalter was paid £300 for the picture in 1854 (WRA). On 14 and 15 July, Winterhalter made sketches in watercolour of the Maharajah, head and shoulders in profile (R.L. no. 13342 and Sotheby's, 19 March 1981, lot 44).

A copy by Janet Hawkins was in the possession of the sitter (*Portraits in Suffolk Houses (West)*; it was sold at Elveden by Christie's, 21 May 1984, lot 70. Koberwein had been paid £84 on 30 June 1865 for a copy (WRA).
OM

## 41

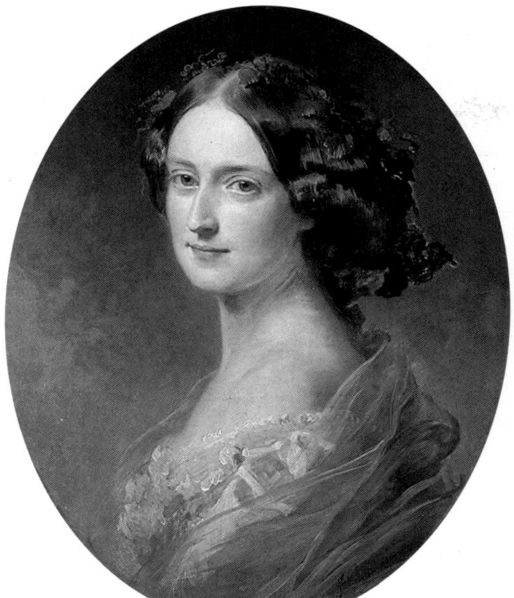

LADY CLEMENTINA AUGUSTA WELLINGTON CHILD-VILLIERS

*Lady Clementina Villiers (1824–58) was one of the three pretty daughters of the Earl of Jersey, twice Master of the Horse to Queen Victoria. She had many admirers, including the future Napoleon III, when he was a pretender in London. However, she never married. The reason may have been that her mother, a celebrated political hostess, had the habit of seizing young men when they entered the ball-room and crying: 'Go and dance with Clemmy!' She died of a fever caught in the country.*
PM

60 × 51 cms, oval
Signed, lower right: *fr Winterhalter*
*The Collection of the Earl of Jersey*

*Provenance*: By descent in the family.
*Exhibitions*: London, Royal Academy, 1856, no. 123.
*Bibliography*: Wild, 1894, no. 396.
See colour plate p. 113.

Winterhalter's portrait of Lady Clementina shows her in a low-cut ball-gown and gauze wrap. The composition concentrates attention on the tilted oval of her head, as she glances backwards over her shoulder to meet the viewer's gaze. The focus of the portrait is on the sitter's serene expression, and the fashionably plain hairstyle which is decorated with a wreath of vine leaves and tendrils (cf. nos. 51, 93).

Together with her sisters, Lady Clementina was much portrayed, as a child, and later: twice by Sir George Hayter, three times by A.E. Chalon in 1832 and 1842, and there is a drawing of her in 1849 by J.B. Swinton which was lithographed by R.J. Lane. Comparison with these earlier portraits shows Winterhalter to have regularized his sitter's features.
CBO

## 42

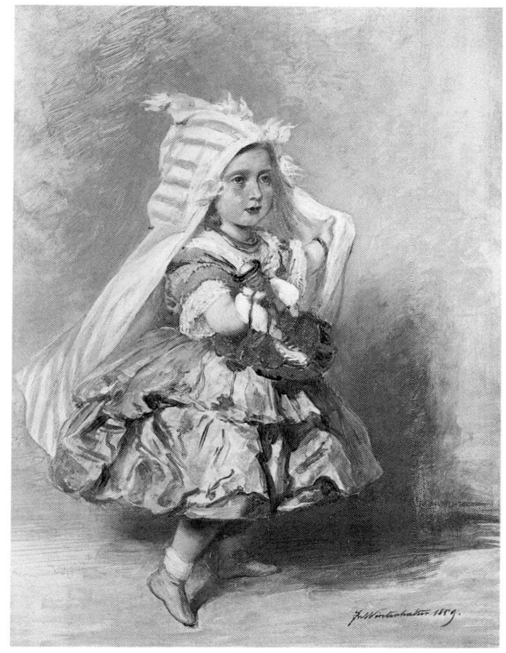

PRINCESS BEATRICE (1859)

*Shy, tactful and musical, Princess Beatrice (1857–1944) was the youngest of the Queen's daughters. She was the Queen's great consolation when Prince Albert died, and grew up to be a close companion and confidante. When she married Prince Henry of Battenberg in 1885, he had to agree to live at his mother-in-law's court. Princess Beatrice inherited her mother's diaries, which she transcribed, edited, and then destroyed.*
PM

50.8 × 41 cms
Signed and dated: *Fr Winterhalter 1859*. Inscribed on the back with the names of artist and sitter and the date, June 1859.
*Her Majesty The Queen*

*Provenance*: Painted for Queen Victoria; placed in the Queen's Bedroom at Buckingham Palace.
*Bibliography*: Millar, *Victorian Pictures*.
See colour plate p. 116.

Princess Beatrice is depicted full-length in a pink dress. She wears an Arab burnous on her head, and clasps a doll which appears to be wearing Russian peasant dress in her right arm.

Painted for Queen Victoria, this was among the 'lovely sketches' which Winterhalter painted for her in the summer of 1859. He was paid £20 for the portrait on 29 June 1859 (WRA).
OM

43

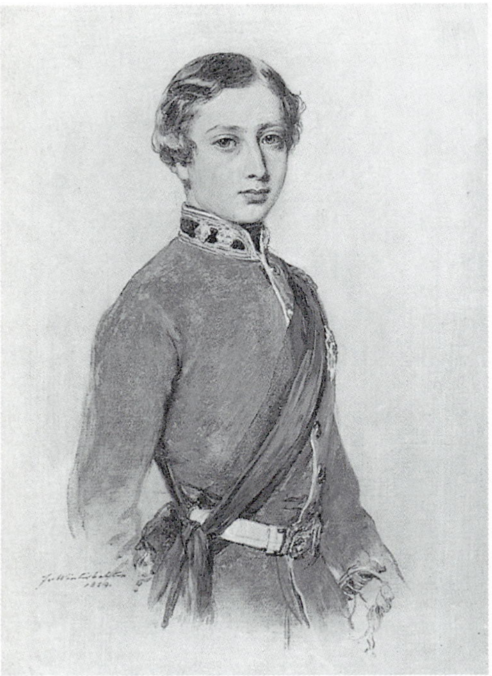

ALBERT EDWARD, PRINCE OF WALES (1859)
(For biography, see no. 31)

40.6 × 30.5 cms
Signed and dated, lower left: *Fr Winterhalter/1859*
Inscribed on the back with the names of artist and sitter and the date, June 1859
*Her Majesty The Queen*

*Provenance*: Painted for Queen Victoria; hung in the Queen's Bedroom at Buckingham Palace.
*Exhibitions*: London, 1956–7, no. 471; National Gallery of Canada, 'A Pageant of Canada', 1967, no. 255; Queen's University, Kingston, Ontario, 'Heritage Kingston', 1973, no. 228.
*Bibliography*: Millar, *Victorian Pictures*.
*Prints after*: Lithograph by J.A. Vintner, pub. 1 June 1860; another was made by J.H. Lynch.
See colour plate p. 117.

The Prince is shown at half-length, against a plain light background, in the uniform of a lieutenant-colonel in the Grenadier Guards with the ribbon and star of the Garter.

The Prince of Wales had been gazetted as a colonel on 9 November 1858. On 2 July 1859, the Queen wrote to the Princess Royal that Winterhalter had 'done such lovely sketches' of sitters who included the Prince of Wales. She had written to her on 29 June describing the Prince as 'a little grown . . . his nose & mouth are much grown also; the nose is becoming the true Coburg nose & begins to hang a little, but there remains, unfortunately the want of chin . . . Winterhalter is making a Sketch of him wh. will be very like'. (WRA.)

Payments to Winterhalter in the quarter ending 30 September 1859 included £30 for a 'Sketch' of the Prince (WRA); another record of payments also at £30 and in 1859, includes 'Head in oils of P^ce^ of Wales'. (WRA.)

A good copy is in the Empress Friedrich's Collection at Schloss Friedrichshof, perhaps the copy for which W. Corden was paid 5 guineas in November 1859.

OM

44

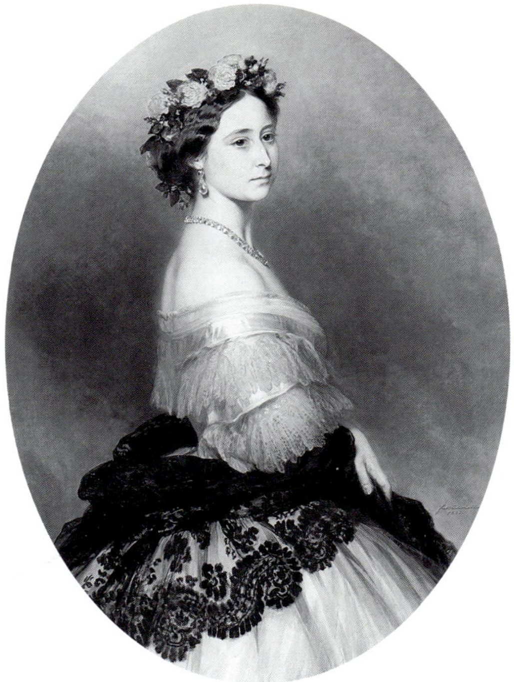

PRINCESS ALICE (1861)

*Princess Alice (1843–78), the second of the Queen's daughters, married Ludwig IV, future Grand Duke of Hesse-Darmstadt and the Rhine in 1862. She went to live in his capital, Darmstadt, where she soon found scope for her interest in welfare, and ability for organization. She started the Alice Hospital, the Alice Sisterhood and the Alice Frauenverein. Her daughter, Alix, married the last Czar, Nicholas II.*
(See nos. 89, 91)
PM

118.7 × 88.9 cms, oval
Signed and dated: *Fr Winterhalter/1861*
*Her Majesty The Queen*

*Provenance*: Painted for Queen Victoria, 1861.
*Bibliography*: Millar, *Victorian Pictures*.
*Prints after*: Lithograph by J.A. Vintner.
See colour plate p. 118.

Princess Alice appears threequarter-length, standing in a dress of white tulle over white silk, a lace turning on the sleeves, and a black silk bobbin lace shawl, with a wreath of flowers in her hair.

This was painted for the Queen, *en suite* with a portrait of the Princess Royal (Her Majesty The Queen). Winterhalter, who had just arrived, began the portrait on 4 June 1861. On 13 June, the Queen recorded in her Journal that he had 'finished Alice's beautiful picture, which is so like & fine'. She had told the Princess Royal the previous day that the portrait was finished and was 'beautiful' (WRA). On 21 June, Winterhalter was paid £150 for the portrait (WRA). At first the Princess held a wreath of flowers in her hand, but this was altered in the course of painting.

A copy by Belli is in the Mountbatten Collection; it may be the copy for which he was paid 30 guineas on 6 August 1861 (WRA).

OM

45

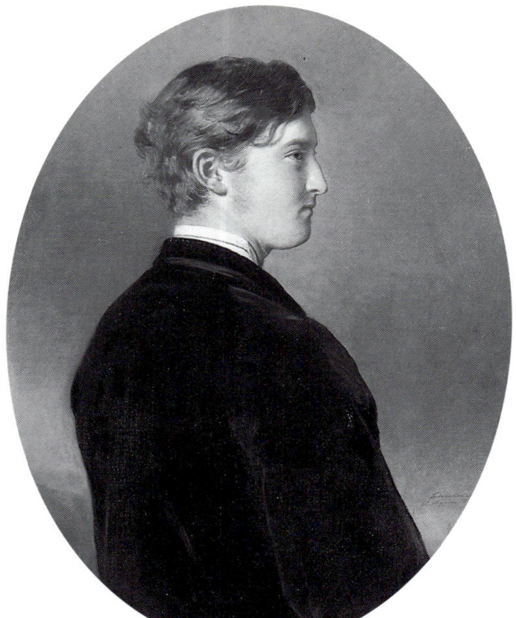

WILLIAM DOUGLAS-HAMILTON, 12TH DUKE OF HAMILTON (1863)

*The Duke of Hamilton (1845–95) was one of the richest peers in Scotland. Through his mother, Princess Marie of Baden, he was a cousin of Napoleon III, who in 1864 revived the ancient Hamilton title of Duc de Châtellerault in his favour. His pursuit of pleasure at home and abroad led him to sell many family possessions at the famous Hamilton Palace sale of 1882. When he died at the age of fifty, the famous Victorian magazine* Truth *wrote that he had been 'beset by all the deadly sins in a far greater degree than perhaps any other young nobleman of his standing'.*
PM

81.3 × 63.5 cms, oval
Signed and dated, lower right:
*F Winterhalter/Baden 1863*
*The National Trust for Scotland, Brodick Castle*

*Provenance*: By descent; passed to the National Trust for Scotland 1958.
*Bibliography*: Wild, 1894, no. 453; A. von Schneider, *Die Pyramide*, 24, 20 January 1935, pp. 9–10.
*Prints after*: Engraving by F. Weber.
See colour plate p. 119.

The Duke of Hamilton is shown at half-length, in an oval format and in profile, his back facing the viewer. He is wearing an informal lounge jacket, probably of velvet, the collar trimmed with braid – a popular feature of men's fashionable dress in the 1860s. The pose and oval format of the portrait of the 12th Duke is one Winterhalter had used for female portraits, but is unusual for a male portrait.

Three portraits by Winterhalter depicting the three children of the 11th Duke of Hamilton are dated 1863, including the present portrait of the 12th Duke who succeeded his father on the former's sudden death from a fall in Paris on 15 July 1863. All three portraits were presumably envisaged as a set, as all are ovals depicting the sitters at half-length, although Winterhalter's portraits of the 12th Duke's brother and sister depict them full-face and wearing Scottish dress. The portraits were probably commissioned by the children's parents: the wife of the 11th Duke of Hamilton was born Princess Marie of Baden, and this portrait of her son was, according to its inscription, painted at Baden. The portraits of Lady Maria and Lord Charles Hamilton (which are not similarly inscribed) were exhibited at Knoedler's in 1936 when they were in the Collection of Viscount Bearsted, but their present whereabouts is unknown. Wild records the portraits of the children of the Duke of Hamilton twice (nos. 431–3, 453 A, B, C), so that it is conceivable that they were painted on more than one occasion – but more probable that the list repeats itself (see p. 226).

The 12th Duke's parents were keen patrons of Winterhalter: a watercolour portrait of the 11th Duke dates from 1850 (Sotheby's, 11 July 1985, lot 93), and Wild (no. 452) mentions a portrait of him 'Commandé de souvenir', presumably a posthumous portrait. A full-length portrait of the Duchess, showing her in profile, shading her eyes, was formerly at Brodick Castle, Isle of Arran. This, or possibly one of the other Hamilton portraits already mentioned, may be the portrait about which the Duchess wrote to Winterhalter from Hamilton Palace in an undated letter (Winterhalter Family Papers):

> *'Sie bitten mir sobald als möglich zu sagen, was wir Ihnen schuldig sind, da wir morgen schon abreisen. Bitte antworten Sie mir sogleich darüber. Der Herzog wünscht auch sehr das Bild nach Hamilton zu schicken. Wenn Sie (wie Sie mir sagten) noch etwas daran ändern wollen, so überlassen wir Ihnen den Zeitpunkt zu bestimmen wann es kann nach Schottland gesendet werden.'*[1]

On another occasion, the Duchess wrote to Winterhalter in Paris to invite him to partake of 'Das vaterländische Sauerkraut'[2] at her children's house in the Avenue des Champs Elysées. (*Die Pyramide*)
SF

1. 'To ask you to tell me as soon as possible what we owe you, as we are going away tomorrow. Please let me know the answer immediately. The Duke also very much wants to send the picture to Hamilton. If (as you told me) you wish to make further changes to it, we will leave it to you to decide upon the time when it can be sent to Scotland.'
2. 'Our native sauerkraut'.

## 46

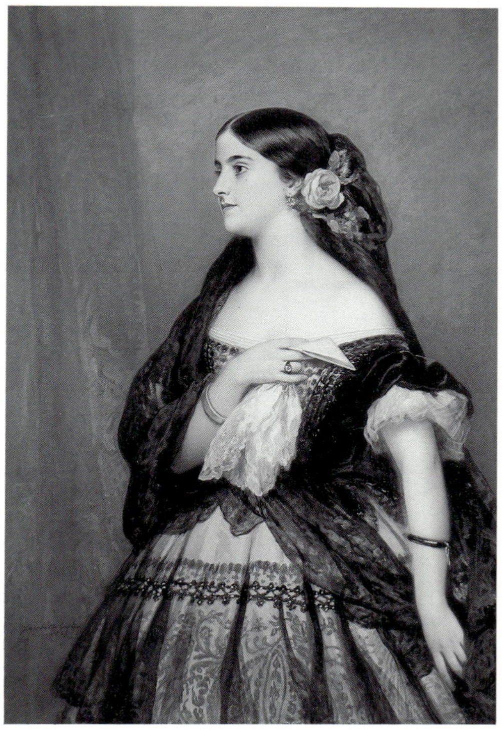

ADELINA PATTI (1863)

*Adelina Patti (1843–1919) was one of the great sopranos of the day. An Italian born in Madrid, she made her début in America. After her triumph as Amina in Bellini's* 'La Sonnambula' *at Covent Garden in 1861, she sang all the great parts in Italian opera, preserving her freshness of voice until her retirement in the late 1880s. She was married to, successively, the Marquis de Caux, a courtier of Napoleon III, the tenor Nicolini, and the Swedish Baron Cederström.*
PM

110 × 77.9 cms
Signed and dated, lower left-hand corner:
*F. Winterhalter 1863*
*Private Collection*

*Provenance*: Baron Olof Rudoph Cederström, third husband of Adelina Patti; by descent in the family.
*Bibliography*: Guy de Charnacé, *A. Patti*, 1868, p. 13; K. Klein, *The Reign of Patti*, 1920, frontispiece; London, Royal Academy, 'The Royal Opera House Retrospective 1732–1982', 1982–3, p. 46.
See colour plate p. 115.

In a bodice of black velvet and pink silk, and a skirt of pink silk trimmed with black Chantilly lace, Adelina Patti is portrayed as Rosina in Rossini's opera 'Il barbiere di Siviglia'. A cluster of pink roses in her hair and a black mantilla allude to the role, while she clasps to her breast the note she will drop for Count Almaviva. There is a suggestion of movement as the soprano, facing the audience by the green curtain of the stage, draws back her mantilla, about to commence the next aria.

Although it was unusual for Winterhalter to enter into the particulars of his sitters' backgrounds, as here, it was appropriate to show Patti in the guise of Rosina. Rossini had rearranged much of the music of 'Il barbiere di Siviglia' especially for her voice, and this was the most popular role of Patti's career. In 1863, she was on tour in Paris, singing the part of Rosina at the Théâtre Italien. The musical critic Scudo wrote:

> *'Cette séduisante sirène a ébloui M. Mario de l'éclat de ses* strillate, *elle l'a étourdi du bruit de ses castagnettes. Aussi n'est-il plus question que d'Adelina Patti, de ses grâces, de sa jeunesse, de sa belle voix, de son instinct merveilleux, de sa bravoure et de ses petites mines d'enfant gâté.'*[1] (*A. Patti*)

It was at this period that Winterhalter first painted her. He painted a second portrait of her *c.*1868 (115 × 81 cms, The Right Hon. The Earl of Harewood), at about the time of her marriage to the Marquis de Caux. In the latter, the classic three-quarter-length, threequarter-face Winterhalter pose, even the magnificent gown of white silk and tulle, possibly by Worth, fail to soften La Patti's somewhat forbidding expression. The 1863 portrait of Patti as Rosina appears all the more engaging by comparison.
CBO

1. 'This alluring siren has dazzled M. Mario [a famous tenor] with her outstanding *strillate*, and has stunned him with the sound of her castagnettes. Henceforth one hears of nothing but Adelina Patti, her charms, her youth, the beauty of her voice, her marvellous feel for music, her fortitude and her spoilt-child affectations.'

## 47

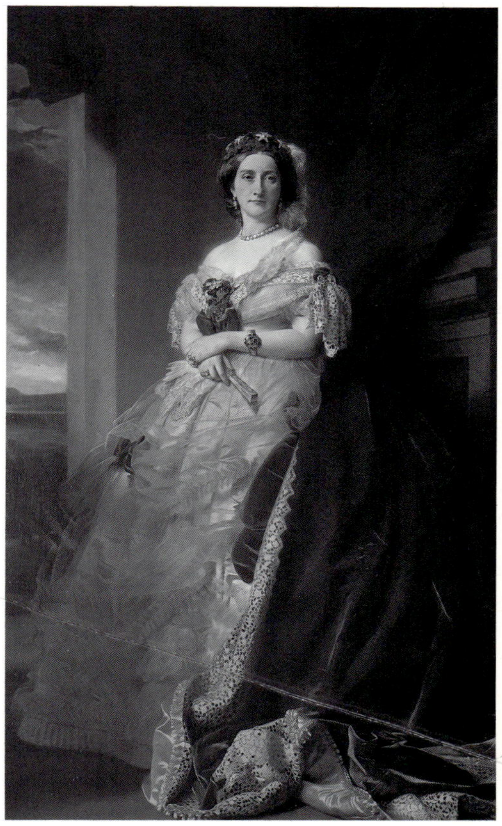

JULIA LOUISA BOSVILLE, LADY MIDDLETON (1863)

*Lady Middleton (1824–1901) married the 8th Lord Middleton. She built luxurious kennels for the Middleton Hunt at Birdsall House in Yorkshire, with an especially wide corridor which enabled her to walk through without hounds jumping over her crinoline. Practical, authoritarian and mother of thirteen children, she led the life of a rich Victorian aristocrat, moving between Yorkshire (Salvin added a storey and two wings to Birdsall House), London, Scotland and Nottinghamshire, where the Middletons owned Wollaton Hall.*
PM

239 × 147.5 cms
Signed, dated and inscribed, base of column to right: *fr Winterhalter/Paris 1863*
*Lord Middleton*

Provenance: By descent in the family.
*Exhibitions*: London, 1956–7, no. 415 (repr.).
*Bibliography*: Wild, 1894, no. 457; Introduction, p. 53.
See colour plate p. 120.

Wearing court dress, Lady Middleton gazes ahead with a commanding expression. The dress, probably by Worth, dominates the picture. White, with swags and puffs of white tulle, it is worn over a dome-shaped crinoline. The bodice is trimmed with ribbon-pleated tulle and lace, probably Honiton. The same lace edges the court train of purple velvet lined with white silk. In her hair, Lady Middleton wears the three feathers (for married women) and two lappets of lace required for court dress. Winterhalter dwells on the differing textures of velvet, lace and tulle with an exactitude rare for his work at this date. As well as the diamond necklace, Lady Middleton wears a bracelet of heavy gold in fashionable neo-Gothic style.

Winterhalter enlivens a somewhat static pose by extending the swirling background drapes with the line of the velvet train. Rich shadows around the figure lend further volume and depth. The noble proportions, drapes, pedestal, and the architecture blending with a distant view are devices borrowed from Van Dyck and Sir Thomas Lawrence. However, the inspired use of viridian for the head-dress and on the corsage, setting off, as it does, the purple of the court train and bows, is the product of a modern and mid-nineteenth-century palette.

The portrait was presented to Lady Middleton by the 'Tenantry and Professional Gentlemen' connected with her husband's estates at Wollaton Hall, on 2 July 1863. A portrait of Lord Middleton by Sir Francis Grant was presented on the same occasion. Slightly smaller in scale, it is an awkward pendant to the more majestic work painted by Winterhalter the same year in Paris.
CBO

## 48

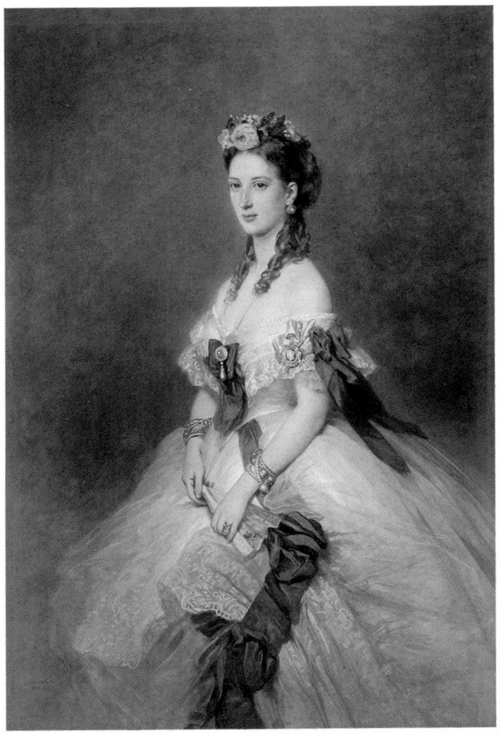

ALEXANDRA, PRINCESS OF WALES (1864)

*The daughter of the future King Christian IX of Denmark, Princess Alexandra (1844–1925) married the Prince of Wales in 1863; they became King and Queen in 1901. Her beauty, charm and elegance made her universally popular and she was also extremely active in charitable work. One of her brothers became the King of Denmark, another King of the Hellenes, and her sister, Dagmar, married Tsar Alexander III of Russia.*
PM

162.6 × 114 cms
Signed and dated, lower left: *Fr. Winterhalter/1864*
*Her Majesty The Queen*

*Provenance*: Commissioned by Queen Victoria and eventually placed in the Crimson Drawing-Room at Windsor.
*Exhibitions*: National Gallery of Canada, 'A Pageant of Canada', 1967, no. 257.
*Bibliography*: M. Alexander, *The Sunday Times Magazine*, 18 November 1973, p. 53, repr.; Introduction, pp. 53–4, 61; Millar, *Victorian Pictures*.
*Prints after*: Lithograph by J.A. Vintner, pub. Colnaghi's, 10 March 1865.
See colour plate p. 121.

The Princess of Wales is shown threequarter-length, standing to the left, in a white silk, lace and tulle dress with blue-green ribbons decorating the bodice, and diagonally holding up the lace skirt at the side; she holds a fan in her hands. She wears the badge of the Order of Victoria and Albert and a wreath of flowers in her hair. Dr Aileen Ribeiro has suggested that the choice of sea-green for the ribbons on the dress might be a reference to the nautical Danish background of the Princess, as in Tennyson's 'Sea King's Daughter from Over the Sea'.

No. 48, together with its pendant, a threequarter-length portrait of the Prince of Wales in the uniform of the 10th Hussars (Her Majesty The Queen), was commissioned by Queen Victoria. The project was discussed in letters to the Princess Royal. At first, the Queen suggested a half-length group for Osborne, with the newly-born Prince Albert Victor in the Princess's lap and the Prince of Wales behind. The alternative was to be a pair of full-lengths for Windsor, 'neither of us can afford'. The Princess Royal replied to the Queen on 4 May 1864: 'I do not know of any particular position Alix should be painted in by Winterhalter, she is prettiest to my taste either quite en face – or quite in Profile. He is sure to do something charming – I am so glad you have got him to come at last.' (WRA.) On his arrival, on or just before 19 May, Winterhalter refused to paint full-lengths, 'so they are to be the size of yours & Fritz's by Lauchert'; the baby was to be omitted. By 26 May, the Queen wrote: 'Winterhalter is painting Bertie and Alix very successfully I hear; – half lengths, I hear. I wonder if he admires Alix.' The Princess Royal had been in no doubt the portraits should be full-length: 'then perhaps a little sketch of her without a background – like Lady Constance Grosvenor Lady Gainsborough & Lady Ely for Osborne.' (WRA.)

Winterhalter was paid £400 for the portraits on 22 August 1864 (WRA). Four years after this commission, in November 1868, the Princess of Wales visited Winterhalter's studio in Paris.
OM

## 49

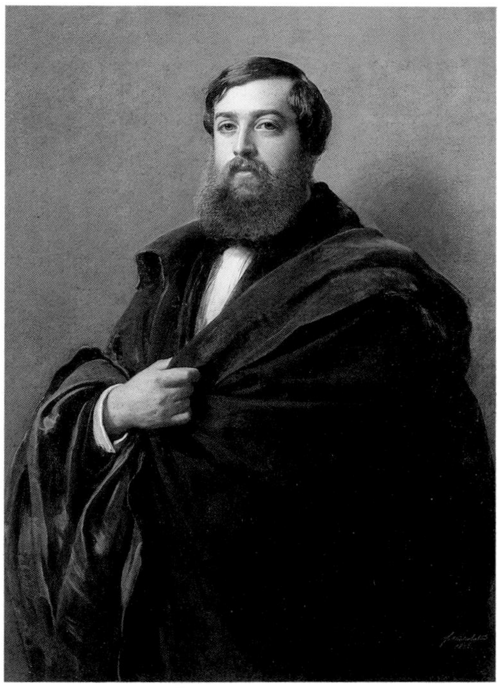

ALFRED-ÉMILIEN, COMTE DE NIEUWERKERKE (1852)

*The Comte de Nieuwerkerke (1811–92) was a member of a Dutch family (allegedly descended from the illegitimate son of a Prince of Orange), which had settled in Paris. He was handsome and charming, and knew how to turn political changes to his own advantage. He was a page of Charles X, King of France (1824–30), and accompanied the King's grandson, the Comte de Chambord, around Italy in 1843. In Florence he met a niece of Napoleon I, Princess Mathilde, and they became lovers. In 1849, after her cousin Louis-Napoleon became President of the Second Republic, Nieuwerkerke was appointed Directeur-Général des Musées Impériaux, and, in 1853, Surintendant des Beaux-Arts. These were positions of great power, which he enjoyed enormously. He had the conventional taste of his day, and was himself a sculptor, but of little originality: he produced equestrian statues of Napoleon I and Napoleon III. Although he acted as host at her parties, he was unfaithful to Princess Mathilde and left her in 1869. After the fall of the Second Empire he settled near Lucca, where he died in 1892.*
PM

118 × 90 cms
Signed and dated, bottom right:
*fr Winterhalter/1852.*
*The Artemis Group*

*Provenance*: Galerie Jean-Françoise et Philippe Heim, Paris.
See colour plate p. 125.

In this threequarter-length portrait, the Comte de Nieuwerkerke stands to the left, wearing a grey travelling cloak with a brown lining.

In 1852, the Comte was in the early stages of his career as Directeur-Général des Musées Impériaux, and collector. However, his rooms in the Louvre housed an already substantial Private Collection of armoury and works of art (Letter from Labouchère to Nieuwerkerke, 2 April 1852, Archives des Musées Nationaux au Louvre o[30]/.356). It must have been a conscious decision to present Nieuwerkerke in the guise of a prince patron of the Renaissance, an effect arrived at by allusion to Titian's portraits in particular. In fact, Nieuwerkerke's ordinary travelling cloak assumes an abstract importance comparable to the quilted sleeve in Titian's *Man in Blue* (National Gallery, London).

In his drawing of Nieuwerkerke of 1856 (Fogg Art Museum, Cambridge, Massachussetts), where the sitter wears decorations and exudes *hubris*, Ingres also used a cloak to expressive effect. But whereas the Ingres drawing represents Nieuwerkerke as a brilliant administrator, Winterhalter's portrait has a Romantic and historical quality which must especially have satisfied its subject. To paint the Directeur-Général des Musées Impériaux in 1852, so soon after the promulgation of the Second Empire, demonstrated Winterhalter's leading position as a portraitist; indeed, the very next year, Winterhalter was given the commission to paint the state portraits of the Emperor and Empress (see Introduction, figs. 33 and 34, pp. 46–7).

Wild fails to mention this portrait, although he records two threequarter-length portraits of a Comte and Comtesse de Neverkerque (*sic*) painted in Paris, in 1840 (nos. 52, 53).
CBO

## 50

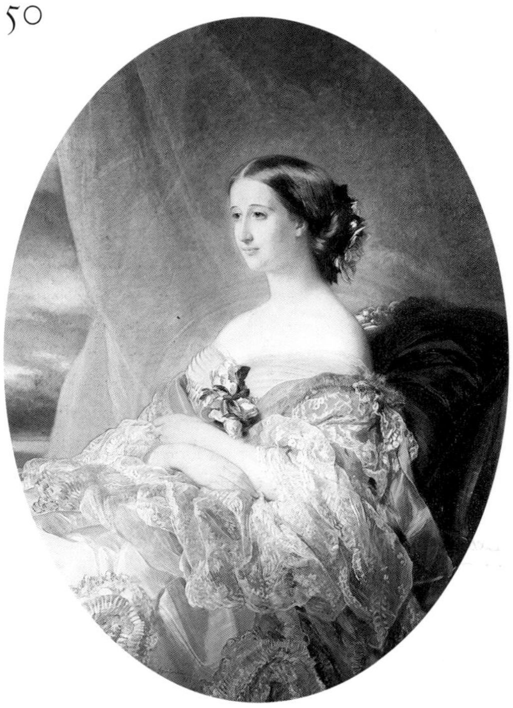

THE EMPRESS EUGÉNIE (1854)

*The Empress (1826–1920) was born Eugénie de Montijo, Comtesse de Teba. Her mother was daughter of a Scottish wine merchant. Her father, a younger son of an ancient Spanish noble family, had supported the French during the Peninsular War and had been a chamberlain of King Joseph Bonaparte. She grew up in France and Spain and married Napoleon III at the age of twenty-seven. She had less influence over government policy, and was less reactionary than was believed at the time.*
(See nos. 52, 53, 54, 58)
PM

125 × 95 cms, oval
Signed, dated and inscribed, bottom centre:
*f Winterhalter Paris/1854*
*Private Collection*

*Provenance*: Presented by the Empress Eugénie to Madame Eugène Rouher, 1884; Artemis Group, London.

*Exhibitions*: Probably Paris, 'Exposition Universelle', 1855, no. 4208; Vienna, Kunstverein, 1856.
*Reviews*: Claude Vignon, *Exposition Universelle des Beaux-Arts*, 1855, pp. 242–3; *Kunstblatt*, 21 March 1856.
*Bibliography*: Wild, 1894, no. 232; Dion Clayton Calthrop, *Connoisseur*, 31, 1911, engraving after, p. 135, repr.; Artemis Group Annual Report, 1983–4, p. 16, repr. facing page; Introduction, pp. 48, 54.
*Prints after*: Engravings by Léon Noël and Faber.
See colour plate p. 126.

Eugénie is seated with folded arms against a green silk cushion on a gilt chair. The dull crimson curtain is lifted to the left to reveal a balustrade and an expanse of sky. She wears a white silk organza ballgown, with what appear to be artificial camellias on her bodice, and in her hair. The dress is probably by Madame Palmyre, who made the 'parures de soirée' for the trousseau of the Empress. The dress is set off by a brilliant lilac shawl. There is a conspicuous lack of jewellery: Eugénie had, according to contemporaries, the perfect bust and shoulders, and she could, therefore, dispense with jewellery in the evenings. Her simple hairstyle, with the wreath of flowers at the nape, was known as 'à l'impératrice', and became the evening style.

This is an early portrait of the Empress, rarely exhibited in public. The flattering curves, encompassed by the oval, allude to a discreet, but unmistakeable sensuousness beneath the formal pose. This recalls another portrayal in early marriage: that of Queen Victoria with unknotted hair (see no. 29).

This painting appears to have been conceived as a foil to the slightly earlier state portrait begun in 1853, completed January 1854 and exhibited in 1855 (see Introduction, fig. 34). In his comparable portrait of the Empress (collection Musée du château de Versailles, MV 5829, 1853), Edouard Dubufe presents her in a conventional threequarter-length pose, as formulated by Winterhalter in the 1840s. As an image, however, Dubufe's work conveys neither the intimate appeal of Winterhalter's 1854 oval, nor the absolute magnificence of the state portrait.

As well as the state portrait and the group of the Empress surrounded by her ladies-in-waiting (no. 53), Winterhalter exhibited a third portrait of the Empress Eugénie at the 1855 'Exposition Universelle': '4208—L'Impératrice'. This was probably no. 50, and not the portrait *à la Marie-Antoinette* (no. 52). Overshadowed by the two other works, it does not seem to have excited any particular comment. Claude Vignon's grudging praise probably summed up the general view, as he surveyed Winterhalter's contribution to the exhibition in *Exposition Universelle des Beaux-Arts*:

> *'M. Winterhalter est décidément le portraitiste des têtes couronnées, et il faut bien avouer, quoique sa peinture soit la plus criarde, la plus lâchée, la plus vulgaire qu'on puisse voir, qu'il est actuellement, de tous nos peintres, le seul qui nous ait donné une image ressemblante de S.M. l'Impératrice.'*[1]

In the spring of 1856, the portrait formed part of a special show of two of Winterhalter's portraits of Eugénie, which took place at the Kunstverein in Vienna. The *Kunstblatt* reported:

> *'Winterhalter's 2 famous pictures, his head & shoulders of the Empress of France, & his Empress surrounded by her Ladies of Honour, are drawing crowds here as they did when shown in Paris. The unsuitable rooms* [in] *the Kunstverein in which since last week the 2 pictures have been shown are crowded from morning till evening. The booking office was*

*nearly overrun in the first few days, so the bookshop & musical instrument shops had to help sell tickets, a phenomenon we have never known here before. The Emperor's entire Household has honoured the exhibition with a long-ish visit, & charming female figures from Winterhalter's brush are the main topic at all the tea-parties & salons.'*[2]

A reduced version of this portrait (51 × 39.5 cms) is now at the Russell-Cotes Art Gallery and Museum, Bournemouth.

CBO

1. 'Mr. Winterhalter is without doubt the painter of crowned heads, and it must be said that although his painting is the most garish, slack and vulgar to be seen, he is nevertheless of all our present-day artists the only one to have produced a true likeness of the Empress.'
2. Information translated and communicated by D. MacAndrew.

## 51

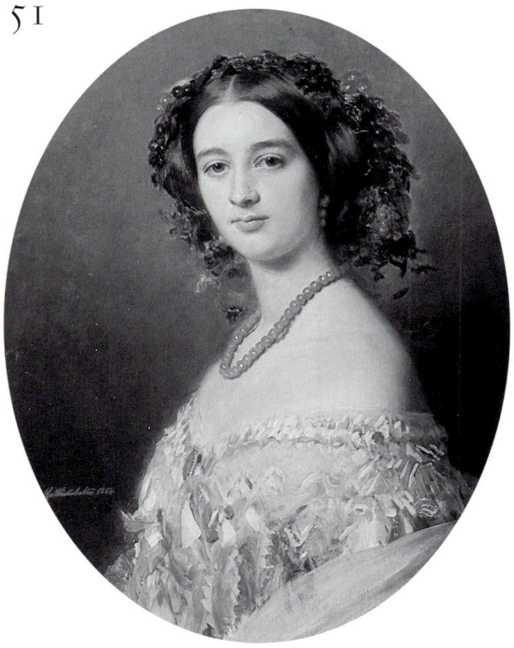

MALCY-LOUISE-CAROLINE-FRÉDÉRIQUE BERTHIER DE WAGRAM, PRINCESSE MURAT (1854)†

*The marriage in 1854 of Malcy-Louise-Caroline-Frédérique Berthier de Wagram (1832–84), a grand-daughter of Marshal Berthier, to Prince Joachim-Joseph-Napoleon Murat, a grandson of Murat, King of Naples, united two of the grandest Napoleonic families at the beginning of the Second Empire. Prince Joachim Murat, although far from brilliant, was described by his cousin Julie as 'joli garçon, fort aimé de toute la famille'.*[1] *He was a favourite of the Empress, served as Colonel of the Guides, and, since he was a cousin of the Emperor, was considered part of his 'civil family'. Their son, Joachim, was one of the best friends of the Prince Imperial.*

PM

73 × 60 cms, oval
Signed and dated, lower left: *fr Winterhalter 1854*
*Prince Louis Murat*

*Provenance*: By descent in the family.
*Exhibitions*: Paris, 1928, no. 9.
*Bibliography*: Wild, 1894, no. 243; E. Schlumberger, *Connaissance des Arts*, February 1961, p. 44, repr; Introduction, p. 51.
See colour plate p. 128.

The Princess is shown at half-length, to the left, in a white satin and tulle ball-dress, the bodice decorated with ribbons. A coral brooch, coral drop earrings and a large coral bead necklace echo Winterhalter's usual red signature on the plain background. Her hair is parted in the middle and dressed with grapes and vine leaves (see no. 41). The realism of the head, with its expression of impassive authority, is off-set by the light and rapid brushwork of the costume.

Winterhalter painted the sitter as a child of five in her father's arms (see no. 10). In the 1837 work, Winterhalter had relied on an intricate composition and a number of well-painted accessories for effect. In the later work, the composition is contained in a simple triangle and all attention is focused on the head at its apex.

Malcy de Wagram's marriage to Prince Murat took place in 1854; the picture is unlikely to have been an engagement portrait, however, as it would have been fairly unusual for an unmarried woman (or a fiancée) to wear such a *décolletage*. Winterhalter makes an undated reference to the portrait in his list ('La Princesse Murat *née* Wagram', Wild, no. 243).

CBO

1. 'a handsome young man, greatly loved by all the family.'

## 52

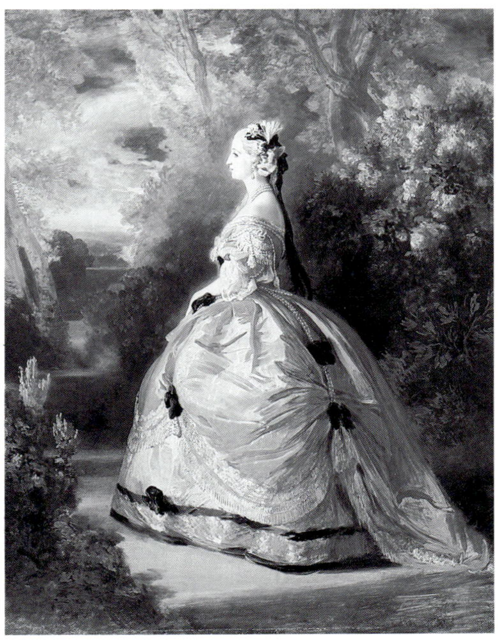

THE EMPRESS EUGÉNIE À LA MARIE-ANTOINETTE (1854)

*In retrospect, the figure of Marie-Antoinette had such glamour that the Empress Eugénie liked to identify herself with the guillotined Queen. She collected objects associated with Marie-Antoinette, housed them in the Petit Trianon, and ordered its restoration. Her favourite decorative style was a version of* Louis Seize *called* Louis Seize Impératrice. *The Empress did, indeed, resemble the Queen in her foreign origin and interest in French politics. In 1870, crowds yelled 'A Bas l'Espagnole' in the streets of Paris, as they had 'A Bas l'Autrichienne', eighty years earlier. Unlike her model, the Empress Eugénie was able to escape and die a natural death.*

PM

92.7 × 73.7 cms
Signed, dated and inscribed, lower right: *fr Winterhalter Paris 1854*
*The Metropolitan Museum of Art, Purchase, Mr and Mrs Claus von Bülow Gift, 1978*

*Provenance*: The Empress Eugénie; Farnborough Hill sale, Christie's, 1 July 1927, lot 99; Seligmann et Compagnie, Paris; Germain Seligmann, New York; E.V. Thaw, New York; no. 1978.403.
*Exhibitions*: Paris, 1928, no. 19; London, M. Knoedler & Co. Inc., 'Beautiful Women of the 19th Century', 1933, no. 3; London, 1936, no. 24; Toronto Art Gallery, 'Paintings of Women from the Fifteenth to the Twentieth Century', 1938, no. 49; New York, World's Fair, 'Masterpieces of Art', 1940, no. 289; San Francisco, California Palace of the Legion of Honor, 'Vanity Fair', 1942, no. 21; New York, Wildenstein, 'Fashion in Headdress', 1943, no. 83; Minneapolis Institute of Arts, 'Great Portraits by Famous Painters', 1952, no. 38; Philadelphia, 1978–9, no. VI–109.
*Reviews*: Armand Dayot, *L'Art et les Artistes*, n.s. XVI, no. 87, 1928, p. 259, p. 262, repr.; A. Flament, *L'Illustration*, 26 May 1928, no. 477, p. 552, repr.; R. Bouyer, *Le Figaro-supplément artistique*, 31 May 1928, p. 528, repr.; Armand Dayot, *International Studio*, XCI, October 1928, p. 41; *La Revue des Deux Mondes*, May–June 1928, p. 911; R. Byron, *Country Life*, no. 80, December 1936, p. 1077, repr.; *Connoisseur*, 99, 1937, p. 44, repr.; *Apollo*, no. 25, 1937, p. 46.
*Bibliography*: S.Z. Levine, *Arts Magazine*, XLIII, no. 4, 1978, p. 8; Carnegie Institute, Pittsburgh, 'Monticelli', 1978, p. 21; J. Richardson, *The Collection of Germain Seligmann*, 1979, no. 89, repr.; B. Scott, *Country Life*, no. 166, December 1979, p. 2160, repr.; Introduction, pp. 48. 53.
See colour plate p. 127.

In this portrait the Empress is portrayed on a relatively small scale, in profile, in a garden. She wears a deep yellow taffeta dress trimmed with black bows and blue ribbon at the hem, pearl ropes, fringes and tassels, and her white powdered hair is decorated with more ribbons and a feather aigrette. Twelve years later, at a ball in February 1866, the Empress wore a dress copied from Madame Vigée-Lebrun's portrait of Queen Marie-Antoinette, 1787 (Versailles; see also no. 58). There is no particular record of Eugénie going to a *bal costumé* disguised as the Queen in 1854, however, and this dress may have been used just for the portrait, to give it a generalized *Louis Seize* effect. Earlier, in 1851, Winterhalter had painted Queen Victoria and Prince Albert in Restoration costume (Her Majesty The Queen); this oil sketch was the record of the actual event, the fancy-dress ball held at Buckingham Palace on 13 July 1851. No. 52 is a more lyrical fancy picture with its pastoral setting, the delicate handling of light and the young woman's abstracted expression. The portrait has recently been compared with the Goncourts's own description of the Empress (Philadelphia, 1978–9, p. 358):

> *'La femme est charmante, après tout. Elle a des yeux qui ne sont que sourire, et de la grâce et de jolis gestes et je ne sais quoi d'aimable dans la façon dont elle passe devant vous. Ni reine ni princesse, – une impératrice des eaux, une impératrice non de France, mais de Bade. Si l'on veut, Marie Antoinette à Mabille.'*[1]

Critics in this century have frequently compared this work to the French eighteenth-century Masters: Fragonard (*La Revue des Deux Mondes*, 1928; *Apollo*, 1937), Watteau (*Country Life*, 1936), Boucher and Van Loo (*The Collection of Germain*

*Seligmann*, 1979). Winterhalter must have looked at these artists, influenced by the revival of interest in eighteenth-century art and the Empress's impassioned identification with Marie-Antoinette. However, the artificial, even introspective, nature of this work sets it unequivocally in the context of the nineteenth century.

This portrait, together with no. 50, is one of the earliest portraits that Winterhalter painted of the Empress. Eugénie appears to have owned it all her life, and it was sold only after her death in 1920.

CBO

1. 'The woman is charming, after all. She has eyes which seem only to smile, grace and prettiness of gesture, and indescribable loveliness in the way she passes before you. Neither a queen nor a princess, – an empress of the watering places, not of France, but of Baden. If you wish, Marie-Antoinette at the Mabille.' (Goncourt & Goncourt, 'Mémoires de la Vie Littéraire', *Journal*, vol. 1, 1956, p. 1219.)

## 53

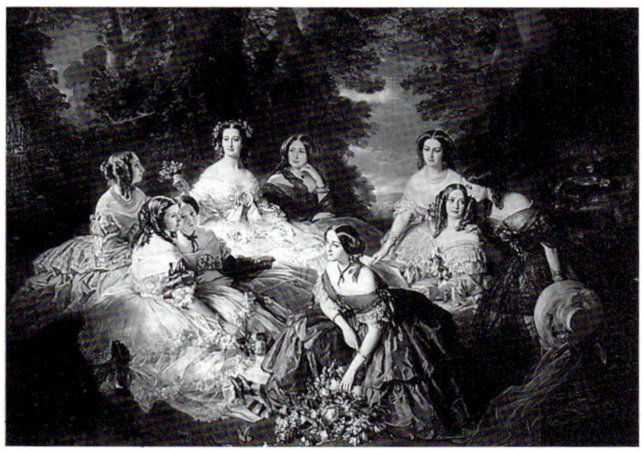

THE EMPRESS EUGÉNIE SURROUNDED BY HER LADIES-IN-WAITING (1855)†

For biography, see no. 50

Signed and dated, lower left: *fr. Winterhalter/1855*

300 × 420 cms

*Musée national du château de Compiègne*

*Provenance*: The Empress Eugénie; Farnborough Hill sale, Christie's, 1 July 1927, lot 98; acquired by Baronne d'Alexandry d'Orengiani, assisted by Vicomte de Noailles, baron de Beauverger and Comte de Cambacérès; presented to Musée national de Malmaison; passed to Musée national du château de Compiègne, 19 December 1952; inv. no. MMPO 941.

*Exhibitions*: Paris, 'Exposition Universelle', 1855, no. 4209; Musée national de Compiègne, 'Le Temps des Crinolines', 1953, no. 257; Philadelphia, 1978–9, no. VI 110.

*Reviews*: T. Gautier, *Les Beaux-Arts en Europe*, I, 1855, pp. 145–6; G. Planche, 'Critique de L'exposition des Beaux-Arts 1855', *La Revue des Deux Mondes* (25th year), pp. 403–4; D. Sébastiani, *Revue Universelle des Arts*, I, 1855, p. 460; C. Vignon, *Exposition Universelle des Beaux-Arts*, 1855, pp. 242–3; C. Delécluze, *Journal des Débats*, 24 November 1855; C. Delécluze, *Journal des Débats*, 30 November 1855; M. du Camp, *Les Beaux-Arts à L'Exposition Universelle de 1855*, 1855, p. 261; A.J. du Pays, 'L'Exposition Universelle des Beaux-Arts', *L'Illustration*, vol. II, 1855, p. 286; E. Loudun, *Exposition Universelle des Beaux-Arts. Le Salon de 1855*, 1855, pp. 149–50.

*Bibliography*: G. Vapereau, *Dictionnaire Universel des Contemporains*, 4th edn. 1870, p. 1863; F. Pecht, *Allgemeine Zeitung*, 8 July 1873; Wild, 1894, no. 388; Armand Dayot, *Le Second Empire*, 1900, p. 23; F. Loliée, *La Vie d'Une Impératrice*, 1905, p. 396; W. Landgraf, *Daheim*, no. 38, 1908, p. 11; Dion Clayton Calthrop, 'Winterhalter and the Crinoline', *Connoisseur*, 31, 1911, no. 123–I, p. 133; A.D. (probably A. Dayot), 'Notes sur des Portraits de S.M. L'Impératrice Eugénie', *Revue de l'Art Ancien et Moderne*, vol. 38, 1920, pp. 312–3; *Le Temps*, 4 July 1927; *Le Figaro*, 23 July 1927; *Gazette de Lausanne*, 21 August 1927; M. Monda, 'Les Meubles et la tapisserie de L'Impératrice Eugénie . . .', *Le Figaro*, 10 July 1927; M. Monda, 'Le Portrait de l'Impératrice Eugénie au Louvre', *Le Figaro*, 11 August 1927; G. Sanvoisin, 'L'Impératrice Eugénie au Louvre', *Le Gaulois*, 19 July 1927; P. Schommer, 'Le Décameron de Winterhalter', *Renaissance*, 1927, pp. 457–9; E.C. Conte Corti, 'Winterhalter, Ein deutsch-französischer Maler', *Velhagen und Klasings Monatshefte*, 53/2, 1938–9, p. 136; M.P. Bolles, *Metropolitan Museum of Art Bulletin*, vol. I, no. 10, June 1943, p. 300; P. Mérimée, *Correspondence Générale*, 1941–61, pp. 480–1; P. Francastel, *Histoire de la Peinture Française*, vol. II, 1955, p. 100; P. Terrier, *Le Second Empire*, Musée national de Compiègne, 1959, no. 10; E. Baader, *Badischer Heimat*, vols. 3, 4, 1960, p. 375; J. Richardson, *La Vie Parisienne*, 1971, p. 44; Introduction, pp. 46, 48–9, 60.

*Prints after*: Lithographs by Léon Noël, pub. 1857, and A. Lemoine, pub. 1858.

See colour plate p. 130.

The Empress Eugénie is seen, slightly raised to the left, wearing a dress of white silk overlaid with white tulle and threaded with lilac silk ribbon. Her hair is centrally parted and turned under in a heavy loop decorated with lilac flowers at each side, and she holds a bunch of honeysuckle towards the Grande-Maîtresse, the Princesse d'Essling, seated in profile wearing pink taffeta, to her right. The Baronne de Pierres (a Dame du Palais) wears a dress of white tulle over white silk, trimmed with broad dark-blue ribbons, with her hair arranged in side ringlets; her companion, the Vicomtesse Lezay Marnésia (a Dame du Palais), wears a black lace shawl over her dress of white tulle (or muslin) striped with red, and holds a book. In the centre foreground, the Marquise de Montebello (a Dame du Palais) wears a tiered and scalloped ball-dress of green taffeta trimmed with white lace; her hair is worn in a low chignon with a red ribbon and she is shown sorting branches of lilac and cabbage roses. The Duchesse de Bassano (the Dame d'Honneur) is seated to the left of the Empress in a red dress with black Chantilly lace, her head resting on her hand. The Baronne de Malaret (a Dame du Palais), full face, standing, wears a yellow silk dress trimmed with heavy lace bands and a corsage of violets. Together with the Marquise de las Marismas (a Dame du Palais), she holds open a large album. The Marquise de las Marismas is seated, wearing a white silk ball-dress with white tulle; the bodice, a double lace bertha, is decorated with a corsage of roses. The Marquise de la Tour Maubourg (a Dame du Palais) closes the composition on the right, standing in a dress of blue silk with tiers of black Chantilly lace; in her left hand she carries a Leghorn straw hat trimmed with roses, ribbons and white tulle.

The most senior among the ladies-in-waiting in the Empress's Household were the Grande-Maîtresse and the Dame d'Honneur, both of whom would only appear with Eugénie on ceremonial occasions. The number of Dames du Palais was raised from seven to thirteen by the decree of 29 January 1855 (Arch. nat. $O^5$ 126), so it is clear that only a small selection was honoured with inclusion in no. 53, painted in the same year. The group is arranged in a grassy clearing overhung by trees; on the right, behind purple lilac branches, a garden urn is filled with honeysuckle. An off-centre vista leads to a distant town while overhead the sky is blue streaked with clouds. The composition is made of two groups of figures, one of five and one of three, which are linked by the figure in green in the foreground. Colours are exuberant and the treatment broad and assured, with none of the awkward passages associated with an earlier portrait group on this scale, *The Royal Family* (see Introduction, fig. 26). For the tradition that links this group with *Florinda*, see no. 38, and for preparatory works, see no 54.

It is likely that the Empress paid for the commission out of her private funds, as it does not appear either among the commissions given by the Ministry of State, or those made by the Ministère de la Maison de l'Empereur. The painting was given a place of honour at the 1855 'Exposition Universelle' in Paris. Winterhalter was awarded a first-class medal for his contribution to the exhibition: altogether four portraits executed for Napoleon and Eugénie.

Most of the critics were silent due to the censorship in force, but a few were openly scornful of the group painting. D. Sébastiani (*Revue Universelle des Arts*) described the quality of Winterhalter's latest works as '. . . ayant l'éclat des papiers peints, toutes les allures de la gouache et la flaccidité de la décoration théâtrale'.[1] Théophile Gautier contrasts the modern French and English Schools of portrait painting, the former dominated by neo-Classicism, the latter exclusive, fashionable and mannered:

> '*M. Winterhalter a toujours cherché la grâce, et il l'a souvent trouvée; sa manière coquette et brillante se rapproche de celle des anglais dont nous parlions toute à l'heure [. . .] peut-être un peu trop préoccupé de l'élégance, M. Winterhalter n'a pas tiré tout le parti possible de ces étoffes aux nuances fraîches et claires, de ces chairs satinées, de ces chevelures brunes ou blondes; il n'a pas donné assez de souplesse aux plis, assez de solidité aux ton; il a fait abus de luisant et de la transparence.*'[2] (Les Beaux-Arts en Europe)

G. Planche was more virulent:

> '*Le portrait de l'impératrice et de ses dames d'honneur est tout bonnement une parodie de Watteau, mais une parodie dont les proportions ne permettent pas l'indulgence. Toutes les incorrections, toutes les omissions qui se peuvent pardonner dans une figure de dix pouces sont inexcusables dans une figure qui a les dimensions du modèle vivant. Les petites filles qui passent devant la toile de M. Winterhalter s'extasient à bon droit devant toutes ces robes qui font le fromage: c'est en effet le seul éloge qui puisse être accordé à cette bizarre composition. Les arbres qui abritent les figures n'ont ni écorce ne feuilles; quant aux figures mêmes, comment en parler sérieusement? Jamais l'ignorance ne s'est affichée avec plus de hardiesse. J'aperçois bien quelque chose que l'auteur a voulu nous donner comme des têtes, et quoiqu'il n'y ait pas une partie du visage modelée d'après nature, je dois lui tenir compte de l'intention; mais la forme du corps n'est pas même indiquée. C'est un défi porté à toutes les lois de la peinture. Ces robes si coquettement étalées ne contiennent absolument rien.*'[3] (La Revue des Deux Mondes)

The painting was displayed at Fontainebleau during the reign of Napoleon III. In 1881, it was returned with other personal possessions to the Empress who was by then at Farnborough Hill in England. There it hung in the main entrance until her death and the sale of 1 July 1927, when it was sold for £3,937. 10s. The heavy gilt frame with the entwined initials of the Empress is the original.

CBO

1. '. . . having the gaudiness of a wall paper, the appearance of a gouache and the flimsiness of a stage set.'
2. 'M. Winterhalter always sought grace, and often found it; his coquettish, sparkling style approaches that of the English artists of whom we were speaking a while ago [. . .] perhaps rather too concerned with elegance, M. Winterhalter has not drawn out the full potential of these fresh, clear materials, these silky complexions, these dark and fair heads; he has not given enough softness to the folds, nor enough strength to the tones; he has used light and transparency to excess.'
3. 'The portrait of the Empress and her ladies-in-waiting is truly a parody of Watteau, but a parody in which the scale allows no room for error. All the mistakes, all the omissions which are forgivable in a ten-inch figure are unforgivable in a figure which is life-size. The little girls who walk past M. Winterhalter's canvas marvel – and with good reason – at these creamy dresses; it is in fact the only praise allowable to this strange composition. The trees which provide shade for the characters have neither bark nor leaves; as for the characters themselves, how can they be seriously spoken of? Never has ignorance been displayed with such defiance. I can perceive something which the artist intended to be heads, and although there is not a single feature of the face which is at all close to nature, I must acknowledge his intention; but the shape of the body is not even so much as indicated. It is a challenge to all the laws of painting. These dresses, so coquettishly displayed, contain absolutely nothing.'

## 54

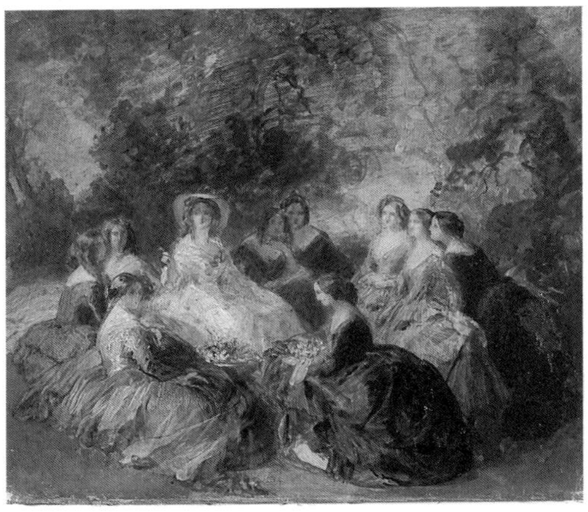

THE EMPRESS EUGÉNIE SURROUNDED BY HER LADIES-IN-WAITING (1855)
For biography, see no. 50

35.5 × 40 cms
*Joachim Egon Fürst zu Fürstenberg, Donaueschingen*

*Provenance*: Unknown.
*Exhibitions*: Karlsruhe, 1965, no. 63 (repr.).
*Bibliography*: Introduction, p. 60.
See colour plate p. 131.

This sketch for *The Empress Eugénie Surrounded by her Ladies-in-Waiting* is one of a number of preparatory works to survive. Of them all, it approximates most nearly to the finished painting. The scale of the figures within the landscape is that of the large painting. The angle of Eugénie's head, and her gesture of holding out honeysuckle, are adopted in the final version, as are the lights and darks of the foliage – similar to those in *Florinda*, 1853 (see no. 38). In this sketch the women appear to be in less formal attire than in the final version, and wear day dresses with long sleeves. The most striking difference between the sketch and the finished painting is in the portrayal of the Empress, however. In the former, she dominates the group of her nine attendants and is the only one in a hat and a light-coloured dress. In the latter, she is no longer instantly recognizable: two of her attendants (now numbering only eight) also wear white dresses, and all are decked in flowers and ribbons.

Winterhalter's brushwork is rapid and assured. The sketch reveals how he organized his vast scene in terms of light and shade, a fact which is lost in the final work. The composition undergoes a small transformation: the group, which is essentially circular in the sketch, is arranged in a looser, more complex (though still circular) pattern in the Compiègne painting.

Two years later, in 1857, Winterhalter painted a particularly distinguished half-length portrait of Eugénie in a straw hat (see Introduction, fig. 36), based on his original pose for *The Empress Eugénie Surrounded by her Ladies-in-Waiting*, as seen in the Donaueschingen sketch.

As well as the final version of 1855 (no. 54), related versions of the sketch are: a pencil sketch, 12.7 × 16.8 cms, Private Collection (1949); and an oil sketch, 38.2 × 46.5 cms, Private Collection (1949). 'The Second Empire' (p. 359) mentions another sketch, very slight, but much closer to the final painting than no. 54, which was sold on the Paris art market (location now unknown).
CBO

## 55

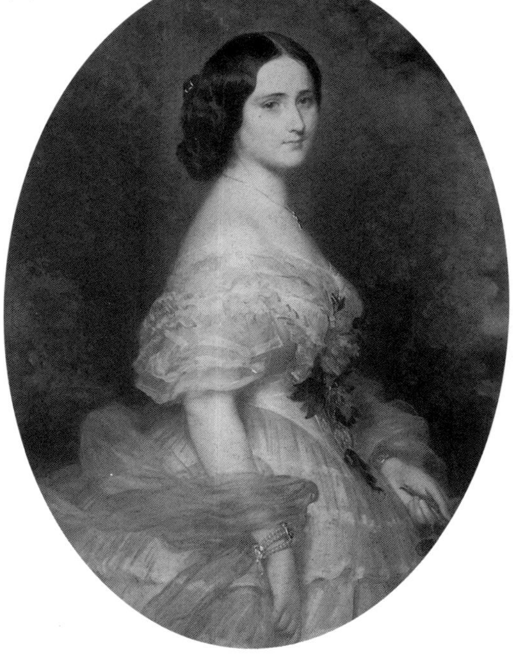

ANNA DOLLFUS, BARONNE DE BOURGOING (1855)†

*Anna Dollfus (1837–1917), the daughter of a rich industrialist from Alsace, married Baron Philippe de Bourgoing, an equerry of Napoleon III, in 1856. They were a very Bonapartist household. The Baronne de Bourgoing was famous for her beauty and the luxury of her* toilettes, *and the Empress made her a lady-in-waiting. Her husband, known at court as 'le beau Philippe', was a devoted Bonapartist Deputy both before and after the fall of the Second Empire, who volunteered to fight as a soldier in the Emperor's Cent-Gardes in the Franco-Prussian War. Their son was a playmate of the Prince Imperial; their daughter married Maréchal Lyautey.*
PM

114 × 98 cms, oval
Signed and dated, lower left: *f Winterhalter/Paris 1855*
*Private Collection*

*Provenance*: By direct descent in the family.
*Exhibitions*: Paris, 1928, no. 7.
*Bibliography*: Armand Dayot, *L'Image de la Femme*, 1899, p. 344, repr.; *Le Figaro*, 31 May 1921, p. 524, repr.
See colour plate p. 129.

The Baronne de Bourgoing is seen threequarter-length, standing to the right, in a white tulle and ribbon ball-gown. Pinned to her pointed bodice front is a corsage of red roses. She wears an emerald cross at her neck and a three-strand bracelet of coral beads on her right wrist. An undulating tulle wrap suggests passing movement, however the billowing contours of the figure are checked in place by the vertical of her right shoulder and arm. Pose and proportions are familiar, without being precisely identical to other portraits of the 1850s. The figure is lit independently of the landscape background.

Painted in the year previous to her marriage to the Baron de Bourgoing, this may have been Anna Dollfus's engagement portrait. Winterhalter recalled painting her father, 'Mr Matthieu Dollfus [*sic*] 1868' (Wild, no. 388), and a portrait of a 'Mme. Dolfuss [*sic*]' (Wild, no. 469). There is no mention of no. 55 in Wild.

The portrait retains its fine original frame, decorated with a wreath of naturalistic flowers.
CBO

56

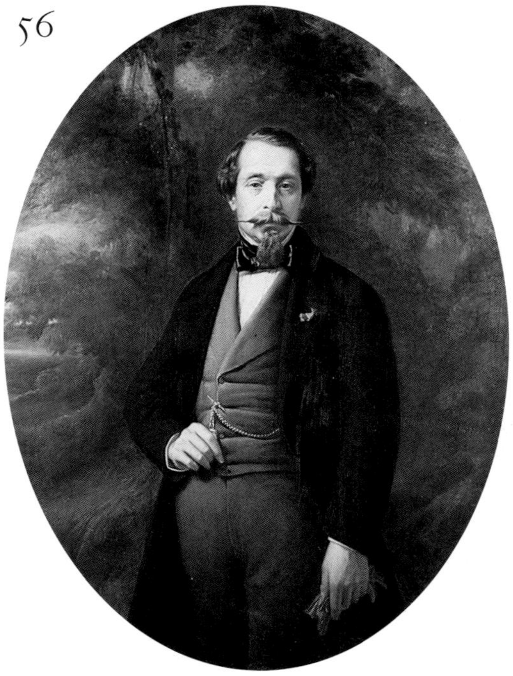

EMPEROR NAPOLEON III

*Astute and idealistic, Louis-Napoleon Bonaparte (1808–73) was first President of the Republic, then Emperor of the French. Although he declared* 'L'Empire c'est la paix', *he led France into wars with Russia, Austria and Mexican nationalists. In pursuit of his ideals of a Europe of nations, and a liberal Empire, he often overlooked matters of detail, even the equipment of the French army. After his defeat in the 1870 Franco-Russian War, he was cursed by his own troops as he was taken to Germany as a prisoner. He died in exile at Chislehurst in Kent.*
PM

140 × 110 cms, oval
*Musée national du château de Compiègne*

*Provenance*: Given by the Comtesse d'Orsetti to the Musée national de Malmaison et Bois Préau; from there on deposit to Musée national du château de Compiègne since 1952; MMPO 1288.
*Bibliography*: Wild, 1894, no. 476; Dr Evans, *Memoirs*, vol. 1, 1905, p. 41; Introduction, pp. 48, 49.
See colour plate p. 132.

Winterhalter's first portrait of Napoleon III, the whole-length state portrait (see Introduction, fig. 33), was greeted with eloquent silence from the critics when it was shown at the 1855 'Exposition Universelle' in Paris. They reserved some acid remarks for Winterhalter's portraits of the Empress instead. Painted about four years later, no. 56 was never exhibited at the time. The Emperor is wearing formal day dress, consisting of a black frock coat with the ribbon of the Légion d'Honneur in his button-hole, a grey waistcoat with a watch-chain looped across, and grey trousers. According to Dr Evans (dentist to the Imperial Family), the Emperor had a stature lower than average, a large head with light brown hair and a waxed moustache: 'He was always carefully dressed and in public, when in plain clothes, usually wore a black frock coat.' (*Memoirs.*) Napoleon had an English tailor, Henry Creed.

Though little-known and unsigned, for stylistic reasons this portrait has always been attributed to Winterhalter. It is typical of his treatment to instinctively 'corriger la nature', so that there is no suggestion here of Napoleon's stocky figure. Nor is there any attempt to characterize the head: Winterhalter's Napoleon is dignified, reserved and impenetrable. No. 56 probably formed a pendant to the 1857 portrait of Eugénie, *Le Chapeau de Paille* (see Introduction, fig. 36). Although the portrait of Napoleon is larger, they share the same oval format, treatment of light, and pastoral background. It is conceivable that the idea of the commission arose during Winterhalter's stay at the Palace of Fontainebleau, where he was a guest of the Imperial couple for a week at the end of November 1856.
CBO

57

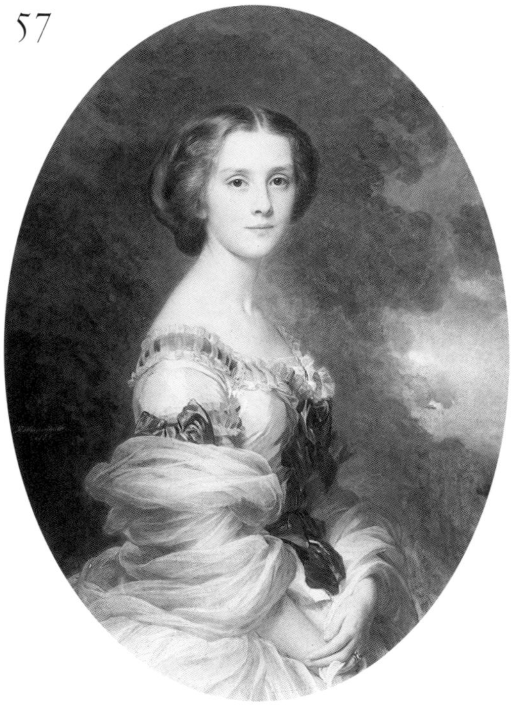

MÉLANIE DE BUSSIÈRE, COMTESSE EDMOND DE POURTALÈS (1857)

*Mélanie de Bussière (1839–1913) was married to Comte Edmond de Pourtalès, a member of a rich Protestant family from Neuchâtel in Switzerland. Beautiful and intelligent, she rapidly became a favourite of the Empress and one of the smartest hostesses of Paris. Her salon remained a centre of Bonapartist social life after the fall of the Second Empire.*
PM

97 × 72 cms, oval
Signed and dated, to left: *F. Winterhalter/1857*
*Collection du Comte de Pourtalès*

*Provenance*: Acquired by the Comte Edmond de Pourtalès.
*Exhibitions*: Paris, 1928, no. 11; London, Knoedler & Company, Inc., 'Beautiful Women of the 19th Century', 1933, no. 16; Maisons-Laffitte, Château de Maisons, 'Exposition de Portraits', 1964, no. 22a.
*Reviews*: A. Dayot, 'A propos de Winterhalter', *L'Art et les Artistes*, no. 87, May 1928, p. 255, repr.; A. Dupouy, 'Winterhalter et ses portraits de femmes', *Le Monde Illustré*, 2 June 1928, p. 354, repr.
*Bibliography*: Wild, 1894, nos. 188, 189; F. Loliée, *Women of the Second Empire*, 1907, repr. facing p. 340.
*Prints after*: Engraved at least once.
See colour plate p. 134.

The portrait of Mélanie de Pourtalès is a deliberate eighteenth-century pastiche. Her white dress, threaded with china-blue bows, is loosely *Louis Seize* in style, and her clear brow and simple hairstyle are echoed by the oval format of the painting. The portrait exudes a direct, natural charm which owes its inspiration to the eighteenth-century French pastel painters. However, the placing of the figure against a leafy background, and the choice of a pose in which the sitter is shown at just over half-length, gazing towards the viewer, are also typical of Winterhalter's treatment, as are the position of the sitter's crossed hands on the crinoline and her somewhat regularized features. The formula must have met with the approval of the Bussière and Pourtalès families, as Winterhalter painted Mélanie on two occasions at least (Wild, pp. 44, 46, nos. 188, 189, 332, 413). Hermann Winterhalter also records painting portraits of the Bussière parents and their daughters (ibid., pp. 49, 50).

Famously beautiful, the Comtesse de Pourtalès was painted by artists such as Carolus Duran as well as Winterhalter. One such portrait inspired the Prince de Vallory to compose the following (undated) sonnet:

> '*A la Comtesse E. de P.*
> *Son portrait*
> *Devant ces grand tableaux de Rome et de Venise*
> *Qui ne s'est cru, parfois, hors du monde emporté*
> *A voir un fier portrait que l'art seul divinise*
> *A force d'idéal, de charme et de beauté?*
> *C'est le front merveilleux et la figure exquise,*
> *Le rêve que l'on fait d'un coeur tout enchanté;*
> *On a les yeux épris, on a l'âme conquise,*
> *Puis on se dit: grand Dieu, si c'était vérité?*
> *Près d'elle, malgré soi tout pâlit dans la toile*
> *La vision regarde avec des yeux d'étoile,*
> *Et l'on voit à jamais le regard éclatant;*
> *Car l'esprit ne peut plus alors s'éloigner d'elle,*
> *D'un beau rêve entrevu, c'est l'image fidèle,*
> *Et l'on repète encore: si c'était vrai pourtant!*'[1]
> (Mélanie de Pourtalès Archive, collection R. Grossmann, Strasbourg)

Mélanie de Pourtalès' first child was born in 1858, and a note from Hermann Winterhalter to Comte Edmond, congratulating him on the birth of his son, is still in the Pourtalès Collection. Family tradition has it that the 1857 portrait was painted to mark this pregnancy.
CBO

1. 'To the Countess of E. de P.
Her portrait
Whilst gazing at these great paintings of Rome and Venice / Who has not, at some point, believed themselves to have transcended the world / At the sight of a noble portrait which art alone has made divine / By strength of its idealism, its charm and its beauty?
The marvellous brow and the exquisite face are creations of / The dream that comes of an enchanted heart; / Eyes are enraptured, the soul is conquered / And then one thinks: Heavens, what if it were true? Beside her, one cannot help but be blind to all other details. / The vision looks with eyes like stars / And the look lives on forever in one's mind; / For the mind can no longer be parted from her, / From a beautiful dream, freshly glimpsed, from an image which is verily like, / And the thought comes again: but what, perhaps, if it were true?'

## 58

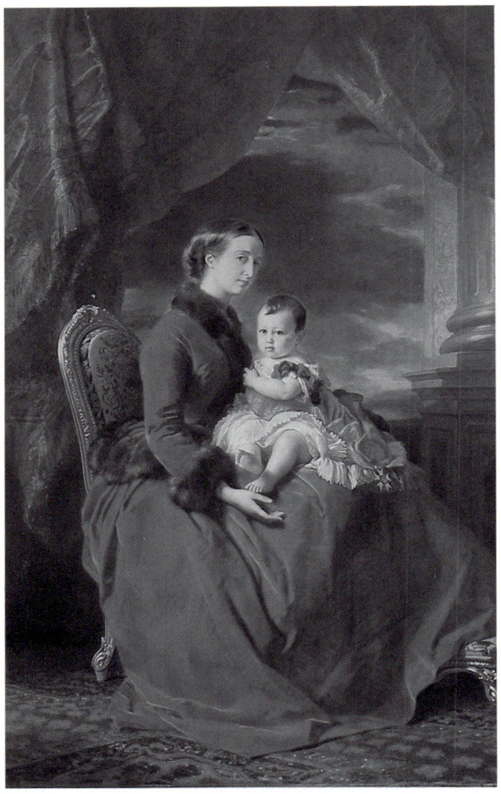

THE EMPRESS EUGÉNIE HOLDING LOUIS-NAPOLEON, THE PRINCE IMPERIAL ON HER KNEES (1857)

*After an agonizing labour, the Prince Imperial was born (1856–79), when the Empress was thirty, in 1856. He was hailed by the diplomats assembled in Paris to negotiate the end of the Crimean War as 'the child of Europe'. The Empress, who could not have any more children, supervised his upbringing and education herself. After the death of Napoleon III in 1873, the Prince Imperial was head of the Bonapartist party, and a potential threat to the Third Republic. However, he felt that as a Bonaparte, he should distinguish himself 'sword in hand'. He died in Zululand in 1879, fighting for England.* (For biography of Eugénie, see no. 50.)
PM

243 × 158 cms
Signed, dated and inscribed, on column to right:
*F Winterhalter Paris 1857*
*LL.AA.II. Le Prince et la Princesse Napoléon*

*Provenance*: The Emperor Napoleon III; returned to the Empress, 1881; from 1979, Musées nationaux de France, on deposit with Prince Napoleon at Château de Prangins.
*Exhibitions*: Paris, Salon, 1857, no. 2695; Château d'Arenenberg, 'Napoleon III', 1949, no. 95; Paris, Grand Palais, 'Cinq Ans d'Enrichissement du Patrimoine National', 1980–1, no. 179.
*Reviews*: Edmond About, *Nos Artistes au Salon de 1857*, 1858, pp. 306, 311; L. Auvray, *Salon*, 1857, p. 56; J. Verne, *Revue des Beaux-Arts*, 1857, p. 252.
*Bibliography*: Wild, 1894, no. 389; A.D. (probably A. Dayot), *Revue de l'Art Ancien et Moderne*, vol. 38, 1920, p. 314; H. Clouzot, *L'Art Décoratif du Second Empire*, 1925, p. 142; A. Castelot, A. Decaux, General Koenig, *Le Livre de la Famille Impériale*, 1969, p. 127, repr.; Introduction, p. 50.
See colour plate p. 133.

The Empress, in a garnet velvet jacket and skirt trimmed with sable, is seated on a Louis XVI-style giltwood chair, her feet resting on a foot stool. The one-year-old Prince Imperial nestles on her knees, his dress trimmed with broderie anglaise and wearing the sash of the Légion d'Honneur. Behind them a rich curtain is looped back to reveal the base of a column and a sheet of sky.

This is the second of the three whole-lengths which Winterhalter painted of the Empress, and the most tender. Although she displays the heir to the throne, she also shields him in her embrace, and looks out not a little diffidently on to the outside world. The composition and the choice of dress have their precedents in the eighteenth century – J.M. Nattier's portrait of Queen Marie Leczinska in red silk trimmed with fur, 1748 (Versailles), and Madame Vigée-Lebrun's portrait of Marie-Antoinette and her children, 1787 (Versailles), in a very similar dress. In 1866, Eugénie gave a fancy-dress ball at the Tuileries, wearing an exact copy of the dress in the Vigée-Lebrun portrait. In 1857, however, Winterhalter probably consulted earlier, Royal portraits. He may also have been inspired by Baron Gérard's portrait of Queen Marie-Louise bearing the one-year-old Roi de Rome in her arms, 1813 (Versailles). The radiant triumphalism of this work differs significantly from Winterhalter's understated portrait, yet both paintings affirm the importance of dynastic continuity. A signed oval of the Prince Imperial, derived from the 1857 portrait, hangs at Compiègne.

Three rare references to Winterhalter's Imperial commissions survive in the Archives Nationales (côte F21–112, Dossier 46: Winterhalter), and concern no. 58. One is a letter to the artist from the Empress's *premier chambellan*, Comte Charles Tascher de la Pagerie, dated 9 January 1858:

> '*Mon cher Monsieur / J'ai pris hier les ordres de S. Majesté l'Impératrice relativement aux deux portraits à payer à Monsieur Winterhalter, et Sa Majesté à daigné décider, que* le chapeau de paille *ayant été donné au Cte Bacciochi serait payé par sa cassette particulière. Le grand portrait avec le Prince Impérial vous revient de droit faisant partie des portraits officiels, et vous voudrez bien vous en charger, et le payer. / Agréer mon cher Monsieur, l'assurance de ma considération la plus distinguée.* Cte de Tascher de la Pagerie.'[1]

A second reference to the commission is in the Minutes of the Decree dated 20 February 1858:

> '*Arrêté: il sera acquis au compte du Ministre d'Etat et moyennant la somme de douze mille francs, imputable sur le crédit des ouvrages d'art et décoration d'édifices publics, exercice 1858, un portrait de S.M. l'Impératrice tenant le Prince Impérial, portrait exécuté par M. Winterhalter.*'[2]

The third reference to the commission is a draft letter from the Ministère d'Etat des Beaux-Arts to Winterhalter, dated 24 February 1858:

> '*Monsieur j'ai l'honneur de vous annoncer que M. le Ministre d'Etat vient de décider, sur ma proposition, que votre portrait de S.M. l'Impératrice tenant le prince impérial, serait acquis au compte du Ministre d'Etat, moyennant une somme de douze mille francs, vous pourrez, en conséquence, vous présenter . . . Agreéz . . .*'[3]

The painting was hung in the library or 'Second Cabinet' in the Emperor's apartments at the Tuileries Palace. In 1881, after a court ruling on the deceased Emperor's effects, it passed to Napoleon III's beneficiaries and thus to his widow in England, along with certain other paintings by Winterhalter. A photograph taken before 1920 shows the portrait of the Empress and the Prince Imperial hanging at Farnborough Hill alongside the threequarter-length portrait by Winterhalter of the Duchess of Alba (now Staatliche Kunsthalle, Karlsruhe).

The portrait was not generally admired at the 1857 Salon. According to J. Verne, the public much preferred the winning grace of the 1855 state portrait, and Louis Auvray complained that the tones lacked Winterhalter's usual light sparkle. But Edmond About, while bracketing Winterhalter with the likes of Court and the Dubufes – sycophantic flatterers – allowed that Winterhalter was not totally devoid of talent, and sometimes even approached the stature of Sir Thomas Lawrence.
CBO

1. 'Dear Sir, / I received yesterday Her Majesty the Empress's orders relating to the two portraits for which M. Winterhalter is to be paid, and Her Majesty has seen fit to decide that the *chapeau de paille*, which has been given to Count Bacciochi, will be paid for from her own privy purse. The large portrait with the Imperial Prince, being one of the official portraits, will be yours by right, and we should be grateful if you would take charge of it and pay for it. / Yours faithfully.'
2. 'Decree: a portrait of Her Majesty the Empress holding the Imperial Prince, painted by M. Winterhalter, will be purchased on behalf of the Secretary of State for the sum of twelve thousand francs, this expense being chargeable to the budget of works of art and decoration of public buildings, financial year 1858.'
3. 'Sir, I have the honour of informing you that the Secretary of State has just decided, upon my suggestion, that your portrait of Her Majesty the Empress, holding the Imperial Prince, will be purchased on behalf of the Secretary of State, upon receipt of the sum of twelve thousand francs, you will consequently be able to present yourself. . . . Yours . . . .'

59

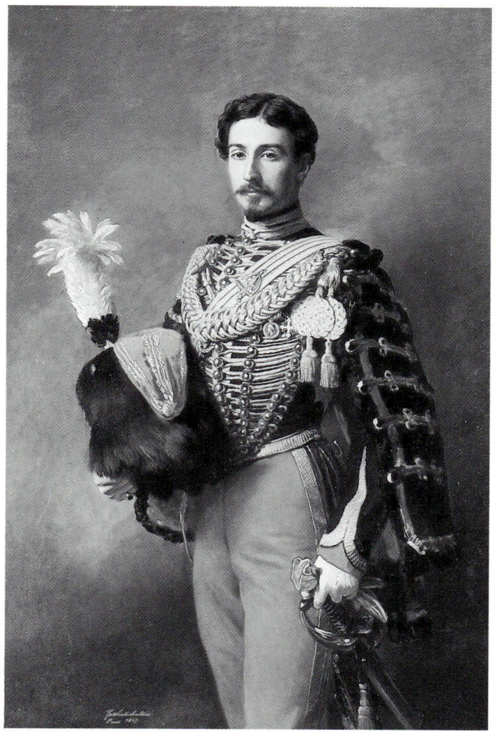

EDOUARD ANDRÉ (1857)

*The son of a rich deputy and banker, Edouard André (1833–94) joined a fashionable regiment, the* Guides *de la Garde Impériale, and served in the Italian and Mexican campaigns. After he left the army, he was a pro-government deputy for the Gard from 1864 to 1870. After his marriage to an artist, Mademoiselle Nellie Jacquemart, he devoted most of his energy to the acquisition of an art collection. He concentrated on acquiring fifteenth-century Italian and eighteenth-century French works which he housed in his splendid* hôtel *on the Boulevard Haussmann – now the Musée Jacquemart-André.*
PM

146 × 102 cms
Signed, dated and inscribed, bottom left:
*fr Winterhalter/Paris 1857.*
*Musée Jacquemart-André, Paris*

*Provenance*: Edouard André; from 1913, Musée Jacquemart-André.
*Exhibitions*: Paris, Musée Jacquemart-André, 'Le Second Empire de Winterhalter à Renoir', 1957.
*Bibliography*: Wild, 1894, no. 475; E. Bertaux, *Revue de l'Art Ancien et Moderne*, vol. 34, 1913, pp. 403–38, p. 407, repr.; J. Mesnil, *Art Flamand et Hollandais*, vol. 21, 1914, p. 41.
See colour plate p. 135.

Edouard André is depicted in full dress uniform of a sous-lieutenant of the Guides de la Garde Impériale. He wears a green dolman with a scarlet collar and cuffs and on his shoulders a scarlet-lined green pelisse. The pantaloons are a complementary deep scarlet with gold stripes. Bare headed, he carries a black busby in one hand and clasps the hilt of a sword with the other. The only medal worn by Edouard André in 1857 was the Médaille d'Italie; the cross of the Knight of the Order of Sts Maurice and Lazare was added subsequently, after 1859.

Light is used more dramatically here than in the male portraits of the 1840s (see *The Duc de Nemours*, 1843, no. 21; *Prince Albert*, 1842, no. 28). It picks out the oval head with its pointed beard, the triangular designs of the cords and buttons and scarlet pouch on the busby: Winterhalter's composition is built on these repeated abstract shapes. The young man's expression is aloof and dignified, the background a cool grey, and the outcome an impressive formal portrait.

The association between the André family and the Winterhalter brothers was a long and fruitful one. Winterhalter painted Edouard's parents in 1843, and a separate portrait of his mother, Madame Louise André, in the same year. Both father and son were painted in the 1850s, and the portrait of Ernest André (half-length, oval) is in the collection of the Musée Jacquemart-André: a letter from Winterhalter to the architect Kreuter, dated 1854, in the Winterhalter Family Papers, refers to Ernest André. A drawing of Madame Ernest André was shown at the Galerie Arnoldi-Livie, Munich in 1977 (no. 35). Hermann Winterhalter also painted several works for the family: 'Mr E. André enfant', 'Mme André mère', 'Mr Louis André' and 'Mme Alfred André' are all listed in Wild as by Winterhalter's younger brother (Wild, pp. 49, 51).
CBO

60

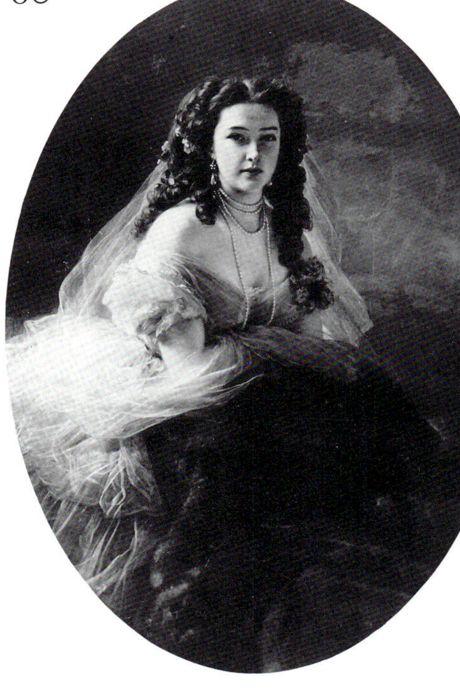

BARBE DMITRIEVNA MERGASSOV,
MADAME RIMSKY-KORSAKOV (1858)

*Madame Rimsky-Korsakov (1833–78) was one of many Russians of noble birth who lent distinction and excitement to Second Empire Paris. She rarely missed a ball or party, was renowned for her wit and beauty, and occasionally caused a sensation with the innovative daring of her costume. At the ball held at the Ministère de la Marine in 1866, she appeared in a chariot drawn by footmen disguised as crocodiles, wearing 'the dress of a savage', which allowed fellow guests ample opportunity to appreciate 'perhaps the most perfectly formed legs in all Europe'.*

*The dashing Rimsky-Korsakovs were said to have been the prototypes for the Korsúnskys in L. Tolstoy's* Anna Karenina, *as in 'the beauty Lida, Korsúnsky's wife, in an impossibly low dress.'* (L. Tolstoy, *Anna Karenina*, 1967, part I, chpt. 22, p. 87, note p. 496.)
(See no. 65)
PM

146 × 114 cms, oval
Signed, dated and inscribed to right:
*f. Winterhalter./Paris 1858*
*The Savitskoy Gallery, Penza, USSR*

*Provenance*: V.D. Rimskaïa Korsakova; A.A. Arapoff; 1917, Museum of Local Lore, Penza; transferred to Penza Picture Gallery Collection.
*Bibliography*: Wild, 1894, nos. 263, 264, 265, 435, 436; *Savitskoy Gallery Catalogue*; Introduction, p. 57.
Not reproduced in colour.

Madame Rimsky-Korsakov is seen threequarter-length, standing to the right, leaning on a fur thrown over the back of a chair.

She wears a silk and tulle ball-gown with *décolletage*, Baroque pearl earrings and pearls around her neck, and pinned to her pleated tulle bodice a corsage of flowers. There is a tulle veil in her hair, which is curled and interlaced with flowers. The figure is strongly lit from the left. The composition was used (in reverse) by Winterhalter in another portrait that year, that of Anna of Hesse, 1858 (see Introduction, fig. 42).

The 1858 portrait emanates an even more powerful sexuality than the portrait *en déshabillé* (see no. 65); Madame Rimsky-Korsakov is shown as the very image of her Parisian sobriquet, 'La Vénus tartare', and Winterhalter did not shrink from painting her as such. Wild records two portraits of her by Winterhalter in one reference (nos. 435, 436) and three in a separate reference (263–5).
CBO

61

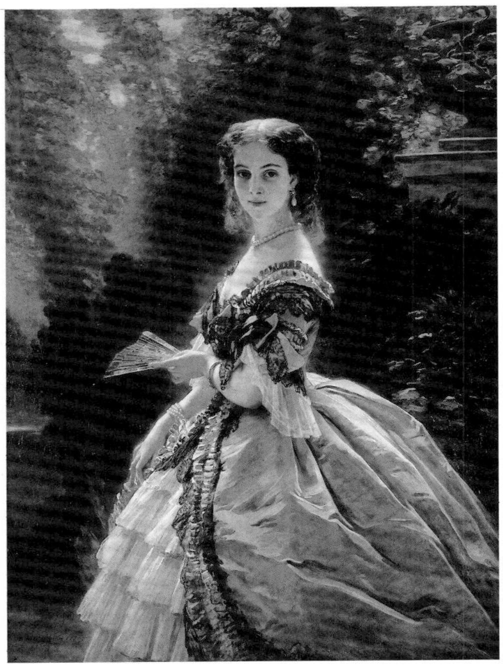

PRINCESS ELIZABETH ESPEROVNA BELOSELSKY-BELOZERSKY, PRINCESS TROUBETSKOÏ

*Born Beloselsky-Belozersky, married to a Master of Ceremonies of the Tsar, Princess Lise Troubetskoï (1834–1907) was one of the many rich and sophisticated Russian nobles who came to live in Paris under the Second Empire. Though her appearance was criticized in Paris, Princess Julie Bonaparte, a cousin of the Emperor, admired the elegance of her clothes and the brilliance of her conversation and found her very well-informed about politics. Wearing wings and a short skirt, she took part in the famous 'Ballet of the Bees' at the Tuileries in 1863.*
PM

147 × 108 cms
Signed, dated and inscribed, bottom left:
*Fr Winterhalter 1859./Paris*
*Private Collection*

*Provenance*: Sir Robert Abdy; Artemis Group, 1986, sold to present owner 1987.
*Exhibitions*: London, 1936, no. 14 (repr.); Plymouth City Art Gallery, 'Art Treasures in the West Country', 1947, no. 48.
*Bibliography*: F. Loliée, *Women of the Second Empire*, 1907, p. 235, repr.; Wild, 1894, no. 406; The Editor, Art Notes round the Galleries, *Apollo*, no. 25, 1937, p. 46; Introduction, pp. 51, 53, 54.
See colour plate p. 138.

Princess Troubetskoï is depicted threequarter-length, standing to the left, in a grey taffeta dress decorated with black lace and coral silk ribbons, over a skirt of white flounced silk.

Winterhalter's backgrounds are frequently little more than formal backdrops to their splendid subjects. Here, however, the choice of a *verdure* tapestry setting is inspired, and in full harmony with the fragile and elegant Princess before it. As usual, Winterhalter provides a faithful record of the costume, which is thoroughly *dix-huitième*, in colour and fabric, as well as in the detail: ruched trimmings ('robings') along the skirt edges, horizontal bands of applied lace and ribbon to the sleeves, and lace sleeve ruffles. Such a mass of eighteenth-century effects would be uncharacteristic of Worth's designs, and this evening gown is probably the work of a less distinguished designer.

Comparisons with eighteenth-century painting spring to mind; with Watteau, say, for the gladed setting, and with Boucher for the colour scheme. However Princess Troubetskoï is a thoroughly up-to-date creature with her fashionably natural hair-style, eighteenth-century revival ball-gown and Japanese fan, and, to a certain extent, Winterhalter's treatment is modern too; for although not true *plein airisme* (it is clearly a studio work), there is an attempt at open-air effects, and the figure is shaped by different light sources.

The chief attraction of the painting resides in its sensuousness, however, which Winterhalter evokes by use of subtle contrasts: an innocent yet alluring expression, and radiant skin juxtaposed to a richly detailed dress.

Wild lists portraits of Prince and Princess Beloselsky (*sic*) for 1865 (Wild, nos. 340–1). These would be relations, but not parents, of Princess Troubetskoï. Her mother, Princess Kotschoubey, remarried after 1846, and her portrait by Winterhalter survives, the threequarter-length painted in Paris in 1860 (Walters Art Gallery, Baltimore). A portrait of Countess Olga Esperovna Schouvalova seated in a white dress, painted in Paris in 1858 (The Hermitage, Leningrad) is presumably that of Lise's sister, Olga. The Schouwaloff family were prolific patrons of Winterhalter (see Wild, passim. and a portrait of another Countess Schouvalova, 1852, Private Collection). This, however, appears to be the only portrait he painted of Princess Lise Troubetskoï.
CBO

62

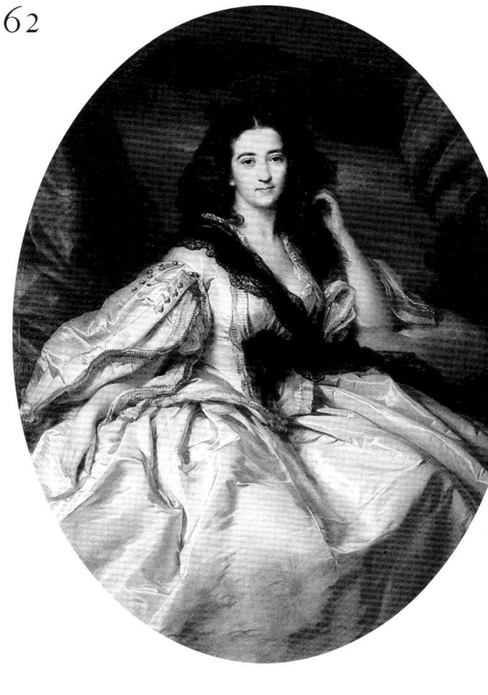

WIEŃCZYSLAWA BARCZEWSKA, MADAME DE JURJEWICZ (1860)

*Wieńczylawa Barczewska's (1854–77) first husband, M. Jurjewicz, was a member of the Polish nobility, like herself, and Marshal of the Nobility for a district near Minsk, in the west of the Russian Empire. Like many Poles who disliked the oppressive government of the Tsar, she spent much time in Paris. Her second husband was a member of the Rodoconachi family settled in France. She died in Odessa.*
PM

156 × 124 cms, oval
Signed, dated and inscribed, bottom centre:
*f. Winterhalter/Paris 1860*
*Baron de Bussière*

*Provenance*: By descent.
*Exhibitions*: Paris, 1928, no. 14; London, 1936, no. 19.
*Reviews*: R.H. Wilenski, *The Listener*, 1936, pp. 1075–7, p. 1077, repr.; 'The Editor', *Apollo*, no. 25, 1937, pp. 46–7, p. 47, repr.
*Bibliography*: Wild, 1894, nos. 254–5, 296; E. Henriot, *Gazette des Beaux-Arts*, vol. VI, 1922, p. 104; Introduction, p. 54.
See colour plate p. 140.

Madame de Jurjewicz wears a voluminous afternoon-dress of white taffeta, with overskirt draped over the hips and open sleeves *à la Juive*, and a floppy ribbon bow on the corsage. She is seated against a backdrop of sky and red drapes.

Madame de Jurjewicz (called in the family 'La Maréchale', owing to her first husband's position as Marshal of the Nobility), is a creature of splendid sophistication. An impression of *ancien régime déshabillé* is conveyed by the loose hair, the casual pose and by the eighteenth-century style of costume. The retrospective impression is enhanced by the handling and composition, and Winterhalter's use of flowing diagonals across the oval is reminiscent of portraits by H. Rigaud, N. de Largillière and other Baroque and early eighteenth-century artists.

Two further portraits of Madame de Jurjewicz by Winterhalter survive in the possession of the family in Poland. One, a roundel, is a study for the head of no. 62. The second, a grand whole-length (probably later than no. 62), shows her in court dress in half-profile to the right, wearing a tiara and the famous Moszynski emeralds, holding a fan and standing against a background of greenery. Wild records several portraits of Madame de Jurjewicz by Winterhalter: '2 portraits, 1 oval, 1 grand en pied', and 'Mme. Jurjewicz, 2 fois en pied' (nos. 254–5, 296). Both references are undated.
CBO

63

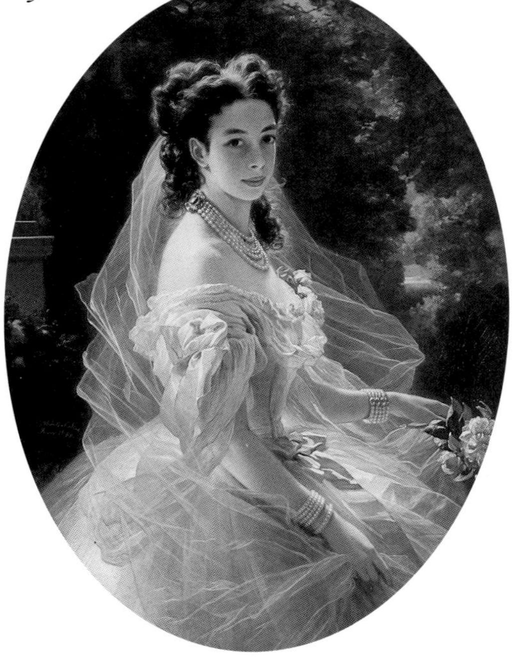

PAULINE SANDOR, PRINCESS METTERNICH (1860)

*Niece and wife of Prince Richard Metternich, Austrian ambassador to France from 1860 to 1871, Princess Metternich (1838–1921) was known as the 'ambassadress of pleasure'. Her vivacity and originality rapidly won her the Empress's favour. She organized charades and* tableaux vivants *to entertain the court at Compiègne. In 'Les Commentaires de César' (1865) she acted, in turn, as a cab-driver, the Spirit of Song and a* vivandière. *She was equally bold as a patron of the arts. She brought 'Tannhäuser' to Paris in 1862 and helped make the great dress-designer Worth fashionable overnight. After the fall of the Second Empire she organized the first contemporary art exhibitions in Vienna. She aroused the enmity of the Empress Elizabeth of Austria and in her memoirs emphasized that she found the court of Napoleon III far more splendid and exciting than that of Franz Joseph I.*

PM

115 × 87.5 cms, oval
Signed, dated and inscribed, lower left: *fr. Winterhalter./Paris 1860*
*Private Collection*

*Provenance*: By descent in the family.
*Bibliography*: Wild, 1894, nos. 298–9, 421–2; F. Loliée, *Women of the Second Empire*, 1907, p. 182, pp. 180–1, repr.; Marcel Dunan (ed.), *Souvenirs de la Princesse Pauline de Metternich*, Paris 1922; A. von Schneider, *Die Pyramide*, 20 January 1935, pp. 9–10; A. von Schneider, *Badenerland*, 'Winterhalter und die Frauen', 2 February 1935; Introduction, p. 63.
See colour plate p. 136.

Princess Metternich wears a dress of white silk trimmed with tulle on the bodice, probably by Worth. A tulle veil is pinned to her hair, and a pearl necklace and bracelets, five strands thick and adorned with massive clasps decorate her neck and wrists. The setting in a glade, with a pillar in the background, and the overhead lighting are close to those in Winterhalter's portrait of Princess Troubetskoï, 1859 (no. 61).

Pauline Metternich is portrayed in the year following her husband's appointment as the Austrian ambassador to Paris. Known as 'le singe à la mode' ('the fashionable monkey', *Souvenirs*), she was a 'jolie-laide' ('plain yet pretty'), rather than a classic beauty, and it is this captivating quality that Winterhalter has sought to convey. Worth had Pauline Metternich in mind when he popularized the word 'chic' in about 1860, and he also used her to make fashionable his new styles in dress, such as the crinoline in 1856. 'When [she] appeared at the Tuileries at a court ball, very slight, even thin, rather tall, her bare shoulders rising from her extremely low dress, her brow ladened with diamonds, her long skirts sweeping the floor, no woman had more distinctly the "grand air".' (*Women of the Second Empire.*)

Wild records Winterhalter painting Princess Metternich twice ('2 fois, une fois profil')[1] (nos. 298–9, 421–2). A profile portrait of 1853 existed at Castle Bajna, near Budapest, until the end of the Second World War. Two letters written on small pink sheets survive from Princess Metternich to Winterhalter (Winterhalter Family Papers). Both undated, it has not proved possible to establish whether they relate to the 1853 or 1860 portraits:

> *'Dienstag*
>
> *Lieber Winterhalter! / Sie beschämen mich mit Ihrem so freundlichen Anerbieten, indessen kann ich Ihnen nur zusagen, indem mir damit Gelegenheit geboten wird, ein Stündchen in Ihrer mir so angenehmen Gesellschaft zuzubringen, und ich zu egoistisch bin, um mir diese Freude zu versagen Befehlen Sie, wann das Modell zu kommen hat! / Ich stehe Ihnen zur Disposition von Donnerstag angefangen. Ich werde sodann mit gewunschter Coiffure und mehreren Kleinigkeiten sowie Blumen erscheinen; ich überlasse Ihnen meinen Kopf und werde meinerseits nur so gut als moglich posieren und sonst keinen Willen haben. / Zu welcher Stunde, an welchem Tage steht Ihnen wie natürlich vollkommen frei. Mit den herzlichsten Grüßen / Fürstin Metternich.'*[2] (Die Pyramide)

In another, still more effusive letter, Princess Metternich writes:

> *'Freitag*
>
> *Lieber Winterhalter, Erlauben Sie Ihrem* Modelle *sich Ihnen in das Gedächtniss zurückzurufen, um Sie zu fragen* wann *Sie uns mit der Übersendung des* chef d'oeuvre*'s beglücken werden*
> *Die Kaiserin war in der That so entzückt darüber, dass sie es selbst* kaufen *wollte. Die Kleine Photographie des Bildes hat Ihre Majestät verlangt, u. ich ihr dieselbe übergeben. – Das* grosse *Bild wurde auf Allerhöchsten Wunsch neulich in die Tuileries (?) gebracht, u.* entzückte beide *Majestäten, die Ähnlichkeit u. dann die bewunderungswürdige Auffassung wurden allgemein anerkannt u. gepriesen. – Ich nehme mir vor Sie nächstens in Ihrem Atelier zu besuchen. – Lord Cowley gedenkt seine beiden allerliebsten Töchter durch Sie malen zu lassen, da ihm mein Porträt so enorme gefällt. – Mit den besten Grüssen*
> *Fstin Metternich'*[3]

CBO

1. 'Twice, once in profile'.
2. 'Tuesday

   Dear Winterhalter, / You put me to shame with your very kind offer, yet I can only agree if I can also have the opportunity of passing a brief hour in your company, which I find so pleasant, and I am too selfish to deny myself this pleasure. – Command your model when she should come! / I am at your disposition from Thursday onwards. I shall then appear with the desired coiffure and several small items, and also flowers; I will leave my head to your care, and I for my part will pose as well as I possibly can, otherwise I shall wish for nothing else. – You are naturally free to determine at what hour and on what day. / With the most cordial regards / Princess Metternich.'
3. 'Friday

   Dear Winterhalter, Permit your model to recall herself to your memory, in order to ask you *when* you are going to delight us by sending your *chef d'oeuvre*. The Empress was indeed so enchanted by it, that she wanted to *buy* it herself. The little photograph of the picture was demanded by Her Majesty and I gave it to her. – The large picture was, by Royal wish, recently brought to the Tuileries (?) and *enchanted both* their Majesties. The likeness and then the admirable conception were appreciated and praised by all. – I intend to visit you shortly at your studio. – Lord Cowley is thinking of having his two extremely sweet daughters painted by you, since he is so enormously taken with my portrait
   With best wishes Princess Metternich.'

64

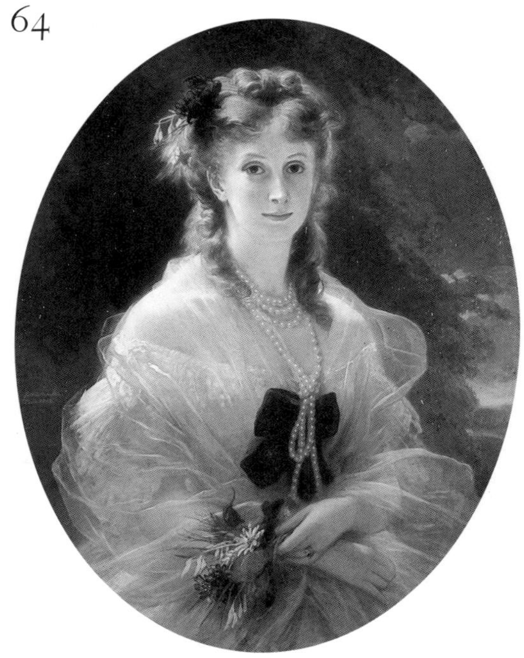

PRINCESS SOPHIE TROUBETSKOÏ, DUCHESSE DE MORNY (1863)

*The Emperor Alexander II himself helped to arrange the marriage of Princess Sophie Troubetskoï (1838–96), a beautiful but in court terms, penniless, Demoiselle d'Honneur of the Empress, to the French ambassador to Russia, the illegitimate half-brother of Napoleon III, the Comte (later Duc) de Morny in 1856.*

*Although devoted to her husband, she disliked having to entertain on his behalf; he was one of the most influential figures of the régime and President of the Corps Législatif. It is said that her discovery of his unburnt love-letters, an impressive and varied collection, after his death in 1865, was a shock. She remarried a cousin of the Empress, the Duke del Sesto, in 1867, and died in Spain in 1896.*

PM

94 × 73 cms, oval
Signed, dated and inscribed to left: *fr Winterhalter 1863*
*Musée national du château de Compiègne*

*Provenance*: Unknown (Fonds de la Récupération Artistique).
*Exhibitions*: Bagatelle, 'Portraits de Femmes', 1907; Paris, 1928, no. 13; London, 1936, no. 23; Musée national de Compiègne, 'Le Temps des Crinolines', 1953, no. 266.

*Bibliography*: Wild, 1894, nos. 314–15, 440; L. Vauxelles, 'Portraits de femmes à Bagatelle', *Les Arts*, no. 66, June 1907, pp. 11–18, p. 17, repr.; Frédéric Loliée, *Women of the Second Empire*, 1907, repr., facing p. 170; *Gazette des Beaux-Arts*, II, vol.VI, 1922, p. 104, repr.; A. Dayot, 'A propos de Winterhalter', *L'Art et les Artistes*, no. 87, 1928, p. 256, repr.; A. Dupouy, 'Winterhalter et ses portraits de femmes', *Le Monde Illustré*, 2 June 1928, pp. 354–5, repr.; Octave Aubry, *Napoleon III*, vol. I, 1932, pl. 5; R.H. Wilenski, 'Winterhalter and Official Art', *The Listener*, 1936, p. 1077, repr.; The Editor, 'Art Notes round the Galleries', *Apollo*, no. 25, 1937, pp. 46–7; J. Laver, 'Winterhalter', *The Burlington Magazine*, 70, 1937, p. 45; *Le Journal de la France*, no. 55, 1970, p. 1520, repr.; J. Richardson, *History Today*, vol. 23, 1973, p. 334, repr.; Grothe Gerda, *Le duc de Morny*, 1966, p. 261; Introduction, p. 53.
See colour plate p. 137.

Sophie de Morny wears a tulle wrap and a white dress with a dark blue bow, possibly by Worth. There is no jewellery other than wedding rings and a loosely knotted rope of pearls at her neck. The fresh simplicity of the sitter is enhanced by her posy of field flowers and by the arrangement in her hair: cornflowers, poppies and daisies, mixed with corn-ears and grasses.

Sophie de Morny's complexion is set off by dark foliage in the background, and dappled light catches her hair, cheeks and shoulders. This natural, outdoor lighting is reminiscent of Winterhalter's great portrait of her namesake, though no close relation, Lise Troubetskoï, 1859 (no. 61).

Although as a likeness no. 64 tends towards the bland and inexpressive, a certain summery charm pervades the picture, which is one of the most popular Winterhalter portraits. The frame, with its knots of flowers which echo those within the painting, is the original.

Several portraits of the Duchesse are recorded by Wild, at least one in profile (Wild, nos. 314–15, 440). The profile version (whereabouts now unknown) is visible in an 1866 watercolour by Jean Sorieul of the bedroom study of the Duc de Morny at the Hotel de Lassay (collection Pierre Fabius, Paris, 1978). An oval half-length of the Duchess, seated to the left, signed and dated 1864, collection M. L., was sold at the Charpentier sale, in Paris, 24–25 May 1934, lot 84. The Duc de Morny's letter to Winterhalter of 17 May 1864 may refer to this rather than to no. 64:

*'CORPS LEGISLATIF/PRESIDENCE*
*Paris le 17 Mai 1864*
*Mon cher Monsieur Winterhalter,*
*J'ai été et je suis encore si occupé par les travaux de la Chambre que vous m'excuserez, je l'espère, d'avoir laissé aussi longtemps sans réponse la question que vous avez addressée à Mme. de Morny.*
*J'ai trouvé le portrait fort bien, ma femme a dû vous le dire, mais pour vous enlever le moindre doute à ce sujet je tiens à vous le répéter. Je suis loin d'en être mécontent comme vous l'avez supposé et si vous voulez me faire savoir quelle somme je vous dois, je m'empresserai de vous la faire parvenir.*
*Croyez, mon cher Monsieur Winterhalter à mes sentiments les plus distingués.*
*Morny.'*[1]
(Winterhalter Family Papers)

CBO

1. Legislative Assembly
The Presidency

Paris, 17 May 1864

My Dear Mr Winterhalter,
I have been and am still so fully occupied by the business of the House, that I trust you will forgive me for not answering your question to Mme de Morny before. I found it a very good portrait, as my wife must have told you, but to remove any lingering doubts I wish to repeat it to you. I am far from being dissatisfied with it, as you imagined, and if you would let me know how much I owe you for it, I shall see that you receive it as soon as possible.
Believe me . . .
Morny.'

## 65

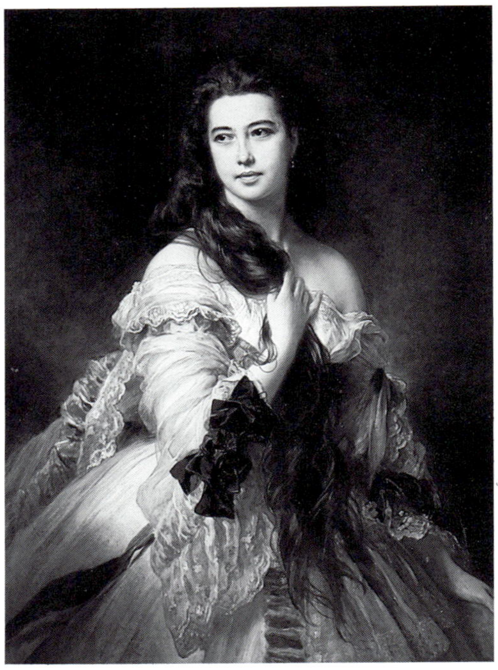

BARBE DMITRIEVNA MERGASSOV,
MADAME RIMSKY-KORSAKOV (1864)†
(For biography, see no. 60)

147 × 90 cms
Signed, dated and inscribed, lower right:
*f. Winterhalter./1864 Paris*
*Musée d'Orsay*

*Provenance*: Given by the sitter's sons to the Louvre, 1879; on deposit at Musée national du château de Compiègne, 1953; on deposit at Musée d'Orsay, 1986, RF 235.
*Exhibitions*: Paris, 1928, no. 1 (repr.); Musée national de Compiègne, 'Le Temps des Crinolines', 1953, no. 270; Rome, Palazzo Venezia, 'Il Ritratto francese da Clouet a Degas', 1962, no. 216.
*Bibliography*: Wild, 1894, nos, 263–5, 435–6; F. Loliée, *Women of the Second Empire*, 1907, p. 14; G. Brière, *Paris, Musée National du Louvre. Catalogue des Peintures*, 1924, no. 993, p. 270; Armand Dayot, 'A propos de Winterhalter', *L'Art et les Artistes*, no. 87, 1928, pp. 260–1, repr.; A. Dupouy, 'Winterhalter et ses portraits de femmes', *Le Monde Illustré*, 2 June 1928, p. 354, repr.; D. Chevalier, 'Une exposition reconstituée, la vie sous le Second Empire', *Jardin des Arts*, 1957, p. 703, repr.; *Le Journal de la France*, 1970, no. 55, p. 1521, repr.; M. Alexander, *The Sunday Times Magazine*, 18 November 1973, p. 48, repr.; C. Simond & M.C. Poinsot, *La Vie Galante aux Tuileries sous le Second Empire*, no date, pp. 160–1, repr.; Introduction, p. 57.
See colour plate p. 139.

Madame Rimsky-Korsakov appears here in a white *robe de chambre*, trimmed with lace and thick blue bows that billows out over a crinoline and dominates the picture. She wears no jewels apart from small drop earrings. She stands with one hand on a red chair, a great coil of loose brown hair clasped in the other.

Madame Rimsky-Korsakov was proud of her figure: in February 1863, she appeared at a court ball disguised as Flaubert's Salammbô, 'draped in gauzes so transparent that the Empress was scandalized, and gave immediate orders to her chamberlain to conduct the new priestess of Tanit out of the imperial ballroom.' (*Women of the Second Empire.*) Watching her emerge from her swim at Biarritz in 1862 was a similar experience: 'focused by a hundred field glasses, she looked as if she had just stepped out of the bath.' (ibid.).

Winterhalter adopted the same *déshabillé* formula in his portrait of Empress Elizabeth of Austria of the same year (see Introduction, fig. 43). The direct physical appeal of these portraits is unusual for Winterhalter, and he seems to have been influenced by Courbet's lush female figures of the 1850s and 60s. The completely unbound hair and loose robe contribute to the impression of sensuality and boudoir intimacy.

In 1982, Stair Sainty Fine Art Inc., New York, was offered a version of no. 65, and a replica was seen in a Private Collection; another replica is believed to be in a Private Collection. An earlier portrait of Madame Rimsky-Korsakov is at Penza Museum, USSR (see no. 60).

Wild lists 'Madame Korsakoff, 2 portraits' (nos. 435–6), but in a separate reference to her, three portraits are mentioned (nos. 263–5); no dates are given, but the latter reference is perhaps to the versions of no. 65. No other portrait type of this sitter by Winterhalter is known.

CBO

66

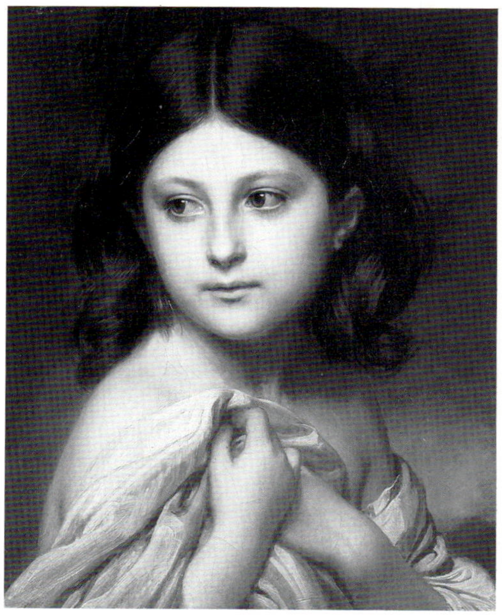

A YOUNG GIRL CALLED PRINCESS CHARLOTTE

46 × 38.5 cms
*Collections royales, Château de Laeken, Belgium*

*Provenance*: King Leopold I, inventory of 1864 as 'Tête de jeune fille', inventory of 1869 as 'tête de jeune fille en déshabillé (*sic*) et se couvrant la gorge'; always in Belgian Royal Collections.
*Exhibitions*: Brussels, 'King Leopold I', 1965, no. 425.
See colour plate p. 143.

This small bust-length study is one of Winterhalter's most attractive depictions of a child. The head is notable for its remarkably fresh, free painting and the delicate flesh tones suggest a face glowing with health. The curling hair and the robe wrapped around her are achieved in a similarly painterly fashion, the brush strokes clearly visible. The sitter is placed in a charming Greuze-like pose, giving point to the comments of those critics who noted in Winterhalter's work its strong affinities with the painting of the eighteenth century. The sitter's pose, although carefully arranged – the hands placed to echo the triangle created by the turning away of the shoulders, the eyes averted in the opposite direction – convincingly suggests spontaneous movement.

The sitter has traditionally been identified as Princess Charlotte of Belgium, whom Winterhalter painted on several occasions, notably in 1842, aged two, in a portrait presented to Queen Victoria (no. 15). This identification is not however supported by the earliest surviving inventories listing the paintings by Winterhalter in the Belgian Royal Collections, where it is referred to only as a portrait of a 'jeune fille'. Despite a slight resemblance between the features of the sitter in this portrait and those of the Princess, it seems highly unlikely that this picture was intended to portray the Princess, and it was probably acquired as a genre work rather than as a portrait. It would seem to date from about 1850.

SF
RLO

67

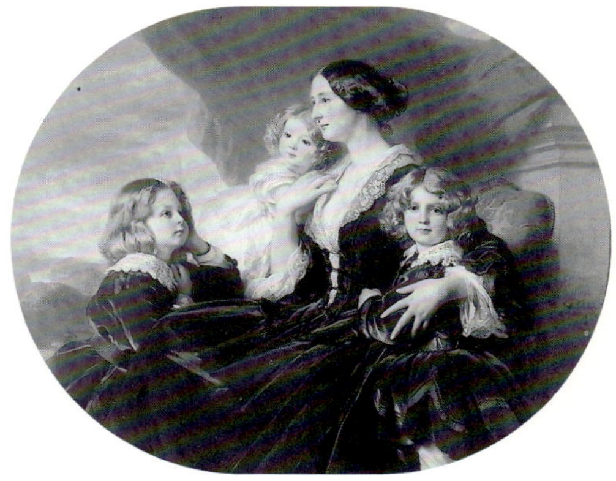

ELZBIETA BRANICKA, COUNTESS KRASINSKA AND HER CHILDREN (1853)

*Elizabeth Krasinska (1820–76) came from one of the families of Polish magnates which, before the Partitions of Poland in the late eighteenth century, had been among the richest, most powerful and most interbred aristocrats in Europe. They felt at home in Paris, Vienna and Saint Petersburg, as well as Warsaw. Her father, Wladislaw Branicki, was Grand Equerry of the Tsar, her mother was a Potocka, and she married Sigismund Krasinski, a godson of Napoleon and one of the great Polish Romantic poets, in 1843. After her husband's death, she married his cousin Ludwik. She was a great patriot whose salon in Cracow was a famous centre of Polish social and artistic life. Her eldest son was a noted bibliophile and writer.*
PM

131 × 163.5 cms, oval
Signed and dated, lower right:
*F. Winterhalter/1853*
*National Museum, Warsaw*

*Provenance*: In the Krasinski Collection; later in the Museum of the Krasinski entailed Estate, Warsaw; National Museum, Warsaw since 1941; in the Gallery at Wilanów no. 185253.
*Bibliography*: Wild, 1894, no. 221; *Portrety Osobistósci Polskich (Portraits of Polish Personalities)*, 1967, no. 88, pp. 89–90, repr. (with Bibliography); *Catalogue of Paintings, Foreign Schools, II, National Museum in Warsaw*, 1970, no. 1496, p. 210, repr.; X. Rey, 'Le Château de Montrésor', *Connaissance de Paris*, no. 43, 1982, p. 35; Introduction, p. 51.
See colour plate p. 144.

The Countess is seated high above the viewer, a rose-coloured curtain linking her figure, dressed in wine velvet and that of her youngest child, Elizabeth, wearing white. The two boys are dressed in contrasting green velvet: Wladislaw on the right, whose glance engages the viewer, wears white trousers, the vertical line of which echoes the stabilizing vertical of the giant column to the right. His brother, Sigismund, acts the role of a donor in a religious composition, gazing adoringly at his mother; behind him is a distant landscape.

The Countess Krasinska was one of Winterhalter's most enthusiastic and devoted patrons, and he portrayed her several times, both alone and with her children, during the 1850s. The present portrait, of 1853, is apparently the second portrait of the Countess and her children which Winterhalter undertook; an earlier (lost) portrait, dated 1850, showed the two elder children before the birth of the daughter Elizabeth, while a watercolour dated 1855 (also lost) showed the Countess with four children. Two further portraits (an oval, National Gallery, Warsaw, and a threequarter-length dated

1857, formerly in the Family Collections) depicted the Countess alone. A copy of the present portrait is in the collection of Comte Rey, Château de Montrésor.

The broadly and confidently handled group of 1853 shows the strong influence of Van Dyck on Winterhalter's portraiture, most apparent in his state portraits, but here evident even in a more intimate family portrait. Echoes of portraits such as Van Dyck's *Marchesa Brignole Sale and Her Son* (National Gallery, Washington D.C.), with its giant columns, are combined with references to religious works in a similar oval format, such as the *Abbé Scaglia adoring the Virgin and Child* (National Gallery, London), where a curtain is placed behind the Virgin in a manner very similar to Winterhalter's positioning of it here.

SF

## 68

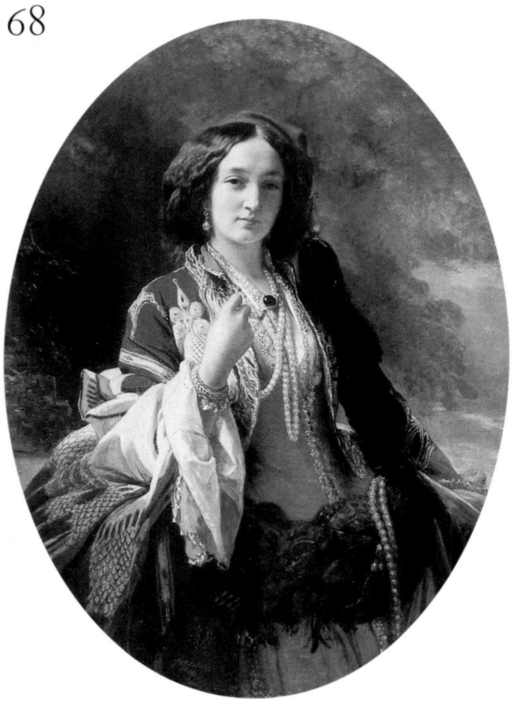

KATARZYNA BRANICKA, COUNTESS POTOCKA (1854)

*Katarzyna Branicka (1825–1907), sister of Elizabeth, married another wealthy magnate, Adam Potocki of Krzeszowice, in 1847. They had seven children, including Artur and Zofia. The lands and power-base of the Potockis were in Galicia, in the part of southern Poland which had been annexed by Austria, and Adam Potocki became a chamberlain of the Emperor of Austria. Katarzyna was beautiful and intelligent and played together with her husband a prominent part in Polish politics. The Potockis were both loyal subjects of the Emperor of Austria. Franz Joseph allowed more freedom in Galicia than the Tsar or the King of Prussia did in their sections of Poland and, being a fellow Catholic, there was no religious hostility.*

PM

116 × 85.5 cms, oval
Signed and dated: *F. Winterhalter 1854*
*National Museum, Warsaw*

*Provenance*: Potocki Collection at Krzeszowice; acquired by National Museum, Warsaw, 1946; no. 1496.
*Bibliography*: Wild, 1894, no. 239; *Catalogue of Paintings, Foreign Schools, II, National Museum in Warsaw*, 1970, no. 1496, p. 210, repr.; Introduction, p. 51.
See colour plate p. 150.

Katarzyna Potocka is seen at threequarter-length, in an oval format, wearing a predominantly red and blue oriental costume with thick ropes of pearls, against a lightly-sketched background of branches.

Winterhalter's portrait of Katarzyna Potocka, sister of his patron, Elzbieta Krasinska (no. 67) and mother of Roza, Zofia, and Artur Potocki (nos. 70, 71 and 72), is one of his most striking female portraits of the 1850s. He portrays her in his favourite oval format, wearing Middle-Eastern dress, the legacy of the period in the Middle East which the sitter and her husband, Count Adam Potocki, had just spent in exile there, after he had wrongly been implicated in a revolutionary bomb plot in 1848. Although oriental dress features in many female portraits of the eighteenth century, when it was worn as fancy-dress, at this period it is highly unusual and lends an exotic air to the portrait, of which Winterhalter makes full use. He places his sitter against a background of foliage, giving a highly dramatic play of light and shadow across the sitter's tilted face, and underlining the slightly secretive, heavy-lidded glance which she throws towards the viewer.

The half-length oval portrait which Winterhalter painted of the same sitter, also in 1854, in conventional European dress (National Museum, Warsaw) is also more conventional in format, and lacks the striking interplay between pose and lighting which characterizes this portrait. Wild records three portraits (nos. 239, 240–1) of Countess Potocka and a third portrait of the Countess, a half-length again, also shows her in conventional dress (location unknown).

A copy of the present portrait is in the collection of Comte Rey, Chateau de Montrésor, France (exhibited Harrods, London, spring 1986).

SF

## 69

SOPHIE GUILLEMETTE, GRAND DUCHESS OF BADEN (1854)*
(For biography, see no. 4)

129 × 91 cms
Signed and dated, lower right: *Fr. Winterhalter 1854*
*Private Collection*

*Provenance*: By descent in the family.
*Exhibitions*: Baden, 1873, no. 2; Karlsruhe, Kunstverein, 'Badische Fürstenbildnisse', 1906–7, no. 21 (repr.); Karlsruhe, 1965, no. 62.
*Bibliography*: W. Brambach, *Bildnisse*, Karlsruhe 1884, no. 669; Hans Müller, *Badische Fürstenbildnisse*, II, Karlsruhe 1893, no. 20, repr. lithograph by F.H. Maguire (listed W. Brambach, *Bildnisse*, no. 667); A. von Schneider, 'Briefe an Franz Xaver Winterhalter', *Die Pyramide*, 3, 20 January 1935, pp. 9–10; A. von Schneider, 'F.X. Winterhalter und die Frauen', in *Badener Land (Beilage der Freiburger Zeitung)*, 2 February 1935; A. von Schneider, *Badische Malerie des 19. Jahrhunderts*, 1935, frontispiece; G.F. Kircher, *Zähringer Bildnissammlung in Neuen Schloss zu Baden-Baden*, Karlsruhe 1958, p. 109, repr.; Emil Baader, 'F.X. Winterhalter, der Europäische Fürstenmaler', *Badischer Heimat*, vols. 3/4, 1960, p. 374, repr.; Introduction, p. 51.
*Prints after*: Lithograph by F.H. Maguire.
Not reproduced.

Grand Duchess Sophie is wearing a black silk dress of half-mourning, trimmed with black ribbon, and with white undersleeves of blonde lace and a ruffle of lace and pearls at the neckline. Her black shawl is probably of embroidered silk. A cap with side lappets, periwinkle-blue flowers and ribbons, frames her head.

It is hard to recognize the sprightly creature of twenty years earlier (see nos. 4 and 95) in this portrait, painted two years after her husband's death. In the intervening time, Grand Duchess Sophie had become a tragic figure, though still beautiful and dignified. Winterhalter's portrait of her is full of sympathy and psychological insight. In spite of the long interval between the early portraits and the 1854 portrait, the friendship was maintained by the artist's summer holidays in Baden and by exchange of letters. The portrait 'in mourning' must have been envisaged for some time, judging by a letter from Sophie to Winterhalter dated 28 September 1853:

> '*Ich hoffe, Sie sind mit Ihrem Bruder glücklich in Paris angekommen und wünsche, dass Sie Zeit finden die vielen Arbeiten zu vollenden. Vergessen Sie nicht, wenn Sie mit allem fertig sind, es mir zu schreiben, damit dann – endlich – ein gewisses versprochenes Bild – ich glaube das meinige – kann gemacht werden.*'[1] (Winterhalter Family Papers, published in *Die Pyramide*, 1935)

No. 69 was the pendant to the posthumous portrait of Grand Duke Leopold of Baden, painted in 1855 by Johann Grund (Private Collection).

CBO

1. 'I hope that you have arrived happily in Paris with your brother and wish that you will find the time to complete your many works. Do not forget to write and tell me when you are done with it all, so that then – at last – a certain picture you promised – I believe it is mine – can be done.'

70

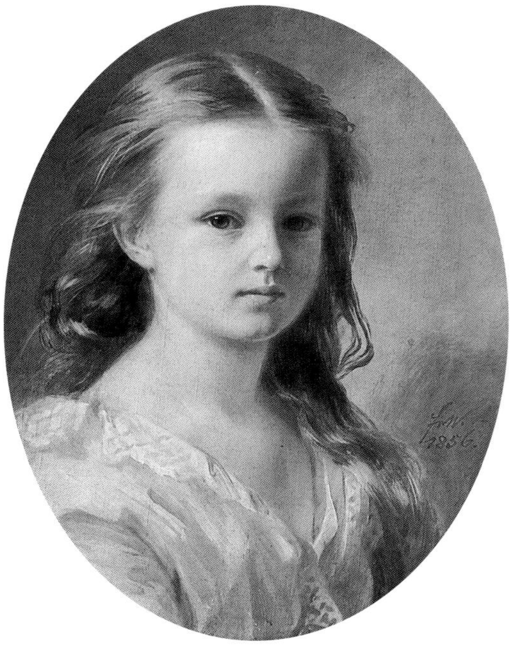

ROZA POTOCKA (1856)

*Roza Potocka (1848–1937) married Count Wladislaw Krasinki first, and second Count Eduard Raczynski, father of the President of the Republic of Poland in exile. She was daughter of Adam and Katarzyna and sister of Artur and Zofia.*
PM

46 × 38 cms, oval
Signed, lower right: *FW./1856*
*National Museum, Warsaw*

*Provenance*: In the Potocki Collection at Krzeszowice; acquired by the National Museum, Warsaw, 1946; Palace at Lańcut; no. 1501.
*Bibliography*: Wild, 1894, nos. 365, 403A, 485; *Catalogue of Paintings, Foreign Schools, II, National Museum in Warsaw*, 1970, no. 1501, p. 211; Introduction, pp. 51, 57.
See colour plate p. 145.

Roza Potocka is seen at bust-length, threequarter-face, wearing a white dress, her long fair hair worn loose.

This is one of a series of three portraits of the children of Katarzyna Potocka (no. 68), painted by Winterhalter in 1856, the year in which he visited Warsaw. All three ovals show head and shoulders only, and are reminiscent of the roundels of Queen Victoria's children which Winterhalter had painted a few years earlier.

The portrait of Roza, the eldest child, then aged seven, shows the sitter as the most poised of the three: Winterhalter places her to the left-hand side of the oval, with her face half-turned into shadow in a manner slightly reminiscent of the dramatic chiaroscuro he had employed in the portrait of her mother two years earlier (no. 68). The calm concentration which Winterhalter depicts on Roza's face contrasts with her slightly ruffled, swept-back hair, glinting with rapidly brushed-on highlights, giving a remarkably fresh portrayal of the child.

Winterhalter painted a second portrait of Roza Potocka, a half-length oval (presumably identical with the portrait of this sitter, dated 1867, in the collection of the National Museum, Warsaw, at Baranów), in Paris in 1867, when the sitter was in her late teens.
SF

71

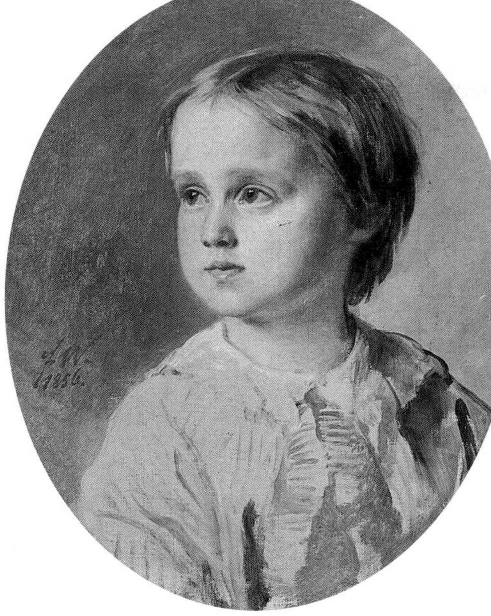

ZOFIA POTOCKA (1856)

*Continuing the tradition of Polish magnate endogamy, Zofia Potocka (1851–1927) married Stefan Zamoyski in 1870. His family was traditionally nationalist and he helped the Polish uprising of 1863. However, he later became a member of the Austrian Herrenhaus (Upper Chamber). They had six children, the last of whom died in 1965.*
(See no. 81)
PM

46 × 38 cms, oval
Signed and dated, lower left: *FW./1856*
*National Museum, Warsaw*

*Provenance*: In the Potocki Collection, Krzeszowice; acquired by the National Museum, Warsaw, 1946; no. 1499.
*Bibliography*: Wild, 1894, nos. 403, 485; *Catalogue of Paintings, Foreign Schools, II, National Museum in Warsaw*, 1970, no. 1499, p. 211; Introduction, pp. 51, 57.
See colour plate p. 147.

Zofia Potocka is depicted bust-length, threequarter-face to left, with short fair hair, wearing a white dress.

In contrast to the portraits of her elder sister and brother (nos. 70 and 72 respectively), Winterhalter portrays the five-year-old Zofia Potocka very much as a small child, her head turned and her large eyes looking out of the picture in a questing manner. This, together with the freedom of Winterhalter's brush strokes, creates a convincing picture of childish animation and charmingly suggests an inability to concentrate on the business of sitting for a portrait.

Winterhalter painted the same sitter, aged twenty, in a half-length oval portrait of 1871 (no. 81).
SF

72

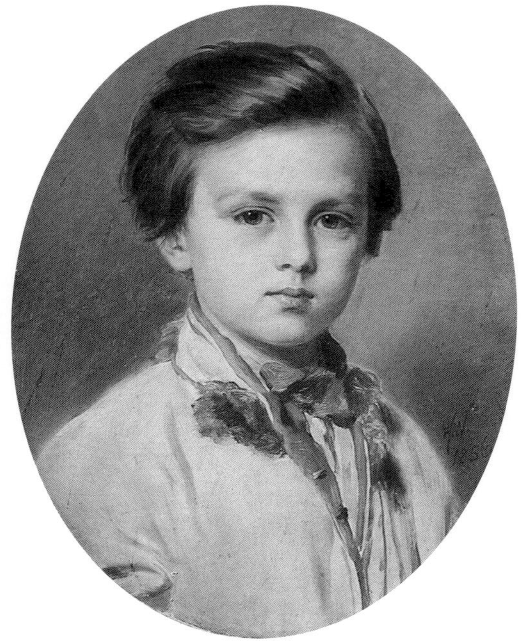

ARTUR POTOCKI (1856)

*Artur Potocki (1850–90), who married a Princess Lubomirska in 1877, was a chamberlain of the Emperor Franz Joseph and a member of the Austrian Herrenhaus. His cousin, Alfred Potocki of Lańcut, was briefly Prime Minister of the Austrian half of Austria-Hungary.*
PM

46 × 38 cms, oval
Signed and dated, lower right: *FW./1856*
*National Museum, Warsaw*

*Provenance*: In the Potocki Collection at Krzeszowice; acquired by the National Museum, Warsaw, 1946; Palace at Lańcut; no. 1500.
*Bibliography*: Wild, 1894, nos. 403B, 485; *Catalogue of Paintings, Foreign Schools, II, National Museum in Warsaw*, 1970, no. 1500, p. 211; Introduction, pp. 51, 57.
See colour plate p. 146.

Artur Potocki is shown at bust-length, full-face with short brown hair, wearing a white jacket with red trimmings and a cravat.

Winterhalter invests his portrayal of the six-year-old Artur Potocki with his usual highly-effective combination of childish innocence, emphasizing the sitter's large, solemn eyes, with a more adult-like dignity and gravity. The portrait forms a pendant to those of the sitter's sisters, Roza and Zofia (nos. 70 and 71).
SF

73

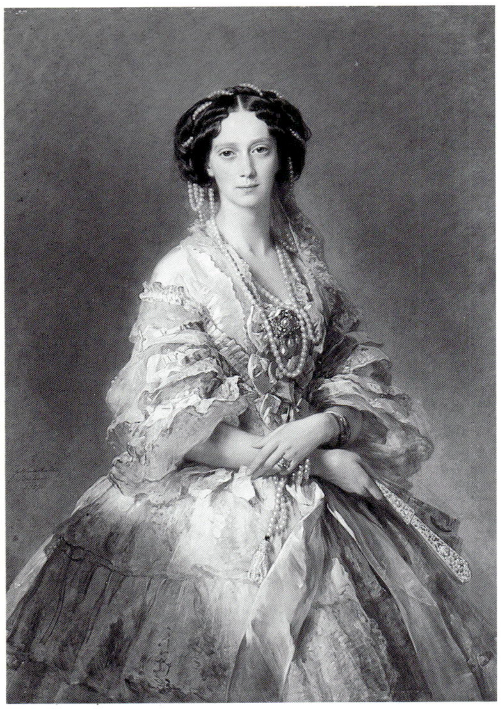

THE EMPRESS MARIA ALEXANDROVNA OF RUSSIA (1857)

*Princess Marie of Hesse-Darmstadt (1824–80) married the Tsar Alexander of Russia in 1841; they ascended the throne in 1855. At first they were devoted and had six children. She was intelligent and liberal and encouraged her husband in progressive measures such as the liberation of the serfs in 1862. Her increasing ill-health and her husband's affair with the ravishing Princess Catherine Dolgoruky, who was installed in the Winter Palace, drove them apart. The Empress died in 1880, a year before the assassination of the Emperor.*
PM

120 × 95 cms
Signed and dated, below centre left:
*Fr. Winterhalter Brückinau 1857*
*The State Hermitage Museum, Leningrad*

*Provenance*: Recorded in the collection of Alexander II in the Winter Palace; acquired by The Hermitage in 1926; no. 7539.
*Exhibitions*: St Petersburg, 1905, no. 1571; Leningrad, 1972, no. 320.
*Bibliography*: Wild, 1894, no. 385; A. von Schneider, *Die Pyramide*, 24, 20 January 1935, p. 15; *Catalogues of the Hermitage Collection*, 3, 1958, p. 342; 2, 1976, p. 244; 1973; Christa von Helmot, 'Der Fürstenmaler Europas', *Frankfurter Allgemeine Zeitung*, 7 July 1973; Introduction, p. 51.
See colour plate p. 158.

The Empress is shown full-face in this threequarter-length portrait; she stands against a grey background, her dark brown hair fashionably adorned with huge pearls, with more ropes of pearls cascading over her white dress.

Winterhalter's portrait of the Russian Empress, painted at Brückinau, the German spa town particularly favoured by the Russian aristocracy, is a study in monochrome. The pale-faced Empress (the strain of ill-health is particularly apparent in contemporary photographs), is dressed entirely in white and posed against a grey background, which hints at a wintry sky. Nothing detracts from the monumentality of the composition, established by the use of a low viewpoint, from which the viewer gazes up at the Tsarina's calm, unsmiling presence. Winterhalter's use of lighting here is particularly subtle and effective: a ray of light strikes the Empress diagonally, lighting up her face and the front of her dress, and playing about her figure to produce something of a haloed effect which adds to the ethereal impression of the portrait. A pendant portrait of the Tsar does not survive.

A letter from the Tsarina's lady-in-waiting, the Countess Tolstoi, told Winterhalter of the delighted reactions to his portraits of the Tsar and Tsarina (*Die Pyramide*; German translation of lost French original): 'Also, Sie müssen zufrieden sein, denn der Kaiser und die Kaiserin waren beide entzückt und wüssten nicht, welchen der zwei Porträts den Vorzug zu geben, jeder begeistert von dem seinigen.'[1] On 12 October 1857, back in Paris, Winterhalter received a letter informing him the Tsar '. . . en témoignage de bienveillance particulière et d'estime pour Votre grand talent a daigné Vous nommer Chevalier de Son Ordre de Ste Anne de la 3e classe.'[2] (Winterhalter Family Papers.)

Further portraits of the Tsar's family from Winterhalter's hand were envisaged: in a letter of 28 June 1864 (Winterhalter Family Papers), Count Alexander Adlerberg, attaché to the Russian legation in Prussia, wrote to Winterhalter regretting that he had departed for Kungen before the Tsarina could commission from him portraits of her children. She was anxious to know if he might carry out these portraits in August or September at Ouchy on Lake Geneva, before his engagement in Vienna to paint the Empress of Austria. Nothing further is known of these portraits.

A signed and dated copy of 1862 was in the collection of T.R.H. Prince and Princess Nicholas of Greece, 1936 (exhibited London, 1936). An unsigned and dated replica is in the Staatliche Kunsthalle, Karlsruhe, and is attributed to Hermann Winterhalter, and another version is in the Schloss Museum, Darmstadt.
SF

1. 'Well, you must be satisfied, for both the Emperor and the Empress were delighted and did not know which of the two portraits to prefer, each being thrilled with his or her own.'
2. '. . . in proof of special benevolence and esteem for your great talent has named you a Knight of the Order of St Anne, Third Class.'

74

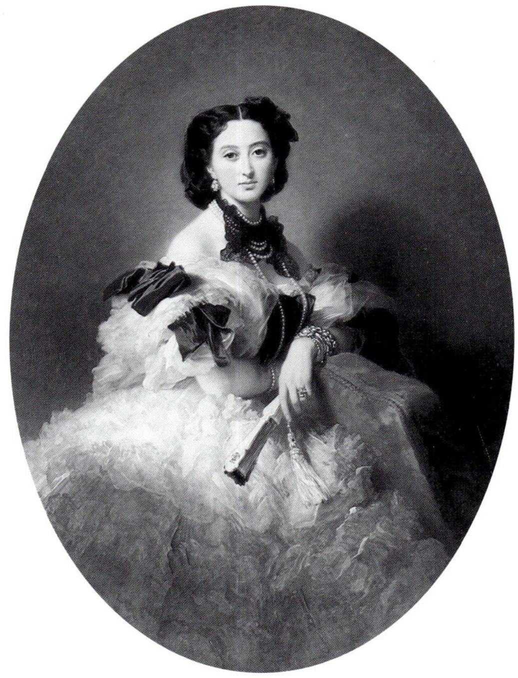

COUNTESS VARVARA ALEKSEYEVNA MUSINA-PUSHKINA

*Born a Sheremeteva (1832–85), she married Count Vladimir Ivanovich Musin-Pushkin in 1857. Both came from the highest ranks of the Russian nobility, which were dedicated to the personal service of the Tsar. Her husband was an officer in the famous regiment of Chevaliers-Gardes and one of the Tsar's equerries.*
PM

147 × 112 cms, oval
Signed right, below centre: *Fr. Winterhalter*
*The State Hermitage Museum, Leningrad*

*Provenance*: Collection of V.V. Musin-Pushkin, St Petersburg (see exhibitions below); 1922 passed from the 'Pokrovskoye' estate, Zvenigorod district via State Museum Fund to Tretyakov State Gallery; 1928 State Museum of Fine Arts, subsequently to the 'Antikvariat' All-Russian Society; 1933 The Hermitage, Leningrad; no. 7382.
*Exhibitions*: St Petersburg, 1905, no. 1570 (Property of Count V. V. Musin-Pushkin in St Petersburg); *Hermitage Travelling Exhibition*, 1954, p. 59.
*Bibliography*: Wild, 1894, nos. 257–8, 300; *Catalogues of the Hermitage Collection*, 2, 1958, p. 343; 1, 1976, p. 244.
See colour plate p. 148.

The sitter is shown threequarter-length, in an oval format, full-face, against a grey background. Her white tulle dress is adorned with blue ribbons and she wears black lace and pearls at her throat; gazing directly at the viewer, her body turning away, she leans against a red velvet-covered chair.

In this portrait of Countess Musina-Pushkina, Winterhalter achieved one of his most effective and alluring balances between a strongly characterized face and an almost fantastically insubstantial costume. The unusually strong gaze of the sitter is emphasized by the careful placing of the catchlights on her large, dark, heavy-lidded eyes, and the shape of her face is outlined by the black lace intertwined with pearls at her neck as well by the arrangement of her dark, wavy hair. The sitter's left hand and right arm are placed exactly at the centre of the oval, and the long, blue-veined hand, its elegant bend at the wrist recalling Van Dyck, holds an ivory fan adorned with a large jewelled tassel. On her wrists she wears thick, gleaming gold bangles, but the viewer's attention is caught chiefly by the huge expanse of what appears to be white froth substituting for a skirt, an outstanding example of Winterhalter's ability to evoke the fashion for filmy tulle dresses, painted with little attention to substance or form, yet superbly effective in the context of the portrait as a whole. The composition is held together by the careful juxtaposition of light and shade, particularly on the sitter's skirt, and by the skilful placing of the sitter and the details of the composition within the oval.

The portrait was, according to Wild, one of two ovals Winterhalter had painted of the Countess, a large and a small version, of which this is presumably the larger. The portrait perhaps dates from the period of the sitter's marriage in 1857.
SF

## 75

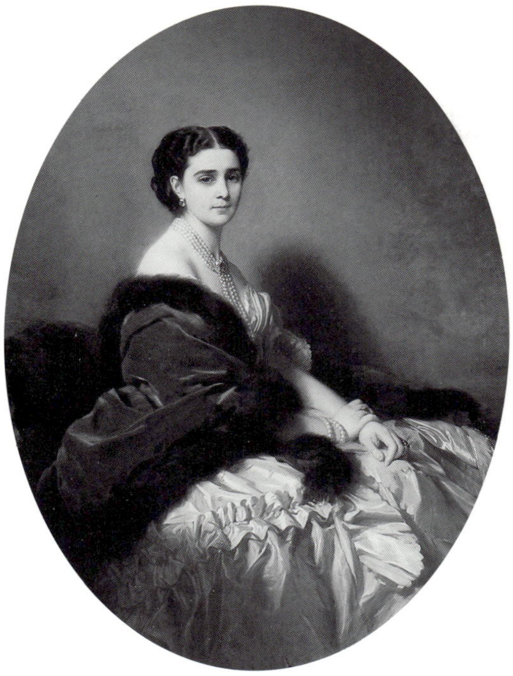

MADAME SOFYA PETROVNA NARYSCHKINA (1858)

*Sofya Petrovna Naryschkina* (née *Ushakova*) *(1823–77), a general's daughter, was wife of Chamberlain Konstantin Pavlovich Naryschkin, a Master of the Household of the Tsar, a Councillor of State and owner of three-thousand serfs. They had no children. The Naryschkins were one of the oldest families of the Russian nobility: Peter the Great's mother was also a Naryschkin. The identification of the portrait was made in 1968.*
PM

150 × 114 cms, oval
Signed and dated, below centre: *Fr. Winterhalter Paris 1858*
*The State Hermitage Museum, Leningrad*

*Provenance*: Acquired by The Hermitage, 1920, from the State Museum Fund; no. 5800.
*Bibliography*: Wild, 1894, no. 259; *Catalogues of the Hermitage Collection*, 2, 1958, p. 342 (as 'Unknown woman of the Naryschkin family'); 1, 1976,' p. 244; A.N. Izergina, *Izergina*, 1969, p. 74; Introduction, p. 51.
See colour plate p. 149.

Winterhalter's portrait of Madame Naryschkina uses the favoured oval format, with a grey background against which the sitter casts a shadow; she is shown threequarter-length, and seated unusually far to one side on a green chair, wearing a red wrap trimmed with brown fur over a yellow dress.

The portrait forms a contrast to other portraits of this period which emphasize light colours and textures (for another portrait of a Russian sitter which uses a similar background to very different effect, see no. 74). No great attention is paid to textures here; the fur is thinly painted, the waves of the hair conveyed schematically by Winterhalter's usual shorthand of a series of short, close strokes of grey paint brushed on over the dark brown hair colour. Instead, Winterhalter sets off the neutral background with bold and unusual contrasts of colour; the sitter's acidic yellow dress, dark red velvet wrap and the vivid green of the chair, which picks up the greenish shadows in the folds of the dress. At her neck and wrist she wears pearls, with the necklace showing an amethyst clasp, and on her right hand a ring with the turquoise stone particularly popular with Russian women; her earrings are probably of crystal. The sitter's face is animated by a suggestion of a dimple in her cheek.

In July 1858, Winterhalter was in correspondence from Interlaken concerning some miniatures for a Monsieur Narischkin by another artist, Herr W–, possibly the miniaturist Hermann Gottlob Wurst (1823–91). He advised that as the miniatures had not been sent to him in Baden as arranged, and Madame Narischkina was about to go to Paris, she would be best to go to the artist himself there; Winterhalter had already paid him (Winterhalter Family Papers). It is conceivable that these miniatures were copies of the present portrait, which was executed in Paris in the same year; alternatively, they might have been for Winterhalter's reference in completing his portrait of Madame Naryschkina.
SF

## 76

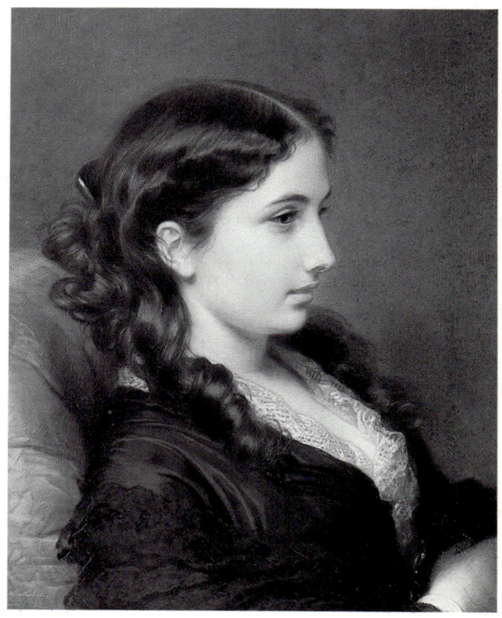

STUDY OF A GIRL IN PROFILE (1862)

58 × 47 cms
Signed and dated, lower right: *Fr Winterhalter 1862*
*Private Collection*

*Provenance*: The artist; his brother Hermann, thence by family descent.
See colour plate p. 157.

This intimate and appealing study of a young girl in black, leaning back against a red cushion, shows Winterhalter in a relaxed vein. Both he and his brother liked to sketch pretty women as an antidote to the demands of formal portraiture, and the Winterhalter *Album* is full of such examples, most of them by Hermann. The sitter is dressed in fashionable day dress, with a black lace shawl and a mood of intimacy is created by the loose hair escaping from the comb. The portrait is unlikely to have been a commission. It is reproduced in the Winterhalter *Album*, 1891, no. 11.
RLO

77

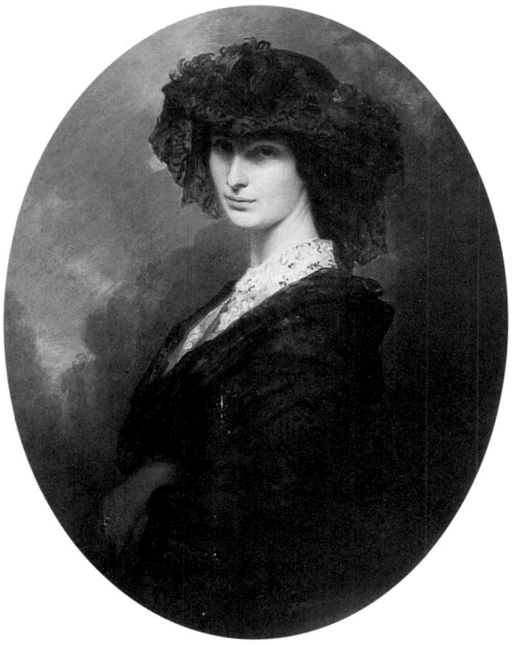

JADWIGA POTOCKA, COUNTESS BRANICKA

*The Branickis were one of the richest Polish magnate families. They had inherited vast estates in Polish Ukraine and had been generously rewarded by Catherine II for their 'realistic' or pro-Russian views. Jadwiga Branicka (1827–1916) was born a Potocka, another traditionally pro-Russian magnate family. Her husband, Konstanty (1824–84), was a keen ornithologist and travelled widely in Africa and Asia.*
PM

79 × 63 cms, oval
Signed, lower right: *Fr. Winterhalter*
*National Museum, Warsaw*

*Provenance*: In the collection at Wilanów since last century; no. 1502.
*Bibliography*: Wild, 1894, no. 307; *Portrety Osobistósci Polskich (Portraits of Polish Personalities)*, 1967, no. 14, p. 33 (with Bibliography), repr.; *Catalogue of Paintings, Foreign Schools, II, National Museum in Warsaw*, 1970, no. 1502, p. 212, repr.; X. Rey, 'Le Château de Montrésor', *Connaissance de Paris*, no. 43, 1982, p. 35; Introduction, p. 51.
See colour plate p. 151.

Jadwiga Branicka is depicted half-length, three-quarter-face, wearing a black hat trimmed with blue ostrich plumes and a black cape, against a background of foliage.

The portrait of Jadwiga Branicka is one of Winterhalter's most expressive and sensitive half-length female portraits. As with other portraits in this oval format, he makes particularly effective use of dramatic contrasts of light and shade, here the shadow thrown across the sitter's eyes by the brim and black lace veiling of her hat; her large eyes are strongly emphasized, and become the focus of the composition. The fragility of the sitter's neck is further emphasized by shadow and by the contrast with her broad-brimmed hat; she half-turns her head as though in mute appeal to the viewer. Winterhalter, for the most part depicting more serene or even blatant beauty, rarely achieved such a successful essay in a more sombre and restrained key.

The portrait is traditionally described as depicting the sitter in mourning for the unsuccessful Polish uprising against Russian rule which took place in 1863. Dr Aileen Ribeiro points out, however, that rather than being signs of mourning, her black dress and feather-trimmed hat are, in fact, highly fashionable.

A second portrait of the sitter by Winterhalter, signed and dated Paris 1862, may be the original of a copy (Wilanów) showing the sitter in a head-and-shoulders portrait, in profile from the back; a profile portrait was recorded in Wild (no. 308).
SF

78

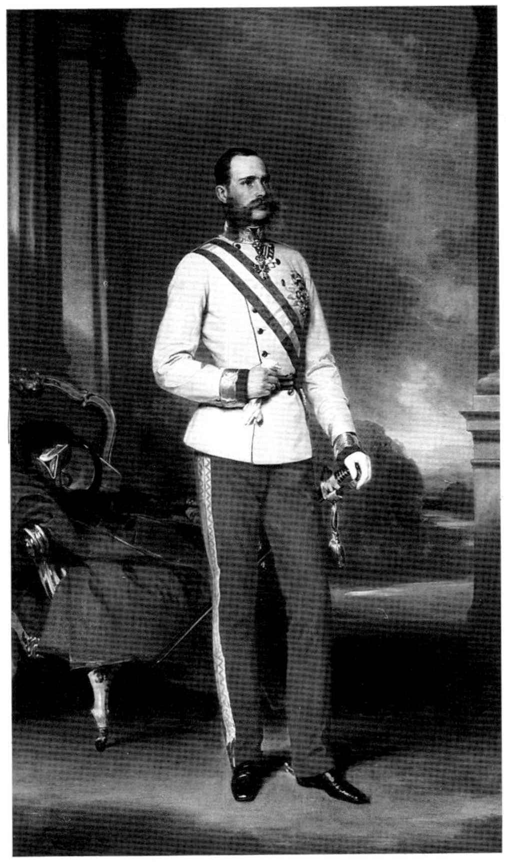

FRANZ JOSEPH I, EMPEROR OF AUSTRIA (1865)*

*Franz Joseph I (1830–1916) succeeded to the throne in 1848, the year of revolutions. He was hard-working and flexible in everything except his sense of duty to his dynasty, his religion and his subjects. Despite defeats by France in 1859 and Prussia in 1866, he held his multiracial empire together until his death. At the time this picture was painted, he was successfully negotiating the transition from absolute monarchy to constitutional government in Austria.*
PM

255 × 133 cms
Signed and dated, lower left: *F.X. Winterhalter. 1865*
*Kunsthistorisches Museum Gemäldegalerie, Vienna*

*Provenance*: Always at the Hofburg, Vienna; no. 7098.
*Exhibitions*: Burgenland, Schloss Halbturn, 'Uniform und Mode am Kaiserhof, Hofkleider und Ornate, Hofuniform und Livreen des 19. Jahrhunderts aus dem Monturdepot des Kunsthistorischen Museums Wien', 1983 (p. 236) (repr.); Niederösterreich, Schloss Grafenegg, 'Das Zeitalter Kaiser Franz Josephs, von der Revolution zur Gründerzeit', 1984, no. 17.72 (p. 343).
*Bibliography*: Wild, 1894, no. 461; *The Imperial Style, Fashions of the Habsburg Era*, 1979, pp. 11, 142; H. Kessler-Aurisch, *Mode und Malerei in Wien vom Wiener Kongress bis zum ersten Weltkrieg*, Dissertation, Freiburg-im-Breisgau 1983, p. 104ff; Introduction, pp. 57, 62.
*Prints after*: Steel engraving by L. Jacobi, undated, pub. P. Kaiser, Vienna (see below).
See colour plate p. 152.

The Emperor is depicted wearing the full dress uniform of an Austrian field marshal with the Great Cross of the Military Order of Maria Theresa, as well as other Austrian Royal orders, and at his neck the insignia of the Order of the Golden Fleece. His elongated figure, the upper part of which is silhouetted against the cloudy sky, is further emphasized by the low viewpoint and by the framing giant columns which enclose a landscape leading off a terrace. This background is echoed in the pendant portrait of the Empress (no. 79), though here the effect of perspective is emphasized rather less, giving the upright figure of the Emperor a more forceful presence. The effect is reinforced by the brilliant reds and golds of his uniform and the adjacent chair. Winterhalter's painting of the head is particularly vigorous.

Winterhalter arrived at the Austrian Court in the autumn of 1864. A letter of 27 September asks for accommodation and a studio to be found for him at the Palace of Schönbrunn (Winterhalter Family Papers, q.v., for all subsequent documentation here). While there, he completed two formal full-length portraits of the Emperor and Empress (the present portrait and no. 79), as well as two further portraits of the Empress (see no. 79). He also portrayed the Emperor's mother, the Archduchess Sophie, and his younger brother, the Archduke Ferdinand Maximilian and his wife Charlotte, who were shortly to leave Austria to rule as the Emperor and Empress of Mexico. Payments disbursed in the summer of 1865 for the dispatch of portraits of the Emperor and Empress to Mexico presumably refer to these portraits. Although no. 78 is dated 1865, it must presumably have been virtually completed when, on 22 December 1864, order was given for Winterhalter to be paid 30,000 florins for portraits of the Emperor and Empress; a letter of 12 December refers to his departure from Vienna and intention to be in Paris by the New Year (see no. 79). On 21 December, Winterhalter received a letter informing him that the Emperor had awarded him the Cross of the Commander of the Imperial Franz Joseph Order. The sculptor, La Vigne, was paid 1800 florins for making the elaborate gilded frames for the portrait pair (not exhibited), which must have been ready at the end of January 1865, when he submitted his account. On 13 January, the Emperor gave instructions for Louis Jacoby to produce engravings of the pair of portraits, and specified that the portraits were not to be removed from the Hofburg for four or five years, so Jacoby was obliged to work there; the engravings ultimately took five years to produce. Arrangements were made to exhibit them in London in 1872.

A copy of this portrait is in the Hofburg, Innsbruck.

SF
RLO

## 79

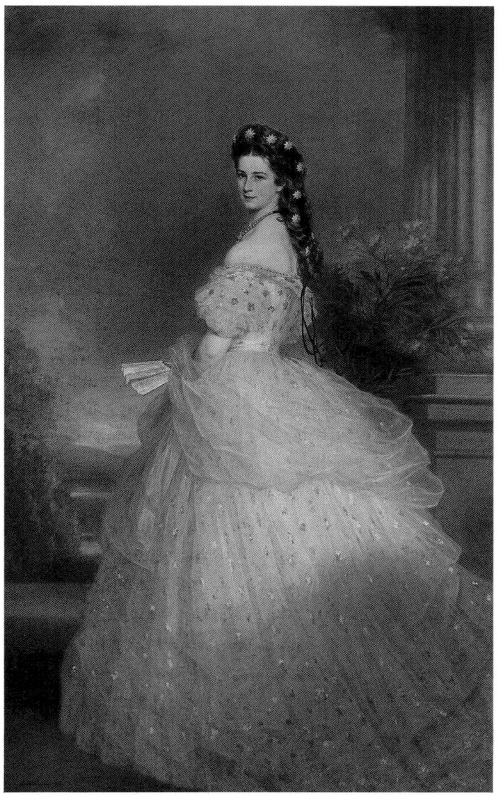

ELIZABETH, EMPRESS OF AUSTRIA (1865)*

*The Empress Elizabeth (1837–98) was one of the most famous beauties of her age. A Wittelsbach and a relation of the King of Bavaria, she was brought up very simply until her marriage to her first cousin, the Emperor Franz Joseph of Austria, at the age of sixteen.*

*At first she seemed happy with her doting husband, and quickly produced three children. However, she disliked Vienna, the court, and her own mother-in-law, the influential Grand Duchess Sophie. Unlike her rival, Princess Pauline Metternich, she did little to lower the barriers surrounding the court and the aristocracy, or to patronize the arts. She found escape in travel, hunting and Hungary, and became very fond of the handsome nationalist politician, Count Andrassy, helping to smooth the way for the compromise of 1867 which created the dual monarchy of Austria–Hungary.*

*Towards the end of her life, saddened by the loss of her looks and the suicide of her son, the Crown Prince Rudolph, and terrified of going mad, she drew closer to her husband: Whilst on holiday in Geneva, she was stabbed by an Italian anarchist.*

PM

255 × 133 cms
Signed and dated, lower left: *F.X. Winterhalter. 1865.*
*Kunsthistorisches Museum Gemäldegalerie, Vienna*

*Provenance*: Always at the Hofburg, Vienna; no. 7099.
*Exhibitions*: London, 1936, no. 1; Metropolitan Museum, New York, 'The Fashions of the Hapsburg Era, Austria–Hungary', 1979–80; Burgenland, Schloss Halbturn, 'Uniform und Mode am Kaiserhof, Hofkleider und Ornate, Hofuniformen und Livreen des 19. Jahrhunderts aus dem Monturdepot des Kunsthistorischen Museums Wien', 1983 (p. 236) (repr.); Niederösterreich, Schloss Grafenegg, 'Das Zeitalter Kaiser Franz Josephs, von der Revolution zur Gründerzeit', 1984, 17.73 (p. 343).
*Bibliography*: Wild, 1894, no. 462; Armand Dayot, 'A propos de Winterhalter', *L'Art et les Artistes*, no. 87, May 1928, p. 257; R. Byron, 'Winterhalter' *Country Life*, no. 80, 5 December 1936, p. 596; R.H. Wilenski, 'Winterhalter and Official Art', *The Listener*, 1936, pp. 1075–7; James Laver, 'Winterhalter', *The Burlington Magazine*, 70, 1937, pp. 44–5; *The Imperial Style, Fashions of the Hapsburg Era*, 1979, pp. 11, 142; Introduction, pp. 53–4 and 62.
*Prints after*: Steel engraving by L. Jacobi, undated, pub. P. Kaiser, Vienna (see no. 78).
See colour plate p. 153.

The present picture, though formal in intention, using the time-honoured formal device of a giant column in the background, which Winterhalter had relied on in earlier court portraits, also presents an appealingly Romantic image of the Empress. Less static and formal than the images of the 1840s, the portrait shows Winterhalter conveying softer textures and working in an altogether more relaxed style. The background includes a terrace looking out on to a distant landscape with trees and hills merging into a cloudy sky, and recalls the informal portrait still at the Hofburg, as well as echoing the background of the pendant portrait of the Emperor (no. 78). Against this, Winterhalter sets the elongated figure of the Empress, emphasizing her well-modelled shoulders which rise out of the white satin and tulle dress dotted with silver foil stars; more stars, this time of diamonds (designed and made by the court jeweller, J.H. Köchert) are worn in her hair. In the 1860s, Worth made spangled tulle all the rage: the sitter here ordered dresses from him, although she never visited him in person. To complete this picture of Imperial allurement, the Empress turns her head to the viewer with a glance which is almost a smile.

This portrait of the Empress Elizabeth is the pendant to the portrait of the Emperor Franz Joseph (no. 78). Winterhalter's chief mission at the Austrian Court seems to have been to portray the Empress, and is referred to as such in a letter of June 1864, written on behalf of the Russian Empress Maria Alexandrovna (Winterhalter Family Papers; see no. 73). As well as this full-length formal portrait, he produced for her husband two strikingly intimate threequarter-length portraits of the Empress. One (The Hofburg, Vienna), showing the Empress gazing out on to a starlit terrace, her long hair loose, still hangs today in its original location in the Emperor's study; the other (unidentified, Private Collection, copy in the collection of Fürst Thürn und Taxis), an oval, signed and dated *Schönbrunn 1864*, shows the Empress with her hair knotted about her shoulders like a thick shawl (see Introduction, fig. 43).

A letter to Winterhalter of 12 December 1864, from Countess Paula König (Winterhalter Family Papers), addressed to him after he had evidently left Vienna intending to be in Paris by the New Year, refers to two photographs of the Empress to be sent on to him in Paris; although it is unclear whether these are simply souvenirs, or were to be of use in producing further portraits. Two sketches apparently by Winterhalter of the dress and of the half-length figure (Winterhalter Family Collection), may have been intended as records of the portraits, rather than working drawings.

A copy of this portrait is in the collection of the Hofburg, Innsbruck.

SF
RLO

80

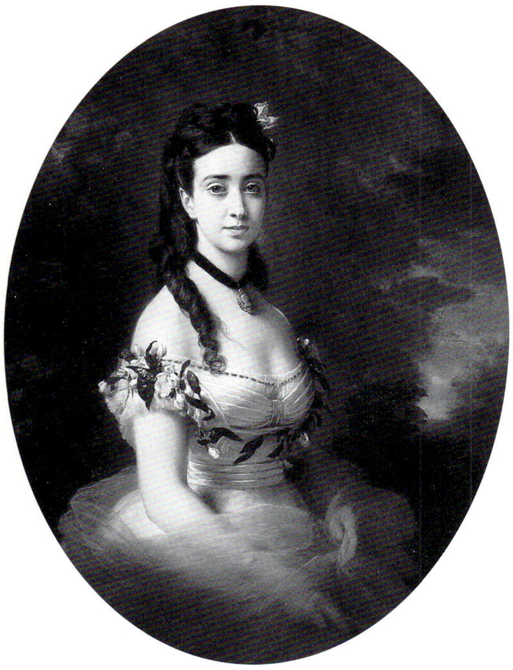

AN AMERICAN LADY (*DIE AMERIKANERIN*)

110 × 85 cms, oval
*Private Collection*

*Provenance*: By descent in the family.
*Bibliography*: Wild, 1894, no. 507; O.E. Sutter, 'Franz Xaver Winterhalter', *Daheim*, no. 25, 1936, p. 373, repr.
See colour plate p. 154.

The sitter wears a ball-gown of white tulle and a tulle stole. A swag connects the bunches of flowers at her shoulders, emphasizing her generous *décolletée*, and a velvet choker holds a cameo at her neck. The elaborate hairstyle is probably supplemented by false hairpieces, as was usual for evening dress in the late 1860s.

Sharply lit, there is no attempt to connect the figure with the sketchy pastoral background. Nor has Winterhalter sought to prettify his model's features; as D. MacAndrew has said, 'the portrait suggests rather one of Henry James's self-possessed heroines from the States whose forthright manner so startled their European sisters'.

According to family tradition, the portrait represents the American who was Winterhalter's last fiancée. There is no evidence to prove that Winterhalter (in his sixties at the time of painting) ever became engaged to a young American, however, or indeed if he did, that this is she. Winterhalter is recorded as painting at least one American sitter, 'Mlle Strahter de Kentucki' in about 1850 (Wild, no. 195), a date which rules out identification with the present portrait. A portrait called *Die Amerikanerin* (Wild, no. 507) is however listed in Winterhalter's nephew's supplement to the artist's own list of portraits painted; no date is given.
CBO

81

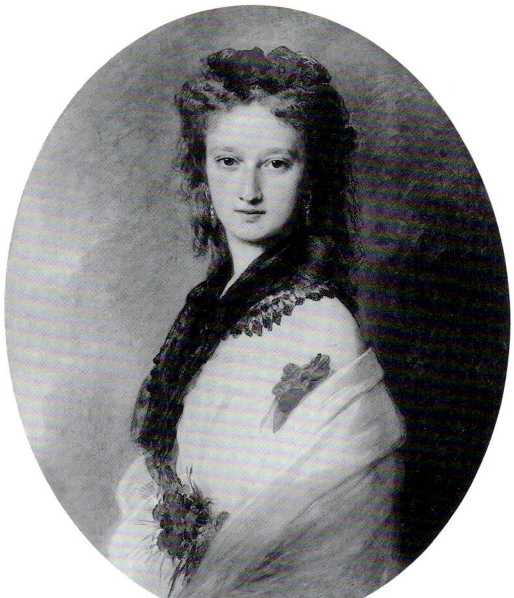

ZOFIA POTOCKA, COUNTESS ZAMOYSKA (1870)
(For biography, see no. 71)

82 × 65.4 cms, oval
Signed and dated, lower right: *F.X. Winterhalter 1870*
*National Museum, Warsaw*
*Provenance*: Acquired by National Museum, Warsaw; no. 128908.
*Bibliography*: Introduction, p. 51.
See colour plate 155.

Zofia Zamoyska is seen half-length, full-face, against a background of hazily suggested distant trees, wearing a white shawl with a black lace scarf at her neck, and a posy of red and blue flowers at her waist.

A late, but very fresh, light-toned portrait of the sitter whom Winterhalter had painted in her native Warsaw at the age of five (no. 71). Using his favoured oval format, Winterhalter places his sitter at a slight angle to the picture plane, so that she appears to look out with a slightly down-turned but steady gaze. The formula Winterhalter had employed so successfully in earlier oval portraits, with background foliage casting dramatic shadows, is here modulated into a more impressionistic background, using more even lighting and a lighter key altogether. The scarf around the sitter's neck and the flowers at her waist evoke a feeling of informality and pastoral life, although her *déshabillé* is actually highly fashionable. This mood, as well as the more muted approach, is reminiscent of some of Winterhalter's rare subject paintings (see no. 39).

The portrait was probably painted in connection with the sitter's marriage, and may possibly have been intended as a pendant to the portrait of her sister, Roza, aged eighteen, which Winterhalter executed in 1867, three years before the present portrait (see no. 70).
SF

82

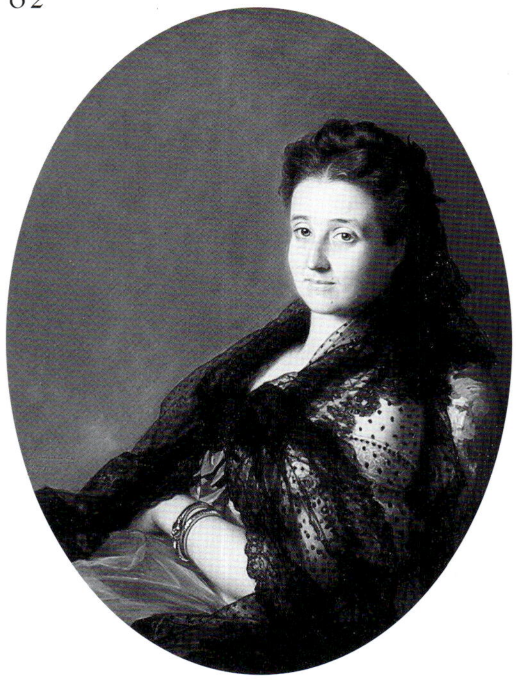

UNIDENTIFIED LADY (1872)*

90 × 70 cms, oval
Signed and dated, lower left: *fr. Winterhalter/1872*
*Private Collection*

*Provenance*: Galerie Bruno Meissner, Zürich, 1982; Bury Street Gallery.
See colour plate p. 156.

The woman is seated on a chintz-covered chair, wearing an off-the-shoulder silk evening dress decorated with lace and a floppy blue bow. Her large mantle of embroidered black net is partly caught up in her hair, and she wears a coiled snake bracelet with a turquoise inset.

In 1871 Winterhalter moved with his brother to Karlsruhe. From this time until his death in 1873, his principal area of patronage was Frankfurt. Here he painted portraits for the city's banking magnates, families such as the Bernus, Grunelius, Guaita, Metzler, Mumm and Passavant. In a letter of 28 October 1872 to his niece's husband, Johann Baptist Schlageter, Winterhalter gives a Frankfurt address. The date of no. 82, together with a label at the back of the contemporary frame (J.P. Schneider jr/16 Rossmarkt/Frankfurt am Main), suggests that the unidentified lady may have belonged to one of these Frankfurt families.

The competent brushwork, delicate pastel tones and the subject's delightful expression show that Winterhalter retained the ability to flatter his female sitters to the very end.
CBO

## 83

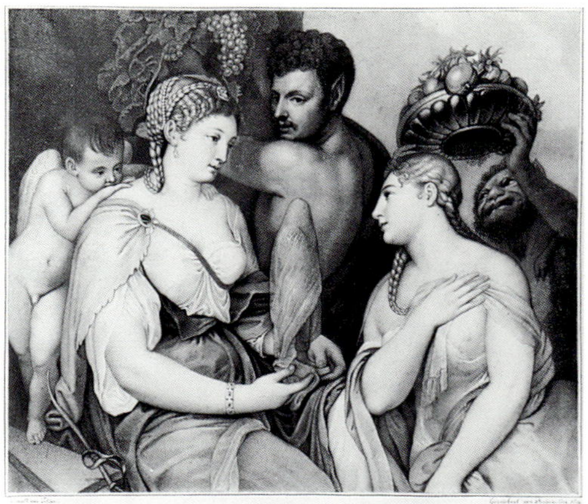

MYTHOLOGY AFTER TITIAN (1824)

Pencil on paper
41 × 47.5 cms
Inscribed on mount: *Gezeichnet von Winterhalter 1824 Gemalt von Titian*
*Private Collection*

*Provenance*: Acquired by the Grand Duke Ludwig of Baden; passed by descent to the present owner.
See colour plate p. 161.

The original picture, now in the Alte Pinakothek, Munich, was in the Munich Royal Collection from 1618. A pastiche, drawn from elements of compositions by Titian, it was evidently produced by a seventeenth-century workshop and is one of several versions of the composition, probably intended to pass as original works by Titian. The subject does not refer to any specific mythological incident: Venus and Cupid hold a mirror to Ceres, while Bacchus looks on, accompanied by a satyr with a basket of fruit.

This highly-finished drawing was apparently made by Winterhalter at the beginning of the period between 1824 and 1832 when he was based at Munich. During this time, he was employed on the volumes of lithographs after Old Masters in the Munich Gallery published by Ferdinand Piloty and Josef Anton Selb. Two lithographs in the volume of 1831, one after a Van Dyck portrait, the other after a *St John* by Maratti, are recorded as Winterhalter's own work. The lithograph after the so-called Titian which appears in the same volume is, however, signed by Piloty himself, and is an altogether weaker rendering of the original than Winterhalter's drawing. This raises the possibility that Winterhalter provided this study, which he must have made in the Munich Gallery, for the volume, but that Piloty was in this case responsible for the actual production of the lithograph, copying Winterhalter's drawing on to the stone, and thereby losing Winterhalter's vigour and fidelity to the original. Alternatively, the drawing may simply have been made by Winterhalter as an academic exercise.

Another drawing by Winterhalter, similar in style to this one, and again with a mythological subject, purporting to be after Raphael, survives in the same Collection, but is not reproduced in Piloty's volume.
SF

## 84

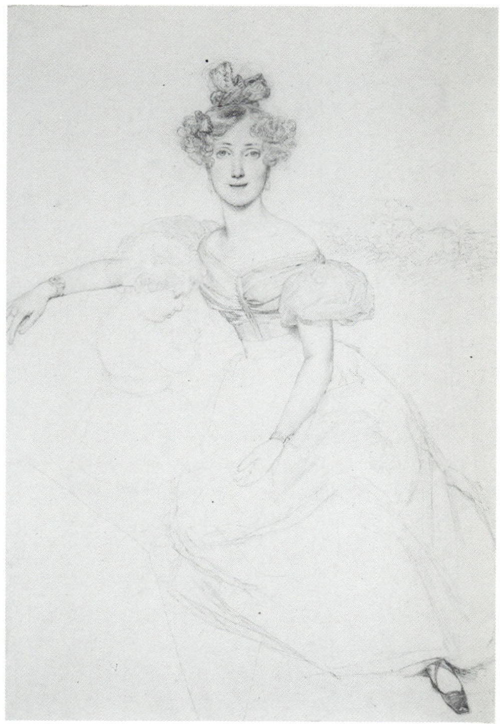

SOPHIE GUILLEMETTE, GRAND DUCHESS OF BADEN AND HER SON PRINCE WILHELM OF BADEN

*Prince Wilhelm (1829–97) was the third surviving son of the Grand Duchess. He later commanded the Baden Army Corps. In 1918 his son, Prince Max of Baden, was the last Chancellor of Imperial Germany.*
(For biography of Sophie, see no. 4.)
PM

Pencil on white laid paper
37.5 × 27.4 cms
Inscribed in pencil, bottom verso: *Je certifie le dessin ci-contre oeuvre originale de Winterhalter. Je l'ai acquis avec une douzaine de portraits à l'huile de cet artiste et deux albums de dessins, croquis et d'études pour ses portraits, de la famille même du peintre, deux vieilles dames, parentes et héritières de Winterhalter, établies à Lausanne et qui, peu avant leur mort m'ont cédé tout le lot restant des oeuvres du maître, cela vers 1930.* Reichlen;[1]

In pencil, bottom right: *181–26 = 21/Dessin original par X. Winterhalter*. Stamp of the Reichlen firm, Lausanne, on the repaired corner.
*Allen Memorial Art Museum, Mrs F.F. Prentiss and Charles F. Olney Funds*

*Provenance*: Descendants of the artist, Lausanne, until *c.*1930; J.L. Reichlen, Lausanne; N. Chaikin, New York, from whom purchased, 1965; no. 65.22.
*Bibliography*: 'College Museum Notes', *Art Journal*, XXV, no. 3, spring 1966, p. 274; Wolfgang Stechow, *AMAM Drawing Catalogue*, 1976, pp. 75–6; 'Accessions of American and Canadian Museums', *Art Quarterly*, nos. 1 and 2, p. 109, p. 118, repr.
See colour plate p. 162.

This is the preparatory drawing for the slightly larger oil painting of Sophie of Baden and her son, Prince Wilhelm of Baden of 1832 (Private Collection). The sitter's head, bust and arms are fully laid in, while the child, skirt of the dress and background are simply sketched. Although unfinished, the drawing is remarkably consistent with the painting, save in some of the accessories (the earrings, necklace and sprig she holds in her left hand, for example), which may have been chosen at a later stage for the oils. Evident empathy existed between artist and sitter, and Winterhalter conveyed Sophie's refined sensibility even more vividly in the drawing than in the finished painting. As well as a preparatory drawing, no. 84 may have been intended as a presentation piece, or served as an exercise in draughtsmanship: Winterhalter had been appointed drawing-master to the young Grand Duchess in 1829. That Winterhalter was in the habit of giving his pupil his own drawings to copy is evident from part of a letter from Sophie, dated 14 May 1829:

*'Only today is it possible for me to express my warmest thanks to you for your letter and the most charming drawing, which earns not just my admiration, but everybody's. I am very pleased with it and will try to see whether my feeble powers permit me to fulfil your wish for me to copy it. It would give me great pleasure if I could at least succeed in achieving a likeness. I fear you would not be entirely satisfied with me if you could see my work, for since your departure I have unfortunately not been very diligent. I have completed only the drawing which you helped me begin, and I have done a few more sketches from memory. Part of the trouble was that my eyes pained me, which naturally persuaded me to spare them, and then time was often too short, which has prevented me from thanking you earlier in the last few days. However you need not fear that I shall give up drawing, for as soon as I have a free moment I at once sit down at my drawing table, which is always there ready to receive me. This week I intend to begin copying your beautiful drawing.'* (Winterhalter Family Papers; published in *Die Pyramide*, 3, 20 January 1935, pp. 9–10)

Other drawings of the Grand Duchess by Winterhalter include: an earlier profile, *c.*1828–9, with a tiara and Classical hairstyle (Staatliche Kunsthalle, Karlsruhe, no. 447), and a threequarter-length finished drawing of Sophie in a shawl seated on a chair (whereabouts now unknown). Another drawing of Grand Duchess Sophie, of 1831, a half-length done in pencil and watercolour, with head resting on hand (see Introduction fig. 9), is in a Private Collection in Germany.

CBO

1. I certify the drawing on the other side to be *an original work by Winterhalter*. I acquired it together with a dozen oil paintings by this artist and two albums of drawings, sketches and studies for his portraits, from the painter's own family, two old ladies, relatives and heiresses of Winterhalter, established at Lausanne and who, shortly before their death, let me have the remaining lot of works by the master, this being about 1930. Reichlen;

## 85

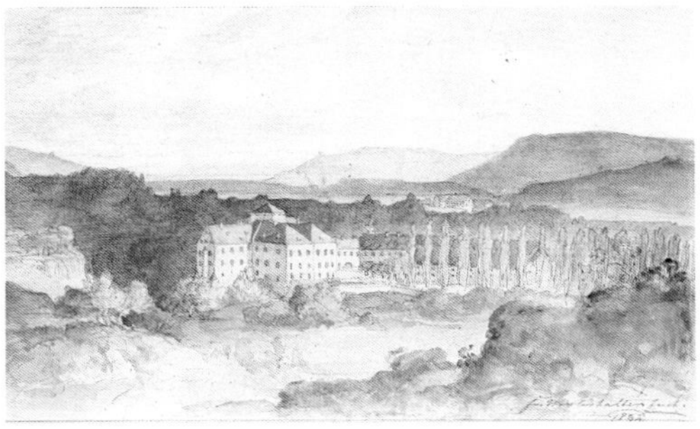

SCHLOSS LANGENSTEIN

Pencil and watercolour on paper
17 × 29.5 cms
Signed and dated, lower right: *Fr Winterhalter fecit/18[?34]*
Private Collection

*Provenance*: By descent to the present owner.
*Bibliography*: *Weltkunst* xxxix, no. 12, 15 June 1969, p. 680; Introduction, p. 26.
See colour plate p. 163.

This represents one of Winterhalter's very few landscape depictions. Schloss Langenstein, near Lake Constance, was the seat of the Grand Duke Ludwig of Baden who died in 1830. Winterhalter was, at this period, the early 1830s, engaged on portraits of the Grand Dukes' mistress, the Countess of Langenstein and their two children (see no. 8).

Winterhalter's handling of the watercolour technique in this landscape study is particularly free: the hilly setting of Schloss Langenstein is evoked in a series of rapidly executed wash outlines over pencil, contrasting with the much tighter handling of the watercolour portraits of this period (see nos. 86 and 87).

SF

## 86

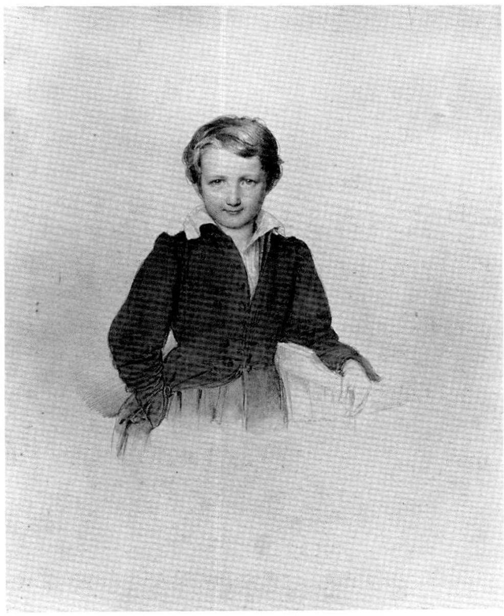

KARL WICH (1833)*

*Karl Wich was the son of the wealthy court doctor, Johann Albert Wich, of Baden-Baden. He was a friend of Winterhalter, who stayed with the Wich family whenever he visited Karlsruhe.*

PM

Ink and brush over pencil on Whatman board, watermarked 1833
37.1 × 30.6 cms
Signed, lower right: *Winterhalter*
*Staatliche Kunsthalle Karlsruhe*

*Provenance*: Acquired by Staatliche Kunsthalle Karlsruhe, 1942, from Gräfin von Lamberg Ortenegg; previously in a Freiburg Private Collection, probably that of Fraulein Aline Leers, 1909; no. 1942–10.
*Exhibitions*: Freiburger Kunstverein, 'Jahrhundert-Austellung, 1780–1880', 1909, no. 195; Karlsruhe, Kunsthalle, 'Deutsche Zeichnungen des 19. Jahrhunderts', 1966, no. 106.
*Bibliography*: C. Sutter, *Die Freiburger Austellungen von 1908 und 1909 in Schau-ins-Land*, 36, 1909, p. 82 and note 83; R. Theilmann and E. Ammann, *Die Deutschen Zeichnungen des 19 Jahrhunderts, Staatliche Kunsthalle Karlsruhe, Kupferstichkabinett*, Karlsruhe 1978, pp. 688–9; Introduction, p. 26.
*Prints after*: Lithograph, Kauffman.
Not reproduced in colour.

Karl Wich is seen at half-length, full-face, with his left hand leaning against a sketchily indicated chair, his right hand in his pocket. He is wearing a blue coat and white shirt.

This is one of two sketches of Karl Wich which Winterhalter made while lodging with the court physician's family at Munich in the early 1830s. The second portrait (Private Collection) shows Karl with his sister, Frida, and the family dog.

Although the portrait is executed in the same meticulous technique as that of Karl's sister, Pauline (no. 87), the more relaxed attitude of the sitter, and in particular his engagingly direct gaze and half-smiling mouth, anticipate the charm of Winterhalter's later watercolour portraits of children.

SF

## 87

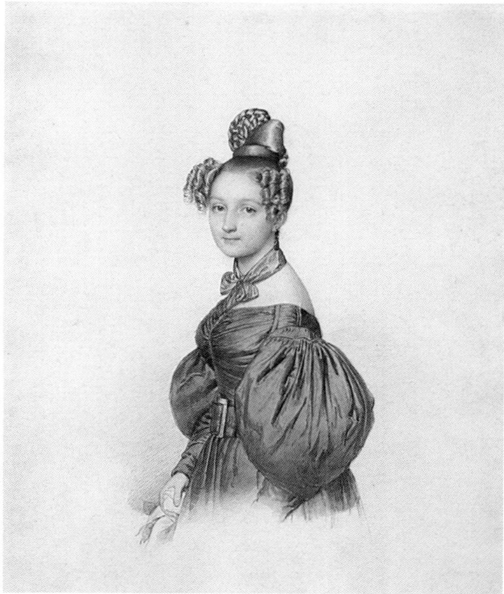

PAULINE WICH, BARONESS SEUTTER VON LÖFZEN (1833)*

*Pauline Wich, later Baroness Seutter von Löfzen, was a daughter of the Privy Court and Medical Councillor Dr Johann Albert Wich. She was the sister of Karl Wich.*
PM

Brush and ink and watercolour over pencil on Whatman card, watermarked 1833
36.8 × 31 cms
Inscribed, lower right (not in Winterhalter's hand): *2/87a*
*Staatliche Kunsthalle Karlsruhe*

*Provenance*: Acquired by Staatliche Kunsthalle Karlsruhe in 1942 from Gräfin von Lamburg Ortenegg; previously in a Freiburg Private Collection, probably that of Fraulein Aline Leers, 1909.
*Exhibitions*: Freiburger Kunstverein, 'Jahrhundert-Ausstellung 1780–1880', 1909, no. 193; Karlsruhe, Kunsthalle, 'Deutsche Zeichnungen des 19. Jahrhunderts', 1966, no. 105.
*Bibliography*: C. Sutter, *Die Freiburger Ausstellungen von 1908 und 1909, Schau-ins-Land*, 36, 1909, p. 82; R. Theilmann and E. Ammann, *Die Deutschen Zeichnungen des 19. Jahrhunderts, Staatliche Kunsthalle Karlsruhe, Kupferstichkabinett*, Karlsruhe 1978, p. 688; Introduction, p. 26.
See colour plate p. 164.

Pauline, Baroness Seutter von Löfzen appears half-length, threequarter-face, holding a handkerchief in one hand. She wears a brown dress with low ballooning sleeves.

This is one of a group of portrait drawings of the Wich family which Winterhalter made during the years in which he lodged with the family of the court physician, Dr Wich, at Karlsruhe. This is the more finished of two portraits of Pauline, who would have been aged about fifteen according to the dating of 1833 or after, provided by the watermarking of the paper.

Winterhalter's extremely closely-worked, highly-finished handling of the watercolour, ink and pencil medium contrasts with his much looser approach to landscape painting in the same period (no. 85), and to the watercolour portraits of the following decades (see nos. 89 and 92). The formality of the pose is emphasized by the meticulous rendering of the gathers of the bodice and shoulders, and the pleats of the set-in sleeves of the dress, as well as of the elaborately curled hairstyle with its 'Apollo' knot and glossy side ringlets.
SF

## 88

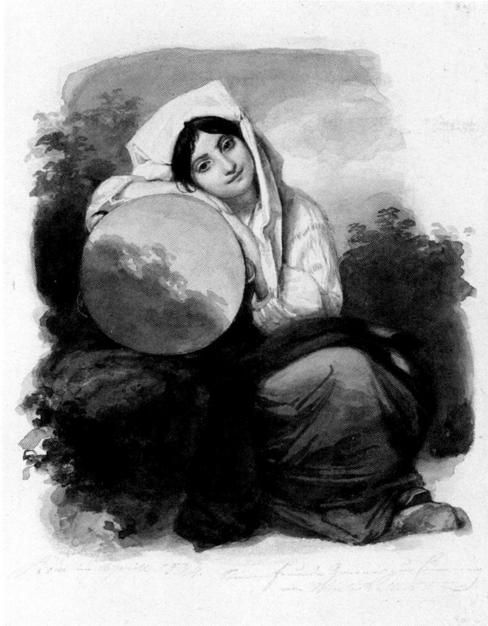

ITALIAN GIRL RESTING WITH A TAMBOURINE (1834)*

Watercolour over pencil on paper
24.1 × 19.5 cms
Signed, dated and inscribed below: *Rom im Aprill 1834. Seinem Freunde* . . . [indecipherable name] *zur Erinnerung von Winterhalter*[1]
*Staatliche Museen zu Berlin, DDR*

*Provenance*: Acquired from Royal Print Room, Berlin, before 1875; earlier provenance unknown.
See colour plate p. 170.

The girl has her head pillowed on her arms, and leans against a tambourine. She wears a white peasant head-dress, a white blouse and a long russet skirt, and she is seated by a rock and some bluish vegetation; foliage is reflected on the drum of the instrument. The background, costume and the hands are freely washed-in by the artist; only the face is painted with small hatching strokes. The girl has wide-set eyes and a haunting expression under the dark fringe.

This is presumably the watercolour preparatory to the oil painting exhibited at the Karlsruhe Art Exhibition in 1835 (present whereabouts unknown). By 1834, Winterhalter was at the end of his stay in Italy, and had thoroughly perfected the type of peasant genre scenes which earned him such popularity. The reviewer from *Kunstblatt* enthused at length about the oil version of no. 88, exhibited at the 1835 Karlsruhe Art Exhibition. Quoting '.. Ein trefflicher Ausleger des Bildes',[2] we read about the conjectured life of the fourteen-year-old waif, and he concludes: 'Für das vorzüglichste Genregemälde halte ich unbedingt Winterhalters ruhende Tänzerin . . . aber sie ist doch das liebste und lieblichste Mädchen, von allen den lockenden Gesichtern, die uns Winterhalter noch gemalt.'[3] The reviewer adds that the oil of the *Italian Girl Resting with a Tambourine* was bought immediately by the Karlsruhe Kunstverein, and that Winterhalter also painted a half-length version for a Karlsruhe collector. A reduced version of the oil was in a Private Collection in Karlsruhe in 1835 (present whereabouts unknown).

A comparable watercolour of a girl and tambourine in the Wallace Collection, London (P669) was formerly attributed to Winterhalter, but is now catalogued as by Hermann Winterhalter.
CBO

1. 'To his friend . . . in memory of Winterhalter.'
2. '. . . one excellent interpreter of the picture.'
3. 'I consider Winterhalter's resting dancer to be without doubt the most superb genre painting . . . she is the dearest and sweetest girl among all the enchanting faces that Winterhalter has so far painted for us.'

89

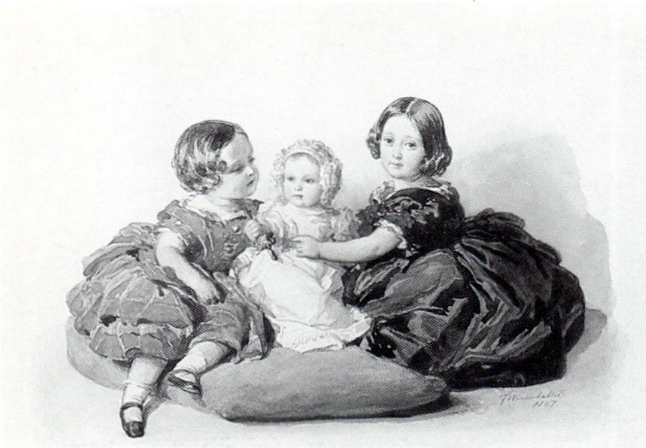

PRINCESS ALICE, PRINCE ALFRED AND PRINCESS HELENA (1847)

*Princess Alice (1843–78) was the second daughter of Queen Victoria; she married Louis, Grand Duke of Hesse-Darmstadt in 1862. Prince Alfred (1844–1900), the second son of Queen Victoria, was created Duke of Edinburgh in 1866 and succeeded as Duke of Saxe-Coburg-Gotha in 1893. Princess Helena (1846–1923), Queen Victoria's third daughter, married Prince Christian of Schleswig-Holstein in 1866.*

Watercolour
24 × 35.4 cms
Signed and dated, bottom right: *F. Winterhalter / 1847*
*Lent by Gracious Permission of Her Majesty The Queen*

*Provenance*: Given to Queen Victoria by Prince Albert, 1847; R.L. 13332.
*Exhibitions*: London, 1956–7, no. 714; London, Queen's Gallery, 'Royal Children', 1963, no. 90.
See colour plate p. 166.

The Prince is seated on the left, wearing a red silk dress, white socks and black patent shoes. His elder sister, Princess Alice, is on the right, wearing a blue silk dress with white collar and cuffs, and supporting the baby, Princess Helena, who wears a white frock and holds a rattle.

The picture was given by Prince Albert to Queen Victoria on their wedding anniversary, 10 February 1847. The Queen found it 'so like, & so pretty', and was herself soon 'trying to copy Winterhalter's beautiful sketch of the children' (Journal, 10 and 22 February 1847). She made another copy of Prince Alfred and the baby in 1850.

The Queen and Prince left Osborne to stay at Arundel Castle from 1–4 December 1846, and Winterhalter may have painted the children during their absence, as a surprise. This is suggested by the date, 1 December 1846, shown on an enamel copy of the watercolour, by Schweizer, made in 1851 (also Her Majesty The Queen). There is no record of Winterhalter being at Osborne at this time, but he was painting the Queen and Prince at Windsor in mid-November and mid-December. A watercolour copy was commissioned from Guglielmo Faija in 1848 for the Queen's albums of portraits (WRA).
DM

90

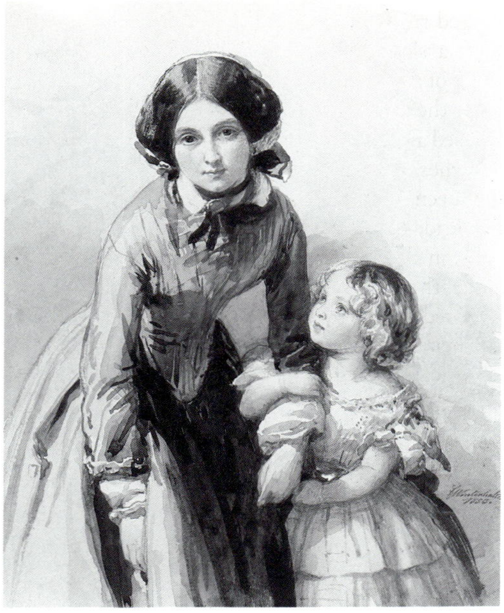

PRINCESS LOUISE WITH HER NURSEMAID ELIZA COLLINS (1850)

*Princess Louise (1848–1939), the fourth daughter of Queen Victoria, married the Marquis of Lorne, later Duke of Argyll, in 1871.*

*Eliza Collins (c. 1832–96) was a Royal nursery maid from at least 1849. She was probably the daughter either of a sergeant footman or a gentleman porter of the name of Collins, in the Queen's employ. She gave up her position and married Prince Albert's valet, Rudolf Löhlein, in July 1850. Their eldest child was born in 1852. For Christmas 1851, the Queen gave Löhlein a copy by G. Faija after Winterhalter's* Sketch of Eliza *(WRA).*

Watercolour on paper
28.4 × 23.7 cms
Signed and dated, lower right: *F. Winterhalter / 1850.*
*Lent by Gracious Permission of Her Majesty The Queen*

*Provenance*: Originally in Queen Victoria's albums of portraits; R.L. 13336.
*Exhibitions*: London, 1956–7, no. 710; London, Queen's Gallery, 'Royal Children', 1963, no. 78.
See colour plate p. 167.

The nurse is shown at threequarter-length, leaning forward and wearing a silk day dress with a pointed bodice, white undersleeves and a white collar; a brooch is fastened on a ribbon at her neck, and a white cap set at the back of her head frames her hair. The Princess is on her right, holding her arm and probably standing on a stool; she wears a white dress with a blue sash.

The Princess was two years and three months old when the painting was made. Winterhalter arrived at Osborne on 5 June 1850, to paint Prince Albert, and that oil painting was completed on 12 June. The watercolour presumably dates from the same week. No payment for it is recorded.

This watercolour and no. 91 (R.L. 13335) were originally in Queen Victoria's albums of portraits. These volumes were being made up from the early 1840s. The Queen showed the first to her uncle, Leopold I, King of the Belgians, in 1844. By the end of 1847, she had three 'really invaluable albums with watercolour portraits' of relations and friends to look through (Journal). She continued to add to the collection until the late 1850s. By then, the volumes of watercolours were being superseded by those with photographic portraits. The albums of portraits were broken up in the early 1930s and the watercolours were mounted separately. In most cases, the titles from the original pages were fixed to the back of the new mounts, so that, although no list of the contents of the original albums survives, it is possible partly to reconstruct them. Many of the drawings in the books were of the Royal children whose appearance the Queen was anxious to record at each stage of their development. Sir William Ross produced for her many small, animated water-colour portraits. Sir George Hayter made a large chalk portrait of the Princess Royal in 1842, but was not invited to portray further additions to the family. Sir Edwin Landseer could, on occasions, capture a good likeness; but it was Winterhalter who succeeded in catching the best likenesses, with speed and spontaneity.
DM

91

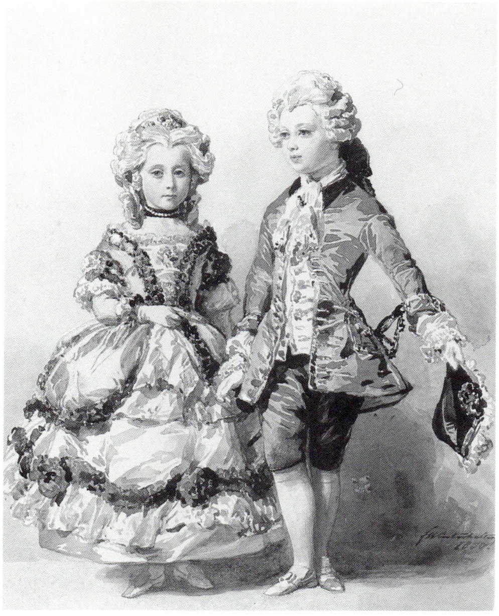

VICTORIA, PRINCESS ROYAL AND PRINCESS ALICE IN EIGHTEENTH-CENTURY COSTUME (1850)

*The Princess Royal (1840–1901) married Prince Frederick William of Prussia in 1858. She became subsequently Crown Princess of Prussia and Empress Frederick of Germany.*

Watercolour
28.8 × 23.8 cms
Signed and dated, lower right: *F Winterhalter / 1850*
*Lent by Gracious Permission of Her Majesty The Queen*

*Provenance*: Originally in Queen Victoria's albums of portraits; R.L. 13335 (see no. 90, R.L. 13336).
*Exhibitions*: London, Queen's Gallery, 'Royal Children', 1963, no. 87.
See colour plate p. 168.

Princess Alice stands to the front, on the left, dressed as a girl in a white dress trimmed with ruched ribbon and flounces, worn over a hoop and with a short yellow silk 'waistcoat', to give the effect of an eighteenth-century overdress, bunched up at the sides. The Princess Royal, on the right, is dressed as a boy, wearing a blue satin coat and knee-breeches, a white waistcoat and lace jabot.

Queen Victoria and Prince Albert enjoyed the whole idea of dressing-up. They gave three costume balls, in 1842, 1845 and 1851, and at the second of these, the guests were asked to wear the dress of a hundred years previously. Their children were frequently dressed by one of their parents in historical or peasant costume, as a surprise for the other. As a birthday treat for the Queen, on 24 May 1850, the Prince arranged that his eldest daughters should be:

> *'dressed as a Lady & Gentleman of the year 1740 or 46, powdered, & both looking so handsome. They danced the Menuet d'Exaudet, beautifully & so correctly. Vicky made a capital boy & looked so tall & dignified, Alice so refined & graceful & her figure looked lovely. The powder was very becoming to both. It was dearest Albert's surprise for me, & I was so pleased & touched. They repeated the Menuet 3 times, & then galopped, &c.'* (Journal.)

The Menuet was the same that their parents had danced at the 1845 ball. It was probably the first year that Prince Albert thought that his two eldest daughters would be competent to cope with its elaborate steps. They had been having dancing lessons with Madame Bourdin who had taught it to the Queen. Its intricacies would probably have defeated the Prince of Wales, so his sisters were chosen to perform it instead. There are records of payments on behalf of the Princesses to M. and Mlle. Vouillon et Laure, who had made the Queen's dress for the 1845 ball. These may relate to the costumes seen here, which are small versions of those worn by their parents on that occasion. Princess Alice's outfit seems to have been worn the following year, by her younger sister, Princess Helena, in a French play.

By 23 July 1850, the Queen recorded in her Journal that Winterhalter had 'made such a beautiful sketch in watercolour of Vicky & Alice, in their powder costumes', and the watercolour was placed in the Queen's albums of portraits (see no. 90, R.L.13336). No payment is recorded for the watercolour.

DM

92

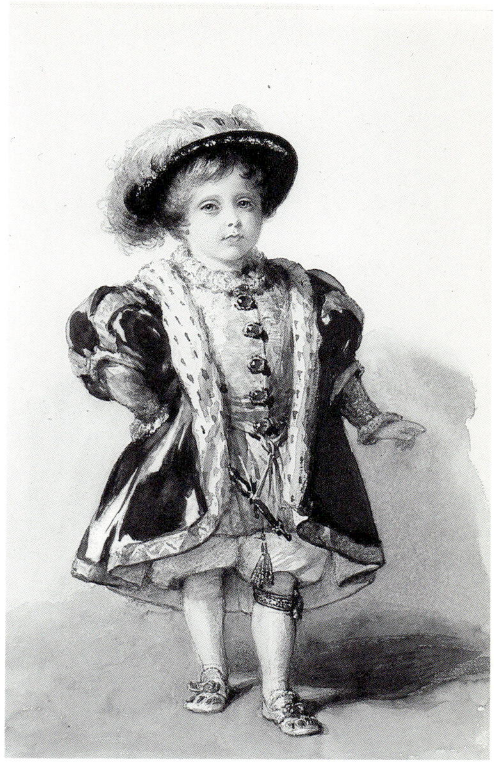

PRINCE ARTHUR DRESSED AS HENRY VIII

*Prince Arthur (1850–1942) was the third son of Queen Victoria, and was created Duke of Connaught in 1874.*

Watercolour with gum arabic on paper
36.5 × 24 cms
*Private Collection: By courtesy of H. Fritz-Denneville Fine Arts Ltd, London*

*Provenance*: Originally in an album of watercolours belonging to Queen Victoria; passed by descent to a member of her family; sold at Sotheby's, 13 March 1986, lot 19.
See colour plate p. 169.

Prince Arthur is seen standing to the front, aged three years, dressed as Henry VIII and wearing a feathered hat, a gold tunic with large buttons and frilled collar and cuffs, puffed knee-breeches, a garter, square-toed shoes of slashed leather in the early sixteenth-century style and a purple and gold ermine-trimmed coat with padded short sleeves.

On 10 February 1847, the Royal wedding anniversary, Prince Arthur's elder brother, Prince Alfred, had been dressed as Henry VIII as a surprise for his father. On 11 January 1853, Prince Arthur appeared, also at the age of three, in the same outfit, 'in which he looked charming. Everybody was much pleased, & so were we'. (Journal). The younger Prince was dressed up in this costume, while elder brothers and sisters performed part of Racine's *Athalie*.

A month later, the Princess Royal, his thirteen-year-old sister, presented her parents, on their anniversary, with a watercolour of 'little Arthur as "King Hal"' which she had drawn, 'almost entirely by herself', as an anniversary present. Winterhalter may also have made his watercolour between 11 January and 10 February. Alternatively, it may have been commissioned by Prince Albert after seeing his daughter's attempt. Apart from the fact that the child wears the same costume, there seems to be no direct link between the two watercolours. Prince Arthur's pose is different in each drawing; Winterhalter uses a more elegant pose, while the

Princess shows her brother full-face with the traditional stance used by Sir Joshua Reynolds in his *Master Crewe as Henry VIII*. That portrait, in Lord Crewe's Collection at Crewe House, had been exhibited at the British Institution in 1843 and the J. Raphael Smith engraving of it (published by John Boydell in 1776) was in the print collection at Windsor Castle.

No. 92 was originally in an album of watercolours belonging to Queen Victoria. An inscription on the original mount described the watercolour as a 'Gift to Queen Victoria from the Prince Consort', which implies that, although painted in 1853, it was not mounted in the album before 1857, when Prince Albert became Prince Consort. There is no recorded payment for the watercolour, but Winterhalter was working for his Royal patrons in oils at this date. Parts of the costume, including the shoes and dagger, remained in the collection of the Duke of Connaught until his death in 1942, when they returned to the Royal Collection (WRA).

DM

## 93

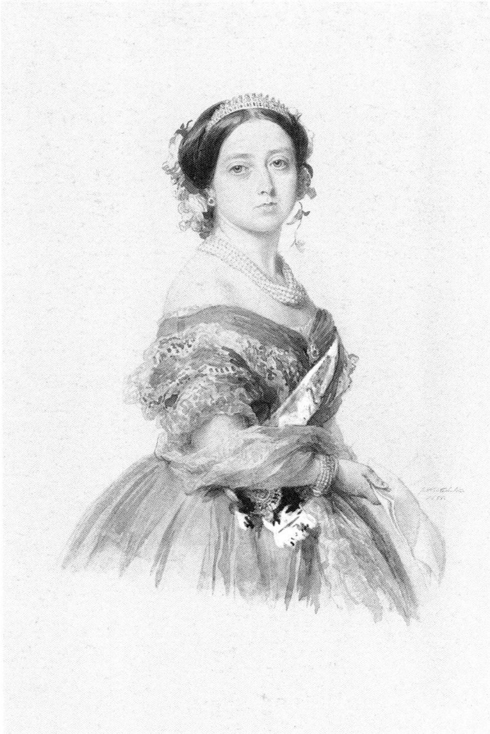

QUEEN VICTORIA (1855)
(For biography, see no. 27)

Watercolour on paper
38.3 × 26.7 cms
Signed and dated, lower right:
*Fr Winterhalter / 1855*
*Lent by Gracious Permission of Her Majesty The Queen*

*Provenance*: Painted for Queen Victoria; R.L. 13344.
*Prints after*: Lithograph by R.J. Lane, 1855; some versions of the chromolithograph have a facsimile of the Queen's signature (*Victoria R*) and the date 1855.
See colour plate p. 165.

Queen Victoria is shown at threequarter-length, standing to the right and looking to the front, wearing a green dress trimmed with lace and the ribbon and star of the Garter, and holding a paper. She wears twisted ropes of pearls around her neck and wrist, and a tiara of diamonds and rubies; her hair is dressed with flowers and leaves at the back.

The painting was made for Queen Victoria, with watercolour portraits of Prince Albert and the Princess Royal (both in Royal Library, Windsor Castle). They were all paid for on 22 June 1855 (WRA). They were originally intended for the Queen's albums of portraits (see no. 90), but proved to be too large and were therefore framed and hung at Windsor Castle until 1913, when they were placed in the Royal Library.

After her visit to Paris in August 1855, the Queen wrote to Lady Cowley, wife of the British ambassador in Paris, promising to send her a print of 'the recent and most like' sketch of herself, which Winterhalter had painted that summer. The lithograph, at that time being made, was not yet completed (WRA).

DM

## 94

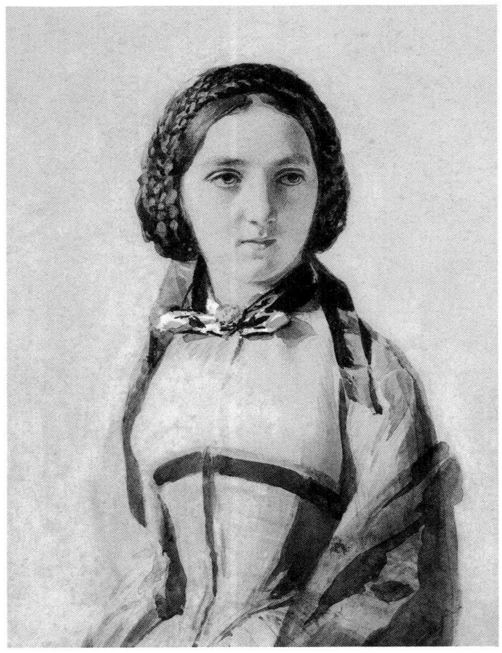

THE DAUGHTER OF MR AEBI (1867)

Pencil and watercolour on paper
Approximately 25.7 × 20.3 cms
*Private Collection*

*Provenance*: Allegedly presented by Winterhalter to Adolphe Ossent, 1867; Charles Ossent; Richard Owen, Paris, 1929; John Nicholas Brown Estate; David Tunick, Inc.
*Exhibitions*: London, 1936, no. 30; Nebraska, Omaha, 'Joslyn Memorial', 1941.
*Prints after*: One of the pair of watercolours was allegedly engraved by O. Weber.
See colour plate p. 171.

The sitter is depicted at half-length, with braided hair, wearing everyday Bernese costume, with a blue knotted scarf at her neck.

This is one of a pair of watercolours, said to be the portraits of the daughters of a hotel owner in Interlaken. One of the two sisters was called Madeleine Aebi. Both portraits were sent in a presentation case of embossed leather with Winterhalter's visiting card (marked in pencil: '2 rue de la Chausée d'Antin – Paris'), to M. Adolphe Ossent, with whom Winterhalter is said to have spent a holiday at Interlaken in about 1867. This might be an error for 1857, the year in which the artist moved to the rue de la Chausée d'Antin, and also visited Switzerland.

The delicate, controlled brushwork is typical of Winterhalter's watercolour portraits, and the small hatching strokes on the face suggest his early training as an engraver. The watercolour of the girl's sister, painted on the same occasion, is in the same Collection as no. 94.

CBO

95

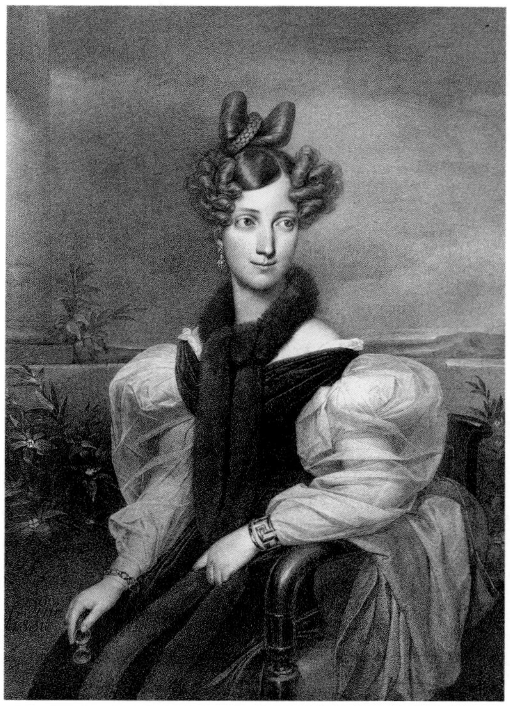

SOPHIE GUILLEMETTE, GRAND DUCHESS OF BADEN*
(For biography, see no. 4)

Lithograph. 48.2 × 34
Inscribed: *Gemalt und auf Stein gezeichnet von Winterhalder* [sic] *Lithographie von J. Velten/Sophie Wilhelmina/Grossherzogin von Baden*
*Staatliche Kunsthalle Karlsruhe*

See colour plate p. 172.
See no. 96.

96

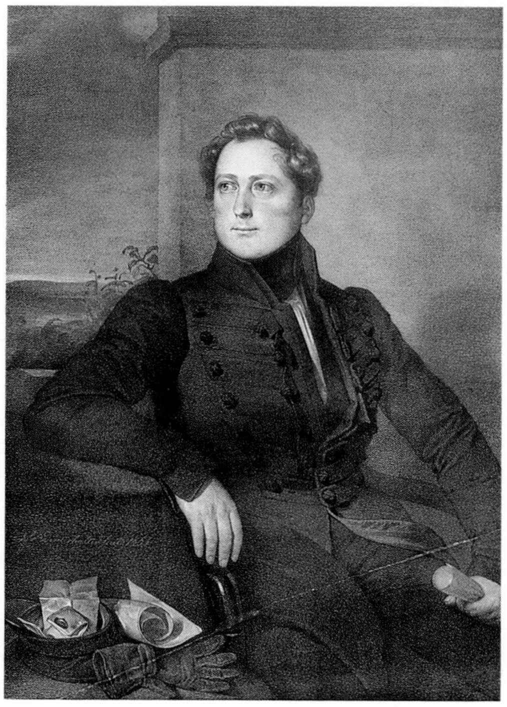

LEOPOLD, GRAND DUKE OF BADEN*
(For biography, see no. 3)

Lithograph. 48.8 × 34
Inscribed: *Winterhalter pinx & del. Lithographie von J. Velten/Leopold/Grossherzog von Baden/Mit Grossherzoglich Badischem Gnädigstem Privilegium*
*Staatliche Kunsthalle Karlsruhe*

See colour plate p. 173.

Leopold is shown in a frock-coat with rather military-looking braid on the chest. He is seated on a balcony, with an assortment of papers and a pair of gloves on a table beside him; in his left hand he clasps another paper. The portrait of Sophie, Grand Duchess of Baden, shows her against a similar background, with a balcony and column. As usual, she is dressed elegantly, here with a fur tippet around her neck. Sleeves were at their widest in the early 1830s: here the sitter's padded puff sleeves can be seen beneath gauze gigot oversleeves, sometimes called 'aerophanes'. Her hair is elaborately dressed with curls, plaits and stiffened loops, and she is depicted with a certain Romantic wistfulness in her gaze.

This lithograph, and its companion (no. 95), were made after small cabinet-sized portraits (present whereabouts of the portrait of Leopold is unknown; the portrait of Sophie, dated 1831, is in a Private Collection). The lithograph of Sophie shows the original painting in reverse. The same is presumably true of that of Leopold, for only in reverse do the two compositions make convincing pendants, with the two sitters facing each other. The portraits were commissioned from Winterhalter at the same time as the 1831 full-length portrait of Leopold (see no. 3). The heads in both portraits of Leopold seem to derive from a single sitting; both lithographs reproduce the date 1831, together with Winterhalter's signature. In this composition, however, Winterhalter appears to have achieved a much greater appearance of naturalness, despite the apparent awkwardness in the drawing of the left arm. The portrait of Sophie is one of several Winterhalter executed of her at this period, all apparently from the life (see nos. 4 and 84 and Introduction, fig. 9).

Winterhalter was, himself, personally responsible for the production of a large number of lithographs after his portraits of the rulers of Baden, a highly successful method of supplementing his income and nos. 95 and 96 are fine examples of his work as a lithographer. The lithograph of the full-length portrait of Leopold (see no. 3) was also published by Velten, but was the work of Sebastian Meier, Winterhalter's contemporary at the Munich Academy.
SF

# The Portraits of Franz Xaver Winterhalter: an annotated edition of Franz Wild's list of 1894

*The Nekrologe und Verzeichnisse der Gemälde von Franz & Hermann Winterhalter* was drawn up by Winterhalter's nephew, Franz Wild, and published in Zürich in 1894. It comprises three lists of paintings by Franz and Hermann Winterhalter. The longest of these includes works by Franz, another, works by Hermann, and one incorporates works by both brothers. The lists are prefaced by five obituaries of the brothers reprinted from contemporary newspapers and other publications, three of Franz, two of Hermann. A list of exhibits at the commemorative exhibition held immediately after Franz's death at the Kunsthalle, Baden, in 1873, is appended, along with a review of the exhibition from the *Karlsruher Zeitung* of the same year.

The main list of paintings by Franz Xaver Winterhalter, published by Wild, is stated to have been taken from Winterhalter's own list of his works, which no longer appears to exist. A manuscript list, now in the possession of his descendants, is similar to that which Wild must have used, but gives only the first third of the published list, and differs from it in several respects. This surviving manuscript consists of a list of sitters and dates, begun in an unknown hand, and completed and annotated by a hand which appears to be that of Franz Winterhalter, with comments as to the nature of the portrait, such as 'buste oval', 'jusqu'aux genoux', etc. This format is echoed in Wild's published list which uses different typography for the names of the sitters, and the comments, suggesting an attempt to make a distinction between hands. However, not only do the order of the sitters and the annotations in this manuscript differ to some extent from Wild's published list; the manuscript also includes a number of annotations concerning the portraits which do not appear in Wild's published version, so that it is unlikely that this is the manuscript which Wild used. Two further manuscripts, again in the possession of Winterhalter's descendants, list Winterhalter's commissions for the French royal family of Orléans, with prices, and appear to be of a different nature from Wild's manuscript.

The manuscript and Wild's published list are both arranged chronologically, grouping the pictures year by year. Whereas the manuscript arranges the pictures in groups under the heading of a single year, the published list (up to 1850) gives each picture a date. Since there are no pictures given dates between the years 1843 and 1849, and some securely identifiable dated pictures are wrongly assigned to 1843 (e.g., nos. 121, 125), this suggests Wild may have misinterpreted his source, and therefore casts some doubt on the reliability of his dating. However, the greater part of the published list gives no dates for any picture after 1850 (except one section which is assigned dates from 1863–8), and the repetition of names in this latter part raises problems which the absence of any manuscript equivalent makes the harder to resolve. The repetitions might indicate that Winterhalter was recording more than one commission by the same sitter, in different years. However, the exact repetition, in some cases, of his annotations regarding the format of the portrait (see nos. 421–2 and 425), would seem rather to indicate either that the manuscript from which Wild was working repeats itself, or that, conceivably, he was conflating two lists into one.

Since the published list is more complete, this is the one now reproduced in italic typeface along with the brief list of paintings by both Franz and Hermann apparently compiled independently by Wild himself, and including a number of subject pictures. We have numbered all entries and included cross-references to other portraits of the same sitter. Since it has not always been possible to establish beyond doubt to which member of a particular family the list refers, these cross-references include references to other portraits of members of the same family. Wherever possible, we have added our own annotations which appear in roman typeface. These give details of the present or last known location of a picture which appears to correspond to that listed by Wild. All locations are assumed unknown unless given. Dimensions are included and given in centimetres. Where a picture is known to be signed and dated this information is also given. It will be seen from Wild's list that the spelling of names is erratic, and modern spellings, where known, appear alongside in square brackets. The annotations 'en buste', 'jusqu'aux genoux', 'en pied' in Wild's list are not translated, but other annotations in French giving further information about the portraits are translated into English and given within square brackets. Other information given includes details of corresponding engravings, where known, and references to pictures exhibited at Paris Salons (and other contemporary exhibitions) which appear to correspond to those listed by Wild. References to all known versions or copies of the pictures are also given, as well as cross-references to exhibition and figure numbers in this catalogue. An index of sitters in this appendix will be found on pp. 238–9 of this catalogue.

The Wild list remains the single most important document concerning Winterhalter, and we felt it essential therefore to see it reprinted, with modern information alongside. We hope that it may serve not only as a record for works which have disappeared, but also as a checklist for future unfamiliar paintings as they emerge.

*Carol Blackett-Ord*
*Susan Foister*
*Richard Ormond*

*Gemälde von Franz Winterhalter (nach eigener Aufzeichnung)*
*(Portraits que j'ai faits et dont je me rapelle)*
[Paintings by Franz Winterhalter
(according to his own record)]
[(Portraits which I remember having done)]

1. *Mr Burkhardt de Bâle, jusqu'aux genoux*
*1835*
Size and present location unknown

2. *Les enfants de Mr le Baron de Schweitzer, Karlsr., tab.*
*1835*
Size and present location unknown

3. *Mlle Tascher de Lapagerie, Baronne de Montbrun, Paris*
*1835*
Size and present location unknown
Baronne Tascher with daughter, Comtesse Jean Pierre de Montalivet, 2 whole-length figures, priv. coll.
See also no. 137

4. *Mr Planat de la Faye, Paris*
*1835*
Size and present location unknown

5. *Le Comte Tascher de Lapagerie*
*1835*
Size and present location unknown
Baronne Tascher with daughter, Comtesse Jean Pierre de Montalivet, 2 whole-length figures, priv. coll.
See also no. 137

6. *Le Comte Jennisson, Mannheim, jusqu'aux genoux*
[Franz Oliver, Graf von Jenison Walworth]
*1835*
Threequarter-length, signed and dated 1837, 131 × 98, Bayerische Staatsgemäldesammlungen, Munich; see fig. 12

7. *Mme Lazaraff, St Petersbourg, Costume fantaisie*
*1836*
Size and present location unknown

8. *Son enfant Dolly, en pied*
*1836*
Size and present location unknown

9. *Mme Smirnoff, St Petersbourg, Costume grec*
*1836*
Size and present location unknown

10. *La Comtesse Foy, Paris, en pied*
*1836*
Size and present location unknown

11. *Le Prince Cimitile de Naples, buste*
[Prince de Cimitile]
*1836*
Size and present location unknown
Engraving by Wagstaff, half-length, 1838, British Museum, London

12. *Le Baron de Montbrun, Paris, jusqu'aux genoux*
*1836*
Size and present location unknown

13. *Mme Delong, Paris, jusqu'aux genoux*
*1836*
Size and present location unknown

14. *Les deux enfants, Paris, en pied*
*1836*
Size and present location unknown
Engraving by L. Noël, pub. Jeanin, inscribed in pencil: 'enfants de M. Delong, 1839', 2 whole-length figures in landscape, Royal Library, Windsor Castle

15. *La Comtesse de Plaisance, Paris, en pied*
[La Comtesse de Plaisance, née Berthier]
*1837*
Whole-length, signed and dated 1838, 226 × 161, priv. coll.
See also no. 24

16. *Mr Dubois d'Angers, demi nature, costume de chasseur*
*1837*
Size and present location unknown

17. *Le Prince de Wagram avec sa fille en pied*
[Alexandre Berthier, Prince de Wagram, and his daughter Malcy-Louise-Caroline]
*1837*
1838 Salon
2 whole-length figures, signed and dated 1837, 198 × 136, priv. coll.; exhibition no. 10; pendant to no. 18; for daughter, see also no. 243

18. *La Princesse de Wagram avec son fils, en pied*
[Zénaïde Clary, Princesse de Wagram]
*1837*
2 whole-length figures, signed and dated 1838, 198 × 136, priv. coll.
Pendant to no. 17

19. *La Princesse de Wagram, en oval*
*1837*
Size and present location unknown

20. *Mme Dubois d'Angers avec son fils*
*1838*
1838 Salon
Size and present location unknown

21. *Le Baron de Sekendorf*
*1838*
Size and present location unknown

22. *La Comtesse Mostrowska*
*1838*
Size and present location unknown

23. *Mme Boscary Villeplaine, Paris, buste oval*
*1838*
Size and present location unknown

24. *La Comtesse de Plaisance, Paris, en oval*
[La Comtesse de Plaisance, née Berthier]
1838
Presumably 1839 Salon
Half-length, oval, priv. coll.
See also no. 15

25. *La Comptesse Jaubert, Paris, buste oval*
*1838*
Size and present location unknown
Drawing of Comte Hippolyte Jaubert, 1842, Kunsthaus Lempertz, Cologne 20.5.85, lot no. 491

26. *Son fils, Paris, buste oval*
*1838*
Size and present location unknown

27. *Sa fille, Paris, buste oval*
*1838*
Size and present location unknown

28. *Mme Akermann, Paris, jusqu'aux genoux*
*1838*
Threequarter-length, signed and dated 1838, seated 50 × 40 approx., present location unknown

29. *La Princesse Clementine d'Orléans, Paris, buste oval*
[Marie-Clémentine-Caroline d'Orléans, later Princess of Saxe-Coburg-Gotha]
*1839*
1839 Salon
Size and present location unknown
Whole-length, 1845, Versailles, MV 5200

30. *Le Duc de Nemours, Chât. de Randau, jusqu'aux genoux*
[Louis-Charles-Philippe d'Orléans, Duc de Nemours]
*1839*
1839 Salon
Size and present location unknown
Whole-length, 1840, Duchesse de Nemours, Versailles, MV 5116
See also no. 84

31. *La Duchesse d'Orléans et le Comte de Paris, en pied*
[Hélène-Louise-Elizabeth de Mecklemburg-Schwerin, Duchesse de Orléans and Prince Louis-Philippe-Albert d'Orléans, Comte de Paris]
*1839*
1839 Salon
Whole-length, signed and dated 1839, 215 × 140, Versailles, MV 5201; exhibition no. 18
See also no. 58 for Comte de Paris

32. *La Duchesse d'Orléans, Paris, en pied*
*1839*
Size and present location unknown
See also no. 31

33. *Le Duc d'Aumale, Paris, jusqu'aux genoux*
[Henri d'Orléans, Duc d'Aumale]
*1839*
Copy, half-length, 92 × 74, Musée Condé, Chantilly
See also nos. 34, 92

34. *Le Duc d'Aumale, Paris, en pied*
*1839*
Size and present location unknown
Copy, whole-length, 215 × 140, Versailles, MV 5201
See also nos. 33, 92

35. *La Reine des Belges avec le Prince Royal*
[Louise-Marie d'Orléans, Queen of the Belgians with her eldest son, the Duke of Brabant]
*1839*
2 threequarter-length figures, signed and dated 1838, 123.2 × 104.1, coll. Her Majesty The Queen, Elizabeth II
Copy, priv. coll.
For Queen Louise-Marie, see also nos. 61, 62
For Duke of Brabant, see also no. 101

36. *Le Roi des Belges, habit bourgeois*
[Leopold I, King of the Belgians, day dress]
*1839*
Half-length, signed and dated 1839, 86 × 66, Royal Coll., Belgium
See also no. 60

37. *La Princesse Marie d'Orléans, de Souvenir*
*1839*
Size and present location unknown

38. *La Princesse Marie d'Orléans en pied*
*1839*
Size and present location unknown

39. *Le Duc Alexandre de Wurtemberg en pied*
[Philippe-Alexandre, Duke, later Prince, of Württemberg]
*1839*
Half-length, signed and dated 1839
Present location unknown
Lithograph by L. Noël, 1843, Württembergisches Museum, Germany

40. *Mlle Audenet en enfant de 6 ans, en pied*
*1839*
Size and present location unknown

41. *Le Roi Louis Philipp en bourgeois, buste carré*
[King Louis-Philippe]
*1839*
Size and present location unknown
See also no. 46

42. *La Jeune Mlle de St-Alégonde, avec un chien*
*1839*
Size and present location unknown

43. *La Comtesse de Montesquiou, Paris*
*1839*
Size and present location unknown
Threequarter-length, *c.*1850, priv. coll.

44. *Les deux Dlles de Rigny, Paris; en pied*
*1839*
Size and present location unknown

45. *idem, une d'elles seule*
*1839*
Size and present location unknown

46. *Le Roi des Français, grande nature en pied*
[King Louis-Philippe]
*1839*
1839 Salon
Whole-length, signed and dated 1839, 260 × 190, Versailles, MV 5219; exhibition no. 17
See also no. 41

47, *Le Duc d'Orléans, un buste bourgeois et un en pied*
48. [Ferdinand-Philippe-Henri, Duc d'Orléans]
*1840*
Size and present location unknown
See also no. 86

49, *Le Prince de Joinville, buste et un en pied*
50. [François-Ferdinand-Philippe d'Orléans, Prince de Joinville]
*1840*
Size and present location unknown
Whole-length, 1843, Versailles, MV 5105, lithograph by E. Lassalle, pub. Goupil & Vibert
See also no. 63

51. *Le jeune Duc de Wurtemberg (Philippe), Londres*
[Philippe-Alexandre, Duke, later Prince, of Württemberg]
*1840*
Two portraits, both signed and dated 1841:
1) Oval, 72 × 58, Versailles, MV 5203, lithograph by Grevedon
2) Oval, 71.5 × 58.5, coll. Her Majesty The Queen, Elizabeth II
See also nos. 386, 387

52. *Le Comte de Neverkerque, Paris, jusqu'aux genoux*
[Alfred-Emilien, Comte de Nieuwerkerke]
*1840*
Size and present location unknown
Threequarter-length, 1852, exhibition no. 49

53. *La Comtesse de Neverkerque, Paris, jusqu'aux genoux*
*1840*
Size and present location unknown

54. *La Duchesse de Vallambrose, Paris, jusqu'aux genoux*
[Duchesse de Vallombrosa]
*1840*
Threequarter-length, signed and dated 1840, 131 × 98, Sotheby's New York, 23.5.85, lot 4, priv. coll.

55. *Le Comte Duchâtel, Paris, buste carré*
*1841*
Size and present location unknown

56. *Mme de Liadières, Paris, buste oval*
*1841*
Size and present location unknown

57. *Mme la Vicomtesse de Bondy, Paris, jusqu'aux genoux*
*1841*
Threequarter-length, signed and dated 1841, priv. coll.
Portrait of Comte de Bondy, *c.*1846, same coll.

58. *Le Comte de Paris, en pied*
*1841*
1842 Salon
Whole-length, signed and dated 1842, priv. coll.
See also no. 31

59. *La Comtesse Duchâtel avec son garçon, Paris, en pied*
[Rosalie, Comtesse Duchâtel, with her son Charles-Jacques-Marie]
*1841*
1842 Salon
2 whole-length figures, signed and dated 1841, 246 × 156
Hôtel Drouot, 3.12.85, lot 31
See also no. 55 for portrait of Comte Duchâtel

60. *Le Roi des Belges, Bruxelles, grand en pied*
[Leopold I, King of the Belgians]
*1841*
Whole-length, signed and dated 1840, 278 × 181, Versailles, MV 6510
Threequarter-length version, 1841, coll. Her Majesty The Queen, Elizabeth II, exhibition no. 14
See also no. 36

61. *La Reine des Belges, un grand en pied*
[Louise-Marie d'Orléans, Queen of the Belgians]
*1841*
Size and present location unknown
Versions:
1) Whole-length, 1844, 215 × 140, Versailles, MV 5110
2) Whole-length, 217 × 128, Brussels, Palais Royal
See also nos. 35, 62

62. *La Reine des Belges, un jusqu'aux genoux*
*1841*
Size and present location unknown
See also nos. 35, 61

63. *Le Prince de Joinville, Paris, buste carré*
[François-Ferdinand-Philippe d'Orléans]
*1841*
Size and present location unknown
See also nos. 49, 50

64. *La Duchesse de Nemours, Paris, en pied*
[Victoire de Saxe-Coburg-Gotha, Duchesse de Nemours]
*1841*
Whole-length, signed and dated 1840, 214 × 140, Versailles, MV 5116
Versions:
1) Whole-length, priv. coll.
2) Half-length, coll. Her Majesty The Queen, Elizabeth II
See also nos. 66, 216

65. *La Reine Marie Christine, Paris, jusqu'aux genoux*
[Maria Cristina de Borbón, Dowager Queen of Spain]
*1841*
1841 Salon
Half-length, signed and dated 1841, 91 × 42, Versailles, MV 4840
Version, Palacio Reál, Madrid

66. *La Duchesse de Nemours, Paris, buste oval*
*1842*
Size and present location unknown
See also nos. 64, 216

67. *La Marquise de Lagrange, Paris, jusqu'aux genoux*
*1842*
Size and present location unknown

68. *La Reine des Français, Paris, grand en pied*
[Marie-Amélie de Bourbon, Queen of the French]
*1842*
1842 Salon
Whole-Length, signed and dated 1842, 215 × 140, Versailles, MV 5111; exhibition no. 19

69. *Mme Adélaïde, Paris en pied*
[Eugène-Adélaïde-Louise d'Orléans, Madame Adélaïde]
*1842*
Whole-length, signed and dated 1842, 215 × 140, Versailles, MV 5101

70. *Le Duc de Chartres, Paris, grand en pied*
[Robert d'Orléans, Duc de Chartres]
*1842*
Whole-length, signed and dated 1843, size and present location unknown
Engraving by L. Noël, 1844, Royal Library, Windsor Castle

71. *Le Maréchal Sébastiani, Paris, grand en pied*
[François Horace, Comte Sébastiani de la Porta]
*1842*
Whole-length, signed and dated 1841, 215 × 139, Versailles, MV 1177
Version, Palais Lantivy, Ajaccio
See fig. 23

72. *La Princesse Charlotte des Belges*
[Marie-Charlotte-Amélie, Duchesse de Saxe, later Empress of Mexico]
*1842*
Whole-length, signed and dated 1842, oval, 72.4 × 58.4, coll. Her Majesty The Queen, Elizabeth II; exhibition no. 15; version, 1843, Versailles, MV 5104
See also nos. 103, 455

73. *La Reine d'Angleterre, Londres, jusqu'aux genoux*
[Queen Victoria]
*1842*
Threequarter-length, signed and dated 1842, 133.4 × 97.8, coll. Her Majesty The Queen, Elizabeth II; exhibition no. 27
Version, Versailles, MV 4675
See also nos. 87, 88, 107, 121, 122, 210, 216, 290, 414

74. *Le Prince Albert, Londres, jusqu'aux genoux*
[Prince Albert of Saxe-Coburg-Gotha]
*1842*
Threequarter-length, signed and dated 1842, 132.7 × 97.2, coll. Her Majesty The Queen, Elizabeth II; exhibition no. 28
Version, Versailles, MV 4676
See also nos. 89, 108, 121, 123, 291, 310, 415

75. *La Princesse Royale, Londres, en pied*
[Victoria, Princess Royal]
*1842*
Whole-length, seated, signed and dated 1842, 79.1 × 61.6, coll. Her Majesty The Queen, Elizabeth II
Engraving by L. Noël, Royal Library, Windsor Castle
See also nos. 121, 150, 280, 321, 362

76. *Le Prince de Galles, Londres en pied*
[Edward, Prince of Wales]
*1843*
Whole-length, signed and dated 1843, 128.3 × 102.9, coll. Her Majesty The Queen, Elizabeth II
Engraving by L. Noël, 1844, Royal Library, Windsor Castle
See also nos. 90, 121, 122, 125, 163, 478

77. *La Duchesse de Saxe-Cobourg (Alexandrine), en pied*
[Alexandrine, Princess of Saxe-Coburg-Gotha]
*1843*
Threequarter-length, signed and dated 1842, 125.6 × 103.5, coll. Her Majesty The Queen, Elizabeth II
1834 portrait, with plaited hair, Neues Schloss, Baden
See also no. 179

78. *Le Duc de Beaufort, costume de la jarretière*
[Henry Somerset, 7th Duke of Beaufort in Garter Robes]
*1843*
Whole-length, 233 × 142, priv. coll.

79, *La Princesse de Wittgenstein, deux portraits, gd en pied*
80. [Princess Leonilla of Sayn-Wittgenstein-Sayn]
*1843*
Whole-length, signed and dated 1843, 142 × 212, J. Paul Getty Museum; exhibition no. 20
See also no. 147

81. *La jeune Comtesse de Langenstein jusquaux genoux*
[Louise, Countess of Langenstein]
*1843*
Half-length, signed and dated 1834, 66 × 51, priv. coll.

82. *Mme de Lesperut, Paris, jusqu'aux genoux*
*1843*
Size and present location unknown

83. *Mlle Hagermann, Paris, jusqu'aux genoux*
[Mathilde Hagerman, Comtesse Renouard de Bussière]
*1843*
Half-length, oval, priv. coll.

84. *Le Duc de Nemours, Paris, grand en pied*
[Louis-Charles-Philippe d'Orléans, Duc de Nemours]
*1843*
1844 Salon
Whole-length, signed and dated 1843, 215 × 140, Versailles, MV 5114; exhibition no. 21
See also no. 30

85. *Le Duc de Montpensier, Paris, grand en pied*
[Marie-Philippe-Louis d'Orléans, Duc de Montpensier]
*1843*
Whole-length, signed and dated 1844, 215 × 137, Versailles, MV 5112
For Duchesse de Montpensier, see also no. 131

86. *Le Duc d'Orléans, Paris, grand en pied*
*1843*
Size and present location unknown
Whole-length, version commissioned by King Louis-Philippe for Algiers, 1842, 218 × 140, Versailles, MV 5228
See fig. 21
See also nos. 47, 48

87. *La Reine d'Angleterre, costume de la jarretière*
[Queen Victoria in Garter robes]
*1843*
Whole-length, signed and dated 1843, 273.1 × 161.6, coll. Her Majesty The Queen, Elizabeth II
Pendant to no. 89
See also nos. 73, 88, 107, 121, 122, 210, 216, 290, 414

88. *La Reine d'Angleterre, buste oval*
[Queen Victoria]
*1843*
Head-and-shoulders, oval, signed and dated 1843, 65.4 × 53.3, coll. Her Majesty The Queen, Elizabeth II; exhibition no. 29
See also nos. 73, 87, 107, 121, 122, 210, 216, 290, 414

89. *Le Prince Albert, en pied costume de la jartière*
[Prince Albert in Garter Robes]
*1843*
Whole-length, signed, 274.3 × 162.6, coll. Her Majesty The Queen, Elizabeth II
Pendant to no. 87
See also nos. 74, 108, 121, 123, 291, 310, 415
See fig. 24

90. *Le Prince de Galles, en pied*
[Edward, Prince of Wales]
*1843*
Whole-length, size and present location unknown
See also nos. 76, 121, 122, 125, 163, 478

91. *La Duchesse de Kent, Château d'Eu, en pied*
[Victoria Mary Louisa Saxe-Saalfeld-Coburg, Duchess of Kent and Strathearn]
*1843*
Whole-length, signed, 238.8 × 148.3, coll. Her Majesty The Queen, Elizabeth II
Engraving by L. Noël, 1846
See also no. 154

92. *Le Duc d'Aumale, Paris, grand en pied*
*1843*
Size and present location unknown
Engraving by L. Noël, Royal Library, Windsor Castle
See also nos. 33, 34

93. *Mme Planat de la Faye, Paris, buste oval*
*1843*
Size and present location unknown

94. *Mr Planat, Paris, buste oval*
*1843*
Size and present location unknown

95. *Mlle de Seilière, Pesse de Bergues, buste oval*
*1843*
Size and present location unknown

96. *La Comtesse Samoloff, Paris, jusqu'aux genoux*
*1843*
Size and present location unknown
Watercolour of Countess Julie Pahlen, Countess Semoiloff, Staatliche Museen, Berlin, DDR

97. *La Princesse Michel Galitzin, Petersbg., jusqu'aux genoux*
*1843*
Size and present location unknown

98. *La Baronne Bartholdy-Walther, Paris, jusqu'aux genoux*
*1843*
Size and present location unknown
See also no. 184

99. *Mme Ernest André, Paris, jusqu'aux genoux*
*1843*
Size and present location unknown
Drawing of Mme Ernst André, exhibited Galerie Arnoldi-Livie, Munich, 1977

100. *Mme Baring, Paris, jusqu'aux genoux*
*1843*
Size and present location unknown

101. *Le Duc de Brabant, enfant du Roi des Belges, jusqu'aux genoux*
[Leopold, Duke of Brabant]
*1843*
Threequarter-length, signed, 142 × 101, Collections royales, Château de Laeken, Belgium; exhibition no. 16; copy, head-and-shoulders, Argenteuil; copy, coll. Her Majesty The Queen, Elizabeth II
Pendant to no. 102
See also no. 35

102. *Le Comte de Flandre, enfant du Roi des Belges, jusqu'aux genoux*
[Prince Philippe, Comte de Flandre]
*1843*
Threequarter-length, Collections royales, Château de Laeken, Belgium; copy, head-and-shoulders, coll. Her Majesty The Queen, Elizabeth II
Pendant to no. 101

103. *La Princesse Charlotte, enfant du Roi des Belges, jusqu'aux genoux*
*1843*
Size and present location unknown
Engraving by D.I. Desvachez of threequarter-length, undated, Witt Print Collection, Courtauld Institute of Art, London
See also nos. 72, 455

104. *Le Comte de Bobrinsky, St-Petersbourg, jusqu'aux genoux*
[Count Aleksander Alekseievich Bobrinski]
*1843*
Threequarter-length, signed and dated 1844, oval, 123 × 93, The Hermitage, Leningrad
See also no. 479

105. *Le Duc de Maillé, Paris, jusqu'aux genoux*
*1843*
Size and present location unknown

106. *La Duchesse de Maillé, Paris, jusqu'aux genoux*
*1843*
Size and present location unknown
See also nos. 132, 134, 135

107. *La Reine d'Angleterre, Isle of Whigt, buste carré*
*1843*
Size and present location unknown
Pendant to no. 108
See also nos. 73, 87, 88, 121, 122, 210, 216, 290, 414

108. *Le Prince Albert, Isle of Whigt, buste carré*
*1843*
Size and present location unknown
Pendant to no. 107
See also nos. 74, 89, 121, 123, 291, 310, 415

109. *La Princesse Alice, London, avec un chien, en pied*
[Princess Alice, whole-length, with a dog]
*1843*
Size and present location unknown
See also nos. 110, 121, 150, 292, 363, 416

110. *La Princesse Alice, costume fantaisie, moitié nature*
[Princess Alice in fancy-dress, half life-size]
*1843*
Size and present location unknown
See above for other portraits

111. *Mr Ernest André, Paris, jusqu'aux genoux*
*1843*
Size and present location unknown
Half-length, oval, *c.*1850, Musée Jacquemart-André, Paris

112. *Mme Louise André, Paris, jusqu'aux genoux*
*1843*
Size and present location unknown

113. *La Comtesse Arthur de l'Aigle, Paris, jusqu'aux genoux*
*1843*
Size and present location unknown

114. *Le Général Comte de Sparre, Paris, jusqu'aux genoux*
*1843*
Size and present location unknown

115. *idem, la Comtesse, Paris, jusqu'aux genoux*
*1843*
Size and present location unknown

116. *Mlle Fontenilliat, Duchesse de Pasquier, jusqu'aux genoux*
*1843*
Size and present location unknown

117. *La Baronne de Bussières, Paris, jusqu'aux genoux*
*1843*
Size and present location unknown

118. *Mlle de Bussières, Paris, en pied*
*1843*
Size and present location unknown
Half-length, 1851, of Mélanie de Bussière, later Comtesse de Pourtalès, see exhibition no. 57
For portraits of the Comtesse de Pourtalès, see also nos. 188, 189, 332, 413

119. *Mme la Comtesse d'Humières, Paris, jusqu'aux genoux*
*1843*
Size and present location unknown

120. *Mme de la Faulette, Paris, jusqu'aux genoux*
*1843*
Size and present location unknown

121. *La Famille Royale d'Angleterre, Isle of Whigt, gd tableau*
[Queen Victoria and Prince Albert, with the Prince of Wales, Princess Royal, Princess Alice, Prince Alfred and Princess Helena]
*1843*
7 whole-length figures, signed and dated 1846, 249.5 × 316, coll. Her Majesty The Queen, Elizabeth II
Lithograph by L. Noël, 1848, pub. Lemercier, Royal Library, Windsor Castle
Engraving by S. Cousins, pub. F. G. Moon
See also nos. 73, 87, 88, 107, 122, 210, 216, 290, 414 for Queen Victoria
See also nos. 74, 89, 108, 123, 291, 310, 415 for Prince Albert
See also nos. 76, 90, 122, 125, 163, 478 for Prince of Wales
See also nos. 75, 150, 280, 321, 362 for Princess Royal
See also nos. 109, 110, 150, 292, 363, 416 for Princess Alice
See also nos. 151, 152, 163, 347 for Prince Alfred
See also nos. 150–2, 342 for Princess Helena
See fig. 26

122. *La Reine Victoria avec le Prince of Wales, en pied*
*1843*
2 whole-length figures, signed and dated 1846, 240 × 152, coll. Her Majesty Queen Elizabeth, The Queen Mother
Pendant to no. 123
See also nos. 73, 87, 88, 107, 121, 210, 216, 290, 414 for Queen Victoria
See also nos. 76, 90, 121, 125, 163, 478 for Prince of Wales

123. *Le Prince Albert, pour Sir R. Peel*
*1843*
Whole-length, signed and dated 1846, 237.5 × 147.5, Lady Lever Art Gallery, Port Sunlight; pendant to no. 122; exhibition no. 32
See also nos. 74, 89, 108, 121, 291, 310, 415

124. *La Princesse de Prusse, jusqu'aux genoux*
[Princess Augusta von Preussen]
*1843*
Threequarter-length, signed and dated 1846, 44.5 × 34.5, coll. Her Majesty The Queen, Elizabeth II
See also nos. 180, 294, 321, 362, 418

125. *Le Prince de Galles, costume de Marin, en pied*
[Albert Edward, Prince of Wales wearing a sailor suit]
*1843*
Whole-length, signed and dated 1846, 127.3 × 88.3, coll. Her Majesty The Queen, Elizabeth II; exhibition no. 31
See also nos. 76, 90, 121, 122, 163, 478

126. *La Princesse Augusta de Cambridge, buste oval*
[Princess Augusta of Cambridge, later Grand Duchess of Mecklenburg-Strelitz]
*1843*
Size and present location unknown
See also nos. 127, 157

127. *Grande Duchesse de Meklenbourg*
[Augusta Caroline, Grand Duchess of Mecklenburg-Strelitz]
Size and present location unknown
Lithograph by T.H. Maguire, 1846, Royal Library, Windsor Castle
See also no. 128 for portrait of sister

128. *La Princesse Marie de Cambridge, London, centre oval*
[Princess Mary Adelaide of Cambridge, later Duchess of Teck]
Head-and-shoulders, oval, signed and dated 1846, 62.5 × 51.4, coll. Her Majesty The Queen, Elizabeth II
Engraving by R.J. Lane, pub. Mitchell, printed by Hanhart, 1851, British Museum, London

129. *Le Baron de Stockmar, London, buste*
[Baron Stockmar]
Half-length, signed and dated 1847, 61.3 × 51.1, coll. Her Majesty The Queen, Elizabeth II

130. *Le Comte Alexandre de Mensdorff, London, buste*
[Count Alexander Mensdorff]
Half-length, signed and dated 1847, 51 × 40.5, coll. Her Majesty The Queen, Elizabeth II

131. *La Duchesse de Montpensier, Paris, en pied*
[Dona Marie-Louise-Ferdinande, Duchesse de Montpensier]
Whole-length, *c.*1847, 215 × 136, Versailles, MV 5113
Lithograph by L. Noël
See fig. 20
See also nos. 144, 145

132. *La Duchesse de Maillé, Paris, jusqu'aux genoux*
Size and present location unknown
See also nos. 106, 134, 135

133. *Le Duc Léopold de Saxe-Cobourg*
Size and present location unknown
See also no. 179 for family portrait

134. *La Duchesse de Maillé, Paris, en costume espagnole*
Size and present location unknown
See also nos. 106, 132, 135

135. *La Duchesse de Maillé, Paris, en ovale*
Size and present location unknown
See also nos. 106, 132, 135

136. *La Comtesse de Mirepoix, Paris, jusqu'aux genoux*
Size and present location unknown

137. *La Comtesse de Montalivet, La Baronne de Tascher, même tableau, grand en pied*
[Baronne Tascher and Comtesse Jean Pierre de Montalivet]
2 whole-length figures, priv. coll.
See also no. 3

138. *Le Comte de Montalivet, La Comtesse de Montalivet, même tableau, grand en pied*
[Comte Camille de Montalivet and Comtesse Camille de Montalivet]
Whole-length and a bust-length, priv. coll.
See also no. 3

139. *La Baronne de Meyendorff, London, costume arabe en pied*
Size and present location unknown

140. *La Comtesse Pozzo di Borgo, Paris, en pied*
[Valentine des Balbes de Berton de Crillon, Comtesse Pozzo di Borgo]
*1849*
Whole-length, priv. coll.
See also nos. 412, 428

141. *La Princesse de Chimay (Alphons), Bruxelles, jusqu'aux genoux*
*1849*
Size and present location unknown
See also no. 214

142. *La Princesse de Chimay (Joseph), jusqu'aux genoux*
[Emilie de Pellapra, Princesse de Chimay, later Comtesse de Brigode]
*1849*
Threequarter-length, signed and dated 1849, 109 × 92, priv. coll.
For the pendant of Prince Joseph de Chimay, 1854, see no. 191
See also no. 213

143. *La grande Duchesse Constantin, London, jusqu'aux genoux*
[presumably Grand Duchess Constantine Nicolaevitch]
*1849*
Size and present location unknown
See also nos. 287, 287A, 410

144. *La Duchesse de Montpensier, Paris, costume espagnol, jusqu'aux genoux*
*1849*
Size and present location unknown
See no. 131 for *c.*1847 portrait
1849 drawing of unknown woman in Spanish costume, possibly the Duchesse de Montpensier, Staatliche Kunsthalle, Karlsruhe

145. *La même, Paris, en pied*
*1849*
Size and present location unknown
See also nos. 131, 144

146. *Le Comte Pozzo di Borgo, jusqu'aux genoux*
[Charles Jérôme, Comte Pozzo di Borgo]
*1849*
Threequarter-length, signed and dated 1849, 157 × 119, priv. coll.; exhibition no. 25
See also no. 428

147. *La Princesse de Wittgenstein, jusqu'aux genoux*
[Princess Leonilla of Sayn-Wittgenstein-Sayn]
*1849*
Size and present location unknown
See also nos. 79, 80

148. *Le Prince de Wittgenstein, jusqu'aux genoux*
[Ludwig Fürst zu Sayn-Wittgenstein-Sayn]
*1849*
Threequarter-length, signed and dated 1850, priv. coll.
Engraving by L. Noël, 1850

149. *La Comtesse Vanderstbraaten Ponthoz, jusqu'aux genoux*
*1849*
Size and present location unknown
Seealso nos. 193, 336

150. *Les quatres Princesses d'Angleterre, Tableau en pied*
[Princess Royal, Princess Alice, Princess Helena and Princess Louise]
4 whole-length figures, signed and dated 1849, oval, 56.5 × 69.2, coll. Her Majesty The Queen, Elizabeth II
Engraving by J. Richardson Jackson, pub. Colnaghi, 1851
See also nos. 343, 344 for Princess Louise
See also nos. 75, 121, 280, 321, 362 for Princess Royal
See also nos. 109, 110, 121, 292, 363, 416 for Princess Alice
See also nos. 121, 151, 152, 342 for Princess Helena

151. *Le Prince Alfred et la Princesse Hélene, London, gd tabl.*
[Prince Alfred and Princess Helena]
*1849*
2 whole-length figures, signed and dated 1849, 127.6 × 87.6, coll. Her Majesty The Queen, Elizabeth II; exhibition no. 33
See also nos. 121, 152, 163, 347 for Prince Alfred
See also nos. 121, 150, 152, 342 for Princess Helena

152. *Le Prince Alfred et la Princesse Hélene, London, buste*
*1849*
Size and present location unknown
Engraving by L. Noël

153. *Le Prince de Cobourg (fils), London, buste*
*1849*
Size and present location unknown

154. *La Duchesse de Kent, jusqu'aux genoux*
[Victoria Mary Louisa Saxe-Saalfeld-Coburg, Duchess of Kent and Strathearn]
1849
Threequarter-length, signed and dated 1849, 141.6 × 97.8, coll. Her Majesty The Queen, Elizabeth II
See also no. 91

155. *Le jeune Comte de Beauford de Bruxelles*
Size and present location unknown
See also no. 197

156. *La Duchesse de Cambridge, jusqu'aux genoux*
[presumably Princess Augusta of Hesse, Duchess of Cambridge]
*1849*
Size and present location unknown
See also no. 126 for Princess Augusta of Cambridge, no. 128 for Princess Mary of Cambridge

157. *La Duchesse de Meklenbourg, buste*
[Augusta Caroline, Grand Duchess of Mecklenburg-Strelitz]
*1849*
Size and present location unknown
See also nos. 126, 127

158. *Le fils de la Duchesse de Meklenbourg, buste*
*1849*
Size and present location unknown
See also no. 237

159. *La duchesse de Sutherland, London, gr. tabl. en pied*
[Harriet Howard, Duchess of Sutherland]
*1849*
Whole-length, 243.8 × 142.2, priv. coll.; exhibition no. 34

160. *Lady Canning, London, buste*
[Charlotte Stuart, Lady Canning, afterwards Countess Canning]
*1849*
Head-and-shoulders, signed and dated 1849, oval, 61.3 × 48.9, priv. coll.; exhibition no. 35

161. *Lady Joutyn, London, buste*
[presumably Lady Frances Jocelyn, Countess of Gainsborough]
*1849*
Size and present location unknown
Whole-length sketch for *Reception of Louis-Philippe*, 1844, priv. coll.
See also no. 171

162. *Lady Douro, Duchesse de Wellington, London, buste*
*1849*
Size and present location unknown

163. *Le Prince de Galles et son frère Alfred, London, en pied*
[Edward Prince of Wales and Prince Alfred]
*1849*
2 whole-length figures, signed and dated 1849, 63.5 × 45.4, coll. Her Majesty The Queen, Elizabeth II
See also nos. 76, 90, 121, 122, 125, 478 for Prince of Wales
See also nos. 151, 152, 121, 347 for portraits of Prince Alfred

164. *La Reine Adélaïde, jusqu'aux genoux*
[Queen Adelaide, queen of William IV]
*1849*
Half-length, signed and dated 1849, 91.5 × 71, coll. Her Majesty The Queen, Elizabeth II
Lithograph by R.J. Lane, 1849

165. *Le Duc de Saxe-Meiningen, buste*
*1849*
Size and present location unknown

166. *La Duchesse de Saxe-Meiningen, buste*
*1849*
Size and present location unknown

167. *Le Prince de Saxe-Meiningen, buste*
*1849*
Size and present location unknown

168. *La Princesse de Saxe-Meiningen, buste*
*1849*
Size and present location unknown

169. *Lady Hove, buste*
*1849*
Size and present location unknown

170. *Le Prince Edouard de Saxe-Weimar, buste*
[Prince Edward of Saxe-Weimar]
*1849*
Size and present location unknown
Engraving by T. Fairland, Royal Library, Windsor Castle)

171. *Lady Gainsborough, buste*
[Lady Frances Jocelyn, Countess of Gainsborough]
*1850*
Half-length, signed and dated 1851, 54 × 43.4, coll. Her Majesty The Queen, Elizabeth II
See also no. 161

172. *Le Prince Hohenlohe Langenbourg, buste*
*1850*
Size and present location unknown
See also no. 233

173. *La Princesse Hohenlohe Langenbourg, buste*
*1850*
Size and present location unknown

174. *Les deux Princesses Langenbourg, leurs enfants, buste*
*1850*
Size and present location unknown
See also nos. 234, 235

175. *La Duchesse de Gloucester, buste*
*1850*
Size and present location unknown

176. *Lady Constance, fille de la Duchesse Sutherland, buste*
[Lady Constance Leveson-Gower, later Duchess of Westminster]
*1850*
Half-length, signed and dated 1850, 54 × 43.4, coll. Her Majesty The Queen, Elizabeth II

177. *Miss Davson*
Size and present location unknown

178. *Le Prince de Saxe-Cobourg (Cadet)*
Size and present location unknown

179. *La Duchesse de Saxe-Cobourg avec 3 enfants*
*1848*
Size and present location unknown
See also no. 77

180. *La Princesse de Prusse, jusqu'aux genoux*
*1850*
Size and present location unknown
See also nos. 124, 294, 321, 362, 418

181. *La Reine de Hollande, aquarelle jusqu'aux genoux*
[Sophia Frederika Mathilda of Württemburg, Queen of the Netherlands]
*1850*
Threequarter-length, signed and dated 1860, seated, size and present location unknown
See also no. 437

182. *La Duchesse de Mouchy*
[presumably Anna Murat, Duchess of Mouchy]
Threequarter-length, signed and dated 1862, priv. coll.
Version, priv. coll.
See fig. 38; see also no. 196

183. *Mme Delesert-François*
Size and present location unknown

184. *Mme Bartholdy, sa fille*
*1850*
Size and present location unknown
See also no. 98 for portrait of Baronne Bartholdy-Walther

185. *Deux enfants de Monsieur Hottinger*
Size and present location unknown

186. *Mme Charles Bethmann*
Size and present location unknown

187. *Mme Metzler*
Size and present location unknown

188, *La Comtesse Pourtalès, 2 portraits, 1 grand*
189. [presumably Mélanie de Bussière, Comtesse Edmond de Pourtalès]
Half-length, signed and dated 1857, oval, 97 × 72, priv. coll.; exhibition no. 57
See also nos. 118, 332, 413

190. *Mme Alphonse Mollet*
Size and present location unknown

191. *Le Prince de Chimay, Joseph*
Threequarter-length, signed and dated 1852, 109 × 92, priv. coll.
See also no. 142 for pendant of Princesse Joseph de Chimay

192. *Le Comte Vanderstraaden Ponthoz*
Size and present location unknown

193. *La Comtesse Vanderstraaden Ponthoz*
Size and present location unknown
See also nos. 149, 336

194. *Mme Malou*
Size and present location unknown

195. *Mlle Strabter de Kentucki*
Size and present location unknown

196. *La Duchesse Noailles (jeune)*
[presumably Cécile, Duchesse de Noailles, later Duchesse de Mouchy]
Head-and-shoulders, oval, 50 × 40, priv. coll.
See also no. 182

197. *Le Petit Duc de Beaufort de Bruxelles*
Size and present location unknown
See also no. 155

198. *Mlle Leclère*
Size and present location unknown

199. *Mlle d'Hulst (Cambray)*
Size and present location unknown

200. *Le petit enfant de la Duchesse de Sutherland*
Size and present location unknown
See also no. 159 for whole-length of Duchess of Sutherland, 1849

201. *Les quatres enfants de la duchesse de Nemours*
Size and present location unknown

202. *Les enfants de la Reine. 1 Mai, (en rond)*
Size and present location unknown

203. *Le Duc de Wellington. (1 Mai)*
[The First of May: Queen Victoria and Prince Albert presenting Prince Arthur to the Duke of Wellington]
4 figures, signed and dated 1851, 106.7 × 129.5, coll. Her Majesty The Queen, Elizabeth II
Engraving, S. Cousins, Royal Library, Windsor Castle
See also nos. 73, 87, 88, 107, 121, 122, 210, 216, 290, 414 for Queen Victoria
See also nos. 74, 89, 108, 121, 123, 291, 310, 415 for Prince Albert
See also nos. 205, 206 for Prince Arthur

204. *Prince et Princesse de Prusse (les enfants)*
Size and present location unknown
Portrait of Prince Frederick William of Prussia, 1851, coll. Her Majesty The Queen, Elizabeth II

205, *Deux Portraits de Prince Arthur*
206. [Arthur, 1st Duke of Connaught and Strathearn]
1) Whole-length with ball, signed and dated 1851, 73.7 × 90.2
2) Whole-length with doll, 1852, oval, 73 × 61
Both coll. Her Majesty The Queen, Elizabeth II
See also no. 203

207. *Mlle de Panisse*
Size and present location unknown

208, *Les enfants de Casimir Perier. 2.*
209. [Jean Casimir-Périer, and his brother]
Pair, ovals, head and shoulders, priv. coll.
For a portrait of Madame Auguste Casimir-Périer in same coll., see no. 225

210. *La Reine Victoria*
Size and present location unknown
See also nos. 73, 87, 88, 107, 121, 122, 216, 290, 414

211. *La Princess Gouruma (le Maharyah grand)*
[Victoria Gouramma of Koorg]
*1852*
Whole-length, signed and dated 1852, 149.5 × 89.5, coll. Her Majesty The Queen, Elizabeth II
Engraving by R. Graves

212. *Mr. Lablache* [Luigi Lablache]
Head-and-shoulders, signed and dated 1852, oval, 62.2 × 50.5, coll. Her Majesty The Queen, Elizabeth II

213. *La Princesse Joseph de Chimay*
[Emilie de Pellapra, Princesse de Chimay, later Comtesse de Brigode]
Size and present location unknown
See also no. 142

214. *La Princesse Alphonse de Chimay*
Size and present location unknown
See also no. 141

215. *Le Duc de Cambridge*
[presumably George William Frederick Charles, 2nd Duke of Cambridge]
Head-and-shoulders, oval, size and present location unknown
See no. 156 for Duchess of Cambridge

216. *La Reine avec la Duchesse de Nemours, tableau*
[Queen Victoria with Princess Victoire, Duchesse de Nemours]
2 half-lengths, seated, signed and dated 1852, coll. Her Majesty The Queen, Elizabeth II; exhibition no. 37
See also nos. 73, 87, 88, 107, 121, 122, 210, 290, 414 for Queen Victoria
See also nos. 64, 66 for Duchesse de Nemours

217 *Mr Baliol Brett*
Size and present location unknown
A portrait of Mrs Baliol Brett exh. RA 1853 (96)

218. *La Marquise Alexandre de las Marismas*
[Carmen Victoire Moreno, Marquise Alexandre de las Marismas]
Size and present location unknown
See also no. 388

219. *Le Comte Olympe Aquado de las Marismas*
Size and present location unknown

220. *Le Vicomte Onesippe Aquado*
Size and present location unknown

221. *La Comtesse Krasinska, avec ses enfants, tableau*
[Countess Elzbieta Krasinska with her children Wladislaw, Elzbieta and Zygmunt]
4 figures, signed and dated 1853, 131 × 163.5, National Museum, Warsaw; exhibition no. 67
See also nos. 275–7

222. *La Reine Isabella d'Espagne*
[Isabella II, Queen of Spain, with Infanta Maria Isabella Francisca]
2 whole-lengths, signed, 275 × 176, Palacio Réal, Madrid
Threequarter-length version, dated 1852, Freiburg-im-Breisgau

223. *La Princesse des Asturies, sa fille*
[Maria Isabella Francisca, Infanta of Spain]
Head-and-shoulders, 29 × 36, priv. coll.
Sketch for no. 222

224. *Mlle de Lagrenée*
Size and present location unknown

225. *Mme Casimir-Perier*
[Madame Auguste Casimir-Périer]
Threequarter-length, priv. coll.
See also nos. 208, 209 for portraits of sons

226. *La Duchesse de Hamilton*
[Princess Mary of Baden, Duchess of Hamilton]
Whole-length, size and present location unknown
See fig. 40

227. *La Princesse Raziwill*
[Princess Sofya Aleksandrovna Radzivill]
Presumably threequarter-length, oval, signed and dated 1864, 126 × 94, The Hermitage, Leningrad

228, *La Comtesse Sophie Schouvaloff. 2.*
229. Size and present location unknown
See also nos. 260–61

230. *La Princesse Marie Woronzoff*
Size and present location unknown
See also nos. 231, 249, 250, 338

231. *idem. un petit*
Half-length, oval, *c.*1858, ex. coll. Irving, T. Bush, New York

232. *L'Impératrice Eugénie*
[Empress Eugénie]
1855 Exposition Universelle
Half-length, oval, signed and dated 1854, 125 × 95, priv. coll., USA; exhibition no. 50
See also nos. 317, 318, 320, 329, 339, 388, 389, 442

233. *Le Prince Hohenlohe Langenbourg*
Size and present location unknown
See also no. 172

234, *Ses filles Adélaïde et Féodora*
235. [Adelaide, Princess of Hohenlohe-Langenburg and Feodora, Princess of Hohenlohe-Langenburg]
1) Half-length, oval, 1853, 35.6 × 30.5
2) Half-length, oval, signed and dated 1855, 35.6 × 30.8
Both coll. Her Majesty The Queen, Elizabeth II
See also no. 174

236. *Le Grand duc de Meklenbourg*
Size and present location unknown
For the Grand Duchess Augusta Caroline see nos. 126, 127, 157

237. *Son fils*
Size and present location unknown
See also no. 158

238. *L'Impératrice de Russie (veuve)*
Size and present location unknown

239. *La Comtesse Cathérine Potocka*
[Katarzyna Branicka, Countess Potocka]
Threequarter-length, oval, signed and dated 1854, 116 × 85.5, National Museum, Warsaw; exhibition no. 68
See also nos. 240, 241

240. *La Comtesse Cathérine Potocka*
Size and present location unknown
Half-length, oval, signed and dated 1854, 75 × 56, National Museum, Warsaw
See also nos. 239, 241

241. *La Comtesse Cathérine Potocka*
Half-length, size and present location unknown
See also nos. 239, 240

242. *Mlle de la Redorte (Madame Commudet)*
Half-length, size and present location unknown

243. *La Princesse Murat née Wagram*
[Malcy-Louise-Caroline-Frédérique Berthier de Wagram, Princesse Murat]
Half-length, oval, signed and dated 1854, 73 × 60, priv. coll.; exhibition no. 51
See also no. 17

244. *Mme Benoit d'Azy*
Size and present location unknown

245. *La Princesse de Hesse, fille de la Pcsse Charles de Prusse*
[Princess Anna von Preussen, Landgräfin von Hessen]
Threequarter-length, oval, signed and dated 1858, 147 × 115.5, Schloss Fasanerie, Fulda, Germany
See fig. 42

246. *La Princesse Jousouloff*
[presumably Princess Tatyana Aleksandrovna Youssoupova]
Threequarter-length, signed and dated 1858, 147 × 104, The Hermitage, Leningrad
See fig. 41

247. *La Princesse Grégoire Gagarine*
[presumably 1859 Salon]
Size and present location unknown
For other Gagarine portraits, see also nos. 248, 348, 399

248. *Ses enfants*
Size and present location unknown

249, *La Princesse Marie Woronzoff, grand 2 fois*
250. [one presumably 1859 Salon]
Formerly coll. Sir Robert Abdy (destroyed by fire)
See fig. 47
See also nos. 230, 231, 338

251. *La Comtesse Alfred Potocka et ses deux enfants*
[Marie Sanguskowa, Countess Alfred Potocka]
Size and present location unknown
Separate roundels of Countess Potocka and her four children, priv. coll.

252. *La Princesse Lubecka*
[Princess Lubika]
Half-length, oval, signed and dated 1853, 102 × 91, formerly coll. Galerie P. Cailleux, Paris

253. *Mme Tschertkoff*
Size and present location unknown

254, *Mme Jurgewicz, 2 portraits, 1 oval, 1 gd en pied.*
255. [Wieńczyslawa Barczewska, Madame de Jurjewicz]
Size and present location unknown
See also nos. 255, 296

256. *Warinka fille de Sophie Schouvaloff*
Size and present location unknown
See no. 269 for portrait of another Schouvaloff daughter

257, *Comtesse Mussine Pouchkim, 2, un petit oval*
258. [Countess Varvara Alekseyevna Musina-Pushkina]
Threequarter-length, oval, 147 × 112, The Hermitage, Leningrad; exhibition no. 74
See also no. 300

259. *Mme Narischkine de Moskou*
[Mme Sofya Petrovna Naryschkina]
Threequarter-length, oval, signed and dated 1858, 150 × 114, The Hermitage, Leningrad; exhibition no. 75

260, *La Comtesse Schouvaloff (2 Paul Biloselska)*
261. [Countess Olga Esperovna Chouvalova]
Threequarter-length, signed and dated 1858, 130 × 97, The Hermitage, Leningrad
See also no. 488

262. *La Comtesse Schouvaloff (Gagarine)*
Size and present location unknown
See also no. 489

263, *Mme Korsakoff, 3*
264, [Barbe Dmitrievna Mergassov, Mme Rimsky-
265. Korsakov]
Threequarter-length, oval, signed and dated 1858, 146 × 114, Savitzkoy Gallery, Penza, USSR; exhibition no. 60; threequarter-length, signed and dated 1864, 147 × 90, Musée d'Orsay, Paris; exhibition no. 65; version, Stair Sainty Fine Art Inc., New York, 1982; two further versions in priv. colls.
See also nos. 435, 436

266. *Le Baron Sina*
Half-length, signed and dated 1867, 86 × 66, location unknown
Sotheby's 11.4.1973, lot 101

267. *Le Comte Pothorski*
[presumably Count Potocki]
Size and present location unknown

268. *Le Comte André Schouvaloff*
Size and present location unknown

269. *Sa fille Lilly*
Size and present location unknown
See also no. 256 for portrait of another Schouvaloff daughter

270. *La Comtesse Alex. Adlerberg*
Size and present location unknown
See also no. 490

271. *L'Empereur des Français*
[Napoléon III]
1855 Salon
Whole-length, size and present location unknown; see fig. 33
See also no. 476

272. *Mr André fils et père*
Size and present location unknown
For André family see nos. 99, 111, 112
See also no. 475 for Edouard André

273, *Mme Romanelli, Ansthruther Winthaw, 2 fois*
274. Size and present location unknown
See also no. 295 for portraits of Mme Anstruther Windham

275, *La Comtesse Krasinska, 3 portraits*
276, [Elzbieta Branicka, Countess Krasinska]
277. 1) Head-and-shoulders, oval, 60.5 × 49.5, National Museum, Warsaw
2) Threequarter-length, ex-Czartoryska coll., Poland
See also no. 221 for 1853 group portrait.

278. *La Princess Sagausko (fille Hèlene)*
[Princess Helena Sanguszkowa]
Threequarter-length, signed and dated 1857, ex-coll. Tarnow, Poland
Size and present location unknown
See also no. 483

279. *La Princesse Odescalcki*
[presumably Sofia Branicka, Princess Odescalchi]
Head-and-shoulders, oval, 61 × 50, National Museum, Warsaw
See also no. 477

280. *La Princesse Royal d'Angleterre (fiancée)*
[Victoria Adelaide Mary Louisa, the Princess Royal]
Threequarter-length, oval, signed and dated 1857, 118.1 × 87.6, coll. Her Majesty The Queen, Elizabeth II
See also nos. 75, 150, 121, 321, 362

281. *La Comtesse Bebrinski*
[presumably Sofya Andreevna, Countess Bobrinskaia]
Threequarter-length, signed and dated 1857, 129 × 97, The Hermitage, Leningrad
See also no. 104 for portrait of Count A. A. Bobrinsky.
See also no. 479

282. *Le Comte Bebrinski père*
Size and present location unknown

283. *La Princesse Bethsy Basatinsky*
[presumably Princess Bariatinsky]
Half-length, oval, signed and dated 1858, 98 × 80, priv. coll., Canada
See also no. 405

284. *La petite Troubezkoy, 6 ans*
Possibly head-and-shoulders, oval, signed and dated 1859, 40.5 × 32.5, The Hermitage, Leningrad

285. *La Comtesse Lamsdorff*
Size and present location unknown
See no. 407

286. *La Comtesse Lottma, mère*
Size and present location unknown

287, *Le Grand-duc et la Grand-duchesse Constantin*
287A. [Grand Duke Constantine Nicolaevitch and Alexandra of Saxe-Altenburg, Grand Duchess Constantine Nicolaevitch]
Threequarter-length of Grand Duchess, late 1850s, priv. coll.
For Grand Duchess see also nos, 143, 410

288. *Comtesse Tchernitschoff*
Size and present location unknown
See also no. 411

289. *La Comtesse Edouard Pourtalès*
Size and present location unknown
See also nos. 188, 189, 332 & 413 for other Pourtalès family portraits

290. *La Reine d'Angleterre, grand en pied*
Whole-length in Coronation Robes, signed and dated 1859, 241.9 × 157.5, coll. Her Majesty The Queen, Elizabeth II; pendant to no. 291
See also nos. 73, 87, 88, 107, 121, 122, 210, 216, 414

291. *Le Prince Albert, grand en pied*
Whole-length in uniform, signed and dated 1859, 241.9 × 158.1, coll. Her Majesty The Queen, Elizabeth II; pendant to no. 290
Replica, NPG 237
See also nos. 74, 89, 108, 121, 123, 310, 415

292. *La Princesse Alice, grand en pied*
Whole-length, signed and dated 1859, 50.8 × 40.6, coll. Her Majesty The Queen, Elizabeth II
See also nos. 109, 110, 121, 150, 363, 416

293. *La Duchesse de Manchester*
[Louisa Frederica Augusta, Duchess of Manchester]
Half-length, profile, signed and dated 1859, 62.4 × 43.2, coll. Her Majesty The Queen, Elizabeth II
See also no. 417

294. *Le Prince et La Princess de Prusse*
Size and present location unknown
For Prince & Princess of Prussia, see also nos. 124, 180, 294, 321, 361, 362, 418

295. *Mme Anstruther Windham. 2*
Size and present location unknown
See also nos. 273–4 for Ansthruther Winthaw portraits

296. *Mme Jurgewicz, 2 fois en pied*
[Wieńczeslawa Barczewska, Madame de Jurjewicz]
Threequarter-length, oval, signed and dated 1860, 160 × 125, priv. coll.; exhibition no. 62
See also nos. 254, 255

297. *La Princesse Obolenski*
[presumably Marie Lvova, Princess Obolenski]
Threequarter-length, oval, 131 × 98, priv. coll., Paris
Exhibited Knoedler, London, 1936, no. 25 B
See also no. 419

298, *La Princesse Metternich, 2 fois, une fois profil*
299. [Pauline Sandor, Princess Metternich]
Half-length, oval, signed and dated 1860, 88 × 115, priv. coll.; exhibition no. 63
See also nos. 421, 422

300. *La Comtesse Pouckim, 1 petit oval, 1 grand*
[Countess Varvara Alekseyevna Musina-Pushkina]
Size and present location unknown
See also nos. 257, 258

301. *Mme Hepting*
Size and present location unknown

302. *La Prince d'Oldenbourg (Pierre)*
Size and present location unknown

303. *La Princesse Marie, fille de la Grande-duchesse Leuchtenbourg*
Size and present location unknown
Lithograph by Selb after a drawing of the Duchess of Leuchtenbourg *c.*1826

303, *Le Comte et la Comtesse Paul Schouvaloff*
304. Half-length of count (304), oval, signed and dated 1860, Demidoff Sale, Nice, 29–30 June 1934
Size and present location unknown
For other Schouvaloff portraits see also nos. 228, 229, 256, 260–1, 262, 268, 325, 326

305. *La Comtesse Maurice Potocka*
Size and present location unknown

306. *La Baronne de Fraenkel*
Size and present location unknown

307. *La Comtesse Branicka (Hedwig)*
[Jadwiga Branicka, Countess Potocka]
Half-length, oval, 79 × 63, National Museum, Warsaw, Wilanòw; exhibition no. 77

308. *idem. en profil*
Copy, half-length, National Museum, Warsaw, Wilanòw
See also no. 307

309. *La Princesse Wassilchikoff, la fille*
Size and present location unknown

310. *Le Prince Albert de Souvenir*
Half-length, signed and dated 28 December 1861, 76 × 63.5, Bonham's, 23.11.83, lot 172
See also nos. 74, 89, 108, 121, 123, 291, 415

311. *Mlle Rogniat. 2*
Size and present location unknown

312. *Le Prince Pierre Troubetzkoi*
Size and present location unknown

313. *Mme Tolstoi*
Size and present location unknown

314, *La Comtesse de Morny, 2, un en profil*
315. [presumably Princess Sophie Troubetskoï, Duchesse de Morny]
Half-length, oval, signed and dated 1863, 94 × 73, Musée national du château de Compiègne, MNR 235; exhibition no. 64
See also nos. 371, 440

316. *La Princesse Anna Murat*
Size and present location unknown
See also no. 319

317. *L'Impératrice Eugénie, en noir, grand*
Whole-length, seated, signed and dated 1862, 229 × 146, priv. coll.
See fig. 37
See also nos. 232, 318, 320, 329, 339, 388, 389, 442

318. *idem. en profil*
Salon 1861
Head-and-shoulders, profile, 1861, ex-coll. Her Royal Highness Princess Beatrice of Great Britain, size and present location unknown
Version, Napoleon Museum, Arenenberg, Switzerland

319. *Mlle la Princesse Murat*
Size and present location unknown
See also no. 316

320. *L'Impératrice des Français (en Robe noir)*
Size and present location unknown
See also no. 317

321. *La Famille du Prince de Prusse*
[presumably Family of Princess Royal: Prince Frederick William, Princess Victoria, Prince William & Princess Charlotte]
4 whole-length figures, signed and dated 1862, 243.5 × 117, coll. Her Majesty The Queen, Elizabeth II
See also nos. 75, 121, 150, 280, 362 for Princess Royal
See also nos. 362 for Prince Frederick of Prussia

322. *Le Roi et la Reine de Prusse, en grand costume*
Size and present location unknown

323. *Mme d'Abaza*
Size and present location unknown

324. *Mlle d'Abaza*
Size and present location unknown

325. *La Comtesse Pierre Schouvaloff. 2*
Size and present location unknown
For other Schouvaloff portraits, see also nos. 228, 229, 256, 260–2, 268–9, 326, 304

326. *avec 5 enfants (separés)*
See above

327. *Mme Auffm'Ordt et sa fille*
Size and present location unknown
See also no. 444

328. *Mme la Princesse de Furstenberg*
Size and present location unknown

329. *L'Impératrice Eugénie, profil*
Size and present location unknown
See also no. 318; and 317 for list of other portraits

330, *Mme Jakounchikoff, 2 fois, un petit oval*
330A. Size and present location unknown

331. *La Princesse Helène Kotchouboy*
[Hélène Bibikoff, Princess Kotschoubey]
Threequarter-length, signed and dated 1860, 129 × 97, Walters Art Gallery, Baltimore

332. *La Comtesse Edmond Pourtalès*
Size and present location unknown
See also nos. 118, 188, 189, 413

333. *La Comtesse Koucheleff*
Size and present location unknown
See also no. 424

334. *La Comtesse Tiesenhausen*
Size and present location unknown
See also no. 420

335. *Mme la Princesse Bibesco (de Souvenir)*
Size and present location unknown
See also no. 425

336. *Mme la Comtesse Vanderstraaten Ponthoz*
Size and present location unknown
See also nos. 149, 193

337. *Mme la Comtesse Swiekoska et son garçon*
Size and present location unknown
For other Swiekowska family portraits, see also nos. 426, 427

338, *La Princesse Marie Woronzoff, 1 grand, 1 petit*
338A. Size and present location unknown
See also nos. 230, 231, 249, 250

339. *L'Impératrice des Français, buste pour son fils 1863*
Salon 1864
Head-and-shoulders, oval, signed and dated 1864, 61 × 54, Musée national du château de Compiègne;
See also nos. 232, 317, 318, 320, 329, 388, 389, 442

340. *Le Prince Beloselsky*
*1865*
Size and present location unknown

341. *La Princesse Beloselsky*
*1865*
Size and present location unknown

342. *La Princesse Helène d'Angleterre*
[Princess Helena, later Princess Christian of Schleswig-Holstein]
*1865*
Threequarter-length, signed and dated 1861, 53.7 × 40.6, coll. Her Majesty The Queen, Elizabeth II
See also nos. 121, 150–2

343. *La Princesse Louise d'Angleterre*
[Princess Louise Caroline Alberta, later Duchess of Argyll]
*1865*
Threequarter-length, oval, 115.9 × 86, coll. Her Majesty The Queen, Elizabeth II
See also nos. 150, 344

344. *La Princesse Louise à Cobourg*
*1865*
Size and present location unknown
See above for other portraits of Princess Louise

345. *La petite Princesse du Grand Duc de Bade*
*1865*
Size and present location unknown

346. *La Princesse Guillaume de Bade*
*1865*
Size and present location unknown

347. *Le Prince Alfred à Cobourg*
[Prince Alfred, Duke of Edinburgh]
*1865*
Size and present location unknown
See also nos. 121, 151, 152, 163

348. *La Princesse Serge Gagarine*
*1866*
Size and present location unknown
For other portraits, see also nos. 247, 248, 399

349. *Richard Burn, petit oval*
*1866*
Size and present location unknown

350. *Mme Boelger Burkhardt*
*1866*
Size and present location unknown

351. *Mme de Dourassoff*
*1866*
Size and present location unknown

352. *Lord Carlo Hamilton*
[Lord Charles Douglas-Hamilton]
*1866*
Size and present location unknown
See also nos. 432, 453

353. *La petite fille de Mr Suermondt*
*1866*
Size and present location unknown

354. *Mme Vanderbyl*
*1867*
Size and present location unknown

355. *Mme Ralli avec son enfant*
*1867*
Size and present location unknown

356. *Mlle Fiocre Eugènie*
*1867*
Size and present location unknown

357. *Mlle Calhoun*
*1867*
Size and present location unknown

358. *Mme Paskiewitch*
*1867*
Half-length, oval, signed and dated 1867, location unknown

359. *Mlle d'Eichthal*
*1867*
Size and present location unknown

360. *Mlle Chégarey*
*1867*
Size and present location unknown

361, *Le Prince et la Princesse Royal de Prusse, 2 portraits*
362. *1867*
Size and present location unknown
See also nos. 124, 180, 294, 321, 418

363. *La Princesse Alice (Louise de Hesse)*
[Princess Alice, Grand Duchess of Hesse]
*1867*
Size and present location unknown
See also nos. 109, 110, 121, 150, 292, 416

364. *Mr Spencer Clifford*
[Sir Robert Spencer Clifford, 2nd Bt.]
*1867*
Priv. coll.

365. *La jeune Comtesse Rose Potocka*
*1867*
Half-length, oval, signed and dated 1867, 81.5 × 65.5, National Museum, Warsaw
See also nos. 403A, 485

366. *La jeune fille du Comte Constantin Branicka*
*1867*
Size and present location unknown

367. *Mme Dreyfuss*
*1867*
Size and present location unknown

368. *Mr Matthieu Dollfuss*
*1868*
Size and present location unknown

369. *Mme Goldschmid*
[Mélanie Biedermann, Madame Goldschmidt]
*1868*
Half-length, signed and dated 1868, 56 × 46, Musée de Louvre, Paris

370. *Mme Demidoff*
[presumably Princesse Mathilde Bonaparte, Comtesse Demidoff]
*1868*
Head-and-shoulders, oval, 60 × 50, priv. coll.

371. *La Duchesse de Morny, velour bleu*
*1868*
Size and present location unknown
See also nos. 314, 315, 440

372. *La Comtesse Pustowska, après la mort*
*1868*
Size and present location unknown

373. *La fille de la Princesse Bethsy Basiatinsky*
Size and present location unknown
For Bariatinsky family portraits, see also nos. 283, 405

374. *La fille de Mr Mumm*
Size and present location unknown

375. *Mme Berrus*
Size and present location unknown

376. *Mr Casso et son fils le jeune Krasinsky, d'après photographie*
Size and present location unknown

377. *Le Prince Cornicheff. d'après photographie*
Size and present location unknown

378. *La Grande-duchesse Olga Princesse Royale de Wurtemberg, 3 p*
[Grand Duchess Olga, Queen of Württemberg]
Whole-length, signed and dated 1865, Württembergisches Landesmuseum, Stüttgart
See also no. 472

379A, *La Grande-duchesse Marie*
379B. [presumably Grand Duchess Maria Nicolayevna]
Threequarter-length, signed and dated 1857, 128 × 97, The Hermitage, Leningrad
See also no. 381

380. *La Grande-duchesse Sophie de Bade*
[Sophie Guillemette, Grand Duchess of Baden]
Threequarter-length, signed and dated 1857, 129 × 91, priv. coll.; exhibition no. 69

381. *La Grande-duchesse Marie, fille de L'Impératrice Marie*
Head-and-shoulders, signed and dated 1869, 50 × 46, Pushkin Museum, Moscow
See also no. 379

382. *La Grande-duchesse Louise de Bade*
Size and present location unknown
Engraving by A. Weger, Leipzig, pub. Verlag Baumgartner

383. *Le Grand-duc Frédéric de Bade*
[Grand Duke Friedrich I von Baden]
Threequarter-length, signed and dated 1855, priv. coll.
Lithograph by S. Meier, pub. Lemercier, Paris, and by J. Velten, St Petersburg and Karlsruhe

384. *La Grande-duchesse Michel (Cécile de Bade)*
Size and present location unknown

385. *L'Impératrice Marie de Russie*
[presumably Maria Alexandrovna, Empress of Russia]
Threequarter-length, signed and dated 1857, 120 × 95, The Hermitage, Leningrad; exhibition no. 73
Version, Staatliche Kunsthalle Karlsruhe

386, *Le Prince Royal de Wurtemberg, 2 portraits*
387. [presumably Philip Alexander, Prince of Würtemberg]
Size and present location unknown
See also no. 51

388. *L'Impératrice Eugènie avec ses Dames, grand tableau*
[Empress Eugénie, Duchesse de Bassano, Princesse d'Essling, Baronne de Pierres, Comtesse Lezay-Marnésia, Marquise le Montebello, Baronne de Malaret, Marquise de Las Marismas, Marquise de la Tour Maubourg]
Exposition Universelle, Paris, 1855
9 whole-length figures, signed and dated 1855, 300 × 420, Musée national du château de Compiègne
Lithograph by L. Noël, 1858, and by Lemoine
Exhibition no. 53
For sketch, see exhibition no. 54
See also nos. 232, 317, 318, 320, 329, 339, 389, 442 for other portraits of Eugénie

389. *L'Impératrice Eugénie avec son enfant*
[Empress Eugénie with Louis-Napoleon, Prince Imperial]
1857 Salon
2 whole-lengths, signed and dated 1857, 240 × 156, priv. coll.; exhibition no. 58
See also no. 443 for Prince Imperial
See also nos. 232, 317, 318, 320, 329, 339, 388, 442 for Eugénie.

390. *Le Maréchal Serrano*
Size and present location unknown

391. *La Comtesse Marie Predziecka*
Size and present location unknown

392. *La Comtesse Lise Predziecka*
Size and present location unknown

393. *Les deux garçons de la Comtesse M. Predziecka*
Size and present location unknown

394. *Mme Schickler*
[Baronne Schickler]
Threequarter-length, signed and dated 1856, 144 × 111, priv. coll.

395. *Mme Tedesco*
Size and present location unknown

396. *Lady Clementine Villers*
[Lady Clementina Child-Villiers]
Head-and-shoulders, oval, signed and dated 1855, 65 × 54.5, priv. coll.; exhibition no. 41

397. *Mlle de Boyen*
Size and present location unknown

398. *Mme de Boyen*
Size and present location unknown

399. *La Princesse Gagarine Lina*
Size and present location unknown
For other Gagarine family portraits, see also nos. 247, 248, 348

400. *Mme Ducos*
[Anne Joly, Comtesse Ducos]
1857 Salon
Threequarter-length, oval, signed and dated 1856, Musée national du château de Compiègne

401, *La Comtesse Alexandre Branicka. Son garçon*
402. Size and present location unknown
See also nos. 445, 484

403, *Les enfants de Mme la Comtesse Cathérine Potocka*
403A, [Zofia (later Zamoyska), Rosa and Artur Potocki]
403B. 3 head-and-shoulders, ovals, each signed and dated 1856, 116 × 38, National Museum, Warsaw; see exhibition nos. 70, 71,
See also nos. 365, 485

404. *Le fils du Comte Pierre Schouwaloff*
Size and present location unknown
See also no. 486

405. *La Princesse Bethsy Bariatinsky*
Size and present location unknown
See also no. 283

406, *La Princesse Troubetzkoi (Lise). Sa fille*
406A. [Princess Elizabeth Esperovna Belosselsky-Belosenki, Princess Troubetskoï]
Threequarter-length, signed and dated 1859, 147 × 108, priv. coll.; exhibition no. 61

407. *La Comtesse Lamsdorff*
[Countess Maria Ivanovna Lamsdorff]
Threequarter-length, signed and dated 1859, 145.4 × 114.9, Metropolitan Museum, New York
See also no. 285

408. *L'Impératrice (mère) de Russie*
Size and present location unknown

409. *La Princesse Putbas*
[Princess Putbus]
Size and present location unknown

410. *Le Grand-duc et la Grand-duchesse Constantin de Russie*
[Grand Duchess Constantine Nicolaevitch]
Size and present location unknown
See also nos. 143, 287, 287A

411. *La Comtesse Tchernicheff Kroyelikoff*
Size and present location unknown
See also no. 288

412. *La Comtesse Pozzo di Borgo*
Size and present location unknown
See also nos. 140, 428

413. *La Comtesse Edmond Pourtalès*
Size and present location unknown
See also nos. 118, 188–189, 332

414. *La Reine Victoria, grand costume*
Whole-length in Coronation Robes, signed and dated 1859, 241.9 × 157.5, coll. Her Majesty The Queen, Elizabeth II
Pendant to no. 415 (probably a repetition of no. 290)
See also nos. 73, 87, 88, 107, 121, 122, 210, 216, 290

415. *Le Prince Albert, grand costume*
Whole-length in uniform, signed and dated 1859, 241.9 × 158.1, coll. Her Majesty The Queen, Elizabeth II
Pendant to no. 414
Version, NPG 237
See also nos. 74, 89, 108, 121, 123, 291, 310

416. *La Princesse Alice*
Whole length, signed and dated 1859, 50.8 × 40.6, coll. Her Majesty The Queen, Elizabeth II
See also nos. 109, 110, 121, 150, 292, 363

417. *La Duchesse de Manchester*
[Louise, Duchess of Manchester]
Half-length, profile, signed and dated 1859, 62.4 × 43.2, coll. Her Majesty The Queen, Elizabeth II

418. *Le Prince et la Princesse de Prusse*
Size and present location unknown
For Prince and Princess of Prussia, see also nos. 124, 180, 294, 321, 361, 362

419. *La Princesse Obolensky*
Size and present location unknown
See also no. 297 for other Obolensky portrait

420. *La Comtesse Tiesenhausen*
Size and present location unknown
See also no. 334

421. *La Princesse Metternich, 2 fois, 1 profil*
422. Size and present location unknown
See also nos. 298, 299

423. *La Comtesse Orloff (Lilly)*
Size and present location unknown

424. *La Comtesse Koucheleff*
Size and present location unknown
See also no. 333

425. *La Princesse Bibesco, de souvenir*
Size and present location unknown
See also 335

426, *La Comtesse Swieykowska. Son fils*
427. Size and present location unknown
See also no. 337

428. *Le Duc et la Duchesse Pozzo di Borgo*
Size and present location unknown
See also nos. 140, 146, 412

429. *La Comtesse Tyzgewich, grand*
Size and present location unknown

430. *La fille de Lady Cowley (Lady Rowston)*
Size and present location unknown
See also no. 441

431, *Les enfants du Duc de Hamilton*
432, [presumably William Douglas-Hamilton,
433. Marquess of Douglas, Lord Charles and Lady Marie Douglas-Hamilton]
Size and present location unknown
See also nos. 352, 453, 474

434. *La Comtesse Stockelbourg, de souvenir*
[presumably Countess Stackelberg]
Half-length, oval, signed and dated 1863, 77 × 62, Palais Galliéra, Paris, 5.3.72, lot 101

435, *Mme Korsakoff, 2 portraits*
436. [Barbe Dmitrievna Mergassov, Mme Rimsky-Korsakov]
Threequarter-length, oval, signed and dated 1858, 146 × 114, Savitzkoy Gallery, Penza, USSR; exhibition no. 60; threequarter-length, signed and dated 1864, 147 × 90, Musée d'Orsay, Paris; exhibition no. 65; version, Stair Sainty Fine Art Inc., New York 1982; two further versions in priv. colls.
See also nos. 263–5

437. *La Reine de Hollande*
[Sophia Frederika Mathilda of Württemberg, Queen of the Netherlands]
Threequarter-length, signed and dated 1863, 132 × 92, Rijksmuseum, Holland
See also no. 181

438. *La Princesse Victor Basiatinsky*
[presumably Bariatinsky]
Size and present location unknown
See also nos. 283, 405

439. *La Princesse Olympe Basiatinsky*
[presumably Bariatinsky]
Size and present location unknown

440. *La Duchesse Morny, en profil*
Size and present location unknown
See also nos. 314, 315, 371

441. *Les deux filles de Lady Cowley*
Size and present location unknown
See also no. 430

442. *L'Impératrice de France*
[Empress Eugénie]
See also nos. 232, 317, 318, 320, 329, 339, 388, 389

443. *Le Prince Impérial*
[Louis-Napoleon, Prince Imperial]
Salon 1864
Whole-length, in hunting costume with gun, priv. coll.
Photographed & pub. by Bingham, 1865, Paris, Royal Library, Windsor Castle
See also no. 389

444. *Mme Hélène Auffm'Ordt*
Size and present location unknown
See also no. 327

445. *La Comtesse Branicka (mère), de souvenir*
Size and present location unknown
See also nos. 401, 402, 484

446, *La Princesse Dadiani, Reine de Mingrelie. Sa fille.*
447. Size and present location unknown

448, *Ses deux garçons*
449. Size and present location unknown

450. *Mme Andréas Achenbach*
Size and present location unknown

451. *Mme Andréas d'Hargivilliers*
Size and present location unknown

452. *Le Duc de Hamilton, de souvenir*
[presumably William Alexander Anthony Archibald, 11th Duke of Hamilton]
Size and present location unknown
For other Hamilton portraits, see also no. 453
A watercolour, threequarter-length, seated, 1850, sold Sotheby's 11. 7. 85, lot 93.

453, *Le jeune Duc de Hamilton, les 3 enfants*
453A, [Marquess of Douglas, Lord Charles and Lady
453B. Marie Hamilton]
Lord Charles, head-and-shoulders, priv. coll.; for William Douglas-Hamilton, 12th Duke of Hamilton see exhibition no. 45; others untraced
See also nos. 352, 431–3, 474

454. *L'Empereur de Mexico*
[Maximilian of Habsburg, Emperor of Mexico]
Half-length, signed and dated 1864, Hearst Museum, San Simeon
Pendant to no. 455

455. *L'Impératrice de Mexico*
[Marie-Charlotte-Amélie, Empress of Mexico]
Half-length, signed and dated 1864, Hearst Museum, San Simeon
Pendant to no. 454
See also nos. 72, 103

456. *Mme Ronay, née Périère*
Size and present location unknown

457. *Lady Middleton, grand*
[Julia Bosville, Lady Middleton]
Whole-length, signed and dated 1863, 239 × 147.5, priv. coll.; exhibition no. 47

458. *Mme Brétonneaux*
Size and present location unknown

459. *Ses deux enfants*
Size and present location unknown

460. *La Baronne de Wächter*
Size and present location unknown

461. *L'Empereur d'Autriche, grand*
[Franz Joseph I, Emperor of Austria]
Whole-length, signed and dated 1865, 255 × 155, the Hofburg, Vienna; exhibition no. 78

462. *L'Impératrice d'Autriche, grand*
[Elizabeth Empress of Austria]
Whole-length, signed and dated 1865, 255 × 155, the Hofburg, Vienna; exhibition no. 79

463. *idem. jusqu'aux genoux*
Half-length, signed and dated 1864, 158 × 117, the Hofburg, Vienna
Copy, coll. Her Majesty The Queen, Elizabeth II

464. *idem. un peu plus petit*
Half-length, oval, signed and dated 1864, priv. coll.
See fig. 43

465. *L'Archiduchesse Marie Therèse, fille de L'Archiduc Albrecht*
Size and present location unknown

466. *L'Archiduchesse Sophie, mère de l'empereur*
Size and present location unknown

467. *Le Prince Wasa*
Size and present location unknown

468. *La Princesse Tour et Taxis, Soeur de l'Impér. d'Autriche*
Size and present location unknown

469. *Mme Dolfuss*
Size and present location unknown

470. *La Comtesse Ladislas Branicka*
[Maria Sapicka, Countess Branicka]
Threequarter-length, signed and dated 1865, 115.8 × 88, Philadelphia Museum of Art

471. *Mme la Comtesse Rembelinska*
Size and present location unknown

472. *La Reine de Wurtemburg, en pied*
[Grand Duchess Olga, Queen of Württemberg]
Size and present location unknown
See also no. 378

473. *La Princesse de Hohenzollern*
Size and present location unknown

474. *Lady Mary Hamilton*
[Lady Marie Douglas-Hamilton]
Size and present location unknown
See also nos. 433, 453

475. *Mr André, fils*
[presumably Edouard André]
Threequarter-length, signed and dated 1857, 141 × 100, Musée Jacquemart-André, Paris; exhibition no. 59
See also no. 272

476. *L'Empereur des Français*
[Emperor Napoleon III]
Threequarter-length, oval, *c.*1857, 160 × 127, Musée national du château de Compiègne; exhibition no. 56
See also no. 271

477. Princesse Odeskalchi
[presumably Sofia Branicka, Princess Odescalchi]
Size and present location unknown
See also no. 279

478. *Le Prince Royal d'Angleterre*
[presumably Edward, Prince of Wales]
Threequarter-length, signed and dated 1864, 162.2 × 114, coll. Her Majesty The Queen, Elizabeth II
See also nos. 76, 90, 121, 122, 125, 163

479. *Comtesse Bobrinsky*
Size and present location unknown
See also nos. 104, 281, 282

480. *L'impératrice de Russie (douarière)*
[presumably Empress Alexandra Feodorovna]
Size and present location unknown

481. *L'impératrice de Russie (régente)*
[presumably Empress Alexandra Feodorovna]
Threequarter-length, signed and dated 1856, 109 × 80, The Hermitage, Leningrad

482. *Mlle von Boiger et la mère, 5 ans avant*
Size and present location unknown

483. *La Princesse Sangusko*
[Princesse Helena Sanguszkowa]
Size and present location unknown
See also no. 278

484. *Mme la Comtesse Alexandre Branicka, et son garçon*
Size and present location unknown
See also nos. 401, 402, 445

485. *Les enfants de la Comtesse Potocka (Cathérine)*
[Zofia, Roza and Artur Potocki]
See also no. 365

486. *Le petit Schouwaloff (Pierre fils)*
Size and present location unknown
See also no. 404

487. *Le Grand-duc de Meklenbourg, son fils de 2 ans*
[presumably: Frederick, Grand Duke of Mecklenburg]
Size and present location unknown

488. *Comtesse Schouwaloff, Olga Biloselska Kotckoubé*
Size and present location unknown
See also nos, 260, 261

489. *Comtesse Schouwaloff Marie (Gagarine)*
Size and present location unknown
See also no. 262

490. *Comtesse d'Adlerberg, sa fille*
Size and present location unknown
See also no. 270

*Gemälde von Franz und Hermann Winterhalter gemalt, die nicht in den eigenen Aufzeichnungen angeführt sind*

[Paintings by Franz and Hermann Winterhalter which have not been listed in their catalogues]

491. *Selbst-Porträt*
*Franz Winterhalter*
Half-length, 1868, 72.5 × 55, Uffizi, Florence
Version at Staatliche Kunsthalle Karlsruhe

492. *Der Frühling Genrebild* [Spring]
*Franz Winterhalter*
Half-length, 116.5 × 89.5, priv. coll.; exhibition no. 39

493. *Das Früchtenmädchen Genrebild* [Young Girl selling Fruit]
*Franz Winterhalter*
Size and present location unknown

494. *Florinde Genrebild* [Florinda]
*Franz Winterhalter*
12 figures, signed and dated 1852, 179.1 × 244.5, coll. Her Majesty The Queen, Elizabeth II; exhibition no. 38
Version, 1853 Salon, signed and undated, 178.4 × 245.7, Metropolitan Museum of Art, New York

495. *Decamerone Genrebild* [The Decameron]
*Franz Winterhalter*
1837 Salon
10 figures, signed and dated 1837, 178 × 243, priv. coll.; see fig. 16
Reduced replica, Staatliche Kunsthalle Karlsruhe
Engravings by F. Girard, pub. Goupil 1840, and A. Martinet

496. *Il Dolce far niente Genrebild* [Il Dolce Farniente]
*Franz Winterhalter*
1836 Salon
12 figures, signed and dated 1836, 160 × 200, priv. coll.; exhibition no. 9
Version, The Hermitage, Leningrad

497. *Der erste Freund Genrebild* [presumably La Siesta]
*Franz Winterhalter*
3 whole-length figures, signed and dated 1841, 55.9 × 43.2, priv. coll.; exhibition no. 12

498. *Drei Italienerinnen Genrebild* [Three Italian Women]
*Franz Winterhalter*
Size and present location unknown

499. *Schweizermädchen von Interlaken* [Swiss Girl from Interlaken]
Threequarter-length, 126 × 93, priv. coll.; exhibition no. 13

500. *Madelaine und Elisabeth (Ritschard)*
*Franz Winterhalter*
Size and present location unknown

501. *F. Chopin Porträt*
*Franz Winterhalter*
Size and present location unknown
A drawing of Chopin, 1847, is said to be at the University of Krakow, Poland

502. *Susanna im Bade* [Susannah and the Elders]
*Franz Winterhalter*
Whole-length figure, size and present location unknown
See fig. 50

503. *Selbst-Porträt*
*Hermann Winterhalter*
Size and location unknown

504. *Hase Stilleben* [Still-life of a Hare]
Size and location unknown

The following paintings are unattributed to either artist:

505. *L'Enfant chéri* [The Beloved Child]
Size and location unknown

506. *Rose naissante* [The Budding Rose]
Size and location unknown

507. *Amerikanerin* [An American Lady]
Half-length, oval, 110 × 85, priv. coll.; exhibition no. 80

508. *Comtesse Canelaux*
Size and location unknown

509. *Le Roi de Portugal* [presumably King Pedro V, King of Portugal]
Presumably threequarter-length, signed and dated F.X. Winterhalter 1854, coll. Her Majesty The Queen, Elizabeth II

510. *Le Duc d'Opporto*
Size and present location unknown

511. *Princesse Louise et sa Bonne* [Princess Louise and her nursemaid]
Size and present location unknown
For watercolour by F.X. Winterhalter, 1850, of Princess Louise and Eliza Collins see exhibition no. 90

# Index to Franz Wild's list

Names and titles in italics are given in the spellings used by Wild but the relevant entries should be consulted for the full descriptions of the pictures given by Wild, as well as for suggested fuller identifications for some sitters.

# Index of Sitters and Subjects

Numbers given below refer to catalogue numbers